Preparing for Certification or Licensure
A Guide

Learning about Statewide Testing for Licensure

Many states require prospective teachers to take standardized tests for licensure. The following questions and answers will help you learn more about this important step to becoming a teacher.

What kinds of tests do states require for licensure?

Some tests assess students' competency in basic skills of reading, writing, and mathematics, often prior to admission to a professional teacher education program. Many states also require standardized tests at the end of a teacher education program; these tests assess prospective teachers' competency and knowledge in their subject area, as well as knowledge about teaching and learning. The tests assess the extent to which prospective teachers meet state and national standards for beginning teachers.

Do all states use the same test for licensure?

No. Many states use the *Praxis Series*™ of tests, published by the Educational Testing Service (ETS). Other states—including Arizona, California, Florida, Illinois, Massachusetts, Michigan, New York, and Texas—have developed their own tests for licensure. You can learn about each state's testing requirements by checking its department of education Web site or contacting the state department of education by mail or telephone. (A table of Web site addresses for all fifty states appears on the next page of this guide.)

What is assessed in the state tests for licensure?

The tests for licensure usually address prospective teachers' knowledge of the teaching-and-learning process and the subjects they will teach. For example, the ETS *Praxis Series*™ includes subtests on Principles of Teaching and Learning and on the content and pedagogy of specific subject areas. Other state tests have similar goals.

How do I know which tests to take?

Contact your advisor or student services center if you are currently a student in a teacher education program. If you are applying for licensure through an alternative licensure program, contact the state department of education's licensure office. ETS describes the topics covered in each category on their Web site (www.ets.org/praxis) or in their free booklet *Test at a Glance*. States that have their own testing requirements also provide information about the tests and preparation materials through their Web sites.

What courses in my teacher preparation program might apply to state tests for licensure?

Almost all of your teacher preparation courses relate to licensure tests in some way. This text, *Teaching in America*, addresses many concepts that are assessed in these tests. You have probably studied or will study concepts and knowledge related to the four content categories in courses such as educational foundations, educational psychology or human growth and development, classroom management, curriculum and methods, and evaluation and assessment. You may have had or will have field experiences and seminars that provide you with knowledge about these concepts as well.

Table 1: Links to Individual State Testing Requirements

States	Contact Web Site	States	Contact Web Site
Alabama	www.alsde.edu	Nebraska	www.nde.state.ne.us/tcert/tcmain.html
Alaska	www.eed.state.ak.us/teachercertification/	Nevada	www.doe.nv.gov/licensure
Arizona	ade.state.az.us/	New Hampshire	www.ed.state.nh.us/
Arkansas	arkedu.state.ar.us/teachers/index.html	New Jersey	www.state.nj.us/njded/educators/license/
California	www.ctc.ca.gov/	New Mexico	sde.state.nm.us/index.html
Colorado	www.cde.state.co.us/	New York	www.nysed.gov/
Connecticut	www.state.ct.us/sde/dtl/cert/index.htm	North Carolina	www.ncpublicschools.org/
Delaware	deeds.doe.state.de.us/	North Dakota	governor.state.nd.us/boards/
Florida	www.fldoe.org/	Ohio	www.ode.state.oh.us/tp/ctp/
Georgia	www.gapsc.com/	Oklahoma	sde.state.ok.us/home/defaultie.html
Hawaii	www.htsb.org/	Oregon	www.tspc.state.or.us/
Idaho	www.idahoboardofed.org/	Pennsylvania	www.pde.state.pa.us/
Illinois	www.isbe.state.il.us/	Rhode Island	www.ridoe.net/
Indiana	www.state.in.us/psb/	South Carolina	www.scteachers.org/
Iowa	www.state.ia.us/educate/stateboard/	South Dakota	wwww.state.sd.us/deca/
Kansas	www.ksbe.state.ks.us/cert/cert.html	Tennessee	www.state.tn.us/education/lic_home.htm
Kentucky	www.kyepsb.net/	Texas	www.sbec.state.tx.us
Louisiana	www.teachlouisiana.net/	Utah	www.usoe.k12.ut.us/
Maine	www.state.me.us/education/	Vermont	www.state.vt.us/educ/
Maryland	certification.msde.state.md.us/	Virginia	www.pen.k12.va.us/VDOE/newvdoe/teached.html
Massachusetts	www.doe.mass.edu/	Washington	www.k12.wa.us/certification/
Michigan	www.michigan.gov.mde/	District of Columbia	www.k12.dc.us/dcps/home.html
Minnesota	education.state.mn.us/html/intro_board_teach.htm	West Virginia	wvde.state.wv.us/
Mississippi	www.mde.k12.ms.us/license/licapndxb.htm	Wisconsin	www.dpi.state.wi.us/dpi/dlsis/tel/licguide.html
Missouri	www.dese.state.mo.us/	Wyoming	www.k12.wy.us/
Montana	www.metnet.state.mt.us/		

What other resources will help me prepare for state tests for licensure?

Several organizations have developed standards for teacher preparation and continued professional development. A consortium of more than thirty states, the Interstate New Teacher Assessment and Support Consortium (INTASC), has developed standards and an assessment process for initial teacher certification. The National Council for the Accreditation of Teacher Education (NCATE) also has developed standards for teacher education programs, and the National Board of Professional Teaching Standards (NBPTS) has developed standards for advanced certification of teachers who possess extensive professional knowledge and the ability to perform at a high level. In addition, most states have developed their own standards for teachers as part of their licensure requirements. As you review these documents, you will find that they contain common expectations of knowledge and skills and can provide a guide for you as you prepare for licensure.

How should I prepare for state tests for licensure?

Tests for licensure are typically integrative tests; you will be asked to apply knowledge learned in several courses and field experiences to realistic situations in case histories and short scenarios. It is important, therefore, that you *understand the concepts* covered in the test, *review the content* from your course work that relates to those concepts, and *apply good test-taking strategies* during the test.

Test Taking Tips for Licensure Tests

Test-Taking Tip # 1: Know the Test

- **Review the topics covered in the exam.** The ETS booklet *Test at a Glance* (available online at www.ets.org/praxis or free by mail) includes detailed descriptions of topics covered in the Praxis tests. States that require their own tests also provide descriptions of the tests and the concepts covered in those tests on their Web sites.

- **Take the sample tests** provided on Web sites and in print materials. Analyze the kind of questions asked, the correct answers, and the knowledge necessary to answer the question correctly.
- **Analyze the sample questions and the standards used for scoring the responses to open-ended (constructed-response) questions.** Carefully read any scoring guides provided in the testing guides. Write your own responses to sample questions and analyze them, using the test-scoring guide. If your responses do not meet all the criteria, revise them.

Test-Taking Tip # 2: Know the Content

- **Plan ahead.** You can begin preparing for standardized teacher licensure tests early in your teacher education program. Think about how each of your courses relates to the concepts and content of the exam.
- **Review what you learned in each course in relation to the topics covered in the test.** Review course textbooks and class notes for relevant concepts and information. At the end of each course, record reminders of how the course's content and knowledge relates to concepts of the test. (*Teaching in America*, Fourth Edition, provides useful review and application activities at the end of each chapter.)
- **Think across courses.** Many of the test items will draw on knowledge from several courses. Think about how knowledge, skills, and concepts from the courses you have taken relate to one another. For example, you might have learned about aspects of working with parents in a foundations course, an educational psychology course, and a methods course. Be prepared to integrate that knowledge.
- **Review the content with others.** Meet with a study group and together review the test and your course work. Brainstorm about relevant content, using the descriptions of each test's categories and representative topics as a guideline.

Test-Taking Tip # 3: Apply Good Test-Taking Strategies

- **Read the test directions carefully.** Even though you have previewed the test format and directions as part of learning about the test, make sure you understand the directions for this test.

For multiple-choice questions:
- **Read each question carefully.** Pay attention to key words such as *not, all, except, always,* or *never.*
- **Try to anticipate the answer to the question** looking at the possible responses. If your among the choices, it is likely to be corr automatically choosing it, however, c alternative answers.

- **Answer questions you are certain of first.** Return to questions you are uncertain of later.
- **If you are unsure of the answer, eliminate obviously incorrect responses first.**

For short-answer open-ended questions:
- **Read the directions carefully.** Look for key words and respond directly to exactly what is asked.
- **Repeat key words from the question to focus your response.** For example, if you are asked to list two advantages to a method, state "Two advantages are (1) . . . and (2) . . . ."
- **Be explicit and concrete.** Short-answer responses should be direct and to the point.

For essay questions:
- **Read the question carefully and pay close attention to key words, especially verbs.** Make sure you understand all parts of the question. For example, if the question asks you to list advantages and disadvantages, be sure to answer both parts.
- **Before you write your response, list key points or make an outline.** The few minutes you take to organize your thoughts will pay off in a better-organized essay.
- **Use the question's words in your response.** For example, if the question asks for three advantages, identify the advantages explicitly: "The first advantage is . . ." "The second advantage is . . ." and "The third advantage is . . . ." Make it easy for the reader to score your response.
- **Stay on topic.** Answer the question fully and in detail, but do not go beyond what the question asks or add irrelevant material.

Sample State Licensure Test Questions

The following sample questions illustrate the kinds of questions that typically appear in state licensure tests. The case study, which focuses on elementary education, contains issues and content related to principles of teaching and learning and professional education. It addresses such issues as organizing the curriculum, creating effective learning environments, effective teaching practices, diversity, and professional practice. These concepts are typical of those found in the Principles of Teaching and Learning test in Praxis and the professional education tests in other state tests.

Following the case study are three related multiple-choice questions, two constructed-response questions, and three additional discrete multiple-choice questions. These sample questions focus on content and issues discussed in *Teaching in America*, Fourth Edition; they are not representative of the entire scope of the actual tests.

Answers with explanations and references to test topics, INTASC standards, and appropriate parts of this text follow the questions.

Sample Case Study and Related Multiple-Choice Questions

Case History: K–6

Columbus, New Mexico, is an agricultural community near the international boundaries separating Mexico and the United States. It's a quiet town, where traditional views of community and territory are being challenged. Just three miles from the border is Columbus Elementary School, a bilingual school for kindergarten through sixth-grade students. Of the some 340 students enrolled at Columbus Elementary, approximately 97% are on free or reduced-price lunches. The school is unique because about 49% of the students live in Mexico and attend Columbus Elementary at U.S. taxpayer expense. Columbus Elementary is a fully bilingual school. In the early grades, basic skills are taught in Spanish, but by the third-grade level, students have begun to make the transition to English. Most of the teachers at Columbus Elementary School are English speakers; some have limited Spanish skills. The school also employs teaching assistants who are fluent in Spanish and can assist the teachers in these bilingual classrooms.

Dennis Armijo, the principal of Columbus Elementary School, describes the unique relationship between Columbus and its neighboring community, Palomas, Mexico. "Most of the people who live in Columbus, New Mexico, have relatives in Palomas, Mexico. At one point or another, many Columbus residents were Mexican residents, and they came over and established a life here. And so they still have ties to Mexico, and a lot of uncles and aunts and grandparents still live in Palomas. They have a kind of family togetherness, where they just go back and forth all the time. The kids who are coming over from Mexico, most of them are American citizens who have been born in the United States. Now, the parents may not be able to cross because of illegal status, but the kids are U.S. citizens; they have been born in U.S. hospitals."

Columbus Elementary School's international enrollment poses special challenges for family and parental involvement. Mr. Armijo notes that parental contact is often not as frequent as he would like it to be. The school occasionally runs into problems reaching parents because many don't have telephones and must be reached through an emergency number in Mexico that might be as far as three blocks away or through a relative on the U.S. side of the border. In many cases, school personnel go into Mexico and talk to the parents or write them a letter so they can cross the border legally to come to the school. Despite these barriers, however, Mr. Armijo says that cooperation from the parents is great. "They'll do anything to help out this school."

The parents who send their children across the border to Columbus Elementary are willing to face the logistical difficulties of getting their children to Columbus each day because they want their children to have the benefits of a bilingual education. Mr. Armijo notes that the only reason that many parents from across the border send their kids to Columbus is to learn English. He describes a potential conflict that sometimes arises from this expectation:

"There's—I wouldn't call it a controversy, but there's some misunderstanding, mainly because parents don't understand what a bilingual program is. Some of them don't want their children to speak Spanish at all; they say they are sending the children to our school just to learn English. A true bilingual program will take kids that are monolingual speakers of any language and combine them together. At Columbus Elementary, for example, if you have a monolingual English speaker and a monolingual Spanish speaker, if they are in a true bilingual program you hope that the Spanish speaker will learn English and the English speaker will learn Spanish. And if they live here for the rest of their lives, they will be able to communicate with anybody. So when the students from Mexico come over, they need to learn the skills and the American way of life that lead to the American dream, if you will, of an education. Because at some point or another, they might want to come over. Remember, these students are U.S. citizens, even though they live with their parents in Mexico. I'm almost sure that most of those kids are going to come over across to the United States and live here, and so they need to have this education.

Perspective of Linda Lebya, Third-Grade Teacher

Linda Lebya is in her third year of teaching third grade at Columbus Elementary School. She lives nearby on a ranch with her husband, who is a deputy sheriff. She speaks conversational Spanish, although she is not a native Spanish speaker. About 95% of her third-grade students are Spanish speaking.

Linda's classroom is small but inviting. Colorful posters and pictures on the wall reflect the students' culture, and many words and phrases are posted in Spanish and English. Desks are grouped in clusters of four so students can sit together facing one another. A list of vocabulary words, written in English and Spanish, is on the blackboard.

Linda describes her teaching approaches and some of the challenges she faces. First, she describes a typical spelling lesson:

On Monday as an introduction for spelling vocabulary we have 10 vocabulary words written in English and Spanish. The intent is for them to learn it in English; I also put up the Spanish words with the intent of helping them to learn what the English word means. We discuss the words in English and Spanish, then use them in sentences in each language.

Columbus Elementary is a poor school, and Linda reports that resources are limited:

Lack of books is a problem because we're supposed to be teaching in Spanish for part of the day but the only thing we have in Spanish are the readers. All the other materials are in English so that is a problem.

One resource that Ms. Lebya does have is a Spanish-speaking instructional assistant. She describes the assistant's role in her classroom:

All of the teachers here at Columbus K–3 have an instructional assistant to help out with different things. My assistant this year is really wonderful; she helps out a great deal. She teaches the Spanish reading to the students because I'm not as fluent to teach it. I can speak it and I can understand, but to actually teach it, I wouldn't know how; my Spanish is not strong enough.

Linda describes her understanding of multicultural education:

Multicultural education here means that most of the students are from a different culture. We have a few Anglos but most of the students are Mexicans or Hispanics, and when you are teaching multicultural education, you want to make sure that the students understand that their culture is just as important as the dominant culture. For example, one of our vocabulary words was fiesta, or party. Some of our students were not in school that day because they were making their First Holy Communion, and their families were having a big celebration. We talked about official fiestas like Cinqo de Mayo and family or traditional fiestas like today, and the students made English and Spanish sentences about fiestas and parties. It all helps them to value their culture while they learn about the culture of the United States.

And as far as the Spanish sentences, that's just giving them an opportunity to do something well because they already know it in Spanish. They have the vocabulary in Spanish, so they're able to do a good job in making the sentences, and that's something they can feel good about, and it helps their self-esteem.

DIRECTIONS: Each of the multiple-choice questions below is followed by four choices. Select the one that is best in each case.

1. Which approach best describes the philosophy of the bilingual program at Columbus Elementary School?

   (a) Children should receive instruction in both English and their native language and culture throughout their school years, making a gradual transition to English.

   (b) Students should make the transition to English through ongoing, intensive instruction in English as a Second Language.

   (c) Students should be removed from their regular classes to receive special help in English or in reading in their native language.

   (d) Students should be immersed in English, then placed in English-speaking classes.

2. Which approach to multicultural education (defined by Sleeter and Grant) best characterizes the Columbus Elementary School program, based on the comments of Ms. Lebya?

   (a) Human Relations

   (b) Single-Group Studies

   (c) Teaching the Exceptionally and Culturally Different

   (d) Education that Is Multicultural and Social Reconstructionist

3. Ms. Lebya's instructional approach to teaching vocabulary could best be described as

   (a) individualized instruction

   (b) cooperative learning

   (c) inquiry learning

   (d) direct instruction

Sample Short-Answer Questions

A well-constructed short-answer response demonstrates an understanding of the aspects of the case that are relevant to the question; responds to all parts of the question; supports explanations with relevant evidence; and demonstrates a strong knowledge of appropriate concepts, theories, or methodologies relevant to the question.

The following sample open-ended questions draw from knowledge and concepts covered in this text only. In an actual state licensure test, respondents should use knowledge and concepts derived from all parts of their teacher education program.

4. Ms. Lebya says that she relies on her instructional assistant to teach reading in Spanish because "I'm not fluent enough to teach it. I can speak it and understand it, but to actually teach it, I wouldn't know how." List at least one positive and one negative possible consequence of this teaching arrangement.

5. Is it possible to teach well without textbooks? If so, when? If not, why not?

Sample Discrete Multiple-Choice Questions

The Praxis Principles of Teaching and Learning tests and other state licensure tests include discrete multiple-choice questions that cover an array of teaching-and-learning topics. In an actual state licensure test, respondents would draw from knowledge and concepts learned in all aspects of an undergraduate teacher preparation program. In this sample test, items are drawn from this text only.

6. The Buckley Amendment

   (a) permits corporal punishment as long as district policies and procedures are in place.
   (b) allows all parents access to their children's academic records.
   (c) establishes that married or pregnant students have the same rights and privileges as other students.
   (d) states that all students with disabilities are entitled to an "appropriate" education.

7. Mr. Williams placed a pitcher of water and several containers of different sizes and shapes on a table. He asked a small group of students, "Which container holds the most water? Which holds the least? How can you figure it out?"

Mr. Williams's philosophical orientation probably is:

   (a) behaviorism
   (b) perennialism
   (c) constructivism
   (d) essentialism

8. Ms. Jackson was planning a unit of study for her 11th grade American History class. She wanted to determine what students already knew and what they wanted to know about the topic prior to beginning the unit. Which forms of preassessment would be most useful?

   (a) a norm-referenced test
   (b) a teacher-made assessment
   (c) a criterion-referenced test
   (d) a summative assessment

Answers

1. **The best answer is (a).** In the Columbus Elementary School's bilingual program, children learn primarily in Spanish during their first few grades, then begin the transition to English in the third grade. They are not experiencing an intensive English instruction or pullout program, nor are they immersed in English.
   Related Praxis and Other State Test Topics: Organizing content knowledge for student learning and needs and characteristics of students from diverse populations; creating an environment for student learning and appropriate teacher responses to individual and cultural diversity
   Related INTASC Standards: Adapting Instruction for Individual Needs.
   Related material in this book: Chapter 4, Teaching Diverse Students: How Does Language Influence Teaching and Learning?

2. **The best answer is (c).** Both Mr. Armijo and Ms. Lebya emphasize that the purpose of their bilingual program is

to help the students assimilate into American culture and acquire language and skills that will help them be successful if they choose to live in the United States.
   Related Praxis and Other State Test Topics: Organizing content knowledge for student learning and needs and characteristics of students from diverse populations; creating an environment for student learning and appropriate teacher responses to individual and cultural diversity
   Related INTASC Standards: Adapting Instruction to Individual Needs
   Related material in this book: Chapter 4, Teaching Diverse Students: How Do Racial and Ethnic Diversity Affect Teaching and Learning?

3. **The best answer is (d).** Ms. Lebya uses a teacher-directed approach, in which she asks specific questions of the students and provides praise or corrective feedback.
   Related Praxis and Other State Test Topics: Organizing content for student learning and creating or selecting teaching methods, learning activities, and instructional materials or other resources that are appropriate for the students and are aligned with the goals of the lesson;

teaching for student learning and repertoire of flexible teaching and learning strategies
Related INTASC Standards: Multiple Instructional Strategies; Instructional Planning Skills
Related material in this book: Chapter 11, Curriculum and Instruction: What Are Some Models of Direct Instruction?

4. A strong response to this open-ended question will explicitly state at least one potential positive consequence and one potential negative consequence to the teaching arrangement. The respondent will use or paraphrase the question and answer explicitly in complete sentences.
Sample Response: One potential positive consequence of having the Spanish-speaking teaching assistant teach reading in Spanish is that the students will acquire better reading skills in Spanish. If they become good readers in Spanish, they may find it easier to become good readers in English later on. One potential negative consequence of having the Spanish-speaking teaching assistant teach reading in Spanish is that she may not have the knowledge or skills to teach reading. (Many teaching assistants have not had the educational preparation that licensed teachers have.) Ms. Lebya's Spanish may not be strong enough to pick up on those problems or correct them. Thus, the children may not become strong readers in Spanish.
Related Praxis and Other State Test Topics: Teaching for student learning and making content comprehensible to students; teacher professionalism and reflecting on the extent to which learning goals were met.
Related INTASC Standards: Multiple Instructional Strategies; Instructional Planning Skills
Related material in this book: Chapter 4, Teaching Diverse Students: How Does Language Affect Teaching and Learning?

5. A strong response to this open-ended question explicitly takes a position on the necessity of textbooks and will defend that position. The respondent will use or paraphrase the question and answer explicitly in complete sentences.
Sample Response: Although it is possible to teach well without textbooks, contemporary textbooks can be an invaluable resource. Most textbooks today include a wealth of teaching aids, both as part of the textbook itself and as accompanying materials for the teacher, and a good textbook can provide a solid foundation for learning. Textbooks, however, should never be the only teaching tool. Teachers might also use a collection of other instructional materials including articles and primary sources, or a variety of multimedia resources including Internet sites, films, DVDs, or CDs. Whatever resources a teacher chooses to use, the teacher must have clear goals and select materials that support those goals.
Related Praxis and Other State Test Topics: Organizing content knowledge for student learning and creating or selecting teaching methods, learning activities, and

instructional materials or other resources that are appropriate for the students and are aligned with the goals of the lesson.
Related INTASC Standards: Multiple Instructional Strategies
Related material in this book: Chapter 11, Curriculum and Instruction: How Do Teachers Plan and Deliver Instruction?

6. **The answer is (b).** Under the Buckley amendment of the Family Educational Rights and Privacy Act of 1974, schools must protect the privacy of student records while affording parents and students over eighteen years of age access to this information.
Related Praxis and Other State Test Topics: Professional responsibilities and communicating with families
Related INTASC Standards: Professional Commitment and Responsibility
Related material in this book: Chapter 8, The Legal Basis for Education and School Law: What Are Students' Legal Rights?

7. **The answer is (c).** Mr. Williams encouraged the students to construct meaning or make sense of information for themselves, one of the characteristics of constructivism.
Related Praxis Topic: Organizing content knowledge for student learning and major theories of human development and learning; teaching for student learning and stages and patterns of cognitive and cultural development
Related INTASC Standards: Knowledge of Human Development and Learning; Instructional Planning Skills
Related material in this book: Chapter 11, Curriculum and Instruction: What Are Some Models of Nondirect Instruction?

8. **The best answer is (b).** Ms. Jackson can best find out what students know and want to know by designing her own instrument.
Related Praxis and Other State Test Topics: Organizing content knowledge for student learning and structuring lessons based on the knowledge, experiences, skills, strategies, and interests of the students in relation to the curriculum.
Related INTASC Standards: Assessment of Student Learning
Related material in this book: Chapter 10, Standards, Assessment, and Accountability in Education Today: Assessing and Reporting Student Achievement

References

Educational Testing Service (2002). *Tests at a Glance: Praxis II Subject Assessments/Principles of Learning and Teaching.* Available online: www.ets.org/praxis/prxtest.html

Kent, T.W., Larsen, V.A., & Becker, F.J. (1998). *Educational Border Culture in New Mexico.* Boston: Allyn & Bacon.

Fourth Edition

Teaching in America

George S. Morrison
University of North Texas

Boston   New York   San Francisco
Mexico City   Montreal   Toronto   London   Madrid   Munich   Paris
Hong Kong   Singapore   Tokyo   Cape Town   Sydney

Executive Editor and Publisher: Stephen D. Dragin
Senior Development Editor: Virginia L. Blanford
Series Editorial Assistant: Meaghan Minnick
Marketing Manager: Tara Kelly
Senior Production Editor: Karen Mason
Editorial Production Service: Trinity Publishers Services
Composition Buyer: Linda Cox
Manufacturing Buyer: Andrew Turso
Electronic Composition: Omegatype Typography, Inc.
Interior Design: Glenna Collett
Photo Researcher: PoYee Oster
Cover Administrator: Linda Knowles
Cover Designer: Studio Nine

For related titles and support materials, visit our online catalog at www.ablongman.com.

Between the time Web site information is gathered and then published, it is not unusual for some sites to have closed. Also, the transcription of URLs can result in typographical errors. The publisher would appreciate notification where these errors occur so that they may be corrected in subsequent editions.

Library of Congress Cataloging-in-Publication Data

Morrison, George, S.
    Teaching in America / George S. Morrison.—4th ed.
        p. cm
    Includes bibliographical references and index.
    ISBN 0-205-45374-0 (pbk.)
    1. Teaching—United States. 2. Teaching—Social aspects—United States.
    3. Teaching—Vocational guidance—United States. 4. Community and school—United States.
    5. Education—United States. 6. Education—Philosophy. I. Title
    LB1025.3.M67 2006
    371.102—dc22
                                                                                    2004061773

Printed in the United States of America

10   9   8   7   6   5   4   3   2   VHP   09   08   07   06   05

Photo credits are on p. 530, which constitutes a continuation of the copyright page.

Brief Contents

Contents

Part THREE   Foundations of Education   223

Part FOUR   Teaching and Learning   367

Preface

*T*eaching is an active process: teachers *think* about what they do, *research about* and *reflect on* their practice, *make decisions*, and *strive to improve* their performance in order to help their students learn. *Teaching in America,* Fourth Edition, embraces this evolving process of professional practice and provides prospective teachers with the professional tools necessary to be high-quality teachers. *Teaching in America* is an *active learning text*—readable, practical, and of course based on current ideas about teaching, but also laced with opportunities for you to *participate* in your own learning. On almost every page, you will find possibilities for reflecting on and writing about what you are learning and applying the content of the book to the real world of schools and classrooms. This revision was guided by advice from teacher educators, experienced teachers, novice teachers, and my own background as a public school teacher and administrator, a professor of education, and a researcher and writer.

Teaching in America is a core text for courses in Introduction to Teaching, Introduction to Education, and Foundations of Education taught within teacher education programs. This text explores the knowledge, attitudes, behaviors, and skills of effective teachers; it also provides a comprehensive background for the foundations of education, with clear and realistic links to actual classrooms and your role as a teacher. Features—Profiles, Education on the Move, You Decide, What Does This Mean for You?—all bring the content of this book into the real world. You will hear real voices of real teachers, explore real programs, and be called on to think about real issues. What I hope this book will do for you is help you make the transition from *thinking* about becoming a teacher to *understanding* what your decision means—so that you can enter the profession of teaching as an active, confident participant. By building a firm foundation—of self-knowledge, knowledge of education as an institution and a career, knowledge of teaching competencies, and knowledge of issues in education—you will grow in your professional development as a teacher.

*W*HAT THIS BOOK IS ABOUT

Teaching in America, Fourth Edition, is built on the ideas of active and interactive learning based on personal reflection. It provides a wealth of opportunities for decision making, collaboration, and creative problem solving. It also asks you to draw on your own prior knowledge—what you have learned about the process of education in your years as a student—and to integrate that knowledge with what you learn from these pages and from the course you are taking. *Teaching in America* is designed as a "working text"—one in which readers reflect and respond on the pages and apply information and ideas in authentic contexts. This working-text format enables you to construct knowledge and ideas about teaching so that you think, plan, and decide as a professional. You'll find several themes occurring frequently in this text:

- Meeting professional standards. Virtually all of you will need to pass some kind of certification examination to become a teacher. More and more, you also will be asked to meet additional standards once you have become a teacher, as you move through your career. Correlation charts at the beginning of each part and marginal icons throughout this text show you specific material that aligns to two important sets of standards for teachers and teacher education—INTASC and NCATE. An eight-page insert at the front of the text, "Preparing for Certification or Licensure: A Guide," provides guidelines for preparing for your initial certification. In addition, you will find a wealth of information in appropriate chapters about the focus on standards and accountability.

- **Understanding classroom realities.**   The United States is a nation of *diversity*, and you will find this reflected in your classroom. Students from a variety of cultures, speaking a variety of languages, and with a variety of abilities will populate your classroom. In addition to a separate chapter on diversity, Profiles and Education on the Move features throughout reflect the diversity of American education. But other realities will also impact your classroom. More and more, parents and communities are involved in educational decision making; education is becoming a *family-centered, community-based* process. You will need to understand and work within that process. Finally, the reality of today's classroom is *accountability.* You will find yourself held accountable for your students' success and for your own progress. This book provides the tools to help you understand the impact of accountability.

- **Making decisions as a teacher.**   Decision making is at the heart of teaching; every minute of every day, you will make decisions large and small. Every chapter of this book models the professional, ethical, practical, and reality-based decision-making processes that are a critical part of the teaching profession. In addition, much of the first part is devoted to exploring the knowledge base that you will need to make decisions effectively, and a new You Decide feature highlights some current issues.

- **Understanding and using technology.**   More and more, technology is central to teaching just as it is to our lives in general. Technology means both the technologies of teaching and learning and the technologies of course management and assessment. In addition to a separate chapter on technology, teaching, and learning, Web icons identify references to useful Web sites in the text, and every chapter includes a resource list of Web Sites Worth Visiting.

*F*EATURES THAT HELP YOU LEARN

Teaching in America provides you with a sound basis for understanding the field of education and what is required to be a teacher today. A number of guideposts support your learning throughout the text.

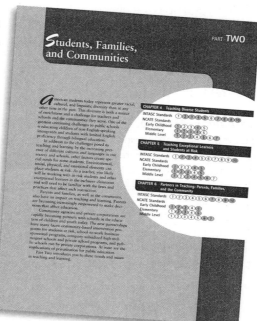

Each of the four parts of the text begins with a brief **part introduction** that explains the content of the chapters that follow, and a **correlation chart** that shows you which chapters align with the important standards of INTASC and NCATE.

A **vignette** written by a classroom teacher, administrator, scholar, or parent emphasizes how the content of that chapter impacts the education process.

Themes of the Times boxes direct you to more information on the text's Companion Web Site.

At the beginning of each chapter, **focus points** highlight the content of the chapter.

Reflect & Write activities appear frequently, both in the text and following every illustration, to encourage you to think about what you are learning and to write a response that applies your own knowledge or explores the issues raised.

Section Summaries, including activities called Thinking Critically, Applying What You've Learned, and Putting Yourself in the Picture, allow you to review information frequently within chapters and check your understanding.

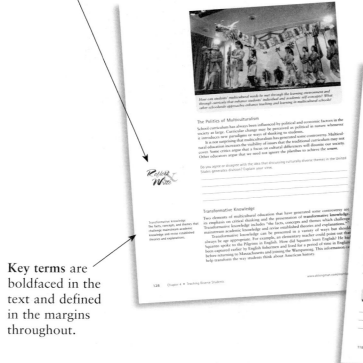

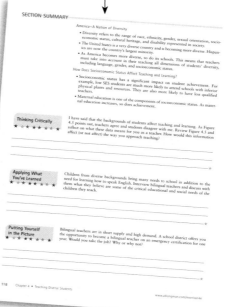

Key terms are boldfaced in the text and defined in the margins throughout.

Profiles are typically of two kinds: first-person accounts from real teachers and educators, and explorations of innovative programs.

Education on the Move boxes highlight current developments in education, such as merit pay for teachers, new grade configurations for schools, and "branding" public school facilities with corporate names.

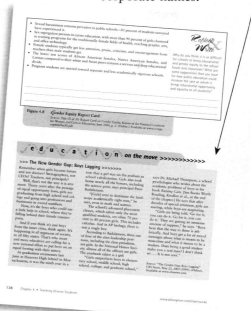

NEW to this edition: You Decide boxes provide overviews of current educational controversies, point you to Web sites with additional information, and ask you to decide what you think.

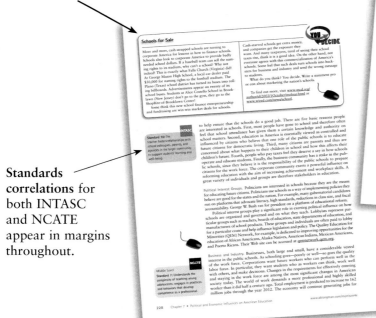

Standards correlations for both INTASC and NCATE appear in margins throughout.

NEW to this edition: What Does This Mean for You? boxes explain how the information in the text about educational philosophy, finance, policy, and so on will impact your life and responsibilities as a teacher.

At the end of every chapter, **Applications for Active Learning** extend the content of the chapter by providing authentic opportunities for you to integrate and apply your knowledge in preparation for teaching. Each chapter concludes with a variety of activities:

> **Connections, Field Experiences, and Personal Research** activities encourage you to make connections between what you are learning from this book and this course and your personal knowledge, knowledge that you acquire through observations and interviews, and knowledge that you acquire through career-related resources.

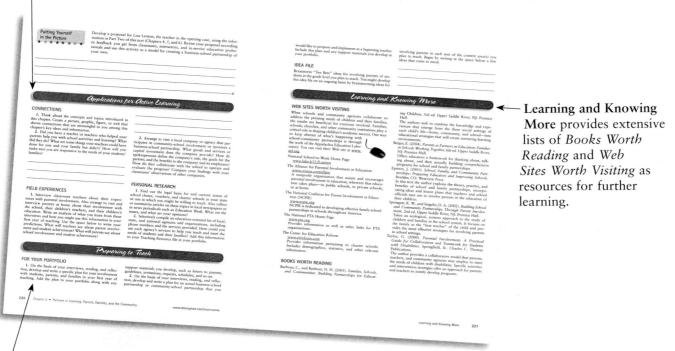

Learning and Knowing More provides extensive lists of *Books Worth Reading* and *Web Sites Worth Visiting* as resources for further learning.

Preparing to Teach activities encourage you to accumulate information and resources to help you find your first job and to teach during your first year. *For Your Portfolio* helps you create a portfolio to document your learning for course assessment, job seeking, and continuing professional development, while *Idea File* allows you to develop and record specific teaching strategies and problem-solving approaches.

✐EW TO THIS EDITION

- **NEW! "Preparing for Certification or Licensure: A Guide"** insert provides useful strategies for studying for the certification exams now routinely required in most states for prospective teachers.
- **NEW! Two new features—You Decide and What Does This Mean for You?—** expand *Teaching in America*'s focus on providing *practical* tools that help you understand the *realities* of teaching.

REVISED! Every chapter in this text has been meticulously updated to make sure that all information is the most current available. Chapter 1 has been entirely rewritten to provide a clear, concise introduction to the book and to the profession of teaching. In particular, the chapters on teaching in diverse classrooms (Chapter 4), students with special needs (Chapter 5), parent and community involvement (Chapter 6), curriculum and instruction (Chapter 11), and technology (Chapter 12) have been extensively revised.

EXPANDED! The emphasis on standards and accountability has also been enhanced, with new material in almost every chapter, particularly on the federal No Child Left Behind law and its impact on schools and teachers. In addition to the correlation charts and marginal icons that appeared in the last edition, the eight-page insert, **"Preparing for Certification or Licensure: A Guide,"** will help any prospective teacher get ready for the national or state certification examination that is required of almost all prospective teachers.

The pedagogical emphasis of the text continues to be on providing practical information and making clear links to actual classroom teaching. These links are supported by the Profiles and Education on the Move features—almost all of which are new in this edition—as well as by the two new features: You Decide and What Does This Mean for You?

SUPPLEMENTS

A wide range of supplementary resources accompany this text, including:

- **For instructors:** A comprehensive Instructor's Manual with Test Bank, a Computerized Test Bank, and the Allyn and Bacon Transparency Package for Foundations of Education and Introduction to Teaching. Also available is Allyn and Bacon's Video Workshop, a total teaching-and-learning system containing almost an hour of video footage, as well as a Student Learning Guide and Instructor's Teaching Guide.
- **For students:** A Companion Web Site (www.ablongman.com/morrison4e), with interactive bonus content and chapter review questions.

ACKNOWLEDGMENTS

Writing a textbook is not a solitary endeavor. Good writing, like all good things in life, involves the cooperation, collaboration, and support of many people. I am blessed to have the care, concern, and help of individuals who want to make *Teaching in America* a book that makes a difference in the lives of teachers. Steve Dragin, executive editor and publisher, has been a key player in always devising ways to make *Teaching in America* better. I always appreciate how Steve watches over and shepherds every facet of writing, design, and production.

Ginny Blanford, senior development editor, is my kind of editor. Ginny has wonderful ideas, is very easy to work with, and knows how to move a project along. With Ginny, there are no problems—only solutions! Thanks, Ginny, for all you did for me.

I am very fortunate to have a group of dedicated and helpful research assistants. Jaime Thomson, Whitney Dwyer, Matthew Bailey, and Matthew MacCarthy are experts at finding information, making figures, and organizing data.

I am also particularly grateful to reviewers, whose suggestions were invaluable in making this edition better than ever. They include Deborah E. Bembry (Albany State University), Margaret M. Denny (Louisiana State University), Barbara C. Jentleson (Duke University), Eileen Mahoney (Hudson Valley Community College), and James W. Stockard, Jr. (Louisiana State University). I am particularly grateful to Michael

Hardman (University of Utah Graduate School of Education) for his close reading of and comments on Chapter 5.

In the course of my research, lecturing, and consulting, I meet and talk with many professionals all across America who are deeply dedicated to doing their best for all students. I am always touched, heartened, and inspired by their openness, honesty, and unselfish sharing of ideas, programs, and practices. I thank all these colleagues who contributed to the many features of this text. Because of them, *Teaching in America* is reality-based and cutting-edge.

Dedication

Finally—but by no means last—for Betty Jane, who provides me with the loving support necessary for all of life's activities.

Coverage of Interstate New Teacher Assessment and Support Consortium (INTASC) Standards for Beginning Teacher Licensing and Development

INTASC Standards

1. The teacher understands the central concepts, tools of inquiry, and structures of the subject being taught and can create learning experiences that make these aspects of subject matter meaningful for students.	Chapters 1, 3, 8, 9, 11
2. The teacher understands how children learn and develop, and can provide learning opportunities that support their intellectual, social, and personal development.	Chapters 4, 5, 8, 9, 10, 11, 13
3. The teacher understands how students differ in their approaches to learning and creates instructional opportunities that are adapted to diverse learners.	Chapters 1, 2, 3, 4, 5, 8, 9, 10, 11, 12
4. The teacher uses various instructional strategies to encourage students' development of critical thinking, problem solving, and performance skills.	Chapters 4, 5, 9, 11
5. The teacher uses an understanding of individual and group motivation and behavior to create a learning environment that encourages positive social interaction, active engagement in learning, and self-motivation.	Chapters 1, 3, 4, 8, 9, 11
6. The teacher uses knowledge of effective verbal, nonverbal, and media communication techniques to foster active inquiry, collaboration, and supportive interaction in the classroom.	Chapters 3, 12
7. The teacher plans instruction based upon knowledge of subject matter, students, the community, and curriculum goals.	Chapters, 1, 3, 4, 6, 10, 11, 12, 13
8. The teacher understands and uses formal and informal assessment strategies to evaluate and ensure the continuous intellectual, social, and physical development of the learner.	Chapters 1, 4, 9, 10
9. The teacher is a reflective practitioner who continually evaluates the effects of his/her choices and actions on others (students, parents, and other professionals in the learning community) and who actively seeks out opportunities to grow professionally.	Chapters 1, 2, 3, 4, 6, 7, 8, 9, 10, 12, 13
10. The teacher fosters relationships with school colleagues, parents, and agencies in the larger community to support students' learning and well-being.	Chapters 1, 2, 3, 4, 5, 6, 7, 12, 13

Coverage of National Council for the Accreditation of Teacher Education (NCATE) Standards

Early Childhood Education Standards

1. Promoting child development and learning.	Chapters 1, 3, 4, 5, 6, 9, 10
2. Building family and community relationships.	Chapters 1, 6, 7, 13
3. Observing, documenting, and assessing to support young children and families.	Chapters 6, 10, 13
4. Teaching and learning (4a: Connecting with children and families; 4b: Using developmentally effective approaches; 4c: Understanding content knowledge in early education; 4d: Building meaningful curriculum).	Chapters 3, 4, 5, 8, 9, 10, 11, 12
5. Becoming a professional.	Chapters 1, 2, 5, 6, 7, 8, 9, 10, 13

Elementary Education Standards (1999, revised 2003)

1. Development, learning and motivation.	Chapters 1, 2, 3, 4, 5, 12, 13
2. Curriculum	
2.1 English language arts.	Chapter 11
2.2 Science.	Chapter 11
2.3 Mathematics.	Chapter 11
2.4 Social studies.	Chapter 11
2.5 The arts.	Chapter 11
2.6 Health education.	Chapter 11
2.7 Physical education.	Chapter 11
2.8 Connections across the curriculum.	Chapters 1, 3, 4, 5, 6, 10, 11
3. Instruction	
3.1 Integrating and applying knowledge for instruction.	Chapters 1, 3, 11, 12, 13
3.2 Adaptation to diverse students.	Chapters 4, 5
3.3 Development of critical thinking, problem solving, and performance skills.	Chapters 4, 5, 11, 12
3.4 Active engagement in learning.	Chapters 4, 5, 11, 12
3.5 Communication to foster collaboration.	Chapters 4, 5, 11, 12
4. Assessment for instruction.	Chapters 3, 4, 5, 10
5. Professionalism	
5.1 Practices and behaviors of developing career teachers.	Chapters 2, 3, 8, 9, 13
5.2 Reflection and evaluation.	Chapters 2, 3, 6, 7, 13
5.3. Collaboration with families.	Chapters 2, 3, 6, 13
5.4. Collaboration with colleagues and the community.	Chapters 2, 3, 6, 13

Middle Level Education Standards

1. Young adolescents' development.	Chapters 3, 4, 5, 8, 9, 11, 12, 13
2. Middle level philosophy and school organization.	Chapters 1, 2, 3, 4, 12
3. Middle level curriculum and assessment.	Chapters 3, 4, 5, 9, 10, 11, 12
4. Middle level teaching fields.	Chapters 3, 5, 10, 11, 12
5. Middle level instruction and assessment.	Chapters 1, 4, 5, 8, 9, 10, 11, 12, 13
6. Family and community involvement.	Chapters 1, 2, 5, 6, 7, 8, 12
7. Middle level professional roles.	Chapters 1, 2, 4, 6, 7, 8, 9, 13

About the Author

*G*eorge S. Morrison is professor of education and holds the Velma E. Schmidt Endowed Chair in Early Childhood Education at the University of North Texas. Dr. Morrison's accomplishments include a Distinguished Academic Service Award from the Pennsylvania Department of Education, an Outstanding Alumni Award from the University of Pittsburgh School of Education, and Outstanding Service and Teaching Awards from Florida International University.

Dr. Morrison is the author of many books on early childhood education, child development, curriculum, and teacher education. As a public school teacher, Professor Morrison taught grades 3–12. At the university level, Professor Morrison has developed and implemented programs for improving urban teaching and learning, alternative models for teacher certification, and staff development with an emphasis on early literacy. Dr. Morrison's professional interests include the application of research to early childhood programs, teacher education, and international education.

George S. Morrison is shown here with 2004 National Teacher of the Year Kathy Mellor at the Annual Velma E. Schmidt Conference on Early Childhood Education at the University of North Texas.

PART ONE

Teachers and Schools

$\mathcal{B}$ecoming and being an effective teacher—a good teacher—is a complex business. The demand for teachers has never been greater. At the same time, teachers are being held to higher levels of accountability than ever before. Teachers are at the forefront of implementing educational reforms, new curricula, and new teaching methods, often at the same time that they are fighting for professional status and pay. And they are doing all this in schools and classrooms that reflect the character, strengths, problems, and expectations of their communities—urban, suburban, rural. Because of their intimate link with society, schools and classrooms reflect broad social issues and social changes.

Part One looks at the choice you are making to become a teacher and provides a context for that choice. We'll look first at what teachers need to know and what they do: the knowledge base good teachers must have, the ways in which teachers put that knowledge base to work in the classroom, and how teachers are held accountable. We'll also explore the profession of teaching—the opportunities and challenges, the realities—and the ways in which educational reform is reflected in today's schools. Finally, we will examine the role of schools in the larger society—how they are organized, and how they are changing.

Will you be one of the teachers who shape public education in the decades to come? Part One will help you explore the world of teaching so that you can answer this question confidently and positively.

CHAPTER 1

*W*hat It Means to Be a Teacher

"Teaching is a way of life."

Betsy Rogers was 2003 U.S. Teacher of the Year.

Teaching is a way of life in my family. For years, I've heard about how my grandmother started teaching in the Alabama hills when she was sixteen, with students older than she was. She and her two sisters all had to quit teaching public school when they married—regulations of the time prohibited teachers from being married—but they continued to teach in Sunday school. My mother joined their ranks, teaching seven- and eight-year-old children in Sunday school for over fifty years. As a child, I attended many a lesson planning meeting, and the commitment of these women to provide inspiring lessons in a caring environment greatly influenced the standards I have set for myself as a teacher.

When I returned to public school teaching myself after an eight-year hiatus to raise my sons and teach in private kindergarten, I was unprepared for the situations faced by the children in my first-grade class. The poverty, neglect, and abuse that they experienced every day overwhelmed me. I wanted to change the world for them—and it took me several years to realize that I could only change a small part of it. From my family, I had learned the value of caring for others: I had watched my parents and grandparents serve their community and church by teaching, visiting the sick, gathering clothes and food for those in need, celebrating births, and grieving deaths. Now I realized that this need to serve, this ability to care, could become my greatest contribution to the children I teach.

For many of the children I teach, school is the best part of their world. I committed myself to making my classroom a haven of safety and an environment full of joy. I also made a commitment to build positive relationships with their families. I realized that many of these families loved their children deeply and were doing the very best they could.

My classroom is learner centered, with an environment of security and positive reinforcement. I believe with William Glasser that teachers need to create warm, supportive climates in their classrooms, and with Nel Noddings that "We should want more from our educational efforts than adequate achievement, and we will not achieve even meager success unless our children believe that they are cared for and learn to care for others." My class is unofficially known as "the nurturing class" in our school; my students are often handpicked, based on their need for extra stability and nurturing. My goal is to make lasting memories for these children. I try to make daily lessons memorable by incorporating art, music, cooking, and literature. For more than a decade, my mother served as our "classroom grannie," coming to class every week with special snacks and sitting in her rocking chair, reading to the children. Her visits were a great highlight; she brought with her the influence of a caring older person that was often lacking in their lives.

Asked to create a school for the workers of Emil Mott's Waldorf-Astoria cigarette factory, Rudolf Steiner tried to build what he called a "third parent" through the cultivation of a long-term teacher-student relationship. I've tried to create this same thing for my students by building strong triangular relationships among students, parents, and myself. I believe strongly that getting to know my students' families is vital: it gives me insight into their backgrounds and the influences in their lives. I send home monthly newsletters and weekly parenting tips, and I provide a parenting backpack with books and brochures. I schedule two conferences each year with all parents (although this is not required in my school) and open my home to students and their families for annual cookouts and swimming parties. As often as possible, I attend students' baptisms, ball games, birthday parties, and graduations. I visit in student homes at times of celebration and sadness. I correspond with many students and their families who have moved away, and when I'm aware of a need, I try to find community or church resources to fill it.

I believe that teachers make a difference—that students' lives can be changed by a classroom that fosters growth and stability. I think the song "Wind Beneath My Wings" must have been written about teachers—I strive to be the wind beneath my students' wings.

How Will This Chapter Help You?

You will learn

★ what makes a good teacher

★ what teachers do

★ why teachers teach

★ how teaching is changing

★ more about your roles as a beginning teacher

*W*HAT MAKES A GOOD TEACHER?

Betsy Rogers's family kindled in her the desire and passion she needed to become a great teacher. But how did Betsy achieve her dream? How will you achieve yours? And how will you know when you have become a good teacher? How is "good teaching" measured?

Most educators agree that good teaching is based on four things: bringing an appropriate core of knowledge into the classroom with you (and being willing to expand that knowledge throughout your career); promoting student achievement through use of your proficiencies and skills (teacher effectiveness); believing in yourself as a teacher and as a person who matters (teacher efficacy); and being accountable for what you achieve (teacher accountability).

Knowledge Base

To become a good teacher, you will need to acquire basic knowledge in a number of areas, and perhaps even more important, you will need to be open to learning more throughout your career. Good teachers are good learners: they reflect on what they do and learn from it; they continue to look for answers as long as they teach.

What is the **knowledge base** that you will need to begin teaching? To be an effective teacher for the students in your classroom, you will need to know

- What to teach. You need to be competent in the subject areas you will be teaching—English, science, math, social studies, or any other subject area in which you intend to teach. Many teacher education programs believe that knowledge of the arts and sciences is essential for all teachers, including prekindergarten and primary-grade teachers. For example, in my program at the University of North Texas, undergraduate teacher education students are not education majors but rather take fifty-nine hours in the university's core curriculum, fifty hours in interdisciplinary studies, and only twenty-four hours of education classes, including student teaching.
- How to teach. Teachers must be skilled in teaching a variety of students from differing cultural and socioeconomic backgrounds, as well as in motivating students and guiding their behavior, managing and organizing classrooms, and using educational technology. Chapter 11 explores the issues of what and how to teach.
- About students. How do students learn? How do children develop? What role do gender, ethnicity, culture, and socioeconomics play in the process of instruction? Today's students represent a more diverse range of backgrounds, languages, and abilities than ever before in this country's history. Good teachers understand all this—and care about individual students within their own classrooms. Chapters 4 and 5 will focus on students.
- About state and local standards. In every school district in every state, standards—statements of what students should know and do—are driving discussions about what and how to teach. You will need to know the standards in the state and district in which you plan to teach. Chapter 10 looks more closely at standards and their impact on individual classrooms.
- About working collaboratively—with parents, families, colleagues, administrators, and community members. Good teachers recognize that parents and other family members play a powerful role in students' learning. Good teachers also understand the need for collaboration within their own school settings. Chapter 6 focuses on these various partnerships.

Your effectiveness as a teacher will also rest on a wider range of knowledge about the context in which you teach—both the professional world of teaching, and the

Standard 1: The teacher understands the central concepts, tools of inquiry, and structures of the subject being taught and can create learning experiences that make these aspects of subject matter meaningful for students.

Knowledge base
The knowledge needed in the process of effective teaching.

Elementary
Standard 2.1–2.8: Understands and uses fundamental concepts and modes of inquiry of all appropriate content disciplines.

Early Childhood
Standard 1: Uses understanding of young children's characteristics, needs, and interacting influences on children's development and learning to create healthy, respectful, supportive, and challenging environments for all children.

INTASC
Standard 10: The teacher fosters relationships with school colleagues, parents, and agencies in the larger community to support students' learning and well-being.

Every day you must ask yourself, "Am I being an effective teacher?" What are some characteristics that all teachers should demonstrate? How do you plan to demonstrate your teaching effectiveness?

foundations of public education in the United States. You will be a better teacher if you know:

- About the profession of teaching. Participating in professional organizations and activities will provide you with a wealth of resources and support beyond what is available to you in your school or district. Professional standards and ethical practices will help shape your professional career. And thinking of yourself as a professional will increase your own confidence in dealing with colleagues, families, and the wider community.
- About the foundations of education. Why learn about the history, philosophy, politics, economics, and legal background of public education in the United States? Why understand the sociocultural role of schools in American society? All of these areas have a direct impact on the classroom in which you teach. Chapter 3 and Chapters 7 through 9 will help explain why.

Finally, becoming a teacher means becoming a lifelong learner. How can you accomplish this? Here are two ways:

- Becoming a reflective practitioner. Self-knowledge and self-assessment are hallmarks of reflective practice. Good teachers are constantly evaluating their own behavior and finding better ways of doing things. Think about your teaching, test new ideas and evaluate the results—and you will improve your teaching practice.
- Becoming a teacher/researcher. Teacher/researchers are active, inquiring producers of knowledge and information who contribute to their own learning and their students' learning by examining how students learn (or don't learn), how to connect curriculum to students' lives and interests, and how to make more and better connections with parents and families. An almost unlimited wealth of research is available. Explore what's already there—or create your own research project to answer a question for yourself.

NCATE

Middle Level

Standard 7: Understands the complexity of teaching young adolescents; engages in practices and behaviors that develop competence as a professional.

INTASC

Standard 9: The teacher is a reflective practitioner who continually evaluates the effects of his/her choices and actions on others.

This list of what you need to know may look daunting, but this is what teacher preparation programs are designed to help you learn. Teachers are evaluated on their proficiencies in these areas as well as on their effectiveness with learners. Many states have adopted standards for preparation and certification as guides to preservice preparation, professional development, and teacher appraisal. These standards for teacher preparation provide you with specific information about what you will be expected to know and be able to do. You will want to be familiar with the standards for your state and the state in which you plan to teach. Figures 1.1 and 1.2 identify the teacher preparation standards for Texas and Kentucky.

Effective Teachers

One measure of good teaching is **teacher effectiveness.** Effective teachers use their proficiencies to promote student achievement in the following ways[1]:

- Communicating positive teacher expectations. Effective teachers have high expectations for learners and believe that all students are capable of learning—and they successfully communicate those expectations to all students. If students do not learn something the first time, effective teachers teach it again or find another way to teach it; if the regular curriculum materials do not do the job, effective teachers find or make other materials.
- Providing students with opportunities to learn. Effective teachers allocate most of their available time to academic instruction rather than to goals in the affective domain. Their students spend more time on academic tasks than do students of teachers less focused on instructional goals. Such teachers provide a mix of academic tasks designed to allow students to comprehend key ideas and connect and apply those ideas, not simply memorize.
- Providing classroom leadership and organization. Effective teachers organize their classrooms as supportive learning environments and use individual and group management approaches that maximize the time students spend on learning tasks. These teachers maintain pleasant, friendly classrooms and are perceived as

INTASC

Standard 2: The teacher understands how children learn and develop, and can provide learning opportunities that support their intellectual, social and personal development.

Teacher effectiveness
How well teachers are able to promote learning in their students.

NCATE

Elementary

Standard 1: Knows, understands, and uses the major concepts, principles, theories, and research related to development of children to construct learning opportunities that support individual students' development, acquisition of knowledge, and motivation.

Standard I.	The teacher designs instruction appropriate for all students that reflects an understanding of relevant content and is based on continuous appropriate assessment.
Standard II.	The teacher creates a classroom environment of respect and rapport that fosters a positive climate for learning, equity, and excellence.
Standard III.	The teacher promotes student learning by providing responsive instruction that makes use of effective communication techniques, instructional strategies that actively engage students in the learning process, and timely, high-quality feedback.
Standard IV.	The teacher fulfills professional roles and responsibilities and adheres to legal and ethical requirements of the profession.

Reflect & Write

State after state is restructuring its requirements for teacher preparation and certification programs. What are the common core requirements for Texas? Why do you think some states emphasize standards that others do not?

_____

_____

_____

Figure 1.1 *Pedagogy and Professional Responsibilities (ECE–12) Standards in Texas*

Source: State Board for Educator Certification, *Pedagogy and Professional Responsibilities (EC-12) Standards, 2002.* (Online). Available at http://sbec.state.tx.us/SBECOnline/standtest/edstandcertfieldlevl.asp and http://sbec.state.tx.us/SBECOnline/standtest/standards/8-12/pdf.

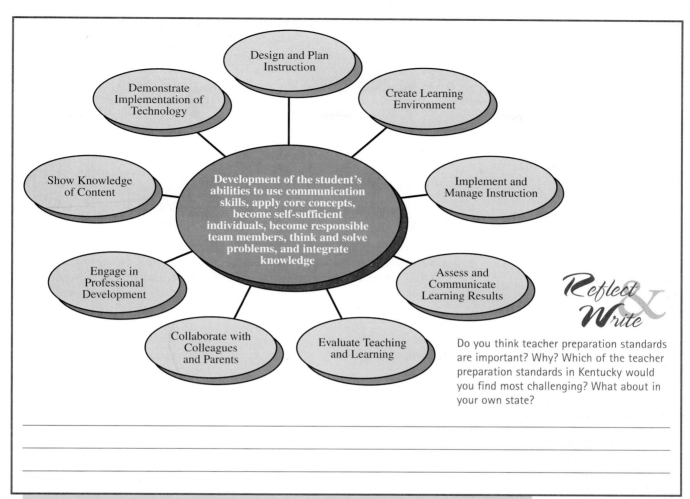

Do you think teacher preparation standards are important? Why? Which of the teacher preparation standards in Kentucky would you find most challenging? What about in your own state?

Figure 1.2 𝒩ew Teacher Standards for Preparation and Certification in Kentucky

Source: Kentucky Department of Education, *New Teacher Standards for Preparation and Certification* (1999). (Online). Available at www.kyepsb.net/standards/new_teach_stds.html.

enthusiastic, supportive instructors. Research suggests that effective teachers tend to show charisma, compassion, a sense of fairness, and a sense of humor.[2]

- Pacing curriculum and instruction for individual learners. Effective teachers move through a curriculum rapidly but in small steps that minimize student frustration and allow continuous progress. They adapt curriculum and pace instruction to meet individual student needs, learning levels, and learning styles. They understand the need for **developmentally appropriate instruction** (see Figure 1.3).

- Teaching actively. Effective teachers demonstrate skills, explain concepts and assignments, conduct participatory activities, and review when necessary. They actively teach rather than expecting students to learn merely by interacting with curriculum materials. Active teachers emphasize concepts and understanding in addition to skills and facts.

- Providing student-centered teaching. Effective teachers focus on student needs and interests, engage students in projects and problem-solving activities, and provide cooperative learning opportunities for students to work with other students.

- Teaching for mastery. Effective teachers provide opportunities for students to practice and apply new content. They monitor each student's progress and provide feedback and remedial or accelerated instruction as needed to make sure that all students achieve mastery and receive enrichment as appropriate.

INTASC

Standard 3: The teacher understands how students differ in their approaches to learning and creates instructional opportunities that are adapted to diverse learners.

Developmentally appropriate instruction
Instruction that is age and individual appropriate for each student in a program. Involves matching teaching practices and curriculum content to the developmental stages of children and adolescents.

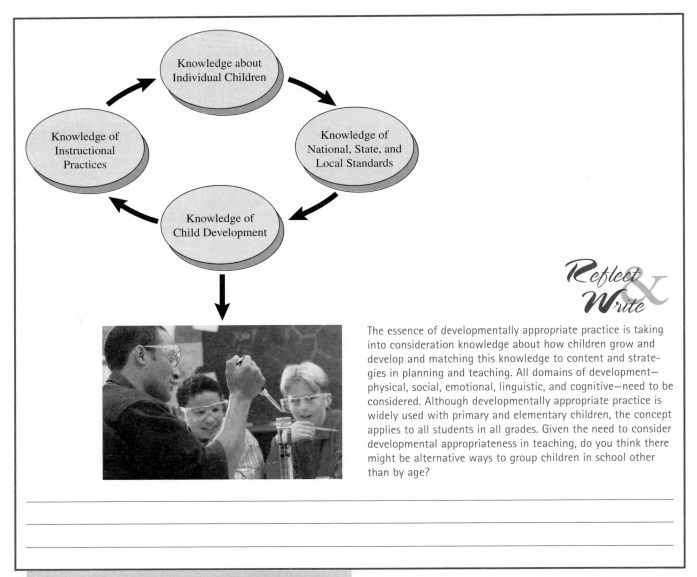

The essence of developmentally appropriate practice is taking into consideration knowledge about how children grow and develop and matching this knowledge to content and strategies in planning and teaching. All domains of development—physical, social, emotional, linguistic, and cognitive—need to be considered. Although developmentally appropriate practice is widely used with primary and elementary children, the concept applies to all students in all grades. Given the need to consider developmental appropriateness in teaching, do you think there might be alternative ways to group children in school other than by age?

Figure 1.3   *D*evelopmentally **Appropriate Practice**

NCATE

Early Childhood

Standard 1: Uses understanding of young children's characteristics, needs, and interacting influences on children's development and learning to create healthy, respectful, supportive, and challenging environments for all children.

Teacher efficacy
Teachers' beliefs about their ability to teach effectively and about the ability of their students to learn.

Special education
A teaching specialty for meeting the needs of exceptional learners.

For one teacher's thoughts about what makes a good teacher, see the Profile on the next page.

Teacher Efficacy

A teacher's belief that he or she can reach and help even difficult students to learn is called **teacher efficacy.** Teachers who believe in themselves and their abilities as teachers—and who believe that their students can learn—generally have students who achieve well. Research shows that teachers who have a high sense of efficacy are "more confident and at ease within their classrooms, more positive (praising, smiling) and less negative (criticizing, punishing) in interactions with their students, more successful in managing their classrooms as efficient learning environments, less defensive, more accepting of student disagreement and challenges, and more effective in stimulating achievement gains."[3] Furthermore, research suggests that teachers with a strong belief in their own effectiveness are more committed to teaching[4] and more likely to use effective motivational strategies with exceptional students. One recent study indicates that general and **special education** teachers with a high sense of per-

Beverly San Agustin, a Guam Teacher of the Year, teaches tenth- through twelfth-grade social studies at Simon Sanchez High School.

This list of what makes a good teacher is based on my experiences and my interactions with many great teachers, but also on input from my students, who have continuously reaffirmed my own sense of good teaching. A good teacher is . . .

- *passionate*—good teachers are always committed to teaching. Their passion is conveyed in every moment in the classroom.
- *resourceful and innovative*—good teachers constantly improve their teaching strategies by taking classes and workshops and seeking new information. They dare to be risk-takers, always willing to try out new ideas.
- *encouraging and optimistic*—good teachers accept challenges as opportunities to make a difference. They exude confidence that things will get better, not worse.
- *flexible*—good teachers improvise in the best interest of their students. They find "teachable moments" in every crisis.
- *entertaining*—the best teachers are hams—willing to make lessons relevant and interesting through drama, comedy, or force of personality.

- *humorous*—good teachers create a classroom conducive to learning, break up the pace to prevent boredom, and are able to defuse stressful or difficult situations through good humor.
- *compassionate*—good teachers nurture all their students with empathy and understanding.
- *a leader*—good teachers support positive ideas, seek creative new strategies, and challenge students to try something different. Good teachers also take active leadership roles in school committees and use the opportunities presented to them to participate in school governance.
- *a mentor*—good teachers promote collaboration, share their own knowledge, and support effective practices among colleagues.

Good teachers do what they do because they love what they do and cannot imagine doing anything else; they are committed to making a difference in the lives of their students. Every teacher begins with that commitment and some of the qualities listed above. The best teachers continue to learn, improve, and acquire more of these qualities throughout their careers.

sonal and teaching efficacy are more likely to agree with general class placement of an exceptional student.[5]

Teacher efficacy stems from teachers' beliefs and attitudes, but it is also influenced by the conditions of the community, school, and classroom. Factors that contribute positively to teachers' sense of efficacy include:

- Moderate and reasonable role demands
- Adequate salaries
- High status
- Recognition for efforts
- Opportunities to interact with other professionals
- Validation from others that what you are doing is right
- Empowerment to make decisions
- The perception that the work you are doing is meaningful
- Good morale within your school and among fellow faculty

Collective Teacher Efficacy. When teachers as a group share the perception that the efforts of the faculty as a whole will have a positive effect on students, the result is **collective teacher efficacy**—a shared sense of efficacy. According to researchers, collective efficacy develops when teachers engage in two key tasks: analysis of the teaching task and assessment of teaching competence.

- Analyzing the task. Faculties that see themselves as effective educators analyze—at both the individual and the school levels—what will be required as they engage in the act of teaching. This analysis provides information about the challenges of teaching in that school—including the abilities and motivations of the students, the availability of instructional materials, the presence of community resources and restraints, and the appropriateness of the school's physical facilities—and what it would take for teachers in that school to be successful.
- Assessing teaching competence. Teachers make explicit judgments about the teaching competence of their colleagues in light of the analysis of the teaching task in

NCATE

Middle Level

Standard 2: Understands the major concepts, principles, theories, and research underlying the philosophical foundations of developmentally responsible middle-level programs and schools; works successfully within these organizational components.

Collective teacher efficacy A group's shared belief in its conjoint capabilities to organize and execute courses of action required to produce given levels of attainment.

INTASC

Standard 9: The teacher is a reflective practitioner who continually evaluates the effects of his/her choices and actions on others (students, parents, and other professionals in the learning community) and who actively seeks out opportunities to grow professionally.

Teachers with high efficacy believe they can teach all students and that all students, regardless of disability, will learn at high levels. High-efficacy teachers use specific instructional processes when teaching students with disabilities, including planning instruction that is based, in part, on state and local standards; explicitly teaching what students are to learn; providing feedback to students about their progress; and individualizing instruction, using methods appropriate for each student.

their specific school. They assess teaching skills, methods, training, and expertise, and they develop strategies for mentoring and correcting perceived weaknesses.

High collective teacher efficacy results, according to research, in the acceptance of challenging goals, strong organizational efforts, and a persistence that leads to better student learning performance.[6]

Teacher Accountability

Elementary

Standard 5.1: Understands and applies practices and behaviors that are characteristic of developing career teachers.

Teachers who bring with them an appropriate knowledge base, who are able to integrate that knowledge into an effective teaching style, and who believe in their own ability to teach and in their students' ability to learn will generally be successful teachers. But how is success as a teacher measured?

One way of defining a "good" teacher is from the *process-product perspective*—that is, a teacher is perceived as effective if students receive high scores on standardized measures of achievement. More and more, teachers are being held to this particular standard of **teacher accountability.** The accountability movement, which began in the late 1970s and continues today, is based on the idea that teachers (and other school personnel) are always accountable to the public—to parents in particular as well as to public agencies such as boards of education, state departments of education, and the federal government.

Teacher accountability
Teachers' responsibility to parents, boards of education, and the general public for student learning.

Performance-Based Teaching. Part of the education reform movement of the last twenty years has focused on performance-based education, meaning that teachers are responsible for ensuring that children learn. The teacher's role has shifted from being responsible only for input—teaching students—to being responsible for output—what students have learned and are able to do. **Performance-based teaching** constitutes a dramatic change in both teacher role and teacher responsibility. It has also dramatically changed how teachers are educated.

Performance-based teaching
Teachers' responsibility to students to ensure that they learn.

Also embedded in the accountability movement is the linking of performance to monetary reward: student achievement can lead to higher pay for teachers (see Education on the Move); for schools, overall student performance attracts more money to operate programs. Tying student achievement to monetary incentives is controversial. For example, teachers who choose (or are assigned) to work with students who perform below grade level will not have the same opportunity for enhanced pay as teachers who work with students who perform above grade level and have a history of outstanding achievement. Similarly, schools in higher socioeconomic districts will typically show higher performance results than schools in districts with fewer resources and less parent involvement.

Over the next decade, more school districts will implement performace-based teacher pay plans similar to the one proposed in Denver in the Education on the Move. Not all teachers agree they are a good idea. Some question the standards by which teachers would be evaluated. Would you welcome the opportunity to teach in a district with a performace-based pay plan? What do you think are some of the pros and cons?

_____

_____

_____

_____

Assessment and Accountability. Recently local, state, and national testing has emerged as a way to help ensure student learning and to promote accountability. Some educators argue that the emphasis on standardized testing has encouraged many teachers to "teach to the test" to boost student achievement—a move that results in a narrow curriculum focus. Achievement is measured only by what is on the test, cheating students of the benefits of a full curriculum. The use of achievement test scores to measure and reward teacher effectiveness poses many challenges and ethical questions for teachers and schools both.

Schools are clearly accountable to state departments of education and federal agencies from which they receive funding. Schools and teachers both are accountable to the students they teach and the parents of those students. But finding an appropriate way to measure success—to hold teachers and students accountable—is very difficult. Despite controversies, the accountability movement continues to exert strong influence on educational practice. The demand for teacher accountability and performance-based teaching will no doubt continue to influence how you and your colleagues teach.

INTASC

Standard 8: The teacher understands and uses formal and informal assessment strategies to evaluate and ensure the continuous intellectual, social and physical development of the learner.

education *on the move* >>>>>>>>>>>>>

>>> Pay Plan Gets a Gold Star >>>>>>>

"The eyes of educators and education policymakers across the nation are on Denver," a jubilant school Superintendent Jerry Wartgow said. "Teachers of Denver, by this vote, you have just opened the doors of opportunity for your fellow teachers."

Teacher salaries have been based almost exclusively on years of experience. A new pay plan would reward teachers who document student growth, sharpen their skills, and agree to work in challenging schools. Denver's new pay plan is called the

Professional Compensation System for Teachers, or ProComp.

Denver teachers said yes to putting the proposal before voters in November 2005. If voters agree, the plan takes off in January 2006. Teachers hired after that date would automatically be enrolled in the new plan. Current teachers would have seven years to opt into the plan, or they could stick with the existing salary system until they retire.

"This is one of the biggest steps we've taken in education in a long

time," said Donald W. Ingwerson, who has talked with educators from California to Washington, D.C., about the pay plan. "Most of all, it is really signaling that our students must learn and that those teachers who are able to help students learn can receive a professional salary."

Source: Created by author from selected information from "Pay Plan Gets a Gold Star," N. Mitchell, *Rocky Mountain News,* March 20, 2004. (Online). Available at www.teacher-leaders.org/TLNEWS/TLN032604.html

Accountability for student achievement can create ethical challenges for teachers. What are some of these challenges? How would you respond to them? Why do you think accountability tied to achievement is so popular with the public?

_____

_____

_____

_____

What Is a Highly Qualified Teacher?

INTASC

Standard 9: The teacher is a reflective practitioner who continually evaluates the effects of his/her choices and actions on others (students, parents, and other professionals in the learning community) and who actively seeks out opportunities to grow professionally.

The answer to this question is provided in part by the No Child Left Behind (NCLB) Act of 2001, a piece of federal legislation that promises almost $3 billion to states through formula grants to prepare, train, and recruit high-quality teachers. NCLB funds can be used in a variety of ways to assist states in preparing teachers, including reforming teacher certification, providing training, developing alternative routes to licensure, developing recruitment and retention strategies, providing high-quality professional development, and supporting activities that improve instructional practices. The NCLB Act is a reauthorization of the Elementary and Secondary Education Act (ESEA) passed by the U.S. Congress in 1965, and it requires that all kindergarten through twelfth-grade students must be taught by "highly qualified teachers" by 2006. (Some rural districts, which historically have had difficulty recruiting teachers, have been given an additional year to comply with this requirement.)

Provisions of NCLB represent the largest and most comprehensive federal investment in preparing, training, and recruiting teachers and administrators in the history of U.S. public education. The act has three goals: (1) to increase student academic achievement through the use of instructional strategies and materials that are proven successful through scientific research; (2) to increase the number of highly qualified teachers and principals (see Figure 1.4 for the act's definition of "highly qualified"); and (3) to hold educational agencies and schools accountable for improvements in teacher quality and student achievement. (We will discuss NCLB in greater detail in Chapter 7.)

NCATE

Elementary

Standard 5.1: Understands and applies practices and behaviors that are characteristic of developing career teachers.

While all teachers must meet the new provisions of the NCLB by 2006, the law leaves to the states to define what a "good" teacher is. Consequently, each state's definition may be unique. And since licensure requirements based on these definitions vary from state to state, what constitutes a "highly qualified" teacher does, too. In twenty-three states, teachers do not need a college degree in the subject that they teach.

A highly qualified teacher
1. Holds at least a bachelor degree
2. Has obtained full state certification or licensure
3. Has demonstrated subject area competence in each of the academic subjects in which the teacher teaches

Look at the criteria that define a "highly qualified teacher," according to the federal government in the No Child Left Behind Act of 2001. Do you think these criteria are sufficient to make a beginning teacher highly qualified? What would you add to this list, if anything?

_____

_____

_____

Figure 1.4 _No_ Child Left Behind: Defining a Highly Qualified Teacher

Source: U.S. Department of Education, Highly Qualified Teachers and Paraprofessionals, Student Achievement and School Accountability Conference, October 2002. *Title I: Defining a Highly Qualified Teacher* (2002). (Online). Available at www.ed.gov/admins/tchrqual/learn/hqt/edlite-slide008.html.

SECTION SUMMARY

What Makes a Good Teacher?

- **Knowledge Base.** To become a good teacher, you will not only need to learn what and how to teach, but you will also need to learn about students, educational settings, the profession of teaching, and the foundations of education. Good teachers are also lifelong learners who work collaboratively with parents, school administrators, and the community; they reflect on their own teaching practices; they are good decision makers and problem solvers; and they engage in research activities.

- **Effective Teachers.** Effective teachers accept responsibility for teaching, allocate most of their time to instruction, organize their classrooms for effective instruction, move through the curriculum quickly but with an understanding of individual student needs, actively instruct, maintain a pleasant learning environment that is student centered, and provide opportunities for practice and feedback on performance.

- **Teacher Efficacy.** Teachers' beliefs about their ability to teach and their students' ability to learn affect the outcomes of teaching. Teachers who believe that they can teach well and that their students can learn generally have high-achieving students. Role demands, salaries, status, recognition, morale, and other conditions in the community, the school, and the classroom all influence teacher efficacy. Collective teacher efficacy is a group's shared beliefs about its capabilities to provide success and is closely linked to student achievement and teaching outcomes.

- **Teacher Accountability.** The teacher accountability movement holds that teachers are responsible for their students' achievements or lack of them. Representing a major shift in the evaluation of teaching, education reform has focused recently on performance-based teaching, which requires teachers to be responsible for output—student learning, as measured by standardized testing—rather than input—the teaching itself. Teacher performance may be linked to monetary incentives. Using test scores to measure and reward teacher effectiveness poses ethical challenges and may motivate teachers to "teach the test."

- **Highly Qualified Teachers.** The No Child Left Behind (NCLB) Act of 2001 requires that all students, prekindergarten through twelfth grade, be taught by "highly qualified teachers" by no later than 2006. NCLB specifies that highly qualified teachers have a bachelor's degree, hold state certification, and have demonstrated subject area competence in the academic areas in which they teach. The NCLB promises funding, most of which has not yet been released, to assist in teacher preparation in a variety of areas.

INTASC

Standard 9: The teacher is a reflective practitioner who continually evaluates the effects of his/her choices and actions on others (students, parents, and other professionals in the learning community) and who actively seeks out opportunities to grow professionally.

NCATE

Early Childhood

Standard 5: Uses ethical guidelines and other professional standards; is a continuous, collaborative learner who demonstrates knowledgeable, reflective, and critical perspectives; is an informed advocate for sound educational practices.

Elementary

Standard 5.1: Understands and applies practices and behaviors that are characteristic of developing career teachers.

Middle Level

Standard 7: Understands the complexity of teaching young adolescents; engages in practices and behaviors that develop competence as a professional.

Thinking Critically

★ ★ ★ ★ ★ ★ ★ ★ ★

Effective teachers

- have high expectations for students
- spend the majority of their time on instruction
- organize their classrooms to support learning
- adapt curriculum and teach to meet individual needs
- are actively engaged in the instructional process
- ensure that students understand, connect, and apply what they learn

What are some things you might do to ensure that these teaching behaviors are part of your own capabilities as a teacher?

Think about the best teacher you had in elementary school and the best teacher you had in middle or high school. What qualities made them good teachers? Did teaching these two different grade levels require similar or different strengths? Identify the characteristics of your good teachers at their particular level.

_____

_____

_____

_____ ★

Putting Yourself in the Picture

You teach at a large suburban high school where students consistently score well on state tests and attend prestigious colleges. You have been offered a challenging job setting up a college-bound program at the inner-city school you attended, and you believe you're the right person to institute some exciting challenges. But there's a catch. In your area, teacher salaries are tied to student scores on state-mandated achievement tests. Because the school offering the job has a history of lower scores on these tests, you and your family will have to take a 10 percent pay cut if you accept the offer. Will you stay in your present job, which bores you, or take the pay cut and teach students who really need you?

_____

_____

_____

_____ ★

*W*HAT DO TEACHERS DO?

INTASC

Standard 9: The teacher is a reflective practitioner who continually evaluates the effects of his/her choices and actions on others (students, parents, and other professionals in the learning community) and who actively seeks out opportunities to grow professionally.

If you asked most teachers what they do, they would tell you that they wear many hats and that their jobs are never done. Teachers are decision makers, planners, creators, organizers, actors, managers, collaborators, evaluators, reporters, community partners, professional learners, and sometimes parent substitutes—and they are teachers. This may sound overwhelming, but remember: you will have a lot of help and support on your journey to becoming a good teacher. The program that prepares you, your instructors, your participating classroom teachers, and this textbook are all designed to help you learn how to meet the many responsibilities of becoming a teacher.

Teachers Are Decision Makers

Decision making may be the single most important function of teachers. Every day is made up of a myriad of decisions—large ones (what to teach, how to teach it) and small ones (which child to call on, what to display on the walls). Making these decisions becomes almost second nature to experienced teachers; first-time teachers will rely on the kind of knowledge base discussed in the first section of this chapter. You will make daily decisions based on your knowledge of the following:

- Basic subjects and core academic content
- Effective teaching methodologies that meet the needs of all learners, including exceptional children
- Child growth and development

- How to assess learning
- Curriculum planning and design
- Effective methods for integrating technology into classrooms
- National, state, and local standards for what students should know and be able to do
- Professional standards, practices, and ethics
- Culturally appropriate curriculum, including bilingual and gender-fair instruction, and how to accommodate children's culture into teaching
- How to create classroom environments and use management strategies that support learning
- The historical, legal, and philosophical foundations of education

The more experienced you become, the more these various pieces of knowledge will integrate into a coherent whole. But before you begin, your competencies in most of these areas will be measured in some way—through the PRAXIS exam, which is required for the certification of teachers in thirty-four states, or through a variety of state-based certification tests. In Texas, for example, you would need to pass the Examination for the Certification of Educators in Texas (ExCET) before being certified to teach. A sample question from that exam, which emphasizes your ability to apply what you have learned, is shown in Figure 1.5.

NCATE

Elementary

Standard 3.1: Plans and implements instruction based on knowledge of students, learning theory, subject matter, curricular goals, and community.

INTASC

Standard 7: The teacher plans instruction based upon knowledge of subject matter, students, the community, and curriculum goals.

Teachers Are Planners

Research points clearly to the importance of planning for student achievement; effective teachers are able to bring about intended learning outcomes.[7] For effective teachers, the planning process is an ongoing one; it involves thinking and making

Students in a middle school class are learning about the westward movement of pioneers in the United States during the nineteenth century. The teacher plans to have students read several selections on this topic and then prepare reports. The teacher is concerned about how meaningful the assignment will be for Alicia, a student whose family moved to the United States from Venezuela a year ago. Alicia's speaking and oral reading skills in English are strong, but she sometimes has comprehension difficulties. The teacher believes that these difficulties often reflect lack of familiarity with the topic of the selection. Which of the following strategies most likely would be effective in helping Alicia complete the assignment successfully and make it a meaningful learning experience for her?

a. Urging Alicia to take detailed notes as she reads to reinforce her understanding of the historical context depicted in the text.
b. Providing Alicia with opportunities to talk about how her own experience of moving to the United States compares with the pioneers' experiences described in the assigned readings.
c. Drawing Alicia's attention to facts and concepts that feature prominently in more than one of the assigned selections to help her recognize which ideas are most important.
d. Encouraging Alicia to write her first draft of the assigned report in Spanish and then translate it into English.

Reflect & Write

Applying knowledge and skills to teaching is a complex process requiring hard work, high levels of education, and an ongoing dedication to improvement. Do you think that test items like this one provide a good evaluation of how effective a teacher might be? Can you think of other ways in which states might maintain high standards for educators?

Figure 1.5 **ExCET Sample Question: Applying Knowledge and Skills to Teaching**

Source: Texas State Board for Educator Certification, *Texas Examinations of Educator Standards Preparation Manual: 110 Pedagogy and Professional Responsibilities, 4–8* (2002), p. 37. (Online). Available at www.excet.nesinc.com/prepmanuals/PDFs/TExES_fld117_prepmanual.pdf.

<table>
<tr><td>

BEFORE TEACHING

What will I teach (content)?
- What do I want my students to learn?
- What is the purpose of what I'm going to do?
- What are the student outcomes?
- How do I integrate content areas?
- How do I make the content multicultural and gender and socioeconomically appropriate?
- What are the needs of my students?

How will I teach?
- What approach/model/style works best with my students (e.g., cooperative learning, Socratic seminar, lecture)?
- How will I group my students?

What resources will I need?
- How much time do I allocate?
- How much space will I need?
- What concrete materials will I need?

What background knowledge do my students have?
- What background knowledge do my students bring to the learning situation?

</td><td>

DURING TEACHING

Have I used the students' prior knowledge to gain their interest and give them a focus?

Am I presenting the lesson well?

Am I constantly evaluating my students?
- Am I providing feedback to my students?
- Am I asking my students open-ended and analytical questions?
- Are my students actively engaged?

Am I responding to the immediate needs of my students?

Am I introducing new concepts and information?

Am I motivating and challenging my students to pursue their own learning and investigation of the topic/subject/theme?

Am I providing my students with the tools to work on their own (e.g., knowing how to find information on their own)?

Am I reviewing and debriefing with my students?

Am I summarizing information for my students?

</td></tr>
</table>

Reflect & Write

Planning for successful teaching involves many dimensions. Consider the process outlined here. Which part of this process do you think is most important? Which is most often ignored?

Figure 1.6 *Pathways to Successful Teaching and Learning*

decisions before, during, and after providing instruction. Figure 1.6 illustrates a teacher's thought process during these three phases of instruction. Reflect on these processes as you develop lesson plans and unit plans, set instructional goals, and create learning objectives and outcomes for your students.

Teachers Build Positive Learning Environments

Teachers spend a huge amount of time in classrooms and schools and, as a consequence, invest a lot of themselves in developing **learning environments** where teaching and learning can become meaningful and rewarding. Today there is a great deal of emphasis on the enriched learning environment, and one indicator of an enriched environment is the quality of the **classroom climate**, or classroom atmosphere. Classroom climate is defined by a number of factors:

- Daily routines and practices
- Approach to classroom management
- Strategies for assessment of students' progress

Learning environments
Environments or settings in which students learn—such as schools, classrooms, community agencies, and homes.

Classroom climate
Includes routines and practices, classroom management approach, assessment of student progress, quantity and quality of instruction, and student-teacher interactions.

- Quantity and quality of instruction
- Number and kind of student-teacher interactions

The classroom atmosphere is also affected by the extent to which teachers and students share common interests and values and have common goals. For example, in classrooms where both teachers and students believe that learning is important and that everyone is capable of learning and where everyone is valued, the classroom atmosphere will promote learning, achievement, and social cohesion.

A positive learning environment also takes into consideration the variety of student learning styles, including both cognitive and cultural styles. For example, many classrooms are highly organized and designed to promote individual achievement. Some children may come from cultures, however, where cooperative involvement is valued; a teacher who doesn't understand this will find progress slow and frustration levels high. In building effective learning environments, teachers consider a number of factors: physical, organizational, sociological, political, economic, and cultural (see Figure 1.7).

Let's look briefly at some of these dimensions. (We will return to these in more depth in later chapters.)

Physical Components. In many ways, classrooms and schools are homes away from homes. They are also places, of course, that must facilitate learning. All teachers must pay attention to the physical components of their workplaces—that is, whether the workplace is safe, comfortable, well-maintained, and well-equipped. Safety is a top concern for all schools today, given the horrific events of the past few years, including the shootings at Columbine High School in Colorado and the terrorist attacks of 9/11. We will take a close-up look at school safety in Chapter 3.

Organizational Structures. Teachers are constantly assessing and making decisions about how school and classroom activities are organized, teaching loads, schedules, and what is included in the curriculum. Educators generally agree that the amount

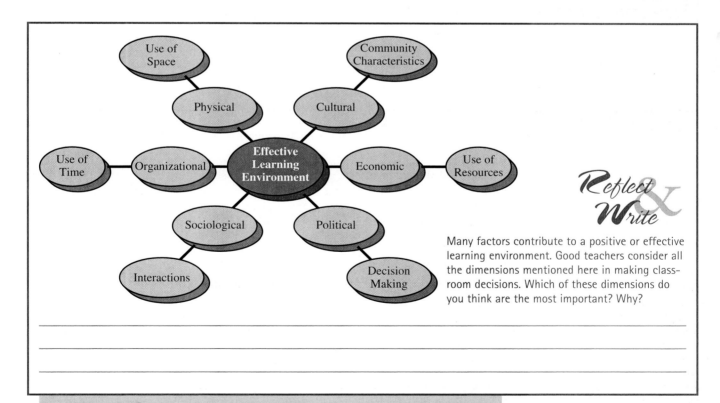

Reflect & Write

Many factors contribute to a positive or effective learning environment. Good teachers consider all the dimensions mentioned here in making classroom decisions. Which of these dimensions do you think are the most important? Why?

Figure 1.7   Dimensions of Effective Teaching and Learning Environments

of time spent on learning tasks has a direct influence on how well students learn, so a major decision you will make as a beginning teacher is how you and your students use time. Teachers who create a positive classroom atmosphere for learning generally try to devote as much time as possible to what is known as *academic learning time*. Making good use of classroom time creates an atmosphere in which learning and student achievement are important and valued. We will explore the importance of classroom organization and management in Chapters 11 and 13.

Sociological Factors. In many ways, teaching is about interpersonal and intrapersonal relationships. Part of building a positive learning environment consists of understanding how you as a teacher relate to and interact with your students, your colleagues, other school staff and administrators, parents and families—and how students relate to one another. You will want to stress the importance of harmony and cooperation in the classroom, and you will want to understand how to arrange your classroom and instructional processes to encourage positive interactions. You will also want to evaluate how your own relationships with others influence learning, especially in terms of your students' perception of the teaching-learning process. We will examine instructional processes based in sociology in Chapter 11.

Political Factors. Schooling is a political process—that is, what happens in schools and classrooms is affected by legislative and administrative processes at national, state, and local levels. Much of what goes on in schools results from political decisions about how schools are governed and operated; the same applies to individual classrooms. In this sense, power and politics are an important aspect of the classroom learning environment. Power frequently becomes an issue in teachers' relationships with students. Positive learning environments are those in which teachers share power with students and try to find a balance between teacher-centered and student-centered learning and decision making. Part of building a positive environment depends on including students in the political process of the classroom; by the same token, teachers who are included in political decisions—such as hiring new faculty, collaborating on curriculum reform, choosing textbooks, and so on—tend to view their own work environments more positively. The role of schools in society is discussed in depth in Chapter 3, and the politics and governance of public education in Chapter 7.

Economic Factors. Funding for schools, classrooms, teachers, and students affects the learning environment in a number of ways, including the nature and content of the curriculum, the quality of the physical plant, the teacher-to-pupil ratio, the number of federally subsidized lunches served daily, teachers' salaries, and the number and quality of curricular and extracurricular programs. Teachers help decide how schools spend their money by working with parent and community groups to advocate for adequate school funding and to raise money for school and classroom projects. Chapter 7 focuses on examples of how political and social factors influence schooling.

Cultural Factors. The learning environment is shaped by the culture of the school and of the surrounding local community. Teachers need to be aware of their school's history and the community's cultural heritages and lifestyles. This knowledge can be used to develop meaningful learning activities and make learning appropriate and relevant for all students; it can also lead to effective collaborative programs with students and families. You also need to consider your own interactions with others in relation to culture, gender, and socioeconomic background—that is, how you as a teacher can provide culturally appropriate instruction and curriculum materials for your students.

Building a positive and effective learning environment and collaborating with colleagues, parents, administrators, students, and others to achieve this goal is a critical part of being a teacher. Such efforts will encourage productive home and school relationships, enhance opportunities for personal growth, and make teaching a rewarding experience for you.

In today's schools, cultural factors are an ever-growing consideration in the learning environment. Explain what you as a teacher will do to use your school's cultural factors to enhance the overall learning environment.

Metaphors for Teaching

Whatever is included in your teacher knowledge base, you will develop a way of thinking about yourself, your students, and what you are doing in your classroom. When you express these thoughts, the words you use will reveal your personal metaphors for teaching.

Every day we use metaphors to describe and compare things and people. The metaphors teachers use to describe themselves and their classrooms reflect their thinking and influence the way they teach. A teacher who sees her classroom as a "workplace," for example, and herself as a "manager" might see students as workers and emphasize on-task behavior and a smoothly functioning, well-managed classroom. On the other hand, a teacher who sees his classroom as a "learning environment" and himself as a "guide" might emphasize cooperative learning and design his classroom as an active learning community.

As a teacher, you will be in a constant process of constructing, changing, and reconstructing your personal metaphors of teaching. It is important that you articulate these metaphors in order to analyze how they influence aspects of your teaching. For example, one preservice teacher described how adopting a different metaphor for classroom management changed the way she did things:

> When I began student teaching, my metaphor for classroom management was a river. Now I believe that management is like [being] a gardener. . . . [The teacher] needs to be able to . . . provide a nurturing, healthy, and learning environment. . . . [Teachers] also need to guide or direct, but you need to specially do things for each child and with each need. You have to be careful not to crush or damage the child (like a flower). You need to tend to each child and be alert to all needs.[8]

During student teaching, this teacher might have used expressions like "going with the flow," "stemming the tide," or "diverting trouble" rather than the metaphor of

INTASC

Standard 9: The teacher is a reflective practitioner who continually evaluates the effects of his/her choices and actions on others (students, parents, and other professionals in the learning community) and who actively seeks out opportunities to grow professionally.

NCATE

Early Childhood

Standard 1: Uses understanding of young children's characteristics, needs, and interacting influences on children's development and learning to create healthy, respectful, supportive, and challenging environments for all children.

Elementary

Standard 5.1: Understands and applies practices and behaviors that are characteristic of developing career teachers.

tending each flower that she uses now. The point is that experience and reflection help teachers change how they view teaching and students and themselves as teachers.

Often teachers think of instruction as a product to be delivered. They deliver a lesson on reading, a module on physics, a unit on social studies, or a problem set in math. This "delivery" metaphor is especially common when educators talk about technology; teachers "deliver" instruction on the Internet or via closed circuit television. The metaphor of teaching as product delivery implies efficiency and views teachers as deliverers and students as recipients.

"Community of learners" is another metaphor often mentioned by those who embrace a constructivist approach to teaching and learning. When teachers see their classrooms as learning communities, they typically see students and teachers as collaborators, working together to support one another's learning and develop solutions to real-world problems.

The ways that teachers see themselves are many and varied—and almost always have implications for what happens in the classroom. As you read the following metaphors that may be used to describe teachers, reflect on the implications they might have for your teaching, your learning, and student learning.

- Teacher as student. Teachers are lifelong learners who grow in their ability to teach as they think actively about their teaching and try out new strategies. Teachers who see themselves as students are open to change and to expanding their own knowledge through their students.
- Teacher as facilitator. Teachers are professionals who set the stage, organize the environment, and make it possible for students to learn. Facilitators view students as active learners who are responsible for their own learning and often capable of learning on their own.
- Teacher as sage. Sages are repositories of knowledge, wisdom, and expertise. Like a tribal elder or a Zen master, the sage challenges learners and models the importance of learning how to think.
- Teacher as coach. Coaches exhort and encourage students to perform to the limits of their individual capabilities, to train for future performance, and to contribute to the team. Coaches also model behaviors and demonstrate skills.
- Teacher as leader. Leaders—ship captains, generals, CEOs, presidents—share a common core of behaviors that includes making decisions, delegating authority, and taking responsibility. Many good leaders share their leadership; similarly, teachers may share leadership with students and colleagues and encourage others to lead, too. Teachers who see themselves as leaders provide opportunities for their students to assume responsibility and often take leadership roles within the school community by participating in action research teams, study groups, and school discussion teams.
- Teacher as researcher. Increasingly, teachers see themselves as researchers; they use research to inform and guide their practice.

Reflect & Write

Pick three of the metaphors above. Do you see teachers in this way? What implications might that have for student learning?

_____

_____

_____

_____

As you read Diane Painter's story (see Profile), reflect on the importance and dimensions of the role teachers play as researchers.

 **Teachers as Researchers: Diane D. Painter**

Diane DeMott Painter, Ph.D., began teaching in 1984. A technology resource teacher in Fairfax County (Virginia), she codirects the Fairfax County Teacher Research Network and is an adjunct professor of education at George Mason University.

On a visit to my special education classroom in the late 1980s, an administrator asked if the computer one of my students was using helped her write. My answer was that something about using the computer somehow enabled her during the writing process, and she wrote better stories. But I realized I didn't know what that something was—and that bothered me.

Soon after that, I enrolled in a teacher-researcher seminar under the Northern Virginia Writing Project at George Mason University to learn how to conduct research in my own classroom. Since 1996, I've been an elementary school technology resource teacher and an active member of several teacher research teams in my district. My first investigation focused on using computers effectively in small writing groups. A National Council of Teachers of English (NCTE) grant supported another study about literacy skills used in research and in creating multimedia presentations.

Our district—Fairfax County, Virginia—began supporting teacher research teams in the late 1990s by forming the Fairfax County Teacher Research Network. Teachers trained in the research process are given small stipends to lead teams, and staff development funds provide release time for meetings, typically a half-day a month. Teams present their findings at faculty meetings at the end of each school year, and these reports often generate new questions for investigation the following year. Reports are also often published on Web sites that support this kind of research or presented at the annual Fairfax County Teacher Research Conference.

Teachers in this area are fortunate to have the resources of George Mason University supporting our work. The University's Web site (http://gse.gum.edu/research/tr/) helps teachers understand how teacher research differs from more traditional "top-down" research (that is, research initiated not by teachers but by universities or educational research organizations) and provides resources and guidelines for conducting site-based action research based on individual needs and curiousities. GMU's Initiatives in Educational Transformation (IET) posts sample action research project papers completed by students in its masters program.

Why bother with this additional work when you are already working hard as a teacher? I do it <u>because it helps me understand what's happening in my classroom and makes me a better teacher.</u> Our district understands that teacher research is far more than staff development; teacher-researchers ask questions based on their own teaching experience and find answers about the teaching and learning that is occurring in their own classrooms and schools. Here are two examples of the many projects in our district that have made a difference throughout our system. Second-grade teacher Michelle Greaver developed a carefully controlled and monitored study of the effect of using books-on-tape for home-based practice in the reading progress of non-native English speakers. The positive correlation that she found has inspired other teachers to incorporate at-home talking books as a central part of their reading programs. And Debbie Seidel, a kindergarten teacher, wanted to find out why her students were not attracted to the literacy center she had created. Her study explored the use of story props; she found that children's story retellings improve when they have the opportunity to use props. But for many of us actively involved in teacher research, the best result may not be from the studies themselves but rather from the opportunities to meet, talk, and share with other teachers in meaningful discourse that often leads to reforms in curriculum and instruction, planning and evaluation, and other staff development initiatives.

SECTION SUMMARY

What Do Teachers Do?

- **Teachers Are Decision Makers.** Every minute of every day, teachers make decisions. To make decisions responsibly, teachers are expected to possess essential knowledge and skills, including knowledge of subject matter, of how to teach appropriately for all students, of the development of children and youth, and of how to evaluate student progress. Together, these form the most important parts of a teacher's knowledge base.

- **Teachers Are Planners.** Teachers who effectively plan their students' learning think about goals, objectives, and outcomes and make decisions about them before, during, and after providing instruction. Through this process, teachers develop insight, knowledge, and skills, and they integrate what they learn into a theory of teaching and a system for applying theory to classroom practice.

- **Teachers Build Positive Learning Environments.** A positive learning environment is reflected in a classroom's climate or atmosphere. Some of the factors that enter into a positive learning environment are a safe physical environment, effective use of classroom time, harmonious and cooperative relationships among students and between students and teachers, a supportive political climate, creative use of economic resources, and respect for and interest in differences in cultural heritage and lifestyle.

- Metaphors for Teaching. Metaphors for teaching and for how teachers view themselves, students, and schools play powerful roles in education. Teacher roles are often described with such terms as student, facilitator, sage, coach, leader, and researcher. Teachers constantly change and reconstruct their personal metaphors.

Thinking Critically
★ ★ ★ ★ ★ ★ ★ ★ ★

If the principal in your school referred to teachers as chief executive officers (CEOs), what behaviors might you feel were expected of you? Are those behaviors consistent with your own metaphor for teaching? What does your own metaphor tell you about the kind of teacher you want to be?

_____

_____

_____

_____ ★

Applying What You've Learned
★ ★ ★ ★ ★ ★ ★ ★ ★

How is the teacher knowledge base defined in your state (or the state in which you plan to teach)? Use the Internet to research this question. How will you acquire the knowledge base required by your state?

_____

_____

_____

_____ ★

Putting Yourself in the Picture
★ ★ ★ ★ ★ ★ ★ ★ ★

You are considering applying for an entry-level teaching position in the middle school of an attractive seaside town that was recently linked to a nearby city by a new train line. To familiarize yourself with the system, you attend a public meeting on the upcoming school budget. At one point, parents and school committee members begin arguing about whether the town's school system is growing too rapidly and is changing from a homelike environment to an education factory. What conflicting characteristics and values are reflected in these two metaphors for this educational environment? What might be the "hidden" arguments of these two positions?

_____

_____

_____

_____ ★

Why DO TEACHERS TEACH?

On your path to becoming a teacher, you will undoubtedly be asked many times why you chose the field. Reflecting on that question will help you work out an honest and reasoned response—and enable you to understand your own motivations more clearly. Typically, people choose to teach because the profession offers a broad array of intrinsic and extrinsic rewards.

Intrinsic Rewards of Teaching

Intrinsic rewards are those based on feelings of personal satisfaction—feelings that stem from individual needs, beliefs, values, and goals—and vary greatly from person to person. Intrinsic rewards for teachers include a love of teaching and learning and of working with children and young people as well as feelings of satisfaction derived from helping others or participating in a public service. Such rewards are powerful motivators for choosing teaching.

Love of Learning. Some like the opportunity for continuous learning, and a teaching career provides this opportunity. Theresa Stapler is a *USA Today* All-USA Teacher; this is how she views teaching:

> As a veteran teacher with twenty-two years experience, I sometimes wonder who is learning more in my classroom, my students or me. There is never a day that passes that I don't learn something from my students. Sitting on my desk is a red apple. The students know that if they teach me a new word or fact, they get the red apple for the day. Sometimes my newfound knowledge may be something I may not want to know! However, most of the time, the students teach me something great. I always seek opportunities for continual growth through learning and will never consider myself to be educationally complacent. My love of learning is what inspires me to greet each new day with vigor.[9]

Love of Teaching. Perhaps when someone asks you why you chose teaching, you will respond, "Because I love to teach." Research shows that many teachers feel this way. Many say it is the love of teaching that keeps them in the profession. But what, really, do we mean by "love of teaching"? As the following comments reveal, for teachers involved in a Boston Public Schools study group, love of teaching means love of their students and of the subjects they teach:

> It seems old-fashioned to speak of teaching as love, yet teachers in the inquiry group often used this word to describe how they feel about their students and the subject matter that they teach. Stephen Gordon observed that preceding everything else in teaching is "a fundamental belief in the lives and minds of students." Love, then, is not simply a sentimental conferring of emotion. Rather, it is a combination of trust, confidence, and faith in students and a deep admiration for their strengths. These teachers demonstrate love through high expectations and rigorous demands on students and by keeping up with their subject matter through professional activities.[10]

Desire to Work with Young People. Wanting to work with children or youth is cited by an overwhelming majority of new teachers as the main reason they choose to teach (see Figure 1.8). Contributing to students' learning and facilitating their achievement and positive behavior are powerful motivating forces for—and one of the major benefits of—teaching. Being around children and youth, developing relationships with them while earning their respect, is a compelling reason to enter the classroom.

Desire to Help Others. Many people choose to teach because they see teaching as a life of service to others. As Sister Alice Hess, a ninth-through-twelfth-grade teacher, puts it, "I make eminently clear to them that [my] classroom

INTASC

Standard 9: The teacher is a reflective practitioner who continually evaluates the effects of his/her choices and actions on others (students, parents, and other professionals in the learning community) and who actively seeks out opportunities to grow professionally.

People choose to teach for a number of reasons. What intrinsic reward is this teacher getting from his job?

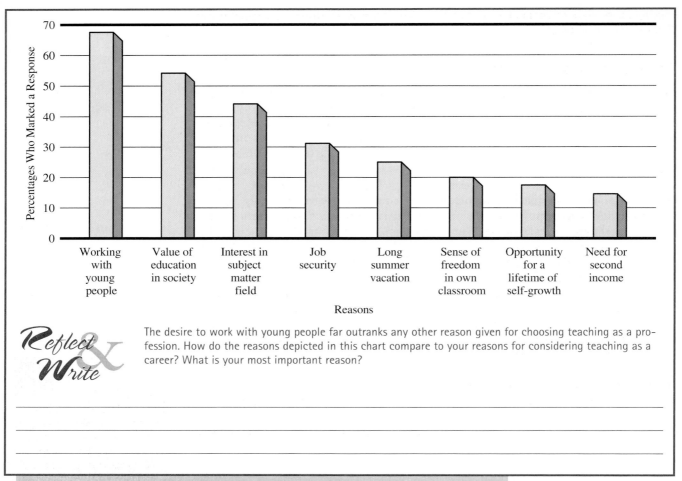

The desire to work with young people far outranks any other reason given for choosing teaching as a profession. How do the reasons depicted in this chart compare to your reasons for considering teaching as a career? What is your most important reason?

Figure 1.8   *W*hy Teachers Choose Teaching

Source: Figure created by author based on data drawn from National Education Association, "Status of the American Public School Teacher, 2000–2001" (2001), table 49. (Online). Available at www.nea.org/edstats/images/status.pdf.

is a room for champions, that I will be content with nothing but their best and that I am ready to go to great lengths to help them learn."

Desire to Provide Public and/or Professional Service. The motivation to make a difference in the world and the lives of others often stems from a commitment to service. The desire to serve and make society and the world a better place is a powerful influence in many people's lives.

The ideal that people should devote part of their lives to helping others has a strong tradition in American culture, and currently a national movement encourages high school students to spend some of their educational time in service activities. For high school students in Delaware, for example, community service is a requirement for graduation.

Teaching offers many lifetime opportunities and rewards to those who seriously dedicate themselves to it. When asked why, after twenty-one years, he was still so enthusiastic about teaching, Leo Ramirez, a math teacher at McAllen High School in Texas, answered without equivocation, "Because of the difference my students are making in the lives of others because of me!" Mr. Ramirez is influencing generations. What a reason to teach!

Extrinsic Rewards of Teaching

Extrinsic rewards include status and material benefits, which also lead to teacher satisfaction. Some cite a teacher's hours and more opportunities for time with their own families; others enjoy the respect the role brings. These external factors can make teaching attractive.

Lifestyle. Teaching appeals to many people as a way of life. The appealing qualities of a teacher's life include a work year of 180 to 210 days, with summers off and long vacations throughout the year, and the correspondence of a school day and year with children's schedules. Being "off" two or three months each year offers teachers opportunities to travel, take on other work, take graduate courses, devote time to their families, or renew themselves for the next school year. The school calendar benefits teachers who are also parents; they find that working in a profession whose hours correspond to their children's school year is ideal. As more and more schools implement new approaches to the school calendar—including year-round schooling and four-day weeks—teachers are beginning to experience shorter vacations spread over longer periods of time. Many teachers initially demonstrate negative feelings toward these changes, but studies show that the more experience they have with this kind of work calendar, the more they begin to prefer it to the traditional system.[11]

Community Respect. Status and respectability contribute to people's decisions to select teaching as a career. While public attitudes toward teachers vary widely, teaching typically brings comparatively high status and community respect. The public generally has high expectations of teachers and places trust in teachers to educate their children. In the eyes of the community, teachers are exemplars.

Security. Material advantages for teachers include a reasonable salary (much improved over the last twenty years in most areas) and benefits, steady employment, and opportunities for advancement. Salaries are rising, and the demand for qualified teachers is growing and will continue to do so. (See Chapter 2 for reasons.) Because most teaching positions are tenured, with guaranteed job security after a certain point except in extraordinary conditions, you could, if you wished, remain a teacher for your lifetime.

For many, teaching is an increasingly attractive career option, since many teachers believe that teaching provides better job security, vacation benefits, and personal satisfaction than other professions.

NCATE

Early Childhood
Standard 2: Understands and values complex characteristics of families and communities; creates respectful, reciprocal relationships that support and empower families; involves families in children's development and learning.

SECTION SUMMARY

Why Do Teachers Teach?

- Intrinsic Rewards. Many people choose to teach because of intrinsic rewards—internal feelings of joy or satisfaction they experience from doing something they love or want to do. For teachers, intrinsic rewards include the satisfactions of continuing to learn, sharing one's learning with others in a career one enjoys, working with children and young people, helping others, performing a public or professional service, and making a contribution to society and the future.

- Extrinsic rewards. Extrinsic rewards are those that are provided by other people for activities they admire and respect. For teachers, extrinsic rewards include the teaching lifestyle—and especially the school calendar—and community respect and professional security.

When did you decide you were interested in teaching as a career? What intrinsic rewards do you expect from this career? What extrinsic rewards?

_____

_____

_____

_____ ★

Everyone is motivated by different rewards. Visit a school in your district and ask several teachers, first, what expectations motivated them to become teachers, and second, whether those expectations were fulfilled. Are the rewards they actually experience from teaching different from the ones they anticipated receiving? How do the rewards they now value compare to your expectations for yourself?

_____

_____

_____

_____ ★

Extrinsic rewards—such as pay for performance, case bonuses based on student achievement, and other monetary rewards—are becoming more common. What is your opinion of such monetary rewards? How would you vote if a plan such as Denver's ProComp (in Education on the Move earlier in this chapter) was proposed in your district? Why?

_____

_____

_____

_____ ★

*H*OW IS TEACHING CHANGING?

Rapid change, a characteristic of American society in general, is also reflected in the teaching profession. The changing nature of teaching results from a variety of factors: new knowledge derived from educational research, changes in society, and state and national school reform efforts, including legislation. (As noted earlier in this chapter and to be explored in other chapters, the No Child Left Behind Act of 2001 is playing a major role in changing the discourse around contemporary educational practice.) All these factors impact one another: changes in society spur new efforts in educational research, which in turn propel reform movements; new legislation derives from perceived problems in the present system and begets yet more research. All of these factors impact the day-to-day lives of teachers and the way that public schools function in the United States. Being a teacher means living with change.

Patterns of Educational Reform

Throughout your teaching career, you will need to respond to change resulting from movements for reform within either the educational community or the political community, or both. Educational reform tends to be cyclical; that is, movements rise, fall, and often rise again in slightly different form twenty or thirty years later. A vocal chorus in the 1980s and early 1990s, for example, decried the traditional use of phonics and decoding and endorsed a **whole language,** or immersion, approach to teaching young children to read. By the mid 1990s, the backlash against whole language propelled phonics once again to the foreground, and the current approach to reading instruction calls for a balanced, or comprehensive, melding of several approaches. Similarly, advocates of **open education** in the later 1960s and 1970s attempted to make learning more student centered and "relevant" by establishing non-graded programs, classrooms without walls, learning stations, multi-age grouping, active learning, individualized instruction, and team teaching. Although some of these practices quickly fell out of favor (classrooms without walls turned out to be noisy and difficult to manage), many of the ideas introduced in this reform movement are now a standard part of the teaching repertory.

We talked earlier about metaphors for teaching. You might picture education reform movements as waves regularly rolling onto the sandy shores of the educational establishment with different effects, depending on the nature and content of the wave itself and the willingness of teachers, administrators, and others to accept what is being proposed. Some reform efforts, like small ripples, leave very little evidence of their existence. Others, like a tsunami, can change the landscape for years to come. Most major reform movements derive, at least initially, from social changes or from reports documenting perceived weaknesses in the current educational system. Figure 1.9 can help you visualize the major educational reform movements since the mid twentieth century.

Whole language
A "top-down" approach to teaching reading that relies on immersion of the child in language.

Open education
A movement toward combining multiage groups in classrooms without walls.

INTASC

Standard 9: The teacher is a reflective practitioner who continually evaluates the effects of his/her choices and actions on others (students, parents, and other professionals in the learning community) and who actively seeks out opportunities to grow professionally.

Reforms of the 1950s and 1960s: Education for Democracy and Educational Opportunity. The first wave of contemporary school reform movements derived from the launching of the first Russian manned spacecraft, *Sputnik,* in 1957. Public outcry over the Russians being first into space led to reform movements focused on improving learning and instruction in math and science; more emphasis on basic skills (reading, writing, and

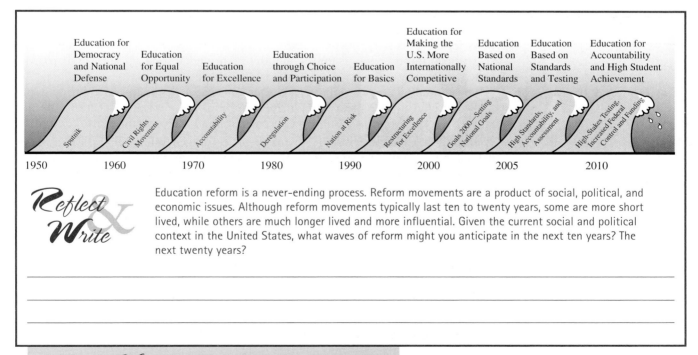

Reflect & Write

Education reform is a never-ending process. Reform movements are a product of social, political, and economic issues. Although reform movements typically last ten to twenty years, some are more short lived, while others are much longer lived and more influential. Given the current social and political context in the United States, what waves of reform might you anticipate in the next ten years? The next twenty years?

Figure 1.9   *Waves of Reform in Education, 1950 to 2010*

mathematics); the development of new curricula (including inquiry-based science); and beginning schooling at an earlier age.

A second wave of reform in the late 1950s and 1960s resulted from the Civil Rights movement and the crises of the Vietnam era and led to major new pieces of national legislation affecting education. The Economic Opportunity Act of 1964 created Head Start, which was designed to provide for the cognitive, social, and health needs of preschool disadvantaged children as a means of helping them succeed in school. The Elementary and Secondary Education Act of 1965 (ESEA) was designed to provide remedial assistance to disadvantaged students who achieved below-grade-level results in math and reading. Legislation with the goal of improving education for children with special needs was also passed. Much of this legislation continues to affect education today. ESEA was substantially amended by the Improving America's Schools Act of 1994 and the No Child Left Behind Act of 2001.

Reforms of the 1980s and 1990s: Accountability and Deregulation. During the tumultuous decades of the 1960s and 1970s, the new national legislation passed in the mid 1960s informed basic changes in American schooling. Then, in 1983, the U.S. Department of Education issued a report called *A Nation at Risk: The Imperatives for Educational Reform*. Highly critical of the nation's schools, the report linked a decline in U.S. economic competitiveness to a decline in the quality of public schooling. "A rising tide of mediocrity . . . threatens our very future as a nation and a people. We have, in effect, been committing an act of unthinking, unilateral disarmament."[12] The idea that America's economic edge in the world depends on the excellence of its schools continues to influence educational reform and practice today.

Although this report again emphasized the need for a focus on basic skills, the responses to *A Nation at Risk* initially focused almost exclusively on test score accountability. Schools and teachers were, for the first time, evaluated and rewarded based on students' test scores. Some districts instituted teacher bonuses for increases in scores. Schools compared test scores among classrooms and teachers; districts compared scores from school to school; states compared districts; and the federal government compared national results to those of students in other countries like Japan and Germany.

This "accountability" movement continues to gain strength today, and each year more and more states institute standardized testing programs at various grade levels, and more and more lists are published evaluating and comparing student performance across schools, districts, states, and the nation. Table 1.1 shows how one school district in Texas meets demands for accountability through testing and informing parents of the results.

Accountability and comparison through testing as a process of reforming and improving education represents a strong tradition in American education and has many adherents. At the heart of this approach lies a strong commitment to centralized control, with authority and power vested in a central administration at the school, district, and state levels. At odds with this emphasis on centralization was another reform movement that grew out of the economic turmoil of the 1980s: restructuring through deregulation. School choice and school restructuring called for teachers, administrators, parents, community members, and even students to participate in decision making about how to improve teaching and learning. Underlying the deregulation movement are calls for school-based management teams and shared decision making; classroom-based approaches, such as cooperative learning; and alternative forms of testing based on performance and product.

Contemporary Reform Movements. **Goals 2000,** part of the Educate America Act of 1994, set standards to be achieved nationwide by the year 2000, including supporting readiness for school and high school completion for all students; setting world-class standards in math and science; establishing adult literacy and lifelong learning opportunities; providing safe, drug-free schools; supporting teacher education and

Goals 2000
Part of the Educate America Act (1994), these goals stressed readiness for school, high school completion, student achievement and citizenship, world-class standards in math and science, adult literacy and lifelong learning, safe and drug-free schools, teacher education and professional development, and parental participation.

Table 1.1 *Annual Performance Report, 2002–2003, Carrollton-Farmers Branch (Texas) Independent School District*

Comparison of TAKS Scores, 2002–2003 Percentage Mastery by Grade and Subject			SAT (Scholastic Aptitude Test) Results			
	C-FB	State		Verbal	Math	Total
Grade 4			**2000**			
Reading	90.0	85.9	District	522	549	1,071
Mathematics	90.1	88.0	Texas	493	500	993
Writing	91.9	86.8	National	505	514	1,019
All tests	82.2	75.8	**2002**			
Grade 8			District	510	535	1,045
Reading	92.5	88.7	Texas	493	500	933
Mathematics	78.5	73.2	National	507	519	1,026
Social Studies	95.6	93.1				
All tests	77.1	69.9				
Grade 10						
English/Language arts	82.2	72.8				
Mathematics	82.2	74.2				
Science	78.6	69.6				
Social studies	90.7	86.8				
All tests	64.7	53.3				

Source: Carrollton-Farmers Branch Independent School District, Annual Performance Report, 2002–2003 (2002). (Online). Available at www.cfbisd.edu/docs/apr.pdf; Texas Educators Association. (2002). (Online). Available at www.tea.state.tx.us.

Reflect & Write

The State of Texas initiated the Texas Assessment of Knowledge and Skills (TAKS) as the 2002–2003 required assessment for public schools. This testing instrument measures the state curriculum in reading, writing, English/language arts, mathematics, science, and social studies. The Texas Education Agency (TEA) provides districts with statistical information concerning TAKS like those shown here, in which the statistics of individual districts are compared to the state and to districts served by the same regional education service center. What use do you think districts might make of this information?

professional development; and providing opportunities for parent participation in education. The Goals 2000 legislation provided a foundation for the No Child Left Behind Act of 2001, which sets standards in many of these same areas.

Another focus in current educational reform is on what the U.S. economy needs. *What Work Requires of Schools: A SCANS Report for America 2000*, a report developed by the Secretary's Commission on Achieving Necessary Skills (SCANS) of the U.S. Department of Labor, identifies five competencies that are important for job performance:

- Knowledge of and use of resources
- Interpersonal skills
- Ability to acquire information
- Ability to understand complex interrelationships
- Ability to work with a variety of technologies

The reform movement based on this report emphasizes the needs and conditions of the workplace and supports a seamless transition from school to workplace; worker training in information technologies; and a curricular emphasis on critical thinking, problem solving, decision making, and group collaboration—all skills that employers say they need in today's workers.

Currently, significant waves of reform, many of which were highlighted in the 2004 presidential election, include accountability through state- and national-level standards and testing programs; high-stakes testing, to ensure that students are achieving on or above grade level, and an end to social promotion; and increased state and federal funding to ensure that districts are meeting the more rigidly defined standards. Perhaps most important is the role that the federal government has begun to play in pre-K–12 education—a role greater than ever before. In fact, federal control of education, especially through the No Child Left Behind Act, is one of the major issues facing U.S. education today.

What Reform Movements Mean to Teachers

Educational reform movement
A comprehensive effort made during the 1980s and 1990s to improve schools and the preparation of teachers.

Restructuring
Reorganizing how schools are controlled at the local level so that teachers, principals, parents, and community members have significant authority.

Whatever **educational reform movement** may be sweeping the shores when you enter teaching, you will need to be able to respond to it. Let's look at trends that will undoubtedly impact your own career in the years to come.

Teaching in Restructured Schools. The waves of educational reform that have rolled onto the beaches of American education over the past fifty years have resulted in a significant restructuring of schools and teaching. **Restructuring**—major changes in the rules, roles, and relationships within an institution—is a common term for changes made in response to reform movements in both business and industry and education. As you might predict, restructuring means that teachers work extra hours planning, communicating with families, teaming, participating in common planning time, and spending what was formerly personal time on school-based activities, helping to ensure that students learn—and will perform well on standardized tests. At the high-school level, for example, participating in a restructuring task force might include making decisions about block scheduling, year-round schooling, common planning time for teachers, and school-to-work transitions programs. Participation at this level may mean more time devoted to work, but it also means empowerment for teachers through enhanced decision-making roles.

INTASC

Standard 3: The teacher understands how students differ in their approaches to learning and creates instructional opportunities that are adapted to diverse learners.

NCATE

Middle Level

Standard 5: Understands and uses major concepts, principles, theories, and research related to effective instruction and assessment; employs a variety of strategies for a developmentally appropriate climate to meet the varying abilities and learning styles of all young adolescents.

Teaching in Diverse Schools. One reality of teaching today is the increasing racial, ethnic, cultural, and socioeconomic diversity of students, their families, and the communities in which they live. Although diversity is greatest in urban areas with high immigration rates—like Dade County (Miami), Florida, where Hispanic Americans comprise the majority of students at all grade levels and 75.2 percent of the student population was enrolled in bilingual programs in 2002–2003—even rural districts are experiencing change. The percentage of the U.S. population who were foreign born reached a peak of 14.7 percent in 1910 and then declined steadily to a low of 4.8 percent in 1970. Since 1970, however, that percentage has almost doubled, and in 2002, 11.5 percent of the U.S. population was foreign born—a figure that continues to grow (see Figure 1.10).

Of the 32.5 million foreign-born residents in the United States, the largest numbers come from Mexico (about 10.2 million) and Asia (about 9.3 million). California has a foreign-born population of about 8 million, or 25 percent of the state's total population. Cultural affinities can be multiple, based on geographic origin, historical origin, national origin, native language, ethnicity, tribal origin, skin color, race, or religion: Ultimately, people belong to a group only to the extent that they define themselves as members.

Schools and teachers must accept, even celebrate, diversity; they must educate all students to their full potential regardless of socioeconomic status, race, ethnicity, language, religion, gender, national origin, or membership in any other category. This means that you as a teacher will need to know and respect your students—their individual differences and the sources of their diversity. You will also need to make sure that your classroom, curriculum, and teaching methods are appropriate for and responsive to students' needs as both individual learners and members of diverse groups.

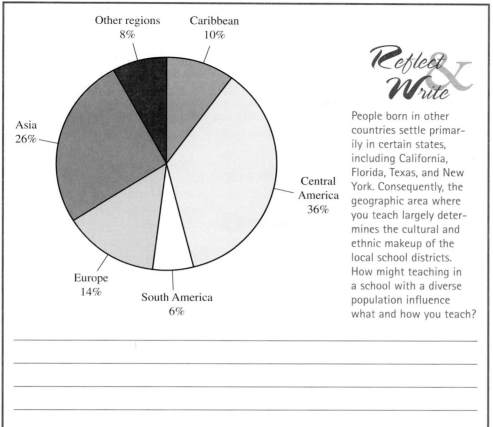

Reflect & Write

People born in other countries settle primarily in certain states, including California, Florida, Texas, and New York. Consequently, the geographic area where you teach largely determines the cultural and ethnic makeup of the local school districts. How might teaching in a school with a diverse population influence what and how you teach?

Figure 1.10 *Foreign-Born U.S. Population, by Region of Birth (2002)*

Source: U.S. Census Bureau, "The Foreign-Born World Population in the United States, 2003" (2003), figure 1. (Online). Available at www.census.gov/prod/2003pubs/p20-539.pdf.

NCATE

Early Childhood

Standard 1: Uses understanding of young children's characteristics, needs, and interacting influences on children's development and learning to create healthy, respectful, supportive, and challenging environments for all children.

Using a Variety of Teaching Methods and Instructional Materials. Reform and restructuring have changed how teachers teach. As a new teacher, you will have available to you a greater variety of instructional methods and materials than did teachers in the past. Today, student assessment is based on the ability to demonstrate mastery through state testing programs, as well as higher-level thinking and problem solving through the completion of projects, performances, written self-assessments, and work samples collected in a portfolio. **Authentic learning tasks and assessments**—that is, tasks that address real needs and problems that students will encounter outside the classroom and assessments that measure the ability to complete those tasks—are valued.

Active learning means that students are out of their seats, working with classmates as evaluators, investigators, decision makers, creative problem solvers, and critical thinkers. Students are also more involved in self-teaching and peer teaching and in **cooperative learning.** Typically, today's students work together on academic tasks in small, mixed-ability groups, sharing responsibility for their own learning.

Using Instructional Technologies. As a beginning teacher, you will teach students who grew up with computers, and you will belong to a generation of teachers who are more computer and multimedia literate than teachers of the past. The vast majority of public schools—87 percent—now have access to the Internet.[13] Clearly, **instructional technologies** will play a larger and larger role in every classroom. You will probably use technologies not only as instructional tools but in other ways as well—for example, to communicate with parents, collaborate with other teachers, assist students with

Authentic learning tasks and assessments
Assignments and assessment that reflect real needs and problems that students will encounter outside the classroom.

Active learning
Process whereby students are mentally and physically active in learning through activities that involve gathering data, thinking, and problem solving.

Cooperative learning
An instructional and learning process in which students work together on academic tasks, help each other, and take responsibility for one another's learning.

Instructional technologies
Any technology—such as computers, video recorders and DVD players, and television—that promotes and supports the teaching-learning process.

Standard 10: The teacher fosters relationships with school colleagues, parents, and agencies in the larger community to support students' learning and well-being.

Professional collaboration
Working cooperatively with teachers, staff, parents, and community members to improve schools and the teaching-learning process.

Disability
A physical or mental impairment that substantially limits one or more major life activities.

Mainstreaming
The educational and social integration of children with special needs into the schoolwide instructional process, usually in the general classroom.

Inclusion
The practice of ensuring that all students with disabilities participate with other students in all aspects of school.

disabilities, and monitor and record student progress and achievement. Chapter 12 will help you learn more about applying technology to your teaching.

Working with Colleagues, Families, and Communities. Teachers have traditionally conceived their role as working with students in a classroom and helping them learn academic material. As a new teacher, however, you will find that there is a growing emphasis on collegiality and on parent and community involvement. Today, teachers might work with entire families to help facilitate student learning; family-based education is becoming the rule rather than the exception. Most teachers recognize the need for family involvement and say they would like to see the level of parental participation increase.[14] Many teachers also work with community leaders to garner support—economic and political—for school projects.

Working with colleagues may involve participating in team teaching (also known as co-teaching), collaborating to integrate curriculum, or planning joint learning experiences. Benefits of **professional collaboration** typically include:

- Increased sense of professional interaction and support
- More effective use of individual teacher talents and abilities
- Opportunities for peer coaching or mentoring and reflective practice
- Opportunities to meet all students' needs more fully and enrich learning
- Increased student achievement and overall student performance

Teaching in Inclusive Classrooms. Reform movements of the last several decades have resulted in the inclusion of more and more students classified with disabilities in the general classroom. A **disability** is a physical, cognitive, or behavioral impairment that substantially limits one or more major life activities. Disabilities include speech and language impairments; hearing and vision impairments, including deafness and blindness; specific learning disabilities; and orthopedic and health impairments, including traumatic brain injury, mental retardation, serious emotional disturbance, and autism.

Collaborative efforts among teachers provide supportive opportunities that promote creativity and problem solving.

Students with disabilities may be taught in special programs but more and more often are part of a **mainstream** or **inclusion** program for all or part of the school day. As a beginning teacher, you can expect to be responsible for one or more students with special needs in your classroom. You will learn more about this in Chapter 5.

We began this chapter with Teacher of the Year Betsy Rogers and her quest to become a teacher. Betsy was fortunate: she had always wanted to teach, and she had focused many of her life activities on achieving that goal. I hope that you follow Betsy's lead and set as your goal to become the very best teacher you can be. Regardless of how you get your first teaching position or where you teach, expect a career full of happiness, challenges, opportunities, and possibilities.

SECTION SUMMARY

How Is Teaching Changing?

- **Patterns of Educational Reform.** Educational reform is a cyclical process, with a new "wave" typically appearing every ten years or so—often in response to some social, economic, or international crisis. General trends in reform over the past fifty years have included efforts to emphasize basics (reading, writing, math, and science), to extend education to all children (including national legislation to address needs of at-risk children and children with disabilities), to make schools and school districts accountable for student learning (generally through state and national standards and standardized testing programs), and to align what schools teach more closely with workplace needs.

- **What Reform Movements Mean to Teachers.** Reforms—and the social, political, and economic context from which they derive—mean a constantly changing environment for teachers. Trends that teachers must respond to now and in the immediate future include:

- **Teaching in restructured schools.** Teachers may work extra hours planning, communicating with families and colleagues, working in teaching teams, and participating in task forces and management committees; in return, they may play enhanced roles as decision makers in their own school environments.

- **Teaching in diverse schools.** As the U.S. population becomes more diverse, so do its schools. Schools and teachers will function most effectively if they incorporate—and celebrate—this diversity in classrooms, curriculum, and teaching methods while also respecting individuals' rights to define their own group memberships.

- **Using a variety of teaching methods and instructional materials.** As a new teacher, your repertoire of potential instructional methods and materials is much greater than that of past generations of teachers. You will no doubt be asked to employ such concepts as active learning, authentic learning and assessment, and cooperative learning.

- **Using instructional technologies.** New teachers will use new technologies at an unprecedented rate, not only for instruction but also to communicate with parents and colleagues, to assist students with special needs, and to maintain student records.

- **Working with colleagues, families, and communities.** Education today is more and more a collaborative effort between teachers and colleagues, teachers and families, and teachers and communities.

- **Teaching in inclusive classrooms.** Classroom teachers are in the forefront of providing all students—exceptional learners, students with average abilities, students with disabilities, students at risk, and students with limited English proficiency—with an education appropriate to their physical, educational, social, emotional, and cultural needs.

Thinking Critically

★ ★ ★ ★ ★ ★ ★ ★

Ernestine Hogan, a math teacher at Southside Comprehensive High School in Atlanta, Georgia, observed:

> Sometimes teachers . . . want to reach everybody in the same way. You lose a lot of students like that, because you are not—I hate to say this, but—you're not teaching. You really aren't teaching. . . . There is a difference between teaching and inspiring, a difference between instructing and enlightening.[15]

How does Ernestine Hogan's statement reflect the challenges that you will probably face as a new teacher?

_____

_____

_____

_____ ★

Applying What You've Learned
★ ★ ★ ★ ★ ★ ★ ★

Interview two or three veteran teachers, either in a local school or in the department offering the course you are now taking. How have educational reform movements changed these teachers' teaching over the years? How have technological changes affected their work and professional development?

_____

_____

_____

_____ ★

Putting Yourself in the Picture
★ ★ ★ ★ ★ ★ ★ ★

Assume that you are teaching second grade and that you have just been notified that one of the students in your class has a life-threatening allergy to peanuts. What other professionals would you want to consult and collaborate with about this, and what measures would you take to try to ensure the child's safety in your classroom?

_____

_____

_____

_____ ★

Applications for Active Learning

CONNECTIONS

1. In every chapter, you will have an opportunity to make a visual representation of significant ideas and information as a learning aid. Create a picture or graphic that shows connections that are meaningful to you from Chapter 1. Here is an example of a graphic representation of some key ideas from this chapter.

2. Create a visual representation of what it takes to become a good teacher. In your visual, show the personal qualities and skills that Betsy Rogers brought to her quest and the events, processes, and programs that enabled her to become U.S. Teacher of the Year.

FIELD EXPERIENCES

1. Teacher stories are a good way to learn about teaching. Ask some teachers to share stories or anecdotes about significant teaching events that helped make a difference in students' lives. Share teacher stories with classmates. What patterns do you observe in teachers who make a difference in people's lives?

2. Interview teachers and ask for or infer their metaphors for teaching and learning. How do their metaphors appear to shape their teaching practice?

3. Share with your classmates your interviews with first-year teachers and teachers with five or more years of experience. What are the reasons they chose teaching as their career? How do their reasons compare with yours?

PERSONAL RESEARCH

1. Recall teachers who were positive influences in your education and your life. What were those teachers like? How did they act as teachers? How did you benefit from knowing them and being their student?

2. What teaching experiences did you have before entering a teacher education program? How did those experiences guide you toward selecting or thinking about teaching as a career?

FOR YOUR PORTFOLIO

In this section, and others like it at the end of every chapter, you will be asked to collect your own writing as well as information you gather about teaching from other sources. The portfolio you develop will be invaluable to you in articulating your own answers to typical interview questions for your first job and will provide resources for your first year of teaching.

1. Collect your Personal Research writings into your teaching portfolio under the heading "What Teaching Means to Me." Incorporate your responses to any questions from this chapter that strike you as particularly meaningful. Later in the course, check back and reflect on your responses to see whether your views of teaching are changing. Keep in mind that you will probably be asked some version of these questions—What does teaching mean to you? Why did you choose to become a teacher?—at job interviews.

2. Collect your information about teacher proficiencies (knowledge and skills) as they are defined in your state and begin developing a plan and timetable for acquiring these proficiencies.

3. Begin a clipping file from the Learning or Education section of local and national newspapers and magazines about changes in public education or new information about teaching methods or learning styles. Explore *Education Week*, a national weekly newspaper devoted entirely to education news. Organize clippings by topic and place them in your portfolio, along with notes about how these changes might affect your own teaching.

IDEA FILE

In this section, and others like it at the end of every chapter, you will be encouraged to create a file of teaching ideas, both general ideas and specific lesson plans, for use in your first teaching position.

1. In what ways do you think teaching will change in the future? What are some advantages and disadvantages of these potential changes? Begin an idea file for ways you might prepare yourself for each change you identify.

2. Join a Future Teachers club, if your school sponsors one, or start a club for future teachers on your own. What three topics might you include on the agenda of your first meeting?

In this section and others like it at the end of each chapter, you will find lists of electronic and print resources that you may find valuable in preparing for a career in teaching.

WEB SITES WORTH VISITING

Pathways to School Improvement. Created and maintained by the North Central Regional Laboratory.
> www.ncrel.org/sdrs
> Lists of topics to explore further including assessment, preservice education, and professional development.

American Association of Colleges for Teacher Education.
> www.aacte.org
> Information about teacher preparation programs and teacher education.

The Four "Sacred Cows" of American Education.
> www.riggsinst.org/cows.htm
> A discussion of educational reform versus tradition in American education.

Kentucky Education Reform Act.
> www.education.ky.gov
> Information and an up-to-date publications list about Kentucky's ongoing reform programs.

Teachers Using the Internet to Conduct Research.
> www.brint.com/research.htm
> List of links for teachers interested in using the Internet to conduct research.

BOOKS WORTH READING

Associates Center. (2001). *First-Class Teacher: Success Strategies for New K–8 Teachers* (rev. ed.). Berkeley, CA: Publishers West. An excellent discussion of teaching strategies for elementary classrooms that can lead to successful teaching and learning experiences.

CHAPTER 2

*T*eaching as a Profession

"I am a professional."

Linda Beck, a ninth- and twelfth-grade Spanish teacher, is a Kentucky High School Teacher of the Year.

Fifteen years ago you could focus on your subject, teach it, and that was it, but that's not true today. Teachers play many different roles, and they are much more involved in many related experiences than ever before.

More and more I find it necessary and advantageous to work with other professionals and my colleagues. For example, other teachers and I work together to develop interdisciplinary units linking my subject area, Spanish, to art and social studies. Integrating content areas is very much in the forefront of what teachers are doing to make curriculum more meaningful and interesting. Team planning plays a bigger role in a teacher's life than it used to.

But you can't just confine your collaborative efforts to those you work with. You have to work with the community as well. I work closely with social workers. We're having a big problem with truancy in my high school because of pregnancy, drugs, alcohol, and runaways. A social worker friend and I asked Kentucky State University to place social work interns in our school. They made home visits, counseled students, and even accompanied them to court. The program makes a big difference in the lives of students.

I attend every possible meeting or program I can if I think it will help students. At one meeting I attended, I found out about Achievement Via Individual Determination (AVID), a national program to help students who might not ordinarily make it into college. The program targets students who are pretty average gradewise and who wouldn't go to college without some additional help. I helped implement it in my school. Each year we identify about thirty students to participate. They have an AVID class once a day, and they are tutored by college students. More than half of them went to college last year.

We have another academic problem that we are trying to solve. Other ninth-grade teachers and I are researching why there is a dramatic drop in ninth-grade student achievement in our schools. We are surveying parents, students, and teachers to try to find out what we can do. It's a challenging problem, but this is what makes action research so interesting. We have a real problem, and we're trying to find an answer to it.

It's important to help students academically, but it's necessary to help in other ways as well. We need to help students become decent human beings. I invited the local director of the National Conference [formerly the National Conference of Christians and Jews] to help implement a Diversity Day at our school. The week before this took place, we conducted a six-hour training program for more than one hundred community members and students to be facilitators. On Diversity Day, we assigned them to small groups of students, and they conducted activities designed to help students grow in their understanding of others. It was so successful that now all the schools in the city do it.

Helping future teachers is important too. I spend about fifty hours a year counseling, coaching, and mentoring a beginning teacher. Being a role model for another teacher is a very rewarding experience. I attend a workshop each summer to help me do a better job.

I also attend professional conferences to keep up with trends and to network. Since I'm the foreign language chairman and I represent my faculty, I have to attend meetings. I belong to the Kentucky Council on Teaching Foreign Languages and the American Association of Teachers of Spanish and Portuguese.

I am a professional. I think a professional is a member of a group that upholds the standards of that group. Previously, teaching had the reputation of being a person's last choice when examining a career. Not anymore. The community is now asking more and has higher standards for teachers, and universities are raising standards. When we become professionals, we are accountable for upholding these standards.

How Will This Chapter Help You?

You will learn

★ how teaching is a profession and how to become a professional

★ about Praxis and other teacher certification testing

★ how to base your teaching practice on ethics and research

★ why and how teacher education programs are changing

★ characteristics of America's teachers

★ about the teaching opportunities available to you

*I*S TEACHING A PROFESSION?

A profession, we learn from the dictionary, is an occupation that requires advanced education and training and involves intellectual skills. Typically, a profession is also an occupation self-governed by standards and requiring some sort of entry certification, like the bar exam for lawyers or medical boards for physicians. Is teaching a profession? The answer is a resounding yes.

You are preparing to be a professional. When you have completed a program of advanced study and practice, you will probably be required to pass a certification exam—and then you will join 4.4 million other teachers, all dedicated to educating America's children to the fullest extent of their abilities. You will have many opportunities and responsibilities that will enrich your life and change the lives of others.

The professionalism of teaching can be measured by the following standards:

- Teachers spend long periods of time gaining the specialized knowledge they must have to ensure that all students learn to their fullest capabilities.
- Teachers pass rigorous state and national examinations to earn an initial certificate to teach.
- Teachers practice under the supervision of mentor teachers and administrators in order to gain a license to teach.
- Teachers continually engage in ongoing study and professional development to renew their licenses to teach and to keep current in their fields.
- Teachers follow codes of ethical conduct established by professional organizations, state departments of education, and local school districts.
- Teachers exercise autonomy by continually making decisions about what and how to teach.
- Teachers belong to professional organizations as a means to professional development.
- Teachers are held in high regard by the communities in which they teach.

Teaching is a helping profession. Teachers are dedicated to helping students learn and grow. Teachers are also committed to helping parents, families, and communities build strong educational programs. The decision to become a teacher—to be able to say, "I am a teacher"—is an ennobling one. You may be pursuing a traditional program moving toward teacher certification and a license to teach, or you may be involved in an alternative, nontraditional program (see Figure 2.1). Regardless of the path you have chosen, you will change your life and the lives of those you teach. In the final analysis, it is what you do with your talents, abilities, and knowledge that will enable you to be called a professional.

Praxis and Teacher Certification Testing

Most professions have specific requirements for licensure. As a requirement for licensure and entry into teaching, you will more than likely have to pass a standardized test as part of your certification process. Many states require a passing score on a state-developed test or on the **Praxis** series of professional assessment for beginning teachers. The Praxis series is developed and administered by the Educational Testing Service (ETS) and consists of academic skills assessments, subject assessments, and classroom performance assessments.

Praxis, which means "theory into practice," is used by nearly 80 percent of the states that require testing as a component of their teacher licensure process, and the exams are given three times annually. Up-to-date information about Praxis is available on the ETS Web site (www.ets.org/praxis).

Praxis is explained in greater detail in Chapter 13, as are other topics relating to teacher certification.

INTASC

Standard 9: The teacher is a reflective practitioner who continually evaluates the effects of his/her choices and actions on others (students, parents, and other professionals in the learning community) and who actively seeks out opportunities to grow professionally.

NCATE

Early Childhood
Standard 5: Uses ethical guidelines and other professional standards; is a continuous, collaborative learner who demonstrates knowledgeable, reflective, and critical perspectives; is an informed advocate for sound educational practices.

Elementary
Standard 5.1: Understands and applies practices and behaviors that are characteristic of developing career teachers.

Middle Level
Standard 7: Understands the complexity of teaching young adolescents; engages in practices and behaviors that develop competence as a professional.

Praxis
A national battery of tests prepared by the Educational Testing Service available for the initial certification of teachers. Consists of assessments in three areas: academic skills, knowledge of subject, and classroom performance.

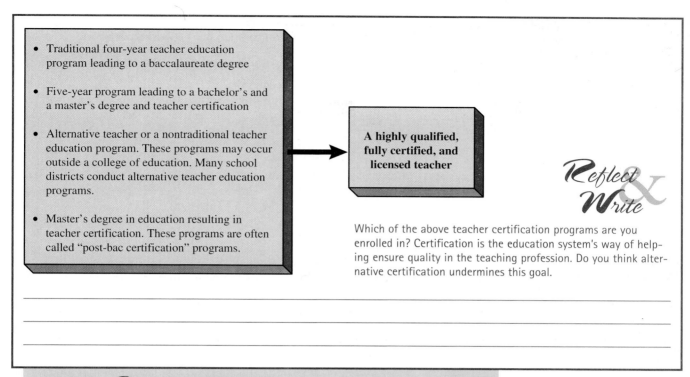

- Traditional four-year teacher education program leading to a baccalaureate degree

- Five-year program leading to a bachelor's and a master's degree and teacher certification

- Alternative teacher or a nontraditional teacher education program. These programs may occur outside a college of education. Many school districts conduct alternative teacher education programs.

- Master's degree in education resulting in teacher certification. These programs are often called "post-bac certification" programs.

A highly qualified, fully certified, and licensed teacher

Reflect & Write

Which of the above teacher certification programs are you enrolled in? Certification is the education system's way of helping ensure quality in the teaching profession. Do you think alternative certification undermines this goal.

Figure 2.1 *P*athways to Becoming a Teacher

Professionals are also subject to ongoing or routine evaluation for quality of performance. As a teacher, you will participate in a performance review at least annually and may be required to take tests at various points during your career.

While some states require Praxis for initial certification, not all do. The chances are good that you will have to pass a state exam for initial certification. For example, while Praxis is required in Connecticut, Delaware, Georgia, and New Hampshire, in Alabama a college or university exam is required, while in Texas, a state exam, the Texas Examinations of Educator Standards (TExES), is required of all who seek initial certification. Initial **teacher certification testing** is, basically, a good idea but is controversial, as the case of Massachusetts demonstrated. When Massachusetts administered its first Massachusetts Educator Certification Test (MECT), 60 percent of the prospective teachers failed. The state threatened to "decertify" a teacher preparation program if it did not produce a passing rate of 80 percent. In response, colleges and universities toughened admission standards to teacher education programs and began "teaching the test." Cases such as Massachusetts will continue to be in the news as teacher preparation programs and states strive to educate highly qualified teachers for the profession.

The Professionalization of Teaching

In the opening case, Linda Beck talked about how teachers' roles have changed and how they are involved in a wide range of responsibilities that involve leadership and decision making. Increasingly, teachers are asked to know and do more and to meet higher standards of preparation and performance. All of this is part of the **professionalization of teaching,** the process of making teaching a better and more authentic profession through agreed-on standards of practice and the regaining of public confidence in the schools' abilities to educate all students well. Some of the components of the professionalism of teaching are shown in Figure 2.2.

INTASC

Standard 9: The teacher is a reflective practitioner who continually evaluates the effects of his/her choices and actions on others (students, parents, and other professionals in the learning community) and who actively seeks out opportunities to grow professionally.

Teacher certification testing
Testing of potential teachers prior to state certification, designed to admit to the profession only those teachers who are competent in basic knowledge and pedagogical skills.

Professionalization of teaching
The process of making teaching a better, more authentic profession through agreed-on standards of practice and thereby regaining public confidence in schools' educational abilities.

NCATE

Elementary

Standard 5.1: Understands and applies practices and behaviors that are characteristic of developing career teachers.

National Commission on Teaching and America's Future. The National Commission on Teaching and America's Future (NCTAF), funded by the Rockefeller Foundation and the Carnegie Corporation of New York, is a blue-ribbon group of public officials, business and community leaders, and educators who are broadly knowledgeable about education, school reform, and teaching.

After careful examination of the field of teaching and teacher preparation programs, the commission issued its report *What Matters Most: Teaching for America's Future.* In it the commission identified as its ultimate goal that "by the year 2006,

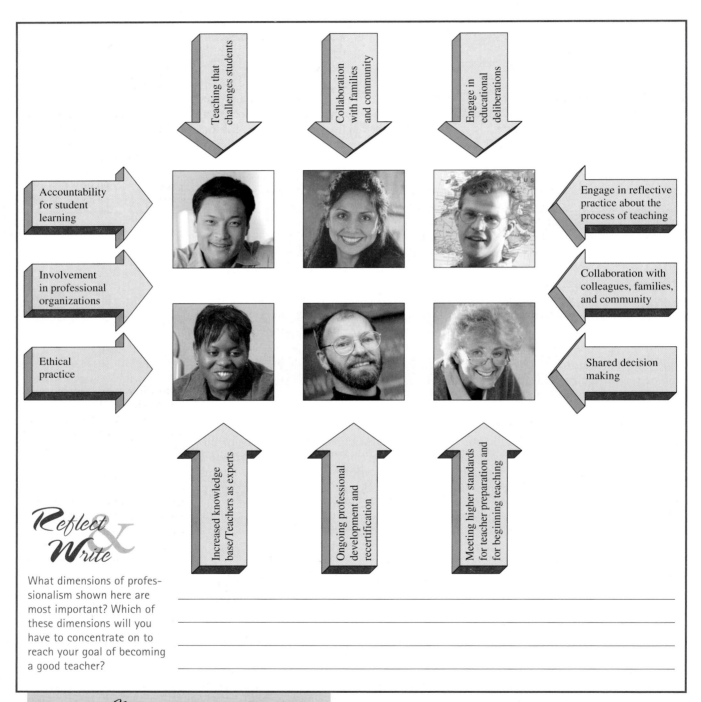

Reflect & Write

What dimensions of professionalism shown here are most important? Which of these dimensions will you have to concentrate on to reach your goal of becoming a good teacher?

Figure 2.2 *M*aking Teaching a Full Profession

America will provide every student with what should be his or her educational birth-right: access to competent, caring, and qualified teachers in schools organized for success" and recommended the following:

1. Get serious about standards, for both students and teachers.
2. Reinvent teacher preparation and professional development.
3. Fix teacher recruitment and put qualified teachers in every classroom.
4. Encourage and reward teacher knowledge and skill.
5. Create schools that are organized for student and teacher success.

NCTAF's recommendations have had a strong impact on teacher preparation and school reform in recent years. For further information about the commission and its work, visit NCTAF at www.nctaf.org and take a closer look at each of the commission's recommendations. Can you cite specific examples from your experiences of how these recommendations are being implemented?

National Council for Accreditation of Teacher Education. The **National Council for Accreditation of Teacher Education** (**NCATE**) is one agency at the forefront of teacher professionalization efforts. NCATE is a teacher education program accrediting agency that acts as "the profession's mechanism to help establish high-quality teacher preparation. Through the process of professional accreditation of schools, colleges, and departments of education, NCATE works to make a difference in the quality of teaching and teacher preparation today, tomorrow, and for the next century."[1] NCATE accreditation is a voluntary process, and 550 of the nation's 1,200 teacher education programs are NCATE accredited. Forty-six states evaluate their teacher preparation programs using NCATE standards. Thirty-six of these states require all teacher preparation programs to earn NCATE accreditation.

Setting standards for teacher education programs, accreditation of programs, and performance standards for courses are important ways of professionalizing teaching. NCATE, like other professional organizations, uses standards to guide the development of teacher preparation programs. These standards also serve as a basis for accreditation of teacher education programs. These NCATE standards (Figure 2.3) represent what high-quality teachers should know and be able to do as a result of participating in an NCATE-accredited teacher preparation program. As you review these NCATE standards, reflect on how your program of teacher preparation is preparing you to meet these standards.

Teacher Education Accreditation Council. The **Teacher Education Accreditation Council** (**TEAC**) was founded in 1997 and is a nonprofit organization dedicated to improving academic degree programs for professional educators. TEAC's primary work is accrediting undergraduate and graduate professional teacher education programs. Its accreditation process examines and verifies the evidence teacher education programs assemble to support their claims that they prepare competent, caring, qualified professionals.

TEAC's accreditation process is based on the questions faculty members ask about the program in which they teach and the program's performance within the context of its mission. TEAC's academic audit verifies evidence that student learning meets high expectations and that the program is following processes that produce quality. For more information about TEAC, visit www.teac.org.

National Board for Professional Teaching Standards. The **National Board for Professional Teaching Standards** (**NBPTS**) is an organization dedicated to professionalizing teaching and raising standards. NBPTS began operation in 1987. In 1995, NBPTS awarded its first **national certification** and to date has certified 20,000 teachers. The assessment is a yearlong process that includes extensive evaluations of classroom performance, portfolio evaluations, and knowledge-based examinations. To be eligible for national certification, teachers must possess a baccalaureate degree from an accredited institution,

INTASC

Standard 9: The teacher is a reflective practitioner who continually evaluates the effects of his/her choices and actions on others (students, parents, and other professionals in the learning community) and who actively seeks out opportunities to grow professionally.

National Council for Accreditation of Teacher Education (NCATE) A teacher education program accrediting agency that encourages "institutions to meet rigorous academic standards of excellence in professional education."

Teacher Education Accreditation Council (TEAC) A nonprofit organization of institutions of higher education and other groups and individuals devoted to the improvement of academic degree programs for professional educators.

National Board for Professional Teaching Standards (NBPTS) An organization dedicated to professionalizing teaching and raising standards by providing certification dependent on extensive evaluations of classroom performance, portfolio evaluation, and knowledge-based examinations.

National certification A certificate awarded by the National Board for Professional Teaching Standards to teachers who possess extensive professional knowledge and the ability to perform at a high level.

Early Childhood Education Standards

1. **Promoting child development and learning**—Candidates use their understanding of young children's characteristics and needs, and of multiple interacting influences on children's development and learning, to create environments that are healthy, respectful, supportive, and challenging for all children.

2. **Building family and community relationships**—Candidates know about, understand, and value the importance and complex characteristics of children's families and communities. They use this understanding to create respectful, reciprocal relationships that support and empower families, and to involve all families in their children's development and learning.

3. **Observing, documenting, and assessing to support young children and families**—Candidates know about and understand the goals, benefits, and uses of assessment. They know about and use systematic observations, documentation, and other effective assessment strategies in a responsible way, in partnership with families and other professionals, to positively influence children's development and learning.

4. **Teaching and learning**—Candidates integrate their understanding of and relationships with children and families; their understanding of developmentally effective approaches to teaching and learning; and their knowledge of academic disciplines, to design, implement, and evaluate experiences that promote positive development and learning for all children.

4a. **Connecting with children and families**—Candidates know, understand, and use positive relationships and supportive interactions as the foundation for their work with young children.

4b. **Using developmentally effective approaches**—Candidates know, understand, and use a wide array of effective approaches, strategies, and tools to positively influence young children's development and learning.

4c. **Understanding content knowledge in early education**—Candidates understand the importance of each content area in young children's learning. They know the essential concepts, inquiry tools, and structure of content areas including academic subjects and can identify resources to deepen their understanding.

4d. **Building meaningful curriculum**—Candidates use their own knowledge and other resources to design, implement, and evaluate meaningful, challenging curriculum that promotes comprehensive developmental and learning outcomes for all young children.

5. **Becoming a professional**—Candidates identify and conduct themselves as members of the early childhood profession. They know and use ethical guidelines and other professional standards related to early childhood practice. They are continuous, collaborative learners who demonstrate knowledgeable, reflective, and critical perspectives on their work, making informed decisions that integrate knowledge from a variety of sources. They are informed advocates for sound educational practices and policies.

Elementary Teacher Standards

1. **Development, learning, and motivation**—Candidates know, understand, and use the major concepts, principles, theories, and research related to development of children and young adolescents to construct learning opportunities that support individual students' development, acquisition of knowledge, and motivation.

2. **Central concepts, tools of inquiry, and structures of content**—Candidates know, understand, and use the central concepts, tools of inquiry, and structures of content for students across the K–6 grades and can create meaningful learning experiences that develop students' competence in subject matter and skills for various developmental levels;

2.1. **English language arts**—Candidates demonstrate a high level of competence in use of the English language arts and they know, understand, and use concepts from reading, language and child development, to teach reading, writing, speaking, viewing, listening, and thinking skills and to help students successfully apply their developing skills to many different situations, materials, and ideas;

2.2. **Science**—Candidates know, understand, and use fundamental concepts in the subject matter of science—including physical, life, and earth and space sciences—as well as concepts in science and technology, science in personal and social perspectives, the history and nature of science, the unifying concepts of science, and the inquiry processes scientists use in discovery of new knowledge to build a base for scientific and technological literacy;

2.3. **Mathematics**—Candidates know, understand, and use the major concepts, procedures, and reasoning processes of mathematics that define number systems and number sense, geometry, measurement, statistics and probability, and algebra in order to foster student understanding and use of patterns, quantities, and spatial relationships that can represent phenomena, solve problems, and manage data;

2.4. **Social studies**—Candidates know, understand, and use the major concepts and modes of inquiry from the social studies—the integrated study of history, geography, the social sciences, and other related areas—to promote elementary students' abilities to make informed decisions as citizens of a culturally diverse democratic society and interdependent world;

2.5. **The arts**—Candidates know, understand, and use—as appropriate to their own knowledge and skills—the content, functions, and achievements of dance, music, theater, and the several visual arts as primary media for communication, inquiry, and insight among elementary students;

Figure 2.3 **National Council for Accreditation of Teacher Education Standards**

Source: National Council for Accreditation of Teacher Education, *Standards* (2003). (Online). Available at www.ncate.org/standard/programstds.htm. Reprinted by permission.

2.6. **Health education**—Candidates know, understand, and use the major concepts in the subject matter of health education to create opportunities for student development and practice of skills that contribute to good health;

2.7. **Physical education**—Candidates know, understand, and use—as appropriate to their own understanding and skills—human movement and physical activity as central elements to foster active, healthy life styles and enhanced quality of life for elementary students;

2.8. **Connections across the curriculum**—Candidates know, understand, and use the connections among concepts, procedures, and applications from content areas to motivate elementary students, build understanding, and encourage the application of knowledge, skills, tools, and ideas to real world issues.

3.1. **Integrating and applying knowledge for instruction**—Candidates plan and implement instruction based on knowledge of students, learning theory, subject matter, curricular goals, and community;

3.2. **Adaptation to diverse students**—Candidates understand how elementary students differ in their development and approaches to learning, and create instructional opportunities that are adapted to diverse students;

3.3. **Development of critical thinking, problem solving and performance skills**—Candidates understand and use a variety of teaching strategies that encourage elementary students' development of critical thinking, problem solving, and performance skills;

3.4. **Active engagement in learning**—Candidates use their knowledge and understanding of individual and group motivation and behavior among students at the K–6 level to foster active engagement in learning, self-motivation, and positive social interaction and to create supportive learning environments;

3.5. **Communication to foster learning**—Candidates use their knowledge and understanding of effective verbal, nonverbal, and media communication techniques to foster active inquiry, collaboration, and supportive interaction in the elementary classroom.

4. **Assessment for instruction**—Candidates know, understand, and use formal and informal assessment strategies to plan, evaluate, and strengthen instruction that will promote continuous intellectual, social, emotional, and physical development of each elementary student.

5.1. **Practices and behaviors of developing career teachers**—Candidates understand and apply practices and behaviors that are characteristic of developing career teachers;

5.2. **Reflection and evaluation**—Candidates are aware of and reflect on their practice in light of research on teaching and resources available for professional learning; they continually evaluate the effects of their professional decisions and actions on students, parents, and other professionals in the learning community and actively seek out opportunities to grow professionally;

5.3. **Collaboration with families**—Candidates know the importance of establishing and maintaining a positive collaborative relationship with families to promote the intellectual, social, emotional, and physical growth of children;

5.4. **Collaboration with colleagues and the community**—Candidates foster relationships with school colleagues and agencies in the larger community to support students' learning and well-being.

Middle-Level Teacher Standards

1. **Young Adolescent Development**—Middle-level teacher candidates understand the major concepts, principles, theories, and research related to young adolescent development, and they provide opportunities that support student development and learning.

2. **Middle-Level Philosophy and School Organization**—Middle-level teacher candidates understand the major concepts, principles, theories, and research underlying the philosophical foundations of developmentally responsive middle-level programs and schools, and they work successfully within these organizational components.

3. **Middle-Level Curriculum and Assessment**—Middle-level teacher candidates understand the major concepts, principles, theories, standards, and research related to middle-level curriculum and assessment, and they use this knowledge in their practice.

4. **Middle-Level Teaching Fields**—Middle-level teacher candidates understand and use the central concepts, tools of inquiry, standards, and structures of content in their chosen teaching fields, and they create meaningful learning experiences that develop all young adolescents' competence in subject matter and skills.

5. **Middle-Level Instruction and Assessment**—Middle-level teacher candidates understand and use the major concepts, principles, theories, and research related to effective instruction and assessment, and they employ a variety of strategies for a developmentally appropriate climate to meet the varying abilities and learning styles of all young adolescents.

6. **Family and Community Involvement**—Middle-level teacher candidates understand the major concepts, principles, theories, and research related to working collaboratively with family and community members, and they use that knowledge to maximize the learning of all young adolescents.

7. **Middle-Level Professional Roles**—Middle-level teacher candidates understand the complexity of teaching young adolescents, and they engage in practices and behaviors that develop their competence as professionals.

Figure 2.3 **Continued**

be state certified, and have three years of teaching experience. National certification is awarded to teachers who possess extensive professional knowledge and the ability to perform at a high level in the five core components shown in Figure 2.4.

NBPTS certification costs $2,300, and NBPTS estimates that most teachers spend approximately 200 to 400 hours on their portfolios. A portfolio consists of videotaped classroom teaching, sample lesson plans, and samples of students' work with commentary by the teacher. NBPTS certification is costly and requires some effort on the part of the teacher, but the certification is valid for ten years. Thirty-one states offer fee support, and thirty-two states provide salary supplements. In addition, NBPTS-certified teachers are eligible to earn up to six hours of graduate credit at hundreds of institutions of higher education. The entire range of NBPTS certification can be found at www.nbpts.org.

Part of the success of NBPTS is that the standards are high. Only about 50 percent of applicants are certified on their first try. In addition, teachers certified by NBPTS are better teachers than those who are not certified.

Teachers are committed to students and their learning.
- Accomplished teachers are dedicated to making knowledge accessible to all students.
- Accomplished teachers understand how students develop and learn.

Teachers know the subjects they teach and how to teach those subjects to students.
- Accomplished teachers have a rich understanding of the subject(s) they teach and appreciate how knowledge of their subject is created, organized, linked to other disciplines, and applied to real-world settings.
- Accomplished teachers command specialized knowledge of how to convey and reveal subject matter to students.

Teachers are responsible for managing and monitoring student learning.
- Accomplished teachers create, enrich, maintain, and alter instructional settings to capture and sustain the interest of their students and to make the most effective use of time.
- Accomplished teachers command a range of generic instructional techniques, know when each is appropriate, and can implement them as needed.
- Accomplished teachers can assess the progress of individual students as well as that of the class as a whole.

Teachers think systematically about their practice and learn from experience.
- Accomplished teachers are models of education persons, exemplifying the virtues they seek to inspire in students—curiosity, tolerance, honesty, fairness, respect for diversity, and appreciation of cultural differences—and the capacities that are prerequisites for intellectual growth: the ability to reason and take multiple perspectives, to be creative and take risks, and to adopt an experimental and problem-solving orientation.
- Accomplished teachers draw on their knowledge of human development, subject matter and instruction, and their understanding of their students to make principled judgments about sound practice.

Teachers are members of learning communities.
- Accomplished teachers contribute to the effectiveness of the school by working collaboratively with other professionals on instructional policy, curriculum development, and staff development.
- Accomplished teachers find ways to work collaboratively and creatively with parents, engaging them productively in the work of the school.

In what ways do you think NBPTS benefits the teaching profession? Is NBPTS certification something to which you will aspire?

Figure 2.4 *N*ational Board for Professional Teaching Standards—Five Components of Accomplished Teaching

Source: National Board for Professional Teaching Standards, *The Five Propositions of Accomplished Teaching.* (2004). (Online). Available at www.nbpts.org/about/coreprops.

National Board certification has its critics. They maintain that certification is too costly, especially in comparison to its outcomes; is time intensive; and does not necessarily result in better student achievement.[2] However, recent research suggests that "the NBPTS certification process does identify teachers who are more effective than their peers at improving student achievement in math and reading (as measured by standardized assessments), particularly for younger students and students in poverty."[3] For an example of a school where NBPTS certification has been emphasized, see Education on the Move.

NCATE

Early Childhood

Standard 5: Uses ethical guidelines and other professional standards; is a continuous, collaborative learner who demonstrates knowledgeable, reflective, and critical perspectives; is an informed advocate for sound educational practices.

Professional Ethics

Professional teachers conduct their practices in ways that are legally and ethically proper. Professionals want to do what is right in their relationships with students,

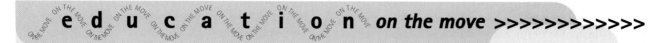

e d u c a t i o n *on the move* >>>>>>>>>>>>

>>> Coventry Leads the Way >>>>>>>

With 10 percent of its 475 teachers NBPTS certified, Coventry school district leads the State of Rhode Island in percentage of its faculty with National Board certification. Approximately 50 percent of its content area leaders are National Board certified, and two recent appointments from the teaching staff to positions in administration were National Board–certified teachers.

Why does Coventry value NBPTS certification? In Coventry, according to superintendent Ken DiPietro, there is an expectation that educational leadership and excellence require a continued commitment to personal growth and development. Educational improvement requires a systemic approach to reforming curriculum, instructional practice, assessment, resources, contract provisions, and community support. Success must be measured by student achievement. Reform must begin by a commitment to teacher quality. The National Board provides an assurance of quality, an incentive for continued growth, and a validation of instructional excellence.

Coventry's success is anchored in using a systemic approach of research-driven practices. The faculty contract includes an incentive of $7,000 per year for the ten years of certification as well as a reimbursement fund for a certain number of National Board application fees annually. The stipend is higher than in most communities—and in return, the contract also requires that National Board–certified teachers mentor new teachers as a service to the school system.

Coventry, a suburban district outside Providence serving 6,000 students, raised the bar for its expectation of teacher quality: stipends for advanced degrees of bachelor's plus thirty credits (B+30) and master's have been eliminated, and advanced degree increments begin only on completion of a minimum of nine credits beyond a master's degree. Coventry also developed a local, performance-based reward system (RHODE) where teachers submit a portfolio of evidence to meet specific criteria of teaching excellence. A team of teachers and administrators score the portfolio against a defined rubric, and successful candidates receive a stipend for four years. A provision in the contract also calls for a professional development center and a professional development coordinator identified from the teaching cadre in lieu of awarding a sabbatical leave. Teachers share in the responsibility of both defining and providing professional development needs at the school and district levels.

These incentives encourage faculty to continually review instructional practice and aspire to meet high standards of excellence in teaching. While the salary scale with advanced degree increments and stipends for National Board and RHODE certifications means that Coventry teachers are among the highest paid in the state, the latest state In$ite report comparing all school districts nevertheless ranks Coventry schools as the sixth lowest overall in cost per student.

Coventry established itself as an innovative school district in the state through its implementation of a teacher evaluation system modeled after Charlotte Danielson's research and a standards-based reform effort linked to the research in *America's Choice—High Skills or Low Wages*. As a skills commission district, Coventry implemented a Certificate of Initial Mastery that requires evidence of achievement, including on-demand tasks, extended tasks, and a capstone project for graduation distinction. Coventry also received a multimillion dollar, multiyear grant from the Bill and Melinda Gates Foundation to promote district excellence and student achievement though the creation of smaller learning communities. Coventry was also awarded a multiyear grant by the Rhode Island Department of Education to operate the state's Rhode Island Teaching and Learning Center. The RI-TLC became the state's center for promoting awareness and preparation for National Board certification.

Source: Ken DiPietro is superintendent of schools in Coventry, Rhode Island, a suburban ring community outside Providence serving some 6,000 students. He is a thirty-year veteran educator and past president of RI-ASCD.

colleagues, parents, and the public. They base their behavior on a code of **professional ethics.** Many professions, such as medicine and law, have a unified code of ethics that governs their practice. The teaching profession does not have a unified code, but professional organizations that represent educators have developed codes of ethics that help inform and guide professional practice. For example, the **National Education Association (NEA)** code of ethics is shown in Figure 2.5.

The NEA code of ethics emphasizes what teachers should not do in their interactions with students and others. However, guiding your behavior as a teacher is not a process of following a recipe. Ethical practice is not just a matter of doing one specific thing and not doing another. Ethical practice means that you will constantly monitor your behavior and think and reflect on your professional practices.

Basing Practice on Evidence-Based Inquiry and Assessment

Teaching is a research-based profession. Strengthening the teaching profession depends on increasing the knowledge base for teaching through research *and* basing professional practices on research and the results of student assessment. Using research to anchor teaching is extremely important to the professionalization of teaching.

> A consistent body of data has developed around a few, well-researched teacher behaviors which show a strong correlation with gains in academic achievement. Research findings have relevance and potential usefulness as a basis for developing prescriptions for practice, but valid use of the findings requires interpretation by educators who are knowledgeable about classroom functioning and mindful of the limitations and qualifications that must be placed on any guidelines induced from such research.[4]

As a beginning teacher, you will be expected to base your teaching on what research says constitutes good teaching and practices that promote quality learning and schools.

As we have discussed, the No Child Left Behind Act of 2001 holds states, school districts, and schools accountable for student achievement. The regular assessment of

On the basis of recent educational research, this teacher is trying out cooperative learning as a means of instructional delivery. What characteristics of professional educators does this action reflect?

The educator, believing in the worth and dignity of each human being, recognizes the supreme importance of the pursuit of truth, devotion to excellence, and the nurture of democratic principles. Essential to these goals is the protection of freedom to learn and to teach and the guarantee of equal educational opportunity for all. The educator accepts the responsibility to adhere to the highest ethical standards.

The educator recognizes the magnitude of the responsibility inherent in the teaching process. The desire for the respect and confidence of one's colleagues, of students, of parents, and of the members of the community provides the incentive to attain and maintain the highest possible degree of ethical conduct. The *Code of Ethics of the Education Profession* indicates the aspiration of all educators and provides standards by which to judge conduct.

The remedies specified by the NEA and/or its affiliates for the violation of any provision of this *Code* shall be exclusive and no such provision shall be enforceable in any form other than one specifically designated by the NEA or its affiliates.

PRINCIPLE I

Commitment to the Student

The educator strives to help each student realize his or her potential as a worthy and effective member of society. The educator therefore works to stimulate the spirit of inquiry, the acquisition of knowledge and understanding, and the thoughtful formulation of worthy goals.

In fulfillment of the obligation to the student, the educator—

1. Shall not unreasonably restrain the student from independent action in the pursuit of learning.
2. Shall not unreasonably deny the student access to varying points of view.
3. Shall not deliberately suppress or distort subject matter relevant to the student's progress.
4. Shall make reasonable effort to protect the student from conditions harmful to learning or to health and safety.
5. Shall not intentionally expose the student to embarrassment or disparagement.
6. Shall not on the basis of race, color, creed, sex, national origin, marital status, political or religious beliefs, family, social or cultural background, or sexual orientation, unfairly—
   a. Exclude any student from participation in any program.
   b. Deny benefits to any student.
   c. Grant any advantage to any student.

7. Shall not use professional relationships with students for private advantage.
8. Shall not disclose information about students obtained in the course of professional service, unless disclosure serves a compelling professional purpose or is required by law.

PRINCIPLE II

Commitment to the Profession

The education profession is vested by the public with a trust and responsibility requiring the highest ideals of professional service.

In the belief that the quality of the services of the education profession directly influences the nation and its citizens, the educator shall exert every effort to raise professional standards, to promote a climate that encourages the exercise of professional judgment, to achieve conditions which attract persons worthy of the trust to careers in education, and to assist in preventing the practice of the profession by unqualified persons.

In fulfillment of the obligation to the profession, the educator—

1. Shall not in an application for a professional position deliberately make a false statement or fail to disclose a material fact related to competency and qualifications.
2. Shall not misrepresent his/her professional qualifications.
3. Shall not assist any entry into the profession of a person known to be unqualified in respect to character, education, or other relevant attribute.
4. Shall not knowingly make a false statement concerning the qualifications of a candidate for a professional position.
5. Shall not assist a noneducator in the unauthorized practice of teaching.
6. Shall not disclose information about colleagues obtained in the course of professional service unless disclosure serves a compelling professional purpose or is required by law.
7. Shall not knowingly make false or malicious statements about a colleague.
8. Shall not accept any gratuity, gift, or favor that might impair or appear to influence professional decisions or action.

—Adopted by 1975 Representative Assembly
© 2002, 2003 nea.org

The NEA code states that professionals "shall not unreasonably deny the student access to varying points of view." What might this mean for you as a teacher? What are some things you can do to ensure that students will have access to varying points of view? Would age and maturity of students be factors in your decisions?

_____

_____

_____

Figure 2.5   NEA Code of Ethics of the Education Profession

Source: National Education Association of the United States, *Code of Ethics.* (Online). Available at www.nea.org/code.html. Reprinted by permission.

Data-driven instruction
The practice of using assessment data measuring student performance to evaluate and change instructional practice so that all students succeed.

Laboratory schools
Schools operated by colleges and universities that conduct research, develop exemplary practices of teaching, and provide opportunities for students to observe and participate in teaching processes.

Professional development school (PDS)
A school that has formed a partnership with a college or university for the purposes of improving teacher preparation programs, student achievement, and reforming schools.

NCATE

Elementary

Standard 5.2: Is aware of and reflects on practice in light of research on teaching and resources available for professional learning; continually evaluates effects of professional decisions and actions on students, parents, and other professionals; actively seeks opportunities to grow professionally.

students provides data that inform decisions about how best to increase achievement. **Data-driven instruction** is based on such data. As Figure 2.6 illustrates, data from assessment can be useful for focusing major stakeholders in the educational process. (We will discuss data-driven instruction in more detail in Chapter 11.)

Laboratory Schools. The close tie between research and practice in education has a long history, beginning with laboratory schools. In 1896, John Dewey established his famous laboratory school at the University of Chicago. The school served as a laboratory for trying out Dewey's ideas about child-centered education.

College and university **laboratory schools** are model programs dedicated to research, teacher training, and noteworthy educational practices. Laboratory schools play an important role in teacher-training programs by providing a clinical setting for students to observe, participate, and benefit from the guidance and direction of teachers and professors.

Professional Development Schools. A **professional development school (PDS)**, also called a professional practice school (PPS) or partner school, is a collaboration between schools, colleges, or departments of education and have four major functions: preparation of new teachers, support of student achievement, teacher induction, and development of school and university faculty practice. According to the American Association of Colleges for Teacher Education, the purpose of professional development schools is to "identify, develop, test, and refine practices that promote student achievement; to support initial preparation and continuing professional development for teachers and other school-based educators; and to support applied inquiry designed to improve pupil and educator development."[5] At the Loyola College–Rockburn PDS in Maryland, students in education from Loyola are matched with faculty members from Rockburn, who become their mentors for the year. During the fall, interns experience life in the classroom through weekly observations. In the second semester, interns do their student teaching. Each intern is involved in two eight-week student teaching assignments. Annually, there is a Loyola-Rockburn retreat, where Loyola's PDS faculty joins with the Rockburn staff to examine and discuss PDS issues.[6] Professional development schools are also places where teachers and professors conduct research about best practices. There are more than 600 PDSs currently in operation that facilitate the development of new knowledge and are an important part of the reform of teacher education.

- **Districts** can use information provided from state and local assessments to determine needs and target resources.
- **Schools** can use information from state and local assessments to provide appropriate professional development for teachers and help meet the needs of all subgroups of students.
- **Teachers** can use information from assessments required under NCLB to inform classroom decisions and provide the best possible instruction for student learning so that all students succeed.
- **Parents** have access to regular school, district, and state report cards so they may monitor progress and make informed decisions.

Reflect & Write

As a beginning teacher, your teaching will be guided by data about what your students know and are able to do. How might assessment data enable you to design your teaching, arrange the classroom, and select instructional strategies and activities to meet the individual needs of all your students?

Figure 2.6 *Why Are Data Important?*

Source: U.S. Department of Education. "Using Data to Influence Classroom Decisions," in *No Child Left Behind* (2004). (Online). Available at www.ed.gov/teachers/nclbguide/datadriven.pdf.

Teacher as Researcher. Individual teachers also conduct classroom research through systematic observation and analysis in decision-making contexts. Chapter 1 introduced the concept of teacher as researcher and pointed out that part of the new teacher's role is to engage in action research. **Action research,** shown in Figure 2.7, is a continuing process whereby teachers identify a problem specific to their own teaching and plan and implement a program to solve the identified problem. Teachers study and reflect on the outcomes of their action research. This reflection produces more questions for teachers to investigate, and the action research cycle begins again. Through action research, teachers seek to solve classroom and school-based problems and apply their solutions to everyday practice.

Action research
The continuing process whereby teachers identify a problem specific to their own classroom situation and plan and implement a program to solve the problem.

Professional Development

As a beginning teacher and throughout your teaching, you will be involved in an ongoing process of **professional development,** which consists of ongoing learning opportunities designed to help you gain new knowledge, skills, and attitudes, resulting in increased effectiveness.

Professional development
The process of growing and becoming a professional.

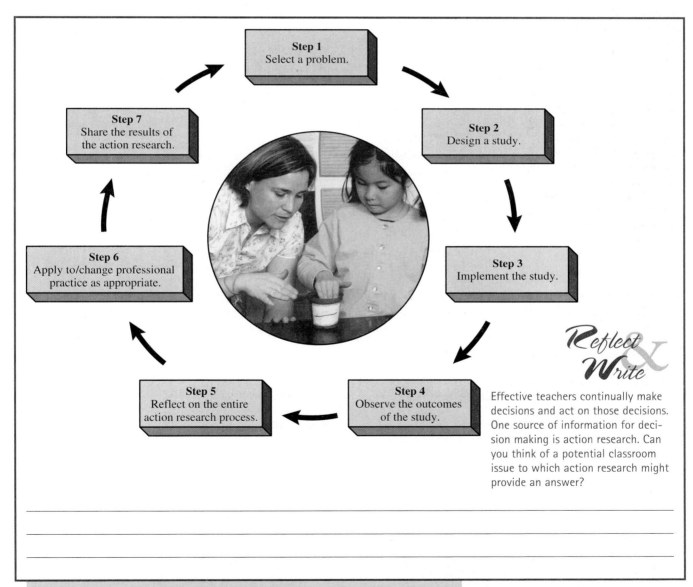

Reflect & Write

Effective teachers continually make decisions and act on those decisions. One source of information for decision making is action research. Can you think of a potential classroom issue to which action research might provide an answer?

_____

_____

_____

Figure 2.7 The Empowerment of Teachers through Action Research

The terms *professional development, staff development,* and *teacher inservice education* are often used synonymously. The No Child Left Behind Act suggests that high-quality professional development includes activities that

- improve and increase knowledge of academic subjects
- are an integral part of schoolwide and districtwide educational improvement plans
- improve classroom management skills
- give teachers knowledge and skills necessary to provide students with the opportunity to meet challenging state academic content and achievement standards
- are sustained, intensive, and classroom focused in order to have a positive and lasting impact on classroom instruction and teacher performance
- advance teachers' understanding of effective instructional strategies
- are developed with the extensive participation of teachers, principals, administrators, and parents
- are designed to give teachers of limited-English-proficient students the knowledge and skills to provide appropriate language and academic support services
- provide training for teachers and principals in the use of technology
- provide instruction in methods of teaching children with special needs
- include instruction in the use of data and assessments to inform classroom practice
- include instruction in the ways in which teachers may work more effectively with parents

Part of your professional development may occur in a **professional learning community,** which includes grade-level teaching teams, school and district committees, and middle and high school department groups.

Professional Organizations for Teachers

Teachers are represented by professional and labor organizations such as the National Education Association (NEA) and the **American Federation of Teachers (AFT).** These organizations exert considerable influence on conditions of employment, organization, governance, compensation and benefits, and curriculum.

The NEA, now with 2.7 million members, was founded in 1857 "to elevate the character and advance the interest of the profession of teaching and to promote the cause of education in the United States." The AFT, founded in 1916, has over 1.3 million members. "The mission of the [AFT AFL-CIO] is to improve the lives of our members and their families, to give voice to their legitimate professional economic and social aspirations, to strengthen the institutions in which we work, to improve the quality of the services we provide, to bring together all members to assist and support one another, and to promote democracy, human rights, and freedom in our union, in our nation, and throughout the world."[7] In 1998, the NEA and AFT formed the NEAFT partnership, an agreement that leaves both groups free to differ and to conduct work separately but also enables them to collaborate on joint projects and expand their areas of cooperation.

Both organizations influence the nature of the relationship among teachers, principals, and boards of education. Unions help set the conditions of employment and the conditions for school-based management and reform.

Both organizations have also moved in recent years to overcome criticism and to be proactive in regard to popular education issues. For example, the NEA supports charter schools and peer review of teachers. The AFT promotes a "zero tolerance" policy that calls for the removal of disruptive students from classrooms.

Unions are also very much involved in the professional development of teachers, informing the public about the nature and needs of public education, and in political activities aimed at influencing the nature and course of education. The NEA and AFT are politically active and support and endorse candidates they believe support their positions on education and will help implement their goals.

NCATE

Elementary

Standard 5.1: Understands and applies practices and behaviors that are characteristic of developing career teachers.

Professional learning community A defined group of educational stakeholders brought together to enable teachers and others to collaborate in support of reflective practice, action research, and ongoing professional development.

American Federation of Teachers (AFT) A national professional association for teachers, affiliated with the AFL-CIO; the second-largest organization of educators.

INTASC

Standard 10: The teacher fosters relationships with school colleagues, parents, and agencies in the larger community to support students' learning and well-being.

Membership in professional organizations offers teachers numerous opportunities for taking part in meetings and conferences that promote professional growth and development and peer networking.

Both presidents—Sandra Feldman of the AFT and Reg Weaver of the NEA—write influential columns published as advertisements in national newspapers and magazines. For example, Feldman, in her column called "Where We Stand," had this to say:

Teacher expertise is one of the most important factors in student achievement. Yet the way we select, prepare, and train teachers often fails to reflect the importance of their role. Fortunately, most teachers do well, but too often, school officials hire individuals who are not adequately prepared to teach, a problem that is especially prevalent in schools with large numbers of poor and minority students. An estimated 6.5 percent of the 200,000 new teachers public schools hire each year are not fully certified. What's more, depending on their discipline, up to a third of public school teachers are teaching subjects in which they didn't major, or minor, when they were in college.

Our nation's public schools need to hire and retain some 200,000 new teachers each year—at a time when fewer graduates are choosing teaching careers. Compounding that challenge is a fast-approaching deadline for schools to meet federally imposed standards for teacher quality or be penalized. This challenge won't be met without careful planning and policy changes. The good news is that there are steps school officials can take immediately to improve teacher quality.

- Strengthen "student teaching." For too many teacher candidates, college course work and student teaching experiences don't provide enough hands-on classroom work with close supervision and constructive feedback. Future teachers need to learn how to handle real classroom situations and challenges before they start teaching.
- Mentoring and peer review. From the start, teachers need ongoing support from skilled veterans who observe them in the classroom and show them ways to improve their work with students. Teachers want to do well. Mentoring and peer review programs across the country are helping to attract and keep good teachers—and to remove from classrooms teachers whose skills aren't up to the task.
- Reduce "out of field" teaching. Teachers should teach subjects they know. It's wrong to have an unprepared teacher take over a math or science class because no one trained in that field is available. Financial incentives for current faculty to take courses in subject areas where the school has a staffing shortage can help.
- Ongoing teacher training. The most successful companies invest in ongoing training and development for their employees, and schools should, too. Professional development in the best and latest techniques helps teachers stay current with their subject areas, learn new teaching methods, and exchange advice and experiences with their colleagues. At

INTASC

Standard 9: The teacher is a reflective practitioner who continually evaluates the effects of his/her choices and actions on others (students, parents, and other professionals in the learning community) and who actively seeks out opportunities to grow professionally.

the Chicago Teachers Union Quest Center, for example, new and experienced teachers alike benefit from the training they receive from their accomplished colleagues, in terms of both strengthened teacher practice and improved teacher retention.

Teacher quality is one very important factor in student achievement, and it is an area in which school districts can made a real and immediate difference.[8]

NEA president Reg Weaver confronted a different issue in this statement about diversity in the teaching force:

Most parents prize diversity within their children's public schools. . . . But how "diverse" and "real-world" is a school that does not have any minority teachers? The bad news is that some 40 percent of America's public schools have no teachers of color. The good news is that we have an opportunity to recruit and encourage more Americans of color to enter the teaching profession. And our success in doing so can have a powerfully positive impact on student achievement.

Bear in mind that teachers do not teach only facts and "content." They also model appropriate behaviors and teach by personal example. . . . So it is important to expose children to a diverse teaching staff within each of our schools. Where we have an urban school with an all-minority staff or a suburban school with an all-white staff, we are giving students a stunted educational experience.

NEA has made it a core strategic priority to increase the recruitment and retention of teachers of diverse backgrounds. Beyond NEA's own programs, we are joining with other organizations to create the National Collaborative on Diversity in the Teacher Workforce. But we can't do it alone. States and school districts need to develop programs to assist teachers' aides—large numbers of whom are minorities—to advance their education and become fully licensed teachers.[9]

NCATE

Elementary

Standard 5.1: Understands and applies practices and behaviors that are characteristic of developing career teachers.

In contrast to their role in social activism, teachers' unions are sometimes seen as preserving the status quo in terms of how schools operate and how teachers are hired and dismissed. Critics of schools frequently cite teachers' unions as a barrier to change. However, teachers' unions are also viewed by their supporters as initiators of change and supportive of teachers who want to engage in new practices and develop new curricula. As a beginning teacher, you may not have a choice of whether or not you want to join the union. In some instances, belonging to a union is part of the contractual process. Nonetheless, you can take your role and responsibilities as a union member seriously and work within the organization for change and for improving the profession.

In addition to NEA and AFT, there are also many large independent teachers' organizations. The largest of these are:

- Association of Texas Professional Educators. Founded 1980, 100,000 members.
- Missouri State Teachers Association. Founded 1856, 43,000 members.
- Professional Educators of North Carolina. Founded 1979, 7,000 members.
- Mississippi Professional Educators. Founded 1979, over 6,500 members.
- Palmetto State Teachers Association (South Carolina). Founded 1976, 6,000 members.

NCATE

Early Childhood

Standard 5: Uses ethical guidelines and other professional standards; is a continuous, collaborative learner who demonstrates knowledgeable, reflective, and critical perspectives; is an informed advocate for sound educational practices.

Other professional organizations reflect interest in particular subject areas or in particular student groups. For instance, in the past decade, professional organizations such as the National Council of Teachers of Mathematics have exerted considerable influence over the content of mathematics and how it is taught. Many organizations that represent professionals in a particular academic area feel that they must take responsibility and initiative for helping determine what should be taught and how the classroom and school should be organized for effective teaching and learning.

The National Association for the Education of Young Children (NAEYC) is the largest professional organization of early childhood professionals, with more than 92,000 members. NAEYC helps improve the professional practice of early childhood educators, sets standards for professional practice, and increases public understanding of high-quality programs for young children and their families.

Many other professional organizations provide teachers the opportunity to be involved with colleagues who are interested in particular career and discipline areas. Some of these are shown in Figure 2.8.

Council for Exceptional Children (CEC)—www.cec.sped.org
National Science Teachers Association (NSTA)—www.nsta.org
National Council of Teachers of English (NCTE)—www.ncte.org
National Council for the Social Studies (NCSS)—www.ncss.org
National Association for Music Education (MENC)—www.menc.org
National Association for the Education of Young Children (NAEYC)—www.naeyc.org
Association of Career and Technical Education (ACTE)—www.acteonline.org
International Reading Association (IRA)—www.reading.org
National Council of Teachers of Mathematics (NCTM)—www.nctm.org
American Council on the Teaching of Foreign Language (ACTFL)—www.actfl.org
American Alliance for Health, Physical Education, Recreation, and Dance (AAHPERD)—
    www.aahperd.org
National Art Education Association (NAEA)—www.naea-reston.org
Association for Education Communications and Technology (AECT)—www.aect.org
National Association for Gifted Children (GIFTED)—www.nagc.org
National Black Child Development Institute (NBCDI)—www.nbcdi.org
National Association for Bilingual Education (BILINGUAL)—www.nabe.org

Reflect & Write

At this stage in your career, what professional organization do you think you will be most likely to join? Give two reasons for how you think a professional organization can help you become a better teacher.

Figure 2.8   *Professional Organizations for Teachers*

SECTION SUMMARY

- Is Teaching a Profession? Linda Beck, whose story opened this chapter, typifies the more than 3 million professional teachers who are involved in a process of career-long learning and are dedicated to keeping abreast of new knowledge in their fields. Today's teachers collaborate with their colleagues and other community members who have a stake in education. They attend professional conferences and meetings to extend and enrich their own knowledge and to learn new ways to benefit students. Like Linda, today's professional teachers mentor and guide the education of future teachers.

- Praxis and Teacher Certification Testing. Teaching is a helping profession. Like other professionals, teachers have specialized skills, and they have met entrance and exit requirements for their scholarly training. They take state examinations and other tests such as Praxis for licensure. Teachers are subject to ongoing reviews of the quality of their performance.

- The Professionalization of Teaching. The professionalization of teaching involves certification, accountability, ethical practice, high practice standards, collaboration and shared decision making, increased knowledge base, and challenging teaching. The NCTAF's recommendations have had a strong impact on teacher preparation and school reform. The New Professional Teacher project of the NCATE is an attempt to transform teaching and enhance the performance of teachers, in part through setting professional standards in collaboration with subject matter associations. The NBPTS program for national teacher certification is another force in the teacher professionalization movement. Teacher organizations such as the NEA, AFT, and TEAC are devoted to improving teaching and learning and the professionalization of teaching.

- Professional Ethics. The teaching profession does not have a unified code of ethics, but professional organizations that represent educators, such as the National Education Association, have developed codes of ethics that help inform and guide teachers in their interactions with students and others. Ethical practice does not stem from a formal list, however; professionals must constantly monitor their own behavior and think and reflect on their own practices.

- Basing Practice on Evidence-Based Inquiry and Assessment. Strengthening the teaching profession means not only increasing the knowledge base for teaching through research but also basing professional practices in research. Laboratory schools and professional development schools are dedicated to enriching teacher training and incorporating current research. Individual teachers also engage in the continuing process of action research, identifying problems specific to their own teaching, reflecting on those problems, and implementing programs to solve them.

- Professional Development. Professional development will be an important part of your teaching career. The kind of activities that will be included in your professional development will be based on what the NCLB identifies as important activities, all designed to increase student achievement and meet state standards. Additionally, your professional development will occur in professional learning communities that promote collaboration and student learning.

- Professional Organizations for Teachers. The two leading professional organizations for teachers are the National Education Association and the American Federation of Teachers. Other independent organizations exist at the state level, and some professional organizations for teachers are focused on a content area or student group.

Thinking Critically
★ ★ ★ ★ ★ ★ ★ ★ ★

What does *professionalism* in teaching mean to you? Begin by defining *professional*. Then list the positive characteristics of professionals you have known, such as doctors, lawyers, and accountants. Reflect on how you can apply these positive attributes to your teaching.

_____

_____

_____

_____ ★

Applying What You've Learned
★ ★ ★ ★ ★ ★ ★ ★ ★

Research to see if your state or district has a code of ethical practice for teachers. What parts of the ethical conduct code do you find most challenging? Interview teachers and ask them what issues they face in their practice of ethical conduct.

_____

_____

_____ ★

Putting Yourself in the Picture
★ ★ ★ ★ ★ ★ ★ ★ ★

Data-driven instruction is an integral part of how teachers teach. While we will discuss this topic more in Chapter 11, begin to put yourself in the picture now by asking teachers for examples of how they use student assessment data to guide their teaching.

_____

_____

_____

_____ ★

HOW ARE REFORM MOVEMENTS CHANGING TEACHER EDUCATION?

The reform of schools and the reform of teacher education go hand in hand. Colleges and universities are changing how teachers are educated to prepare them for their new roles in schools and to ensure the success of educational reforms.

Just as school reform was and is influenced by reform reports (see Chapter 1), so teacher education reforms are fueled by similar reports. The **Carnegie Task Force on Teaching as a Profession**—which authored *A Nation Prepared: Teachers for the 21st Century*[10]—has been particularly influential. This report was critical of how the nation's colleges and universities prepare teachers and recommended more rigorous education in their preparation. As a result, an increasing number of the 1,300 teacher-training programs in the United States are seeking ways to better train teachers so that they are equipped with the knowledge and skills for both effective teaching and effective participation in school restructuring activities. Some colleges of education have formed and joined organized reform groups specifically designed to promote teacher education reform. Some of these are:

- Holmes Partnership. The Holmes Partnership (originally the Holmes Group) is named after Henry W. Holmes, former dean of the Harvard Graduate School of Education. The Holmes Partnership, a consortium of research universities, public school districts, and organizations that represent professional educators, has six principal goals:

  Goal 1: High-quality professional preparation. Provide exemplary professional preparation and development programs for public school educators.
  Goal 2: Simultaneous renewal. Engage in the simultaneous renewal of public K–12 schools and teacher education programs.
  Goal 3: Equity, diversity, and cultural competence. Actively work on equity, diversity, and cultural competence in the programs of K–12 schools, higher education, and the education profession.
  Goal 4: Scholarly inquiry and programs of research. Conduct and disseminate educational research and engage in other scholarly activities that advance knowledge, improve teaching and learning for all children and youth, inform the preparation and development of educators, and influence educational policy and practice.
  Goal 5: School and university-based faculty development. Provide high-quality doctoral programs for the future education professoriate and for advanced professional development of school-based educators.
  Goal 6: Policy initiation. Engage in policy analysis and development related to public schools and the preparation of educators.[11]

  One of the major accomplishments of the Holmes Partnership has been the creation of the professional development school (PDS), as discussed in the previous section.

- Project 30 Alliance. This organization endeavors to erase the lines between education and liberal arts courses and to add more liberal arts courses to teacher training. The concept is that teachers should have a thorough knowledge of the subject disciplines they teach. (More information is available at http://astecproject30.org.)

- Renaissance Group. This group believes teacher training programs must have the full support of colleges and universities and that classroom experiences for prospective teachers must begin before their senior year. (More information is available at www.empharia.edu/rengroup/index.htm.)

While all teacher education reform efforts differ in their details and the priorities they advocate, they all have some common themes, as depicted in Figure 2.9.

Carnegie Task Force on Teaching as a Profession
This group issued the report *A Nation Prepared: Teachers for the 21st Century* criticizing how the nation's colleges and universities prepare teachers and recommending more rigorous teacher education.
A Nation Prepared: Teachers for the 21st Century
A Carnegie Foundation report that criticizes how the nation's colleges and universities prepare teachers and recommends more rigorous teacher preparation.

INTASC

Standard 9: The teacher is a reflective practitioner who continually evaluates the effects of his/her choices and actions on others (students, parents, and other professionals in the learning community) and who actively seeks out opportunities to grow professionally.

NCATE

Early Childhood

Standard 5: Uses ethical guidelines and other professional standards; is a continuous, collaborative learner who demonstrates knowledgeable, reflective, and critical perspectives; is an informed advocate for sound educational practices.

Middle Level

Standard 7: Understands the complexity of teaching young adolescents; engages in practices and behaviors that develop competence as a professional.

FORCES THAT CAUSE AND INFLUENCE TEACHER REFORM	HOW TEACHER EDUCATION REFORM IS IMPLEMENTED	PRODUCTS OF TEACHER EDUCATION REFORM
• Federal legislation, such as NCLB • State standards for what students should know and do • State standards for the licensing and certification of teachers • Standards set by national organizations, such as INTASC • Standards of national professional organizations, such as the National Council of Teachers of Mathematics	• Colleges of education change/modify their programs in response to legislation, standards, and public pressure • Colleges of education raise standards for admission • Colleges of education emphasize teaching content and pedagogy teacher education students need to pass university and state teacher tests • Other agencies, such as private, for-profit universities and intermediate units, enter the field of teacher preparation • Federal and state politicians lobby colleges of education to reform their programs • Federal agencies and state governments provide grants to entice and encourage colleges of education to reform their programs	• More rigorous teacher education programs • Teacher education programs based on national and state standards • Testing programs for licensure and certification • Higher standards (e.g., higher GPA) for admission to teacher education programs • Creation of alternative and multiple types of programs for teacher education and certification • Colleges of education engage in collaborative programs with public schools, such as professional development schools • Five-year teacher education programs • Emphasis on performance-based teaching

Reflect & Write

Your teacher education program likely has been influenced by some of the reform initiatives. Identify two ways your program has changed. As a future teacher engaged in some form of teacher preparation, you probably have some ideas about how to reinvent the process. What two recommendations would you make?

Figure 2.9   *Reforming Teacher Education*

Changing Standards for Teacher Education

One way states are seeking to change and improve teacher education is through new and higher standards. This is reflected through new certification standards that specify what teachers should know and be able to do. Although there is an arbitrary standard for what teachers should know, various organizations also have specific standards for what teachers should know and be able to do.

The Interstate New Teacher Assessment and Support Consortium (INTASC) is a consortium of state education agencies, higher education institutions, and national educational organizations dedicated to the reform of the education, licensing, and ongoing professional development of teachers. Created in 1987, INTASC's primary constituency is state education agencies responsible for teacher licensing and professional development. Its work is guided by one basic premise: an effective teacher must be able to integrate content knowledge with pedagogical understanding to ensure that

NCATE

Elementary

Standard 5.1: Understands and applies practices and behaviors that are characteristic of developing career teachers.

all students learn and perform at high levels.[12] INTASC identified ten basic standards (see Figure 2.10) that beginning teachers should be able to meet.

NCATE's role in reforming teacher education and what the new professional teacher knows and is able to do was discussed earlier in the chapter. Some of these efforts will be touched on throughout the book. Together, NCATE and INTASC are helping to change the professional expectations and landscape for today's educators.

Standard	Description
1—Content Pedagogy	The teacher understands the central concepts, tools of inquiry, and structures of the discipline he or she teaches and can create learning experiences that make these aspects of subject matter meaningful for students.
2—Student Development	The teacher understands how children learn and develop and can provide learning opportunities that support their intellectual, social, and personal development.
3—Diverse Learners	The teacher understands how students differ in their approaches to learning and creates instructional opportunities that are adapted to diverse learners.
4—Multiple Instructional Strategies	The teacher understands and uses a variety of instructional strategies to encourage students' development of critical thinking, problem solving, and performance skills.
5—Motivation and Management	The teacher uses an understanding of individual and group motivation and behavior to create a learning environment that encourages positive social interaction, active engagement in learning, and self-motivation.
6—Communication and Technology	The teacher uses knowledge of effective verbal, nonverbal, and media communication techniques to foster active inquiry, collaboration, and supportive interaction in the classroom.
7—Planning	The teacher plans instruction based upon knowledge of subject matter, students, the community, and curriculum goals.
8—Assessment	The teacher understands and uses formal and informal assessment strategies to evaluate and ensure the continuous intellectual, social, and physical development of the learner.
9—Reflective Practice: Professional Growth	The teacher is a reflective practitioner who continually evaluates the effects of his or her choices and actions on others (students, parents, and other professionals in the learning community) and who actively seeks out opportunities to grow professionally.
10—School and Community Involvement	The teacher fosters relationships with school colleagues, parents, and agencies in the larger community to support students' learning and well-being.

Reflect & Write

Which of the INTASC standards do you think you may need the most help in meeting? What can you do now to become more proficient in all the ten standards?

_____

_____

_____

Figure 2.10   INTASC Standards: What Beginning Teachers Should Know and Be Able to Do

Source: Interstate New Teacher Assessment and Support Consortium, *Model Standards for Beginning Teacher Licensing and Development: A Resource for State Dialogue* (Washington, DC: Council of Chief State School Officers, 1991). (Online). Available at www.ccsso.org/content/pdfs.corestrd.pdf. Reprinted by permission.

More than likely, your teacher preparation program has been and is being influenced by the INTASC and NCATE standards. As the author of this textbook, which is helping you prepare for your teaching career, I have integrated the INTASC and NCATE standards into every chapter and topic. Margin notes alert you to content that addresses INTASC and NCATE standards. In addition, state and national teacher exams are written to test your and your classmates' knowledge of what both sets of standards say teachers should know and be able to do.

In addition to national organizations setting standards for new teachers, states are also increasing the requirements of teacher education programs. For example, in Georgia, elementary education candidates are required to have an academic minor in reading and math; middle school teachers must have a concentration in language arts, math, science, and social studies; and high school teachers need to complete expanded requirements in the subjects they expect to teach. Maryland requires that teacher education graduates complete twelve hours of reading instruction. These are typical of the ways states and colleges of education are helping ensure that teachers will have sufficient knowledge of the areas in which they will teach.

The American Council of Education (ACE), in its influential report "To Touch the Future: Transforming the Way Teachers are Taught," challenges colleges and universities to reform teacher education. "Colleges and universities have educated virtually every teacher in every classroom in every school in the country; thus, it is colleges and universities that must take responsibility for the way teachers are taught, and ultimately the way children are taught."[13]

The report charges colleges and universities with teacher preparation programs to (1) move the education of teachers to the center of their institutional agenda; (2) connect teacher education to the mission of the institution, with the full support and coordination of the academic departments; (3) conduct third-party and internal evaluations of the quality of their teacher education programs; (4) ensure that graduates of their programs are supported, monitored, and mentored; and (5) ensure that future teachers are educated in the uses of technology.

What Does This Mean for You?

The INTASC and NCATE standards have implications for you as a teacher education student and as a beginning teacher. You will receive much more extensive and specialized preparation based on theory, research, content area methods, and guided practice than teachers of the past. Furthermore, you will be more accountable for student success, as measured by local, state, and national standards and tests.

What Does This Mean for You?

The reform movement in teacher education will profoundly affect your career as a teacher in a number of ways.

- Both as a preservice teacher and as a beginning teacher, you will have to meet the definition of "highly qualified" that is in place at the national level and in your state and local school district.
- You may have to meet recertification standards at regular intervals. A major trend is for teachers to periodically renew their license to teach through ongoing education. Lifetime licenses to teach are being replaced by periodic demonstrations that teachers meet the "highly qualified" standard.
- As school districts constantly monitor and upgrade their teaching staffs, you will participate in staff development designed to ensure that you and your colleagues are in fact highly qualified, and that you are teaching in ways that will ensure student learning.

A teacher is never finished with her professional education. Current forces of teacher education reform probably will mean that your education is never entirely complete.

Politics and Teacher Education Reform

The whole school accountability movement has encouraged and promoted reform in teacher education. The public and politicians have demanded more accountability of schools and classroom teachers to increase student achievement and to ensure that all students learn. This school-based accountability movement has in turn beamed the spotlight of accountability on colleges of education to educate more highly qualified teachers.

The No Child Left Behind Act of 2001 is also playing a significant role in the reform of teacher education by its call to raise the quality of the nation's teachers. NCLB requires that every student be taught by a highly qualified teacher by 2006. Consequently, colleges of education are under significant pressure to ensure that all of their graduates are "highly qualified." This accounts, in part, for the increased emphasis on testing of teachers to help ensure that they are qualified to teach. The current emphasis on improving the nation's schools by providing every student with a "highly qualified" teacher will have an impact that should not be underestimated.

Changing Teacher Education Programs

Reverend Samuel Hall established the first private normal school, or standard teacher-training school, in 1823 in Concord, Vermont. Horace Mann helped establish the first state-supported normal school in 1839 (some sources say 1837) in Lexington, Massachusetts. Formal teacher education began with Henry Bernard in 1867, with the first Department of Education in the federal government and the first normal teaching programs in 1896. Teacher education lasted two years and consisted mainly of learning how to teach. Beginning in the 1950s, many normal schools made the transition to state teacher colleges. Gradually, the "teacher" designation was dropped, and today many former normal schools are state universities. So, change in teacher education as in all of education is a natural and evolutionary process. We would expect teacher education to change as society changes and as the public, politicians, and educators develop new visions for what teaching is and what it should be like.

Four-Year Programs. Today, many teacher education programs are four-year programs. Generally, the first two years are devoted to general studies at the "lower division" consisting of arts and sciences courses. Students then meet teacher education admissions requirements—usually grade-point averages and basic skills tests—and are admitted to the teacher education program and "upper-division" courses. The last two years are devoted to professional studies and clinical field experiences culminating in a semester-long student teaching experience.

Five-Year Programs. Some professional schools of education, especially those that belong to the Holmes Partnership, have five-year teacher education programs. These programs are generally of two kinds. The teacher-training program is extended across five years, providing for more arts and sciences courses, especially in a content area, and for more field experiences. In these programs, students graduate with a bachelor's degree. In other five-year programs, students earn a bachelor's degree, which includes only arts and sciences courses, or a combination of arts and sciences classes and education courses as well as field experiences. Students then apply for admission to teacher education and take education courses culminating in a master's degree.

> **NCATE**
> Elementary
> **Standard 3.2:** Understands how elementary students differ in development and approaches to learning; creates instructional opportunities that are adapted to diverse students.

There are a number of pros and cons to various teacher training programs, depending on whose point of view is considered. Four-year programs enable students to enter teaching sooner and cost students less money. They also supply more teachers to meet the rising demand for teachers. Five-year programs provide a more rigorous preparation and a solid grounding in the liberal arts. Not all students agree that entering the teaching field with a master's degree is an advantage. They argue that they have a better chance of getting a job without the master's because they will be hired at a lower level on the salary scale than will a person with a master's degree. Also, they argue that many school districts will reimburse for master's-level courses and provide a salary increment for earning the master's.

Preparation for Teaching in Diverse Schools. Students in schools represent the diversity of the population as a whole. They bring varied cultural and ethnic backgrounds and differences in values, learning expectations, and family expectations to the classroom. Some of your students—about one in five—will speak a primary language other than English. Some of your students will be new immigrants who will need your help to make sense of a new language, culture, and behavioral standards.

Student teachers gain valuable experience in the classroom through observation and hands-on experiences with children. How might education reforms and the raising of professional standards affect teacher education programs?

Standard 3: The teacher understands how students differ in their approaches to learning and creates instructional opportunities that are adapted to diverse learners.

INTASC

All students have the same basic needs—for food, clothing, shelter, safety, belonging, and affection. Students also have individual needs based on their individual histories, backgrounds, and how well their basic needs have or have not been met. Your students will also have needs based on their abilities, achievements, and learning styles.

Being aware of the various dimensions of diversity that students have will enable you to better address their educational needs. One of your biggest challenges will be to provide a variety of worthwhile and growth-producing experiences for all your students. The following are best practices for preparing teachers for multicultural teaching and learning:

- Multicultural education must be infused throughout the entire preservice program. Courses that have multicultural education throughout the curriculum and instructional methods are important building blocks for helping preservice students acquire an acceptance of multicultural knowledge and knowledge about their personal and professional awareness of diversity. But alone these courses are not sufficient for preparing students to teach in urban schools or to teach all students.
- Workshops on multicultural education offer some benefit for preservice students, but in and of themselves, they are not adequate for preparing students to teach all students.
- Preservice programs that have multicultural education infused throughout and that include a field experience in which student teachers are immersed in a culturally diverse community help prepare teachers to work in urban schools or to teach all students. When providing preservice programs with experiences in culturally diverse communities, it is important to understand the total student and to put curriculum and instruction in a context familiar to students.
- Preservice teachers need to be placed with cooperating teachers who have a thorough knowledge of multicultural education, accept a multicultural focus as a classroom need, and advocate multicultural education throughout their teaching. Also, the university supervisor must be informed about multicultural education.
- Instruction about multicultural education needs to take place in many forms—for example, readings, preservice experience in multicultural schools, and living in a multicultural community. Students need to do projects or complete assignments that require them to critically analyze race, class, and gender issues.[14]

In what ways is your teacher-training program preparing you to teach in diverse settings? How might the program better prepare you?

_____

_____

_____

_____

SECTION SUMMARY

How Are Reform Movements Changing Teacher Education?

Reform movements are sparked by reports such as the Carnegie Task Force on Teaching as a Profession's *A Nation Prepared: Teachers for the 21st Century.*

Several organizations are attempting to change how teachers are prepared and are advocating more rigorous standards and longer periods of training in professional development schools. Among them are the Holmes Partnership, a consortium that encourages and supports the creation of professional development schools as a means of enhancing the quality of teacher preparation; the Project 30 Alliance, which proposes that teachers should have a thorough knowledge of the subjects they teach; and the Renaissance Group, which believes that teachers must begin their classroom experiences before their senior year.

- Changing Standards for Teacher Education. States are improving teacher education, in part through setting higher standards for teacher certification. NCATE and INTASC have set standards for the preparation of teachers that are influential in determining what teachers should know and be able to do and in how colleges of education prepare teachers. States are also increasing requirements for teacher education programs. Because of the more rigorous standards, this generation of teachers will receive much more extensive and specialized preparation based on theory, research, content area methods, and guided practice than did the teachers of the past. And today's teachers will be held more accountable for student success.

- Politics and Teacher Education Reform. The public and politicians are demanding more accountability from schools and teachers for higher student achievement. This school-based accountability means that teacher education programs are being held accountable for educating highly qualified teachers who can increase student achievement. In addition, the No Child Left Behind Act's provisions for all students to be taught by "highly qualified teachers" creates pressure for teacher education programs to reexamine their programs.

- Changing Teacher Education Programs. Currently, teacher education programs tend to be four-year programs, with the first two years devoted to general studies and the last two years devoted to professional studies and clinical field experiences, ending with one semester of student teaching. Where five-year programs are implemented, students may graduate with a bachelor's degree but may include additional field experience or additional arts and science courses or both. Four-year and five-year programs each have their own advantages. All teacher-training programs must prepare teachers to work with and respect the multicultural classrooms that characterize today's diverse society.

Thinking Critically
★ ★ ★ ★ ★ ★ ★ ★

Experienced teachers often say that teaching is not just a job or even just a career; it is a way of life. What do you think these teachers mean? Do you agree with this statement? Do you plan to make teaching your way of life? How?

_____

_____

_____

_____ ★

Applying What You've Learned
★ ★ ★ ★ ★ ★ ★ ★

How have recent teacher education reform proposals affected your teacher preparation program? How is your teacher education program accredited? Is it approved by NCATE or by another agency? What professional standards does your teacher education program strive to uphold? In what ways is your program preparing you to compete with applicants from other colleges and universities for teaching jobs?

_____

_____

_____

_____ ★

You are a faculty member in a teacher education program. You have just been selected as a member of the team that will review the program to ensure that it is preparing future teachers to take an active part in multicultural education when they become teaching professionals. What will you want to know about the courses currently being taught in your school's program? What guidelines will you recommend for any future courses that faculty members want to add to the present course listing?

*W*HO ARE TODAY'S TEACHERS?

When you think about teachers, of whom do you think? Perhaps you think about your favorite teacher from high school or the teacher who helped you learn to read. Perhaps you picture the teacher you want to be. Whatever your vision, the fact is that the nation's 4.4 million teachers are a diverse group. One way of looking at teachers is to examine their characteristics. The following information about teachers and the teaching force will help you understand who teachers are.

Characteristics of the Teaching Force

Table 2.1 reveals two striking characteristics about today's teaching force: It is female and white. Seventy-five percent of all teachers are female, and the overwhelming majority are white or Anglo-European American. Approximately one-third of the entire teaching force is between the ages of 40 and 49, and a third of the teaching force is over 50 years old.[15] The graying of the teaching force means that the demand for teachers will be greater as more teachers approach retirement age. Many people think that the teaching force should be more balanced—that because the student population is more diverse, so too should be the teaching force. What are some implications for having a teaching force that is not as diverse as the student population?

Teacher Diversity

While the nation's population becomes more multicultural and multiethnic, the teaching force remains nondiverse, much as it was two decades ago. Forty percent of the student population is multicultural—African American, Hispanic American, Asian American, and Native American—but only 15 percent of the teaching force is multicultural.[16] For the first time in the nation's history, the number of Hispanic children under age 18 surpasses African American children. Hispanic children are the largest minority group. The impact of the lack of minority teachers to teach minority students—or indeed students of any culture—stands out in sharper contrast when we look at teacher-to-student ratios. For example, in the Miami-Dade County School System, there is one white teacher for every five white students, one black teacher for every nineteen black students, and one Hispanic teacher for every twenty-five Hispanic students.[17]

The comparative lack of racial and ethnic diversity among teachers has a number of implications. First, colleges of education and school districts must increase their efforts to recruit and attract minorities into the profession. Second, public and private schools and other agencies must implement programs to attract minority students to teaching as a career.

Table 2.1 *T*eachers in Public and Private Elementary and Secondary Schools, 1999–2000

Total	3,451,315
Men	861,067
Women	2,590,249
Race/ethnicity	
White	2,933,590
Black	244,035
Hispanic	190,049
Asian or Pacific Islander	55,293
American Indian or Alaskan	28,349
Age	
Less than 30	595,987
30 to 39	761,461
40 to 49	1,084,136
50 to 59	891,251
60 or more	118,480

Source: National Center for Education Statistics, *Digest of Education Statistics, 2002,* table 68. (Online). Available at www.nces.ed.gov/pubs/digest.

Mildred Hudson, CEO of Recruiting New Teachers, Inc., says, "A student today could go through twelve years of education without ever seeing a teacher of color. One-third of public school students are children of racial or ethnic minority, while only 13 percent of educators are teachers of color. Forty percent of U.S. schools have no minority teachers at all. That's just not good enough." Hudson thinks it is time to focus sustained attention on new models for recruiting and retaining a qualified, diverse teacher work force. Some of Hudson's suggestions are:

What skills do new professional teachers need to teach diverse students? What reasons are given for seeking to increase racial and ethnic diversity in the teaching force? What reasons are given for seeking to increase the proportion of male teachers in the teaching force?

- **Acknowledge the problem.** The misperception has been that minorities don't want to go into the profession. But when you see the obstacles as real—the lack of scholarship support, low retention rates of minority teacher education students, the test-score gap in teaching licensure—you can begin to remove them and be effective.
- **Open the pipeline early.** It's too late if you try to recruit in college. Establish middle and high school teaching academies to introduce teaching as a career choice early.
- **Expand the teacher candidate pool.** Target paraeducators, midcareer adults, community college students, recent graduates in liberal arts, and specific populations who have the potential of staying in urban and rural communities. Many paraeducators have been in the classroom for a lifetime but don't have the support they need if they want to become teachers. Former Peace Corps volunteers are excellent candidates, because many have teaching credentials and experience working in multicultural environments and speak a second language.
- **Shun stop-gap measures.** Stop bringing unqualified teachers in through the back door—those without knowledge, certification, or classroom experience. Uncertified teachers are more often than not placed in high-poverty communities, and this exacerbates the problem for students and staff alike.
- **Provide quality induction programs.** Create a continuous network of support, mentorship, and professional development. Minority educators have high retention rates when given the proper support systems, and paraeducators from the community tend to stay there.
- **Provide alternative compensation.** Commit to meaningful financial support, such as scholarship support for teacher prep programs, housing allowances, and signing bonuses. Loan forgiveness is a key incentive for minority educators.[18]

Phi Delta Kappa, the professional fraternity in education, sponsors Future Educators of America (FEA), an organization designed to provide middle and high school students with opportunities to explore teaching as a career option and to help students gain a realistic understanding of the nature of education and the role of the teacher. FEA also helps encourage students from diverse backgrounds to think seriously about the teaching profession. Additionally, FEA offers a chance to shape our nation's future by shaping the future of the education professional and gives teachers opportunities to examine, clarify, and explain their role in students' lives. For colleges, FEA expands the pool of applicants to teacher education programs and provides early identification of potentially excellent future teachers.

Some states, such as South Carolina, have statewide programs to recruit students into teaching, especially minority students. For example, the Teacher Cadet Program for High School Students and the Pro Team Program for Middle School Students actively involve students in opportunities to consider teaching as a career. More information is available online at www.cerra.org/teachercadet.asp.

What are some reasons why there are not more men and minorities in teaching? In addition to what Mildred Hudson proposes, what would you propose to attract minorities and men to the profession?

_____

_____

_____

_____

SECTION SUMMARY

Who Are Today's Teachers?

Today's teachers do not reflect the multicultural and multiethnic characteristics of the U.S. population.

- Characteristics of the Teaching Force. Today's teaching force is overwhelmingly female, white, and middle aged.
- Teacher Diversity. Colleges and schools of education must work with private and public schools to increase efforts to attract more men and minorities to the teaching profession. The teaching profession itself must address shortages of teachers in particular fields and in urban areas.

Thinking Critically
★ ★ ★ ★ ★ ★ ★ ★

Review and reflect on the opening case. How might Linda Beck's plans for her school's Diversity Day have altered if her students were primarily bilingual, first-generation Latino Americans and Asian Americans and her school was located in a West Coast urban center?

_____

_____

_____

_____★

Applying What You've Learned
★ ★ ★ ★ ★ ★ ★ ★

What are school districts in your area doing to attract men and minority students to the teaching profession?

_____

_____

_____

_____★

While teacher education reform comes from many sources, as discussed, other forces are at play as well: the teaching force is getting older, is predominantly female, and lacks diversity, and there is an ongoing teacher shortage. These demographic factors have created a need for more and different kinds of teachers than those educated by traditional colleges of education. One result is the tremendous growth of alternative teacher education programs. Put yourself in the picture now by making a list of different kinds of alternative teacher education programs. Begin by logging on to the Troops to Teachers Program at www.proudtoserveagain.com and the National Teacher Recruitment Clearing House at www.rnt.org/.

WHAT JOB OPPORTUNITIES DO YOU HAVE AS A TEACHER?

As a prospective teacher, you will analyze job opportunities in terms of a number of key factors: salaries offered, benefits available, and vacancies reflecting teacher demand in different parts of the country and in different subject areas. You will balance these factors with your own feelings about where you want to teach and the students you are most comfortable teaching. The following sections will give you an idea of what to expect.

Salaries and Benefits

Teachers' salaries vary greatly from state to state and region to region. Table 2.2 shows teachers' salaries by state. The lowest-paying states are North Dakota and South Dakota, and the highest-paying states are Connecticut and New Jersey, but salaries must be evaluated in relation to differences in the cost of living, which is higher in states like Connecticut and New Jersey. In other words, a teacher in Connecticut earns more but has to pay more for food, clothing, and housing. By region, the southern states are the lowest paying, and the northeastern the highest paying. On the other hand, southern states on average provide less support to public education.

The conventional view that public school teachers are woefully underpaid may be wrong according to a report by Michael Podgursky, an expert on teacher pay. Contrary to popular belief, teachers' salaries compare favorably to the salaries of other professions and occupations. When salaries are computed on an hourly basis, teachers generally earn more than registered nurses, accountants, engineers, and other middle-class workers.[19]

Do teachers in some areas make more money than teachers in other areas? Yes. Teachers who teach in big school districts—districts with more than 10,000 students—make less than teachers in smaller districts. There are a number of reasons for the lower salaries in urban districts. First, many urban districts are faced with declining tax bases and therefore are trimming budgets. This accounts for why urban teachers' salaries are often below those of their suburban counterparts. Second, urban school districts tend to have younger and less experienced teachers, and their salaries are lower than those of the older and more experienced teachers in suburban districts.

Table 2.2 *What* Teachers Earn (estimated teacher salaries by state)

State	Average Annual Teacher Salary 2001–2002	Percentage Change, 1989–1990 to 2001–2002 (in constant dollars)	State	Average Annual Teacher Salary 2001–2002	Percentage Change, 1989–1990 to 2001–2002 (in constant dollars)
United States	$44,604	1.3	Missouri	37,695	−0.9
Alabama	39,268	12.7	Montana	34,379	−2.3
Alaska	49,418	−18.4	Nebraska	36,236	1.2
Arizona	36,966	−10.4	Nevada	41,524	−3.3
Arkansas	35,389	12.8	New Hampshire	38,911	−4.3
California	53,870	1.0	New Jersey	54,575	9.0
Colorado	40,222	−6.8	New Mexico	36,490	5.0
Connecticut	54,300	−4.4	New York	53,081	−2.8
Delaware	48,363	3.3	North Carolina	42,959	9.8
District of Columbia	47,049	−12.7	North Dakota	31,709	−1.8
Florida	38,719	−4.2	Ohio	44,492	1.6
Georgia	44,073	12.1	Oklahoma	35.412	9.4
Hawaii	41,951	−6.7	Oregon	43,886	1.4
Idaho	37,482	11.9	Pennsylvania	50,599	8.2
Illinois	50,000	8.6	Rhode Island	49,758	−1.7
Indiana	44,195	1.9	South Carolina	38,943	2.0
Iowa	38,230	1.8	South Dakota	31,295	4.7
Kansas	36,673	−9.1	Tennessee	38,554	1.6
Kentucky	37,847	2.6	Texas	39,293	1.8
Louisiana	35,437	3.9	Utah	37,414	12.6
Maine	37,100	−1.7	Vermont	38,802	−4.7
Maryland	46,200	−9.4	Virginia	41,262	−5.0
Massachusetts	50,293	3.2	Washington	43,483	1.7
Michigan	52,037	7.4	West Virginia	36,751	14.6
Minnesota	43,330	−4.1	Wisconsin	43,114	−3.8
Mississippi	32,800	−3.8	Wyoming	37,841	−4.2

Source: National Center for Education Statistics, *Digest of Education Statistics,* 2002 (Washington, DC: U.S. Government Printing Office, 2000).

The geographic region in which you teach also determines the salary you will receive as a teacher as Figure 2.11 illustrates. There are a number of reasons why salaries vary based on metropolitan and geographic area. Most school boards operate within budgets that depend on income from property taxes. Most property owners don't like to see their property taxes raised. So, as long as the majority of a school's budget comes from property taxes, there will always be pressure to keep school expenses and expenditures as low as possible, including teachers' salaries. In addition, many inequalities exist when schooling is financed through property taxes. Districts in suburban areas, where incomes and property values are higher, have more dollars to spend on their schools. The opposite is true in less affluent rural and inner-city neighborhoods. In many respects, teaching is a two-tiered profession. Teachers of poor and minority students teach in schools with more teacher turnover, more teacher vacancies, less parent involvement,

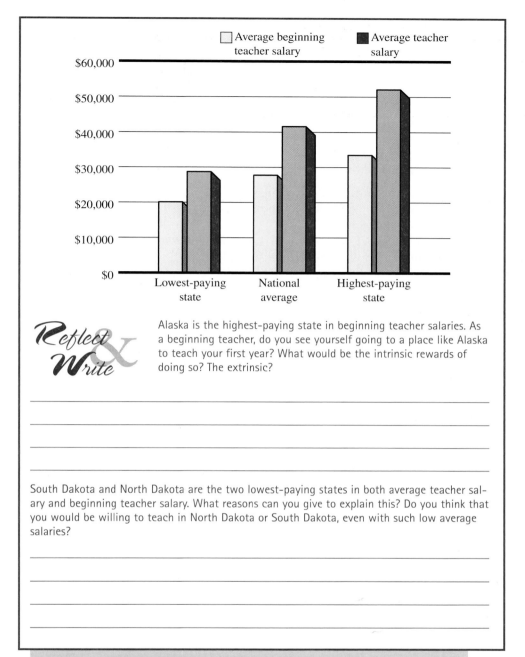

Reflect & Write

Alaska is the highest-paying state in beginning teacher salaries. As a beginning teacher, do you see yourself going to a place like Alaska to teach your first year? What would be the intrinsic rewards of doing so? The extrinsic?

_____

_____

_____

_____

South Dakota and North Dakota are the two lowest-paying states in both average teacher salary and beginning teacher salary. What reasons can you give to explain this? Do you think that you would be willing to teach in North Dakota or South Dakota, even with such low average salaries?

_____

_____

_____

_____

Figure 2.11 _Average Teacher Salaries_

Note: Connecticut is the highest paying state in teacher salaries; South Dakota is the lowest. In beginning teacher salaries, Alaska is the highest, and North Dakota is the lowest.

Source: American Federation of Teachers, "Survey & Analysis of Teacher Salary Trends, 2000" (2000). (Online). Available at www.aft.org/research/survey00/salarysurvey00.pdf.

and fewer textbooks and other learning materials. Where you teach does indeed influence not only how much you get paid, but other conditions of teaching as well.[20]

What salary will you earn as a beginning teacher? Figure 2.11 helps answer this question. As a beginning teacher, you should receive a salary schedule by which you can quickly determine the salary you will receive after five, ten, and thirty years of teaching. In addition, some school districts are implementing **merit pay,** or **performance pay**—an

Merit pay
Pay based on meritorious service, performance, and/or special assignments.

Performance pay
Salary increases based on student achievement and classroom performance. Gradually replacing the term _merit pay._

incentive system that rewards teachers for extra service, an exceptionally well-done job, or increases in student achievement. Increasingly, performance pay plans are gaining in popularity, as discussed earlier. Iowa became the first state to base teacher pay on classroom performance and student achievement rather than years spent in teaching.

Georgia has put in place a merit pay program based on four goals designed to reward overall school improvement. These goals are:

- Academic achievement
- Resource development
- Educational programming
- Client involvement[21]

Increasingly, other incentive pay plans are based on higher levels of education, different levels of teaching responsibilities, more professional responsibilities, and additional certifications.

Benefits are another part of a salary package, and when you are considering a teaching position, you will want to inquire about benefits. Major benefits that are part of a salary package include health and life insurance and a retirement plan. For example, the Houston (Texas) ISD provides these benefits: medical plan, dental plan, life and accidental death insurance, income replacement plan, cancer care plan, hospital indemnity plan, group legal services, flexible spending accounts, and a health connection plan. For a description of the benefits, access www.hisdbenefits.org/.

School districts are also becoming more creative in their benefits to attract and keep quality teachers. The Santa Clara (California) Unified School District, in a first-of-a-kind effort, built lower-cost housing for teachers on school property. A lottery was held to determine which teachers would get one of the forty slots in the new apartment building in Casa del Maestro. Rents run at about half the price of regular apartments.[22]

Also, California has what is believed to be the first income tax credit for teachers in the country. Public and private school teachers with at least four years of service are eligible to receive credits ranging from $250 to $1,500, depending on how long they have taught."[23]

Teacher Supply and Demand

You are probably asking, "Will I be able to get a job?" The answer to this question is an optimistic yes, if you are willing to go where the jobs are and if your teaching field is in demand. Projections indicate that over the next ten years, the nation will need 2.2 to 2.4 million teachers. The needs are greatest in curricular areas such as special education, mathematics, science, bilingual education, and English as a second language.

Teacher shortages are particularly acute in urban and rural areas, where there is an immediate need to fill teaching positions in all subject areas, from elementary grades to high school classes. In addition, states with rapidly growing populations, such as California, Texas, Nevada, North Carolina, and Florida, are experiencing chronic shortages, especially to meet the challenges of their increasing numbers of students of color.[24]

Teaching in Private, Independent, and Parochial Schools

About 15 percent (449,057) of the nation's teachers choose to teach in private schools.[25] The average salary for private school teachers is $29,822, well below the $44,604 average salary for public school teachers. Although salaries in private schools are lower than those in the public sector, some teachers prefer private settings because they feel they have more autonomy and more to say about what should be taught and how it will be taught. The Profiles of Sister Alice Hess and Fraser Randolph will help you capture the essence of what teaching in independent schools is like and what motivates these teachers as professionals.

Is Teaching for You?

In Chapter 1 and this chapter, you have read and thought about what teaching means and about teaching as a profession. Now is a good time to pause and reflect more about choosing teaching as a career. The self-analysis in Figure 2.12 provides a basis for further clarifying your motivations for teaching and can assist you in identifying those areas you want to strengthen throughout this course and your teacher education program.

Profile   Teaching in a Parochial School: Sister Alice Hess, I.H.M.

Sister Alice Hess teaches high school math at Archbishop Ryan, a Catholic high school with about 2,650 students in north-eastern Philadelphia.

With no formal academic entrance requirements and generous charitable contributions, Archbishop Ryan serves a wide range of students with varying abilities, learning styles, and economic backgrounds. Most Ryan parents are blue-collar workers; many are police officers and fire fighters. Most are not college graduates but aspire to college for their children. Recently, more and more students with learning disabilities (both documented and undocumented) have begun to arrive at our door. As a result, our faculty must understand various learning styles and be flexible in classroom management.

I encounter the whole spectrum within a typical teaching day, from the at-risk freshmen in my algebra classes to the more settled students in my precalculus and advanced placement calculus and statistics classes. More than anything, our students need structure (often missing at home) and a reason to learn. From the first day they enter my classroom, whatever their abilities, I make eminently clear that I will go to great lengths to help them—as long as they give me nothing but their best. Sometimes it takes weeks or even months for new students to get the message (*"I say what I mean, and I mean what I say"*). But given more structure, consistent discipline, individualized learning opportunities, group activities, after-school extra help and parent-student conferences, they do get it eventually, and from that day on, my students and I both have fun learning in my classroom.

Making a difference—this is what Catholic schools are all about, and this is what I strive to do in my classroom every day. It's the message I constantly repeat, plain and simple, to teachers I mentor. Here's what I say:

Know what you are about. The power and beauty of mathematics enables students to move toward these goals. A rapidly changing, computerized world needs citizens who can and will function ethically in a global economy—citizens who will probably change jobs and perhaps professions several times; who are capable of reasoning logically and communicating effectively; who recognize mathematical applications in the world around them; and who approach mathematical problems with confidence. Mathematics instruction can teach coping skills through perseverance in problem solving.

Get yourself organized. Teaching effectively is more than simply transmitting knowledge about your content area. You need to know how to structure your classroom to minimize routine tasks and maximize your teaching time. Distribute a copy of your expectations—make your list positive, short, comprehensive, and easy to understand. Above all, say what you mean, and mean what you say.

Establish a plan for the year. Break the instructional material into semester-long portions, six-week units, weekly lessons—but be sure to allow for flexibility to follow students' interests or to include new ideas that you create from professional readings and discussions with colleagues. Since most students perform better when they can use a range of strengths rather than a narrow set of skills, create open-ended, multidisciplinary projects. Mathematics is connected to virtually everything, and good teaching constantly reveals these connections.

Know your students as learners of mathematics. Believe that all students can learn mathematics (in spite of how they feel or what their parents' experience was) and learn it well, given the opportunity—which it is our job to provide.

Help students use technology to become problem solvers. Let problem solving be primary in your classroom and exploit computers and inexpensive graphing calculators to help accomplish this. Invite students to speculate and pursue their hunches, thus capturing their curiosity and providing valuable experiences with the scientific method.

Assess what you value. See that your classroom models a mathematical community in which students articulate, communicate, and make connections and be sure that your assessment reflects these values.

Finally, when you meet resistance from students or parents, remember that one of the best-kept secrets in this country is that youth want to learn. They may not like to work—but an effective teacher strives to get them so involved in learning that they forget that they are working. Technology can help students become imaginative, adventuresome learners rather than assembly-line robots. A real-world, problem-solving environment allows students to gain self-confidence and learn to accept responsibility for their own learning—and to be transformed into lifelong learners.

Fraser Randolph teaches at New Canaan Country School, an independent school in Connecticut with about 600 students, prekindergarten through ninth grade.

I really did love my eighth-grade English position at an urban Connecticut junior high school. I was challenged; I felt I was making a difference in some kids' lives; I enjoyed the subject matter. On the other hand, in 1989 I was in my mid thirties, and it was beginning to look as though all I would ever do in my life was teach English to thirteen-year-olds. Union regulations made it impossible for me to change grade levels or schools, and my school was becoming increasingly "burned out." Discipline loomed larger and larger, and the administration was uninspired and ineffective.

A year's leave of absence during which I taught fifth grade at New Canaan Country School convinced me I was ready for a change. At Country School, I was greeted by teachers who welcomed me as if to their family and offered advice and material to ease my transition. I was immediately given a key that opened virtually every door on the campus, as well as social studies and math classes, in addition to English, to teach. I also was able to coach basketball and baseball during the school day.

Both students and teachers are serious about education at Country School. My students expect to work and are truly curious about everything that goes on in the classroom. They supplement the curriculum with materials from home and shared experiences, and needless to say, parents are eager to know what is going on as well—how their children are faring, how they can facilitate the learning process. In my fifteen years at Country School, I have always found parents available and willing to do whatever was needed to help their children succeed.

Country School is a community where everyone shares a common philosophy about children and how they learn. While many instructional methods are practiced here, you will not find busy work, tedious drills, and "teaching to the test." Classes are rigorous and interactive. The walls and lobbies are festooned with the creative and intellectual products of students in all subjects. This is a progressive school, but one with a traditional background. Teachers practice Piagetian methods, offering children concrete experiences with new ideas and skills and gradually leading them into abstract ideas. Teachers often compare our children to flowers, each blossoming in his or her own time.

Country School is "formal" about the job of educating children but informal in its administrative approach. Forms and bureaucracy are kept to a minimum. Nor must teachers wrestle with the stifling demands of discipline, tracking down absent children, and taking attendance each and every class. The small corps of administrators, who all also teach, make teachers' lives easier by identifying tutorial, emotional, and psychological help for students who need it and by keeping abreast of the ever-changing daily schedule.

Is there a downside to this experience? There are certainly challenges: demanding parents, a frenetic pace, and "entitled" children who always expect more. Country School is also challenged by its own mission statement to diversify the student body and faculty. With limited space and great demand, the competition for admission is intense, and we are constantly looking at ourselves to find other avenues to attract students and teachers of more diverse cultures.

Am I glad that I made this decision to leave public education? Perhaps at the end of my career I will return to the public schools and rejoin the fight for quality education there. But I have learned in my fifteen years at New Canaan Country School that all children have this need. It's the service that counts.

SECTION SUMMARY

What Job Opportunities Do You Have as a Teacher?

- **Salaries and Benefits.** Generally, teachers' salaries compare favorably with those of other professions and occupations, and they are on the rise. Salaries vary with size of school (highest in suburban schools, lowest in urban) and with geographic region (highest in the Northeast, lowest in the South). Increasingly, pay for performance, based on student achievement and other quality indicators, is growing in popularity. Most schooling is financed through property taxes and varies as property values vary.

- **Teacher Supply and Demand.** Demand for teachers is high for those in fields such as special education, bilingual education, the sciences, and Spanish and for those who are willing to relocate, often to rural or urban areas.

- **Teaching in Private, Independent, and Parochial Schools.** About 15 percent of the nation's teachers teach in private schools. Of those, about three out of four teach in Catholic or other religious schools, with the remainder teaching in nonsectarian private schools. Private school teachers' average salaries are significantly lower than those of public school teachers. Nevertheless, some teachers prefer what they experience as greater freedom to decide what to teach and how to teach.

- **Is Teaching for You?** This is a very personal question, one that can only be answered through careful reflection.

The following self-analysis will help you reflect on your choice of teaching as a career. You might want to discuss with friends, classmates, colleagues, and instructors any items that you answer "no" or "undecided."

	Yes	No	Undecided
1. Do I believe that all children can learn?	☐	☐	☐
2. Do I have high expectations for myself and others?	☐	☐	☐
3. Am I dedicated to learning the necessary content knowledge and teaching skills?	☐	☐	☐
4. Do I see myself as a professional?	☐	☐	☐
5. Do I look forward to reading professional journals?	☐	☐	☐
6. Do I look forward to participating in professional organizations for teachers?	☐	☐	☐
7. Am I willing to uphold high ethical and professional standards for myself?	☐	☐	☐
8. Am I willing to learn new things and to change?	☐	☐	☐
9. Am I willing to devote myself to ongoing professional development as a teacher?	☐	☐	☐
10. Do I see myself as a lifelong learner?	☐	☐	☐
11. Am I willing to continue my teacher education to improve my knowledge and skills?	☐	☐	☐
12. Am I committed to basing my classroom practice on education research?	☐	☐	☐
13. Do I want to spend my days in close contact and interaction with children and young people?	☐	☐	☐
14. Are teachers the kind of people with whom I want to work?	☐	☐	☐
15. Am I willing to invest time and energy in professional collaborations?	☐	☐	☐
16. Am I willing to do more than what is "required" of me?	☐	☐	☐
17. Am I willing to give more time to students than a teaching contract may specify?	☐	☐	☐
18. Am I willing to communicate my teaching philosophy and practices to parents and others?	☐	☐	☐
19. Am I willing to work at developing parent-school and community-school partnerships?	☐	☐	☐
20. Am I willing to teach children of all cultures and racial and ethnic backgrounds?	☐	☐	☐
21. Do I have the energy, sense of humor, enthusiasm, and outgoingness teachers need?	☐	☐	☐
22. Am I a flexible person and able to deal with situations in highly active environments?	☐	☐	☐
23. Do I have good organizational, managerial, and leadership skills?	☐	☐	☐
24. Do I have a strong sense of self-efficacy as a teacher?	☐	☐	☐
25. Am I willing to undertake periods of apprenticeship as a preservice and novice teacher?	☐	☐	☐
26. Am I willing to undergo periodic formal evaluations of my teaching performance?	☐	☐	☐
27. Am I willing to explore many alternatives in finding job opportunities as a teacher?	☐	☐	☐
28. Will I be willing to relocate to take advantage of teaching opportunities?	☐	☐	☐
29. Can I initially meet my needs on a teacher's starting salary and benefits?	☐	☐	☐
30. Will I be satisfied with a salary based on educational attainment and years of service?	☐	☐	☐

Reflect & Write

After reading Chapters 1 and 2, and after completing Figure 2.12, you have some pretty good answers to the question: "Is teaching for me?" Write your personal statement about why teaching is or is not for you.

_____

_____

_____

Figure 2.12   Is Teaching for Me?

Thinking Critically
★ ★ ★ ★ ★ ★ ★ ★ ★

Historically, teachers' salary increases have been based on years in service. Do you agree with this? Is this how you want to be paid? What are criteria you think should be used to increase teachers' salaries?

_____

_____

_____

_____★

Applying What You've Learned
★ ★ ★ ★ ★ ★ ★ ★ ★

What are the pros and cons of teaching in private schools and parochial schools? Do you "connect" more to Sister Alice's views or to Fraser Randolph's?

_____

_____

_____

_____ ★

Putting Yourself in the Picture
★ ★ ★ ★ ★ ★ ★ ★ ★

You have been offered two jobs, equally attractive except in one area: salary and benefits. The first job, which offers a relatively low salary and benefit package, is in your home town. You like the school system, and your family and friends live nearby. But property taxes are low in your home town, and there is little hope that teachers' salaries will rise in the near future. The second job offer is several states away, in a more prosperous community that is conducting a national search for talented and qualified new teachers. The cost of living is higher in that state, but your salary will more than cover the difference. What do you think?

_____

_____

_____

_____ ★

Applications for Active Learning

CONNECTIONS

1. Think about how teacher education is being reformed. Create a graphic that shows these reforms and the resulting changes. Figure 2.9 (p. 56) can help you get started.

2. What it means to be a professional will be an ongoing theme of your teaching career. Write five "guideposts to professionalism" based on your ideas of professionalism, those of Linda Beck, and the information presented in this text so far. You can refer back to these guideposts—and adapt them as you learn more—on your journey to becoming a teacher.

3. The whole "pay-for-performance" issue will continue to be contentious and hotly debated in the years to come. Make a connection to this topic by gathering information about the pros and cons of the issue. You can begin by logging onto www. educationworld.com and searching for "pay for performance."

FIELD EXPERIENCES

1. Interview teachers to learn how they found their jobs. What tips do they have for you as you begin to think about where you might want to teach?

2. Research the following question: What have been some positive and negative influences of teachers' unions nationally? Begin now by making a few predictions about what you think you will find.

_____

_____

_____

PERSONAL RESEARCH

1. Gather information about your state certification exam, including sample outcomes, performance criteria, and test items.

2. Gather information about alternative and national certification programs in your state. What are the pros and cons of these programs compared to the traditional teacher certification process?

3. Research projections of teaching opportunities, salaries, and benefits in the state or region in which you plan to teach. What preparation is required or recommended? How will this information influence your decisions about becoming a teacher?

FOR YOUR PORTFOLIO

1. Extend the clipping file you started in Chapter 1 by reviewing articles from education and professional journals in your subject area. Consider, for example, the following publications:

American Educator

American School Board Journal

Childhood Education

Educational Leadership

Elementary School Journal

Exceptional Children

High School Journal

Instructor

Kappa Delta Phi Record

Phi Delta Kappan

PTA Today

Teacher Magazine

Young Children

2. Keep selected results of your pers[...] your portfolio, especially information about te[...] fessional standards, organizations, state requirements, a[...] job opportunities. Also include any personal checklists you develop from the following Idea File activities.

IDEA FILE

1. Develop a list of tips for becoming a professional and share your ideas with classmates.

_____

_____

_____

2. Using your research on the state certification exam, develop a personal checklist of what you will need to know and be able to do before you take the exam.

3. Review the INTASC and NCATE standards and underline those terms and phrases whose meanings and implications are not clear. Using these underlinings, develop a list of specific questions about becoming a teacher that you would like answered by the time you finish this course.

Learning and Knowing More

WEB SITES WORTH VISITING

If you have not already done so, now would be a good time to visit the Allyn and Bacon Web site (www.ablongman.com) to access information about teaching. The federal government is also a valuable source of information. For example, the Department of Education maintains a constantly updated Web site with current news and information regarding federal programs and government decisions on the subject of schools and education. Their Web site is www.ed.gov/index.jsp.

Teaching as a Profession
http://gateway.library.uiuc.edu/schoolreform/teaching.htm
A gateway site with links to a series of helpful Web sites.

The Praxis Home Page
www.ets.org/praxis
Detailed information about all aspects of Praxis.

Teachers' Professional Development in a Climate of Education Reform
www.ed.gov/pubs/EdReformStudies/SysReforms/little1.html
Essay by Judith Warren Little stating that the current model of professional development is inadequate to support reform initiatives.

BOOKS WORTH READING

Diaz-Maggioli, Gabriel. (2004). *Teacher-Centered Professional Development*. Alexandria, VA: Association for Supervision and Curriculum Development Press.
This book provides the framework and steps to help teachers choose the right professional development strategies for their needs; collaborate with their peers in mentoring, planning, and scheduling professional development events and experiences; and evaluate the effect of their efforts.

Levine, S. L., McKay, S., and Frost, K. (1999). *A Passion for Teaching*. Alexandria, VA: Association for Supervision and Curriculum Development Press.
This book celebrates teachers and teaching. Through stories, poems, plays, and artwork, forty-two experienced teachers express their thoughts about students, other teachers and mentors, and the power of teaching and learning.

Stronge, James H. (2002). *Qualities of Effective Teachers*. Alexandria, VA: Association for Supervision and Curriculum Development Press.
For any educator who has wanted real proof of which teacher qualities are most apt to lead to higher student achievement, here, at last, is a book that synthesizes decades of research into clear guidelines.

How Schools Are Organized and Linked to Society

RULES
1) Follow directions the first time given.
2) Mutual Respect.

:Media
any means of communication that reaches or influences large numbers of people

"Public schools are the most important institutions in a democratic society."

George Albano is principal of Lincoln Elementary School, Mount Vernon, New York.

If democracy is going to succeed, each and every member of that democracy must receive an equitable, quality education. It has been fifty years since the Supreme Court ruled on *Brown v. Board of Education.* As a result of that decision, minority students have equal access to public schools—but the question we must ask today is, are they receiving equal education?

An April 7, 2002, *New York Times* story headlined "Using love and chess lessons to defy theories about race and test scores" featured Lincoln Elementary School, in Mount Vernon, New York, where I am principal. The writer first demonstrated that when New York State elementary and middle school test results were filtered through the prisms of race, gender, ethnicity, and socioeconomic background, they showed a yawning achievement gap between whites and minority students. And the gap existed across the demographic spectrum, from wealthy suburbs to big cities. But some schools, the article pointed out, seem to defy assumptions about race and income. The article describes Lincoln as "a school that outperformed some of the elite public schools in the country."

Lincoln's 800 students are 60 percent minorities (40 percent African American, 20 percent Hispanic, and a small Asian population). Over 50 percent of the students are eligible for free or reduced lunch. Yet their performance on all state assessments is high, and the gap between blacks/Hispanics and whites is negligible. Over the last four years, over 98 percent of our students have performed at or above the New York State average on all state tests.

What is Lincoln doing differently? Closing the achievement gap did not just happen by chance. At Lincoln, every staff member has an unwavering commitment to educate every child to his or her fullest potential: we will do whatever is necessary to promote achievement and development of all our students. The school culture is dominated by teamwork. At Lincoln, our mission statement is very simple: "We have a commitment to educational equality and excellence by consistently acting on the belief that all students can, must, and will learn; no exceptions." We set goals and maintain high standards; we implement strategies and put standards in place that allow us to accomplish our mission.

The school curriculum plays an integral part in our success. We believe the arts are important. All children are exposed to classical music and fine arts activities. The arts program is integrated into the curriculum, enhances students' abilities to make connections, and supports accelerated learning. Systematic and frequent collection of assessment data and a consistent process for using this information for individual student planning, grade-level planning, and school improvement are also important ingredients in the Lincoln success story.

At Lincoln, teachers attend frequent staff development workshops, and young teachers are mentored by more experienced teachers on a regular basis. Part of Lincoln's success story is our ability to attract and retain an extremely talented, highly qualified staff. There is very little turnover in personnel. The average teacher has been here for over fifteen years. Why would teachers want to work in an urban setting, where they are paid 10 to 20 percent less than their counterparts in wealthier suburbs? Because they want to teach in an environment where they truly feel they are making a difference. Why does the staff stay at Lincoln? Because every staff member knows that what he or she is doing is important—and appreciated. At Lincoln, the administration empowers the staff. Faculty members are part of the decision-making process. There is a high degree of accountability, and this leads to high morale—and when morale is high, a school will be successful.

At Lincoln, parents are also held accountable. Parents must come in personally to sign for report cards and confer with teachers. Monthly calendars of events, phone calls in the evening, progress reports, schoolwide reading incentive programs, a science fair where parents are invited to participate—all these things encourage parental involvement.

A Lincoln teacher, interviewed on television after the article appeared, put it this way: "If you expect the best from children, that's what you'll get." We expect the best at Lincoln. And we achieve it. For more information about Lincoln Elementary, go to www.georgealbano.com.

How Will This Chapter Help You?

You will learn

★ the basic purposes of schools and schooling

★ how schools are organized

★ what it is like to teach in urban, suburban, and rural schools today

The New York Times
expect the world®
nytimes.com

Themes of the Times

Expand your knowledge of the concepts discussed in this chapter by reading current and historical articles from *The New York Times* by visiting the "Themes of the Times" section of the companion Web site.

*W*HAT IS THE PURPOSE OF SCHOOLING*?*

Surely you and I agree with George Albano that schools play an important role in American society. But just what is that role? And what should it be? Take a minute to reflect on this question. Jot down your answers, and keep them in mind as you read this chapter.

Here are some things that I think American public education should accomplish. Compare your thoughts with mine. I think public schools in the United States should

NCATE

Middle Level

Standard 2: Understands the major concepts, principles, theories, and research underlying the philosophical foundations of developmentally responsible middle-level programs and schools; works successfully within these organizational components.

- educate all students to their fullest potential regardless of race, culture, gender, and socioeconomic status
- instill a love of learning
- prepare students for responsible democratic living
- educate students of good moral character
- ensure that student educations are well rounded

Federal and state laws also mandate certain roles for public education, including:

- To have all children reading at grade level by grade 3
- To ensure that students pass state achievement tests
- To have students master rigorous content and achieve high standards

As you can see, while we might all agree that the role of the school is to teach students, the issues are in the details. Because of differences in our beliefs about the purposes and functions of schooling, the role of education varies from state to state and from school to school.

What schools teach is what teachers, parents, the community, states, and the federal government think students should know and do in order to lead meaningful and productive lives in the twenty-first century. If schools are not successful in achieving this goal, then children, youth, and society are the losers. That makes it doubly important that you as a teacher understand how education is organized and linked to American society. How schools are organized and linked to society determines to a large extent what is taught, how teachers teach, and if students learn.

Aims of Education

An aim is a purpose, intention, or goal. Many schools and school districts have aims that guide their teaching and help determine what students will learn. For example, the aims of one school might be to help students become responsible, encourage habits of organization, and involve them in setting personal and academic goals. Because educational aims reflect the dominant values and beliefs of the society, they change over time as society's goals shift and change. Aims also vary according to the beliefs and values of specific communities (see Figure 3.1).

One of the most influential sets of aims was issued in 1918 by the National Education Association's (NEA) Commission on the Reorganization of Secondary Education. The commission's report, *Cardinal Principles of Secondary Education,*[1] recommended that the high school curriculum be organized around "seven cardinal principles":

- Health
- Command of fundamental processes
- Worthy home membership
- Citizenship

- Ethical character
- Vocational preparation
- Worthy use of leisure time

Many think these seven cardinal principles still are appropriate for guiding decisions about what to teach. However, what society thinks the aims of education are or should be in one decade is not necessarily appropriate for another.

The seven cardinal principles were influential in the decades from 1920 through the late 1950s, when education emphasized a decidedly utilitarian purpose. In the late

[The mission of the Peters Township (Pennsylvania) schools, a rural/suburban district, is] to ensure that all students acquire the knowledge base and skills necessary to become contributing members of society and lifelong learners by providing the highest-quality resources and staff within a comprehensive, result-oriented program implemented by caring people.

Source: Peters Township School District Web site, available at www.ptsd.k12.pa.us.

Klein Oak is committed to excellence in education and believes that all students possess inherent worth and the ability to learn. Based on this premise, its purpose is designed to help students reach their full potential as individuals and become happy, competent, productive members of society. Pursuing this goal, Klein Oak teaches those skills necessary for success in a competitive world. Students are taught to think for themselves, apply their knowledge, and develop an appreciation of the world around them. To instill these abilities, Klein Oak High School provides a broad spectrum of educational opportunities designed to meet various students' needs. Professional educators present programs in a manner that creates a learning environment in which students can enhance their abilities. In doing so, young people acquire the discipline and sensitivity needed to become responsible citizens.

Source: Klein Oak High School Mission Statement, available at http://kleinoak.kleinisd.net/about/missionstatement.html.

Reflect & Write

If you were a faculty member asked to help draft a mission statement for your school, whom might you want on the committee with you? Why?

Figure 3.1   School Mission Statements

1950s and early 1960s, after the Soviet Union launched the space satellite *Sputnik,* national defense became a top priority. The aims of education consequently shifted toward science and an emphasis on teaching students how to think. In the late 1960s and 1970s, the emphasis moved to promoting equal educational opportunity, making education "relevant," and promoting awareness of ecological issues. In the 1980s, academic excellence was stressed, and schools emphasized basic skills. As society's goals shifted again in the 1990s, educational aims followed suit; excellence was to be achieved through high "standards" in all the content areas in order to make the United States economically competitive. As discussed earlier, standards-based education is the center of many political and educational debates.

Standards–Based Education

Today, reforming schools and setting high standards for what students should know and be able to do dominates educational discussion. The standards movement became popular because its advocates believe that having standards for what should be taught in the nation's schools will increase achievement and quality. The rationale for standards is best articulated by Rod Paige, former secretary of the U.S. Department of Education: "States, districts, and schools should first have high standards for all of their students. When we expect more from our children, we will get more."[2] For more on standards and expectations, see the Profile of Mesa Verde Middle School, p. 79. The assumption is that higher standards will improve the quality of education.

Standards-based education draws, in part, on content standards developed by professional groups for history, geography, the arts, science, math, and other subjects. Opponents of standards maintain that they could become what amounts to a national curriculum controlled by federal bureaucrats and could erode the right of states and

NCATE

Elementary

Standard 3.1: Plans and implements instruction based on knowledge of students, learning theory, subject matter, curricular goals, and community.

Standards–based education Instruction aimed at providing students the specific skills and levels of competency necessary to move through the educational system.

local schools to set their own curriculum guidelines and standards and make decisions about what our children should learn. Furthermore, critics maintain that standards will promote inequality, diminish cultural diversity, and force students into a "one size fits all" curriculum. Also, many are fearful that the federal government will put in place a system of national testing and comparison.

Current public sentiment is that citizens are willing to support national and state standards but still want the option to teach at the local level what communities think is important. Americans still value local control of schools and the freedom to make decisions about what is best for children at the local level. At the present time, current educational reform is focused on three issues: high standards, testing to ensure standards of achievement and accountability, smaller schools, smaller classes, alternative approaches to education, and national efforts to reform the basic purposes of American education. Chapter 10 discusses in detail standards and assessment.

Which three of the reforms discussed above do you think are the most essential? The most controversial?

_____

_____

_____

_____

SECTION SUMMARY

What Is the Purpose of Schooling?

The purposes of schools are varied, but all include teaching students to lead meaningful and productive lives.

- Aims of Education. The NEA Commission's report, *The Cardinal Principles of Secondary Education,* recommends the aims of education be health, command of fundamental processes, worthy home membership, citizenship, ethical character, vocation, and worthy use of leisure time. The aims of education reflect changes in society. In the United States, those aims have included perpetuating national defense goals by emphasizing science education; promoting equal opportunity; making education "relevant"; preserving the environment; promoting basic skills; maintaining high academic standards; and increasing America's competitiveness.

- Standards-Based Education. Currently, national, state, and local aims of education are expressed through standards—statements of what students should know and be able to do.

Thinking Critically

★ ★ ★ ★ ★ ★ ★ ★

Log on to the Web page of your local school district and review its aims and purposes. Do you agree with these aims? What would you delete or add?

_____

_____

_____

_____ ★

Juanita Lampi has been principal since 2000 at Mesa Verde, a middle school in fast-growing Moorpark, California, which serves over 1,000 students from a wide range of economic backgrounds. (This profile was submitted by Dr. Tina Cantrell, Assistant Superintendent of Moorpark Unified School District.)

Of the over 1,100 middle schools in California, those that stand out have one trait in common; they recognize the uniqueness of students who are neither the youngest nor the oldest, and who function like the proverbial cream in the cookie—caught between two competing worlds. Dealing with students who act like children one day and young adults the next is a situation many educators choose to avoid. But some seek it out, and Mesa Verde has risen to the challenge. Principal Juanita Lampi's office is inviting—a place where parents, students, and teachers talk, solve problems, and plan exciting events for the school community. She believes strongly in students first; "They don't care how much we know until they know how much we care." She tries to make sure that that belief is supported in every aspect of the school, integrated into the curriculum, and practiced in all school activities.

Mesa Verde draws children from a wide variety of ethnic and economic backgrounds—from students who live in the sprawling, expensive developments near the school to students who are considered homeless. Almost 30 percent qualify for free/reduced lunch programs, 14 percent are second-language learners, 8 percent are classified as gifted, and 10 percent receive special education services.

The education for every Mesa Verde student is rigorous and demanding. Standards, an integral part of every teacher's repertoire, provide a coherent, consistent teaching vision and drive classroom instruction. They appear everywhere—posted on daily whiteboards, at the top of assignment sheets—and are translated into "kidspeak" to make sure that students understand them. Every child is enrolled in the core areas (math, English, science, and social science) as well as an elective and physical education; "safety nets" help struggling students close the gap by targeting specific skills and remediation. Within the core curriculum, teachers blend music, film, painting, photography, and other artistic media to create links to all areas of students' experiences. Students read and perform roles in stories, engage in courtroom-type procedures, and create artistic expressions of their learning.

A major challenge at Mesa Verde is to remedy the academic disparity between high-income, English-speaking students and those who come from poverty and whose native language is not English. Mesa Verde has confronted this aggressively, offering sheltered and ESL classes, programs that support first-generation students preparing for college admission, and counseling services for at-risk students. As a result, test scores have consistently risen. In one year, test scores for minority students rose 61 points and for socioeconomically disadvantaged students an astonishing 77 points (an increase of five points is typically noteworthy).

Lampi and her staff believe in personalizing the middle school experience. A team of teachers serves each grade level, so teachers can develop close relationships with students, and lots of exploratory opportunities are available for students. All teachers are expected to differentiate instruction at both ends of the learning spectrum, and the staff meets regularly to talk about the progress of at-risk students and share successful strategies. Mesa Verde is even sensitive to students' "internal clocks." Some kids do better in the morning, while others seem to "wake up" after lunch, so Mesa Verde operates on a rotating schedule: Each day, subject periods shift one hour later until the cycle of six periods has been completed.

Classroom discussions frequently explore the "So what?" question—that is, "How is this relevant to real life?" Students often speak about their personal lives, listen to others, and raise and resolve questions. In fact, student voices are heard in a variety of ways. All students are paired with counselors, who are available whenever students feel a need. Counselors not only provide guidance on academic issues but also offer emotional support for students when they are struggling. Mesa Verde has a part-time counselor to whom at-risk students can talk in groups or individually. Lampi often spends the lunch period with students, listening to their concerns and helping them with their schoolwork, and so do many teachers.

Each year, Portfolio Sharing Day serves as a kind of "exit interview" for eighth-graders. Students collect work throughout the year and then select their best work to present to a panel of community and district personnel. This allows students both to understand the process of evaluating their own work and to share that work with adults; it also gives students a comfortable context to talk with adults and peers about their middle school experiences and their future plans. The day gives each eighth-grader a chance to shine, to hone oral expression skills, and to gain confidence.

The challenging task for middle school educators is easily matched by the challenges these children themselves face every day as they figure out how to become adults. The goal at Mesa Verde is to make sure each student is an individual, not just a name on a teacher's roster. Teachers are listeners; they make themselves available to all students; they embrace the middle school concept and provide a warm, caring climate. What happens at Mesa Verde does not happen by accident. Success has emerged from careful planning, ongoing collaboration, and a profound commitment to the students. At Mesa Verde, the administration and faculty share the belief that this is a journey, and they celebrate the many accomplishments along the way. Their goal is to take students who are caught in the middle and help them move to center stage.

NCATE

Middle Level

Standard 2: Understands the major concepts, principles, theories, and research underlying the philosophical foundations of developmentally responsible middle-level programs and schools; works successfully within these organizational components.

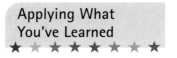
In newspapers, magazines, and journals, politicians discuss the educational system, either local or national. What goals or aims do these decision makers have for the educational system they describe?

_____

_____

_____

_____ ★

Putting Yourself
in the Picture
★ ★ ★ ★ ★ ★ ★ ★

By now, I'm sure you have developed some fairly clear ideas of what you think the purposes of education should be. For example, perhaps you think all students should graduate knowing how to read on their grade level, use technology to learn, and possess certain character traits. Put yourself in the picture now by listing your top three purposes of American education.

_____

_____

_____

_____ ★

Organization
The structure and administration of education.

*H*OW ARE PUBLIC SCHOOLS ORGANIZED*?*

Organization, or structure and function, is a characteristic of education as a social institution. School organization makes it possible for schools to achieve their purposes and goals. Organization also brings order to students, teachers, and staff members who are responsible for school operation and gives them a framework within which to work. In this sense, organization enables schools to be effective and enhances student learning. The structure of schooling, the establishment of grade levels and schedules, and schools as physical plants are all part of organization.

How schools are organized depends in part on where they are located. Factors that contribute to and affect how schools are organized include location and geography (urban, suburban, or rural), number and kind of students in a district, monetary and other resources available, and the goals of the district and communities for their schools. How schools are organized—range of grades included, ratio of students to teachers and administrators, and so on—impacts student learning in a variety of ways.

The Structure of Schooling in the United States

Figure 3.2 shows how schooling is structured in the United States. This figure shows the progression of education for students at different ages from preschool through kindergarten and the elementary grades through secondary and postsecondary education. Consider how much you have learned about the structure of schooling through your personal experience as a student. As a teacher, you will view education from the broader perspective of an organizational structure that accomplishes specific educational goals. From this view, the organization of schooling is influenced by administrative needs; the nature of the faculty; students' ages, experiences, and cultural backgrounds; time and resources available for teaching; and the size of the student body.

Organization at the District Level. A **school district** is an administrative unit empowered by a state to run a community's school system. While school districts differ across the United States, most are similarly organized—namely, with top-down administrative structure, grade-level organization, and individual teachers teaching groups of students in self-contained classrooms. However, each school district provides education in a unique way, and each is structured to achieve its particular purposes. The nature of the local community—how big, small, rural, or urban it is—shapes and defines the nature of the educational enterprise. (You will read about district organizations in greater detail in Chapter 7 on governance and finance.)

> **School district**
> An administrative unit empowered by a state to run a community's school system.

School districts are often compared on the basis of size, but this can be misleading. Over 30 percent of the school districts in the United States have enrollments of under 300 students. While megaschools exist—for example, Belmont Senior High School in Los Angeles has 5,410 students in grades 10 to 12—there are 5,196 public schools in the United States that operate pre-K–12 programs as one unit.[3] The size of a district influences the way it is organized and the number and kinds of staff it employs.

Grade-Level Organization. Think about the buildings in which you attended school and about the schools of today. To what extent are they the same? Many schools are square or rectangular, with classrooms for each grade level opening onto a main corridor leading to offices, cafeterias, libraries, and gymnasiums. The architecture of most schools reflects an **age-graded approach** to schooling. In this organization, when children enter school in the fall, they are assigned to a grade level according to their age. The graded approach to school organization was introduced by Horace Mann in 1848 at the Quincy Grammar School in Boston. Mann thought the graded approach, which he observed in Prussia, would bring efficiency to American education. The age-graded approach is reflected in the structure of education in the United States. Note from Figure 3.2 that education is now P–12, meaning that public school education for three- to four-year-old children has become almost universal.

> **Age-graded approach**
> Assigning children to a grade level according to their age.

Criticisms of the graded approach have led to **multi-age/multi-ability grouping,** the mixing or integration of students of different ages and abilities in one classroom or learning setting. Multi-age/multi-ability grouping is becoming popular in the United States and Canada, especially in grades pre-K–3. British Columbia has mandated multi-age grouping in K–3 for the entire province, and Kentucky recommends it for the whole state. While Kentucky leaves the choice of multi-age/multi-ability or graded classes to individual schools, the majority of primary programs use multi-age/multi-ability classes. Teachers and schools elect to use multi-age/multi-ability classes because they

> **Multi-age/multi-ability grouping**
> The mixing or integration of students of different ages in one classroom or learning setting.

- enable teachers to use a wide variety of curricula and materials so that each student's needs are met
- enable students to help and learn from each other
- promote a positive feeling of success and accomplishment
- are designed to prevent grade and school failure. Lisa Gross of the Kentucky Department of Education notes: "Children who experience failure in the early grades of school tend to view education bleakly. The nongraded primary program removes the possibility of early failure and enables children to learn at their own pace."[4]

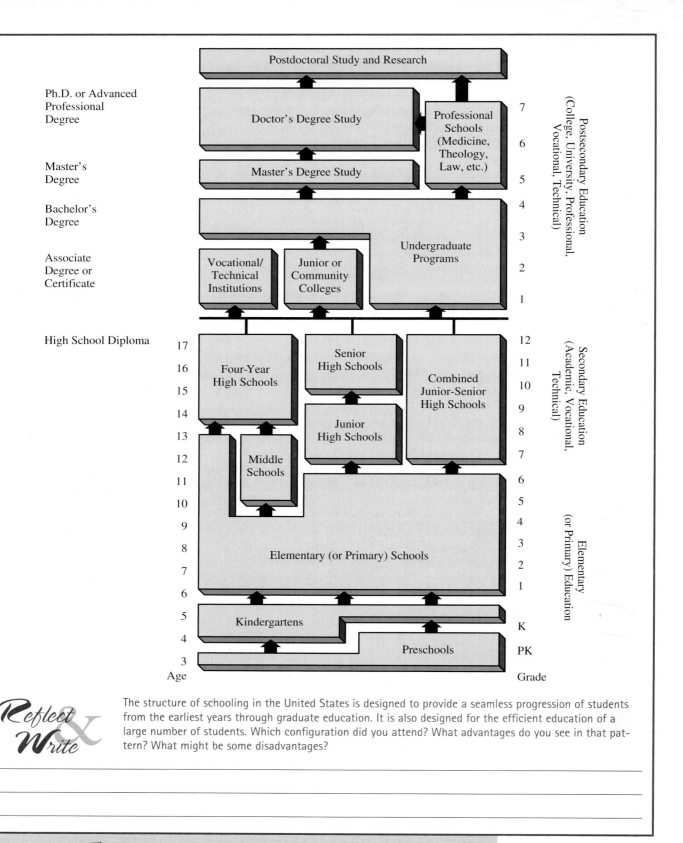

The structure of schooling in the United States is designed to provide a seamless progression of students from the earliest years through graduate education. It is also designed for the efficient education of a large number of students. Which configuration did you attend? What advantages do you see in that pattern? What might be some disadvantages?

Figure 3.2   The Structure of Education in the United States

Source: National Center for Education Statistics, *Digest of Education Statistics, 2003* (2003). (Online). Available at http://nces.ed.gov.

Some schools have tried to get away from the "egg carton" approach to architecture and organization that has characterized the graded approach. In the 1970s, many schools were built and organized on the "open" design—large open-space rooms without walls—with the intent of accommodating and encouraging multi-age grouping and open education practices. Not all such plans were successful, however, because teachers were not always comfortable teaching in open settings. A number of these schools subsequently put up walls to create individual classrooms. Education in many ways is a conservative process, and even when changes are made, they are often reversed. Even so, many of these open classroom schools still exist across America.

Looping breaks the traditional mold of a teacher teaching a different class of students each year. Looping enables teachers to spend two or more years with the same group of same-age children. In other words, a teacher involved in looping might begin teaching a group in kindergarten and then teach the same group as first-graders, and perhaps as second-graders. Another teacher might do the same with second-, third-, and fourth-graders. Other names for looping are *student-teacher progress, multi-year instruction,* and *multi-year grouping.* The advantages of looping are that it

- enables teachers to develop a family atmosphere for teachers and children to develop long-term relationships
- provides a sense of stability and security, especially for young children
- provides freedom to expand and enrich the curriculum vertically and horizontally over a two-year period
- enables teachers to gain weeks of instructional time at the beginning of the school year because they already know the children
- supports individualized instruction because teachers are more familiar with the strengths and weaknesses of each child

The Profile gives you a firsthand glimpse of how looping works.

Time and School Organization. Time and the scheduling of time also influence the organization of schooling, primarily through the six-hour day and 180-day school year. Some reformers are campaigning for longer school days and school calendars. Proponents of a longer school day believe that if schools opened at 7:00 A.M. (or before) and stayed open until 6:00 P.M. or later, they could provide before- and after-school care for students and other community services as well. Teachers would also have more preparation time, and students would have more time to learn. Proponents of **year-round schooling** say that extending the school year calendar to twelve months has several advantages, including making better use of facilities, preventing "summer drop-off" in student achievement, providing a solution to overcrowding, better reflecting parents' work schedules, and allowing more time for teaching and learning.

Many argue that the traditional school calendar, based on the needs of an agrarian society, no longer meets the needs of today's technological society. To respond to today's schedules, many school systems have instituted a number of changes:

1. After-school programs. After-school programs are also referred to as after-school time and out-of-school time. Such programs are becoming increasingly common and popular. **After-school programs** not only extend the day, they meet other legitimate educational and social needs as well. They help maintain, extend, and enrich skills learned in the classroom, offer extracurricular opportunities and participation, and provide after-school care for children and youth. According to Joyce Shortt, codirector of the National Institute of Out-of-School Time, "Having a safe place with constructive activities and nurturing adults can be a very positive experience for kids."[5]
   - 21st Century Community Learning Centers (21st CCLC). This program is a key component of the No Child Left Behind Act. It is an opportunity for students and their families to continue to learn new skills and discover new abilities after the school day has ended. **21st Century Community Learning Centers** provide expanded academic enrichment opportunities for children attending low-performing schools.

Looping
A nontraditional approach to learning in which the teacher moves from grade to grade with the students.

INTASC

Standard 3: The teacher understands how students differ in their approaches to learning and creates instructional opportunities that are adapted to diverse learners.

NCATE

Elementary
Standard 5.3: Knows importance of establishing and maintaining positive collaborative relationships with families to promote the academic, social, and emotional growth of children.

Year-round schooling
Educational programs that run through the summer months as well as during the academic year.

After-school programs
Programs provided by schools that extend the school day and provide programs and activities to support student social and educational needs.

21st Century Community Learning Centers (21st CCLC)
A component of the No Child Left Behind Act, this program provides opportunities for students and their families to learn new skills and abilities after the school day has ended.

Team Looping: Vicki Sheffler and Christa Pehrson

Vicki Sheffler and Christa Pehrson, 2002 USA Today's First Team Teachers, collaborate on the faculty of Amos K. Hutchinson Elementary School, Greensburg, Pennsylvania.

Our first-to-second-grade team-looping classroom is innovative and unique because, as teachers, we live by and teach by the creed, "effort creates ability." Our beliefs about learning and daily practice are clearly focused. We teach our students in the ways in which we would want our own children to be taught. In one large classroom, we have taught the same forty children for the past two years as their first- and second-grade teachers. This environment is extremely beneficial because it has helped us to develop meaningful relationships with students, understand how they learn, and determine how to best provide instruction. By having the same children for two years, we gain about six weeks of instructional time. We already know our students' strengths and weaknesses, and at the beginning of the second year we simply continue the previous year's work. Some of our students just need extra time, not an extra year in the same grade, and our team loop is an alternative to retention. Our parents gain a greater understanding of their children's academic and social needs and become more active participants in their education. By planning picnics, potluck dinners, dessert socials, and in-class luncheon dates with family members, we form a bond of trust and confidence with our parents. Forming that bond provides us with the necessary insight to further improve our teaching methods and student learning.

Because we share a classroom, we must also share the responsibility of sharing strategies and processes that help us to identify student needs and create an innovative approach to team teaching in a looping classroom. We use various methods to identify student needs. These methods include verbal and written assessments, running records and portfolios, rubrics, writing samples, diagnostic testing, and teacher observation. Once student needs are identified, we seek assistance from our school and community. Title 1 Reading and Mathematics programs assist our students who need more reinforcement and review to master necessary skills. Our program for gifted students provides enrichment and acceleration. Our comprehensive counseling therapists help children resolve issues that hinder their learning, and our after-school programs provide maintenance of skills in most subject areas.

Because children come to school with their own strengths and interests, we have integrated the process of compacting into the curricula. Compacting is a process that involves pre-assessing students, giving them credit for what they already know and allowing them to move ahead in the curricula. In spelling, our students are given a pretest at the beginning of each five-day week. If the students achieve 100 percent accuracy, they are permitted to choose their own list of words to be studied for the week.

By far, the best advantage to our team-loop approach has been the building of significant relationships with our students. Whether we were working with a gifted child, an overachiever, an average student, or one who required many repetitions, learning evolved in our classroom according to the student's personal continuum, not by a rigid agenda. No child is left behind.

Tutorial services and academic enrichment activities help students meet local and state academic standards in subjects such as reading and math. In addition, the 21st CCLC program provides youth development activities; drug and violence prevention programs; technology education programs, art, music, and recreation programs; and counseling and character education to enhance the academic component of the program. About 6,800 rural and inner-city public schools in 1,420 communities participate as 21st Century CLCs. For more information about 21st CCLCs, log on to www.ed.gov/21stcclc.

2. *Summer school.* Summer school is becoming commonplace for more students. Forty-six percent of students in Chicago, 44 percent in St. Louis, and 41 percent in Miami-Dade County, Florida, attend summer school.[6]

3. *Flex high school graduation programs.* The Rochester (New York) and the Chicago School Districts graduate students in three, four, or five years. The districts design curriculum and programs that enable incoming freshmen to meet their individual graduation target.

4. *Year-round education.* Also called extended year programs and year-round schooling, these arrangements work in several ways. Year-round education (YRE) centers on reorganizing the school year to provide more continuous learning by breaking up the long summer vacation into shorter, more frequent vacations throughout the year. The National Association for Year-Round Education promotes year-round education by providing leadership and service to individuals and organizations on all aspects of time and learning. Teachers at Dooly County (Georgia) Middle School praise the year-round calendar for its potential to help students retain what they learn. Dooly County high school teacher Deborah Heckwolf says, "We get

more and more kids who come to us who don't have the skills they're supposed to. We need that extra time."[7] Nationally, 3,184 year-round schools enrolled about 2.3 million students in 2003, or about 4 percent of U.S. schools.[8] For more information about year-round education, log on to www.nayre.org/us.

5. Eliminating the Senior Year. Some question the usefulness and importance of the senior year. The National Commission on the High School Senior Year calls for a transformation that will result in a more productive senior year. As an alternative, Florida has a fast-track graduation law that allows students to graduate with six fewer credits as long as they take at least four credits' worth of English and study a foreign language for two years. Students are allowed to skip several elective credits, including physical education, art, and life management courses.[9] The purpose of this program is twofold: to give students the option of graduating earlier and to reduce class size by moving students out of the school more quickly.

Regardless of whether such changes are implemented, school organization is affected by how time is used throughout the school day and the school year. High schools, for example, typically use the **Carnegie Unit** of instructional time. Under this system, teachers have five classes, each forty-five minutes in length, and students enroll in six courses that meet daily for 180 days. Recognizing that forty-five-minute classes effectively prevent many kinds of learning enterprises, educators are now devising alternative ways of scheduling the school day, such as **block scheduling.** In block scheduling, students attend four ninety-minute classes each day, changing classes in the middle of the year. Block scheduling frees students from "seat time" defined in Carnegie Units, allows students to complete eight classes a year rather than seven, and enables students to investigate subjects in more depth.

Other scheduling variations, such as the trimester system, are being tried by many school districts. By dividing the school year into three twelve-week terms (trimesters), students can take three or four classes a term, earning nine or more credits a year. At Angola High School in Indiana, there are four ninety-minute periods in the school day. More efforts likely will be made to organize the school day into longer periods.

Carnegie Unit
A credit awarded for successfully completing a high school course and used in determining graduation requirements and college admissions.

Block scheduling
School class schedules that provide students longer periods of time, for example, four ninety-minute classes each day.

What are your thoughts about year-round education? Would you want to teach in a year-round school? Why? Why not?

_____

_____

_____

_____

Where Do You Stand on High Schools' Shifting Mission?

America's high schools are in transition. Pressure to reform high schools is coming from all sectors of society. Across the country, there is a general consensus that the comprehensive high school that has served America over the last fifty years is in need of restructuring and reform. In addition to reform efforts that create smaller, more personalized learning communities aimed at increasing student achievement, school reformers also want to change the basic mission of the comprehensive high school. The federal government is leading the charge on high school reform. It wants to ensure that students are prepared to enter the nation's work force. Examples of these federal reform initiatives are found in *Preparing America's Future,* a plan to reduce dropout rates and educate students for the twenty-first-century work force, and *Jobs for the 21st Century,* a plan for spending over $100 million on remedial reading and math programs to prepare students for the nation's fastest-growing occupations. Reform efforts to prepare students for the future work force focus not on technical and vocational preparation, but on academic preparation that will enable all students to succeed in college and the workplace. Some reformers believe high schools should prepare all students for college. What do you think?

Visit www.ed.gov for more information on *Preparing America's Future* and *Jobs for the 21st Century.*

School Size and School Organization. The size of schools is another factor that influences organization. There are 423 one-teacher schools in the United States.[10] The average size of enrollment in elementary schools is 477. While the average size of high school enrollments is 785, there are nearly 200 high schools with more than 3,000 students.[11] Large schools enable educators to provide more varied curriculum offerings than would be possible in smaller schools. However, research indicates that large school size adversely affects attendance, school climate, and student involvement in school activities and that it contributes to higher rates of dropping out, vandalism, and violence.[12] One response to the disadvantages of large schools has been to organize them into smaller units of subschools, called *learning communities*, or *schools within schools*, with their own principals and teachers. This organization provides for a feeling of community and caring.

Is Smaller Better? Approximately 70 percent of high school students attend schools enrolling over 1,000 students, and 50 percent attend schools of over 1,500.[13] However, the public and many parents and educators believe that smaller is better. As a result, interest in small schools as a way of addressing problems of schooling has been growing over the past decade.

While small schools are schools of under 1,000 students, at the same time, the term *small school* is applied to those enrolling 400 to 600 students.[14] Some of the issues small schools hope to address are student achievement, safety, anonymity, and social alienation. In a study of schools in Georgia, Montana, Ohio, and Texas, researchers found that poor students do better in smaller schools and worse in larger schools. On the other hand, students in affluent communities do better in larger schools.[15]

The U.S. Department of Education's Smaller Learning Communities Program is a $142 million competitive grant program that enables school districts to develop and implement smaller learning communities in large high schools of over 1,000 students. The Web address for more information is http://www.ed.gov/offices/OVAE/HS/SLCP/slcpgrntinfo.html.

Creekland Middle School in Georgia is one school that has implemented the program. With 3,100 students, Creekland—which may be the largest middle school in the country—still tries to feel small. Creekland is divided into five "communities"(also called "houses" or "schools within a school") each of which has its own administration. Creekland's teachers work in teams of two, with each teacher responsible for two subjects. Teachers believe the two-team approach enables them to get to know their students better than if they were in teams of four. The communities are integrated for elective classes thus enabling students to meet other students outside their communities. For a closer look at Creekland Middle School, log on to www.coopercarry.com/casestudies/00Educationk-12/Creekland1.html. Education on the Move focuses on one effort to support small schools.

Just making schools smaller, however, is not necessarily sufficient in and of itself, since simply reducing class size does not necessarily result in increased learning and achievement. In the case of smaller schools, the following are necessary to support student learning:

INTASC

Standard 10: The teacher fosters relationships with school colleagues, parents, and agencies in the larger community to support students' learning and well-being.

- Relationships between students and adults are strong and ongoing. These relationships develop most often through extensive advisory systems.
- Relationships with parents are strong and ongoing. In most small schools, advisors and parents communicate regularly, not simply when a student experiences problems.
- The school's organization is flat, with broadly distributed leadership. Small schools have a leaner administrative structure, without specialized academic departments.
- The school does not attempt to be comprehensive. Most small schools concentrate on a few goals and insist that all students meet them, finding ways to honor student choice through the development of projects or other learning activities within a course rather than through an extensive course catalog.
- The school develops its own culture. The culture of small schools typically revolves around the expectations of hard work, high aspirations, respect for others, and success for all students.[16]

>>> Gates Foundation Says Small Schools Are Key to Education >>>>>>>

Efforts to reform public schools by creating small learning communities are receiving a fiscal shot in the arm from the Bill and Melinda Gates Foundation. Convinced that high schools are too big and that efforts need to be found to create smaller learning communities, the Gates Foundation has given a total of $1.9 billion in grants to support small school initiatives. For example, the state of Texas has initiated the Texas High School Project, which is designed to increase high school graduation and college attendance rates, particularly among underserved students. The Gates Foundation is providing $35,000,400 over five years to create seventy-five to eighty new and redesigned small schools in high-minority areas along the Texas-Mexico border and in the state's large inner-city schools, primarily targeting San Antonio, Dallas–Ft. Worth, and Houston. In San Diego, the Gates Foundation has given $11 million to the San Diego city schools to transform three large high schools into high-performing, small learning communities. According to the Gates Foundation, "We know where we need to start. We need to redesign large, ineffective schools, create new, small high schools, and replicate proven models."

Source: For more information on the Bill and Melinda Gates Foundation's support of small school initiatives, visit www.gatesfoundation.org.

Reflect & Write

Schools are organized to achieve their purposes and support effective teaching and efficient learning. Would you prefer to work in a large school, a mid-sized school, a small school, or a large school organized into learning communities? Why?

_____

_____

_____

_____

Pre-K Programs

Today, it is common for many children to be in a school of some kind beginning as early as age 2 or 3, and child care beginning at six weeks is commonplace for many children of working parents. Forty-three states currently invest in preschool, or pre-K, education, whether as public preschools or as support for Head Start. Since 1997, New York has provided free early childhood education to every four-year-old whose parents want it. In Georgia, preschool programs are provided for all children. Annually, the United States spent $4.6 billion on preschool care and education. Preschool education continues to grow, with greater numbers of four-year-olds entering preschools. Currently, about 7.6 million three- to five-year-old children are in some kind of preschool program.

A number of reasons help explain the current popularity of preschool programs:

- Many parents view public schools as the agency that can and should provide child care and education for their children.
- More parents are in the work force than ever before. This places a great demand on the early childhood profession to provide more programs and services, including programs for three- and four-year-olds.
- Parents, public policy planners, and researchers believe intervention programs designed to prevent such social problems as substance abuse and school dropout work best in the early years. Research supports the effectiveness of this early intervention approach.
- Brain research makes it clear that the foundation for learning is laid in the early years and that three- and four-year-old children are ready and able to learn.

As preschool programs have grown in number and popularity over the last decade, they have also undergone significant changes in purpose. Previously, the predominant purposes of preschools were to help socialize children, enhance their social-emotional

> **NCATE**
>
> Early Childhood
>
> **Standard 4:** Integrates understanding of children and families, of developmentally effective approaches to teaching and learning, and of academic disciplines to design, implement, and evaluate positive learning experiences for all children.

development, and get them ready for kindergarten or first grade. Today, there is a decided move away from socialization as the primary function of preschool. Preschools are now promoted as places that accomplish the following:

- **Support and develop children's innate capacity for learning.** The responsibility for "getting ready for school" has shifted from being primarily children's and parents' responsibilities to being a cooperative venture between the child, family, home, schools, and communities.
- **Provide academic, social, and behavioral skills necessary for entry into kindergarten.** Today, a major focus is on developing children's literacy and math skills.
- **Solve or find solutions for pressing social problems.** The early years are viewed as a time when interventions are most likely to have long-term positive influences. Preschool programs are seen as a way of lowering the number of dropouts, improving children's health, and preventing serious social problems such as substance abuse and violence.

The goals of the "new" preschool are dramatically changing how preschool programs operate and teachers teach. Given the changing nature of preschool, it is little wonder that the preschool years are playing a larger role in early childhood education.

Pre-K programs come in many different formats, depending on their purposes, the children served, and funding agencies. Preschools may be either public or private and are operated by many different agencies. Although a common goal of all programs is to provide quality education and services for all children, how they achieve this goal depends on the children served, the parents, and the philosophies of teachers' programs. As pre-K programs admit more two- to four-year-olds nationwide, opportunities for teachers of young children will grow.

Head Start. Head Start has had more influence on early childhood programs than any other single program or agency. **Head Start** began in 1965 as a program to help children from low-income families who would enter first grade. Now it is a year-round program for children ages 3 to 5. Head Start has a federal budget of $6.4 billion and enrolls 909,608 children in 19,200 centers.[17] Early Head Start, initiated in 1994, serves children six weeks to two years. Currently, low-income families are served in more than 708 Early Head Start Programs, with an annual enrollment of 61,500 children. Head Start components include:

- Education
- Parent involvement
- Health services (including psychological services, nutrition, and mental health)
- Social services
- Staff development to provide the knowledge and skills needed for administration and management of programs

How do current changes in early childhood education reflect the link between society and education? Why is pre-K of growing importance in education? Does pre-K teaching appeal to you? Why? Why not?

_____

_____

_____

_____

Kindergartens

Perhaps you have heard the saying, "Everything I need to know in life I learned in kindergarten." This pretty well sums up the view that kindergarten plays an important role in many children's lives. Kindergartens are sponsored by private and public schools and enroll four- and five-year-old children, although the ages of kindergarten children vary from state to state depending on entrance age cutoff dates. Many school districts require children to be five years old by September 1 of the school year in order to be eligible to enter kindergarten. Most kindergartens provide for the academic, intellectual, social, emotional, and physical development of children.

Just as there is growing support for universally available public preschools, there is wide public support for compulsory and tax-supported public kindergarten. In keeping with this national sentiment, most children attend kindergarten, though it is mandatory in only thirteen states (Arkansas, Connecticut, Delaware, Louisiana, Maryland, New Mexico, Ohio, Oklahoma, Rhode Island, South Carolina, Tennessee, Virginia, West Virginia) and the District of Columbia. In many ways, kindergarten is now considered the first grade of school.

The kindergarten of today is not the same as the kindergarten of five years ago. Kindergarten is now a program that focuses primarily on academics, especially early literacy, math, and science and activities that prepare children to think and problem solve. These changes represent a transformation of great magnitude and will have a lasting impact on kindergarten curriculum and teaching in the future.

Kindergarten is either a half- or whole-day program. Texas, for example, leaves the decision to districts to provide full- or half-day programs. However, Florida has compulsory full-day kindergarten for all children. Full-day kindergartens are becoming more common because they better meet the needs of children and working parents than do half-day programs.

The National Education Association (NEA) believes that kindergarten attendance should be mandatory and supports full-day—as opposed to half-day—kindergarten and prekindergarten. In addition, the NEA supports the establishment in every state of two years of universal prekindergarten for all three- and four-year-old children.[18]

Public support for compulsory and tax-supported public kindergartens and preschool programs is widespread, as a recent Gallup poll indicates. Of those responding

Early Childhood

Standard 1: Uses understanding of young children's characteristics, needs, and interacting influences on children's development and learning to create healthy, respectful, supportive, and challenging environments for all children.

Standard 4: Integrates understanding of children and families, of developmentally effective approaches to teaching and learning, and of academic disciplines to design, implement, and evaluate positive learning experiences for all children.

A concern in early childhood education is that programs, materials, and instructional methods be appropriate to children's levels of physical, cognitive, and social development. Aside from "developmentally appropriate education," what other concepts are issues in preschool education?

to the poll, 85 percent support making kindergarten mandatory and 82 percent support making preschools part of the public school program.[19]

Primary and Elementary Schools

Grades K through 3 are known as the primary grades, while grades 4 through 6 are referred to as the elementary grades, although it is common to refer to grades 1 through 6 as the elementary school years. This structure is somewhat fluid, however, with many middle schools enrolling sixth-graders and many elementary schools enrolling children in grades K through 5. Within a school, the typical organization reflects the graded approach, with fifteen to twenty-five students and a teacher in a self-contained classroom. In the primary grades, teachers sometimes have aides to assist with instructional activities and classroom routines.

Elementary schools come in all shapes and sizes and have different purposes, depending on the school district and the neighborhood they serve. For example, Casimir Pulaski Elementary School in Meriden, Connecticut, is a nationally recognized Blue Ribbon School of Excellence, with about 720 students in K through 5. The teachers believe that students should be given the opportunity to maximize their ability to learn, and the key to success in education is through cooperation with others, including parents, students, teachers, and community citizens. Special activities at Pulaski include the Pulaski Academy, Safety Patrol, Sign Language Club, Special Chorus, Pulaski PALS, Student Council, Mathletix, Green Thumb Club, and the Pulaski Press. Directly behind the school is a nature trail to encourage students, teachers, and area residents to learn more about the habitats and wildlife found within the area. To learn more about Casimir Pulaski Elementary School visit their Web site at www.meriden.k12.ct.us/pulaski/index.html.

Alianza School (*alianza* means alliance), a two-way bilingual immersion elementary school in Watsonville, California, is designed to address another mission. Alianza is a magnet school and a key element in the Pajaro Valley Unified School District's Desegregation Plan. This area is primarily low income and 98 percent Latino. Alianza's mission is to teach understanding and respect for racial, cultural, and linguistic diversity. This is accomplished though a model bilingual/immersion program for all students that emphasizes the acquisition of a second language, high academic standards, cooperation with others, and the appreciation of each individual's uniqueness.[20] Alianza has implemented a schoolwide two-way immersion in Spanish program. Two-way immersion programs integrate language-minority and language-majority students, providing instruction in both English and the native language of the language minority students. The structure of these programs varies, but they all integrate students for most content instruction and provide this instruction in the non-English language for a significant portion of the school day. Two-way bilingual immersion programs strive to promote bilingualism and biliteracy, grade-level academic achievement, and positive cross-cultural attitudes and behaviors in all students.

Clearly, the definition of what elementary schools are for and how they should operate is changing. (See, for example, Education on the Move about K–8 schools.) Schooling in the primary and elementary grades has become a serious enterprise, for political and social reasons. It is in the primary grades, especially grades 3 and 4, where state and national testing begins. There is therefore an emphasis on ensuring that children know what will be tested and that they will do well on the tests. For example, the federal government and many states (including Texas and California) have a goal that all children will read on grade level by grade 3. This goal makes the teaching of reading a high priority. The National Assessment of Educational Progress (NAEP), known as the "nation's report card," is given in grades 4, 8, and 12. The NAEP project is carried out by the Commissioner of Educational Statistics in the Department of Education. The No Child Left Behind Act requires states to participate in NAEP in order to validate student progress. The pressure for high performance on state and national tests begins early in children's school careers. For more information, visit the NAEP Web site at http://nces.ed.gov/nationsreportcard/sitemap.asp.

>>> K–8 Schools—Popular Again! >>>>>>>

Cincinnati, Cleveland, Milwaukee, New York, and Philadelphia are among the states in which some school districts are restructuring to include K–8 schools—an idea that went out of fashion some years ago. But they are making the change driven by research and a rising pile of anecdotes suggesting that K–8 configurations help academic performance, decrease discipline problems, enhance parent involvement, and save money.

The wave of K–8 reorganization comes as educators, pressured by new federal mandates, are seeking ways to boost student achievement. Most district leaders who favor the K–8 model see it as one part of an overhaul that includes smaller, more personalized schools able to meet the needs of varying age groups with improved curricula and better staff training.

In New York City, a three-year plan envisions creating 200 or more smaller schools in K–8, 6–12, and 9–12 configurations, including fifteen elementary schools that will convert to K–8s in the fall.

Michele Cahill, a senior policy advisor to school chancellor Joel I. Klein, said the plan is part of an effort to create schools "at a more human scale," forge strong pupil-teacher connections, and minimize school-to-school transitions.

Milwaukee now has thirty K–8 schools, with another twenty in various stages of transition. Milwaukee is adding thousands of seats in city schools to enable all children to attend neighborhood schools, a policy that answers parents' desire to have children close by and addresses the district's difficulty in shouldering massive transportation costs to bus students to schools of choice.

According to the administrators, the decision to pursue K–8 configuration is part of the 97,000-student district's drive to meet parents' needs and save money.

Source: F. Schouten, "Kids Like Get-Out-of-Junior-High Card," *USA Today,* October 16, 2002. (Online). Available at www.middleweb.com/MGNEWS/MGN1019.html. Copyright 2002 by USA Today. Reprinted by permission.

Middle Level

Standard 2: Understands the major concepts, principles, theories, and research underlying the philosophical foundations of developmentally responsible middle-level programs and schools; works successfully within these organizational components.

Over the years, the new "vision" in elementary schools has included a movement toward investigation and collaboration. What do you see as the advantages of this movement in children's learning?

There are also changes in physical structure and in teachers' roles. Changes in curriculum and instructional methods have affected how classrooms are organized. Instead of sitting in seats in straight rows and engaging in solitary learning activities, students are now out of their seats, discussing projects with classmates and collaborating on completing them. While the elementary teacher's roles of facilitator, learning collaborator, and coach are still popular, direct systematic instruction is becoming preferred as teachers strive to teach children the skills they need for school and life success.

The reforms taking place at Casimir Pulaski and Alianza reflect a nationwide movement toward a new vision of the elementary school: one that centers on giving children of all abilities many opportunities and ways to achieve state standards and be successful socially and academically. Such schools shun practices that march every child of the same age through the same drill at the same time. Instead, these schools group pupils in ways that allow them to move at their own rates while working cooperatively with peers of different ages and abilities. They also keep children with the same teacher for more than one year, promoting a view of teachers as children's guides and coinvestigators, and integrate subjects around themes and principles and through technology. The tools of the teaching trade have also changed—from textbooks to technology.

Middle and Junior High Schools

Junior high schools enroll students in grades 7 and 8 or 7 through 9. In 1909, the first junior high schools opened in Columbus, Ohio, and Berkeley, California, and this organizational structure has been an important feature of American education ever since. Beginning in the 1960s, middle schools have been gradually replacing junior high schools as the organizing model for educating young adolescents. (For a new idea about organizing midlevel education, see Education on the Move.)

Middle schools typically serve children in grades 6 through 8 (ages 10 through 14) and provide an earlier transition from the elementary school. Other grade configurations for middle schools include grades 5 through 7 and 7 through 9. Some junior high schools have changed their names to "middle schools." The organization, operation, and curriculum of middle schools are receiving a lot of attention. The following issues are some that confront middle schools:

- Finding a balance between providing for academics and students' social-emotional development.
- The preparation and certification of middle school teachers specifically to teach middle school students. Many middle school teachers hold elementary and senior high school certification. Many colleges of education offer middle-grade certification for teachers who are entering teaching in middle schools.
- A curriculum that fails to meet the academic needs of students. Some call the curricula of many schools "shallow, fragmented, and unchallenging" and claim that middle schools are "caught between the warmth of a good elementary school and the academic seriousness of a good high school and that middle school students often get the least of both and the best of neither."[21]

The contemporary middle school is designed to address the unique developmental needs (cognitive, psychosocial, and physical) of emerging adolescents. Many adolescents change schools during these formative years, moving from the comforting confines of a neighborhood elementary school to a large middle school, junior high school, or high school. Such moves have important consequences for young people. These changes disrupt familiar peer group structures, introduce youth to different standards and achievement expectations, and provide opportunities for new extracurricular activities as part of both the planned curriculum and the hidden curriculum (what students learn simply because they attend school).

The concept of **middle-level education** denotes attempts to provide unique experiences for young adolescents in response to their developmental needs and particular environments and to accomplish a gradual, peaceful transition to later adolescence

Middle-level education
Reflects attempts to provide unique experiences for young adolescents in response to their developmental needs and unique environments for gradual, peaceful transitions to later adolescence and high school education.

>>> Schools for Ninth-Graders Only >>>>>>>

Ask middle school and high school teachers about ninth grade and they will probably tell you, "It's a make or break year." As a former teacher of ninth graders, I agree with this assessment! Ninth grade is known as a slump year. It is the grade when students can lose their confidence, become disillusioned, and drop out of school. One solution to the pivotal year? Schools for ninth-graders only.

Texas is in the forefront of a national trend school leaders think will make the transition to high school smoother: special schools for freshmen only. Six Dallas-area districts have ninth-grade-only schools, and more are likely to appear in the coming years. *Texas Construction* magazine recently cited the freshman school trend as one of the reasons the state's builders are expected to keep busy during the next few years.

"I've been in education for thirty years, mostly at four-year high schools," said Jim Yakubovsky, principal of DeSoto High School's fresh-man campus. "And you really notice how much a freshman matures from August to May, physically, emotionally, socially. Separating them out gives these kids a chance to mature."

Steve Payne, principal of the Lowery Freshman Central in Allen (Texas), said the school was created in response to concerns about a higher-than-desired failure rate in the ninth grade. "We thought that once kids get through freshman and sophomore year, they can get all the way through," he said.

In the 6,000-student Rush-Henrietta Central School District outside Rochester, New York, ninth-graders also attend a separate facility. The separate school gives ninth-graders "an environment that addresses their unique needs," says Superintendent Kenneth Graham. As he puts it, ninth grade should fit ninth-graders—not the other way around.

According to the U.S. Department of Education's National Center for Education Statistics (NCES), ninth-grade-only schools, often housed on a separate campus, are catching on, especially in urban school districts. Some 128 separate ninth-grade schools were operating in 2000, NCES says, with more in the planning stages.

Source: J. N. Reents, "Isolating Ninth-Graders: Separate Schools Ease the Academic and Social Transition for High School Bound Students," *School Administrator*, March 2002. (Online). Available at www.aasa.org/publications/sa/2002_03/reents.htm; National Center for Education Statistics. *National Digest of Education Statistics, 2002* (2002). (Online). Available at http://nces.ed.gov/programs/digest/d02/. Reprinted with permission from the March 2002 issue of *The School Administrator.*

Middle Level

Standard 1: Understands the major concepts, principles, theories and research related to young adolescent development; provides opportunities that support student development and learning.

and high school education. Probably more than any other school configuration, the middle school is perceived as focusing on the characteristics and needs of its students as a way to provide an arena of comfort to young teenagers at a time when they need it most. For this reason, middle schools are increasing in popularity and number. They are now the predominant form of school organization for early adolescents. There are currently over 14,000 middle schools in the United States, over five times the number in existence in 1970. Three essential features characterize quality middle schools: guidance programs; transition programs; and instructional organization that includes team teaching, career exploration, and athletics.

Middle Level

Standard 2: Understands the major concepts, principles, theories, and research underlying the philosophical foundations of developmentally responsible middle-level programs and schools; works successfully within these organizational components.

1. Effective guidance systems provide adult mentors and guidance counselors who give advice on academic, personal, social, and vocational matters. When the counselor-student ratio is too high to provide the quality of services necessary, a number of alternatives exist. One alternative is the home base plan in which each teacher works with an assigned group of advisees. Classrooms serve as a "home base" where students receive daily counseling. Generally, students are assigned to the same home base over the three years of their middle school experience, for consistency and continuity.

2. Transition programs help children (and often their parents) make the passage from one educational setting to another—from the elementary grades to the middle school, and from the middle school to the senior high school. **Transition programs** are designed to help minimize confusion or distress. Activities include orienting students before their arrival at the new school, informing parents of the philosophy of the school and providing them with opportunities to visit classes,

Transition programs
Programs designed to help children and parents make the passage from one program or educational setting to another, for example, from the elementary grades to the middle school and from the middle school to the senior high school.

inviting students already enrolled at the new school to talk to arriving students, and having teachers visit new students' homes.

3. Instructional trends in middle-level schooling include block scheduling, cross-disciplinary or thematically integrated curricula, and teaching to students' individual learning styles. Teaching strategies emphasize inquiry teaching, cooperative learning, independent study, and exploratory opportunities. Career exploration and athletics programs give middle school students opportunities to make informed choices, which helps them become more independent and self-reliant. Courses that provide exploratory opportunities include computer education, industrial arts, music, home economics, technology education, typing, fine arts, career education, and community service.

The National Forum to Accelerate Middle Grades Reform helps middle schools achieve three goals: academic excellence, developmental responsiveness, and social equity. The forum sponsors a "Schools-to-Watch" program to call attention to high-performing schools, such as Thurgood Marshall Middle School in Chicago, Illinois; Jefferson Middle School in Champaign, Illinois; Barren County Middle School in Glasgow, Kentucky; and Freeport Intermediate School in Freeport, Texas. You can take a virtual tour of theses schools at www.schoolstowatch.org/visit.htm. The forum maintains that youth in the middle grades are capable of learning and achieving at high levels and is working to see that high-performing schools with middle grades become the norm, not the exception. For more information, visit their Web site at www.mgforum.org/Improvingschools/Improveschools.asp.

Do you think all the changes occurring in middle schools are good for students and teachers? Why or why not? On a scale of 1 (low) to 10 (high), rank your desire to teach in a middle school.

_____

_____

_____

_____

High Schools

High schools serve students in grades 9 or 10 through 12 and vary in size from a few hundred students to almost 5,000. Today's **comprehensive high schools** serve a large and diverse student body and provide a range of services and curricula to students. The typical organization of a comprehensive high school is shown in Figure 3.3.

Richard Schafer, principal at Ft. Myers High School, says that running a high school today is a lot different from the way it was twenty years ago when he entered the profession. He identifies the following ways that things have changed:

- Politics. There is much more politics involved in providing education to students. As a consequence, a principal has to spend a lot of time being a politician and being involved in political affairs.
- Business affairs. More and more, schools are being run like businesses, and principals are more responsible for the financial affairs of the school than ever before.
- Activities. Schools today provide a wider range of activities and services for their students. Some schools have staff members whose sole job is to coordinate, supervise, and facilitate student activities.
- Collaboration and cooperation. Schools are no longer run by the principal. Today, teachers, students, staff, parents, community members, and others are included in decisions about what is taught and how it is taught.
- Community issues and concerns. Community needs, educational needs, and professional needs have to be balanced and evaluated so that community needs alone don't run the school. Certain community advocacy groups can be very powerful and exert tremendous influence. Some special interest groups are designed to protect the rights of children—for example, children with disabilities. Others are designed to promote

NCATE

Middle Level

Standard 2: Understands the major concepts, principles, theories and research underlying the philosophical foundations of developmentally responsible middle-level programs and schools; works successfully within these organizational components.

Comprehensive high schools
High schools that serve a large and diverse student body and provide a wide range of services and curricula to students.

INTASC

Standard 10: The teacher fosters relationships with school colleagues, parents, and agencies in the larger community to support students' learning and well-being.

INTASC

Standard 1: The teacher understands the central concepts, tools of inquiry, and structures of the subject being taught and can create learning experiences that make these aspects of subject matter meaningful for students.

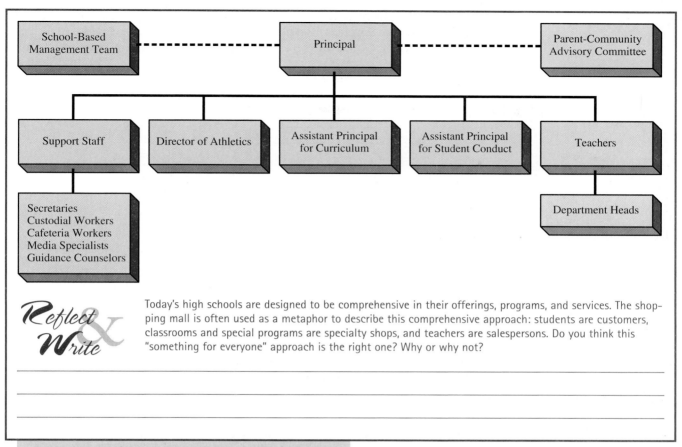

Today's high schools are designed to be comprehensive in their offerings, programs, and services. The shopping mall is often used as a metaphor to describe this comprehensive approach: students are customers, classrooms and special programs are specialty shops, and teachers are salespersons. Do you think this "something for everyone" approach is the right one? Why or why not?

Figure 3.3 *Organization at the High School Level*

INTASC

Standard 10: The teacher fosters relationships with school colleagues, parents, and agencies in the larger community to support students' learning and well-being.

the teaching of certain topics in the public schools, for example, school prayer. Advocacy groups are intent on making their positions known and on advancing their particular agendas. Today, schools are literally surrounded by such groups, and school personnel have to determine the best way to work with them.

- Public relations. Today, many school personnel are public relations experts. They are involved in speaking to groups and community agencies about community and school issues. How well the schools get along with stakeholders and how well they articulate their programs to them determines to some degree how successful schools are as educational agencies.

- Delivering a quality education program. Although some educators may lose or have lost sight of it, the primary goal of schools is to provide their students with a quality educational program that will serve them well in the world after grade 12, whatever that world may immediately be. Because of the constant criticisms of the schools, more and more professionals are concentrating their efforts on basic skills training. They are intent on ensuring that they are capable of delivering a quality product, in this case, students who can read, write, compute, and think; who are technologically literate; and who can take their place in the nation's work force.[22]

Schools today offer students a wide range of services and programs. Such opportunities promote curiosity and allow students to explore various interests and to broaden their awareness and knowledge.

Principal Richard Schafer offers some interesting comments about how high schools are changing. How do these changes compare to the high school you attended? How will these changes affect how you will teach?

_____

_____

_____

_____

_____

Alternative Learning Programs and Schools

Alternative schools
Schools formed by public schools and private groups as alternatives to existing public schools.

Social and educational change is reflected in the creation of alternative learning programs or **alternative schools.** Alternative schools are designed to provide alternatives to the regular or typical school program. Alternative schools come in many configurations.

At-Risk Students. One type of alternative school is specifically designed to meet the needs of students who are at risk for some reason, such as constant truancy, drug use, and having been expelled from the regular school program. This school can be in a separate building from the regular school or a school within a school. In this type of alternative school, teachers provide remedial programs as well as individualized and specialized counseling services, and the class size is generally small. The goal of the alternative approach is to keep students in school (in most states students have to stay in school until they are 17), help students address and overcome their problems, and assist students to graduate.

Parental Choice. A second kind of alternative school is designed to provide parents with choices relating to their expectations of curriculum and schooling. For example, the Poudre School District in Ft. Collins, Colorado, has elementary alternative schools open to any student in the district, depending on space. These schools include:

NCATE

Middle Level

Standard 2: Understands the major concepts, principles, theories, and research underlying the philosophical foundations of developmentally responsible middle-level programs and schools; works successfully within these organizational components.

INTASC

Standard 3: The teacher understands how students differ in their approaches to learning and creates instructional opportunities that are adapted to diverse learners.

1. **The Traut Core Knowledge School,** a school of choice, uses the cultural literacy curriculum developed by E. D. Hirsch (this approach is discussed in Chapter 10). This back-to-basics elementary school stresses character education, parent partnerships, and literacy instruction.
2. **The Lab School for Creative Learning** is at the opposite end of the educational continuum. It offers a nontraditional school setting that emphasizes a small pupil-teacher ratio and a child-centered, developmental curriculum.
3. **The Harris Bilingual Immersion School** offers strong bilingual language skills and cross-cultural knowledge to a balanced mix of predominantly Spanish-speaking and predominantly English-speaking elementary students.

Magnet schools
Designed to attract diverse students from all over a district or attendance area and to address issues of equity in course and program offerings. Many magnet schools have a particular curriculum or program emphasis.

Magnet Schools. **Magnet schools** are designed to address issues of equality and are often viewed as an alternative to busing. The curriculum and programs of these schools are so appealing that they attract students from across the district.

Many magnet schools have a particular curriculum or program emphasis. The Chicago Public School District has more than 300 magnet schools and programs. Some of the magnet themes are:

Agricultural sciences
Dual language
Humanities
Mathematics and science
Montessori program

Open classroom
Paideia program (see Chapter 9)
Scholastic academics
World language

The effectiveness of magnet schools as a means of integrating schools and reducing segregation is being questioned. Recent research indicates that there is no "conclusive evidence that magnet schools significantly bolster districtwide efforts to reduce racial isolation, improve racial balance, or stem white flight." On the other hand, magnet schools are effective in improving student learning. Urban high school students in magnet schools make greater gains in reading, social studies, and science.[23]

Private For–Profit Schools. A fast-growing segment of the educational enterprise is private for-profit schools. Many of these schools serve an increasing number of students who have been expelled for violating drug and weapons policies and for other disciplinary reasons. There were over 1.4 million incidents of violence occurring in public schools in 1999–2000 school year, and the expulsion rate for students violating school policies is up dramatically due, in large measure, to the 1996 zero-tolerance laws adopted by the majority of public schools. Zero-tolerance laws require schools to expel students who bring guns to school; otherwise schools lose their federal funding.

Some states require school districts to provide alternative schools and programs for expelled students. For example, Texas requires that each of its twenty-two counties with populations of 125,000 or more provide alternative schools. Many districts find it easier and more cost-effective to let for-profit companies provide the services. These privately operated alternative schools are both day and residential schools. Additionally, more affluent parents are turning to private alternative schools to help their children overcome addiction and other problems. While some alternative schools receive support from tax revenue, tuition for private alternative schools can be quite expensive.

Charter Schools. One of the most talked-about innovations in public education, charter schools, or "contract" schools, are custom designed by individuals or groups and are a major aid in reforming public education. Charter schools have a great deal of public and political support. Funding for charter schools comes from the district that granted the charter and from states, foundations, and individuals. Although they are considered independent, these schools are not exempt from state laws governing education. Charter schools:

- Seek to realize an alternative vision of schooling
- Provide local, autonomous control of education
- Free teachers and schools from cumbersome, bureaucratic state and local board of education red tape (though they remain subject to all state laws applying to public education)
- Provide parents and students with alternative choices to public education
- Respond to the needs of an increasingly diverse student population
- Serve a special student population
- Bring accountability and excellence to the educational process through improved student learning and achievement
- Are innovative in curriculum, teaching, and delivery of services
- Guarantee educational outcome for students
- Create improved opportunities for teachers

Minnesota was the first state to approve charter schools in 1991. There are many kinds of charter schools, designed to meet many different purposes. For example, the Vivian Banks Charter School of the Bonsall Union School District in Bonsall, California, is a K–5 school on the Pala Indian reservation north of San Diego. The main goal of Vivian Banks is to achieve literacy for all children in reading, writing, speaking, and listening. Computers are used for instruction, and there is an emphasis on small class size and parent participation. Nationwide, more than 3,000 charter schools operate

INTASC

Standard 3: The teacher understands how students differ in their approaches to learning and creates instructional opportunities that are adapted to diverse learners.

Standard 7: The teacher plans instruction based upon knowledge of subject matter, students, the community, and curriculum goals.

Charter schools
Provide free public elementary/secondary education under a charter granted by the state legislature or other appropriate authority.

Have Charter Schools Lived Up to Their Promise?

Charter schools have their supporters and detractors. Here are two news stories—pro and con—about the success or lack of success of charter schools. Read these accounts and then you decide—Have charter schools lived up to their promise?

"Charter School Test Scores Highest in NY"

Long Island's first charter school, which only a year ago appeared in administrative disarray, has bounced back under new leadership this year with the highest elementary test scores for any charter school in the state.

Latest results show that 87 percent of fourth-graders at Roosevelt Children's Academy scored at the proficient level or higher on state-administered English tests. That's the highest rate among more than thirty charter schools operating statewide and is competitive with scores in many of [Long] Island's more affluent school districts.

"Charter Schools Not as Integrated as Many Would Like"

When the Reverends Michael Nickleson and Vernon Graham set out to start a local charter school, they wanted to offer a choice to families in the southwest part of East Allen County Schools.

But now, after years of fighting with local school districts to make sure schools are integrated, the two men find themselves on the board of directors for the Timothy L. Johnson Academy, a charter school on South Anthony Boulevard with a student body experts call "hypersegregated"—95 percent of the students are black.

Need help making up your mind? Here are some links to help you.

- USCS: United Charter Schools homepage— www.uscharterschools.org
- National Education Association— www.nea.org/charter/
- Charter Schools USA—www.charterschoolsusa.com/
- National Charter School Institute—www.nationalcharter-schools.org/

Source: Adapted from selected information from J. Hildebrande, "Charter School Test Scores Highest in NY," *NY Newsday,* June 8, 2004. (Online). Available at www.nynewsday.com/; K. Stockman, "Charter Schools Not as Integrated as Many Would Like," *The Journal Gazette,* May 16, 2004. (Online). Available at: www.fortwayne.com/mld/fortwayne/news/local/8680900.htm.

in forty-one states and the District of Columbia. Table 3.1 shows the top ten states for charter schools. Charter schools are not large, with an average enrollment of 475. Nationwide, 703,089 students attend charter schools. For more information about charter schools, visit www.uscharterschools.org and www.NCSC.info.

What Does This Mean for You?

Choice seems to be a major theme of contemporary society. Schooling choices include home schooling, private schools, charter schools, magnet schools, and alternative schools. Some of these choices come with a price tag (my neighbors spend $10,000 a year in tuition to send their son to a faith-based school). Public school districts are also responding to choice demands and are providing parents with more choices. For you as a teacher, this means that

- you will probably teach in a school with programs that appeal to parents as well as their children
- if you are proficient in specialty areas such as technology, foreign languages, and Montessori, you will be in high demand to teach in schools of choice
- you will engage in high levels of collaboration with colleagues and parents to help ensure that the specialization of the school is maintained and enhanced
- over your career, school options for parents and their children will increase, and choice will be more common and expected

Table 3.1   *Top Ten States for Charter Schools, 2004*

State	*Number of Charter Schools*
Arizona	495
California	471
Florida	258
Texas	241
Michigan	210
Wisconsin	147
Ohio	142
Pennsylvania	103
North Carolina	94
Colorado	93

Source: See www.uscharterschools.org.

SECTION SUMMARY

How Are Public Schools Organized?

A school's organization is aimed at achieving the school's purposes, establishing order, and enabling effective teaching and learning.

- The Structure of Schooling in the United States. Most schools have similar organization patterns: a top-down administrative structure and an age-graded approach to instruction. *Looping* expands on the age-graded approach. To gain more time for teaching, many schools are experimenting with longer school days and school years or new approaches, such as block scheduling, extended day programs, summer school, flex high school graduation, and year-round education. Size affects school organization, and more efforts are being made to develop smaller schools and learning communities.

- Pre-K Programs. Preschool (pre-K) programs are becoming a more important part of public schools because of their ability to remediate learning and social problems, thereby helping children to get a good start in school. Preschools are seen as providing children the academic skills needed for success in kindergarten. Head Start has had a significant impact on preschool education.

- Kindergartens. Most children attend kindergarten, and these programs are now considered the first grade in the public school system. Kindergarten curriculum emphasizes literacy, math, and science.

- Primary and Elementary Schools. Primary and elementary schools are changing their curricula and instructional methods to meet the needs of children and society. These are responding to pressure for high student performance on national tests.

- Middle and Junior High Schools. Middle schools have undergone the greatest restructuring of all the levels of schooling. Middle schools are being specifically redesigned to meet the needs of emerging teenagers. These schools emphasize transition programs, interdisciplinary teaching, and attention to adolescents' special needs.

- High Schools. High schools are changing in order to teach a wider range of curricula and to provide more social services. High schools are also more of a business than ever before, and they are adopting and using business practices to help achieve their goals.

- Alternative Learning Programs and Schools. Alternative schools, such as magnet schools and charter schools, increase parents' choices about where to send their children to school. Chartering literally creates new schools by allowing schools to operate independently of the traditional public school system.

Thinking Critically

★ ★ ★ ★ ★ ★ ★ ★

Increasingly, schools are called on to address and solve many of society's problems relating to violence, substance abuse, crime, and teenage pregnancy. Many believe that the schools have strayed too far from their mission of teaching basic skills. Why are schools asked to solve society's problems? Do you think the schools are being asked to do too much for too many students? What do you believe should be the primary mission of schools?

If you could make only one recommendation for the restructuring of schools, what would that recommendation be? Why?

_____

_____

_____

_____ ★

You are a teacher member of a districtwide planning committee charged with designing a new middle school to house 900 students. What three reforms would you recommend from the middle or junior high school you attended?

_____

_____

_____

_____ ★

INTASC

Standard 3: The teacher understands how students differ in their approaches to learning and creates instructional opportunities that are adapted to diverse learners.

NCATE

Middle Level

Standard 3: Understands the major concepts, principles, theories, and research related to middle-level curriculum and assessment; uses this knowledge in practice.

*W*HAT IS IT LIKE TO TEACH IN URBAN, RURAL, AND SUBURBAN SCHOOLS?

You have read how schools are organized. Another way to look at public schools is according to population densities and other characteristics (such as cultural diversity, socioeconomic status, and funding available for education) of the communities in which they are located. Geography provides another lens through which we can look at schools. Where schools are located frequently determines their nature, curriculum, and purpose. In this kind of classification, there are three types of schools—urban (also called inner-city and metropolitan), suburban, and rural. Each type has its unique student populations, features, and cultures. Even within each type individual schools differ. For example, the Laredo (Texas) Independent School District is 13.83 square miles. It has 24,000 students and 3,500 full-time employees on thirty campuses. This district has all categories of schools—urban, suburban, and rural. The unique differences of individual schools arise not only from the American tradition of local control of schools but also from each school's responsiveness to the nature and character of the local community. Figure 3.4 shows some of the sources of differences among urban, rural, and suburban schools.

Which type(s) of schools have you attended? Consider the sources of differences displayed in Figure 3.4, and then answer this question: How did the characteristics of the schools you attended affect your learning and school life?

_____

_____

_____

_____

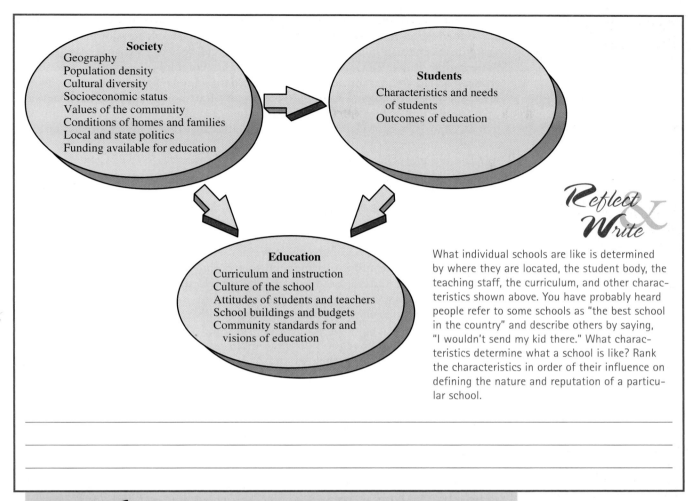

Figure 3.4   Sources of Differences among Urban, Rural, and Suburban Schools

Urban School Districts and Schools

An urban school district is one in which 75 percent or more of the households served are in the central city of a metropolitan area. Urban schools take their character from the cities of which they are a part. Urban schools tend to be large, and student bodies tend to reflect the diversity of urban communities. Miami, for example, has large populations of Cubans, Haitians, and Central Americans. Los Angeles has large populations of Hispanic and Asian Americans. Approximately 70.8 percent of the Los Angeles school district is Hispanic American. Belmont High School in downtown Los Angeles is a year-round school with an enrollment of 5,410 students. Over 50 percent of the students are classified as English learners. Urban schools like Belmont enroll one-quarter of all students—35 percent of the poor students and 43 percent of the minority students in the United States.

The social problems of urban areas and the educational needs of students exert great influence on the curriculum, the learning environment, and the day-to-day operation of schools. Despite the pressures and challenges of urban districts, many urban schools are excellent, with vibrant school cultures, outstanding curricula, and highly dedicated teaching professionals. For example, Reading, Pennsylvania, a city of over 81,000, has only one high school with a population of 3,862 in grades 9 through 12, making it Pennsylvania's largest. It provides a full range of programs including advanced placement classes, a jazz ensemble, and on-site child care for the 60 to 100 girls who get pregnant each year.[24]

INTASC

Standard 10: The teacher fosters relationships with school colleagues, parents, and agencies in the larger community to support students' learning and well-being.

A central issue for schools is how to ensure the safety of their students. Providing a safe learning environment is a key to fulfilling the academic mission of all schools. Some districts are employing prevention design and devices to ensure safer schools. For example, Town View Magnet School in Dallas combines the latest in safe school design (barriers to keep intruders out) with modern school security technology. Thirty-seven surveillance cameras are monitored twenty-four hours a day, and each student wears a photo identification card. Five full-time campus security officers monitor the school. Many schools use metal detectors to help ensure that weapons are not brought to school, and security officers patrolling the halls are almost commonplace.

The national School Security Technologies and Resource (SSTAR) Center, a Department of Energy (DOE) research and development laboratory based at Sandia, Albuquerque, advises schools about security technologies. This advisement stresses low-tech approaches that are both cost-effective and safety effective. Some of the low-tech approaches include radios and communication devices, intrusion detection systems, hand-held metal detectors, ID badging systems, and visitors' passes that expire after one day. Sandia also advises on nontechnology approaches that contribute to safe schools, including campus cleanliness, crime-reporting hotlines, crisis intervention programs, drug dogs, fences, and school design. For more information about Sandia's security work, go online at www.sandia.gov/media/sch/sec.htm.

In addition to using zero-tolerance, expulsions, metal detectors, and security guards to ensure safety, some schools are turning to other means. There are other methods that work. Safe schools depend on safe communities. For one teacher's view about teaching in urban schools, see the Profile on p. 103.

Rural Schools

Rural schools reflect a sense of community and are often the center of community life. Just how much of a sense of community is conveyed in rural schools was impressed upon new high school principal Hasse K. Halley of Cabot, Vermont. "At the annual Fourth of July parade, she was introduced to the village atop a red Chevy pickup. . . .

Rural communities have a culture very different from urban and suburban communities, and the schools reflect this culture. What considerations might a teacher in a rural community have to make that would be unique to the setting?

Marty Walker teaches at H. Grady Spruce High School in the Dallas Independent School District and was the Dallas Golden Apple Teacher of the Year and is a Texas Outstanding Teacher of Humanities. Spruce is located in a changing neighborhood in which middle-income families are moving out, and low-income families are moving in. These new families are less educated, and many are single parents. Many of the students receive free breakfasts and lunches.

Marty teaches regular English IV (seniors), English IV AP, and is chairman of the English department, trains new teachers for the Dallas School System, and serves on the Campus Leadership Instructional team.

I choose to be in an urban school. I've been asked to change jobs and go to other schools, but I feel a calling to my school. I have a lot to offer my students, and there is a need for role models in my school. I grew up disadvantaged and lived on the "other side of the tracks." I am what I am because of my teachers, and I want to return the opportunity to my students to have good teaching. Perhaps some of them will be inspired to select teaching as a career and teach in the inner city.

It's different teaching in an urban school. Every morning every student must go through a metal detector—they are located at every entrance. Also, the assistant principals and aides are at tables, and they go through all book bags and purses in order to keep guns out of schools. We have a "youth action officer," a plainclothes police officer who is in the school all the time. We also have a female uniformed police officer in the school all the time. She patrols the halls and lunchroom to help maintain order. If there is a rumor of any impending school disturbance, then we have more police officers. We do all we can to have a safe and violence-free school for our students.

I really and truly love the kids. That's why I choose to be here at Spruce. You need to have a calling to help students, and you have to look beyond the poverty and look beyond the surface and have a great desire to help students become all that they can become.

As you work with inner-city students, you are always looking for a hook to get them interested in learning. I do a lot of praising in my teaching. The students need to hear words of praise. They do not get many words of encouragement in their homes, so I have to provide it in school. I also do a lot of correcting; it is one way of letting students know I care. You must care about students. You have to have a vision for the kids. If you don't, you shouldn't be teaching. If you are a person who doesn't care for kids who don't look right and act right all the time, then chances are you wouldn't be happy teaching in an inner-city school. You have to see persons, not color, and look at character, not just the surface.

Teaching in an urban school is stressful. You have to give 150 percent. Every day, I come home from school wiped out. I am a high-energy person, and I put a lot into my teaching. I tell new teachers that some things they can do to handle stress are to take vitamins, to go to bed as early as possible, and to be good to themselves.

They want the school to be the heart of the community . . . that's the old way, and that's the way they are going to keep it."[25] While by no means free of social problems, rural communities and families tend to have close ties, and children often attend the same school their parents and grandparents attended.

Many rural school districts cover hundreds of square miles. Outside of small community centers, people often live far from each other, and students travel long distances to and from school. Rural schools are found primarily in the Midwest, West, and South. *Rural* is defined by the Census Bureau as communities with fewer than 2,500 people. North Carolina has 257,417 rural students, the greatest absolute number found in any state. Vermont has the highest proportion of rural students, with 92 percent of its students attending rural schools. Rural students make up more than 30 percent of the enrollment in twelve other states. More than 30 percent of rural schools serve fewer than 200 students, while fewer than 25 percent serve 800 or more.[26] For example, Pennsylvania's smallest school is in Austin and has seventy-two students in grades 9 through 12; the district's entire student body of 128 is housed in one building. Students participate in distance education classes through cable television. In such a school, strong relationships are possible.

Rural students' test scores are at or near the top of national averages according to the report *The Conditions of Education in Rural Schools*.[27] In addition, small rural schools in the Midwest and West register the highest Scholastic Aptitude Test (SAT) scores in the nation. School size is the primary reason that students in small schools achieve so well, with schools of fewer than 300 students doing the best. In small schools, students, teachers, and administrators tend to know one another. Rural schools also seem to place more emphasis on core subjects and to see themselves as "places of learning."[28]

The nature and character of rural life affects teachers, who are expected to support community values, adhere to community standards, and participate in community affairs and activities. For one teacher's view on teaching in rural schools, see the Profile on p. 104.

Teaching in Rural Schools: Juanita Wilkerson

Juanita Wilkerson taught preschool (four-year program) and kindergarten at the Paris, Kentucky, Elementary School, which has an enrollment of 500 students.

I designed the four-year program, wrote the goals and objectives and the curriculum. I even painted the furniture! My husband helped me prepare my room before school started. In a rural school we are expected to do more. Because of a limited budget, I spend a lot of my own money. I supplemented my classroom supplies by going to yard sales and buying toys and other materials to put into my learning centers. As a rural teacher, I also save everything, because sooner or later I will find a use for it.

Teaching in a rural school is very challenging. Teachers are very important in the rural community, and parents expect us to teach the basics and we do. Many of the new teaching ideas are unfamiliar to parents, and some do not approve of them. We have to try to preserve the best of the old while educating parents to new ideas and practices that will help their children to learn better. Things happen slower in a rural school and evolve in a slower way. For example, we have site-based management.

This means the teacher and parents are involved in discussions about how the school operates. It took the faculty and administration a lot of time and effort to get parents involved.

One of the best things about teaching in a rural school is parent support. When I teach, I always tell parents it is their classroom, too. My students' parents help with everything—arts and crafts activities, musical programs, physical activities, cooking, parties, and field trips.

The kids are great in rural schools. They love to learn, and I try to provide experiences that they might not otherwise have had. Some of the children have limited opportunities, so I try to provide a variety of classroom experiences.

New teachers need to get to know the parents and the children, so parent conferences are very important. In past years, about three-quarters of the parents came in for conferences, and if they didn't, I made home visits. In this regard, teachers can expect to spend more time with parents than they might otherwise anticipate. Also, teachers should not expect to change everything during their first year of teaching. Change is much slower in rural schools.

Suburban Schools

World War II marked the beginning of the suburban school movement in the United States. The years after the war were prosperous, giving rise to a large middle class that could afford to move out of the cities. This population migration led to the building of suburban school systems.

Suburban areas, and therefore suburban schools, are adjacent to large cities. While people move to suburbia to escape some of the problems frequently associated with city life, the problems of city life have frequently followed people to suburbia. Today, violence, substance abuse, teenage pregnancy, and other "urban" problems are as prevalent in suburbia as they are in the inner city.

As more people live in less space in older suburbs, these areas become more city-like. Many suburbs are served by local and regional shopping malls, where youth can spend their money and time, socialize, and be free of parental supervision.

Suburban curricula tend to be geared toward college preparation. Many schools measure success by average SAT scores and the number of students accepted to colleges. One other measure of school quality is the number of students taking advanced placement courses. Teachers are expected to help parents achieve academic success for their children. For one teacher's view on teaching in suburban schools, see the Profile on p. 105.

What Makes a Good School?

Regardless of where a school is located, everybody wants children to go to "good" schools, and every teacher wants to teach in one. But what are the characteristics of a good school? Over the past decade, researchers have conducted many studies on what makes good or effective schools.

Effective schools are those that have been successful in teaching the adopted curriculum to all students. These schools have adopted both quality and equity standards. The quality standard expects the highest levels of performance of every student, and the equity standard ensures that student achievement is not a function of gender, economic status, or ethnicity.[29] Effective schools have

Don Bott teaches different levels of English at Amos Alonzo Stagg High School in Stockton, California. He is also the advisor to the school newspaper, the Amos Alonzo Stagg Line. *Stagg High has an enrollment of 3,001 students, most of whom are Anglo-European American, African American, and Hispanic.*

I feel there are so many discrepancies between what you hear about schools and what schools are really like. I don't feel unsafe nor have I encountered students who feel unsafe at school. For some students, the climate of the school is the safest they have.

Students are the one thing that makes me love teaching. The kids do not automatically respect you because you are a teacher. They want a reason to respect you and to come to school to learn. Students today have a "show me" attitude, and you have to prove to them that they have a reason to be at school. I would prefer it if students had a little more giving attitude, but teachers have to deal with reality. Some teachers are working hard and trying to make it worthwhile for students. They really want to be good teachers.

A basic problem with suburban schools—and perhaps inner-city schools as well—is that it is very hard to get consistency in instruction and to get professionals to agree on what students should be learning.

When deciding where to teach, new teachers need to consider the kind of school they attended. Teachers have to build on what they know. Going from a rural school to an inner-city school can be very different. I'm not saying that you have to teach in the kind of school you went to, but you do need to consider the contrast between your school and another school where you might want to teach. I've seen young teachers, who have a vision of what school should be like, get discouraged because the students were not like the ones they went to high school with or the ones they encountered in their field experiences. We have to teach the students who come to us. Being nostalgic or wishing students would change to fit a stereotype doesn't get the job done.

- a clear school mission
- high expectations for success
- instructional leadership
- frequent and appropriate monitoring of student progress
- opportunity to learn
- a safe, orderly, and productive environment
- positive home-school relations

How these characteristics are translated into practice depends on the staff and the setting of each school. A study of highly effective urban high schools in four states identified these common characteristics:

- Teachers described the schools as pleasant environments where goals and rules were well articulated.
- Teacher turnover rates were low.
- Principals were instructional leaders.
- Teachers felt they had a meaningful role in school decision making.
- Teachers felt the support of administrators, parents, and community.
- Students were positive about the learning and social atmosphere.
- Parents were proud of the school and praised teachers and principals.
- The community provided support in the form of college scholarships and sponsorship of school activities.[30]

How Schools Are Changing

This chapter has identified many changes and trends in the organization of schooling in the United States. These include:

- Larger schools (for the sake of economy)
- Smaller schools (for improved student performance)

Schools also are involved in providing services for adults in the community. To what extent do you think public schools should serve the communities of which they are a part? What are some issues involved in providing such services? What would be some benefits?

- Different approaches to the use of time in the school year and school day
- Merged school districts and schools within schools
- Better use of instructional time through flexible scheduling and block scheduling
- Multi-age grouping
- Integrated or interdisciplinary curricula
- More academically oriented elementary and early childhood education
- Middle-level schooling and transition programs designed to meet students' unique needs
- Alternative public schools, magnet schools, and charter schools
- Community-based and full-service schools
- Instructional technologies and distance learning
- National and state standards that specify what students should know and be able to do
- Testing and comparisons of student achievement
- Distance education
- Privatization of education (for-profit public and private education)
- Schools as marketplace (increased choice regarding school purposes and curricula)
- Full-service schools

Some dimensions of schooling, such as the age-graded approach and the self-contained classroom, have changed little over the years. But other aspects have changed dramatically and will continue to do so in response to changing expectations, social issues, and needs of students. One thing is certain: change is the driving force that reforms and transforms schools to fit and respond to society's needs.

Reflect & Write

Schools change in response to changing public and political expectations, social issues, and student needs. What are the most important educational changes you have witnessed in your lifetime, both in your community and in the United States? What changes can you add to those identified in this chapter?

_____

_____

_____

_____

Reflect & Write

Effective schools pay attention to academics and show high levels of achievement, distributed fairly equally among the student population. They are also places that care about students and try to meet their needs. What qualities would make a school attractive to you as a teacher?

_____

_____

_____

_____

SECTION SUMMARY

What Is It Like to Teach in Urban, Rural, and Suburban Schools?

Teaching experiences in urban, rural, and suburban schools are different for students and teachers, but in general teachers enjoy the particular aspects that make their schools unique. Population density, geography, and other factors determine the type of school and its curriculum.

- **Urban School Districts and Schools.** These schools tend to be large and are found in metropolitan areas. They serve a diverse student population, many of whom are from minority populations, and the curriculum is designed to meet the needs of these urban students. Urban schools can reflect the problems associated with big-city living, such as crowding, crime, and violence. Many teachers feel called to teach in urban schools and enjoy the students and the challenges.

- **Rural Schools.** Like urban and suburban schools, rural schools reflect the values of the citizens, students, and teachers. Rural teachers say they like the sense of community that is reflected in rural life and schools.

- **Suburban Schools.** These schools generally have students from more affluent neighborhoods, and the curriculum is oriented toward the college-bound and other postsecondary education. Suburban schools face overcrowding, and many schools encounter problems of crime, drugs, and violence that parents thought they were leaving behind when they moved to the suburbs. Teachers at suburban schools like the challenge of meeting the academic needs of students and addressing their other needs as well.

- **What Makes a Good School?** Effective schools are orderly and purposeful and have high expectations for their students, a clear mission, and high levels of parent involvement. The school climate is not oppressive and is conducive to learning and teaching. The principal is an instructional leader, and teachers allocate a significant amount of time to instruction.

- **How Schools Are Changing.** Schools are changing to meet the unique needs of today's students and to address society's needs. Schools are offering more services and more choices.

Thinking Critically
★ ★ ★ ★ ★ ★ ★ ★

When you teach, it is important for you to be happy and for you to like the colleagues you teach with and the students you teach. What factors do you think are critical for your success and happiness as a teacher, regardless of whether the school is urban, suburban, or rural?

_____

_____

_____

_____ ★

Applying What You've Learned
★ ★ ★ ★ ★ ★ ★ ★

Interview teachers in your area. Ask them what makes them happy in their teaching. What factors do they believe contribute to their success as teachers? Compare the teachers' answers to what you listed in the above question.

_____

_____

_____

_____ ★

1. Marty Walker stated that to be happy teaching in an inner-city school, a teacher has to "see persons, not color, and look at character, not just the surface." Many people tend to think of other social, economic, ethnic, or gender groups in terms of *stereotypes*—a set of shared beliefs about what individuals in those groups must be like. Stereotypes describe people in terms of a category rather than their individual characteristics. Think back to an occasion when a teacher reacted to you in a stereotyped way, perhaps because of your gender or the neighborhood where you lived. Then write your impressions of children who attend urban schools, those who attend suburban schools, and those who attend rural schools. After doing that, reread your impressions and explain how you would prove your assertions. If you can't prove them, you may be in danger of overlooking students' individual characteristics.

2. Visit a school in your area and identify its characteristics as rural, suburban, or urban. Interview teachers regarding their beliefs about the major issues facing their school. What do they regard as the major advantages of teaching in their school?

Applications for Active Learning

CONNECTIONS

1. The values and beliefs of teachers, parents, the community, and other interested parties help determine the aims of education—its purposes, intentions, or goals—and what is taught in our schools. Review your own beliefs and values and connect them to the aims of education you consider most important—the ones you would choose for a school where you would want to teach.

2. Although each school is a unique entity, schools share some characteristics based on the kinds of communities they represent—urban, suburban, and rural. Teachers do not necessarily have to teach in the same type of community in which they grew up, but they must be realistic about their role as teacher in that community. Considering your own background and skills, would your best match be an urban, suburban, or rural school? Create a profile of your characteristics in relation to the three types of schools.

3. Think about the concepts and topics introduced in this chapter. Create a picture, graphic, or figure that shows connections that are meaningful to you among this chapter's key ideas and information. Show how you expect those elements to change in the next decade or two.

FIELD EXPERIENCES

1. Collect data on the structure of schooling in a district in your area. How many students are served? What is the size of the teaching force and the pupil-to-teacher ratio? How are grade levels organized? What alternative schools are offered? How are the uses of time and space in schools

organized? Analyze your data in light of the information in this chapter.

2. Visit a school in your area and identify its characteristics as rural, suburban, or urban. Interview teachers regarding their beliefs about the major issues facing their school. What do they regard as the major advantages of teaching in their school?

_____

_____

_____

3. Collect data on the availability and use of computer and telecommunications technologies in your school district. What recommendations might you make on the basis of your research?

PERSONAL RESEARCH

1. Collect news clippings from the "Education" or "Learning" sections of newspapers that describe schools in which you think you would enjoy teaching. What patterns do you observe in the qualities you will be looking for in a school?

2. Research alternative schools and charter schools in your state or region. Who attends them? On what basis were they founded? Would you ever be interested in teaching in an alternative school? In a charter school? Why or why not? Note your current opinions here.

_____

_____

_____

Preparing to Teach

FOR YOUR PORTFOLIO

Develop position statements explaining your beliefs about the aims of education and your reasons for choosing the type of school, size of school, and grade level in which you plan to teach. Add these documents to your teaching portfolio.

IDEA FILE

1. The following are some ways that teaching may be different in rural schools. How might you address these differences as a teacher?

- Students may lack experiences often associated with urban and suburban living. They may have few opportunities to visit zoos, museums, or other educational attractions.
- Student populations may be comparatively homogeneous and lack experience with cultural and ethnic diversity.

- Many districts transport students long distances. Students spend long periods of time on school buses coming to school.
- Many districts have a small or shrinking tax base and therefore have less money to provide materials.

2. The following are some ways that teaching may be different in inner-city schools. How might you address these differences as a teacher?

- Students may not have had the opportunity, resources, or encouragement to have the cultural and educational experiences often associated with urban living.
- Students may come from comparatively homogeneous neighborhoods and lack experience with cultural and socioeconomic diversity.
- Students may bring concerns about personal safety in getting to and from school, being on school grounds, or moving from place to place within the school.
- Many districts have low socioeconomic populations and therefore have less money to provide a quality learning environment.

Learning and Knowing More

WEB SITES WORTH VISITING

National Center for Family and Community Connections with Schools
www.sedl.org/connections/welcome.html
The National Center for Family and Community Connections bridges research and practice, linking people with research-based information and resources that they can use to effectively connect schools, families, and communities.

National Center for Restructuring Education, Schools, and Teaching (NCREST)
www.tc.columbia.edu/~ncrest/
NCREST works to develop understandings that help schools become learner centered, by focusing on the needs of learners in school organization, governance, and pedagogy; knowledge based, by restructuring teacher learning and professional development; and responsible and responsive, by restructuring accountability and assessment practices.

Distance Learning on the Net
www.hoyle.com/distance.htm
    Numerous links to other sites and searchable online repositories of information about distance education.

BOOKS WORTH READING

Kralovec, Elta. (2003). *Schools That Do Too Much: Wasting Time and Money in Schools and What We Can All Do About It*. Boston: Beacon Press.
    Kralovec argues that American schools systematically misspend their two most precious resources—time and money—and end up delivering too little by way of real teaching and learning.
Toch, Thomas. (2003). *High Schools on a Human Scale: How Small Schools Can Transform American Education*. Boston: Beacon Press.
    Thomas explores the power of small schools, perhaps the nation's fastest-growing reform idea. This book is sponsored in part by the Bill and Melinda Gates Foundation's $40-million effort to support small schools nationwide.
Schneider, Mark, Teske, Paul, and Marschall, Melissa. (2000). *Choosing Schools: Consumer Choice and the Quality of American Schools*. Princeton, NJ: Princeton University Press.
    The authors ask the question: Will parents be able to function as "smart consumers" on behalf of their children? This highly respected team of social scientists provides extensive empirical evidence on how parents do make these choices.

Students, Families, and Communities

merican students today represent greater racial, cultural, and linguistic diversity than at any other time in the past. This diversity is both a source of enrichment and a challenge for teachers and schools and the communities they serve. One of the greatest continuing challenges to public schools is educating children of non-English-speaking immigrants and students with limited English proficiency through bilingual education.

In addition to the challenges posed to teaching and learning by the increasing presence of different cultures and languages in our society and schools, other factors create special needs for some students. Environmental, social, physical, and emotional elements can place students at risk. As a teacher, you likely will be working with at-risk students and other exceptional learners in the inclusive classroom and will need to be familiar with the laws and practices that affect such instruction.

Parents and families, as well as the community, also have an impact on teaching and learning. Parents are becoming increasingly empowered to make decisions that affect education.

Community agencies and private corporations are rapidly becoming partners with schools in the education of children and youth today. The new partnerships have many faces: community-based intervention programs for students at risk, school-to-work business-sponsored programs, company-subsidized high-tech magnet schools and private school programs, and public schools run by private corporations. At issue are the implications of privatization for public education.

Part Two introduces you to these trends and issues in teaching and learning.

CHAPTER 4 Teaching Diverse Students

INTASC Standards ① ② ③ ④ ⑤ ⑥ ⑦ ⑧ ⑨ ⑩
NCATE Standards
  Early Childhood ① ② ③ ④ ⑤
  Elementary ① ② ③ ④ ⑤
  Middle Level ① ② ③ ④ ⑤ ⑥ ⑦

CHAPTER 5 Teaching Exceptional Learners and Students at Risk

INTASC Standards ① ② ③ ④ ⑤ ⑥ ⑦ ⑧ ⑨ ⑩
NCATE Standards
  Early Childhood ① ② ③ ④ ⑤
  Elementary ① ② ③ ④ ⑤
  Middle Level ① ② ③ ④ ⑤ ⑥ ⑦

CHAPTER 6 Partners in Teaching: Parents, Families, and the Community

INTASC Standards ① ② ③ ④ ⑤ ⑥ ⑦ ⑧ ⑨ ⑩
NCATE Standards
  Early Childhood ① ② ③ ④ ⑤
  Elementary ① ② ③ ④ ⑤
  Middle Level ① ② ③ ④ ⑤ ⑥ ⑦

Teaching Diverse Students

"I consider this ESL program my greatest accomplishment."

Kathy Mellor, 2004 National Teacher of the Year, teaches English as a second language at Davisville Middle School in North Kingstown, Rhode Island.

When I was four years old, I entered a private kindergarten before it was required as part of the public school program. I loved the activities, the learning, and the way my teacher made everyone feel—smart and special. We played, we worked, and we learned a lot. I learned to read. I was impressed by my teacher. What a great job being a teacher must be! For the next five years in elementary school, I was blessed with teachers who had the same effect on me. Each of those classes was large—well over forty students. There was less play and a lot more work, but just as much excitement in learning.

In third, fourth, and sixth grades, I was assigned to split grades, where I learned a lot by osmosis, watching the teacher work with the other group or as she taught us together. I had the same teacher for third, fourth, and fifth grades. Early on, I experienced the benefits of multi-aged groupings and looping—moving up a level with a class and then returning to the lower grade to do the same with another class. With such wonderful experiences as a student, I knew that I would love being a teacher myself.

My parents valued education. Like many of their contemporaries, they had to leave school to go to work to help support their families. My parents spoke openly about how important schooling was. "A house without books is like a house without windows," proclaimed my father, who encouraged me on my first day of first grade to stay in school so my hands wouldn't look like his. It was a defining moment in my life. Before I completed elementary school, I had decided that I would become a teacher.

Mainstream teachers and ESL/bilingual teachers must function as a team, fully sharing responsibility for the students they have in common. They need each other's expertise, and the students need them to work toward the same goals, reinforcing each other's efforts on behalf of the students. Today, ESL instruction in my district has evolved into a program set up to deal successfully with the many variables the students present. Children remain integrated in their home schools. They are a shared responsibility between the ESL and content-area teachers. As a result, the program is cognitively demanding, and the students are not isolated from their English-speaking peers, so a great deal of natural language acquisition takes place. The ESL component of the program is a developmental language program that provides each student with one to three periods of instruction per day according to the child's proficiency level in the areas of listening, speaking, reading, and writing.

I consider this ESL program to be one of my greatest accomplishments in education. Unlike many districts, the students are not segregated into separate classrooms or schools. They are integrated into all programs within the district and are held to the same high standards. The program, the students, and their families are accepted and respected.

ESL is acknowledged as an effective program by the students, their families, other teachers, and administrators. Many students surpass more than a year's growth in a year's time, making honor roll or honor society while in and after being exited from the ESL program. I delight in observing the students' growth, their increased confidence, and their ultimate academic independence. I appreciate the continued support of my colleagues. After many years, I still look forward to Monday mornings. Working with this diverse community of learners and their supportive families is one of the most rewarding things I have ever done or ever could do.

Academically, teaching is the challenge of maximizing student growth regardless of ability level or previous achievement. It requires teachers to be responsible for and responsive to every child in the classroom. I believe that my achievement as a teacher is directly related to the success and achievement of my students. Effective teaching establishes goals and expectations that are clear, consistent, and attainable.

I believe the teaching environment must be conducive to learning. It is our job as educators to see that it is. I strongly believe that teachers are responsible for every child enrolled in their classroom and must be each child's advocate. Isn't that what we would want for ourselves?

How Will This Chapter Help You?

You will learn

★ how diversity in America's schools influences what you will teach and how you will teach

★ how to teach diverse students

★ about multicultural education and how to implement it

★ how socioeconomic class influences learning and achievement

★ how teacher quality affects student achievement

★ about bilingual and ESL programs that help students learn English and maintain their native languages

★ how gender influences teaching and learning

AMERICA—A NATION OF DIVERSITY

Diversity
The range of race, ethnicity, sexual orientation, socioeconomic status, cultural heritage, gender, and ability or disability represented in society.

INTASC

Standard 3: The teacher understands how students differ in their approaches to learning and creates instructional opportunities that are adapted to diverse learners.

Kathy Mellor's opening vignette clearly demonstrates the importance of helping children learn English. It also emphasizes that America is a land of immigrants and that **diversity** is the norm in America's schools as well.

As Figures 4.1 and 4.2 aptly illustrate, America is a diverse country and is becoming more so all the time. We can count on the fact that an increase in diversity will be the demographic norm rather than the exception. When we talk about diversity, we often think of race and ethnicity, but these are only part of what diversity is. More and more students come to school speaking a language other than English. You will be confronted with a wide, rich variety of native languages and will need to consider what programs will help your students learn what they need to know to succeed in school and life. Your students will represent a spectrum of socioeconomic backgrounds. Socioeconomic status (SES) affects and influences students' achievement. This chapter explores what schools, and teachers, can do to help students overcome the debilitating effects low SES has on their achievement.

It seems obvious that students are also male and female. Yet we often overlook the impact of this fact on our teaching. Despite best efforts, boys and girls are often reared and educated differently. These differences in child rearing and education have a profound influence on school achievement and on career and life outcomes. You will also teach gay and lesbian students and will have opportunities to interact with their parents, who also may be gay or lesbian. Gay and lesbian students bring diverse needs to the classroom. One of your responsibilities as a high-quality teacher is to provide a nonthreatening and safe learning environment and to protect all your students from harassment. (Legal issues relating to gays and lesbians are covered in Chapter 8.)

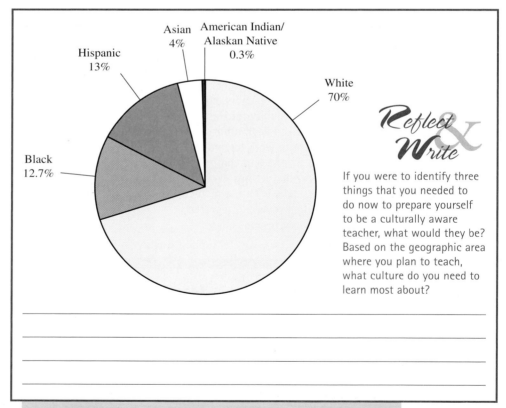

Reflect & Write

If you were to identify three things that you needed to do now to prepare yourself to be a culturally aware teacher, what would they be? Based on the geographic area where you plan to teach, what culture do you need to learn most about?

Figure 4.1 *Diversity in the United States*

Source: U.S. Census Bureau, *Census 2000*. (Online). Available at www.census.gov.

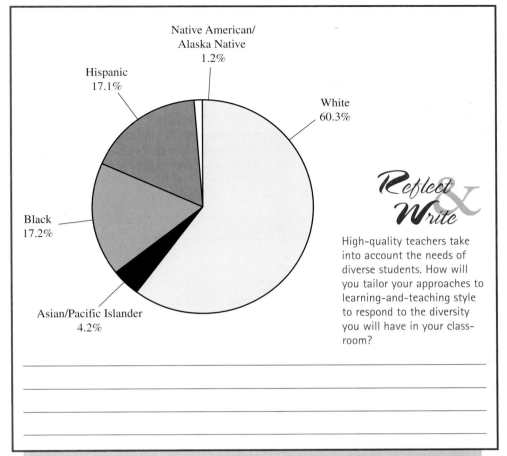

Native American/
Alaska Native
1.2%

Hispanic
17.1%

White
60.3%

Black
17.2%

Asian/Pacific Islander
4.2%

Reflect & Write

High-quality teachers take into account the needs of diverse students. How will you tailor your approaches to learning-and-teaching style to respond to the diversity you will have in your class-room?

Figure 4.2 *Diversity in U.S. Schools*

Source: Figure created by author from selected data from "Back to School: The American Student." (Online). Available at www.cnn.com/SPECIALS/2003/back.to.school/overview/. © 2004 Cable News Network LP, LLLP. A Time Warner Company.

Students bring particular needs to the classroom, in part as a result of their different racial, ethnic, cultural, and socioeconomic backgrounds and in part because of their gender and sexual orientation. They bring different approaches to learning as well as a variety of aspirations for achievement. This academic diversity is a given in today's classroom. You likely will spend many hours planning for how to best provide academic and extracurricular programs that will meet your students' particular needs, learning styles, and abilities. (Issues of academic diversity are addressed further in Chapter 11.)

INTASC

Standard 3: The teacher understands how students differ in their approaches to learning and creates instructional opportunities that are adapted to diverse learners.

How Does Socioeconomic Status Affect Teaching and Learning?

The socioeconomic backgrounds of students have a significant effect on the type and quality of teaching they receive as well as on their ultimate academic achievement. Socioeconomic level affects the funding of school districts and, since students are typically assigned to schools based on where they live, the kind of school they attend. Students who live in upper-income neighborhoods generally have access to better schools and more highly educated teachers, while students from lower-income neighborhoods are much more likely to be in schools that lack the material infrastructure necessary for quality education. The United States still has a long way to go in establishing equity within public schools.

Socioeconomic status (SES)
The social and economic background of an individual or individuals.

Socioeconomic status (SES) is a reflection of family income, maternal education level, and family occupation. You may be surprised by the inclusion of maternal education level in this list, but in fact it is a powerful predictor of how well students do in school. As a mother's education increases, so does student achievement (see Figure 4.3). This helps explain why, from a social and educational policy perspective, a U.S. priority is to prevent teenage mothers from dropping out of school.

Family income also correlates with how well students do in school, whether or not they drop out, the kind and type of schools they attend, and the quality of their teachers. Students' socioeconomic status is used to determine eligibility for many state and federal programs such as Head Start and Title I programs. One Head Start eligibility criterion, for example, is that the child's family meets federal poverty income criteria for enrollment, and many schools provide free or reduced school lunches based on family income. Table 4.1 shows the 2004 Department of Health and Human Services (HHS) poverty guidelines.

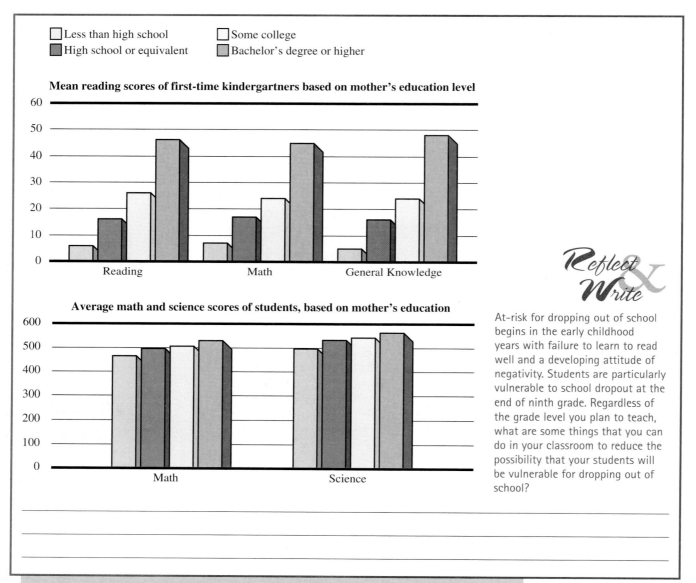

Reflect & Write

At-risk for dropping out of school begins in the early childhood years with failure to learn to read well and a developing attitude of negativity. Students are particularly vulnerable to school dropout at the end of ninth grade. Regardless of the grade level you plan to teach, what are some things that you can do in your classroom to reduce the possibility that your students will be vulnerable for dropping out of school?

Figure 4.3   The Effects of Maternal Education on Student Achievement

Source: K. Denton and E. Germino-Hausken (2000). *America's Kindergartners* (NCES No. 200-070). Washington, DC: National Center for Education Statistics, U.S. Department of Education; *Mathematics and Science in the Eighth Grade: Findings from the Third International Mathematics and Science Study* (NCES No. 2000-014). Washington, DC: National Center for Education Statistics, U.S. Department of Education.

Table 4.1   2004 U.S. Health and Human Services Poverty Guidelines

Size of Family Unit	Forty-eight Contiguous States and DC	Alaska	Hawaii
1	$ 9,310	$11,630	$10,700
2	12,490	15,610	14,360
3	15,670	19,590	18,020
4	18,850	23,570	21,680
5	22,030	27,550	25,340
6	25,210	31,530	29,000
7	28,390	35,510	32,660
8	31,570	39,490	36,320
For each additional person, add	3,180	3,980	3,660

Source: U.S. Department of Health and Human Services, *The 2004 HHS Poverty Guidelines—One Version of the [U.S.] Federal Poverty Measure* (2004). (Online). Available at http://aspe.hhs.gov/poverty/04poverty.shtml.

How does socioeconomic status affect the kind of school a student attends? First, it can affect the quality of teaching. Schools in low-income neighborhoods often have a high percentage of teachers teaching "out of field"—that is, teaching subjects they are not academically prepared for or certified to teach. (See Figure 4.4.) The No Child Left Behind Act seeks to remedy this situation.

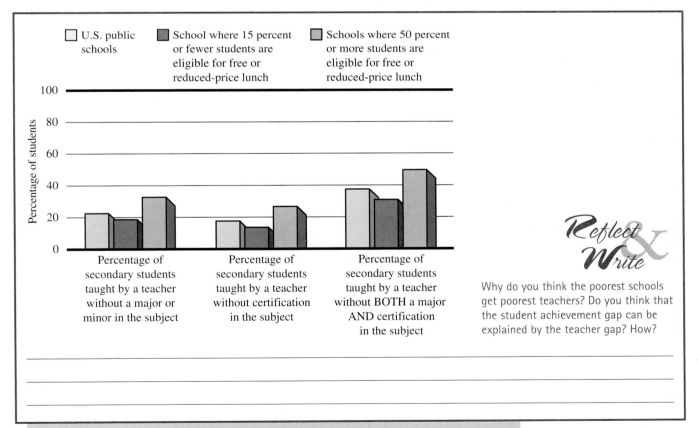

Reflect & Write

Why do you think the poorest schools get poorest teachers? Do you think that the student achievement gap can be explained by the teacher gap? How?

Figure 4.4   Quality of Teachers Based on Income Level of Districts

Source: Richard M. Ingersoll, "Quality Counts: Special Analysis of National Center for Education Statistics, Schools and Staffing Survey (1999–2000)," *Education Week*, January 9, 2003.

America—A Nation of Diversity

- Diversity refers to the range of race, ethnicity, gender, sexual orientation, socio-economic status, cultural heritage, and disability represented in society.
- The United States is a very diverse country and is becoming more diverse. Hispanics are now the country's largest minority.
- As America becomes more diverse, so do its schools. This means that teachers must take into account in their teaching all dimensions of students' diversity, including language, gender, and socioeconomic status.

How Does Socioeconomic Status Affect Teaching and Learning?

- Socioeconomic status has a significant impact on student achievement. For example, low SES students are much more likely to attend schools with inferior physical plants and resources. They are also more likely to have less qualified teachers.
- Maternal education is one of the components of socioeconomic status. As maternal education increases, so does achievement.

Thinking Critically

★ ★ ★ ★ ★ ★ ★ ★

I have said that the backgrounds of students affect teaching and learning. As Figure 4.5 points out, teachers agree and students disagree with me. Review Figure 4.5 and reflect on what these data means for you as a teacher. How would this information affect (or not affect) the way you approach teaching?

_____

_____

_____★

Applying What You've Learned

★ ★ ★ ★ ★ ★ ★ ★

Children from diverse backgrounds bring many needs to school in addition to the need for learning how to speak English. Interview bilingual teachers and discuss with them what they believe are some of the critical educational and social needs of the children they teach.

_____

_____

_____★

Putting Yourself in the Picture

★ ★ ★ ★ ★ ★ ★ ★

Bilingual teachers are in short supply and high demand. A school district offers you the opportunity to become a bilingual teacher on an emergency certification for one year. Would you take the job? Why or why not?

_____

_____

_____★

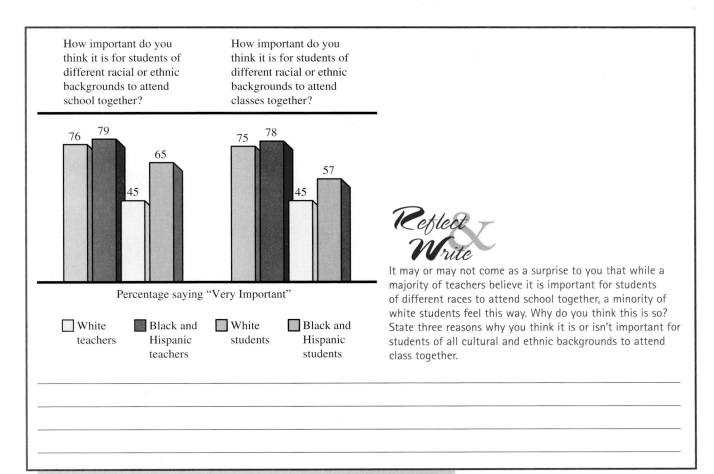

How important do you think it is for students of different racial or ethnic backgrounds to attend school together?

How important do you think it is for students of different racial or ethnic backgrounds to attend classes together?

76 79 45 65

75 78 45 57

Percentage saying "Very Important"

☐ White teachers ■ Black and Hispanic teachers ☐ White students ■ Black and Hispanic students

Reflect & Write

It may or may not come as a surprise to you that while a majority of teachers believe it is important for students of different races to attend school together, a minority of white students feel this way. Why do you think this is so? State three reasons why you think it is or isn't important for students of all cultural and ethnic backgrounds to attend class together.

Figure 4.5 *Does Diversity Matter?*

Source: Figure created by author from selected data from National Survey of Public School Teachers and Students on Race and Education, *Education Week,* May 12, 2004, p. 16.

HOW DO RACIAL AND ETHNIC DIVERSITY AFFECT TEACHING AND LEARNING?

Research in the area of school and classroom climate has consistently shown that students of different genders, races, and ethnicities receive different treatment in schools. Teachers interact more often with, call on with greater frequency, praise more highly, and intellectually challenge more students who are middle class, male, and white.[1]

Cultural Impacts on Teaching and Learning

All students and teachers bring a cultural frame of reference to school. For some students, the frame of reference is very similar to the culture they encounter in schools. School culture, or the way schools actually operate, has emanated largely from a cultural context involving Anglo-European American values. Students from this background typically experience the greatest familiarity with the way schools operate and with school norms.

Students who come from cultural and language backgrounds that vary significantly from traditional school culture often feel unfamiliar with the school environment and school norms. In a sense, these students have a double task: (1) to learn the

Early Childhood

Standard 1: Uses understanding of young children's characteristics, needs, and interacting influences on children's development and learning to create healthy, respectful, supportive, and challenging environments for all children.

Elementary

Standard 2.1–2.8: Understands and uses fundamental concepts and modes of inquiry of all appropriate content disciplines.

Issues of diversity greatly influence the direction of education, as cultural needs and traditions of diverse populations offer wonderful learning opportunities for students and teachers alike.

NCATE

Elementary

Standard 3.2: Understands how elementary students differ in development and approaches to learning; creates instructional opportunities that are adapted to diverse students.

norms of a school environment that are already familiar to others and (2) to learn the same academic content that all students are expected to master.

Teachers who recognize that the complexity of learning tasks increases for students who are less familiar with traditional school culture provide a variety of teaching approaches as well as ample time for instruction. The goal for these teachers is not *equal* treatment but *equitable* treatment—that is, providing students with teaching approaches and attention that are proportional to their academic needs.

The proportion of minority students in this nation's schools in 2000 was 39 percent.[2] Table 4.2 shows the racial or ethnic composition of students in the nation's eleven largest school districts for the school year 1999–2000. As you can see from the table, these school districts have a majority of students who are classified as minorities. In these cases, minorities are actually majorities. Two realities of changing demographics of school populations are that (1) you and other beginning teachers will, in all likelihood, teach minority students, and (2) school districts and colleges of education will have to increase their efforts to recruit minority teachers. Teachers who have the skills to succeed in culturally and linguistically diverse classrooms will be in ever-greater demand. Teacher education programs that prepare teachers for the multicultural classroom will be producing graduates with the right backgrounds for teaching in the twenty-first century.

The cultural backgrounds of students play a major role in the learning process. Culture frequently influences how students respond to various teaching approaches. Students from Native American cultures will often not respond to questions posed openly before the entire class. What may be viewed as disinterest is actually a cultural norm that one should not venture answers in public before one is certain. For another example, a classroom that is highly teacher centered and structured may be effective with Asian immigrant students who were accustomed to this model in their countries of origin. However, the same approach may be ineffective with Mexican American students, who prefer cooperative learning environments.

While there is no single teaching approach that is uniformly effective with all students, teachers often rely heavily on one method. This is increasingly true as grade

Table 4.2 *Proportion of Minority Students in the Eleven Largest Public School Districts in the United States, 1999–2000*

Name of Reporting District	State	Percentage of Minority Students
New York City Public School District	NY	84.7
Los Angeles Unified School District	CA	90.1
City of Chicago School District	IL	90.4
Dade County School District	FL	88.7
Broward County School District	FL	58.8
Clark County School District	NV	50.1
Houston Independent School District	TX	90.0
Philadelphia City School District	PA	83.3
Hawaii Department of Education	HI	79.6
Hillsborough County School District	FL	48.2
Detroit City School District	MI	96.3

Source: National Center for Education Statistics, *Digest of Education Statistics, 2002* (Washington, DC: Office of Educational Research and Improvement, 2002). Available online at www.nces.ed.gov.

levels get higher. What is most beneficial is to use a variety of instructional approaches that are reflective of the different learning modalities present in every classroom.

Helping Immigrant Students Learn

The No Child Left Behind (NCLB) Act of 2001 requires that all children, including English language learners (ELLs), reach high standards by demonstrating proficiency in English language arts and mathematics by 2014. Schools and districts must help ELL students, among other subgroups, make continuous progress toward this goal, as measured by performance on state tests, or risk serious consequences. Through these mandates, NCLB establishes high expectations for all students and seeks to reduce the achievement gap between advantaged and disadvantaged students.

A goal of all schools and teachers is to help ensure that all children learn. Here are some things you can do to make the goal a reality:

- **Reduce the cognitive load.** One very important step teachers can take is to make every effort to reduce the cognitive load of the lessons they teach. The key is to choose activities and assignments that allow students to draw on their prior knowledge and life experiences. It is crucial during the process of lesson planning that teachers take into account the capacities of the students involved.
- **Evaluate teaching strategies and approaches.** Teachers also need to pay attention to how they run their classrooms. Some students may have difficulty coping with the style of classroom management that the teacher has chosen. For example, in many countries, students are not to speak unless the teacher asks them a question directly. To volunteer answers might be considered boastful or conceited. Many students will not question what the teacher says even if they know it to be wrong.
- **Reduce the cultural load.** Showing respect for the immigrant child's life begins by building personal relationships with the students and their families and by making an effort to include aspects of each child's culture in the classroom on a regular basis. Some simple actions each teacher can take include learning to pronounce each student's name correctly, finding out where each student is from, and gathering a little background information about each one.
- **Reduce the language load.** Teacher talk is often filled with words that are unfamiliar to English language learners, which can put a great deal of pressure on students

INTASC

Standard 10: The teacher fosters relationships with school colleagues, parents, and agencies in the larger community to support students' learning and well-being.

NCATE

Elementary

Standard 3.2: Understands how elementary students differ in development and approaches to learning; creates instructional opportunities that are adapted to diverse students.

Middle Level

Standard 5: Understands and uses major concepts, principles, theories, and research related to effective instruction and assessment; employs a variety of strategies for a developmentally appropriate climate to meet the varying abilities and learning styles of all young adolescents.

as they try to process what the teacher says or what they have to read. To lighten this heavy language load for the student, teachers can employ a number of strategies. They can rewrite difficult texts using simpler terms or at least explain the original language simply. They can also break up complex sentences into smaller sentences. They can point out new and particularly difficult words, define them, and explain how they are used.[3]

Academic Achievement and Race

One of the great hopes of proponents of school integration is that as African American and Hispanic American students receive more opportunities, gaps in academic achievement among racial and ethnic groups will diminish and eventually disappear. This goal has been only partly fulfilled, as the following data indicate:

- Only 70 percent of all students in public high schools graduate, and only 32 percent of all students leave high school qualified to attend four-year colleges.
- Only 51 percent of all black students and 52 percent of all Hispanic students graduate, and only 20 percent of all black students and 16 percent of all Hispanic students leave high school college ready.
- The graduation rate for white students is 72 percent; for Asian students, 79 percent; and for American Indian students, 54 percent. The college readiness rate for white students is 37 percent; for Asian students, 38 percent; for American Indian students, 14 percent.
- Graduation rates in the Northeast (73 percent) and Midwest (77 percent) are higher than the overall national figure, whereas graduation rates in the South (65 percent) and West (69 percent) are lower than the national figure. The Northeast and the Midwest have the same college readiness rate as the nation overall (32 percent), whereas the South has a higher rate (38 percent) and the West has a lower rate (25 percent).
- The state with the highest graduation rate in the nation is North Dakota (89 percent); the state with the lowest graduation rate in the nation is Florida (56 percent).[4]

At the beginning of this century, students who failed to succeed in school were not regarded as a problem. They were defined as "school leavers," not "high school dropouts." Today, however, in this technological age, literacy is key to survival, and educators must consider that "disposable" students do not exist.

Diversity Issues in School Life

Schools tend to be microcosms of the communities in which they are situated. If a community exhibits diversity and is open and receptive to it, schools in that community tend to emulate that pattern. In communities where diversity is not found, or where it is present but not valued, schools frequently play down or ignore diversity issues.

A common issue involving diversity is social acceptance. To what extent do the racial, ethnic, or socioeconomic groups to which students belong affect their acceptance among peers, faculty, and staff in our schools? This is an important issue, since "children who have trouble being accepted are two to eight times as likely to drop out."[5] Consider the case of Jana Elhifny who came to Reno, Nevada, from Egypt with her family a year ago seeking the freedoms promised to all Americans. Instead, the sixteen-year-old Muslim girl, who wears a scarf as a symbol of her religion, faced a death threat and harassment at North Valley High School. She said she was so frightened of continued mistreatment that she stopped going to school. "I'm so scared of going back to high school," Elhifny said. "I don't want to do it all over again. I don't want to try. I can't have it 24/7. I can't."[6] This example illustrates that when students of diverse backgrounds are harassed, their personal and educational lives suffer.

Other diversity issues can have an impact on classroom procedures. You might be asked by one student to postpone an exam because of a religious observance,

INTASC

Standard 10: The teacher fosters relationships with school colleagues, parents, and agencies in the larger community to support students' learning and well-being.

NCATE

Middle Level

Standard 1: Understands the major concepts, principles, theories and research related to young adolescent development; provides opportunities that support student development and learning.

Standard 2: Understands the major concepts, principles, theories, and research underlying the philosophical foundations of developmentally responsible middle-level programs and schools; works successfully within these organizational components.

for example. Do you respond to this request with equal or equitable treatment? To what extent should classroom procedures accommodate different student needs? One principle to keep in mind is: Does the accommodation being requested affect *process* (procedures) or *product* (academic outcome)? Educators usually can be flexible in areas of process while still maintaining high academic standards for all students.

Another principle to consider is: Are classroom and school rules enforced equitably regardless of gender, race, ethnicity, or social class? Students recognize when one group is favored over another. Fairness, however, does not always mean treating all students identically. For example, a teacher or administrator might offer students choices of two or three alternative penalties for a rule infraction. There will likely be different choices made by students of different cultural backgrounds, but the same options should be presented to all students.

School culture is composed of the values and norms of a school as well as a school's operating procedures. Students enter schools in the United States with different levels of familiarity with school culture. Students discover whether or not beliefs and values that are important in their home cultures are reflected in the overall school culture. When both the school's culture and student population are multicultural, students of diverse backgrounds feel vital and included in school life. Even when the school's student population is not diverse, a multicultural school culture prepares students as citizens of a culturally diverse nation. When the student population is diverse but the school's culture reflects only one cultural perspective, some students feel like outsiders in their own school. Schools like these may be desegregated, but they are not integrated. Even if the faces at a school assembly reflect a rainbow of colors, certain groups of students may not feel like an integral or valued portion of that school's community. Multiculturally aware teachers look for new ways to expand a sense of community and inclusion in their classrooms.

School culture
The collective "way of life" characteristic of a school; a set of beliefs, values, traditions, and ways of thinking and behaving that distinguishes one school from another.

Based on your past experiences, identify two school cultural factors that affected how teachers taught and how and what students learned.

_____

_____

_____

_____

Should Race Be Used to Assign Students to Schools?

YOU DECIDE

Race-based student assignment systems are controversial, as the case of Lynn, Massachusetts, attests. "In Lynn, students are guaranteed seats in their neighborhood schools. If students want to enroll elsewhere, their choices are based on where they live, the availability of space, and their race—in that order. Transfers that worsen the racial balance of either the receiving or the sending school are prohibited" (*Education Week*, June 9, 2004, p. 6). According to Nicholas P. Kostan, the district superintendent, "The plan has enhanced the feeling of acceptance among students. I think it would be a mistake for Lynn to abandon this plan."

Of the district's 15,000 students, 38 percent are white, 34 percent are Hispanic, 16 percent are black, and 12 percent are of Asian origin. About 65 percent are eligible for free or reduced-price lunches. Roughly 4,000 students took

advantage of the transfer policy this school year, and eleven of the district's twenty-six schools, including all three high schools, are deemed racially balanced.

Some argue that Lynn's student assignment system plan violates the U.S. Constitution's guarantee of equal protection of the law. On the other hand, a U.S. District judge maintains that "K–12 schools have a compelling interest in promoting diversity to promote good citizenship" (*Education Week*, June 9, 2004, p. 6).

What do you think?

Find more information about this at http://aad.english.ucsb.edu/docs/xmay4.

Diversity Issues in the Curriculum

Eurocentric
Focusing on European and European-American history and culture.

Four decades ago, the public school curriculum was almost entirely **Eurocentric,** reflecting the European roots of the majority culture in the United States. Today, the school curriculum reflects the more diverse society of the United States. Beginning in the 1960s, monoethnic units such as Black History or Hispanic Literature were added to the high school curriculum mainly to benefit students from these groups. In elementary schools, heroes and holidays representing minority groups were added to the curriculum and school calendar. While monoethnic materials added diversity to the school curriculum, they reached relatively few students and teachers. Multicultural education, by contrast, attempts to broaden the perspectives of all students at all grade levels.

Global education
An effort to ensure that information and perspectives emanating from outside the United States are brought to bear in the classroom.

Global education (or international education) is an effort to ensure that information and perspectives emanating from outside the United States are brought to bear in the classroom. This is particularly true for non-Western content, which historically has been underemphasized. Multicultural education is linked with global education because students must understand cultural diversity in a national context before they can understand diversity in a more complex global setting.

SECTION SUMMARY

How Do Racial and Ethnic Diversity Affect Teaching and Learning?

Human differences are real, but American education continues to expect equal treatment for all students. Adhering to this rationale contributes to significant instructional and curricular problems for nontraditional students.

- **Cultural Impacts on Teaching and Learning.** Cultural background plays a major role in the learning process. The proportion of minority students in American schools is projected to rise steadily. Teachers must recognize and address the needs of these nontraditional students.

- **Helping Immigrant Students Learn.** The No Child Left Behind Act of 2001 requires that all students, including English language learners (ELL), demonstrate proficiency in Language Arts and mathematics. Teachers can help all immigrant students learn by reducing cognitive load, evaluating teaching strategies and approaches, reducing the cultural load, and reducing the language load.

- **Academic Achievement and Race.** While African American and Hispanic American students have narrowed the academic gap with their white counterparts, a significant difference in achievement remains.

- **Diversity Issues in School Life.** Diversity issues, such as social acceptance, can affect academic achievement and classroom procedures. School and classroom procedures should be handled equitably for all students.

- **Diversity Issues in the Curriculum.** In the past, public school curriculum was Eurocentric. Multicultural education examines curriculum and diversity within the context of the student's nation. Global education examines these topics in nations and places that are outside the student's nation.

Thinking Critically
★ ★ ★ ★ ★ ★ ★ ★ ★

Given the effects of socioeconomic status and race and ethnicity on learning, do you believe most schools are providing equal educational opportunities for all of their students? Why or why not?

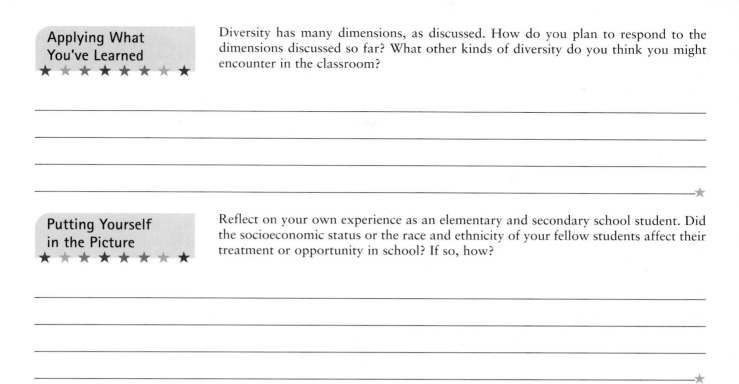

**Applying What
You've Learned**
★ ★ ★ ★ ★ ★ ★ ★ ★

Diversity has many dimensions, as discussed. How do you plan to respond to the dimensions discussed so far? What other kinds of diversity do you think you might encounter in the classroom?

_____

_____

_____

_____★

**Putting Yourself
in the Picture**
★ ★ ★ ★ ★ ★ ★ ★

Reflect on your own experience as an elementary and secondary school student. Did the socioeconomic status or the race and ethnicity of your fellow students affect their treatment or opportunity in school? If so, how?

_____

_____

_____

_____★

*W*HAT IS MULTICULTURAL EDUCATION*?*

Multicultural education is designed to ensure that all students receive equal opportunities regardless of socioeconomic status, gender, sexual orientation, and racial and cultural backgrounds.

Multicultural education looks at academically relevant knowledge and events from the perspectives of all ethnic or cultural groups. While not everything taught in our schools has a multicultural dimension, most topics do. Even subjects that are perceived to have little cultural content, like mathematics and science, have multicultural dimensions. For example, the multicultural and global history of mathematics is seldom presented when that subject is taught strictly from a problem-solving perspective. But mathematics has a cultural aspect too. *Algebra* is an Arabic word meaning "restitution." Al-Khwarizmi, an early mathematician, acknowledged that in an equation one adds and subtracts identical quantities on both sides. One tries to keep an equation like a scale—in perfect balance. Similarly, when studying science, students can learn about scientific contributions made by peoples of other cultures. Topics such as Native American knowledge of the medicinal qualities of plants or the contributions of the physician Ar-Razi to the field of medicine can be included in the science curriculum.

In teaching language or literature, teachers using a multicultural approach explore the richness of African, Hispanic, Asian, and Native American literature. Multicultural and global teachers of history present events from diverse perspectives. For example, the American Revolution would be examined from the perspectives of the loyalists, African Americans, and Native Americans, along with the traditional focus on the revolutionaries. Likewise, in a social studies class, the concept of western expansion would be traced and analyzed from the views of European settlers and Native American groups.

In order for multicultural education to really work and be effective, it must become an integral part of the curriculum and school life. Figure 4.6 shows guidelines for embedding multicultural education in the fabric of school life and for making it

Multicultural education
Education designed to ensure that all students receive equal opportunities regardless of socioeconomic status, gender, sexual orientation, and racial and cultural backgrounds.

INTASC

Standard 2: The teacher understands how children learn and develop, and can provide learning opportunities that support their intellectual, social and personal development.

Standard 3: The teacher understands how students differ in their approaches to learning and creates instructional opportunities that are adapted to diverse learners.

NCATE

Elementary
Standard 3.2: Understands how elementary students differ in development and approaches to learning; creates instructional opportunities that are adapted to diverse students.

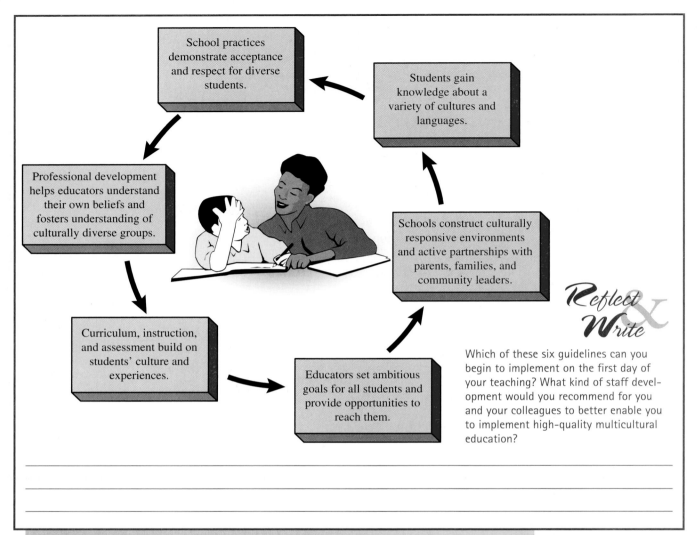

Reflect & Write

Which of these six guidelines can you begin to implement on the first day of your teaching? What kind of staff development would you recommend for you and your colleagues to better enable you to implement high-quality multicultural education?

Figure 4.6 *G*uidelines for Developing Authentic Multicultural Education

Source: Figure created by author based on information drawn from "Promising Program and Practices in Multicultural Education" (1995), North Central Regional Educational Library. (Online). Available at www.ncrel.org.

explicit to students, teachers, administrators, and the public. This figure can help you understand what you can do to be a multiculturally aware teacher and to ensure that multicultural education is integrated into your curriculum and teaching.

What Are Models of Multicultural Education?

INTASC

Standard 2: The teacher understands how children learn and develop, and can provide learning opportunities that support their intellectual, social and personal development.

Another important dimension of multicultural education is how it broadens the academic achievement of all students.

There are five basic approaches to multicultural education (see Figure 4.7). The first approach is teaching exceptional and culturally different students, which targets students who are behind academically. The curriculum is made relevant to the students' background, and instruction often focuses on student learning styles. Examples of this approach are a dropout prevention program, a transitional bilingual program, or classes for students with special learning disabilities.

The second approach targets human relations. The goals of this approach are to enhance student self-concept, reduce prejudice, and promote positive feelings among

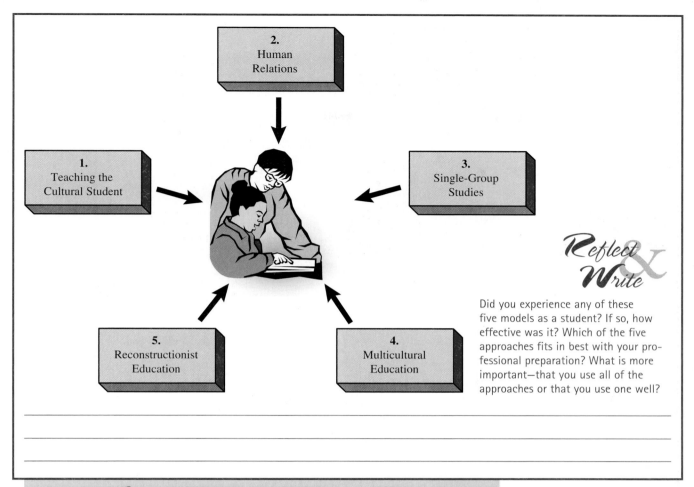

Figure 4.7   *F*ive Models of Multicultural Education

Source: Figure was created by the author based on selected information from C. Grant and C. Sleeter, *Making Choices for Multicultural Education: Five Approaches to Race, Class, and Gender,* 4th ed. (Englewood Cliffs, NJ: Prentice Hall, 2002). Available online at www.prenhall.com/search.html.

Reflect & Write

Did you experience any of these five models as a student? If so, how effective was it? Which of the five approaches fits in best with your professional preparation? What is more important—that you use all of the approaches or that you use one well?

students. Common activities used in this model to help promote positive feelings are cooperative learning, role reversal, and simulation. This approach is more frequently found in elementary classrooms.

The third approach is single-group studies. In this case, the curriculum focuses on the background of one group. Examples of this are Afroamerican or Native American studies. Implicit in single-group studies is that students not only learn about but also work toward social change that benefits the identified group.

The fourth approach is multicultural education. This approach targets all students and organizes curriculum to provide culturally relevant activities in all subjects. Critical thinking and instruction tailored to student learning styles are key elements of multicultural education. In addition, multicultural education stresses that evaluation procedures should assess a variety of abilities and that the community be included as an integral part of the school.

The fifth approach is education that is multicultural and social reconstructionist. This approach shares many curricular principles with multicultural education. The major difference is the high degree of emphasis on social action and having students work toward promoting equal opportunity and equality.

How can students' multicultural needs be met through the learning environment and through curricula that enhance students' individual and academic self-concepts? What other schoolwide approaches enhance teaching and learning in multicultural schools?

The Politics of Multiculturalism

School curriculum has always been influenced by political and economic factors in the society at large. Curricular change may be perceived as political in nature whenever it introduces new paradigms or ways of thinking to students.

It is not surprising that multiculturalism has generated some controversy. Multicultural education increases the visibility of issues that the traditional curriculum may not cover. Some critics argue that a focus on cultural differences will disunite our society. Other educators argue that we need not ignore the *pluribus* to achieve the *unum*.

Do you agree or disagree with the idea that discussing culturally diverse themes in the United States generates division? Explain your view.

_____

_____

_____

_____

Transformative Knowledge

Transformative knowledge
The facts, concepts, and themes that challenge mainstream academic knowledge and revise established theories and explanations.

Two elements of multicultural education that have generated some controversy are its emphasis on critical thinking and the presentation of **transformative knowledge.** Transformative knowledge includes "the facts, concepts and themes which challenge mainstream academic knowledge and revise established theories and explanations."[7]

Transformative knowledge can be presented in a variety of ways but should always be age appropriate. For example, an elementary teacher could point out that Squanto spoke to the Pilgrims in English. How did Squanto learn English? He had been captured earlier by English fishermen and lived for a period of time in England before returning to Massachusetts and joining the Wampanoag. This information can help transform the way students think about American history.

When middle and high school teachers discuss the Mexican War, they can look at the conflict from the perspective of Mexico as well as that of the United States. What did each nation have to gain or lose from this conflict? How did Mexico respond to efforts by the United States to purchase the northern territories? What was the U.S. administration's response when Congressman Abraham Lincoln challenged President Polk to point out where on American soil American blood had been spilled? The answers to these questions provide students with transformative knowledge. Such knowledge helps engage students in the subject and encourages them to be participants in learning.

Whenever students are presented with information unfamiliar to their parents, there is a potential for controversy. However, change must occur or the curriculum will remain static. Teachers who encourage critical thinking and present transformative knowledge must be sure that the new information is accurate and well documented so that they can support their position.

NCATE

Middle Level

Standard 7: Understands the complexity of teaching young adolescents; engages in practices and behaviors that develop competence as a professional.

The Multiculturally Aware Teacher

How can you become a culturally relevant teacher? **Multicultural awareness** is a characteristic of educators who perceive and acknowledge differences among their students without making value judgments about these differences. Teachers must resist the tendency to see themselves, their values, and their way of life as the standard against which all others are to be judged. Teacher-training programs recognize the importance of multiculturally aware teachers. The National Council for Accreditation of Teacher Education (NCATE) defines a "multicultural perspective" as a recognition of (1) the social, political and economic realities that individuals experience in culturally diverse and complex human encounters and (2) the importance of culture, race, sex and gender, ethnicity, religion, socioeconomic status and exceptionalities in the education process."[8]

The multiculturally aware teacher actively seeks out experiences that lead to increased understanding and appreciation of other cultures. The more you can learn about the backgrounds and cultures of the students you will teach, the more culturally aware you will be. Learning about the student's home environment also helps teachers see through their students' eyes.

> Multicultural awareness
> Ability to perceive and acknowledge cultural differences among people without making value judgments about those differences.

Multiculturally aware teachers

- take the time to learn about students' backgrounds and cultural characteristics of their families and community
- respect and accommodate students' individual and culture-based learning styles
- provide accurate and age-appropriate multicultural information and instructional materials
- challenge and avoid using stereotypes
- use culture-fair and gender-fair language and examples
- integrate multicultural perspectives throughout the curriculum

Your attitude regarding diversity will have a strong influence on your ability to address diversity issues, reach all your students, and deliver a multicultural curriculum.

INTASC

Standard 9: The teacher is a reflective practitioner who continually evaluates the effects of his/her choices and actions on others (students, parents, and other professionals in the learning community) and who actively seeks out opportunities to grow professionally.

Reflect & Write

What qualities and experiences do you possess or lack that might affect your ability to be a multiculturally aware teacher?

_____

_____

_____

_____

- What Is Multicultural Education? Multiculturalism is an approach to education in which all peoples of the United States are given proportional attention in the curriculum. Multicultural education injects new knowledge into the study of Western tradition and presents non-Western concepts and cultural perspectives. Multicultural education is not intended strictly for minority and/or at-risk students; it is intended for *all* students.

- What Are Models of Multicultural Education? There are basically five models of multicultural education: teaching culturally diverse students, the human relations approach, single-group studies, multicultural education, and reconstructionist education.

- The Politics of Multiculturalism. Multicultural education has been labeled by its critics as divisive to national unity. Multicultural education, as all change, has generated some controversy.

- Transformative Knowledge. Transformative knowledge provides students with alternative ways of looking at established theories and explanations and encourages them to be participants in learning.

- The Multiculturally Aware Teacher. Your attitude toward diversity will influence your ability to address diversity issues, reach all your students, and deliver a multicultural curriculum.

Thinking Critically
★ ☆ ★ ★ ★ ☆ ★ ☆ ★

Multicultural education contains significant European and European American content. Why do you think it has been criticized for this? Do you believe this criticism is fair?

_____

_____

_____

_____

_____ ★

Applying What You've Learned
★ ☆ ★ ★ ★ ☆ ★ ☆ ★

Consider the examples of transformative knowledge provided in this section. Make a list of other examples of transformative knowledge you can use in your classroom.

_____

_____

_____

_____

_____ ★

Examine some books for students on African American and Hispanic themes. Would you feel comfortable teaching this content in your class? If so, why? If not, what would you need to do to become comfortable with this content?

_____

_____

_____

_____

_____ ★

How DOES LANGUAGE INFLUENCE TEACHING AND LEARNING?

Nothing is more fundamental to instruction than full communication and comprehension between teacher and student. When understandable instruction is a problem, academic achievement declines.

America is a land of diverse culture. With cultural diversity comes diversity of language. There are over 5.5 million limited-English-proficient (LEP) students in the United States. Florida's school-age population speaks over 150 languages, with Spanish being the most prominent. Other widely spoken languages are Haitian, Creole, Portuguese, French, Vietnamese, and Chinese. The Los Angeles Unified School District has 320,594 students in LEP programs.

Few issues in education today are as controversial as the use of non-English languages as the languages of instruction. While there is little disagreement that all students in the United States should try to reach the goal of full fluency and literacy in English, for students whose native language is not English, a vital issue is whether learning a second language means losing proficiency in their native language. Language is an

Early Childhood

Standard 1: Uses understanding of young children's characteristics, needs, and interacting influences on children's development and learning to create healthy, respectful, supportive, and challenging environments for all children.

Elementary

Standard 1: Knows, understands, and uses the major concepts, principles, theories, and research related to development of children to construct learning opportunities that support individual students' development, acquisition of knowledge, and motivation.

Middle Level

Standard 1: Understands the major concepts, principles, theories and research related to young adolescent development; provides opportunities that support student development and learning.

Table 4.3 *Number and Proportion of Limited-English-Proficient Students Receiving Services*

State	Number of Students Receiving LEP Services	Percentage of Students Receiving LEP Services
California	1,510,859	24.6
Texas	601,791	14.5
Florida	204,208	8.2
New York	193,711	6.7
Arizona	148,861	16.1
Illinois	136,295	6.6
Colorado	71,011	9.6
New Mexico	66,035	20.6
Georgia	63,272	4.3
New Jersey	56,712	4.2

Source: National Center for Education Statistics, *Overview of Public Elementary and Secondary Schools and Districts* (Washington, DC: U.S. Government Printing Office, 2002), table 10.

In families where English may be a second language, homework has additional challenges. What types of programs are available for students with limited English proficiency? What are their advantages and disadvantages for teachers and students?

integral part of culture and identity. If the native language is lost, the individual is hampered from participating in vital cultural activities such as social gatherings, religious observations, and family exchanges that occur within the ethnic community.

Bilingual Education Legislation and Court Cases

The **Bilingual Education Act** (Public Law 90-247) was enacted in 1968 to provide funds to assist local school districts in carrying out elementary and secondary programs for students whose first language is not English.

In 1974, a landmark U.S. Supreme Court decision in *Lau v. Nichols* stated that equal educational opportunities are denied when non-English-speaking students receive the same English language instruction as that given to all students. The Court did not mandate **bilingual education** but required that special programs providing understandable instruction be made available to limited or non-English speakers.

In 1979, the Supreme Court ruled in *Dyrcia S. et al. v. Board of Education of New York City* that students with disabilities who have limited English proficiency have the same rights as their English-proficient peers to receive special educational services. Schools could meet this requirement using a bilingual or **English as a second language** (ESL) approach to special education services.

In 1998, the voters of California passed **Proposition 227**, which outlawed bilingual education in California schools. The proposition did provide for a waiver process if enough citizens in a school district wished to retain some form of bilingual education.

The legislation concerning bilingual education illustrates that efforts to address the educational needs of LEP students have brought many gains.

NCLB and English Language Learning

The No Child Left Behind (NCLB) Act of 2001 has significantly transformed the ways in which language-minority students are educated. NCLB replaced the Bilingual Education Act with the English Language Acquisition, Language Enhancement, and Academic Achievement Act. "The purpose of this act is (1) to help ensure that children who are limited English proficient, including immigrant children and youth, attain English proficiency, develop high levels of academic attainment in English, and meet the same challenging State academic content and student academic achievement standards as all children are expected to meet" (NCLB Act, Sec. 3101a and c).

Under NCLB, the term *bilingual* is seldom used. In its place, the term **English language learner** (ELL) is used instead. The new terminology reflects NCLB's intent to teach students English as rapidly as possible.

As you can see, NCLB brings ELL students into the same context of standards and accountability as their native English-speaking peers. NCLB has major implications for mainstream teachers. As Kathleen Leos of the Office of English Language Acquisition states:

> The role of every teacher in every classroom in the nation has never been more important than today. The teacher, who is the key component within the standards reform model, must link core academic instruction to the content standards set by the state. In classrooms with language diverse populations, teachers must also ensure that the curriculum and teaching strategies reflect an alignment with English Language Proficiency Standards.[9]

Methods for Promoting English Language Learning

There are many approaches to promoting programs for ELLs. Table 4.4 depicts some of these. Keep in mind that these are descriptions only and there are many variations on these themes across the landscape of American education.

Reflect & Write

What steps might you take to help students in your class who have not yet achieved cognitive academic language proficiency in English?

_____

_____

_____

_____

Table 4.4 Types of Programs for English Language Learners

Program	Description	Goal
English as a second language (ESL)	Students receive specified periods of instruction aimed at the development of English language skills, with a primary focus on grammar, vocabulary, and communication rather than academic content areas. Academic content is addressed through mainstream instruction, where no special assistance is provided.	English language fluency
Structured immersion (or "sheltered immersion")	Students are limited English proficient, usually from different language backgrounds. Instruction is in English, with an adjustment made to the level of English so that subject matter is more easily understood. Typically, there is no native language support.	English language fluency
Transitional bilingual programs	Most students are English language learners. They receive some degree of instruction through the native language. However, within the program there is a rapid shift toward using primarily English.	Transition to English as quickly as possible
Maintenance bilingual education	Most students are English language learners and from the same language background. They receive significant amounts of instruction in the native language.	Academic proficiency in both languages
Two-way bilingual programs	About half of students are native speakers of English; the other half are English language learners from the same language group. Instruction is in both languages.	Proficiency in both languages
English language development or ESL Pull Out	Students are usually at beginning-level proficiency. Students are integrated in mainstream, English-only classrooms in other subjects with no assistance. Students are pulled out for instruction aimed at developing English grammar, vocabulary, and communication skills, rather than academic content.	English language fluency
Submersion with primary language support	Used when only a few students in each grade level are English-language learners. Bilingual teachers tutor small groups of students by reviewing particular lessons covered in mainstream classes, using students' primary language.	English language fluency

Source: Table was created by author based on selected information from K. Hakuta, "Population Characteristics, Social Goals, and Educational Treatments for English-Language-Learning Students" (1999). (Online). Available at http://www.stanford.edu/~hakuta/Docs/BOTAForum.PDF; R. Linquanti, "Types of Instructional Program Models" (1999). WestEd. Available at www.wested.org/policy/pubs/fostering/originals/models.doc.

Research on English Language Learning

Research in the area of English language acquisition over the past two decades has shown some encouraging results. Among the major findings:

- There is steady growth in the number of immigrant children in the nation's schools and therefore a growth in the English-language-learner (ELL) population.
- Spanish speakers are increasingly predominant in this population. While there are more foreign-born immigrant children in the high school population (5.7 percent) than in the elementary school population (3.5 percent), spending on language acquisition programs is focused on elementary schools.
- A significantly smaller number of ELL students receive some form of bilingual instruction in either middle or high school than in elementary school.[10]
- No clear consensus exists on the length of time ELLs need to become proficient in English.
- Individual differences among children and their family situations make generalizations about ELLs difficult.
- English-based instruction is more common than instruction in which a student's native language is used.
- Between 46 and 90 percent of ELL students in Arizona, Florida, Illinois, New Jersey, Texas, and Washington spent four years or less in bilingual programs.[11]

The question of how to best teach students whose first language is something other than English can be expected to remain a front burner topic for some time to come, especially when this country's role in the wider world is hotly debated. For an interesting note on this, see Education on the Move.

education on the move >>>>>>>>>>>>

>>> Who Is Learning Arabic? >>>>>>>

Since terrorists from Arab countries attacked the United States on Sept. 11, 2001, the U.S. government has been desperately seeking to hire Arabic speakers. But even now, the nation has only a small pool of students who are seriously studying the language.

Yet only a smattering of public elementary and secondary schools across the country—perhaps no more than two dozen—teach the language as part of the regular curriculum.

Arabic is still one of the nation's least commonly studied languages of those spoken worldwide, according to the Modern Language Association.

If the U.S. government really wanted to increase the number of Arabic speakers, argues Ahmed Elghotni, a native of Egypt and an American citizen, it would provide more grants for programs such as the one he runs at North Atlanta High School. Mr. Elghotni teaches four Arabic classes at differing levels of

difficulty at North Atlanta High, part of the 51,000-student Atlanta district.

The students come from varied backgrounds. Some are immigrants or second-generation Americans. Others are African American. About a third who take Arabic at North Atlanta are Muslim. Three of the five students in Mr. Elghotni's Arabic 3 class say they are taking the course so they can better understand their religion, Islam. The Quran is written in Arabic, and Muslims believe it should be read in that language.

Shamima Begum, a Muslim who immigrated to the United States from Bangladesh four years ago, learned to read Arabic as a child. Ms. Begum said she's studying Arabic in high school because "I want to know more about other countries."

Language experts say that it's best for people to start studying Arabic as young as possible because it is a difficult language to learn.

It is no coincidence that the school system with the most students enrolled in Arabic classes is in Dearborn, Michigan. The 17,600-student Dearborn district is located in the greater Detroit area, home to the nation's largest community of Arab Americans. Six public schools in the district offer Arabic, with 1,000 students participating.

Finding Arabic teachers certified at the K–12 level can also be an obstacle. That's the case in Stuyvesant High School in New York City, where the Muslim students' association helped raise $15,000 to launch an Arabic program. Rolf M. Schwagermann, the assistant principal supervising foreign languages for Stuyvesant, said, "We want to run the class, but I cannot find a qualified teacher at this point."

Source: M. A. Zehr, "Arab Offerings Rare in Schools," *Education Week* May 26, 2004, pp. 14–16. Available online at http://www.edweek.org/ew/ewstory.cfm?slug=38Arabic.h23. Reprinted by permission.

In our discussion of ELL, it is evident that most everyone agrees that LEP students should become fully literate in English. Differences exist over how to accomplish this goal.

SECTION SUMMARY

How Does Language Influence Teaching and Learning?

Students with limited English proficiency are increasing in U.S. schools. Students who have not mastered the language of instruction face additional challenges. Controversy exists over how to remedy these challenges.

- Bilingual Education Legislation and Court Cases. The *Lau v. Nichols* 1974 decision mandated that limited-English-proficient students must receive understandable instruction. Other court cases supported bilingual education. Funding for bilingual education was provided by the 1968 Bilingual Education Act. California Proposition 227 outlawed bilingual education and points to continued controversy in this area.

- NCLB and English Language Learning. The No Child Left Behind Act requires that all children attain English proficiency, develop high levels of academic attainment in English, and meet state standards. NCLB also introduces the term *English language learner* in place of *bilingual*.

- Methods for Promoting English Language Learning. Programs to serve ELL students include: English as a second language (ESL), structural immersion, **transitional bilingual programs, maintenance bilingual education,** two-way bilingual programs, ESL pull-out programs, and submersion.

- Research on English Language Learning. Research on second language learning indicates that there is a steady growth in the number of immigrant students and ELL programs. Spending on ELL programs is focused on elementary schools. English-based instruction is based, more commonly than not, in native language instruction. Generally, students spend less than four years in ELL programs.

Transitional bilingual programs English-as-a-second-language programs that use the second language to teach English while using the first language to teach other subjects.
Maintenance bilingual education Transitional bilingual programs that also infuse English into content area instruction with the goal of biliteracy.

Thinking Critically
★ ★ ★ ★ ★ ★ ★ ★ ★

If native English speakers in the United States routinely graduated from high school as bilingual and biliterate persons, do you think this would affect the level of opposition faced by bilingual education? Give two reasons to support your response.

_____

_____

_____ ★

Applying What You've Learned
★ ★ ★ ★ ★ ★ ★ ★

How are limited-English-proficient students taught in the school districts near where you live? How long is mediated language instruction available for LEP students? What is the rate of high school graduation for LEP students compared to the graduation rate for native English speakers?

_____

_____

_____

_____ ★

Find a simple children's book written in a language you don't understand. Pretend this book was your first reading text in first grade. Do you think learning to read in a second language, when you couldn't read in your first, would have affected your current literacy level?

_____

_____

_____

_____ ★

$\mathcal{H}$OW DOES GENDER AFFECT TEACHING AND LEARNING?

In an ideal gender-fair school, teachers would have similar high expectations of all students in all subjects. Male and female students would participate equally in classroom discourse. Students of both genders would receive a similar amount and quality of attention from teachers. Counselors would advise on career choices based on student interest, aptitude, and academic achievement. Administrators would have similar leadership expectations of male and female students.

Do you recall any incidents of gender bias toward you or your classmates in school? If you do, please explain. If you do not, what made those teachers gender fair?

_____

_____

_____

_____

NCATE

Middle Level

Standard 3: Understands the major concepts, principles, theories, and research related to middle-level curriculum and assessment; uses this knowledge in practice.

Elementary

Standard 1: Knows, understands, and uses the major concepts, principles, theories, and research related to development of children to construct learning opportunities that support individual students' development, acquisition of knowledge, and motivation.

Academic Achievement and Gender

When we examine how gender and achievement interact, we find on the one hand that it is a complex issue, with very few differences apparent. On the other hand, the differences are rather striking.

A review of gender differences in elementary and secondary education achievement reveals the following:

- Reading. In grades 4, 8, and 12, females scored higher than males across all racial and ethnic groups, with the gap widening for most groups as the student progressed through the school.
- Writing. In grades, 4, 8, and 12, females scored higher than males across all racial and ethnic groups.
- Science. At age 9, there were no statistically significant score differences in 1996 between males and females in all ethnic groups—black, Hispanic, Asian/Pacific Islander, and white. At age 13, white males scored higher than white females, whereas the other groups demonstrated no gender difference. At age 17, white males again outscored white females, Hispanic males outscored Hispanic females, and blacks and Asian/Pacific Islanders still exhibited no gender gap.
- Mathematics. At grade 4, white males scored higher than white females; there was no gender difference within the other groups. At grades 8 and 12, no group demonstrated a gender gap.
- Advanced placement. The advanced placement (AP) program, which enables high school students to take courses that earn college credits, has grown dramatically.

Student participation across all racial and ethnic groups has increased in excess of group growth in the U.S. population at large, most dramatically for Chicano/Mexican American females (308 percent). White male participation has increased least (79 percent). Female participation in the program is increasing, and the gender gap is widening; over the last decade, across all ethnic groups, more females have taken AP examinations than males.

- High school completion. The overall high school completion rate for females was 90 percent; for males, 87 percent.[12]

When examining the role of gender in academic achievement, care must be taken to note that gender interrelates with race, ethnicity, and socioeconomic class. Female students who are African American, Hispanic American, Asian American, or from low-income households face additional challenges. European American female students may encounter challenges based on gender but not typically because of cultural background. Female students from racial or ethnic minority backgrounds often encounter challenges based on gender and culture that impact their academic achievement.[13]

What gender issues affect student achievement and school life? How can teachers and schools provide education that is gender fair?

Gender Issues in School Life

The school provides an academic and social milieu in which male and female students interact with each other and with faculty and staff. A gender-fair school environment provides equitable educational opportunities to students of both genders. In addition, **gender-fair schools** provide social climates where students may interact without encountering sexism or sexual harassment in nonacademic activities or in interpersonal interactions.

One of the most influential forces in establishing a more gender-fair school environment was the passage of **Title IX** of the Education Amendments of 1972, which banned discrimination on the basis of gender. This legislation states:

> No person in the United States shall, on the basis of sex, be excluded from participation in, be denied the benefits of, or be subjected to discrimination under any educational program or activity receiving Federal financial assistance.[14]

Gender-fair schools
Learning environments in which male and female students participate equally and respond to similar high expectations in all subjects.

Title IX
Part of the Education Amendments of 1972 that prohibits exclusion on the basis of sex from participation in or benefits of any education program or activity receiving federal funding.

However, when we consider that it has been over fifty years since the *Brown v. Board of Education* Supreme Court decision and over thirty years since the passage of Title IX barring discrimination by gender, a glance at the gender equity report card in Figure 4.8 indicates that we still have a long way to go to providing equal opportunity and education for all students.

Gender remains a salient factor in school life. You must take care to ensure that female and male students are given equitable academic and extracurricular opportunities in schools. One issue that is in the forefront currently is the question of gender equity for boys. After years of focusing on the needs of girls, many now contend that it's boys who are being short-changed. (See Education on the Move.)

INTASC

Standard 2: The teacher understands how children learn and develop, and can provide learning opportunities that support their intellectual, social and personal development.

- Sexual harassment remains pervasive in public schools—81 percent of students surveyed have experienced it.
- Sex segregation persists in career education, with more than 90 percent of girls clustered in training programs for the traditionally female fields of health, teaching graphic arts, and office technology.
- Female students typically get less attention, praise, criticism, and encouragement from teachers than male students get.
- The lower test scores of African American females, Native American females, and Latinas compared to their white and Asian peers remains a serious and deep educational divide.
- Pregnant students are steered toward separate and less academically rigorous schools.

Reflect & Write

Why do you think it is so difficult for schools to bring educational and gender equity to the school house and classroom? What are some suggestions that you have for how public education could increase the rate at which it brings educational opportunity and equality to all students?

Figure 4.8 *Gender Equity Report Card*

Source: *Title IX at 30: Report Card on Gender Equity,* Report of the National Coalition for Women and Girls in Education, June 2002, p. 2. (Online.) Available at www.ncwge. org/title9at30.pdf.

education on the move >>>>>>>>>>>>

>>> The New Gender Gap: Boys Lagging >>>>>>>

Remember when girls became nurses and not doctors? Stenographers, not CEOs? Teachers, not principals?

Well, that's not the way it is anymore. Thirty years after the passage of equal opportunity laws, girls are graduating from high school and college and going into professions and businesses in record numbers.

Now, it's the boys who could use a little help in school, where they're falling behind their female counterparts.

And if you think it's just boys from the inner cities, think again. It's happening in all segments of society, in all fifty states. That's why more and more educators are calling for a new national effort to put boys on an equal footing with their sisters.

At graduation ceremonies last June at Hanover High School in Massachusetts, it was the ninth year in a row that a girl was on the podium as school valedictorian. Girls also took home nearly all the honors, including the science prize, says principal Peter Badalament.

"[Girls] tend to dominate the landscape academically right now," he says, even in math and science.

The school's advanced placement classes, which admit only the most qualified students, are often 70 percent to 80 percent girls. This includes calculus. And in AP biology, there is not a single boy.

According to Badalament, three out of four of the class leadership positions, including the class presidents, are girls. In the National Honor Society, almost all of the officers are girls. The yearbook editor is a girl.

"Girls outperform boys in elementary school, middle school, high school, college, and graduate school,"

says Dr. Michael Thompson, a school pyschologist who writes about the academic problems of boys in his book *Raising Cain.* [See Books Worth Reading, Kindlon et al., at the end of the chapter.] He says that after decades of special attention, girls are soaring, while boys are stagnating.

"Girls are being told, 'Go for it, you can do it. Go for it, you can do it.' They are getting an immense amount of support," he says. "Boys hear that the way to shine is athletically. And boys get a lot of mixed messages about what is means to be masculine and what it means to be a student. Does being a good student make you a real man? I don't think so . . . It is not cool."

Source: "The Gender Gap: Boys Lagging" *CBS News,* May 25, 2003 (2004). (Online). Available at www.cbsnews.com.

Providing a Gender-Fair Education

Providing a gender-fair curriculum is far more than injecting a vignette about Madame Curie into a science class or giving students a glimpse of the life of Harriet Tubman or Sojourner Truth during Women's History Month. Gender-fair treatment involves a reconceptualization of subjects, gender issues, and how to best meet the needs of boys and girls. Providing a gender-fair education can take many forms:

INTASC

Standard 7: The teacher plans instruction based upon knowledge of subject matter, students, the community, and curriculum goals.

1. Being aware of your patterns of discussion in the classroom. As a beginning teacher, some questions to ask yourself are:

   - Do I pay more attention to boys than girls, or vice versa?
   - When selecting students for participation in events and activities, do I favor one sex over the other?
   - Do I give more constructive feedback to boys than girls, or vice versa?

2. Making classroom arrangements gender fair so that both genders are represented fairly in books, displays, and study materials.

3. Putting into practice gender-fair special education and gifted programs so that neither boys nor girls are over- or underrepresented in special education programs. For example, some maintain that special education is the newest boys' club. Figure 4.9 shows the enrollment of boys and girls in special education.

4. Conducting high-quality programs that help ensure that all students graduate from high school. High school graduation rates for males are lower than for females, as Table 4.5 illustrates. In addition, as Table 4.5 shows, the high school graduation rate for all students is much lower than it should be. Failure to graduate from high school is a waste of talent and fails to give boys and girls the foundation they need for life success.

NCATE

Early Childhood

Standard 1: Uses understanding of young children's characteristics, needs, and interacting influences on children's development and learning to create healthy, respectful, supportive, and challenging environments for all children.

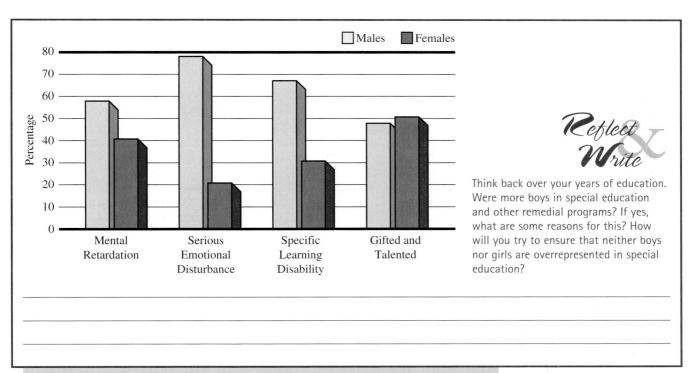

Reflect & Write

Think back over your years of education. Were more boys in special education and other remedial programs? If yes, what are some reasons for this? How will you try to ensure that neither boys nor girls are overrepresented in special education?

Figure 4.9   Enrollment of Boys and Girls in Special Education

Source: Office for Civil Rights, U.S. Department of Education, "OCR Elementary and Secondary School Survey," *OCR Reports* (1998). (Online). Available at http://205.207.175.80/ocrpublic/wds_list98p.asp.

Table 4.5   National Graduation Rates by Race and Gender

Race/Ethnicity	Nation	Female	Male
American Indian/AK Nat	51.1	51.4	47.0
Asian/Pacific Islander	76.8	80.0	72.6
Hispanic	53.2	58.5	48.0
Black	50.2	56.2	42.8
White	74.9	77.0	70.8
All Students	68.0	72.0	64.1

Source: Table was created by author based on selected information from G. Orfield, D. Losen, J. Wald, and C. Swanson, *Losing Our Future: How Minority Youth Are Being Left Behind by the Graduation Rate Crisis* (Cambridge, MA: The Civil Rights Project, Harvard University, 2004). Available online at www.civilrightsproject.harvard.edu.

Single-Sex Schools and Classes

Educators, politicians, and the public are constantly seeking new ways to provide opportunities for boys and girls to excel. Single-sex schools, while not new, are now being tested as one way to ensure that boys and girls get the most of their educational opportunities. Single-sex classrooms and programs in existing middle and high schools are another way. At Arapahoe High School in Littleton, Colorado, Principal Ron Booth comments:

> A lot of people deny the difference between boys and girls. It's denied because who would know what to do with it? It's politically incorrect even to say boys and girls are different.[15]

As a beginning teacher, you will be involved in educational and political issues relating to how best to educate boys and girls. For more about single-sex schools, see Education on the Move.

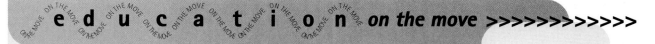

education *on the move* >>>>>>>>>>>

Single-Sex Schools Stage a Comeback

On March 3, 2004, the U.S. Department of Education published new regulations governing single-sex education in public schools. The new regulations allow coeducational public schools (elementary and secondary schools) to offer single-sex classrooms, provided that the schools

1. Provide a rationale for offering a single-gender class in that subject. A variety of rationales are acceptable (e.g., if very few girls have taken computer science in the past, the school could offer a girls-only computer science class).
2. Provide a coeducational class in the same subject at the same school.

3. Conduct periodic reviews to determine whether single-sex classes are still necessary to remedy whatever inequity prompted the school to offer the classes in the first place.

Just as important, the new regulations clear the way for single-sex schools—schools that are all girls or all boys. In fact, the new regulations provide some incentive for school districts to offer single-sex schools rather than single-sex classrooms within coed schools. Single-sex schools are specifically exempted from two of the three requirements above. They do not have to provide any rationale for their single-sex format, and they do not have to conduct any periodic review

to determine whether single-sex education is "necessary" to remedy some inequity. They will have to offer "substantially equal" courses, services, and facilities at other schools within the same school district, but those other schools can be single-sex or coed. In other words, a school district may offer a single-sex high school for girls without having to offer a single-sex high school for boys. A school district can offer an all-boys elementary school without having to offer an all-girls elementary school.

Source: "New Regulations Released March, 2004" (n.d.). (Online). Available at www.singlesexschools.org.

Reflect & Write

All across the country, from Camden to Denver to Los Angeles, almost one hundred public schools now offer single-sex education. Proponents argue that single-sex classes provide a better learning environment for both boys and girls. Critics argue that such classes undermine civil rights gains and promote discrimination. What do you think? Should boys and girls be educated separately? What reasons can you give?

_____

_____

_____

_____

SECTION SUMMARY

How Does Gender Affect Teaching and Learning?

Boys and girls do not have identical experiences in school. There are many significant differences. One of your jobs as a beginning teacher is to minimize these differences.

- **Academic Achievement and Gender.** The differences in boys' and girls' educational achievement are much less pronounced than they were a decade ago. In fact, in many indicators of school success, boys now lag behind girls.

- **Gender Issues in School Life.** Title IX of the Education Amendments of 1972 banned discrimination on the basis of gender. Yet, when we examine a current Title IX report card, the schools and the nation still have a long way to go in providing equal opportunity for all.

- **Providing a Gender-Fair Education.** You will want to provide a gender-fair program for your students. You can begin by being aware of your patterns of discourse and asking yourself key questions about how you treat boys and girls. You and the schools must put into practice procedures that help ensure that neither boys nor girls are over- or underrepresented in special education. In addition, you and your school should conduct high-quality programs that will help all students graduate from high school.

- **Single-Sex Schools and Classes.** Educators are implementing single-sex schools and single-sex classrooms as two ways of helping ensure that education for boys and girls is gender fair and equal in opportunity. Critics of such programs claim they prove unequal opportunity and undermine civil rights advances.

Thinking Critically
★ ★ ★ ★ ★ ★ ★ ★

Critics of gender-fair education argue that women's perspectives on issues and events do not differ fundamentally from those of men. Therefore, presenting knowledge with particular attention to women's perspectives is using an "artificial prism" on knowledge. Do you agree or disagree with this position? Explain why.

_____

_____

_____

_____★

Research the literature pro and con on single-sex schools and classrooms. Do the data support the implementation of these programs?

_____

_____

_____

_____ ★

**Putting Yourself
in the Picture**

★ ★ ★ ★ ★ ★ ★ ★ ★

Observe in a classroom. Note the interactions between male and female students and the attention the teacher gives to students of each gender. After summarizing the patterns observed, what conclusions can you draw?

_____

_____

_____

_____ ★

Applications for Active Learning

CONNECTIONS

1. In the chapter opener, Kathy Mellor passionately conveys her strong support of programs to help students learn English. What are your beliefs about ELL programs? What kind of ELL programs will you advocate for as a beginning teacher?

_____

_____

_____

2. How does the information in this chapter relate to the discussion of urban, rural, and suburban schools in Chapter 3? Write a paragraph using the concepts in this chapter to describe the differences among schools presented in the previous chapter.

_____

_____

_____

FIELD EXPERIENCES

1. Interview teachers about their views on multicultural education and their experiences with multicultural cur-

ricula. How do you account for the range of views you find? Which views do you think are most constructive in promoting both quality and equity in the education of culturally diverse learners? Relate the teachers' views and experiences to the five models of multicultural education presented in this chapter. From a practical standpoint, what seem to be the requirements, benefits, and challenges of each approach?

2. Observe students in a culturally diverse school. How, if at all, do race, ethnicity, language, gender, and culture seem to influence students' interactions and social relations? On the basis of your observations, what recommendations might you make for improving learning environments for diverse learners?

_____

_____

_____

PERSONAL RESEARCH

1. Research the demographics of the student population in the school, district, or state in which you plan to teach.

2. Collect information about resources for multicultural education in the school, district, or state in which you plan to teach. Consider human resources as well as community

sites, historical and art institutions, and civic organizations and also print and media resources. How might you integrate the resources for multicultural education you find into the curriculum you will be teaching?

FOR YOUR PORTFOLIO

Getting to know—I mean really know—English-language learners is one way to enhance your professional growth. You can achieve this goal by developing a "Portrait" of an ELL. Here are some things to include in your ELL Portrait:

- a word picture of the student
- a brief description of culture and language
- a description of family and home background
- a description and analysis of how and in what way the student's home language is influencing—positively or negatively—school performance
- your recommendations for how to enhance the student's language and school achievement

Place your ELL Portrait in your portfolio.

IDEA FILE

1. Think of two or three creative and effective strategies you could use in each of the following situations to achieve multicultural education goals. In each situation, the students are in the process of entering or leaving your classroom.

- Students of different races use racial epithets in talking with one another.

- Students of the same race use racial epithets in talking with one another.
- A male student makes unwanted, aggressive, or inappropriate physical contact with a student of the opposite sex.
- A male student makes unwanted, aggressive, or inappropriate physical contact with a student of the same sex.
- A teacher reprimands a student for disturbing the class. The student challenges the teacher by saying his cultural background is the only reason he is being singled out.

2. A new student who does not speak English is transferred to your class from another state with very little notice. What are the first five things you will do to set the stage for this student's social integration and academic success? What are the next five things you will do? Note your ideas here.

_____

_____

_____

WEB SITES WORTH VISITING

As we have discussed in this chapter, many of your students will benefit from a number of different kinds of programs. Fortunately, many programs exist to help students who need special help and support. One of these is the School Development Program: The Comer Process. A primary goal of this program is to promote the overall development of students, including significant gains in academic and social behavior skills, by providing enriched school experiences. Comer is at the Yale Child Study Center, which you can visit online at http://info.med.yale.edu/comer. Also, you can learn more about multicultural education online at the Pathways to School Improvement project at www.ncrel.org/sdrs/

Electronic Magazine of Multicultural Education
www.eastern.edu/publications/emme
This electronic journal provides articles, instructional ideas, reviews, and literature for young readers in the area of multicultural education.

Multicultural Awareness in the Language Classroom
www.wfi.fr/
This site contains excellent sources for language arts and English teachers.

Multicultural Perspectives in Mathematics Education
http://jwilson.coe.uga.edu/DEPT/Multicultural/mathED.html
Explores multicultural dimensions of mathematics, a field often regarded as difficult to teach multiculturally.

National Association for Multicultural Education
www.nameorg.org
The Web site of this national organization provides a free sample of its journal, *Multicultural Perspectives*.

National Multicultural Institute
www.nmci.org
This site is operated by the Washington-based National Multicultural Institute and explores many facets of diversity.

North Central Regional Education Laboratory
www.ncrel.org
This Web site contains links to multicultural school initiatives, professional development programs, organizations, and curricula.

National Women's History Project
www.nwhp.org
This site contains excellent resources for faculty or students wishing to research women's history or gender issues.

Multicultural Book Reviews
www.isomedia.com/homes/jmele/homepage.html
This is a useful site for educators to preview existing and new titles in multicultural education.

BOOKS WORTH READING

Banks, J. A., and Banks, C. A. (Eds.). (2004). *Multicultural Education: Issues and Perspectives* (5th ed.). New York: Wiley.
Articles treat characteristics, goals, content, and methods in multicultural and multilingual education, including gender equity. This book offers research-based perspectives on issues and controversies in the field of multicultural education.

Baruth, L. G., and Manning, M. L. (2004). *Multicultural Education of Children and Adolescents* (4th ed.). Boston: Allyn & Bacon.
This books focuses on multicultural education theory and methods and their applications in classroom practice across the curriculum at all grade levels.

Bennett, C. I. (Ed.). (2002). *Comprehensive Multicultural Education: Theory and Practice* (5th ed.). New York: Allyn & Bacon.
Comprehensive Multicultural Education provides a curriculum model with six goals and numerous lesson plans illustrating how each goal can be implemented in the classroom. The text includes conceptual frameworks from the social sciences and historical backgrounds. Both theory and practice in the text present interdisciplinary content through primary source material and vignettes of actual teachers and students and encourage interaction between students' cultural and individual differences.

Blair, T. (Ed.). (2002). *New Teachers' Performance-Based Guide to Culturally Diverse Classrooms.* New York: Allyn & Bacon.
The text clearly presents the latest information on teacher effectiveness and providing "culturally responsive instruction" in today's classrooms. Cultural differences influence classroom instruction and the performance of all students. Teachers need to understand diversity and to develop a teaching style that both respects and capitalizes on the strengths of all students. Practical lists are provided throughout the text to demonstrate exactly how teachers can accommodate their teaching styles to meet the diverse learning styles of students who speak a nonstandard dialect and those students whose native language is not English.

Davidman, L. (Ed.). (2001). *Teaching with a Multicultural Perspective* (3rd ed.). New York: Allyn & Bacon.
This title empowers future teachers to develop and embrace a multicultural perspective. It provides a clear seven-goal model for creating effective instruction in culturally diverse environments. Based on a set of field-tested planning questions and linked to a series of curriculum case studies, educator profiles, and activities, this practical text makes clear and convincing connections between multicultural practice and theory.

Davidman, L., and Davidman, P. (2001). *Teaching with a Multicultural Perspective: A Practical Guide* (3rd ed.). New York: Longman.
This source examines the conditions necessary for creating an equitable education and gives numerous examples useful for creating a multicultural curriculum.

Diaz, C., Massialas, B., and Xanthopoulos, J. (Ed.). (1999). *Global Perspectives for Educators.* New York: Allyn & Bacon.
This text fills a void by focusing on global education and its definition, purposes, and methods of inquiry. It offers a logical conceptual framework and category system through which to analyze global issues, such as the environment, population, and nutrition. Options in curriculum development and activities, designed for K–12 students, provide practical information to implement global education.

Garcia, E. (2002). *Hispanic Education in the United States.* Blue Ridge Summit, PA: Rowman and Littlefield.
This book examines the nature and characteristics of Hispanics in the United States. It contains chapters on what works for Hispanic students in the early and adolescent years. The subtheme of this book, "Raices y Alas," refers to "Roots and Wings."

Irvine, J., and Banks, J. (Ed.). (2003). *Educating Teachers for Diversity: Seeing with a Cultural Eye (Multicultural Education, No. 15).* New York: Teachers College Press.
Educating Teachers for Diversity addresses the complex issues of how culture, race, ethnicity, and social class influence the teaching-learning process. The author provides not only an analysis of current conditions and reforms in education but also offers suggestions and practices for improving educational outcomes for all children.

Kindlon, D. J., Thompson, M., Kindlon, D., and Barker, T. (Eds.). (2000). *Raising Cain: Protecting the Emotional Life of Boys.* New York: Ballantine Books.
In *Raising Cain,* two of the country's leading child psychologists share what they have learned in more than thirty-five years of combined experience working with boys and their families. They reveal a nation of boys who are hurting—sad, afraid, angry, and silent.

Manning, M. Lee. (Ed.). (2004). *Multicultural Education of Children and Adolescents* (4th ed.). New York: Allyn & Bacon.
This text expands the definition of multicultural to include gender, disability, and sexual orientation. It is an invaluable resource, providing suggestions for working with families of culturally diverse backgrounds as

well as with school administration and special school personnel.

Nieto, S. (Ed.). (2004). *Affirming Diversity: The Sociopolitical Context of Multicultural Education* (4th ed.). Boston: Allyn & Bacon.

The text looks at how personal, social, political, cultural, and educational factors affect the success or failure of students in today's classroom. It examines the lives of eighteen real students who are affected by multicultural education, or a lack of it. Social justice is firmly embedded in this view of multicultural education, and teachers are encouraged to work for social change in their classrooms, schools, and communities.

Schrag, P. (Ed.). (2004). *Final Test: The Battle for Adequacy in America's Schools*. New York: New Press.

This book is designed to help present and future educators acquire the concepts, paradigms, and explanations needed to become effective practitioners in culturally, racially, and language diverse settings for the education of students from both genders and from different cultural, racial, ethnic, and language groups.

CHAPTER 5

*T*eaching Exceptional Learners and Students at Risk

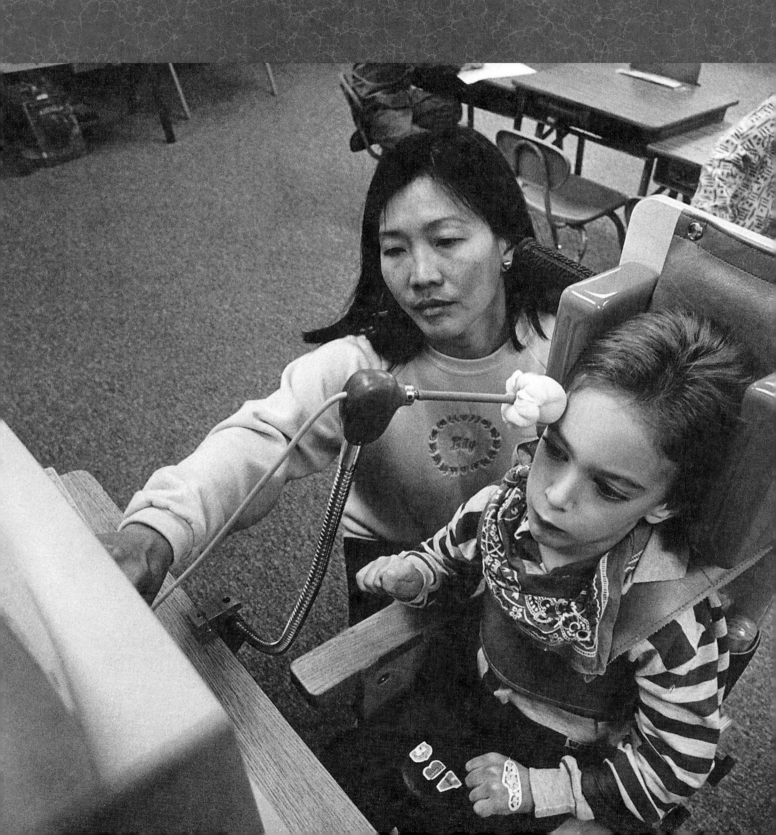

"High expectations, safe environments, and parent collaboration."

Susan Hentz is the Florida Council of Exceptional Children's 2003 Teacher of the Year.

Congratulations! You are about to embark on a career that has a direct impact on every facet of our society. Yes, teaching is the only career in the world that touches every individual's life. Children who will ultimately become nurses, teachers, lawyers, sanitation workers, builders, cosmetologists, and firefighters will walk through your door as students. Regardless of ability or disability, these children come to school highly receptive to the learning process.

As a special educator for the past twenty-one years, my experience has afforded me the opportunity to work with students ranging from birth through adult. I believe my greatest contribution to the field of education is my personal dedication and enthusiasm in working to positively influence the life of each and every student that walks through my classroom door. My experience has taught me that fostering positive self-esteem within my students ultimately results in future academic successes and sustained motivation to learn. By setting standards of behavior and high academic expectations, I have given my students the opportunity to continually succeed, which in turn helps to develop and maintain positive self-worth. My teaching environment for students from birth through adults has been consistent: high expectations in a safe environment with teacher and parent collaboration focusing on student achievement.

As a beginning teacher, it is your responsibility to have an awareness of the diverse learning styles and influences that will affect the learning process of each student. It is imperative that you respect and value your students while having a clear vision and high expectations for all. Additionally, you must be prepared to utilize a variety of teaching strategies to address the physical, behavioral, intellectual, and cultural differences of each individual student. Three questions you can use to guide your teaching are these: What do I expect my students to learn? How will I assess my students to determine if learning occurred? What will I do when students do not learn the material? If you can consistently provide answers to these three questions, you will be well on your way to helping your students reach their full potential. Needless to say, the challenges you will face are extreme. However, the positive educational outcomes are equally extreme and professionally rewarding. The adventure of teaching will enable you to touch your students, both mentally and emotionally, so they achieve and become contributing members of our society.

NCATE

Middle Level

Standard 6: Understands the major concepts, principles, theories, and research related to working collaboratively with family and community members; uses that knowledge to maximize learning of all young adolescents.

NCATE

Early Childhood

Standard 4: Integrates understanding of children and families, of developmentally effective approaches to teaching and learning, and of academic disciplines to design, implement, and evaluate positive learning experiences for all children.

Elementary

Standard 5.3: Knows importance of establishing and maintaining positive collaborative relationships with families to promote the academic, social, and emotional growth of children.

How Will This Chapter Help You?

You will learn

★ about mainstreaming and inclusion

★ how to teach mainstreamed and inclusive classrooms

★ about students with ADHD

★ how to consult and collaborate with special education teachers and other professionals

★ about assistive technology and its applications to classroom practice

★ how to identify and teach gifted students

★ about six basic approaches to educating students at risk

The New York Times
expect the world®
nytimes.com

Themes of the Times

Expand your knowledge of the concepts discussed in this chapter by reading current and historical articles from *The New York Times* by visiting the "Themes of the Times" section of the companion Web site.

$\mathcal{W}$HAT LAWS AND DEFINITIONS PROVIDE FOR THE EDUCATION OF EXCEPTIONAL LEARNERS?

Middle Level

NCATE

Standard 6: Understands the major concepts, principles, theories, and research related to working collaboratively with family and community members; uses that knowledge to maximize learning of all young adolescents.

Students with special needs are in every school and in every classroom in the United States. As a beginning teacher, you will teach students who have special needs for a variety of reasons. They may come from low-income families and different racial and ethnic groups; they may have exceptional abilities and disabilities. Students with special needs are often discriminated against because of their disability, socioeconomic background, language, race, or gender. Your challenge will be to provide for all students an education that is appropriate to their physical, mental, social, and emotional abilities and to help them achieve their best. Your challenge also includes learning as much as you can about the special needs of your students and collaborating with other professionals to identify and develop teaching strategies, programs, and curricula for them. Most of all, you need to be a strong advocate for meeting all students' individual needs.

Students with Disabilities and the Individuals with Disabilities Education Act (IDEA)

Early Childhood

NCATE

Standard 1: Uses understanding of young children's characteristics, needs, and interacting influences on children's development and learning to create healthy, respectful, supportive, and challenging environments for all children.

Individuals with Disabilities Education Act (IDEA)
A federal act providing a free and appropriate education to disabled youth between ages 3 and 21.

Students with special needs and their families need education and services that will help them succeed. You will be a part of the process of seeing that they receive such services. Unfortunately, quite often students with disabilities are not provided appropriate services and fail to reach their full potential. This is one reason for laws to help ensure that schools and teachers will have high expectations for these students and that they will have special education and related services. The federal government has passed many laws protecting and promoting the rights and needs of children with disabilities. One of the most important federal laws is the **Individuals with Disabilities Education Act (IDEA)**, originally passed in 1975 as the Education for All Handicapped Children Act. The law was renamed IDEA in 1990. Congress has periodically updated IDEA, with the latest revision in 2004.

The purpose of the Individuals with Disabilities Education Act, as amended in 1997, is to ensure that all children with disabilities have available to them a free appropriate public education that emphasizes special education and related services designed to meet their unique needs, to ensure that the rights of children with disabilities and their parents or guardians are protected, to assist states and localities to provide for the education of all children with disabilities, and to assess and ensure the effectiveness of efforts to educate children with disabilities."[1]

Students with disabilities
Children with physical impairments (hearing, speech or language, visual, orthopedic) or mental/emotional impairments (mental retardation, autism, emotional disturbance, traumatic brain injury) or specific learning disabilities and who, by reason thereof, need special education and related services.

IDEA defines **students with disabilities** as "those with mental retardation, hearing impairments (including deafness), speech or language impairments (including blindness), serious emotional disturbance, orthopedic impairments, autism, traumatic brain injury, other health impairments, or specific learning disabilities; and who, by reason thereof, need special education and related services." IDEA also allows states the option of classifying students between the ages of 3 through 9 who have disabilities as developmentally delayed. Developmental delays may be in one or more of the following areas: physical development, cognitive development, communication development, social or emotional development, or adaptive development. About 10 to 12 percent of the nation's students have some type of disability and need special education services. Table 5.1 lists the number of persons from birth to age 21 with disabilities in the various categories covered under IDEA.

IDEA establishes seven basic principles to follow as you provide educational and other services to children with special needs:

1. Zero reject. IDEA calls for educating all children and rejecting none from an education. Whereas before IDEA many children were excluded from educational programs or were denied an education, this is not the case today.
2. Nondiscriminatory evaluation and multidisciplinary assessment. A fair evaluation is needed to determine whether a student has a disability, and, if so, what the

Table 5.1 **Children with Disabilities Served in Federally Supported Programs**

	Numbers Served	Percentage Served
All disabilities	5,775,722	100.00
Learning disabilities	2,887,217	49.99
Speech or language disabilities	1,093,808	18.94
Mental retardation	612,978	10.61
Emotional disturbance	473,663	8.20
Hearing impairments	70,767	1.23
Orthopedic impairments	73,057	1.26
Autism	78,749	1.36
Deaf-blindness	1,320	0.02
Traumatic brain injury	14,844	0.26
Developmental delay	28,935	0.50
Other health impairments	291,850	5.05
Multiple disabilities	122,559	2.12

Source: U.S. Office of Special Education and Rehabilitation Services, *Twenty-Fourth Annual Report to Congress on the Implementation of the Individuals with Disabilities Education Act* (Washington, DC: U.S. Department of Education, 2002).

student's education should consist of. IDEA specifies the use of nondiscretionary testing procedures in labeling and placement of students for special education services. These include:

- Testing of students in their native or primary language, whenever possible
- Use of evaluation procedures selected and administered in such a way as to prevent cultural or racial discrimination

3. Multidisciplinary Assessment. This is a team approach in which a group of people use various methods in a child's evaluation. Having a **multidisciplinary assessment (MDA)** helps ensure that a child's needs and program will not be determined by one test or one person.

4. Appropriate education. Instruction and related services need to be individually designed to provide educational benefits to students in making progress toward meeting their unique needs. Basically, IDEA provides for a **free and appropriate education (FAPE)** for all students between the ages of 3 and 21. *Appropriate* means that children must receive an education suited to their age, maturity level, condition of disability, past achievements, and parental expectations.

5. Least restrictive placement/environment. All students with disabilities have the right to learn in the **least restrictive environment (LRE)**—an environment consistent with their academic, social, and physical needs. Such a setting may or may not be the general classroom, but 95 percent of children with disabilities spend at least part of their school day in general classrooms.

6. Procedural due process. IDEA provides schools and parents with ways of resolving their differences by mediation and/or hearings before impartial hearing officers or judges.

7. Parental and student participation. IDEA specifies a process of shared decision making whereby educators, parents, and students collaborate in deciding a student's educational plan.

Referral Process. Under the provisions of IDEA and other guidelines that specify the fair treatment of children with disabilities and their families, educators must follow certain procedures in developing a special plan for each child. These procedures occur through the school referral planning and placement process (see Figure 5.1). Referral

INTASC

Standard 8: The teacher understands and uses formal and informal assessment strategies to evaluate and ensure the continuous intellectual, social and physical development of the learner.

Multidisciplinary assessment (MDA)
A team approach using various methods to conduct a child's evaluation.

Free and appropriate education (FAPE)
Children must receive education suited to their age, maturity, condition of disability, past achievements, and parental expectations.

Least restrictive environment (LRE)
The principle that, to the maximum extent appropriate, students with disabilities are to be educated with their peers who are not disabled.

PHASE 1 **Initiating the referral**	PHASE 2 **Assessing student eligibility and educational needs**	PHASE 3 **Developing the individualized education program (IEP)**	PHASE 4 **Determining the least restrictive environment (LRE)**
• School personnel or parents indicate concern about student's learning, behavior, or overall development.	• Multidisciplinary and nondiscriminatory assessment tools and strategies are used to evaluate student's eligibility for special education services.	• Appropriate professionals to serve on an IEP team are identified. A team coordinator is appointed.	• Identify potential education placements, based on student's annual goals and special education services to be provided.
• If referral is made by school personnel, parents are notified of concerns.	• Child-study team reviews assessment information to determine (1) whether student meets eligibility requirements for special education services under one of twelve disability classifications or meets the definition of developmentally delayed (for students between ages 3 and 9), and (2) whether the student requires special education services.	• Parents (and student when appropriate) participate as equal members of the team and are provided with written copies of all assessment information.	• Adhering to the principle that students with disabilities are to be educated with their nondisabled peers to the maximum extent appropriate, justify any removal of the child from the general education classroom.
• Child-study team decides to provide additional support services and adapt student's instructional program prior to initiating formal assessment for eligibility. (This step may be bypassed, and team may choose to immediately seek parental permission to evaluate the student's eligibility for special education.)		• Team meets and agrees upon the essential elements of the student's individualized education program plan.	• With parents involved in the decision-making process, determine student's appropriate educational placement.
• School seeks and receives parents' permission to evaluate student's eligibility for special education services.	• If team agrees that the student is eligible for and needs special education services, then the process moves to phase 3, developing the IEP.		• Document, on the student's IEP, justification for any removal from the general education classroom.
			• Team members agree in writing to the essential elements of the IEP and to the education placement where special education and related services are to be provided.
			• As members of the IEP team, parents must consent in writing to the agreed-upon educational placement for their child.

This four-phase process of the referral and placement procedure will help you understand the seriousness and the responsibilities of ensuring that all children with disabilities receive a free and appropriate education. After reviewing this process, did you have any "surprises"? What were they? Which of these phases is the most critical? In what way?

Figure 5.1 The Four-Phase Special Education, Referral Planning, and Placement Process

Source: Adapted from M. Hardman, C. Drew, and M. Egan, *Human Exceptionality: School, Community, and Family,* 8th ed. (Boston: Allyn & Bacon, 2005), fig 2.2, p. 37. Copyright 2005 by Pearson Education. Reprinted by permission of the publisher.

of the student for special services can be made by a teacher, parent, doctor, or some other professional. The referral is usually followed by a comprehensive individual assessment in order to determine if the child possesses a disability and is eligible for services. In order for testing to occur, parents or guardians must give their consent.

If the child is eligible for special education services, the **child study team** meets to develop an **individualized education program (IEP)**. IEPs are discussed in more detail in the following section, but essentially the IEP is a contract or agreement that specifies how the child will be educated and what services will be provided. The IEP is a binding legal document. Consequently, teachers, administrators, and others cannot simply say, "I don't have time for this."

The child study team consists of a parent or parent representative; the student, when appropriate; a representative of the school district; and a principal, assistant principal, or coordinator of exceptional student services. The IEP must be renewed annually and revised as appropriate.

The child study team is also responsible for dismissing students from special education services when they are able to function in a regular classroom without the services.

Individualized Education Programs and Individualized Family Service Plans

Because IDEA requires **individualization of instruction**, schools must provide for all students' specific needs, disabilities, and modes of learning, as well as those of their parents. Individualization of instruction also means developing and implementing an **individualized education program (IEP)** for each student. The IEP must specify what will be done for the child, how and when it will be done, and by whom it will be done. This information must be in writing. Figure 5.1 shows a sample IEP form. In developing the IEP, a person trained in assessing disabling conditions, such as an evaluation specialist, must be involved, as well as a general education teacher, a special education teacher, the parent, and, when appropriate, the student.

In 1986, Congress passed PL 99-457, the Education of the Handicapped Act Amendments, which was landmark legislation relating to infants, toddlers, and preschoolers with disabilities. This law extends to children with disabilities between the ages of 3 and 5 the same rights that are extended to children with disabilities under IDEA and establishes a state grant program for infants and toddlers with disabilities. Most states participate in the infant and toddler grant program.

The process of helping infants and toddlers through age 2 with disabilities begins with referral and assessment and results in the development of an **individualized family service plan (IFSP)**, which is designed to help families reach the goals they have for themselves and their children. The law provides for:

- Multidisciplinary assessment developed by a multidisciplinary team and the parents. Planned services must meet developmental needs and can include special education, speech and language pathology and audiology, occupational therapy, physical therapy, psychological services, parent and family training and counseling services, transition services, medical diagnostic services, and health services.
- A written IFSP, which must contain a statement of the child's present levels of development; a statement of the family's strengths and needs in regard to enhancing the child's development; a statement of major expected outcomes for the child and family; the criteria, procedures, and timelines for determining progress; the specific early intervention services necessary to meet the unique needs of the child and family; the

Child study team
A group of individuals responsible for seeing that the four-phase process of referral and placement is implemented fairly for every student referred for evaluation and services. Also referred to as the *intervention assistance team*.

Individualization of instruction
Students' educations are individualized by providing for their specific needs, disabilities, and preferences.

Individualized education program (IEP)
A plan for meeting an exceptional learner's educational needs that specifies goals, objectives, services, and procedures for evaluating progress.

Individualized family service plan (IFSP)
A plan designed to help families reach their goals, for themselves and for their children, with the following support services: special education, speech and language pathology and audiology, occupational therapy, physical therapy, psychological services, parent and family training, and counseling.

Collaboration among colleagues and specialists helps all parties working with students with special needs identify strategies most beneficial for these students' progress. What kind of information can you gain from such collaboration?

Sample Form

Individualized Education Program (IEP)

_____ Student Name   _____ Date of Meeting to Develop or Review IEP

Note: For each student with a disability beginning at age 14 (or younger, if appropriate), a statement of the student's **transition service needs** must be included under the applicable parts of the IEP. The statement must focus on the courses the students needs to take to reach his or her post-school goals.

[a general statement of the transition needs of the student; must be updated annually]

Present Levels of Educational Performance

[includes a description of how the disability affects involvement and progress or (for preschool children) how the the disability affects participation.]

Measurable Annual Goals (Including Benchmarks or Short-Term Objectives)

[clearly stated goals that lay out the plan for meeting the child's needs for improvement as well as all other educational needs]

Special Education and Related Services	Start Date	Frequency	Location	Duration
Supplementary Aids and Services	Start Date	Frequency	Location	Duration
Program Modifications or Supports for School Personnel	Start Date	Frequency	Location	Duration

[listing of all services, aids, and special modifications needed along with specific details]

Explanation of Extent, if Any, to Which Child Will Not Participate in Regular Education Classroom

[description of child's lack of interaction with other children in regular class setting]

ADMINISTRATION OF STATE AND DISTRICT-WIDE ASSESSMENTS OF STUDENT ACHIEVEMENT

Any Individual Modifications in Administration Needed for Child to Participate in State or District-wide Assessment(s)

[a listing of any special requirements needed for child to participate in assessments]

If IEP Team Determines That Child Will Not Participate in a Particular State or District-Wide Assessment

- Why isn't the assessment appropriate for the child?
- Describe alternative assessment.

How Child's Progress Toward Annual Goals Will Be Measured

[clear statement of measurement procedures]

How Child's Parents Will Be Regularly Informed of Child's Progress Toward Annual Goals and Extent to Which Child's Progress Is Sufficient to Meet Goals by End of Year

[description of plan for working with parents and informing them of child's progress]

[Beginning at age 16 or younger if determined appropriate by IEP team] Statement of Needed Transition Services (Including, If Appropriate, Statement of Interagency Responsibilities or Any Needed Linkages)

[takes into account special considerations involved with older children, including student preferences and interests]

[In a state that transfers rights to the student at the age of majority, the following information must be included beginning at least one year before the student reaches the age of majority]
The student has been informed of the rights under Part B of IDEA, if any, that will transfer to the student on reaching the age of majority. Yes

[guarantees that student is fully informed of rights regarding services available under IDEA]

Figure 5.2   Sample IEP Form

Source: Adapted from U.S. Office of Special Education Programs, "A Guide to the Individualized Education Program." (2000). (Online). Available at www.ed.gov/offices/OSERS/OSEP/Products/IEP_Guide/.

projected dates for initiation of services; the name of the case manager; and transition procedures from the early intervention program into a preschool program.

Reflect & Write

Now that you know more about IDEA and exceptional student education terms, how will these influence you as a beginning teacher? Why?

_____

_____

_____

_____

SECTION SUMMARY

What Laws and Definitions Provide for the Education of Exceptional Learners?

Students come to school with special needs because of their socioeconomic and cultural backgrounds, gender, family situation, and abilities and disabilities. As a teacher working with special needs students, you will need to know the vocabulary, definitions, and laws governing the education of students with disabilities.

- Students with Disabilities and the Individuals with Disabilities Education Act (IDEA). The Individuals with Disabilities Education Act (IDEA), as amended in 1997, ensures that students with disabilities be provided a free and appropriate education in the least restrictive environment, the environment in which their specific needs will be met and in which they can learn best. IDEA has six basic principles, which include zero reject, nondiscriminatory evaluation and multidisciplinary assessment, appropriate education, education in a least restrictive environment (LRE), procedural due process, and parent and student participation.

- Individualized Education Programs and Individualized Family Service Plans. Individualized education programs (IEPs) are required by IDEA for all students with disabilities. Individualized family service plans (IFSPs) are individualized programs designed to help families reach the goals set for themselves and for the students.

Thinking Critically
★ ★ ★ ★ ★ ★ ★ ★

Why do you think laws are necessary to help ensure that all students receive an appropriate education?

_____

_____

_____

_____

Applying What You've Learned
★ ★ ★ ★ ★ ★ ★ ★

What steps should you take to prepare for teaching students with disabilities? Interview teachers to find out their views about how you can prepare for teaching students with disabilities.

_____

_____

_____

_____

Assume that you have been notified that Kim Sue, a child with a disability, has been placed in your classroom for the school year. Kim is of above-average intelligence, but two years ago she suffered a spinal cord injury that left her with no movement or sensation from the waist down. What else do you want to know about Kim, and what other professionals or community members will you want to consult?

★

Adaptive education
An educational approach aimed at providing learning experiences that help each student achieve desired educational goals.

Full inclusion
An approach whereby students with disabilities receive all instruction in a general classroom and support services are provided in that context.

Partial inclusion
An approach whereby students with disabilities receive some instruction in a general classroom and some in a specialized instructional setting.

INTASC
Standard 3: The teacher understands how students differ in their approaches to learning and creates instructional opportunities that are adapted to diverse learners.

NCATE
Middle Level
Standard 1: Understands the major concepts, principles, theories and research related to young adolescent development; provides opportunities that support student development and learning.

*W*HAT ARE MAINSTREAMING AND INCLUSION?

A variety of adaptations are used to ensure that all students, regardless of abilities, have equal access to a quality education. **Adaptive education** is an educational approach aimed at providing learning experiences that help each student achieve the desired educational goals. Education is adaptive when school learning environments are modified to respond effectively to student differences and to enhance the individual's ability to succeed in learning in such environments.

Mainstreaming implies the placement of students with disabilities in general classrooms, called natural environments. (Natural environments are the ones in which students would be if they did not have a disability.) Today most educators agree that special needs should be met as much as possible in the general education classroom.

The Full Inclusion Debate

Inclusion supports the right of all students to participate in natural environments. **Full inclusion** means that students with disabilities receive the services and supports appropriate to their individual needs entirely in the general classroom. **Partial inclusion** means that students receive some of their instruction in the general classroom and some in pull-out classrooms or resource rooms, where they work individually or in small groups with special education teachers. Full inclusion receives a lot of attention and is the subject of debate for several reasons:

- Court decisions and state and federal laws mandate, support, and encourage full inclusion. Many of these laws and court cases relate to extending to children and parents basic civil rights. For example, in the 1992 case of *Oberti v. Board of Education of the Borough of Clementon School District*, the judge ruled that Rafael, an eight-year-old child with Down syndrome, should not have to earn his way into an integrated classroom but that it was his right to be there from the beginning.
- Some parents of children with disabilities are dissatisfied with their children's attending separate programs. They view separate programs for their children as a form of segregation. In addition, they want their children to have the social benefits of attending classes in general education classrooms.
- Some parents believe their children are best served in separate special education settings. Many members of the public also do not support full-inclusion programs. In one public opinion poll, 65 percent of respondents believed children with learning problems should be placed in special classrooms. Thirty-seven percent said

that if students with learning problems are included in the same classrooms with other students, the effect of their inclusion on other students would be negative; 36 percent thought it would not make much difference. Forty percent believed that inclusion would have a negative effect on the students with learning problems.[2]

- Some teachers feel they do not have the training or support necessary to provide for the disabilities of children in full inclusion classrooms. These teachers also believe they will not be able to provide for children with disabilities, even with the assistance of aides and special support services.
- Some people believe the cost of full inclusion outweighs the benefits. There is no doubt that it costs more to educate students with disabilities than students who have no disabilities. The average cost of educating a regular classroom student nationally is $8,177[3] compared to $13,801 (1.69 times) for educating an exceptional education student in a special education program.[4] (This cost can be more for some individual students and can cost more in some school districts.) Some professionals think that the money spent on separate special education facilities and programs can be better used for full inclusion programs.

Many educators and special education advocates support providing special needs children a continuum of services. A **continuum of services** means that a full range of services is available for individuals, from the most restrictive to the least restrictive placements. This continuum implies a graduated range of services, with one level of services leading directly to the next. For example, a continuum of services for students with disabilities would be an institutional placement, as the most restrictive, to a placement in a general education classroom, as the least restrictive (see Figure 5.3).

Part of the controversy over full inclusion comes over the interpretation of IDEA, which requires that:

> to the maximum extent appropriate, children with disabilities . . . are educated with nondisabled children, and that special classes, separate schooling, and the removal of children with disabilities from the regular educational environment occurs only when the nature or severity of the disability is such that education in regular classrooms with the use of supplemental aids and services cannot be achieved satisfactorily.[5]

As a teacher, you will be expected to provide for all of the students assigned to you. Figure 5.3 will give you an idea of the options available to you for achieving this goal.

Given the great amount of interest in full inclusion, discussions regarding its appropriateness and how best to implement it will continue. As a beginning teacher, you will have many opportunities to participate fully in this discussion and to help shape the policies of implementation and classroom practice. (See the Profile on p. 157)

Continuum of services
A full range of educational services available for individuals from the most restrictive to the least restrictive placements.

Early Childhood
Standard 1: Uses understanding of young children's characteristics, needs, and interacting influences on children's development and learning to create healthy, respectful, supportive, and challenging environments for all children.

Elementary
Standard 1: Knows, understands, and uses the major concepts, principles, theories, and research related to development of children to construct learning opportunities that support individual students' development, acquisition of knowledge, and motivation.

Middle Level
Standard 1: Understands the major concepts, principles, theories and research related to young adolescent development; provides opportunities that support student development and learning.

Reflect & Write

What are your beliefs about full inclusion views and practices?

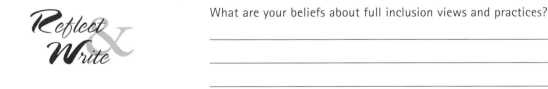

Teaching Students with Learning Disabilities

As Table 5.1 shows, students with learning disabilities comprise the largest number of students with disabilities. It is possible that you will have one or more students

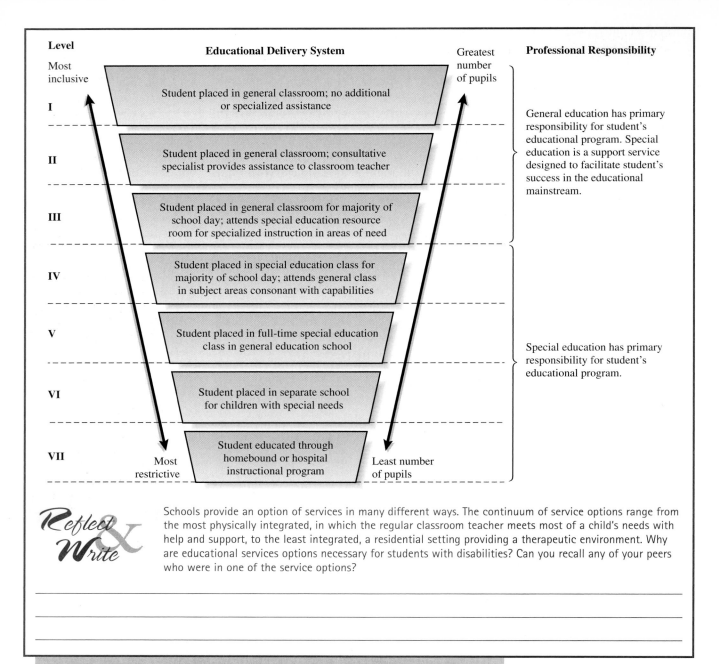

Level	Educational Delivery System	Greatest number of pupils	Professional Responsibility
Most inclusive			
I	Student placed in general classroom; no additional or specialized assistance		General education has primary responsibility for student's educational program. Special education is a support service designed to facilitate student's success in the educational mainstream.
II	Student placed in general classroom; consultative specialist provides assistance to classroom teacher		
III	Student placed in general classroom for majority of school day; attends special education resource room for specialized instruction in areas of need		
IV	Student placed in special education class for majority of school day; attends general class in subject areas consonant with capabilities		Special education has primary responsibility for student's educational program.
V	Student placed in full-time special education class in general education school		
VI	Student placed in separate school for children with special needs		
VII	Student educated through homebound or hospital instructional program	Least number of pupils	

Most restrictive

Reflect & Write

Schools provide an option of services in many different ways. The continuum of service options range from the most physically integrated, in which the regular classroom teacher meets most of a child's needs with help and support, to the least integrated, a residential setting providing a therapeutic environment. Why are educational services options necessary for students with disabilities? Can you recall any of your peers who were in one of the service options?

_____

_____

_____

Figure 5.3   Educational Service Options for Students with Disabilities

Source: Extracted from M. L. Hardman, C. Drew & M. Egan, *Human Exceptionality: School, Community, and Family,* 8th ed. (Boston: Allyn & Bacon, 2005). Copyright 2005 by Allyn & Bacon. Reprinted by permission of Pearson Learning, Inc.

with learning disabilities in your classroom. The federal government defines a learning disability this way:

> The term "specific learning disability" means a disorder in one or more of the basic psychological processes involved in understanding or in using language, spoken or written, which disorder may manifest itself in an imperfect ability to listen, think, speak, read, write, or spell, or do mathematical calculations.[6]

Profile   Opening Doors: Chris

Chris is a student with an emotional disability and has required a self-contained special education classroom since the third grade. He has a great smile but otherwise is disheveled and has poor personal hygiene. He is a large student and tends to be verbally impulsive. Chris has poor interpersonal skills and therefore has difficulty being accepted by his peers. He often exhibits angry inappropriate behavior and annoys his peers and teachers; Chris seems to thrive on the negative and positive attention.

In the tenth grade, Chris was given a variety of accommodations, including one-on-one intervention strategies coupled with positive reinforcement and the opportunity to participate in a vocational program half-day. This experience has been pivotal in Chris's school success. Chris has excelled in the "hands-on" active learning environment of the half-day vocational program. Chris feels valued as a member of the program, and he is valued by his teachers, who give him many chances to succeed.

Teaching exceptional students involves constantly finding ways to open new doors to new programs and new accommodations.

Figure 5.4 displays areas of knowledge and skills needed for teaching students with learning and other disabilities in the inclusive classroom.

Teaching Students with Attention Deficit Hyperactivity Disorder (ADHD)

Students with **attention deficit hyperactivity disorder (ADHD)** generally display cognitive delays and have difficulties in three specific areas: attention, impulse control, and hyperactivity. To be classified as having ADHD, a student must display for a minimum of six months before age 7 at least eight of the characteristics outlined in Table 5.2.

ADHD is diagnosed more often in boys than in girls and occurs in about 3 to 5 percent of all students. About half of the cases are diagnosed before age 4. Frequently, the term *attention deficit disorder* (ADD) is used to refer to ADHD, but ADD is a form of learning disorder, whereas ADHD is a behavioral disorder.

> **INTASC**
>
> **Standard 3:** The teacher understands how students differ in their approaches to learning and creates instructional opportunities that are adapted to diverse learners.

Attention deficit hyperactivity disorder (ADHD)
Children with ADHD have an unusual degree of difficulty with attention and self-control, which leads to problems with learning, social functioning, and behavior that occur in more than one situation and that have been present for a significant length of time.

SECTION SUMMARY

What Are Mainstreaming and Inclusion?

Mainstreaming offers a continuum of placements and services. *Inclusion*, particularly *full inclusion*, refers to the practice of including all children with disabilities in all natural environments, such as playgrounds, child-care centers, and general education classrooms.

- The Full Inclusion Debate. The full inclusion movement has been the topic of much debate by professional groups and the public, mainly over where money for exceptional education is best spent. Court decisions and federal and state laws mandate full inclusion.

- Teaching Students with Learning Disabilities. Most teachers will at some point have in their classrooms a child with learning disabilities. The National Joint Committee on Learning Disabilities defines *learning disability* as disorders that are characterized by "significant difficulties in the acquisition and use of listening, speaking, reading, writing, reasoning, or mathematical abilities" and that are "intrinsic to the individual and presumed to be due to central nervous system dysfunction." Learning disabilities are not the same as behavioral problems or

KNOWLEDGE OF STUDENTS AND THEIR NEEDS

- Learn characteristics of students with special needs.
- Learn legislation regarding students with special needs.
- Develop a willingness to teach students with special needs.
- Foster social acceptance of students with special needs.
- Use assistive and educational technologies.

CLASSROOM LEADERSHIP AND CLASSROOM MANAGEMENT SKILLS

- Plan and manage the learning environment to accommodate students with special needs.
- Provide inclusion in varied student groupings and use peer tutoring.
- Manage the behavior of special needs students.
- Motivate all students.

KNOWLEDGE AND SKILLS IN CURRICULUM AND INSTRUCTION

- Develop and modify instruction for students with special needs.
- Use a variety of instructional styles and media and increase the range of learning behaviors.
- Provide instruction for students of all ability levels.
- Modify assessment techniques for students with special needs.
- Individualize instruction and integrate the curriculum.

PROFESSIONAL COLLABORATION SKILLS

- Work closely with special educators and other specialists.
- Work with and involve parents.
- Participate in planning and implementing IEPs.

There is a lot to know and do when teaching in an inclusive classroom or other setting. As this figure indicates, you will need special kinds of knowledge and skills about students, the curriculum, and working with others. Which of the above knowledge and skills do you possess? Which ones will you have to make a special effort to acquire?

_____

_____

_____

_____

Figure 5.4 *Effective Teaching in Inclusive Classrooms*

Table 5.2   *D*iagnostic Criteria for Attention Deficit Hyperactivity Disorder

A. Either (1) or (2)

(1) six (or more) of the following symptoms of inattention have persisted for at least 6 months to a degree that is maladaptive and inconsistent with developmental level:

Inattention

(a) often fails to give close attention to details or makes careless mistakes in school-work, work, or other activities
(b) often has difficulty sustaining attention in tasks or play activities
(c) often does not seem to listen when spoken to directly
(d) often does not follow through on instructions and fails to finish schoolwork, chores, or duties in the workplace (not due to Oppositional behavior or failure to understand instructions)
(e) often has difficulty organizing tasks and activities
(f) often avoids, dislikes, or is reluctant to engage in tasks that require sustained mental effort (such as schoolwork or homework)
(g) often loses things necessary for tasks or activities (e.g., toys, school assignments, pencils, books, or tools)
(h) is often easily distracted by extraneous stimuli

(2) six (or more) of the following symptoms of hyperactivity-impulsivity have persisted for at least 6 months to a degree that is maladaptive and inconsistent with developmental level.

Hyperactivity

(a) often fidgets with hands or feet or squirms in seat
(b) often leaves seat in classroom or in other situations in which remaining seated is expected
(c) often runs about or climbs excessively in situations in which it is inappropriate (in adolescents or adults, may be limited to subjective feelings of restlessness)
(d) often has difficulty playing or engaging in leisure activities quietly
(e) is often "on the go" or often acts as if "driven by a motor"
(f) often talks excessively

Impulsivity

(g) often blurts out answers before questions have been completed
(h) often has difficulty awaiting turn
(i) often interrupts or intrudes on others (e.g., butts into conversations or games)

B. Some hyperactive-impulsive or inattentive symptoms that caused impairment were present before age 7 years.

C. Some impairment from the symptoms is present in two or more settings (e.g., at school or work and at home).

D. There must be clear evidence of clinically significant impairment in social, academic, or occupational functioning.

E. The symptoms do not occur exclusively during the course of a Pervasive Developmental Disorder, Schizophrenia, or other Psychotic Disorder and are not better accounted for by another mental disorder (e.g., Mood Disorder, Anxiety Disorder, Dissociative Disorder, or a Personality Disorder).

Source: Table created by author from data drawn from American Psychiatric Association, *Diagnostic and Statistical Manual of Mental Disorders*, 4th ed., text rev. (Washington DC: American Psychiatric Association, 2000).

difficulties in social adjustment, though those problems may coexist with learning disabilities.

- Teaching Students with Attention Deficit Hyperactivity Disorder (ADHD). Students with ADHD tend to display cognitive delays and difficulties in attention, impulse control, and hyperactivity. ADHD occurs in about 20 percent of the student population, more often in boys than in girls.

<table>
<tr><td>

Thinking Critically
★ ★ ★ ★ ★ ★ ★ ★

</td><td>

Some teachers feel they do not have the training or support necessary to provide for the disabilities of children who will be placed in their classrooms as a result of full inclusion. Do you feel the same way? Why?

</td></tr>
</table>

_____

_____

_____

_____ ★

<table>
<tr><td>

Applying What You've Learned
★ ★ ★ ★ ★ ★ ★ ★

</td><td>

Visit several schools in your area and determine if they are providing for full inclusion. After visiting these classrooms, identify some issues of inclusion based on your observations.

</td></tr>
</table>

_____

_____

_____

_____ ★

<table>
<tr><td>

Putting Yourself in the Picture
★ ★ ★ ★ ★ ★ ★ ★

</td><td>

You have noticed that one of your students frequently engages in small skirmishes with his classmates and moves about the classroom and playground at high speed. He has trouble following directions, is often out of step with class activities, and tends to change the subject when you try to engage him in conversation. How will you decide whether this is a normal behavioral problem or the symptoms of attention deficit hyperactivity disorder? What will you do about the situation?

</td></tr>
</table>

_____

_____

_____

_____ ★

Consultation
Seeking advice and information from colleagues.

Collaboration
To work jointly and cooperatively with other professionals, parents, and community members.

How CAN PROFESSIONAL COLLABORATION ENHANCE EDUCATION IN INCLUSIVE CLASSROOMS?

As a beginning teacher in an inclusive classroom, you will want to participate in **consultation,** seeking advice and information from colleagues. You will also engage in **collaboration,** working cooperatively with a range of professionals, special educators, parents, and administrators to provide services to students with disabilities and students at risk. Some of your collaboration will involve working with

- **itinerant teachers,** who travel from school to school and provide assistance and teach students
- **resource teachers,** who provide assistance with materials and planning
- diagnosticians, who are trained to test and analyze students' strengths and weaknesses
- physical therapists, who treat physical disabilities through nonmedical means
- occupational therapists, who direct activities that develop muscular control and self-help skills
- special educators, who are trained to instruct students with special needs
- speech and language pathologists

Consultation and Collaboration

Consultation with experienced teachers, experts in the field of special education, and administrators will enable you to see your options more clearly, gain important knowledge and insight, and consider teaching and learning strategies you might not have thought of on your own. Collaboration will enable you to implement intervention strategies and try new approaches with the help and support of others. Such collaboration and consultation will enable you to gain the knowledge and skills you need to modify curricula, teaching strategies, and your classroom environment for students with disabilities. Refer to Figure 5.3 (p. 156) for areas of skills and knowledge needed in teaching all students in inclusive classrooms.

Consultation and collaboration will also enable you to work with others in planning what you will do and how best to meet the needs of students in your classroom. Discussing students' needs and how best to meet them with other colleagues, especially exceptional education educators, is an essential component of successful teaching and learning in the inclusive classroom. As a classroom teacher, you will be expected to provide information and ideas about content knowledge, curriculum objectives, curriculum sequence, and content evaluation. Exceptional education educators can be expected to contribute information about disabilities, learning and motivational strategies that work with students with disabilities, and ideas about how to adapt curriculum to meet students' special needs.

Consultation and collaboration also include working with and involving parents, families, and members of community agencies. The development of an IEP requires that you work closely with parents in developing learning and evaluation goals for students with disabilities. Also, some parents may want to spend time in your classroom to help you meet the needs of their children. All parents have information about their children's needs, growth, and development that will be helpful to you as you plan and teach. Here are some things you will want to consider when you collaborate in developing an IEP or IFSP:

- Involve parents. Involving and working with parents is an absolute must for every classroom professional. You should learn all you can about parent conferences and communication, parent involvement, and parents as volunteers and aides. IDEA emphasizes parent participation as well as that of children.
- Collaborate and cooperate. Working with all levels of professionals offers a unique opportunity for you to individualize instruction. Since it is obvious that all professionals need help in individualizing instruction, it makes sense to involve all professionals in this process.
- Assess needs. As individual education becomes a reality for all children and families, you will want to develop skills in assessing student behavior and family background and settings.
- Consider students' learning styles. Taking into account the visual, auditory, and tactile/kinesthetic learning styles of all students helps to provide for special

Itinerant teachers
Professionals who travel from school to school or district to district and provide assistance and teach students.

Resource teachers
Professionals who provide assistance with materials and planning for teachers of exceptional students and teachers in mainstreamed classrooms.

INTASC

Standard 10: The teacher fosters relationships with school colleagues, parents, and agencies in the larger community to support students' learning and well-being.

Middle Level
Standard 6: Understands the major concepts, principles, theories, and research related to working collaboratively with family and community members; uses that knowledge to maximize learning of all young adolescents.

Early Childhood
Standard 5: Uses ethical guidelines and other professional standards; is a continuous, collaborative learner who demonstrates knowledgeable, reflective, and critical perspectives; is an informed advocate for sound educational practices.

Elementary
Standard 5.2: Is aware of and reflects on practice in light of research on teaching and resources available for professional learning; continually evaluates effects of professional decisions and actions on students, parents, and other professionals; actively seeks opportunities to grow professionally

needs. Some students may learn best through one mode; other students, through another.

You may have one or more full- or part-time aides in your classroom, depending on the number of students with disabilities and the nature of their disabilities. Classroom assistants can help you in providing multimodal instruction and assessing students' skills. Consultation and collaboration with aides is a key part of your being a successful teacher and providing the best for your students.

Administrators also play a key role in professional consultation and collaboration. Administrators can help you with the legal, political, and procedural matters of teaching students with special needs in your classroom. Administrators also can help you with planning by providing more planning time, making opportunities for special education and general education teachers to plan together, and employing a "floating substitute" to aid teachers and increase release time for teacher planning. In supporting co-teaching partnerships, administrators also can give you access to a network of additional services, information, and resources.

Cooperative teaching
The process by which a regular classroom teacher and a special educator or a person trained in exceptional student education team teach, in the same classroom, a group of regular and mainstreamed students.

Co-Teaching

Cooperative teaching, also known as co-teaching or collaborative teaching, is the process by which a classroom teacher and a special educator trained in exceptional student education teach together in the same mainstreamed classroom. Both professionals consult and collaborate to plan instruction and teach in the mainstreamed setting, and both are responsible for the instructional process. (See the Profile.)

SECTION SUMMARY

How Can Professional Collaboration Enhance Education in Inclusive Classrooms?

Teachers consult and collaborate with a range of other professionals in educating students with disabilities in the general education classroom. As a beginning teacher, you will consult and collaborate with itinerant and resource teachers, diagnosticians, physical and occupational therapists, special educators, and parents.

- Consultation and Collaboration. Teachers consult with colleagues to gain advice and information, and they collaborate with a wide range of professionals to provide services to students with disabilities and students at risk. Teachers also consult and collaborate with administrators, parents, and school aides. Things to consider in developing an IEP or IFSP include involving parents, collaborating with professionals, assessing needs, and considering student learning styles.
- Co-teaching. In cooperative teaching, also known as co-teaching or collaborative teaching, a classroom teacher and a special educator trained in exceptional student education share responsibility for the instructional process. They consult and collaborate to plan instruction and teach in a mainstreamed setting.

Thinking Critically
★ ☆ ★ ☆ ★ ☆ ★ ☆ ★

What main concern would you have about co-teaching a class? How would you address that concern?

_____

_____

_____

_____ ★

It Takes Two! Co-Teaching and Collaboration: Susan Heintz and Kim Richardson

Susan Heintz, a special educator, and Kim Richardson, a classroom teacher, developed and nurtured a classroom environment in their Florida school conducive to meeting the needs of all students.

Before developing this model classroom of inclusion, Susan was delivering her services through a traditional resource pull-out program—students would attend her classroom for a portion of their academics and spend the remainder of the day in the general education classroom—and Kim, a first-grade teacher, sent students to Susan's room. As a special educator, Susan felt that the students' learning was fragmented and that they appeared to miss social opportunities in their classroom during their scheduled time with her. It was difficult to work on a reading strategy when these students knew their classmates were outside for an extra recess or having a party! Kim felt the students had limited classroom time with their peers and had difficulty with general classroom behaviors. She also experienced frustration with the scheduling challenges and the fragmentation of learning opportunities.

Susan and Kim felt the best way to meet students' needs was to increase their success level in their general education classroom. Both highly innovative educators brought varied expertise to their classroom. Combining and sharing their methods in the environment in which the student was expected to learn became the viable solution. Kim and Susan merged their strategies into one unified system structured to meet the unique needs of all students. The result, called co-teaching, created a dynamic, fun, high-energy classroom environment that promoted increased learning for the students and teachers.

Initially, Susan observed in Kim's general education classroom to obtain information about the current instructional environment. Susan and Kim met prior to the school year to define their roles and academic and behavioral expectations. Parent involvement was identified as an important aspect of their program. Both educators began planning and scheduling on a weekly basis, discussing curriculum and instructional strategies to address all learning styles. Kim and Susan agreed to share ownership of all students in the classroom. This would offer the teachers the opportunity to use their skills with a wide range of students and to integrate the students with disabilities successfully. Individualized educational programs (IEPs), parent input, and informal observations of the learners were all tools used in developing effective instructional strategies at the beginning of the year. Susan worked daily with Kim in the general education classroom with twenty-four students: four identified as specific learning disabled, two with emotional disabilities, and one with hearing impairment.

Co-teaching requires organizing, sharing, committing, planning, understanding, and supporting in a flexible learning environment. It encourages teachers to take risks together. Susan assisted with the room arrangement in the general education classroom, incorporating learning centers to address the learning styles of all students. These learning centers became an integral component of the inclusion classroom, providing students with interactive tasks based on their learning needs and addressing varying needs by emphasizing visual, auditory, and kinesthetic pathways to learning. This kind of differentiated instruction meets all the instructional needs of every student in the classroom. Susan, the special educator, assumed responsibility for teaching students how to use the centers and provided Kim with resources based on preplanned objectives. The strategies and techniques Susan brought into the classroom varied depending on the needs of the individual students. Flexible instructional groupings were formed, based on a variety of assessment data, formal and informal. The lessons often incorporated cooperative learning strategies, multisensory learning centers, auditory/visual cues for comprehension of directions, creative learning, problem solving, and computerized instruction to be carried out by both instructors through student-centered learning.

The students in this inclusive environment were encouraged to work together and be resources for one another just as the teachers were modeling this behavior on a daily basis. The auditory input coupled with visual stimuli to increase the comprehension of directions for independent tasks was quite beneficial for all students. The changes in classroom practice required Kim and Susan to use a full circle process in evaluation of the program. Instructional strategies were evaluated, modifications made if necessary, and a new action plan implemented. This continual collaborative evaluation of instruction and student learning determined strategies needed for mastery. If and when any of the students did not experience success or mastery of a specific skill, Kim and Susan reevaluated the mode of delivery and retaught the skill before moving on—so mastery was an expected outcome for all students. The assessment methods drove the changes in instruction to revolve around learning and, ultimately, increased student achievement.

Kim and Susan developed an appreciation for each other's talents and challenges. All students benefited from having two teachers in the classroom because it reduced the student/teacher ratio and provided various instructional strategies that addressed all learning styles. Students became risk takers and intrinsically valued their achievements because of their teachers' and peers' encouragement. Students given this opportunity have shown significant academic and behavioral growth through their academic careers.

NCATE

Elementary

Standard 5.1: Understands and applies practices and behaviors that are characteristic of developing career teachers.

Early Childhood

Standard 5: Uses ethical guidelines and other professional standards; is a continuous, collaborative learner who demonstrates knowledgeable, reflective, and critical perspectives; is an informed advocate for sound educational practices.

The range of school-community partnerships and community-based programs that cooperate with public schools is increasing. Many agencies, such as the Urban League, work with schools to help provide special funding and support. Visit several local schools in your area and determine the kinds of community-based programs that are used to help provide for the special needs of students. In addition, investigate the sources of information about students with disabilities available through the ERIC Clearinghouse on Disabilities and Gifted Education (www.ericec.org).

★

Envision that prior to the beginning of the school year, Kim took a leave of absence from teaching, and you were placed in the program to co-teach. What steps would you take to begin this collaborative process with Susan?

★

*H*OW CAN YOU TEACH EXCEPTIONAL LEARNERS IN YOUR CLASSROOM*?*

You will need to make adjustments in your classroom arrangement, curriculum, and teaching plan to provide for the special needs of all your students. Here are some of the things you can do:

- Assess the individual learning needs of all your students and determine which students' needs require special attention and accommodation. In some cases, your students' assessments may already be made, but you will be involved in determining how to meet needs and how they change during the school year. Like all classroom teachers, you will be involved in evaluating all students' abilities, referring students for further evaluation, and participating in the planning and writing of IEPs.
- Determine which special needs of your students you can meet without assistance and which you may need help with. You will want to learn all you can about the particular disabilities of your students. For example, you can learn about the causes of Down syndrome and about interventions and accommodations. You can consult with the former teacher of your students, with other exceptional student educators, and school district specialists for advice and for collaborative planning. Also, be sure to consult with and involve your students' parents. They have a wealth of knowledge about the teaching and parenting of their children.
- Determine what special training you may need. You may need to attend workshops on classroom management strategies and behavior management techniques for mainstreamed and inclusive settings. Getting the appropriate training and education is an important part of learning how to help students with special needs. Most school districts have staff development programs designed to help school faculty

and staff meet job demands. District 24, in Queens, New York, employs full-time inclusion facilitators who are in the classroom every week. Facilitators regularly address teacher attitudes, beliefs, and practice issues where they are teaching.[7] In this way, facilitators can affect how teachers do their job, provide meaningful support, and address both school culture and quality of teaching. An excellent site that offers information, guidelines, and techniques for teachers and parents is the Circle of Inclusion Web site, sponsored by the U.S. Department of Education, Office of Special Education and available online at http://circleofinclusion.org. At Dorseyville Middle School in Pittsburgh, staff development has been a key to successful inclusion. Teacher training was provided through Gateways: Pennsylvania Statewide System Project, whose staff provided on-site technical assistance to support inclusion efforts.[8]

- **Determine what instructional accommodations you must make for individual students.** You will need to be creative and flexible in adapting curriculum and instruction for all students. For instance, you can use small-group and large-group instruction, cooperative learning, opportunities for individualized instruction, and self-paced student learning.
- **Determine what accommodations you must make in the classroom environment to provide for students' special needs.** You will need to be aware of all of the needs of the students in your classroom.
- **Determine what you must do to educate students to be accepting of and helpful toward students with special needs.** Social acceptance is often the key to success for students with disabilities in mainstreamed settings. Educate your class about student disabilities, the special accommodations needed for learning and for behaving well, and how they can help all their classmates be fully functioning members of the class.

Using Assistive Technology

Public Law 100-407, the Technology-Related Assistance for Individuals with Disabilities Act (Tech Act), defines an **assistive technology device** as "any item, device or piece of equipment, or product system, whether acquired commercially off the shelf, modified, or customized, that is used to increase, maintain, or improve functional abilities of individuals with disabilities."[9]

Assistive technology covers a range of products and applications from simple devices, such as adaptive spoons and switch-adapted battery-operated toys, to recordings for the blind, to complex devices, such as computerized environmental control systems. You will have opportunities to use many forms of assistive technology and modified educational software with all ages of students with special needs.

Assistive technology is particularly important for students with disabilities who depend on technology to assist them to communicate, learn, and be mobile. (See the Profile.) For example, closed-circuit television can be used to enlarge print, a Braille printer can convert words to Braille, and audiotaped instructional materials can be provided for students with vision impairments. Closed-captioned television and FM amplification systems can assist students who are deaf or hard of hearing. Classroom amplification systems are becoming more common in classrooms to assist all students in hearing and listening. Touch-screen computers, augmentative communication boards, and voice synthesizers can assist students with limited mobility or with disabilities that make communication difficult. In addition, computer-assisted instruction provides software tools for teaching students at all ability levels, including programmed instruction for students with specific learning disabilities. (See Profile of Jonathan.)

Teaching Gifted Learners

The Jacob K. Javits Gifted and Talented Students Education Act of 2001 (originally passed in 1988) defines gifted and talented children as those who "give evidence of

Meet Jonathan, a five-year-old kindergarten student with a quick, engaging smile. Jonathan also has lots of courage and is a power user of technology. Medically speaking, Jonathan is ventilator dependent and has quadraplegia. He is able to move his head, but has no movement from his neck down. A nurse is with him at school, assisting with his physical needs. With the help of a committed family and school team, positive attitudes, and some adaptive technology, Jonathan has successfully been included in a general education kindergarten classroom in the Charlotte-Mecklenburg (North Carolina) schools.

When Jonathan began attending a preschool exceptional children's classroom at Reid Park Preschool, his school-based team included his parents, the teacher, the physical therapist, and myself, the occupational therapist. We all immediately began working on low- and high-tech strategies that might allow Jonathan to experience success with the curriculum and participate equally with his fellow students.

Jonathan, his mother, nurse, and the rest of the team visited CCAC (Carolina Computer Access Center) in October of that year to determine the most effective way for him to use a computer. A sensitive switch mounted on the end of a flexible gooseneck rod (Ultimate Switch by Enabling Devices) was felt to be the easiest for Jonathan to use at that time, since his neck muscles were weak. The switch was positioned so that he pushed it with his chin. With the addition of a Macintosh interface and switch-compatible software (Blocks in Motion by Don Johnston, Inc.), Jonathan used the classroom computer as well as other electronic devices, like a tape player. In fact, Jonathan was the "music master" when the class played musical chairs, and he operated the blender for many cooking activities.

His long-awaited power wheelchair came in February of 1995. Using a chin control (he was a pro by then), he practiced cruising down the school hallways with his physical therapist

by his side. As his neck strength and head control improved, the team decided a head pointer would give Jonathan a more direct option for using the computer keyboard. He had already tried a commercially available (Zygo) head pointer for manipulating materials in class and for doing art work. I collaborated with another local occupational therapist to make a customized one. This gave Jonathan even more opportunities to use the computer, turn book pages, activate push-button toys, and play games.

Now he became a real technology power user. He worked with his head pointer throughout the summer and started kindergarten in 1996, excited and anxious about new adventures.

In his Reid Park Elementary School classroom this year, Jonathan participates in the usual kindergarten activities, including circle time, centers, and French. He answers questions, recites, and directs his classmates (although never out of turn). Some of his high-tech tools are a Ke:nx interface by Don Johnston, Inc., and a Tash mini-keyboard, used with his customized head pointer. Often Jonathan works cooperatively with a friend at the computer for literacy and math activities. He is also learning to maneuver his power wheelchair carefully within his classroom. Sometimes he even plays "catch me" during recess with his friends and teachers.

I think I can speak for Jonathan's team when I say that he truly is an example of the power that technology can bring to a child with a severe physical disability. Our team will continue to learn and adapt to Jonathan's changing needs, helping him to participate to his maximum potential in each new school adventure. As technology advances and the academic demands of each grade level change, we all will be seeking even better ways for him to become a successful and contributing student. Jonathan and his team are looking forward to the challenge![15]

Gifted
Students with the potential for high performance because of strengths in one or more of the following areas: general intellectual ability, specific academic aptitude, creative or productive thinking, leadership ability, ability in the visual or performing arts, and psychomotor ability.

Talented
Exceptional students who demonstrate excellence in drama, art, music, athletics, or leadership.

Acceleration
Involves moving students through the curriculum as rapidly as they are able and to the extent that acceleration is in their best interests.

high performance capability in areas such as intellectual, creative, artistic, or leadership capacity, or in specific academic fields, and who require services or activities not ordinarily provided by the school in order to fully develop such capabilities."[10] The definition distinguishes between **gifted,** referring to above-average intellectual ability, and **talented,** referring to excellence in drama, art, music, athletics, or leadership. Students can have these abilities separately or in combination. About 10 to 20 percent of students are gifted. States and local school districts have varying definitions of gifted and talented. They also have different criteria for determining how gifted and talented is evaluated. It seems clear that districts tend to be very inclusive of identifying students as gifted and talented.

Students with disabilities are among the gifted and talented. A talented five-year-old may have a learning disability, for example, and a student with physical disabilities may be gifted. Like low-income and minority students, students with disabilities are disproportionately underrepresented in the ranks of students identified as gifted and talented.

Acceleration and enrichment are two traditional ways of providing for the needs of students who are gifted and talented. **Acceleration** involves moving students through the curriculum as rapidly as they are able and to the extent that acceleration is in their best interests. Some approaches to acceleration include early entrance into programs—for example, early entrance to kindergarten and first grade, middle school, high school, and college. Other acceleration methods include skipping grades, taking extra courses or honors courses, participating in advanced placement programs, and completing high school in two or three years.

In inclusive schools, acceleration is provided in the general education classroom through special instructional programs such as **curriculum compacting** and accelerated integrated learning. In these programs, students who are gifted and talented study the same themes and topics as their classmates but in greater depth or detail and with greater opportunities for real-world applications. Also, in inclusive schools, all students may have access to activities for gifted and talented learners through schoolwide enrichment programs.

Enrichment is the process of offering students additional activities and experiences not usually found in the curriculum. Enrichment activities occur through many arrangements in addition to enrichment within the classroom. These arrangements include the use of a resource teacher who consults and plans with the classroom teacher; pull-out programs, in which students go to a resource room where they are taught by a resource teacher; independent study; group instruction of students who are gifted across grade levels; special classes outside of the school setting; and apprenticeship and mentorship programs. For more information about the changing rules for gifted programs, see Education on the Move.

Apprenticeship programs pair students with people in the community for periods of time; students acquire knowledge and skills through direct observation and practice. **Mentoring programs** provide students with adults who can offer them assistance in learning inside or outside of the classroom. Mentoring is a growing option for all students with special needs. Mentors can supply what students need most—the support, encouragement, assistance, and guidance that make it possible for them to succeed. Mentoring can take many forms. Typically, students set the agenda based on their own goals and interests. The relationship can focus on career goals, community service, cultural enrichment, common heritage, social skills, or talents such as art or sports. Although mentoring does not necessarily focus on academic achievement, and

Curriculum compacting
Students who are gifted and talented study the same themes and topics as their classmates but in greater depth or detail than their classmates and with greater opportunities for real-world applications.

Enrichment
The process of offering students additional activities and experiences not usually found in the curriculum.

Apprenticeship programs
Programs that pair students with people in the community for periods of time during which students acquire knowledge and skills through direct observation and practice.

Mentoring programs
Support systems aimed at enhancing academic success and self-esteem of at-risk students, also programs to help new teachers.

---

e d u c a t i o n *on the move* >>>>>>>>>>>>

>>> Increasing Minorities in Gifted Programs >>>>>>>

TiShanna Smith is an eleven-year-old African American from a single-parent family who was identified as gifted by a special test intended to boost minorities. Under South Carolina's old rules, TiShanna wouldn't be considered gifted. Under its new rules, she is. Every Tuesday, the fifth-grader at Greenview Elementary, in Greenville, South Carolina, attends a three-hour advanced class in which she studies algebra and researches topics such as the history of hot air balloons.

Around the country and especially in the South, new tests are propelling more minority students into predominantly white gifted education programs. Proponents applaud what they say is an overdue easing of racial disparities in gifted education, stressing that the special classes can open greater opportunities for blacks, Hispanics, and Native Americans.

But it's not that simple. By changing the standards for gifted education, traditionalists say, school districts seeking classroom equity are undermining academic excellence.

Aided by the new test, Greenville has nearly doubled the numbers of black gifted students to 606, or 7.6% of gifted students, up from 320 in 1999–2000. Gifted white students have increased 43.4%, to 7,027, from 4,904 in 1999–2000.

Greenville has also tailored its gifted curriculum to students who have difficulty reading by emphasizing hands-on lessons. In math, third- through fifth-graders simplify algebraic equations by removing number cubes and chess pawns, which stand for the unknown X, from either side of a scale. Once they have mastered this approach, it is easier for them to make the leap to abstract equations and working on paper.

Source: D. Golden, "Boosting Minorities in Gifted Programs Poses Dilemmas," *Wall Street Journal*, April 7, 2004, pp. A1–A14. Reprinted by permission.

Gifted and talented students provide many challenges for teachers. Generally, the gifted are very bright and quickly grasp ideas and concepts. Many schools have programs specifically designed to meet their needs. Identify some things you will be able to do to meet the needs of the gifted and talented in your classroom.

hus differs from tutoring, the student and mentor may jointly decide to work on study skills or classroom projects. For example, Joyce Stoneham, director of the Mentor-Works program in Fairfax County Public Schools in Virginia, pairs student council members with corporate executives to enhance the students' leadership skills.[11]

Differentiated instruction (DI) is another means of providing for the needs of all students. In differentiated instruction, teachers use a variety of methods, materials, and activities to meet the needs of all students. In addition, teachers offer students a number of learning options that will enable students to meet learning goals. Carol A. Tomlinson, a twenty-year classroom veteran, states that teachers need to envision their classroom as an "escalator" going higher and higher, not as a "stairwell" that takes students to a certain grade-level landing where they stop. Tasks have to be "respectful of kids, hands-on, engaging, and thought provoking."[12] The following guidelines will help you prepare for using differentiated instruction in your classroom.

1. Differentiated instruction is *proactive*.
   The teacher assumes that different learners have differing needs and proactively plans a variety of ways to "get at" and express learning.
2. Differentiated instruction is more *qualitative* than quantitative.
   Differentiated instruction focuses more on understanding concepts than on producing work. However, it does not necessarily mean giving some students less work to do. Rather, the emphasis is on adjusting the nature of an assignment to match students' learning characteristics as opposed to merely increasing the quantity of the assignment.
3. Differentiated instruction provides *multiple* approaches to assessment, process, and product.
   Teachers offer different practices and approaches based on how individual students learn and how they demonstrate what they have learned. What these different practices and approaches must have in common, however, is that they are

Differentiated instruction (DI)
Using a variety of methods, materials, and activities to meet the learning needs of all students.

crafted to encourage substantial growth in all students and are based on high standards for all students.

4. Differentiated instruction is *student centered*.

   Learning experiences are most effective when they are engaging, relevant, and interesting. All students will not always find the same avenues to learning equally engaging, relevant, and interesting. Understandings must be built on previous understandings, and not all students possess the same background knowledge at the outset of a given investigation.

5. Differentiated instruction is a *blend of instruction*, including whole-class, group, and individual instruction.

   There are times in all classrooms when it is more effective or efficient to share information or use the same activity with the whole class. Such whole-group instruction establishes common understandings and a sense of community for students by sharing discussion and review.

Kari Sue Wehrmann teaches English at Hopkins West Junior High School in Minnetonka, Minnesota. She relates one way that she differentiates instruction for some of the gifted students in her class. In differentiating content for a small group, her objective was to create an individualized, alternative learning experience for talented writers during a formula essay unit so that gifted students might show growth and retain an interest in writing.

> Four of my English 9 students had demonstrated their mastery of the formula essay, so I gave them the option to demonstrate their growth in writing in an independent study format or to do a series of formula essays with the general class. All four students chose the independent study option.
>
> Each student developed a different project. One student penned an essay and entered it in a creative writing contest. Another student wanted to work on using colorful details in her narrative writing. Her incredible first draft was ten single-spaced pages. The third student read *A Prayer for Owen Meany* and wrote a comparison/contrast paper of the book and the movie *Simon Birch*. The fourth student researched influential figures from the Civil Rights movement and wrote a historical fiction piece.
>
> This learning opportunity allowed four students to work on the same concept that the rest of the class was working on but allowed for individual differentiation of curriculum in content and process. The product, a paper, was the same for all students.[13]

Some Web sites that can help and inform you about differentiated instruction are http://web.uvic.ca/~jdurkin/edd40isu/Differentiated.html and www.ascd.org/pdi/demoe/diffinstr/differentiated1.html.

As a beginning teacher, you will want to be aware of the characteristics of gifted learners. Students who are gifted tend to get their work done quickly, often seek additional work, ask probing questions, prefer to select their own learning activities, have a greater depth of understanding of topics, and have interests in areas that are more like the interests of older students. Some gifted learners may have difficulty with social adjustment or may be underachievers, but research shows that students who are gifted and talented tend to be successful in a range of contexts.

More likely than not, you will have to provide for students who are gifted and talented in your classroom. Here are some of the things you can do to help meet their needs:

- Avoid treating their probing questions as challenges to your authority or expertise.
- Provide alternative projects and activities that introduce greater novelty and complexity.
- Help students achieve a level of sophistication on advanced material.
- Arrange independent studies based on, but extending, the curriculum.
- Arrange for students to self-select and self-monitor alternative assignments.

NCATE

Middle Level

Standard 5: Understands and uses major concepts, principles, theories, and research related to effective instruction and assessment; employs a variety of strategies for a developmentally appropriate climate to meet the varying abilities and learning styles of all young adolescents.

INTASC

Standard 4: The teacher uses various instructional strategies to encourage students' development of critical thinking, problem solving, and performance skills.

- Arrange for students to contract for specific projects and grades.
- Allow students the extra time they may need to explore a topic to a satisfying depth.
- Connect students with opportunities to participate in science fairs and similar programs that give them opportunities to use their talents and abilities.
- Connect students with opportunities to contribute to others or to the community through their talents and abilities, such as arranging for them to be peer or cross-age tutors or creative contributors to community service initiatives.
- Encourage and reward creativity and critical thinking in all your students.

Reflect & Write

What other steps could you take to meet the needs of gifted and talented students while teaching all students in your class?

_____

_____

_____

_____

SECTION SUMMARY

How Can You Teach Exceptional Learners in Your Classroom?

To provide for the special needs of all students, teachers must adjust their classroom environment, curricula, and teaching approach. Among other things, teachers must (1) assess the needs of all students, (2) determine which needs students can meet without assistance and which will require special help, (3) consider areas in which students need special training, (4) determine what instructional and classroom accommodations are necessary for individual students, and (5) decide what to do to educate other students to be accepting of and helpful toward their classmates with special needs.

- Using Assistive Technology. Assistive technology covers a range of products and applications, from low technology, such as modifications of writing surfaces, to high technology, such as computers with synthesized speech. As a beginning teacher, you will want to use assistive technology and computer-assisted instruction that is appropriate for students and helps them learn.

- Teaching Gifted Learners. Acceleration, enrichment, curriculum compacting, integration, apprenticeship and mentoring programs, and differentiated instruction are among the approaches used in educating students who are gifted and talented. Students with disabilities can also be among the gifted and talented.

Thinking Critically

★ ★ ★ ★ ★ ★ ★ ★ ★

Which do you think would be more challenging—teaching gifted and talented students, or teaching students with learning disabilities? Does your answer give you any insight into your strengths as a teacher?

_____

_____

_____

_____ ★

How might a school identify gifted and talented students? To find out, observe a class or program for gifted and talented students. Start by recording characteristics of student communication and performance that may have contributed to their being identified as exceptional learners. Then talk with the teacher of that class and ask how that school identified those students.

Read through the Profile in this section and imagine that you have Jonathan in your class. Design an activity or class project that Jonathan and all the other students in your class could carry out, using the tape recorder.

WHAT FACTORS PLACE STUDENTS AT RISK AND AFFECT TEACHING AND LEARNING?

Students with disabilities are, as discussed, at risk because of their disabilities and many other factors as well, such as socio-economic status and other risk factors shown in Figure 5.5. Students without disabilities face these same risk factors. You can expect to have in your classroom **students at risk**—children and youth who are in danger of failing in school and/or dropping out. Children and youth are at risk from certain life experiences that can negatively impact the processes of development and maturation. Risk factors affect students' academic performance and may become serious or long-term problems for the student. Before going further, list some risk factors in students' lives. Then compare your response to the risk factors listed in Figure 5.5.

Children and youth are placed at risk by economic and political forces and social problems in their families and communities. The effects of risks on children's health, safety, growth, and development and on their learning and academic success depend mainly on their age, the number of risk factors in their environment and degree of exposure to them, and family and community resources for reducing or eliminating the sources and effects of those risk factors. Supportive families, good schools, caring teachers, and responsive communities can make all the difference in the world to students when they are at risk.

The risks that American children and youth face today are a national concern. According to the Centers for Disease Control and Prevention, the youth of today face risk factors that include tobacco use; unhealthy dietary behaviors; inadequate physical activity; alcohol and other drug use; and sexual behaviors that may result in HIV infection, other sexually transmitted diseases, and unintended pregnancies. The National Middle School Association has developed the program Safe Passage: Voices from the Middle School in order to help young people navigate though their

NCATE

Early Childhood

Standard 1: Uses understanding of young children's characteristics, needs, and interacting influences on children's development and learning to create healthy, respectful, supportive, and challenging environments for all children.

Elementary

Standard 1: Knows, understands, and uses the major concepts, principles, theories, and research related to development of children to construct learning opportunities that support individual students' development, acquisition of knowledge, and motivation.

Middle Level

Standard 1: Understands the major concepts, principles, theories and research related to young adolescent development; provides opportunities that support student development and learning.

Students at risk
Students whose living conditions and backgrounds place them at risk for dropping out of school.

Risk Factors	Characteristics

Risk Factors

- Alienation from school (feelings of not belonging)
- Low SES—lives below the poverty level
- Minority status
- Non-English or limited English speaking
- Dysfunctional family (abuse, drug use, etc.)
- Lives in community/neighborhood with gang activity, high crime, drug use, etc.
- Transient (moves a lot, unstable home life)
- Families have low educational levels
- Poor health and nutrition
- Teenage pregnancy
- Single-parent family

Characteristics

- Truancy/poor school attendance
- Suspension/expulsion from school
- Delinquency
- Grade failure
- Poor school achievement/low test scores
- Low or no involvement in school activities
- Drug use
- School behavior problems
- Not interested in school
- Not cooperative in class

Reflect & Write

The growing number of students who are defined as at risk presents challenges to all educators. Do you think society asks too much of teachers and schools in the prevention and controlling of student risk factors? State your reasons, pro and con.

Figure 5.5 *R*isk Factors and Characteristics of Students at Risk

adolescent years safely and securely. Safe Passage calls for schools that are safe, adults who are caring and involved, safety nets that are in place when things get difficult, elimination of the power of the bully, and reaching high academic goals. You can read more about the Safe Passage program at www.courttv.com/safepassage/index.html.

Many students, individually and as groups, face barriers to learning and developing to their full potential. Review once again risk factors and characteristics of students at risk in Figure 5.5. Students can come to school tired, hungry, abused, neglected, and from homes where adults are not supportive of children or their learning. Other students live in poverty, have AIDS, suffer from substance abuse, or live in fear of neighborhood violence. Teenage students may have children at a young age and before they graduate from high school. These and other factors place students at risk for failure and affect their development toward a mature and productive adulthood. In addition, these students often deal with their problems in ways that negatively influence their attitudes and values, their mental and physical health, and their outlook on life, thus further increasing their chances of failure, both in school and long term.

Poverty

Almost 17 percent (more than 12 million) of all children in the United States under age 18 live in poverty. About 30 percent of African American children live in poverty. Poverty rates for Hispanic American children are 28.6 percent overall.[14]

Living in poverty means families do not have the income to purchase adequate health care, housing, food, clothing, and education services. In 2004, poverty for a nonfarm family of four meant an income of less than $18,307. The federal government annually revises its poverty guidelines, which are the basis for distribution of federal aid to schools and student eligibility for services such as Head Start, and free and reduced school breakfasts and lunches.

Homelessness can be a consequence of poverty. The Stewart B. McKinney Homeless Assistance Act protects the right of homeless children to attend public school. The act also established the Education of Homeless Children and Youth (EHCY) program. This program provides grants to school districts to provide additional ser-

>>> Finding Ways to Educate Children of Homeless Families >>>>>>

The Thomas J. Pappas School in Tempe, Arizona, founded in 1989, now comprises two schools: the new Pappas School built for children kindergarten through fifth grade, and the old location, now the Pappas Junior High and High School.

The Pappas schools are accommodation public schools for children from homeless families. Throughout the school year, the Pappas teachers will educate over 2,000 children, with as many as 750 enrolled on a daily basis. It is the only school of its kind in the United States.

T. J. Pappas provides a wide array of services for its students, and the community helps a great deal by volunteering, mentoring, and providing us with donations of money, school supplies, clothing, shoes, socks,

underwear, and hygiene items for the clothing room. Also, food items are donated for food boxes that are available for families in need. Gifts for birthday parties are also generously given.

The medical clinic has doctors who donate their valuable time to help the children get the medical attention they otherwise would not have. Dentists are also kind in donating office visits to the children. Generous companies also provide vision services.

The library is equipped with over 13,000 donated books. The children use the library as their public library. Computers in the reading lab allow the children an opportunity to get caught up to their grade level.

One reason Pappas is so successful is due to the transportation provided

by nine buses. They collectively travel 350 miles to pick up the children, no matter where they are or how often they move. There could be fifteen to thirty changes a day because of the transitional lifestyles of the families. The outreach department locates families, makes home visits, and keeps up with all of the bus changes. The beauty of Pappas is that the families do not have to continually enroll their children in different schools. During a school year, over 1,200 students and their families will receive services through the outreach department. Visit the Pappas School at www. tjpappasschool.org/.

vices for homeless children. The Thomas J. Pappas School in Tempe, Arizona, is the largest school for homeless children in the United States, with 500 children in grades K through 12. Education on the Move discusses one community's efforts to make sure homeless children maintain their right to an education.

Children and youth have no control over the social, economic, and family conditions that contribute to the conditions of poverty. Living in a rural community and in a rural southern state increases the likelihood that families will live in poverty. Cities with the highest number of school-age children living in poverty are in the South and East. Also, living in the inner city means that the chances of being poor are higher. With increases in rural and urban poverty go decreases in wealth and support for education. This, in turn, means that as a whole, children living in poverty will attend schools that have fewer resources and poorer facilities.

The effects of poverty are detrimental to students' achievement and life prospects. For example, children and youth from low-income families are often older than others in their grade level, move more slowly through the educational system, are more likely to drop out, and are less likely to find work.[15] Poor children are more likely to be retained in school, and students who have repeated one or more grades are more likely to become school dropouts.[16] Poverty affects students' health prospects as well. For example, more than one-half of all children who lack insured health care come from poor families.[17]

Substance Abuse

Substance abuse includes the use of illicit drugs, alcohol, and tobacco. Some students abuse multiple substances. Drug use among teenagers has been on the rise since 1992. In 2002, 47.8 percent of high school seniors reported using marijuana at least once. Overall, 53.0 percent of all high school seniors have used some form of illicit drug. Drinking is also a serious drug problem, with 30 percent of twelfth-graders engaging

> **INTASC**
>
> **Standard 2:** The teacher understands how children learn and develop, and can provide learning opportunities that support their intellectual, social and personal development.

Students face a number of factors that put their learning at risk. What are some factors not discussed here? What can and should teachers and schools do to help students at risk?

NCATE

Elementary

Standard 3.2: Understands how elementary students differ in development and approaches to learning; creates instructional opportunities that are adapted to diverse students.

in this activity.[18] Clearly, alcohol and drugs are among the foremost student problems facing schools and society. Another problem with binge drinking and early drinking is that it leads to alcoholism. Young people who start drinking before age 15 are four times more likely to become alcoholics than those who begin drinking at age 21.

Smoking is a serious health hazard for many students. While the use of tobacco is down for the population as a whole, its use by teenagers, especially female teenagers, is on the rise. Each year more than a million young people start smoking.[19] Cigarette smoking is seen as a "gateway function" to the use of other drugs, and programs designed to inhibit, prevent, or stop smoking are seen as critical in helping students lead healthy lifestyles.[20]

Society looks to schools and teachers to play a major role in the delivery of programs to prevent substance abuse. As a result, schools are a major factor in the delivery of programs to prevent the use of drugs, alcohol, and tobacco. These programs help students be informed and empowered to decide not to use harmful substances. In Richardson, Texas, administrators, teachers, and students have established a Student Assistance Program designed to prevent substance abuse and assist students and their families, through teacher referral, to an intervention team of teachers, administrators, and counselors. Teachers use a Referral Concern Form to identify students who exhibit "signs of concern," which include low grades and achievement, absenteeism, tardiness, increased visits to the school nurse, erratic behavior, and sleeping in class.

HIV/AIDS

Acquired Immune Deficiency Syndrome (AIDS)

Acquired immune deficiency syndrome is caused by the human immunodeficiency virus (HIV). HIV weakens or destroys the immune system, thus allowing diseases and infections to develop.

AIDS, or **Acquired Immune Deficiency Syndrome,** is caused by the human immunodeficiency virus (HIV). HIV weakens or destroys the immune system, thus allowing diseases and infections to develop. The number of students with AIDS increases every year. The Centers for Disease Control (CDC) note that the number of AIDS cases reported each year among U.S. adolescents ages 13 to 14 has increased from one case in 1981 to 3,610 through 2002. In addition, CDC reports that AIDS incidence increased throughout the 1980s, declined from the mid 1990s through 2001, and increased 2 percent in 2002 (compared with 2001). During 1998–2002, the estimated number of deaths among persons with AIDS declined 14 percent. At the end of 2002, however, an estimated 384,906 persons in the United States were known to be living with AIDS.[21] While the number of AIDS cases may seem small, the problem is that the incubation period between infection and diagnosis is many years; therefore, it is likely that many more adolescents are infected than diagnosed. A further problem, according to the Centers for Disease Control, is that older teens, males, and racial and ethnic minorities are disproportionately affected.

The treatment of students with AIDS includes medical care, education, and support services. For all students, AIDS education is an essential and, in some school districts, a mandatory part of the curriculum. Many AIDS prevention programs and curricula stress abstinence, safe sex, avoidance of drugs, and nonsharing of drug equipment. Many school AIDS prevention programs begin in the elementary grades, and some states, such as Florida, have mandatory AIDS education programs that begin in kindergarten. As a beginning teacher, you will want to familiarize yourself with the AIDS policy in your school and district as well as the AIDS prevention curriculum.

Truancy and Delinquency

Being absent from school, dropping out of school, and juvenile delinquency go hand in hand. **Delinquency** is behavior that violates the rules and regulations of society. The economic consequences to individuals and society of delinquency and dropping out are very high.

Delinquency
A behavior that violates the rules and regulations of society.

Every year an increasing number of students drop out of high school. In 2001, over 200,000 students dropped out of high school. It is estimated that 4.2 percent of young adults (ages 16 to 24) were not enrolled in high school or had not completed high school. Hispanic (11 percent), African American (10 percent), and Asian American (12 percent) students are more likely to drop out of school than are white students (9 percent).[22] School dropouts represent a national tragedy of lost potential and wasted lives. High school graduates earn over $7,000 per year more than high school dropouts.[23] There are a number of risk factors that account for dropping out of school:

- Low SES quartile
- Single-parent family
- Older sibling(s) dropped out of school
- Changed schools two or more times
- Average grades of C or lower from sixth to eight grade
- Repeated a grade

Dropout rates vary by race and ethnicity. For Anglo-European Americans, it is 7.3 percent; for African Americans, 10.9 percent; and for Hispanic Americans, 27.0 percent.

Some schools are turning to **peer mediation** to prevent at-risk students from dropping out of school. Mediation is a process for resolving disputes and conflicts in which a neutral third party (or parties) acts as a moderator for the process. In mediation, the goal is to work out differences constructively. Trained students help their classmates identify the problems behind the conflicts and find solutions. Peer mediation is not about finding out who is right or wrong. Instead, students are encouraged to move beyond the immediate conflict and learn how to get along with each other—an important skill in today's world. Peer mediators ask the disputing students to tell their stories and ask questions for clarification. The mediators help the students identify ways to solve the conflict. Common situations involving name calling, spreading rumors, bumping into students in the hallways, and bullying have been successfully resolved though peer mediation. The Web sites of the Center for the Study and Prevention of Violence (www.colorado.edu/cspv) and the School Mediation Center (www.csmp.org) will help you learn more about peer mediation and other violence prevention programs.

Peer mediation
Programs in which students interact, work with, and counsel other students in solving social and behavioral problems.

Clearly, there is much the schools and the public must do to help all students, but particularly minority students, graduate from high school. Money for such efforts is well spent when such programs are successful, since 60 percent of prison inmates are school dropouts and 79 percent of teenage parents become dropouts.

Delinquent gangs are a major concern in many cities and towns across the United States. Once confined primarily to the inner city, gangs are now also active in suburban and rural areas. Reports of gang vandalism, crime, and warfare, and the resulting violence, are common on nightly television and in the daily newspapers. Schools have responded to gangs by banning gang attire in the schools, offering programs to take the place of gang participation, and educating parents and the public about the necessity for expanded school-based programs for at-risk students.

What problems can a high dropout rate lead to for a community?

_____

_____

_____

_____

Teen Pregnancy

About 1 million teenagers (11 percent of fifteen- to nineteen-year-old girls) become pregnant each year. The bad news is that the United States has the highest teenage pregnancy rate of the developed countries in the world[24]. It is twice as high as England and three times as high as France and Canada.

But there is good news. Beginning in 1991, the teenage pregnancy rate has declined. The birthrate for U.S. teenagers in 2000 was 48.7 births per 1,000 for women ages 15 through 19, the lowest level ever reported for the nation. Reasons for the declining teen pregnancy rates are multiple and interrelated. They include decreased sexual activity, reflected in public attitudes toward premarital sex; increases in condom use; and the adoption of newly available hormone contraception, implants, and injections.[25]

Consequences of Teenage Pregnancy. The consequences of teenage pregnancy, like the reasons for the decline in the pregnancy rate, are also multiple and interrelated. Teenage pregnancy has health, educational, and societal consequences.

In many regards, teenagers are children themselves and are still in the process of growing up and developing. Consequently, a pregnancy places them at a greater risk for complications relating to pregnancy and birth. In addition, unhealthy lifestyle habits and risky behaviors, such as drug use, place the child at risk as well, resulting in low birth weight, premature birth, lower cognitive functioning, and overall poor health and development of the child. Poor child health and development have many negative educational outcomes. These include lack of readiness for school, school failure, increased need for special services, and school dropout.

Public schools have many programs designed to reduce teenage pregnancy. These include sex education programs and programs designed to enhance the overall health and wellness of all students. Child abuse and prevention programs are another way to reduce teenage pregnancy. The Center on Adolescent Sexuality, Pregnancy, and Prevention reports that roughly half of teenage mothers report they had been sexually abused as children.[26] In addition, schools provide parent education classes for teenage mothers and child care for their children.

Many school districts offer teenage parenting programs (TPPs) to meet the needs of adolescent parents. These programs unite young families, teach them parenting skills, and help them achieve the goals they have set for themselves and their families. As a result, teen parents are less likely to drop out of school. Although this picture shows only teenage mothers, teenage fathers are often also included in TPP programs. Today, there is a national effort to keep teenage fathers engaged and active in the lives of their children and to have them assume responsibility for parenting.

Most teachers of adolescents can expect to have in their classroom students who are pregnant and who are parents. These young mothers are generally at risk for educational, occupational, and financial difficulties. How can you as a beginning teacher help meet the needs of teenage parents?

_____

_____

_____

_____

Violence

Violence in children's lives occurs in many forms. Child abuse and neglect have become serious problems in the United States. The Child Abuse Prevention and Treatment Act of 1974 (PL 100-294) defines abuse and neglect as the "physical or mental injury, sexual abuse, or exploitation, negligent treatment, or maltreatment of a child by a person who is responsible for the child's welfare, under circumstances which indicate the child's health or welfare is harmed or threatened."[27] There were an estimated 2.6 million reported cases of child abuse in 1999. About 900,000 children were confirmed victims of abuse or neglect in 2001.[28] The law requires that teachers report any signs or symptoms of child abuse or neglect in their students.

The National Center for Education Statistics reports that violent crimes (such as murder and assault) committed by juveniles increased steadily between 1988 and

Over the years, there has been a lot of discussion about how clothes make a difference in how students behave and achieve. Many schools and parents have jumped on the school uniform bandwagon. However, as you might suspect, the topic of school uniforms has supporters and detractors. Those who favor uniforms agree that they increase self-esteem; improve learning by focusing on academics, not fashion; level the outward appearances of social class; and save parents (and students) money. On the other hand, opponents of uniforms contend they violate students' freedom of choice, promote conformity, make more problems rather than solve them, and are an added economic burden for poor families. I'm sure you have an opinion too! You decide—what do you think about school uniforms?

Visit the National Association of Elementary School Principals (www.naesp.org/misc/uniforms.htm) for more information on this topic.

NCATE

Elementary

Standard 3.2: Understands how elementary students differ in development and approaches to learning; creates instructional opportunities that are adapted to diverse students.

2001. In the 2000–2001 school year, there were 2.7 million crimes committed at school, including over a quarter of a million serious crimes (assault, rape, and robbery) and sixty violent deaths.[29] Firearm deaths are particularly lethal for minority males who live in low-income neighborhoods. The ten- to fourteen-year-old age group has a death rate of almost 12 per 100,000 deaths, and the rate skyrockets to 140 per 1,000 deaths in the fifteen- to nineteen-year-old age group.[30]

Schools across the country are responding to school violence. These responses include violence prevention and reduction programs, discipline codes, dress codes, school uniforms, school suspension and expulsion, zero tolerance, and increased security measures. The use of violence prevention curriculum programs is one of the most popular methods. Forty-two percent of all school districts have put such programs in place to help students learn nonviolent ways to resolve disputes. Many view school uniforms as a means of dealing with school violence and other school problems. According to the National Association of Elementary and Secondary Principals, about 20 percent of the nation's schools have uniform policies in place (www.naesp.org).

In Long Beach, California, students, teachers, parents, and school officials worked together to establish a uniform code for all elementary and middle schools. Each school chooses what its uniform will look like. In addition, students can "opt out" of wearing a uniform if they have their parents' approval. The Long Beach program involves 58,000 students and includes assistance for families that cannot afford to buy uniforms. In many Long Beach schools, graduating students donate or sell their used uniforms to needy families.

In the year following the establishment of the uniform policy, Long Beach school officials found that overall school crime decreased 36 percent. Fights decreased 51 percent, sex offenses decreased 74 percent, weapons offenses decreased 50 percent, assault and battery offenses decreased 34 percent, and vandalism decreased 18 percent. Less than 1 percent of the students chose not to wear uniforms.[31]

SECTION SUMMARY

What Factors Place Students at Risk and Affect Teaching and Learning?

Many children and youth today are at risk because of their behavior or are placed at risk by forces in their environments. The effects of these risk factors make it more difficult, and in some cases impossible, for these students to learn. As a teacher you will need to make extra efforts and take extra care in meeting the needs of students at risk.

- Poverty. More than 12 million American children under the age of 18 live in poverty. Many of these children live in single-parent homes headed by women.

Poverty rates are especially high among children living in inner-city, single-parent African American and Hispanic American homes.

- **Substance Abuse.** Alcohol, drugs, and smoking are serious problems in U.S. schools. Binge drinking and cigarette smoking are on the rise among young people. Schools are a major factor in the delivery of programs to prevent the use of drugs, alcohol, and tobacco.

- **HIV/AIDS.** Teachers need to familiarize themselves with AIDS policies in their schools and districts. AIDS prevention programs are a common part of the curriculum because, although the actual number of AIDS cases is small in most schools, AIDS is now the sixth leading cause of death among fifteen- to twenty-four-year-olds in the United States.

- **Truancy and Delinquency.** Dropout rates vary by race and ethnicity. Because of the enormous difference a diploma or college degree makes in earning power in our society, schools make great efforts to help students graduate from high school. Some schools have instituted peer mediation programs to address student dropout and violence issues. Delinquent gangs are a major concern in many inner-city, suburban, and rural schools.

- **Teen Pregnancy.** The U.S. teenage pregnancy rate is higher than that of any other developed country. Since 1991, however, that rate has begun to decline. Among the many reasons for this decline are increased use of birth control methods, school sex education programs, and greater attention to preventing child abuse.

- **Violence.** Violence, both against children and by children, is an unfortunate but common occurrence in the United States. Teachers are required by law to report signs of child abuse or neglect in their students. As violent crimes (such as murder and assault) committed by juveniles have increased, many schools have instituted violence prevention programs to help students learn nonviolent ways to resolve disputes. Other schools are requiring students to wear uniforms to reduce some forms of conflict.

Thinking Critically
★ ★ ★ ★ ★ ★ ★ ★

During your childhood and adolescence, did you or anyone close to you face any of the risk factors described in this chapter? If yes, how will your understanding of those risk factors make you a better teacher? If not, how can you learn more about risk factors and their effects on your students?

_____

_____

_____

_____★

Applying What You've Learned
★ ★ ★ ★ ★ ★ ★ ★

What factors do you think contribute to school violence? What actions can you take to help ensure the safety of your students?

_____

_____

_____

_____★

Reflect on students who dropped out of school when you were in high school. What might you have done as a teacher to help prevent dropouts? At what ages do you think students can benefit most from help designed to prevent dropping out?

_____

_____

_____

_____ ★

NCATE

Elementary

Standard 1: Knows, understands, and uses the major concepts, principles, theories, and research related to development of children to construct learning opportunities that support individual students' development, acquisition of knowledge, and motivation.

Middle Level

Standard 1: Understands the major concepts, principles, theories and research related to young adolescent development; provides opportunities that support student development and learning.

*W*HAT CAN SCHOOLS DO TO HELP STUDENTS AT RISK?

Schools can help educate students at risk by providing a school environment and climate that make it possible for students to learn. Table 5.3 identifies some school characteristics that support learning and staying in school, namely, safety, community feeling, positive attitude, respectful treatment, focus on academics, high standards, and parental involvement.

In reducing the risks and enhancing the opportunities for at-risk students, there is often a tendency to focus on a particular problem (such as preventing violence) in isolation from other risk factors. However, according to the Carnegie Council on Adolescent Development:

> One of the important insights to emerge from scientific inquiry into adolescence in the past two decades is that problem behaviors tend to cluster in the same individual and reinforce one another. Crime, school dropout, teenage childbearing, and drug abuse typically are considered separately, but in the real world they occur together. Those who drink and smoke in early adolescence are thus more likely to initiate sex earlier than their peers; those who engage in these behavior patterns often have a history of difficulties in school. When young people have a low commitment to school and education, and when teachers or parents have low expectations for the children's performance, trouble lurks. Once educational failure occurs, then other adverse events begin to take hold.[32]

Generic interventions address some reasons for the underlying or predisposing factors that increase the likelihood that an adolescent will engage in high-risk or problem behaviors. These factors include low self-esteem, underdeveloped interpersonal and decision-making skills, lack of interest in education, inadequate information regarding

Table 5.3 *S*ome Characteristics of Schools That Support Learning and Staying in School

Schools can help at-risk students by

- providing a safe, violence-free, orderly school environment
- providing a caring, familylike school and classroom and a source of community
- developing positive teacher, administrator, and staff attitudes toward all students
- treating all students with respect
- focusing on academic and school achievement
- setting high standards and expecting all students to meet them
- conducting and providing a comprehensive program of parent involvement
- acknowledging your students' self-worth and their value to your class

health matters, low perception of opportunities, the absence of dependable and close human relationships, and meager incentives in delaying short-term gratification.

Given the tremendous risk factors facing children and youths today, schools are challenged to provide curricula and services that go beyond the traditional. Whether generic or targeted to specific risk factors, a number of models exist that schools and social service agencies use to help at-risk students in some way. Five basic approaches to educating students at risk are compensatory, prevention, intervention, and transition programs and providing separate schools and other facilities for at-risk students. Keep in mind that these approaches represent alternatives that are often applied sequentially or in combination (see Figure 5.6).

Compensatory Education

Compensatory programs are designed to compensate or make up for existing or past risk factors and their effects in students' lives. For example, as you have read, Head Start and Title I are designed to help children overcome the negative effects of poverty on their academic achievement and future school success.

The concept of remediation and the traditional practice of providing remedial instruction are also expressions of the compensatory approach. Many school districts run after-school programs or summer programs that are designed to help students

Compensatory programs
Programs that provide students from low-income families with additional education opportunities beyond those offered in the school's standard program in order to compensate or make up for factors missing in these students' lives.

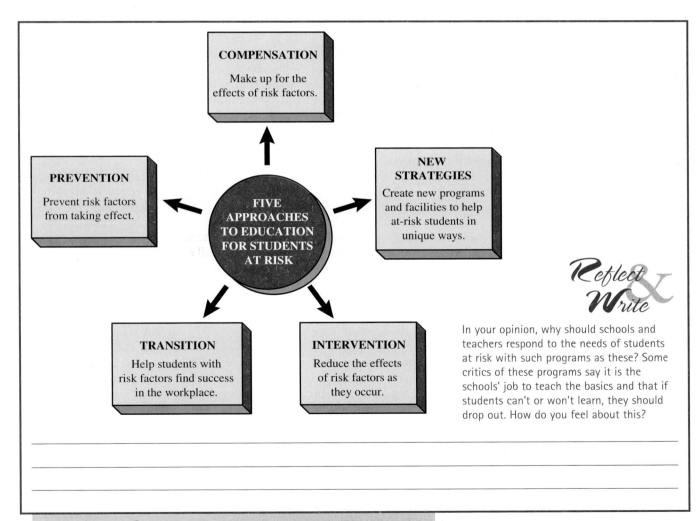

Reflect & Write

In your opinion, why should schools and teachers respond to the needs of students at risk with such programs as these? Some critics of these programs say it is the schools' job to teach the basics and that if students can't or won't learn, they should drop out. How do you feel about this?

Figure 5.6   *Five* **Approaches for Education for Students at Risk**

compensate for or overcome poor academic performance. Programs often include special classes for school dropouts to help them achieve and receive their high school diplomas.

Prevention Programs

Prevention programs
Programs intended to prevent or inhibit certain behaviors, for example, drug prevention programs, sex education programs, and AIDS education programs.

Prevention programs, as the name implies, are intended to prevent or inhibit certain behaviors. Drug prevention programs, sex education programs, and other education programs are examples of programs designed to prevent student behavior from being affected adversely by such risk factors. In addition, curriculum and instruction in values clarification or character training, self-esteem, decision making, interpersonal problem solving, social skills, communication skills, conflict mediation, and life skills are all part of a preventive approach.

For example, life skills training usually aims to provide students with the awareness and skills necessary for resisting social pressures to smoke cigarettes, drink alcohol excessively, or use marijuana. Training provides accurate information about the negative consequences of high-risk behaviors and about hidden pressures, such as the influence of advertising. Providing experiences that allow students to build self-confidence and self-esteem, to reduce anxiety and stress, and to develop greater autonomy and social competency decreases students' susceptibility to social pressures to engage in high-risk behaviors. Proponents of prevention programs argue that it is easier and less costly to prevent problems than it is to make up for their negative effects.

In preventive health programs, there increasingly is an emphasis on preventing some risk factors even before children are born. Many major childhood risk factors that affect learning ability, such as poor prenatal nutrition and lead poisoning, can be prevented. Many school- and community-based health clinics conduct outreach and education programs to promote maternal, infant, and family health as a way of ensuring healthy children who are ready for school.

Intervention Programs

Intervention programs
Programs provided by schools and social service agencies designed to provide support and services to students and their families to help eliminate risk factors and/or reduce their influence.

Intervention programs are provided by schools and social service agencies and are designed to provide support and services to students and their families to help eliminate risk factors and/or reduce their influence. The hoped-for effect in intervention programs is enhanced student and family functioning. For example, teenage parenting programs are designed to intervene in the lives of teenagers by teaching them the parenting skills they will need to be good parents and providing them with other information that will enable them to be better-functioning adults.

Intervention programs are frequently found in early childhood programs. **Early intervention** programs are implemented on two basic assumptions. One is that the effects of risk factors can be more easily overcome in the early years than in the teenage or adult years, because young children are thought to be more resilient to negative environmental influences than are youth or adults. The second assumption is that it is more cost-effective to intervene in the early years.

Early intervention
Providing care and support from the prenatal period through the first years of life to enable children to enter school ready to learn.

Research supports both assumptions in the education of young children. Children who attend quality preschool programs outperform their peers who did not attend preschool in terms of both educational and life success. Furthermore, over participants' lifetimes, quality preschool programs are estimated to yield economic benefits to the public of $98,000 per participant, in the form of savings in schooling, welfare, and legal costs.[33] Head Start is an excellent example of a national early intervention program.

Transition Programs

Approximately three-quarters of all high school graduates do not go on to a four-year college program. One of the problems many of these students face is how to make the transition from school to work. An educational trend is to help students see the relevance between what they are learning in the classroom and the world of work. The linking of work-based learning and classroom-based learning is also seen as one way to keep students in high school and help them move into meaningful employment opportunities. For example, in a school-based morning program, students might learn academic skills such as mathematics used in building construction, and in a job-related afternoon program, students might apply that learning in helping to build a homeless shelter.

New Strategies

One of the problems educators and public policy developers encounter in their efforts to help at-risk students is the "same-old-thing" phenomenon. Doing the same thing over and over can be self-defeating and not provide children and youth the desired outcomes. In other words, programs don't deliver the benefits promised. As a result, community and educational leaders try to engage in "out-of-the-box" thinking that leads to new approaches and programs. Some of these approaches are evident in **alternative schools,** often called second-chance schools, designed to provide the school climate, services, and support that at-risk students need. Many alternative schools target students who are habitually truant, at risk for dropping out, low achievers, and juvenile offenders. More school districts are building separate facilities specifically designed as alternative schools.

In addition to the instructional and curriculum modifications discussed in this chapter, there are a number of other actions you can take as a teacher to help students with special needs and students at risk.

As a teacher of at-risk students, you will need to

- get the specialized training you may need to respond appropriately to students' needs and problems
- be willing to work cooperatively and collaboratively with others to address the instructional needs of all students
- actively seek assistance from others in your school, district, and community to fully serve students and their families
- report signs of abuse or neglect promptly and refer students to special programs or for evaluation for special education or related services
- be an advocate for students and their families by encouraging other individuals and agencies to act on these students' behalf
- help educate parents and others about how to prevent risk factors from developing or from adversely affecting their children and their children's life chances and success in school
- keep parents informed on a regular basis about their children's progress and needs
- work with parents to help them connect with their children's development and lives and help their children with school work and life problems
- engage students so that they trust you and believe you are doing your best for them
- communicate to students that you have respect and high expectations for them and that you believe they are capable of learning
- provide instruction designed to help all students learn to the best of their ability, develop positive self-concepts, and build resilience against negative life experiences

Meeting the needs of students with special needs and students at risk makes teaching a challenging and rewarding profession. As more laws are passed protecting the rights of students with disabilities and more initiatives are taken to reduce risk factors for students, the role of the schools and teachers will be expanded and reconceptualized in new and rewarding ways. As society, families, children, and youth change, so will schools and teaching have to change. In a sense, schools and teachers

INTASC

Standard 10: The teacher fosters relationships with school colleagues, parents, and agencies in the larger community to support students' learning and well-being.

Alternative schools
Programs designed to give students special services, programs, and support necessary for them to be successful in school.

NCATE

Early Childhood

Standard 4: Integrates understanding of children and families, of developmentally effective approaches to teaching and learning, and of academic disciplines to design, implement, and evaluate positive learning experiences for all children.

Elementary

Standard 3.1: Plans and implements instruction based on knowledge of students, learning theory, subject matter, curricular goals, and community.

Standard 3.2: Understands how elementary students differ in development and approaches to learning; creates instructional opportunities that are adapted to diverse students.

Standard 3.3: Understands and uses a variety of teaching strategies that encourage students' development of critical thinking, problem solving, and performance skills.

Standard 3.4: Uses knowledge and understanding of individual and group motivation and behavior among students at K–6 level to foster active engagement in learning, self-motivation, and positive social interaction and to create supportive learning environments.

Standard 3.5: Uses knowledge and understanding of effective verbal, nonverbal, and media communication techniques to foster active inquiry, collaboration, and supportive interaction.

NCATE

Middle Level

Standard 5: Understands and uses major concepts, principles, theories, and research related to effective instruction and assessment; employs a variety of strategies for a developmentally appropriate climate to meet the varying abilities and learning styles of all adolescents.

are constantly catching up with the demands of society for meeting societal problems as they affect students and their success in school and in later life.

Part of the challenge for schools and teachers is how to constantly improve their responses to students' problems and improve the condition and quality of education. As more students come to school with special needs, schools will have to continually seek creative responses, including new and different curricula and restructured educational settings, that give teachers more decision-making power and more support to do their jobs.

As a prospective teacher, you are entering a prime time to be in the teaching profession. The opportunities for service and creativity have never been greater. Your students are waiting for you to make a difference in their lives and to help them fulfill their highest potential.

SECTION SUMMARY

What Can Schools Do to Help Students at Risk?

Schools can be a crucial factor in creating a positive learning climate. Rather than focusing on a single problem, schools and other agencies are taking a more holistic approach and are considering generic interventions that address underlying problems that predispose students to risk. As a beginning teacher you can be an advocate, get specialized training, and take other actions to assist students with special needs and students at risk. Four basic approaches exist for designing educational programs for at-risk students.

- Compensatory Education. Compensatory programs attempt to make up for existing or past risk factors and their effects in students' lives. Head Start, Title I, and traditional remedial instruction are examples of compensatory programs.

- Prevention Programs. Prevention programs educate students about the dangers of high-risk behaviors and help reduce students' susceptibility to social pressures. Such programs may stress values clarification or character training, self-esteem, decision making, interpersonal problem solving, social skills, communication skills, conflict mediation, and life skills. The basic idea of prevention programs is that it is easier and less costly to prevent problems than to deal with their negative effects.

- Intervention Programs. Early intervention programs assume that the effects of risk factors are more easily overcome in the early years, when children are more resilient, and that intervention is more cost-effective at this time.

- Transition Programs. Transitions of any kind are difficult for all students. The purpose of transition programs is to make it easier for students to move effortlessly from school to work. Increasingly, educators talk about a seamless transition from school to appropriate work. As a result, more schools are conducting orientation awareness and training programs designed to help students get the skills they need for employment following graduation.

- New Strategies. One trend in developing new approaches to helping students at risk is to create new facilities designed to meet their specific learning and behavioral needs. As schools develop even more sophisticated ways to help students who are at risk, it is likely that we will see an increase in separate facilities for them. One reason for this is to help ensure that these students receive the support they need. A second reason is that separate facilities help provide smaller learning environments. However, an issue associated with separate facilities is the issue of exclusion, which has been discussed at length in this chapter.

Thinking Critically
★ ★ ★ ★ ★ ★ ★ ★

Do you think sex education programs should be taught in public schools? Would you help teach such a program?

_____

_____

_____

_____ ★

Applying What You've Learned
★ ★ ★ ★ ★ ★ ★ ★

What steps should you take to prepare yourself for teaching students at risk? As part of developing answers to these questions, interview a school psychologist or social worker, a special education teacher, and others, such as a juvenile officer, who might be involved with this student population. As you develop your list of steps, identify your goal in each step and any specific resource, such as courses you could take, that seem to match that goal.

_____

_____

_____

_____ ★

Putting Yourself in the Picture
★ ★ ★ ★ ★ ★ ★ ★

You have been asked to design a smoking prevention program for middle school students. Draw up a proposal to present to your colleagues and the administration.

_____

_____

_____

_____ ★

Applications for Active Learning

CONNECTIONS

1. Think about the concepts and topics introduced in this chapter. Create a picture, graphic, or figure that shows connections that are meaningful to you among this chapter's key ideas and information.

2. A major theme that runs through Susan Hentz's opening chapter vignette is high expectations. Why do you think Susan places so much emphasis on high expectations? Why is it so important to have high expectations for exceptional

learners? Do you think it would be "easier" if teachers had lower expectations for exceptional learners? What can you do to help ensure that you have high expectations for all the students you will teach?

_____

_____

_____

3. Think about a student in your school experiences who was an exceptional learner. How did teachers accommodate that student's needs?

_____

_____

_____

FIELD EXPERIENCES

1. How is curriculum and instruction in a class for gifted and talented students different from that in other classes? Get permission to visit and observe such a class. Then compare that class with others you have observed or experienced. On the basis of your observations, describe how you might teach a student who is gifted and talented within your inclusive classroom.

2. Contact local schools in your area and ask them what activities and services they provide for students before and after school. How are these designed to meet students' special needs?

PERSONAL RESEARCH

1. How can a teacher modify the classroom environment, classroom routines, learning activities, student groupings, teaching strategies, instructional materials, assessments, and homework assignments to meet all students' needs? What human and material resources for successful inclusion are available to teachers and to students with special needs? How do students show social acceptance for their classmates with special needs? Visit an inclusive classroom and take notes on what you observe. Compare and discuss your observations with classmates who have visited different settings across all grade levels.

2. Visit the teacher resource center of a local school district or in the district where you plan to teach. Develop a list of resources that would be available to you in teaching students with special needs in your class.

Preparing to Teach

FOR YOUR PORTFOLIO

1. Place in your portfolio the teaching applications you have developed on the basis of your field observations and the plan you have outlined for your professional development as a teacher of students with disabilities, exceptional learners, and students at risk.

2. Collect in your portfolio information you believe will help you teach effectively in an inclusive classroom. For example, include the list of resources you researched at a school district's teacher resource center. Also review articles in journals such as the *Journal of Exceptional Children* and the *Journal of Learning Disabilities* and use the electronic search facilities of your library to locate articles that relate to teaching students with special needs. You might also write

to the Council for Exceptional Children (1920 Association Drive, Reston, VA 22091) and ask for sources of information that will be useful to you as a beginning teacher.

IDEA FILE

Develop an instructional plan for students whose learning is affected by one of the disabilities or risk factors described in this chapter. Include specific instructional activities and ideas for working with resource people and agencies as well as with the students' parents. Extend your idea file by repeating this procedure for other categories of disabilities or risk factors, and then amend your plans according to feedback you get from classmates, teachers, and professors.

Learning and Knowing More

WEB SITES WORTH VISITING

Valuable information relating to exceptional education, at-risk students, risk factors for students, and other areas of education can be found at the following Web sites on the Internet. For example, the Web site at the Curry School of Education, University of Virginia, contains much information about special education, including the history of the field and types of disabilities. It also offers discussion groups, electronic addresses of special educators, and much more. Visit the World Wide Web site at http://curry.edschool. virginia.edu/go/specialed.

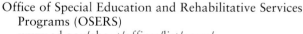

Council for Exceptional Children
www.cec.sped.org

Office of Special Education and Rehabilitative Services Programs (OSERS)
www.ed.gov/about/offices/list/osers/programs.html

Alan Guttmacher Institute
www.agi-usa.org

National Committee to Prevent Child Abuse
www.childabuse.org

Federal Resource Center (FRC) for Special Education
www.dssc.org/frc

School-to-Work Outreach Project
www.ici.umn.edu/schooltowork

BOOKS WORTH READING

Culatta, R., and Tompkins, J. R. (2002). *Fundamentals of Special Education: What Every Teacher Needs to Know* (2nd ed.). Upper Saddle River, NJ: Prentice Hall.
Delivers concise coverage of exceptionalities, educational programs, and issues driving the field of special education, without extraneous information that can detract from the real issues. Includes only the most essential facts and concepts needed to understand children with exceptionalities.

Davis, G. A., and Rimms, S. B. (2004). *Education of the Gifted and Talented* (5th ed.). Boston: Allyn & Bacon.
The authors provide a broad overview of the gifted and talented field, including an introduction to giftedness, characteristics, program types, curriculum, identification, and program evaluation.

Friend, M., and Bursuck, W. (2001). *Including Students with Special Needs* (3rd ed.). Boston: Allyn & Bacon.
This is a practical guide for classroom teachers on teaching all students in inclusive classrooms. This book explains how to modify curricula, textbooks, classrooms, student groupings, assessments, and instruction to meet all students' learning needs.

Garrett, A. G. (2001). *Keeping American Schools Safe: A Handbook for Parents, Students, Educators, Law Enforcement Personnel, and the Community*. Jefferson, NC: McFarland.
The state of violence in American schools today and methods for making and keeping schools safer places are the topics of this book. The author discusses characteristics of children with violent tendencies and includes profiles of potentially dangerous children.

Hallahan, D. P., and Kauffman, J. (2003). *Exceptional Learners: Introduction to Special Education* (9th ed.). Boston: Allyn & Bacon.
This book is a general introduction to the characteristics of exceptional students and their education and is written with both special education and general education in mind. The authors' clear and concise writing style makes research and theoretical issues easily understood.

Henley, M., Ramsey, R. S., and Algozzine, R. (2002). *Characteristics of and Strategies for Teaching Students with Mild Disabilities* (4th ed.). Boston: Allyn & Bacon.
This book describes characteristics of mild disabilities in an easy-to-read-and-understand format. It includes the best teaching practices for inclusion, behavior management, and classroom instruction.

Strichart, S. S., and Mangrum, C. T. (2002). *Teaching Study Skills and Strategies to Students with Learning Disabilities, Attention Deficit Disorders, or Special Needs* (3rd ed.). Boston: Allyn & Bacon.
Featured are 169 reproducible activities that provide opportunities for active learning and student practice in the study skills and strategies most important for students with special needs.

CHAPTER 6

Partners in Learning: Parents, Families, and the Community

"A business–school partnership—what a great idea!"

Lisa Lenton, a beginning eighth-grade math teacher, is on her way to a meeting with José Cardinez, her mentor teacher. Lisa is concerned about her students' math achievement and their overall attitude toward math.

"I have to do something, José. It's six weeks into the term and a number of my students aren't doing well at all. I've tried things like cooperative learning, grouping, and incentive systems. But they're not working as well as I expected. The kids are just not doing as well as I know they can. And I have to do something about it. Fast. Or else some of them won't have the skills they need for high school. Or for the world of work, for that matter."

José Cardinez understands the pressure Lisa feels to make sure students are ready for the future. "I know what you are talking about, Lisa. I have the same concern about my students' reading skills. Part of my solution has been to get the parents involved. The students read to parents at home and parents log the assignments. Would something like that work with your students in math?"

"Well, any reinforcement of math skills at home would certainly help. The kids could do math in authentic contexts like shopping and family finances. I'll have to think about that. But, you know, I also think they need more direct help in the classroom. They would benefit from role models in math, especially adults who use math in their work and in their everyday lives. If students could see the importance of math through others, José, they might be more motivated to learn math."

"Hmmm. I was reading in *Education Week* about a school that's working with a local business to improve achievement in math. Employees go to the school and tutor students in the classroom. Would something like that work here for your students?"

"A business–school partnership—what a great idea! I've read about them too, but I never thought. . . . Whom do you think we could get? What if we could get Sterling Scientific involved? They're the town's biggest employer. What do you think?"

"I think it's a good idea. You should talk to Mr. Matz and find out how to go about it and what all the ins and outs are of corporate involvement. Also, you might want to talk to Sheila Bronkowsky down in the business lab. She gets local businesses to come in and give workshops on retailing. Her students also visit the stores and make observations. Maybe your students could shadow some of Sterling's employees to see how they use math on the job."

"Wow—I love it! You know, I think this is something that could really turn my kids on to math. It is starting to sound a little complex though. I'd better do some homework and get some ideas down on paper. Will you review my proposal, José, before I start the ball rolling?"

"Sure will, Lisa. Looking forward to it. And good luck."

NCATE

Middle Level

Standard 6: Understands the major concepts, principles, theories, and research related to working collaboratively with family and community members; uses that knowledge to maximize learning of all young adolescents.

INTASC

Standard 10: The teacher fosters relationships with school colleagues, parents, and agencies in the larger community to support students' learning and well-being.

How Will This Chapter Help You?

You will learn

★ how families and the community influence teaching and learning

★ how federal and state laws shape and influence parent involvement

★ how you can involve parents, families, and the community in your teaching

★ how you can collaborate with the community to help you teach and your students learn

★ how school choice is influencing education reform and parent involvement

The New York Times
expect the world®
nytimes.com

Themes of the Times

Expand your knowledge of the concepts discussed in this chapter by reading current and historical articles from *The New York Times* by visiting the "Themes of the Times" section of the companion Web site.

Standard 10: The teacher fosters relationships with school colleagues, parents, and agencies in the larger community to support students' learning and well-being.

Elementary

Standard 5.3: Knows importance of establishing and maintaining positive collaborative relationships with families to promote the academic, social, and emotional growth of children.

Standard 5.4: Fosters relationships with school colleagues and agencies in the larger community to support students' learning and well-being.

Middle Level

Standard 6: Understands the major concepts, principles, theories, and research related to working collaboratively with family and community members; uses that knowledge to maximize learning of all young adolescents.

HOW DO PARENTS, FAMILIES, AND COMMUNITIES INFLUENCE TEACHING AND LEARNING?

One thing we can say with certainty about the educational landscape today is that parents, families, and communities are as much a part of the educational process as are the students, teachers, and staff. Efforts to involve families and communities in the process of educating the nation's youth are at an all-time high. One primary reason for these renewed efforts to involve parents is the overwhelming evidence that the effect of involving parents, families, and communities in the schools increases student achievement and promotes positive educational outcomes. A summary of over eighty research studies regarding parent involvement confirms the benefits of parent/community support.

> The research found that there is a positive and convincing relationship between family involvement and benefits for students, including improved academic achievement. This relationship holds across families of all economic, racial/ethnic, and educational background and for students at all ages: students with involved parents, no matter their background, are more likely to earn higher grades and test scores, enroll in higher-level programs, be promoted and earn credits, adapt well to school and attend regularly, have better social skills and behavior, and graduate and go on to higher education. Family involvement also has a protective effect; the more families can support their children's progress, the better their children do in school and the longer they stay in school.[1]

In fact, the public believes that nothing has a greater effect on students' level of achievement than parents (see Figure 6.1). This makes it even more critical that schools make efforts to see that parents are involved in their children's education in school.

Changing Families Affect Parent Involvement

The family of today is not the family of yesterday, nor will the family of today be the family of tomorrow. For example, households with children, which comprised 45 percent of total U.S. households in the 1970s, comprised only 33 percent in 2000.

Who has the greatest effect on a student's level of achievement in school? The response is—parents!

	National Totals (%)
Parents	53
Teachers	26
Students	17
Don't know	4

Which is a more important factor in determining whether students learn in school—the school or the parents? Once again, the answer is—parents!

	National Totals (%)
The school	30
The students' parents	60
Don't know	10

Reflect & Write

What are your feelings about the importance of parents to student achievement? If a pollster asked you these questions, how would you respond?

Figure 6.1 *The Public's View of the Importance of Parents*

Source: Figure created by author from data drawn from L.C. Rose and A. M. Gallup, "The Thirty-Second Annual Phi Delta Kappa/Gallup Poll of the Public's Attitudes Toward the Public Schools," *Phi Delta Kappan,* 2000. (Online.) Available at www.pdkintl.org/kappan/kpol0009.htm.

Table 6.1 *How* Families Have Changed

Types of Families	1970 (%)	2000 (%)
Households with own children	45	33
Married-couple families	87	69
Single-mother families with children	12	26
Single-father families with children	1	5
Children living with relative	2	3
Children living with nonrelative	1	1

Source: U.S. Census Bureau. (Online). Available at www.census.gov/population/www/socdemo/ hh-fam.html; J. Fields and L. M. Casper, *America's Families and Living Arrangements,* March 2000; Current Population Reports, No. P20-537 (Washington, D.C.: U.S. Census Bureau, 2001). Available online at www.census.gov/prod/2001pubs/p20-537.pdf.

Table 6.1 shows some of the other ways families have changed over the years. In addition, more mothers are entering the work force than ever before. This means that at an early age, often as young as six weeks, many children are spending eight hours a day or more in the care of others.

The need for early childhood care has meant a blossoming of opportunities for child-serving agencies—child-care centers and preschools, for example. A major trend in the next decade will surely be that more programs will provide more parents with child development and child-rearing resources and information.

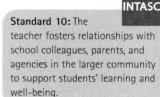

Grandparents as Parents. Grandparents who take on primary parenting roles for their grandchildren are a growing reality in the United States today. Since the millennium,

Increasing numbers of grandparents, by default and by choice, find themselves in the parenting role. Grandparents assume the primary parent role for a number of reasons: to provide a homelike atmosphere, to prevent placement of children in foster care, to protect children against the effects of divorce and single parenthood, and to protect children from abuse and neglect. You will want to work with these grandparents as parents and involve them in your programs and their grandchildren's education.

more grandparents have stepped into parenting roles than ever before: Four million children, or 5.5 percent of all children under 18, are living in homes maintained by 2.5 million grandparents. These numbers should come as no surprise when we realize that one of every four adults is a grandparent.

Many of the children in homes headed by grandparents are "skipped-generation" children—neither parent is living with them, perhaps because of drug abuse, divorce, mental and physical illness, abandonment, teenage pregnancy, or child abuse and neglect, incarceration, or even the death of the parents. Grandparent-parents in these skipped-generation households must provide for their grandchildren's basic needs and care as well as make sure that they do well in school. Grandparents who are raising a new generation, often unexpectedly, need your support. Keep in mind that they are rearing their grandchildren in a world very different from the one in which they reared their children. You can help grandparents with this responsibility in a number of ways, including linking them with support groups such as Raising Our Children's Children (ROCC) and the American Association of Retired Persons (AARP) Grandparent Information Center (www.aarp.org/contacts/programs/gic.html).

How Does the Federal Government Influence Parent Involvement?

Given the key role that parents play in student education, it should come as no surprise that federal and state governments are taking a leading role in ensuring that parents are involved in schools. The No Child Left Behind Act of 2001 (NCLB) has changed the way schools need to interact with parents. Prior to NCLB, parental involvement was largely determined by school district policies and administrator and teacher discretion. This is no longer the case: NCLB mandates a wide range of required procedures and activities relating to parental involvement.

The extent and range of parental involvement under NCLB is specific and comprehensive, both at the district level and in the schoolhouse. At the district level, NCLB requires that

- programs, activities, and procedures be planned and implemented with meaningful consultation with parents of participating children
- each district develop jointly with parents a written parent involvement policy describing how the district will involve parents in a wide variety of areas, including curriculum, physical plant, decision making, and evaluation of the district on various levels

At the schoolhouse level, each school must

- convene an annual meeting at a convenient time, to which all parents of participating children shall be invited and encouraged to attend; inform parents of their school's participation; and explain the requirements and the right of the parents to be involved
- involve parents in an organized, ongoing, and timely way in the planning, review, and improvement of programs, including the planning, review, and improvement of the school parental involvement policy and the joint development of the schoolwide program plan
- provide parents with timely information about programs, a description and explanation of the curriculum, and the forms of academic assessment used to measure student progress and the proficiency levels students are expected to meet
- provide opportunities, if requested by parents, for regular meetings to formulate suggestions and to participate, as appropriate, in decisions relating to the education of their children and respond to any such suggestions as soon as practicably possible

The School Compact. NCLB also requires that the district, parents, schools, and students enter into a compact of shared responsibility for ensuring high student achievement. The school compact describes the school's responsibility to provide high-quality curriculum and instruction in a supportive and effective learning environment that enables the children served to meet the state's student academic achievement standards and to inform parents of the ways they will be responsible for supporting their children's learning (such as monitoring attendance, homework completion, and television watching; volunteering in their child's classroom; and participating, as appropriate, in decisions relating to the education of their children and positive use of extracurricular time). The compact also addresses the importance of communication between teachers and parents on an ongoing basis through

- parent-teacher conferences in elementary schools, at least annually, during which the compact shall be discussed as the compact relates to the individual child's achievement
- frequent reports to parents on their children's progress
- reasonable access to staff, opportunities to volunteer and participate in their child's class, and observation of classroom activities

Finally, NCLB requires that districts help parents understand both the system of public education and their role in it through a program called Building Capacity for Involvement. In order to build parental capacity, both school districts and local schools must

- provide assistance to parents of children served by the school or local educational agency, as appropriate, in understanding such topics as state academic content standards, state student academic achievement standards, state and local academic assessments, how to monitor their children's progress, and how to work with educators to improve the achievement of their children
- provide materials and training to help parents to work with their children to improve their children's achievement, such as literacy training and using technology, as appropriate, to foster parental involvement
- educate teachers, pupil services personnel, principals, and other staff, with the assistance of parents, in the value and utility of contributions of parents and in how to reach out to, communicate with, and work with parents as equal partners; implement and coordinate parent programs; and build ties between parents and the school
- coordinate and integrate parent involvement programs and activities with Head Start, Reading First, Early Reading First, Even Start, the Home Instruction Programs for Preschool Youngsters, the Parents as Teachers Program, and public preschool and other programs and conduct other activities, such as parent resource centers, that encourage and support parents in more fully participating in the education of their children
- ensure that information related to school and parent programs, meetings, and other activities is sent to the parents of participating children in a format and, to the extent practicable, in a language the parents can understand

In addition, the Building Capacity for Involvement process allows school districts and schools, at their discretion, to support parent involvement through resources, including funds and training, and even to bring parents into the process of developing training for teachers and administrators. Districts are asked to arrange school meetings at a variety of times or to conduct in-home conferences between teachers and working parents who may be unable to make scheduled school conferences. Finally, districts are encouraged to establish a districtwide parent advisory council to provide advice on all matters related to parental involvement in programs, to develop appropriate roles for community-based organizations and businesses in parent involvement activities, and to provide any other reasonable support that parents may request.[2]

Other Legislation and Laws

Numerous other federal and state laws recognize the importance of meaningful parental involvement and require that parents take responsibility for helping ensure that their children learn. The National Head Start program requires that all local Head

NCATE

Early Childhood

Standard 2: Understands and values complex characteristics of families and communities; creates respectful, reciprocal relationships that support and empower families; involves families in children's development and learning.

Elementary

Standard 5.3: Knows importance of establishing and maintaining positive collaborative relationships with families to promote the academic, social, and emotional growth of children.

Start agencies have procedures to ensure that parents are involved. From our discussions in Chapter 5, recall that IDEA gives parents many rights and responsibilities relating to their involvement in their children's education. Parental involvement occurs in other ways, some that you might not have thought about. For example, thirty-nine states and the District of Columbia require school districts to permit parental involvement in sexuality and STD/HIV education. Some of these states require parental consent for students to participate in the programs, while thirty-six states allow parents to remove their children from the programs.

Florida law requires that each parent of a child within a compulsory attendance age shall be responsible for such child's school attendance. The absence of a child from school is evidence of a violation of this law. Furthermore, the law states that parents who refuse or fail to have a child under their control attend school regularly shall be guilty of a misdemeanor of the second degree, punishable by law.[3]

SECTION SUMMARY

How Do Parents and Families Influence Teaching and Learning?

A majority of parents believe there should be more parental involvement with the public schools. Research also shows that schools that reach out to and welcome parents, families, and communities into the decision-making process are more successful than other schools.

- Changing Families. Today's families differ from traditional families of earlier generations. Many parents, even of very young children, both work. Almost half of all children have divorced parents. Families now also tend to have less time to spend with and on behalf of their children. Families' needs for child-rearing assistance and support have never been greater. Additionally, grandparents are assuming a greater role in their grandchildren's education. Over 4 million children are being parented by grandparents. It is essential for you as a beginning teacher to be sensitive to the parental needs of grandparents and to seek ways to involve them in their grandchildren's education.

- How Does the Federal Government Influence Parent Involvement? The federal government is playing a major role in making mandatory parents' involvement in their children's education. In addition, the federal government is specifying the nature and extent of parent and family involvement, particularly through the No Child Left Behind Act of 2002. This federal involvement in parent education will continue well into the future.

- Other Legislation and Laws. Many federal laws, such as IDEA, require the involvement of parents of children with disabilities in their children's education. State laws also require parental involvement in such matters as sex education programs and in matters relating to compulsory school attendance.

Thinking Critically

★ ★ ★ ★ ★ ★ ★ ★

Given the fact that parents now spend increasingly longer work days on the job, how can working parents be involved in their children's education in school and at home?

_____

_____

_____

_____ ★

To what extent do the schools in the area where you live implement the parental involvement provisions of NCLB? Interview local school principals and find out how they support parent/family involvement.

_____

_____

_____

_____ ★

Based on what you have read so far, and given your knowledge about parent involvement, what are some topics you feel you need to know more about in order to effectively involve parents and families?

_____

_____

_____

_____ ★

*W*HAT ARE FAMILY-CENTERED PROGRAMS *?*

Education starts in the home, and what happens there profoundly affects the trajectory of children's development and learning. According to the U.S. Department of Education, education is a family affair: The greater the family's involvement in children's learning, the more likely it is that students will receive a high-quality education. Following are ways families can play a critical role in children's education:

- Three factors over which families have control—student absenteeism, variety of reading material in the home, and amount of television watching—explain differences in students' mathematics achievement. School attendance rates, exposure to print in the home, and restricted television time all correlate with higher achievement, as measured by the National Assessment of Educational Progress.
- While math and science achievement is based on learning activities in the home, literacy is even more dependent on home life. The single most important activity for building the knowledge required for eventual success in reading is reading aloud to children.
- What the family does with and for its children is more important to student success than family income or education. This is true whether the family is rich or poor, whether the parents finished high school or not, or whether the child is in preschool or in the upper grades.[4]

The central role families play in children's education is a reality that teachers and schools must address as they make plans for how to reform schools and increase student achievement. Developing a partnership with families is of crucial importance. The benefits of these school-home alliances far outweigh any inconveniences or barriers that may stand in the way of bringing teachers and parents together.

NCATE

Early Childhood

Standard 2: Understands and values complex characteristics of families and communities; creates respectful, reciprocal relationships that support and empower families; involves families in children's development and learning.

Elementary

Standard 5.3: Knows importance of establishing and maintaining positive collaborative relationships with families to promote the academic, social, and emotional growth of children.

How will you involve parents and families in your planning as a teacher?

_____

_____

_____

_____

Family-centered teaching Instruction that focuses on the needs of students through the family unit, whatever that unit may be, and is designed to help both generations while strengthening the family unit.

INTASC

Standard 7: The teacher plans instruction based upon knowledge of subject matter, students, the community, and curriculum goals.

Family-centered teaching and learning focuses on meeting the needs of students through the family unit. Education professionals recognize that to most effectively meet the needs of students, they must also meet the needs of family members and the family unit. **Family-centered teaching** and learning makes sense for a number of reasons. First, the family unit has the major responsibility for meeting children's needs. Children's development begins in the family system, and the family system is a powerful determiner of developmental processes, both for better and for worse. Therefore, helping individuals in the family unit become better parents and family members benefits children and consequently promotes their success in school.

Second, it is frequently the case that to help children effectively, family issues and problems must be addressed first. For instance, helping parents gain access to adequate and affordable health care increases the chances that the whole family, including the children, will be healthy.

Third, teachers can do many things concurrently with children and their families that will benefit both at the same time. Literacy is a good example. Adopting a family approach to literacy means that helping parents learn to read, build literacy, and read aloud to their children helps ensure children's literacy development as well. Figure 6.2 summarizes the concept of family-centered programs.

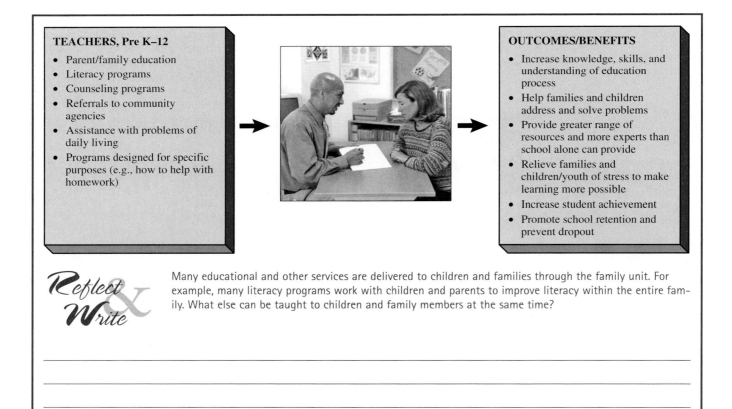

TEACHERS, Pre K–12
- Parent/family education
- Literacy programs
- Counseling programs
- Referrals to community agencies
- Assistance with problems of daily living
- Programs designed for specific purposes (e.g., how to help with homework)

OUTCOMES/BENEFITS
- Increase knowledge, skills, and understanding of education process
- Help families and children address and solve problems
- Provide greater range of resources and more experts than school alone can provide
- Relieve families and children/youth of stress to make learning more possible
- Increase student achievement
- Promote school retention and prevent dropout

Reflect & Write

Many educational and other services are delivered to children and families through the family unit. For example, many literacy programs work with children and parents to improve literacy within the entire family. What else can be taught to children and family members at the same time?

_____

_____

_____

Figure 6.2   Family-Centered Teaching

An example of family-centered education is the William F. Goodling Even Start Family Literacy Program, a federally funded family literacy program that combines adult literacy and parenting training with early childhood education to break cycles of illiteracy that are often passed on from one generation to another. Even Start is funded under Title I of the No Child Left Behind Act of 2001 and operated through the public school system and provides family-centered education. In particular, Even Start helps parents become full partners in the education of their children, assists children in reaching their full potential, and provides literacy training for their parents. (See Education on the Move.) Even Start projects are designed to work cooperatively with existing community resources to provide a full range of services and to integrate early childhood education and adult education.

Family-Centered Curriculum and Instruction

Family-centered curriculum and instruction exists at three levels. At the first level, it consists of programs and materials designed to help parents be better parents to and teachers of their children. To support parents in these roles, schools and teachers provide materials on parenting, conduct parenting classes, and furnish ideas about teaching their children reading and math skills through daily living activities. At the second level, family-centered curriculum and instruction focuses on helping parents with everyday problems and issues of family living. Classes and information on tenant rights, nutritious meals, the importance of immunizations, and access to health services are examples of

education *on the move* >>>>>>>>>>>>

>>> Even Start Gives Everyone a Fair Chance >>>>>>>

Even Start, a family literacy program, supports over a million children in over 800 locations and helps ensure that all children in the United States who are starting school are ready to learn. It does that by enlisting parents as "first teachers" and educating parents about how to accomplish that.

To be eligible for Even Start, an adult must be a parent of a child who is 7 or younger and must demonstrate a need for literacy skills that make that adult eligible for a literacy program under the Adult Education Act. Children are eligible for Even Start if they are younger than 7, have an eligible parent, and live in an elementary school attendance area designated for participation in programs under Title I. Even Start children take part in early childhood reading activities. Parents take adult literacy, parent training, and job training classes; study for the General Equivalency Diploma (GED); and learn how to teach their children in their homes.

Even Start work focuses on four areas: adult education (including English as a second language), childhood education, parenting education, and PACT (parent and child together) time. Here is how these goals are accomplished in the District of Columbia Public Schools Even Start program.[5]

Adult Education. Adult literacy education provides classes to enhance reading, math, language skills, GED preparation, and/or English as a second language (ESL). Parents are encouraged to set goals for their educational achievement, to design their own work plans, and to collaborate with their peers. They develop skills to enhance their lives, secure employment, and thrive in society.

Childhood education. The childhood education component is designed to promote the growth and development of young children from infancy to age 9. The focus is on everything from motor skills to language development to attendance at school and social interactions.

Parenting education. Even Start offers a variety of topics of study

and discussion. Parents learn about their child's developmental stages and strategies to support their children's education at home and at school. These classes also create an atmosphere among members that promotes group identity and peer support. This component not only provides instruction in areas such as child development and time management but also connects parents with a wide array of community resources and teaches them to become advocates for their child's education.

PACT Time. PACT Time is a time set aside for parents and children to take part in child-led activities together. Parents actually learn how to teach their children during work-play activities, fulfilling their role as their child's most important teacher. Parents and children develop new interaction patterns and often a more positive, supportive relationship.[6]

Reflect & Write

areas that address families' daily living needs. At the third level, family-centered curriculum and instruction attempts to integrate students' classroom learning with learning in the home. For example, such efforts as providing parents with books to read to their children, loaning computers, and offering ideas for helping children with homework all work to link school learning with learning in the home.

Working with and through families is an ideal way to support students' learning at all grade levels, including the middle school years. As a beginning teacher you might consider some of the strategies shown in Figure 6.3. Engaging all parents is a productive way to help both parents and their children succeed in school and life.

Do you know as much as you will need to about children and families? In what ways do you think teaching goes beyond the classroom?

_____

_____

_____

_____

Intergenerational programs
Programs promoting cooperation, interaction, and exchange between two or more generations.

Intergenerational programs are those that promote cooperation, interaction, and exchange between two or more generations. Intergenerational programming is becoming a popular way of bringing younger and older generations together. There are a number of reasons for efforts to join generations. First, Americans tend to become segregated by age and life stages. The young are in child care and school, adults are

---

Family Involvement Activities

- Provide information about child rearing and how to guide and manage behavior.
- Inform parents about programs and students' progress on a weekly basis through newsletters, e-mail, etc.
- Provide specific suggestions for ways parents can assist with homework and other learning activities at home.
- Educate parents about the school curriculum.
- Involve parents in classroom activities.
- Include parents as appropriate in decisions regarding their children.
- Create family resource centers that provide educational programs for parents, including computer literacy, job-employment counseling, English as a second language, health promotion, and citizenship.

Reflect & Write

As a beginning teacher, how can you be prepared to promote family involvement in educational processes? Which of the suggestions listed above do you think are most important? Which of these, if any, have you seen successfully used in schools you attended?

_____

_____

_____

Figure 6.3   *Effective Family Involvement*

in workplaces, and the elderly are in age-segregated housing and nursing homes. Second, with cutbacks in federal support for health and social programs, the young and the old especially are in competition for funds and services. One way to reduce this competition and to use existing funds effectively is to provide intergenerational programs for the mutual benefit of all. Most often, intergenerational programming focuses on young people below age 25 and adults over age 60.[7]

Intergenerational programming also includes programs in which young people provide services to older persons, in which older persons provide services to youth, and in which two generations work cooperatively on a project. Providing community service is increasingly a part of school-based curricula and a requirement of graduation in some schools. Such community service involvements often team youngsters with the elderly. (See Education on the Move.) As a beginning teacher, you might want

NCATE

Elementary
Standard 2.1–2.8: Understands and uses fundamental concepts and modes of inquiry of all appropriate content disciplines.

Standard 5.4: Fosters relationships with school colleagues and agencies in the larger community to support students' learning and well-being.

education *on the move* >>>>>>>>>>>>

>>> A Partnership for Literacy >>>>>>>

Located in Oakland's largely Latino Fruitvale neighborhood, Hawthorne—with more than 1,200 children—is the largest elementary school in the district. Eighty-five percent of the students qualify for a free or reduced lunch. The student population mirrors the state's diverse population. Students come from at least twelve different ethnic and cultural groups, and 74 percent of them speak only a limited amount of English. All district communications go home in Spanish, Vietnamese, Cantonese, Cambodian, English, and Lao.

Hawthorne's school reform history dates back more than fifteen years and spans three principals. With support from the state and the district, the school has implemented a wide range of programs for families and students in an effort to build a responsive, caring, and inclusive community. Programs and services include TRIBES (a process that builds respect for diversity and communication skills among children and adults), conflict mediation, a health and dental clinic, mental health services, and a parent center. As a result of these efforts, Hawthorne now serves as a model for how a school can meet the varied needs of its community in a respectful and resourceful way.

Hawthorne is a Leadership School in the Bay Area School Reform Collaborative, the regional Annenberg reform initiative. This collaborative has stimulated and supported

Hawthorne's reform work, in part with its vision for mutually accountable partnerships between school and community. The School Reform Collaborative's highest standards for partnerships serve as Hawthorne's guides:

- Whole community consensus building
- Partners in decision making and accountability
- Two-way communication and mutually beneficial relationships
- Partners in the substantive work of the school

An opportunity to build such a partnership has occurred recently at Hawthorne. In separate meetings with teachers and administrators, parents of Vietnamese and Cambodian students expressed concern about losing touch with their children as their children lose touch with their native language. In some cases, families literally could not communicate across the generations because the children now spoke only English and the parents spoke only their native language.

As a result of the meetings, the school has begun to offer after-school Vietnamese and Cambodian language classes. The school encourages children as well as parents to join the classes to build literacy skills.

Parents need to be informed about progress toward reform goals, but they also need to play a part in achieving them. To that end,

Hawthorne has begun to test the theory that parents are more likely to become involved in the school and in their child's education if they develop a strong, trusting relationship with the child's teachers. Four teachers piloted an effort in this direction last year. The teachers were already working closely together to create a seamless continuum of expectations, curriculum, and relationships among their K–3 Spanish bilingual classes. The next step was to involve the parents of their students in a project they called Home-School Connections.

Activities included frequent information updates via phone and mail; family homework projects that encouraged reading at home; a series of family seminars on such topics as homework help, discipline, and reading; and social events. Parents felt free to visit the classrooms during and after school and to communicate with the teachers by phone. Through this pilot effort, parents got to know not only their child's current teacher but also the teachers their child would have in the next several years. Although it is difficult to assess the direct impact of this close family connection, last year the students in these classrooms had some of the highest reading scores in the school.

Source: K. Grosse et al., "A Partnership for Literacy." *Educational Leadership*, May 1998, pp. 45–48. Reprinted by permission.

to explore the many learning opportunities that community service projects offer as a way of promoting active learning and problem solving with your students.

SECTION SUMMARY

What Are Family-Centered Programs?

Family-centered teaching and learning focuses on meeting the needs of the family as a unit in the belief that to help children effectively, family issues and problems must be addressed first. Programs focus on family-centered curriculum and instruction and two-generation or intergenerational delivery of services.

- Family-Centered Curriculum and Instruction. Family-centered education supports parents in their roles as parents and teachers. Efforts include helping parents with educating their children, with daily living needs, and with integrating student classroom learning with learning in the home.

Thinking Critically
★ ★ ★ ★ ★ ★ ★ ★

Sandra Pritchard, director of an Even Start program in Mississippi, states that teachers "need to get into the community and homes and know what [families] are like." How could you do this in your school district?

_____

_____

_____

_____ ★

Applying What You've Learned
★ ★ ★ ★ ★ ★ ★ ★

Literacy—reading, speaking, writing, and listening—is a major theme in American education today. The continuing challenge is how to provide children and youth the literacy skills they need. Many schools encourage teachers to work with families to increase their awareness of the importance of literacy in children's lives and in the home. What are some things you could do to help families value and support literacy in the home?

_____

_____

_____

_____ ★

Putting Yourself in the Picture
★ ★ ★ ★ ★ ★ ★ ★

You are determined to implement family-centered curriculum and instruction in your classroom. You have just discovered that the father of a student in your second-grade class was recently laid off from his minimum-wage job. The mother is pregnant, and the other children are ages 2 and 4. What could you do to help this family? Where would you start?

_____

_____

_____

_____ ★

WHAT IS PARENT INVOLVEMENT?

In our discussion of parent and family involvement, it is important for us to have a clear understanding of what we mean when we say parent involvement. Title I of NCLB defines parent involvement as

> the participation of parents in regular, two-way, and meaningful communication involving student academic learning and other school activities, including ensuring—
> - that parents play an integral role in assisting their child's learning;
> - that parents are encouraged to be actively involved in their child's education at school;
> - that parents are full partners in their child's education and are included, as appropriate, in decision-making and on advisory committees to assist in the education of their child.[8]

Three things are significant about this definition. First is the definition itself. This marks the first time that the federal government has defined parent involvement in public education. Second, the definition gives parents "full partnership" in the education of their children. And third, the definition provides the context by which schools and school districts will implement programs, activities, and procedures by which parents will be involved.

As you think more about your role in involving parents, review and reflect on Figure 6.4, which outlines six types of family/parent involvement.

Six Types of Parent/Family Involvement

The following real-life examples of parent involvement in the six areas show what is possible when determined and dedicated teachers and administrators resolve to make meaningful parent involvement a reality. (For another example, see Education on the Move, p. 207.)

1. Parenting. Assist families with parenting and child-rearing skills, understanding child and adolescent development, and setting home conditions that support children as students at each age and grade level. Assist schools in understanding families.

   Magnet Middle School, Stamford, Connecticut

   The Action Team made transportation and babysitting services available to families who want to come to school events but do not have transportation or a babysitter. The Action Team surveyed the school's families and discovered that over twenty families would use the transportation and babysitting services. Parents volunteered to pick up those parents who needed rides, and seventh- and eighth-grade students served as babysitters.

2. Communicating. Communicate with families about school programs and student progress through effective school-to-home and home-to-school communications.

   Freedom Elementary School, Freedom, Wisconsin

   Everyone has heard the saying, "Serve food, and they will come." Freedom Elementary proved that this strategy continues to be successful. In September, the school hosted a family-school picnic supper immediately preceding open house night. Nine hundred people attended, and they all visited classrooms for open house. This rural school has 730 students enrolled in pre-K to grade 5.

3. Volunteering. Improve recruitment, training, work, and schedules to involve families as volunteers and audiences at the school or in other locations to support students and school programs.

   Clover Street School, Windsor, Connecticut

   Every year it is difficult to recruit enough parents to volunteer for the library, classrooms, and other activities. The Action Team for Partnerships (ATP)

Early Childhood

Standard 2: Understands and values complex characteristics of families and communities; creates respectful, reciprocal relationships that support and empower families; involves families in children's development and learning.

Middle Level

Standard 6: Understands the major concepts, principles, theories, and research related to working collaboratively with family and community members; uses that knowledge to maximize learning of all young adolescents.

Elementary

Standard 5.3: Knows importance of establishing and maintaining positive collaborative relationships with families to promote the academic, social, and emotional growth of children.

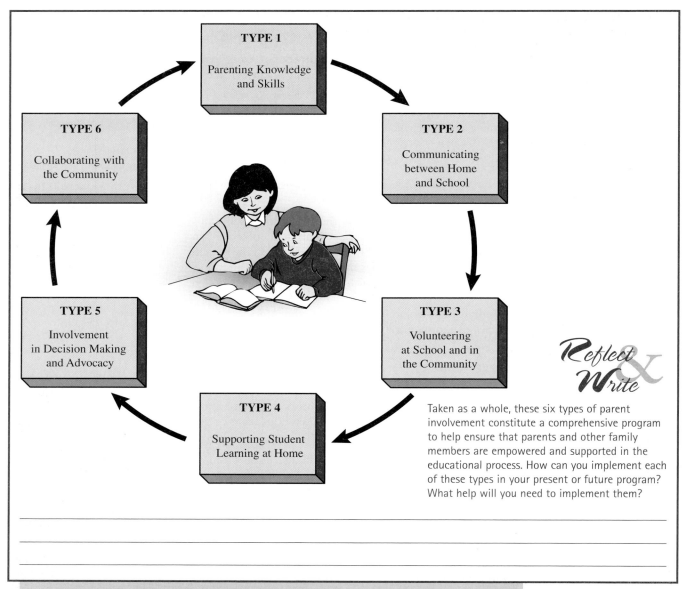

TYPE 1
Parenting Knowledge
and Skills

TYPE 6
Collaborating with
the Community

TYPE 2
Communicating
between Home
and School

TYPE 5
Involvement
in Decision Making
and Advocacy

TYPE 3
Volunteering
at School and in
the Community

TYPE 4
Supporting Student
Learning at Home

Reflect & Write

Taken as a whole, these six types of parent involvement constitute a comprehensive program to help ensure that parents and other family members are empowered and supported in the educational process. How can you implement each of these types in your present or future program? What help will you need to implement them?

Figure 6.4   Six Types of Parent/Family Involvement

Source: J. Epstein, *School, Family, and Community Partnerships: Preparing Educators and Improving Schools* (Boulder, Colo.: Westview Press, 2001).

worked to solve this challenge by reaching out to an untapped source—fathers and other male relatives. The goal was to involve men in the learning community and provide opportunities for them to be role models for students. Having men participate in school activities also helps break the stereotype that only mothers volunteer and monitor student progress.

4. Learning at home. Involve families with their children in learning activities at home, including homework and other curriculum-related activities and decisions.

Glenville High School, Cleveland, Ohio

At Family Nights Out for Fun and Learning, teachers inform and involve families of students who are required to pass the Ninth Grade Ohio Proficiency Test (OPT). Parents learn about the high school's practices, their children's status on the OPT, and what they can do at home to prepare for the test. The program also offers vision screenings and tips on stress reduction, nutrition, and time management. The number of parent/family encouragers continues to increase; and the number of ninth- and tenth-grade students completing the graduation test requirements has also increased.

5. Decision making. Include families as participants in school decisions, governance, and advocacy through PTA/PTO, school councils, committees, and other parent organizations.

James Ford Rhodes High School, Cleveland, Ohio

James Ford Rhodes High School recently formed the Teacher-Alumni-Parent Partnership (TAPP) to help guide students down the road of success. TAPP's first objective targeted boosting school spirit by recognizing student success. This was done by developing the Rhodes to Success Wall. At the end of every month, teachers selected three students from each of the four grades to receive an award for their excellence in academics, attitude, or athletics and have their pictures displayed on the Success Wall. These award-winning students had their names announced over the PA system and received a certificate designed by a TAPP member. At the end of the year, the students also were recognized in the local newspaper. TAPP hopes that these students' families and the community will see the children's accomplishments, know of the pride TAPP feels in them, and be inspired to become more involved with the school.

6. Collaborating with the community. Coordinate resources and services for families, students, and the school with businesses, agencies, and other groups and provide services to the community.

Chaska Middle School, Chaska, Minnesota

Involvement Coordinators at Chaska Middle School partnered with community agencies to develop Club Mid—an exciting opportunity to keep young adolescents out of trouble by engaging them in after-school activities. Club Mid serves as an alternative to traditional competitive athletics by offering different types of clubs during the school year to middle school students, such as computers, board games, party cooking, video, drama, stock market game, police detectives, snowboarding, and weight lifting clubs. Teachers or other adults with an interest in the activity lead the clubs. Club Mid has about 150 sixth-, seventh-, eighth-, and ninth-grade students registered in the program. As promotion efforts improve, parents are beginning to call ahead to find out what is being offered so they can guide their students' upcoming season.[9]

Parent/Family Conferences

There is a range of ways parents can be involved, depending on their needs and their willingness and inclination to be involved and the motivation and resources of teachers and schools. Parents and families can be involved by attending school functions, supervising homework, assisting with home-based learning activities, participating in school events and programs, attending school-based parenting classes and other adult education programs, volunteering time and expertise, serving as classroom aides, being an advocate for children and schools, and serving on advisory boards and decision-making committees.

Parent/family conferences are an effective way to communicate with parents and other family members about their children's achievement and behavior and to assess parents' needs as they relate to supporting their children's learning. Significant parent involvement can be facilitated through well-planned and well-conducted parent-teacher conferences. Such conferences are often the first contact many families have with schools. Conferences are critical from a public relations point of view and as a vehicle for helping families, teachers, and other school personnel accomplish their

INTASC

Standard 10: The teacher fosters relationships with school colleagues, parents, and agencies in the larger community to support students' learning and well-being.

NCATE

Middle Level

Standard 6: Understands the major concepts, principles, theories, and research related to working collaboratively with family and community members; uses that knowledge to maximize learning of all young adolescents.

INTASC

Standard 10: The teacher fosters relationships with school colleagues, parents, and agencies in the larger community to support students' learning and well-being.

NCATE

Early Childhood

Standard 2: Understands and values complex characteristics of families and communities; creates respectful, reciprocal relationships that support and empower families; involves families in children's development and learning.

goals. The following guidelines will assist you as you prepare for and conduct parent/family conferences:

1. Plan ahead. Be sure of the reason for the conference. What are your objectives? What do you want to accomplish? List the points you want to cover and think about what you are going to say.
2. Get to know the parents. This is not wasted time; the more effectively you establish rapport with parents, the more you will accomplish in the long run.
3. Avoid an authoritative atmosphere. Do not sit behind your desk while parents sit across from you. Treat parents and others like the adults they are and sit next to them or in an arrangement that is comfortable for you and them.
4. Communicate at parents' levels. Do not condescend or patronize. Instead, use words, phrases, and explanations that parents understand and that are familiar to them. Do not use jargon or complicated explanations and speak in your natural style.
5. Accentuate the positive. Make every effort to show and tell parents what their children are doing well. When you deal with problems, put them in the proper perspective. Relate what a student is able to do, what the goals and purposes of the learning program are, what specific skill or concept you are trying to get a student to learn, and what problems the student is having in achieving. Most important, explain what you plan to do to help a student achieve in school and what specific role the parents can have in meeting these achievement goals.
6. Give parents a chance to talk. You will not learn much about parents if you do all the talking; neither are you likely to achieve your goals. If you dominate a conversation, you may put some parents off.
7. Learn to listen. An active listener makes eye contact, uses body language such as head nodding and hand gestures, does not interrupt, avoids arguing, paraphrases as a way of clarifying ideas, and keeps the conversation on track.

Early Childhood

Standard 2: Understands and values complex characteristics of families and communities; creates respectful, reciprocal relationships that support and empower families; involves families in children's development and learning.

Educators have long recognized that parent involvement in schools and classrooms increases student achievement. Parents have a great deal of influence over whether or not students succeed in school. Parents are their children's first teachers and play a primary role in socializing children. Because of the similarity between parents' and teachers' roles, teachers can benefit greatly by involving parents in their classrooms.

8. **Follow up.** Ask parents for a definite time for the next conference as you are concluding the current one. Another conference is the best method of solidifying gains and extending support, but other acceptable means of following up are telephone calls, written reports, mailed letters or notes sent home with students, or brief visits to the home. While these types of contacts may appear casual, they should be planned for and conducted as seriously as any regular parent-teacher conference. No matter which approach you choose, the advantages of a parent-teacher conference follow-up are these:
   - Families see that you genuinely care about their children.
   - Everyone can clarify problems, issues, advice, and directions.
   - Parents, family members, and children are encouraged to continue to do their best.
   - Follow-up offers further opportunities to extend classroom learning to the home.
   - You can extend programs initiated for helping families and formulate new plans.
9. **Develop an action plan.** Never leave parents with a sense of frustration, not knowing what you are doing or what they are to do. Every communication with families should end on a positive note, so that everyone knows what can be done and how to do it.

Home Visits

Home visits are becoming more commonplace for early childhood professionals. In fact, California has a $15 million initiative to pay teachers overtime for visiting students' homes. Teachers who do home visiting are trained prior to going on the visits.

A home visiting program can show that the teachers, principal, and school staff are willing to "go more than halfway" to involve all parents in their children's education. Home visits help teachers demonstrate their interest in students' families and understand their students better by seeing them in their home environment.

These visits should not replace parent-teacher conferences or be used to discuss children's progress. When done early, before any school problems can arise, they avoid putting any parents on the defensive and signal that teachers are eager to work with all parents. Teachers who have made home visits say they build stronger relationships with parents and their children and improve attendance and achievement. Guidelines for planning and implementing successful home visits can be found on this book's Web site at www.ablongman.com/morrison4.

Involving Single-Parent Families

Many of the students you teach will be from single-parent families. Based on where you teach, as many as 50 percent of your children could be from single-parent families. Here are some things you can do to ensure that single-parent families are involved.

First, many adults in one-parent families are employed during school hours and may not be available for conferences or other activities during that time. You must be willing to accommodate family schedules by arranging conferences at other times, perhaps early morning (breakfast), midmorning, noon (lunch), early afternoon, late afternoon, or early evening. Some employers, sensitive to these needs, give release time to participate in school functions, but others do not. Professionals and principals need to think seriously about going to families rather than having families always come to them. Some schools have set up parent conferences to accommodate families' work schedules, while some professionals find that home visits work best.

Second, remember that single parents have a limited amount of time to spend on involvement with their children's school and with their children at home. When you talk with single-parent families, make sure that (1) the meeting starts on time, (2) you have a list of items (skills, behaviors, achievements) to discuss, (3) you have sample materials available to illustrate all points, (4) you make specific suggestions relative to the one-parent environment, and (5) the meeting ends on time. One-parent families are more likely to need child-care assistance to attend meetings, so child care should be planned for every parent meeting or activity.

Third, suggest some ways that single parents can make their time with their children meaningful. If a child has trouble following directions, show parents how to use home situations to help in this area. Children can learn to follow directions while helping with errands, meal preparations, or housework.

Fourth, get to know families' lifestyles and living conditions. For example, you can recommend that every child have a quiet place to study, but this may be an impossible demand for some households. Before you set meeting times, you need to visit some of the homes in your community, decide what family involvement activities to implement, and what you will ask of families during the year.

Fifth, help develop support groups for one-parent families within your school, such as discussion groups and classes on parenting for singles. Include the needs and abilities of one-parent families in your family involvement activities and programs. After all, single-parent families may be the majority of families represented in the program.

Involving Language-Minority Parents and Families

Language-minority parents are individuals whose English proficiency is minimal and who lack a comprehensive knowledge of the norms and social systems in the United States. Language-minority families often face language and cultural barriers that greatly hamper their ability to become actively involved, although many have a great desire and willingness to participate in their children's education.

Because the culture of language-minority families often differs from the majority in a community, those who seek truly collaborative community, home, and school involvement must take into account the cultural features that can inhibit collaboration. Traditional styles of child rearing and family organization, attitudes toward schooling, organizations around which families center their lives, life goals and values, political influences, and methods of communication within the cultural group all have implications for parent participation.

Language-minority families often lack information about the U.S. educational system, including basic school philosophy, practice, and structure, which can result in misconceptions, fear, and a general reluctance to respond to invitations for involvement. Furthermore, this educational system may be quite different from what these families are used to. They may have been taught to avoid active involvement in the educational process, with the result that they prefer to leave all decisions concerning their children's education to professionals and administrators.

The U.S. ideal of a community-controlled and community-supported educational system must be explained to families from cultures in which this concept is not as highly valued. Traditional roles of children, professionals, and administrators also have to be explained. Many families, especially language-minority families, are willing to relinquish to professionals any rights and responsibilities they have for their children's education and need to be taught to assume their roles and obligations toward schooling.

Culturally Appropriate Family Involvement

Regardless of culture, here are some things that will help you:

- Know what parents want for their children. Find out families' goals for education, careers, and accomplishments. The more you talk to parents, the more you will be able to help them and their children.
- Be clear about your own educational values and goals. Share with parents what you believe are the purposes of schooling. At the same time, help parents see how

their goals for their children fit with your goals and the school's goals. Remember, all parents want the best for their children.

- Help parents learn to participate in the system of schooling. The process of schooling is complex and is confusing for parents. Provide specific examples of how you and the school are working to help them and their children.
- Build relationships with parents. Building relationships takes time, but it is worth the effort, because good relationships enhance communication and understandings. You communicate better when you have a relationship, and learning to communicate builds relationships.
- Learn to be an effective cross-cultural communicator. Learn about communication styles that are different from your own. What you think a person of another culture means may not be what he or she *really* means. Listen carefully and ask for clarification. When you are clear about what parents mean, then you can be more confident about helping them and their children.
- Clarify with parents what they think their roles are in educating children. These roles vary by culture. Once you learn what parents believe about appropriate roles, you will be better able to help meet parents' expectations for schooling.
- When interacting with parents, use a *problem-solving* rather than a *power* approach. Working together is the key. Be willing to include parents in setting goals, developing plans, and solving problems. Sharing power with parents is the foundation for working collaboratively for the common purpose of helping all students achieve.
- Commit yourself to education—both your own and that of the families. Sometimes lack of information or understanding of each other's perspective is what keeps the conflict going.

Elementary

Standard 5.3: Knows importance of establishing and maintaining positive collaborative relationships with families to promote the academic, social, and emotional growth of children.

e d u c a t i o n *on the move* >>>>>>>>>>>>

>>> New York City Gets Serious about Parent Involvement >>>>>>

For the three years Francine O. Honegan was a leader of the Parent Teacher Association at Middle School 144 in the Bronx, the group tried everything to get more than the same two dozen parents to attend meetings. There were raffles featuring $50 gift certificates for CDs, electronics, and Oprah's Book Club novels; there were potluck dinners with steaming stewed chicken and macaroni and cheese. But even hours spent calling no-show parents did not draw more than ten or so new faces—and most never returned.

Now, increasing parental involvement at M.S. 144 is Ms. Honegan's full-time job. She is the school's new parent coordinator, one of the 1,200 who represent perhaps the biggest gamble in New York City's overhaul of its public schools. In a year of budget cuts, the New York City Department of Education is spending $43 million to hire a parent coordinator in every school to encourage parents to

participate in their children's education. Each parent coordinator will be paid between $30,000 and $39,000 annually.

On another front, Learning Leaders, a forty-eight-year-old organization with more than 14,000 volunteers, is enlisting parent volunteers to dedicate six weeks to helping children who are attending summer school sharpen their skills in English. "It's the first time we've had a summer initiative of this kind," said Digna Sánchez, the group's executive director, noting high interest among parents. "Clearly, the so-called end of social promotion for third-graders is a controversial issue."

The new initiative, Volunteers for Summer School Success, trained more than four hundred volunteers. The training was developed in conjunction with the Department of Education in April, shortly after the promotion policy was approved. Under the

policy, more than 9,000 third-graders who did not achieve a level 2 score or above on standardized reading or math state tests faced repeating the grade. (A level 1 score is the lowest of four rankings.) They are being encouraged to attend summer school and to take the exams again.

The Volunteers for Summer School Success will focus on English language skills and building students' confidence and skills in the hope that they will pass the English exam at the end of the summer.

Source: E. Gootman, "In Gamble, New York Schools Pay to Get Parents Involved," *New York Times.* August 30, 2003. (Online). Available at www.nytimes.com/2003/08/30/nyregion/30PARE.html; A. N. Stevens, "Parents Join Effort to Help Pupils Reach Fourth Grade," *New York Times,* June 27, 2004. (Online). Available at www.nytimes.com/2004/06/27/education/27learn.html. Reprinted by permission.

Teachers can also help parents support, extend, and enrich their children's learning in the home. For example, parents can be homework helpers, co-authors of books and stories, and partners with their children in learning. Some things you can do to help parents be homework helpers are:

- Send home guidelines for being a homework helper. Guidelines can include how to answer children's questions, how to help but not do the homework, how to help students see how the homework fits in with real-life applications, and what to review for in a well-done and complete homework assignment.
- Send textbooks and other materials home for parents to use as resources.
- Help parents plan ahead for homework assignments by providing weekly or even monthly schedules and topics.
- Suggest to parents that they use television, newspapers, and magazines as sources for connecting homework to everyday events and activities.
- Provide parents with guidelines when helping with their children's homework, such as be positive, listen to each other, work together, set a time limit for doing homework, and review finished homework together.

How confident are you about conducting parent/family conferences? What are some things you will have to do to prepare for this important role?

_____

_____

_____

_____

SECTION SUMMARY

What Is Parent Involvement?

Parent involvement is an excellent way to maximize students' benefits from schooling. It is important, among other things, to approach contact with parents with cultural sensitivity and communicate in a natural and positive way.

- Six Types of Parent/Family Involvement. Six types of involvement include parenting knowledge and skills, communicating between home and school, volunteering at school and in the community, supporting student learning at home, involvement in decision making and advocacy, and collaborating with the community. You will want to do your best to involve your families in all six of these types of parent involvement. Activities for helping you do this are found on this book's Web site at www.ablongman.com/morrison4e.
- Parent/Family Conferences. Conferences are a good way to communicate with parents/families and enlist their involvement. Important elements in these conferences are giving parents a chance to talk, following up, and developing an action plan.
- Home visits. Home visits are becoming more commonplace as a means of getting to know and involve parents. These visits enable you to see the context in which children are reared and how conditions of the home affect their learning and behavior.
- Involving Single Parents. Part of your role as a high-quality teacher will be to involve single parents. Since as many as half of your students may come from single-parent homes, it is essential for you to know how to involve single parents and to be sensitive to their needs.
- Involving Language-Minority Parents and Families. Many of your students will come from language-minority homes. Language-minority families often face language

and cultural barriers that interfere with their ability to become actively involved. You must take into account language and cultural factors as you seek to implement an effective family involvement program.

- Culturally Sensitive Family Involvement. Knowing and understanding the cultural identities of your students and their families will be a critical part of your responsibilities as a teacher.

Thinking Critically
★ ★ ★ ★ ★ ★ ★ ★

Which form of follow-up are you most comfortable with—a telephone call, a letter sent home with a student, or a brief visit to the family's home? What might your choice reveal about your strengths or weaknesses as a teacher?

_____

_____

_____

_____ ★

Applying What You've Learned
★ ★ ★ ★ ★ ★ ★ ★

Homework is a challenge for students, teachers, and parents. One solution is to provide online help. B. J. Pinchbeck, in 1996 (when he was nine years old), launched B. J. Pinchbeck's Homework Helper, a Web site that lists over 700 links to educational sites on the Internet and is affiliated with the Discovery channel. Subjects include art, computer science, current events, English, foreign languages, history, math, music, and science. Visit this Web site at http://school.discovery.com/Schoolhome.html. Review the Web site and tell how you could use it in your work with parents.

_____

_____

_____ ★

Putting Yourself in the Picture
★ ★ ★ ★ ★ ★ ★ ★

You are asking the parents of your class of middle-class, suburban seventh-graders to take a more active role in helping their children learn at home. Construct a two-page letter offering tips and advice to parents about ways they can help their children with homework assignments.

_____

_____

_____

_____ ★

𝒲HAT EDUCATIONAL REFORMS ARE PROMOTING GREATER PARENT EMPOWERMENT?

Empowering parents is both a process and a product. As a process, **parent empowerment** provides parents with decision-making and participation opportunities as they become involved with the school as partners in their children's education. As a

Parent empowerment
Provides parents with decision-making and participation opportunities; represents the collaborative achievements of parents and school personnel.

NCATE

Elementary

Standard 5.4: Fosters relationships with school colleagues and agencies in the larger community to support students' learning and well-being.

Middle Level

Standard 7: Understands the complexity of teaching young adolescents; engages in practices and behaviors that develop competence as a professional.

Site-based management
Process that empowers those who are affected by school decisions by including them in the decision-making process.

School choice
Various proposals that allow parents to choose the schools their children will attend.

INTASC

Standard 10: The teacher fosters relationships with school colleagues, parents, and agencies in the larger community to support students' learning and well-being.

product, parent empowerment represents the concrete achievements of parents and school personnel as they cooperatively and collaboratively work together.

The involvement of parents in schools and school-related activities is accelerating and will likely continue in the future. It is also likely that as society continues to expect schools to solve more social problems, teachers and other school leaders will expend increasing efforts to reach out to parents, the community, and the public to assist them in their efforts to address social issues. At the same time, schools will be continually under pressure to improve their services and performance.

Site-Based Management

In many school districts across the United States, administrators, teachers, parents, and community members are participating in forms of school governance that are changing how decisions are made and how schools operate. One form of governance is known by a number of names, including **site-based management.** This approach is intended to empower those who are affected by school decisions by including them in the decision-making process. The process and influence of site-based (or school-based) management are discussed in greater detail in Chapter 7. Parents and community members participate in site-based decision-making processes, and their opinions are increasingly influential in determining how schools operate and how teaching and learning occur. Often, the involvement of parents on site-based committees is mandated by school district policy or state law.

School Choice

School choice programs are designed to enable parents to choose the school their children will attend, with certain limitations and within certain constraints. **School choice** is defined in a number of ways. At its most controversial level, it means giving families public funds to send their children to private schools. It also means giving parents the choice to send their children to other public schools in the district and across district lines and/or school attendance patterns. This process of giving parents the opportunity to choose schools for their children—and providing the means to do so through tax dollars—is a major political issue in education today. In addition to creating much discussion, the school choice controversy has also reinforced and emphasized parents' roles and responsibilities for the education of their children. Furthermore, the debate has placed parents at the center of decision making about where children will attend school and what they will study and learn.

School Choice and NCLB. Under the No Child Left Behind Education Act (NCLB) of 2001, students are eligible for public school choice when the Title I school they attend has not made adequate yearly progress (AYP) for two consecutive years or longer and is therefore identified as needing improvement, corrective action, or restructuring. Any child attending such a school in a district must be offered the option of transferring to a public school in the district—including a public charter school—not identified as needing improvement. NCLB requires that priority in providing school choice be given to the lowest-achieving children from low-income families. This school choice option really means that parents have the responsibility for making the choice for their children.

One goal of the choice option is that as academically deficient schools lose students, they will be motivated to improve in order to retain students and even attract other students. In addition to the choice option of NCLB, more than one-half of the states have laws supporting school choice. However, merely having laws that permit choice does not necessarily mean that school choice will work. For example, a problem with many choice plans is that some schools will not accept students because their

Parents and community members across the country have become involved in the school reform movement. What options of educational empowerment are available to parents today?

schools are already full, because of a negative effect on racial balances, or because many local boards have policies of not accepting students from outside the district.

Vouchers. Another expression of school choice is the voucher system. **Vouchers** are certificates good for certain amounts of money that parents can use to pay for some or all of their children's tuition at a private or public school. Milwaukee has had a voucher system since 1990, and currently, over 11,000 low-income students are attending a variety of public, private, and parochial schools at state expense.

Vouchers are designed to support efforts at providing parents with choice. Proponents of vouchers say that vouchers are a means of school reform and that they return decision making to parents. Opponents counter that the goal should be to make public schools better rather than going outside the public system. Critics also maintain that vouchers erode public school support and drain needed tax dollars from schools. Some opponents also claim that vouchers lead to resegregation of the schools.

Public opinion about school choice is mixed. Generally, the public is supportive of the concept of allowing parents to choose the school their children will attend. However, many people do not support allowing parents to send their children to private or church-related schools at public expense. Additional controversy surrounds the issue of accountability. Historically, private and church-affiliated schools have had more flexibility than publicly funded schools with regard to the rules and requirements they establish. Publicly funded schools must abide by the strict constructs of state and federal law or face the threat of losing funding. Many argue that private schools receiving any public monies should be accountable to the same laws.

In the recent Supreme Court case *Zelman v. Simmons-Harris*, the court held that a state-enacted voucher program in Cleveland does not violate the U.S. Constitution's prohibition on government establishment of religion. The court found that the program "is entirely neutral with respect to religion" since it permits the "participation of all schools within the district, religious or nonreligious." The court also ruled that

Vouchers
Funds allocated to parents to be used to purchase education for their children at public or private schools in the area.

Elementary
Standard 5.4: Fosters relationships with school colleagues and agencies in the larger community to support students' learning and well-being.

School Vouchers

The issues of using vouchers to enable parents to send their children to private schools and public charter schools are many and contentious. As a beginning teacher, you will be asked questions about and be involved in discussions relating to school choice. Reformers see school choice as one way of encouraging low-performing schools to bring their programs up to a higher level. Opponents of school choice believe that allowing parents to send their children, at public expense, to any school they desire erodes or detracts from the role of public education and lets tax dollars flow from the public to the private sector. In a recent public opinion poll, here is how the public responded to a question about school vouchers.[10]

YOU DECIDE

Do you favor or oppose allowing students and parents to choose a private school to attend at public expense?

	2003 (%)	2002 (%)	2001 (%)	2000 (%)	1999 (%)	1998 (%)	1997 (%)	1996 (%)
Favor	38	46	34	39	41	44	44	36
Oppose	60	52	62	56	55	50	52	61
Don't know	2	2	4	5	4	6	4	3

Now, it's your turn! How do you decide? Answer the same question. Write a short paragraph expressing your views pro or con regarding vouchers and their use.

For more information about vouchers and choice, visit www.schoolchoices.org.

the government provision of funds to religious schools through voucher programs does not violate stands on church-state separation.[10]

The voucher movement is very much a part of the educational landscape and is a "hot" topic politically and educationally. As a beginning teacher, you will be involved in discussions about school choice and vouchers with administrators, colleagues, parents, and the public. Parental choice and voucher systems will continue to be topics of debate in the years to come.

Charter Schools

In Chapter 3 charter schools were discussed as independent public schools designed to enhance efforts at improving and reforming public schools. St. Paul City Academy in Minnesota was the nation's first charter school. It opened its doors in 1992. One of the purposes of charter schools is to provide parents and pupils with more alternatives to public schools, both within and outside of existing school districts. Advocates of charter schools say that these schools encourage innovative teaching, promote performance-based accountability, expand choices of type of public school, create new professional opportunities for teachers, improve student learning, and promote community involvement.[12]

Many states have approved charter school legislation, and more are doing so each year. Arizona has the most (495) charter schools, followed by California, Florida, and Texas.[13] Charter schools may be new schools or conversions of existing schools. The legal basis for the authority of charter schools varies from state to state. In Arizona, Massachusetts, Michigan, and Minnesota, for example, charter schools are legally independent of school districts. On the other hand, in Colorado, Georgia, Kansas, New Mexico, and Wisconsin, charter schools are legally part of the traditional school district.

In spite of all of the discussion of and publicity about charter schools over the last decade, the public does not appear to be well informed about them. Only 55 percent of the public says they have read about or heard of charter schools. At the same time,

On Our Own: Karen Butterfield

Karen Butterfield is an Arizona Teacher of the Year and founder of the Flagstaff Arts and Leadership Academy. Its motto is: "Arts in education, leadership as an art, in order to make a difference in the community and world in which we live." According to Karen:

The charter school movement is growing by leaps and bounds in Arizona, and there are many opportunities for teachers and parents to come together to form the kind of school they want which will meet the needs of students. In Arizona, charter schools are free and are considered to be public schools. They are exempt from all regulations except those dealing with health, safety, insurance, and civil rights.

I wanted to start this charter school, in part, to help meet the needs of my Navajo students. There really needs to be more of an opportunity for Navajo students to succeed. About 25 percent of the students are Navajo, and they need alternatives. Several years ago I attended a Navajo cultural training session, and it really opened my eyes about what I could do for and with students by focusing on and supporting their culture. I'm also partnering with a local university for teacher training. I saw the charter school as an ideal opportunity to tie in teacher training at the secondary level. I believe more secondary teachers have to be sensitive to the cultural and life needs of students and their families, so I want to include a strong emphasis on parent and community involvement in the training of teachers.

I am dedicated to leadership. So, the main focus of the charter school is to educate creative and productive leaders for the future. The core of the curriculum is an integrated arts program

with emphasis on the visual and performing arts. Students will take at least a dozen hours of art, music, and drama classes each week, and these will be integrated with core classes of science, math, and English. In addition, all students have to engage in community service as part of their graduation requirements. The parents really love the community service component. A lot of parents and students don't like what they see happening in society today with the decline in moral values and lack of care about others. Parents think that civic duty and leadership are essential parts of educating youth.

I have a great deal of faith in parents participating in school decisions and in helping make schools better. A lot of parents believe there is a need for developing ways for teaching students that may not be found in traditional schools. When other teachers ask me how I manage to get parents so involved, I tell them it's because I seek parents out and I ask them for help and advice. I tell teachers, "Don't be afraid to ask." I have never been turned down by a parent or community leader when I have asked them to help.

I think charter schools represent a good way for teachers, parents, and community leaders to come together to try something new and to provide an education for students that is really in keeping with agreed-upon goals and values. I hope that beginning teachers see the value of working with and in the community to make a difference. It is a wonderful time to be a teacher because of the opportunities available for those who are willing to lead.

82 percent of the public believes that any private or charter school that receives public monies should be accountable to the public in the same way that the public schools are accountable.[14] (See the Profile.)

SECTION SUMMARY

What Educational Reforms Are Promoting Greater Parent Empowerment?

Today parents are more empowered than ever before to participate in schools as full partners through site-based management, school choice, and vouchers.

- Site-Based Management. Many site-based management committees have specific provisions for parent membership. As a result, parents' voices and opinions are increasingly influential in determining how schools operate.

- School Choice. School choice is a controversial and politically "hot topic." In considering school choice, the attitudes and desires of parents are important to consider. The No Child Left Behind Act requires that children attending a substandard school be offered school choice options. Vouchers provide many parents the opportunity to send their children to an alternative public or private school, which further empowers parents.

- Charter Schools. Charter schools are independent public schools designed to improve on public school offerings. These schools provide parents with greater choice opportunities, making them key players in the operation of these schools. Legislation in many states supports charter schools.

Thinking Critically

★ ★ ★ ★ ★ ★ ★ ★

If you knew that the families of students in your classroom could exercise their right to remove their children and send them across district lines to another school, how do you think this knowledge might affect your teaching and your relationships with your students?

_____

_____

_____

_____ ★

Applying What You've Learned

★ ★ ★ ★ ★ ★ ★ ★

Choice is a major theme that pervades all of education today. Students want choice, teachers, parents, and families want choice. Why do you think there is so much emphasis on choice? Do you think that the federal government, states, and school districts are going "overboard" and giving parents too much choice?

_____

_____

_____ ★

Putting Yourself in the Picture

★ ★ ★ ★ ★ ★ ★ ★

You have been offered a position at a charter school. A friend tells you that there is also an opening for someone with your background in the public school in which he teaches. Which option seems most attractive to you? Why?

_____

_____

_____

_____ ★

INTASC

Standard 10: The teacher fosters relationships with school colleagues, parents, and agencies in the larger community to support students' learning and well-being.

NCATE

Middle Level

Standard 6: Understands the major concepts, principles, theories, and research related to working collaboratively with family and community members; uses that knowledge to maximize learning of all young adolescents.

*H*OW CAN YOU USE THE COMMUNITY TO TEACH *?*

The community offers a vital and rich array of resources for helping you teach better and for helping you meet the needs of parents and their children. Schools and teachers cannot address the many issues facing children and youth without the partnership and collaboration of powerful sectors of society, including community agencies, businesses, and industry. Here are some actions you can take to help you make use of resources in the community:

- Know your students and their needs. By knowing your students through observation, conferences with parents, and discussions with students, you can identify any barriers to their learning. In this way, you know what kind of help to seek.
- Know your community. You can learn about your community by walking or driving around in it. Ask parents to introduce you to community members and agencies. Other good ways of learning about a community are reading the local newspaper and attending events in the community.
- Ask for help and support from parents and the community. Keep in mind that many parents will not be involved unless you ask them directly. The only encouragement many need is your personal invitation.

- Develop a directory of community agencies. You can make such a directory by consulting the yellow pages of the local phone book, contacting the local chamber of commerce, and asking parents what agencies are helpful to them.
- Compile a list of people willing to speak to or work with your students. You can start by asking parents to volunteer and for their suggestions and recommendations of others who might help.
- Join and/or network with community-based social and civic organizations. Many of these service agencies, such as the Kiwanas and Rotary International, actively seek out collaborative opportunities to serve children and youth.

Communities have much to offer teachers who are willing to seek out and build relationships that support collaborative and cooperative ventures. You and your students will be richly rewarded by your efforts in using the community to help support teaching and learning.

Developing Community–School Partnerships

Many of the pressures that influence a community have implications for schools and teaching. Community pressures stem from such issues as how best to pay for schools, what curriculum best fits student and community needs, what kinds of schools are worth supporting, and how to educate students who are able to be productive as citizens and in the work force. As you work in and through the community, you will have many opportunities to take the pulse of parents and community leaders on these and other issues. It is important for you to be in touch with your school's community so that you can be fully informed and make wise teaching decisions.

Working arrangements and exchanges between school districts and schools and community agencies and businesses are termed **community-school partnerships.** Increasingly, community-based groups are forging relationships that support schools, make the community a better place, and prepare students for work and life. In developing connections with the community, consider all agencies that are potential sources of partnership. Groups to consider include professional associations of doctors, lawyers, architects, nurses, and accountants. For example, an architect might work with your students on issues of public housing and neighborhoods. Also, museums, colleges and universities, ethnic and cultural groups, senior citizens' centers, religious groups, health organizations, and social and civic groups are all potential collaborators. (See the Profile.)

Linking Schools, Communities, and Businesses

Critics of the schools frequently complain that many students are cut off from the "real" world and that what students do in school has little application to life and work. The contention is that owing to a lack of real-life connection, students view school as irrelevant. Another concern is how students move from high school into the work world. Approximately three-quarters of all high school graduates do not go on to a four-year college program. These students therefore face the difficulties of making the transition from school to work. The School-to-Work Opportunities Act of 1994 provided states and local communities with venture capital to form partnerships among schools, parents, students, employers, organized labor, and community organizations. These partnerships connect the classroom with the world of work to show students how academic achievement is crucial to their success as working adults. The School-to-Work Opportunities Act expired in 2001. Schools used school-to-work funds to build a foundation for many of their work-based learning programs.

School-to-work (STW) programs help students see the relevance between what they learn in the classroom and the world of work, develop career-specific skills, and integrate classroom and on-the-job instruction. Other terms for STW are *school-to-careers* and *learning-to-work, work-based learning,* and *tech prep.* School-to-work programs serve a broad cross-section of students, including those who are from low-income families and/or those who are low achieving. The linking of work-based and

Community-school partnerships Working arrangements or exchanges between school districts and/or schools and community agencies and/or businesses.

School-to-work (STW) programs Partnerships among schools, parents, students, employers, organized labor, and community organizations that help students make the transition from the school world to the work world.

It Takes a 'Hood: The Harlem Children's Zone

Geoffrey Canada is a man with a vision—a vision as big as New York City. His vision is that if you really want to change the lives of inner-city children, you change everything—their schools, their families, their neighborhood—all at once. No piecemeal approaches, no one program at a time. You do it all—all at once. Canada was profiled in a New York Times Magazine *article by P. Tough on June 20, 2004.*

Geoffrey Canada's new program, the Harlem Children's Zone, combines educational, social, and medical services. It starts at birth and follows children to college. It meshes those services into an interlocking web, and then it drops that web over an entire neighborhood. It operates on the principle that each child will do better if all the children around him are doing better. So instead of waiting for residents to find out about the services on their own, the organization's recruiters go door-to-door to find participants, sometimes offering prizes and raffles and free groceries to parents who enroll their children in the group's programs. What results is a remarkable level of "market penetration," as the organization describes it. Eighty-eight percent of the roughly 3,400 children under 18 in the twenty-four-block core neighborhood are already served by at least one program, and this year Canada began to extend his programs to the larger sixty-block zone. The objective is to create a safety net woven so tightly that children in the neighborhood can't slip through. At a moment when each new attempt to solve the problem of poverty seems to fall apart, what is going on in Harlem is one of the biggest social experiments of our time.

The programs that the Harlem Children's Zone offers are all carefully planned and well run, but none of them, on their own, are particularly revolutionary. It is only when they are con-sidered as a network that they seem so new. The organization employs more than 650 people in more than twenty programs.

At Harlem Gems, a program for forty prekindergarten students at a public school on 118th Street, five-year-old Keith sits at a computer working away at "Hooked on Phonics," while Luis, a nineteen-year-old tutor, gives him one-on-one instruction. A few blocks up Lenox Avenue, at the Employment and Technology Center, thirty teenagers who are part of the organization's new investment club are gathered around a conference table, listening to an executive from Lehman Brothers explain the difference between the Dow Jones and the NASDAQ. At P.S. 76 on West 121st Street, fifth-grade students in an after-school program stand in front of their peers, reading aloud the autobiographies they wrote this afternoon. And over at Truce, the after-school center for teenagers, a tutor named Carl helps Trevis, a student in the eighth grade, with a research project for his social studies class, an eight-page paper on the life of Frederick Douglass.

In a nearby housing project, a counselor from the Family Support Center pays a home visit to a woman who has just been granted legal custody of her two grandchildren; in other apartments in the neighborhood, outreach workers from Baby College, a class for new parents, are making home visits of their own, helping teach better parenting techniques. A few blocks away, at the corner of Madison Avenue and 125th Street, construction is under way on the organization's new headquarters, a six-story, $44-million building that will also house the Promise Academy, a new charter school opening in the fall.

Source: P. Tough, "It Takes a 'Hood: The Harlem Children's Zone," *New York Times,* June 20, 2004. Reprinted by permission.

---

classroom-based learning is seen as one way to keep students in high school and help them move into meaningful employment opportunities. For example, in a morning school-based program, students might apply mathematics skills in learning about building construction, and in an afternoon job-related program, students might apply this learning in helping build a shelter for the homeless.

In Wisconsin, school-to-work is a system of education-related opportunities that center on actively preparing all students to enter the global work force of the future. These opportunities provide students with strong academic, technical, and life skills deemed by both business and educational leaders to be necessary skills for the future. The partnerships between business and education that have been developed throughout the state are the foundations of the school-to-work system and connect the classroom to the community and the world of work.

Students in Wisconsin's 426 school districts have access to school-to-work opportunities. The programs are coordinated locally by school-to-work, youth apprenticeship, tech prep, and vocational educational coordinators located in elementary, middle, and high schools, technical colleges, the University of Wisconsin system, cooperative educational service agencies (CESA), chambers of commerce, and other community organizations.[15]

Developing Social Capital

We can further appreciate the value of school-community partnerships by emphasizing a banking metaphor and introducing a concept from macroeconomics.

Social capital is a concept from economics meaning socially valued goods and services that are exchanged in the social transactions within a family or community. For example, in a family social capital can consist of the attention, nurturance, support, and help family members can provide children in their learning and development. When family members provide these things to children, social capital is strong. Low socioeconomic status and family problems—such as substance abuse, unemployment, spousal abuse, divorce, employment stress, lack of education, and the like—weaken social capital. The same concept can be applied to the community. A community with strong social capital has systems in place for children and families, such as parks and playgrounds, senior citizen and community centers, violence- and drug-free environments, and a caring attitude.

When families and communities are weak, the school lacks resources central to its role of effectively educating children. When social capital of the family and the community are weak, it is necessary to rebuild that capital. Such rebuilding can be done by agencies other than the school, but it is in the school's interest to generate activities and programs to accomplish this task. If children are to learn and not merely be taught, the school must help in rebuilding family and community social capital.

Social capital can be built through family-centered programs that acknowledge parents as the first teachers of their children; help them develop skills, knowledge, and abilities; and link them to community agencies. The social capital of the school's neighborhood can be enhanced through community-centered programs linking school programs with community agencies. The Profile of Geoffrey Canada is very illustrative of developing social capital to improve the lives of children, youth, and families. You and your school can work with families and communities to help develop social capital and the means to use it in the education and development of children and families.

> **Social capital**
> Concept from economics meaning socially valued goods and services that are exchanged in the social transactions within a family or community.

> **INTASC**
> **Standard 10:** The teacher fosters relationships with school colleagues, parents, and agencies in the larger community to support students' learning and well-being.

Working with Community Agencies

The range of community groups that you can work with in partnerships includes community agencies; professional associations; and local, state, and federal organizations. For example, the National Coalition for Parent Involvement in Education consists of more than one hundred groups, including parents, schools, community and religious groups, and businesses. Community alliances can tackle almost any problem impacting school effectiveness and student learning, often with spectacular results.

Using School-Linked Services. Many school districts provide **school-linked services** for students and families. These services can be provided either at the school building, near the school site, or at another agency. A key factor is that they be coordinated between the school and the agencies providing the services. Funding for these linked services generally comes from federal funds, local government agency funds, private donations, fund-raisers, and grants.[16] The most frequently provided linked services are shown in Table 6.2.

Working with Parent Organizations. Many parents and families experience involvement at the local level through parent-teacher organizations. Many of these are represented at the national level by the National Parent-Teacher Association (PTA), which has 6 million members in 23,000 local units.

The PTA has developed National Standards for Parent/Family Involvement Programs, outlined in Figure 6.5.

> **School-linked services**
> Services coordinated between schools and agencies providing the services, for example, health, psychological, family welfare, housing, and other services.

Table 6.2   School-Linked Services Provided by School Districts

School-Linked Service	Percentage of Districts
Substance abuse services	62.90
Psychological services	56.85
Education services	58.60
Health services	51.95
Social services	51.25
Job training	49.55
Teen pregnancy	47.20
Child welfare	44.80
Juvenile probation	43.75
Family welfare	33.00
Housing services	27.10

Source: Adapted from P. M. Hardiman, J. L. Curcio, and J. C. Fortune, "School-Linked Services," *American School Board Journal,* *185* (9), 37–40. Copyright 1998 by the National School Board Association. All rights reserved. Reprinted by permission.

Standard I	Communicating—Communication between home and school is regular, two-way, and meaningful.
Standard II	Parenting—Parenting skills are promoted and supported.
Standard III	Student Learning—Parents play an integral role in assisting student learning.
Standard IV	Volunteering—Parents are welcome in the school, and their support and assistance are sought.
Standard V	School Decision Making and Advocacy—Parents are full partners in the decisions that affect children and families.
Standard VI	Collaborating with Community—Community resources are used to strengthen schools, families, and student learning.

Reflect & Write

These PTA Standards incorporate all of the dimensions of a successful parent-family involvement program. List five specific things you will do as a classroom teacher to try and make parents full partners in decision making.

Figure 6.5 *National Standards for Parent/Family Involvement Programs*

Source: National Parent and Teacher Association, *National Standards for Parent/Family Involvement Programs: An Implementation Guide for School Communities* (Bloomington, IN: National Educational Service, 2004). Available at www.pta.org/parentinvolvement/pfistand.htm. Reprinted with permission of National PTA.

What Parents Can Do

NCATE

Early Childhood

Standard 2: Understands and values complex characteristics of families and communities; creates respectful, reciprocal relationships that support and empower families; involves families in children's development and learning.

As a beginning teacher you will have many opportunities to advise parents about how they can help their children learn and succeed. Figure 6.6 outlines some of the things you can share with families about the role of successful parenting.

Not all parents will be able to do all of the suggestions listed in the figure. Also, some parents will be more adept in some areas than in others. Some parents will have more time than other parents. What is important is that you encourage and support all parents in being involved in their children's lives and education in the best ways they can.

- Help children set daily and weekly routine. Routines need to be established for most activities including going to bed, eating, and doing homework.
- Help children manage their time.
- Know where children are.
- Know who children's friends are and whom they are spending time with.
- Monitor children's television and reading habits.
- Be interested in school affairs, what is going on at school, what the child is learning, and the child's successes and difficulties.
- Attend school events and activities.
- Communicate with teachers.

Reflect & Write

Parents have many responsibilities for helping their children be successful in school and life. What are two specific things you can do to help parents assume the above roles? List two other responsibilities you would add to the list.

Figure 6.6 *Suggestions for Successful Parenting*

SECTION SUMMARY

How Can You Use the Community to Teach?

Teachers can make use of community resources by taking action to know students' needs, investigate community and parent resources, ask for help, and compile lists of agency and individual resources.

- Developing Community-School Partnerships. Teachers who know students' and parents' needs and who understand community pressures are better equipped to use community resources to address those needs. Community pressures can stem from financial, curricular, and philosophical issues. A strong community that supports the schools is a key factor to the success of the school and of its students. There are many community groups that are potential partners.

- Linking Schools, Communities, and Businesses. Many businesses and industries recognize that public school education largely determines how successful students will be in the future and in the workplace. Such organizations may offer partnerships or grants or encourage employee participation as students, volunteers, aides, and tutors. School-to-work programs play a key role in these linkages and help students make the transition from school to work.

- Developing Social Capital. A community with strong social capital provides children and families with such things as parks and playgrounds, community centers for young and old, environments free from violence and drugs, and a caring attitude. Social capital is a key component in effective education.

- Working with Community Agencies. Teachers have access to many community resources in forming alliances to improve school effectiveness and create a better environment for student learning. These exist at all levels of government, and many are affiliated with religious groups and businesses. Particularly noteworthy are school-linked services and parent organizations, such as the National Parent-Teacher Association.

- What Parents Can Do. Teachers can encourage parents to be as involved as possible in their children's lives and education. It is important that parents help their children establish good daily routines and study habits.

Thinking Critically
★ ★ ★ ★ ★ ★ ★ ★ ★

Why is it important to gather information about company or agency goals and priorities before attempting to craft a successful partnership?

_____

_____

_____

_____

Applying What You've Learned
★ ★ ★ ★ ★ ★ ★ ★ ★

What agencies function as resources for the community in which your college or university is located? Using the yellow pages, compile a directory of these agencies. You can also contact the local chamber of commerce about community resources, and you can consult faculty members, librarians, friends, and family members for their ideas. When you finish, donate your directory to a local school.

_____

_____

_____

_____

Develop a proposal for Lisa Lenton, the teacher in the opening case, using the information in Part Two of this text (Chapters 4, 5, and 6). Revise your proposal according to feedback you get from classmates, instructors, and in-service education professionals and use this activity as a model for creating a business-school partnership of your own.

_____

_____

_____

_____★

Applications for Active Learning

CONNECTIONS

1. Think about the concepts and topics introduced in this chapter. Create a picture, graphic, figure, or web that shows connections that are meaningful to you among this chapter's key ideas and information.

2. Did you have a teacher or teachers who helped your parents help you with school activities and learning? What did they do? What are some things your teachers could have done for you and your family but didn't? How will you make sure you are responsive to the needs of your students' families?

_____

_____

_____

FIELD EXPERIENCES

1. Interview classroom teachers about their experiences with parental involvement. Also arrange to visit and interview parents at home about their involvement with the school, their children's teachers, and their children's education. Write an analysis of what you learn from these interviews and how you might use this information in your first year of teaching. Use the space below to write your predictions. What will teachers say about parent involvement and student achievement? What will parents say about school involvement and student achievement?

_____

_____

_____

2. Arrange to visit a local company or agency that participates in community-school involvement or sponsors a business-school partnership. What goods and services or capital investment does the company provide? How do spokespersons define the company's role, the goals for the partner, and the benefits to the company and its employees? How do they collaborate with the school to operate and evaluate the program? Compare your findings with your classmates' observations of other companies.

PERSONAL RESEARCH

1. Find out the legal basis for and current status of school choice, vouchers, and charter schools in your state or one in which you might be willing to teach. Also collect or summarize articles on these topics in local newspapers or in news periodicals such as _Education Week_. What are the issues, and what are your opinions?

2. Selectively compile an education-oriented list of local, state, and national agencies and organizations, including phone numbers and the services provided. How could you use each agency's services to help you teach and meet the needs of students and their families? Add this information to your Teaching Resource file in your portfolio.

Preparing to Teach

FOR YOUR PORTFOLIO

1. On the basis of your interviews, reading, and reflection, develop and write a specific plan for your involvement with students, parents, and families in your first year of teaching. Add the plan to your portfolio along with any

support materials you develop, such as letters to parents, guidelines, invitations, requests, schedules, and so on.

2. On the basis of your interviews, reading, and reflection, develop and write a plan for an actual business-school partnership or community-school partnership that you would like to propose and implement as a beginning teacher. Include this plan and any support materials you develop in your portfolio.

IDEA FILE

Brainstorm "Ten Best" ideas for involving parents of students at the grade level you plan to teach. You might develop this idea file on an ongoing basis by brainstorming ideas for involving parents in each unit of the content area(s) you plan to teach. Begin by writing in the space below a few ideas that come to mind.

_____

_____

_____

Learning and Knowing More

WEB SITES WORTH VISITING

When schools and community agencies collaborate to address the pressing needs of children and their families, the results are beneficial for everyone involved. Families, schools, churches, and other community institutions play a critical role in shaping children's academic success. One way to keep abreast of what's happening with school-community partnerships is through the work of the Appalachia Education Laboratory. You can visit their Web site at www.ael.org.

National School-to-Work Home Page
www.lake.k12.fl.us/stw

The Alliance for Parental Involvement in Education
www.croton.com/allpie
A nonprofit organization that assists and encourages parental involvement in education, wherever that education takes place—in public schools, in private schools, or at home.

The National Coalition for Parent Involvement in Education (NCPIE)
www.ncpie.org
NCPIE is dedicated to developing effective family-school partnerships in schools throughout America.

The National PTA Home Page
www.pta.org
Provides information as well as other links for PTA organizations.

The Center for Education Reform
www.edreform.com
Provides information pertaining to charter schools. Includes demographics, statistics, and other relevant information.

BOOKS WORTH READING

Barbour, C., and Barbour, N. H. (2005). *Families, Schools, and Communities: Building Partnerships for Educating Children*, 3rd ed. Upper Saddle River, NJ: Prentice Hall.
The authors seek to combine the knowledge and experiences that emerge from the three social settings of each child's life—home, community, and school—into educational strategies that will create nurturing learning environments.

Berger, E. (2004). *Parents as Partners in Education: Families in Schools Working Together*, 6th ed. Upper Saddle River, NJ: Prentice Hall.
Offers educators a framework for thinking about, talking about, and then actually building comprehensive programs for school and family partnerships.

Epstein, J. (2001). *School, Family, and Community Partnerships: Preparing Educators and Improving Schools*. Boulder, CO: Westview Press.
In this text the author explains the theory, practice, and benefits of school and family partnerships, incorporating ideas and lesson plans that teachers and school officials may use to involve parents in the education of their children.

Springate, K. W., and Stegelin, D. A. (2002). *Building School and Community Partnerships Through Parent Involvement*, 2nd ed. Upper Saddle River, NJ: Prentice Hall.
Takes an ecological, systems approach to the study of children and families in the school system. It focuses on the family as the "first teacher" of the child and provides the most effective strategies for involving parents in school settings.

Taylor, G. (2000). *Parental Involvement: A Practical Guide for Collaboration and Teamwork for Students with Disabilities*. Springfield, IL: Charles C. Thomas Publications.
The author provides a collaborative model that parents, teachers, and community agencies may employ to meet the needs of children with disabilities. Specific activities and intervention strategies offer an approach for parents and teachers to jointly develop programs.

PART THREE

*F*oundations of Education

*E*vents and ideas that shape teaching and learning are influenced by local, state, national, and international politics and economic conditions. These influences are reflected in school budgets, in efforts of education lobbies, and in legislation and court rulings on matters such as school finance reform, home schooling, and charter schools.

Time and place also link the events and ideas that shape teaching and learning. Today's schools reflect historical developments in education, from the Socratic method of classical Greece to the school desegregation movement of the 1950s. In the classroom you will see educational philosophy in action, translated into classroom arrangements, expectations for teaching and learning, instructional methods, communication patterns, and curriculum materials and activities.

The chapters in Part Three explore how the historical and philosophical roots of the Western world support the environment and outlook of education in America today. You as a teacher will experience directly the impact of these historical, philosophical, and legal influences as you work with students, parents, colleagues, administrators, and other professionals in the field of education.

CHAPTER 7 Political and Economic Influences on American Education

INTASC Standards ① ② ③ ④ ⑤ ⑥ ⑦ ⑧ **⑨ ⑩**

NCATE Standards
Early Childhood ① **②** ③ ④ **⑤**
Elementary ① ② ③ ④ **⑤**
Middle Level ① **②** ③ ④ ⑤ **⑥ ⑦**

CHAPTER 8 The Legal Basis for Education and School Law

INTASC Standards ① **②** ③ ④ **⑤** ⑥ ⑦ ⑧ **⑨** ⑩

NCATE Standards
Early Childhood ① ② ③ **④ ⑤**
Elementary ① ② **③** ④ **⑤**
Middle Level **①** ② ③ ④ **⑤ ⑥ ⑦**

CHAPTER 9 Historical and Philosophical Influences on Teaching and Learning in America

INTASC Standards ① **②** ③ ④ ⑤ ⑥ ⑦ **⑧** ⑨ ⑩

NCATE Standards
Early Childhood ① ② ③ **④ ⑤**
Elementary ① ② **③** ④ **⑤**
Middle Level **①** ② ③ ④ **⑤** ⑥ **⑦**

CHAPTER 7

Political and Economic Influences on American Education

"I'm very interested in school-based decision making."

Carol Braca, in her first year of teaching, and Dorrit McCormick, who has been in the classroom almost fifteen years, are both sixth-grade teachers. At their suburban school, many students are from well-to-do homes with parents whose jobs are very demanding. Students sometimes reflect a sense of entitlement, and classroom management can be a problem. The current discipline system used in the school gives individual teachers little freedom but rather relies on a fairly rigid point structure.

As Carol finished another fast-paced day, she sat at her desk and added entries to her journal, revising her lesson plans for the following day based on her thoughts about today's events. The day had gone well—for the most part it had been extremely fulfilling, as most days had been in the five months she had been teaching. She was beginning to see real results—not always easy with hormonally charged sixth-graders! But one thing bothered her. Alec had misbehaved, talking out of turn and responding with wisecracks when she called on him. Because the school's discipline system made teachers rather than students responsible for managing behavior, Carol had not been able to work out a classroom "code" with her students, which she believed would have helped control Alec's disruptions by showing him how other students felt.

She went next door to Dorrit's classroom. Dorrit, her first-year mentor, was happy to listen.

"I'm concerned about the discipline policy," Carol began. "I really think it's too restrictive for these kids. It doesn't give them enough responsibility for their own behavior. One of the things we talked about in classroom management courses at college was that open communication between students and teachers is important—it helps kids understand their roles and responsibilities in class. I just don't see that happening here."

Dorrit was interested. "I've actually been thinking about the same thing. It concerns me, too. The discipline policy is new. It was just put in place last year, and frankly I'm not sure the faculty or students really understand or agree with it. And it actually seems like I spend more time on discipline and less on instruction since we started it. How about if you and I bring this up at faculty council and see if we can get a committee formed to try to find ways to improve our discipline policies? If we could get buy-in from teachers, students, administrators, and parents, we could definitely make a change."

"I'd really like that! The whole management area is one I'm really interested in—and as a first-year teacher, it would be great to have an opportunity to get involved and make a difference outside my own classroom. I'm very interested in school-based decision making. I think I can contribute."

Dorrit grinned. "Terrific. I think teacher involvement in policy changes is really important—and the administration here supports it."

"I'll start doing some research. I'll see what I can find in the literature and check out programs that other schools are using. Then we can come to the council with some support for our ideas."

INTASC

Standard 9: The teacher is a reflective practitioner who continually evaluates the effects of his/her choices and actions on others (students, parents, and other professionals in the learning community) and who actively seeks out opportunities to grow professionally.

NCATE

Early Childhood

Standard 5: Uses ethical guidelines and other professional standards; is a continuous, collaborative learner who demonstrates knowledgeable, reflective, and critical perspectives; is an informed advocate for sound educational practices.

NCATE

Elementary

Standard 5.4: Fosters relationships with school colleagues and agencies in the larger community to support students' learning and well-being.

Middle Level

Standard 7: Understands the complexity of teaching young adolescents; engages in practices and behaviors that develop competence as a professional.

How Will This Chapter Help You?

You will learn

★ about the political and social influences that affect school governance and finance and shape the culture of education

★ how schools are governed and financed

★ about the roles of the national, state, and local governments in the control and governance of public education

★ about issues associated with school governance and funding

★ how you as a teacher are affected by issues of school governance and finance

The New York Times
expect the world®
nytimes.com

Themes of the Times

Expand your knowledge of the concepts discussed in this chapter by reading current and historical articles from *The New York Times* by visiting the "Themes of the Times" section of the companion Web site.

WHAT FORCES INFLUENCE SCHOOL GOVERNANCE AND FINANCE?

Just as Dorrit and Carol are affected by how schools are governed, you, too, will be affected by the **governance**, financial, and political decisions made by school boards, administrators, and others. Every day, decisions are made about what to teach, how to teach, and what programs should and should not be funded. All of these decisions are based on the politics and finance of schooling. For example, some school districts may decide to implement sex education and teenage pregnancy prevention programs, while other districts may feel such programs are politically disadvantageous. Figure 7.1 lists sixteen characteristics identified by the American Association of School Administrators that schools will need for success in the future. To meet these needs, political and financial decisions will be required. In this chapter, you will learn about the reasons for how and why schools are governed and financed.

Public Opinion and Social Issues

The public is always interested in and concerned about how schools spend their taxes. The public wants to make sure they are getting the biggest bang for their tax bucks. Taxpayers want the schools to educate all students so they achieve the high standards prescribed by the federal government and the states. They want their children educated for responsible citizenship. They also want the schools to address and prevent major social problems such as violence, substance abuse, teenage pregnancy, crime, racism, sexism, and a deteriorating environment. Parents and the public also are increasingly interested in promoting patriotism and character. In addition to all this, as Table 7.1 shows, the public believes the biggest problem facing the public schools today is lack of money. How to get the money they need is a constant challenge for schools. There are never enough resources to achieve all the goals. As a result, school governance and finance is a constant balancing act of how to allocate limited resources in the face of voracious demand.

Public opinion plays a powerful role in what schools teach and how they operate. For example, as Table 7.1 also shows, the public believes that lack of discipline is also a major problem. This concern is reflected in the emphasis on providing gun-free schools and reducing school violence. The public believes that until and unless schools are safe and orderly, they will not be able to provide a high-quality education for the nation's students. In addition, issues of how to finance and support education are reflected in increased federal funding, more state control of education, and higher local taxes.

Social issues also affect how schools operate and what schools teach. This is evident in schools' efforts to address such social concerns as violence, substance abuse, teenage pregnancy, and single parenting. Political and economic issues impact schools as well. For example, the current perception that public schools fail to educate students adequately for the workplace is a concern of business and industry. Comparisons of U.S. students' achievement with the achievement of students in other developed countries reveal that U.S. students' performance falls short. This has led to calls for educational reform. Some reformers recommend decentralizing authority and control of education and making local schools and faculty more responsible for their organization and operation. On the other hand, one of the major trends of the last decade is the increased involvement of the federal and state governments and departments of education in educational matters. This centralized, top-down state involvement will likely continue well into the future. Previous discussions have illustrated how vast and influential the federal role is in education. You will get a better and deeper appreciation of this federal control in this chapter.

Stakeholders in Education

People and agencies with a particular interest in the schools are called **stakeholders.** Stakeholders are interested in and concerned about the process of schooling and want

- [ ] The definitions of *school, teacher,* and *learner* are reshaped by the digital world.
- [ ] All students have equal opportunity for an outstanding education, with adequate funding, no matter where they live.
- [ ] Educators are driven by high expectations and clear, challenging standards that are widely understood by students, families, and communities.
- [ ] A project-based "curriculum for life" engages students in addressing real-world problems, issues important to humanity, and questions that matter.
- [ ] Teachers and administrators are effectively prepared for the global knowledge/information age.
- [ ] Students, schools, school systems, and communities are connected around the clock with each other and with the world through information-rich, interactive technology.
- [ ] School systems conduct, consider, and apply significant research in designing programs that lead to constantly improving student achievement.
- [ ] Students learn to think, reason, and make sound decisions and demonstrate values inherent in a democracy.

- [ ] School facilities provide safe, secure, stimulating, joyous learning environments that contribute to a lifelong passion for learning and high student achievement.
- [ ] Leadership is collaborative, and governance is focused on broad issues that affect student learning.
- [ ] Students learn about other cultures, respect and honor diversity, and see the world as an extended neighborhood.
- [ ] Schools promote creativity and teamwork at all levels, and teachers help students turn information into knowledge and knowledge into wisdom.
- [ ] Assessment of student progress is more performance based, taking into account students' individual talents, abilities, and aspirations.
- [ ] A student-centered, collaboratively developed vision provides power and focus for education communitywide.
- [ ] Continuous improvement is a driving force in every school and school system.
- [ ] Schools are the crossroads and central convening point of the community.

Reflect & Write

All sixteen of the characteristics listed here are dependent on political and economic factors. Without political and economic support, it would be difficult, if not impossible, to translate these characteristics into classroom, school, district, and community practice. Which of these characteristics do you think are most important? Rank them from 1 to 16, with 1 being the most important, in terms of their importance to public schooling.

Figure 7.1   Sixteen Characteristics of Schools for the Twenty-First Century

Source: American Association of School Administrators, "AASA Online, Issues and Insights." (Online). Available at www.aasa.org/issues_and_insights/district_organization/preparing_21stcentury.htm. Reprinted by permisson.

Table 7.1   Biggest Problems Facing Local Public Schools

Problems	National Totals (percentage)	Respondents with No Children in School (percentage)	Public School Parents (percentage)
Lack of financial support/funding/money	25	26	24
Lack of discipline, more control	16	17	13
Overcrowded schools	14	12	16
Use of drugs	9	10	7
Difficulty getting good teachers/quality teachers	5	5	5
Standards/quality/basics	4	5	2
Fighting/violence/gangs	4	3	5
Low pay for teachers	4	4	3

Source: L. C. Rose and A. M. Gallup, "The 35th Annual Phi Delta Kappan/Gallup Poll of the Public's Attitudes toward the Public Schools," *Phi Delta Kappan,* 2003, p. 50. Reprinted by permission.

Schools for Sale

More and more, cash-strapped schools are turning to corporate America for lessons in how to finance schools. Schools also look to corporate America to provide badly needed school dollars. If a baseball team can sell the naming rights to its stadium, why can't a school? Why not indeed! This is exactly what Falls Church (Virginia) did! At George Mason High School, a local car dealer paid $50,000 for naming rights to the football stadium. The Plano (Texas) school district has turned its buses into rolling billboards. Advertisements appear on twenty of its school buses. Students at Alice Costello School in Brooklawn (New Jersey) don't go to the gym, they go to the ShopRite-of-Brooklawn Center!

Some think this new school finance entrepreneurship and fundraising are win-win market deals for schools.

Cash-starved schools get extra money, and companies get the exposure they want. And many taxpayers, tired of seeing their school taxes rise, think it is a good idea. On the other hand, not everyone agrees with this commercialization of America's schools. Some feel that such deals turn schools into hucksters for business and industry and send the wrong message to students.

What do you think? You decide. Write a statement pro or con about marketing the nation's schools.

To find out more, visit www.ascd.org/author/el/2002/1October/molnar.html or www.wired.com/news/school.

---

to help ensure that the schools do a good job. There are five basic reasons people are interested in schools. First, most people have gone to school and therefore often feel that school attendance has given them a certain knowledge and authority on school matters. Second, education in America is essentially viewed as controlled and influenced by citizens who believe that one role of the public schools is to educate future citizens for democratic living. Third, many citizens are parents and thus are concerned about what happens to their children in school and how this affects their children's future. Fourth, people who pay taxes feel they deserve a say in how schools operate and educate students. Finally, the business community has a stake in the public schools, since they believe it is the responsibility of the public schools to prepare citizens for the work force. The corporate community exerts a powerful influence on reforming education with the aim of increasing achievement and workplace skills. A great variety of individuals and groups are therefore stakeholders in education.

Political Interest Groups. Politicians are interested in schools because they are the means for educating future citizens. Politicians use schools as a way of implementing policies they believe are good for the states and the nation. For example, many gubernatorial candidates run on platforms that advocate literacy, high standards, reductions in class size, and fiscal accountability. George W. Bush ran for president on a platform of educational reform.

Political interest groups play a significant role in exerting political influence on how schools are organized and governed and on what they teach. Lobbyists represent particular groups such as teachers, boards of education, state departments of education, and manufacturers of school products. These groups and individuals are often paid to lobby for a particular cause and help influence legislation and policy. The Quality Education for Minorities (QEM) Network, for example, is dedicated to improving opportunities for the education of African Americans, Alaska Natives, American Indians, Mexican Americans, and Puerto Ricans. Their Web site can be accessed at qemnetwork.qem.org.

Business and Industry. Businesses, both large and small, have a considerable vested interest in the public schools. As schooling goes—poorly or well—so goes the quality of the work force. Corporations want future workers who can perform well in the labor force. In particular, they want students who as workers can think, work well with others, and make decisions. Changes in the requirements for effectively entering and staying in the work force are among the most significant changes in American society today. The world of work demands a more professional and highly skilled worker than it did half a century ago. Total employment is predicted to increase to 162 million jobs through the year 2012. The economy will continue generating jobs for

Contracts with soda companies can generate thousands of dollars in revenue for cash-strapped schools. Opponents of this practice, however, feel it promotes unhealthy habits and compromises student health. School administrators claim they can't do without the revenue. What do you think?

workers at all levels of education and training, although average growth is predicted to be greater for occupations requiring at least an associate's degree than for occupations requiring less training.[1] Because of these trends and changes, business and industry are in the forefront of current education reform efforts. Many business and industry leaders want schools to teach thinking and decision-making skills as well as basic skills. Consequently, high school programs are more geared to the world of work than they were in past decades. Business and industry are often integrally involved with schools through partnership programs, such as those discussed in Chapter 6.

However, there continue to be conflict and tension over the purposes of the American high school. Some think high school should prepare all students for college; others think the primary emphasis should be on preparing students for the world of work; still others think it should be both.

Professional Organizations and Teachers. Teachers are major stakeholders in education policy and finance. They are involved in school governance and, at the same time, are influenced by it. Teachers are represented by labor organizations such as the National Education Association (NEA) and the American Federation of Teachers (AFT) and by other professional associations (see Chapter 2). These organizations exert considerable influence on conditions of employment, organization, governance, compensation and benefits, and curriculum.

In the past decade, professional organizations such as the National Council of Teachers of Mathematics (NCTM) have greatly influenced the content of the mathematics curriculum and how it is taught. Another professional organization, the National Association for the Education of Young Children (NAEYC), has helped improve the professional practice of early childhood educators (see Chapter 2).

Parents, Students, and Community Groups. Parents represent a significant source of the political power influencing the educational process (see Chapter 6). As stakeholders, parents are interested in having schools that meet their perceived needs of helping children learn basic skills as well as other academic skills and social behaviors necessary for

NCATE

Early Childhood

Standard 5: Uses ethical guidelines and other professional standards; is a continuous, collaborative learner who demonstrates knowledgeable, reflective, and critical perspectives; is an informed advocate for sound educational practices.

Elementary

Standard 5.4: Fosters relationships with school colleagues and agencies in the larger community to support students' learning and well-being.

successful work and living. Parents are also very much in the forefront of efforts to restructure and reform education. Parents and parent groups influence what goes on at the classroom and district levels as well as what goes on at the state and national levels.

Parents are organized at the local level into groups such as parent-teacher organizations. Many of these local groups are represented at the national level by the National Parent-Teacher Association (PTA), which we discussed in Chapter 6.

Because students are the primary consumers of the educational process, they are most often affected by the rules, regulations, organization, governance, and funding of the schools. Students exert considerable influence through the behaviors, backgrounds, and diverse cultures they bring to school. Many schools have organizations such as student councils that provide students opportunities for a voice in school decisions and policies. Students are often interested in governance issues that directly affect them, such as rules for behavior, dress codes, and curriculum.

Parents and students are members of a community. Many community groups are focused on particular, or single, school-related issues. Groups organize to change attendance boundaries, teaching practices, curriculum content, school policies, and school-funding issues. As stakeholders in education, community groups reflect and influence local issues and priorities. Special interest groups often are successful in electing proponents of their points of view to boards of education.

In your experience, what stakeholder groups most influenced your education? How? What are some of the most influential stakeholder groups today? What are they advocating? Why?

_____

_____

_____

_____

SECTION SUMMARY

What Forces Influence School Governance and Finance?

Some of the forces that influence school governance and finance are public opinion, social issues, and the interests of various stakeholders in the education process.

- Public Opinion and Social Issues. Public opinion plays a powerful role in determining what schools teach and how schools operate. Polls show that public concern currently focuses on reducing violence, providing a safe environment in which children can learn, adequately funding education, and making the standards of education in U.S. schools more competitive with those of other developed countries.

- Stakeholders in Education. Stakeholders are people who have an interest in education and are involved in decisions about how schools operate. Stakeholders include political interest groups; business and industry; professional organizations and teachers; and parents, students, and community groups.

Thinking Critically

★ ★ ★ ★ ★ ★ ★ ★ ★

One of the problems every representative democracy must solve is ensuring the rights of minorities while respecting the decisions of the majority. How do special interest groups reflect this problem in the area of public education?

_____

_____

_____

_____ ★

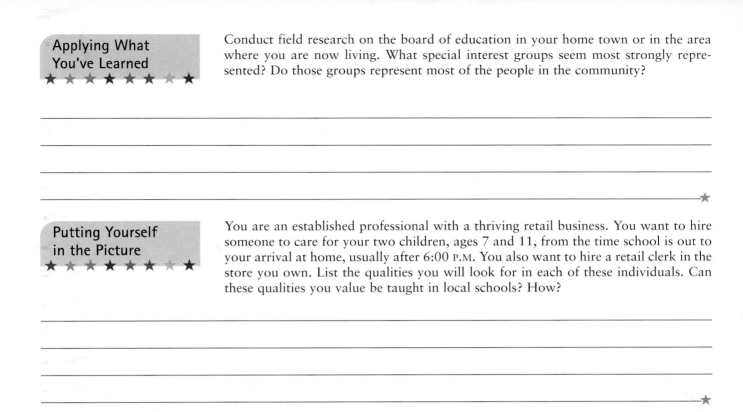

Conduct field research on the board of education in your home town or in the area where you are now living. What special interest groups seem most strongly represented? Do those groups represent most of the people in the community?

_____

_____

_____

_____★

Putting Yourself in the Picture
★ ★ ★ ★ ★ ★ ★ ★

You are an established professional with a thriving retail business. You want to hire someone to care for your two children, ages 7 and 11, from the time school is out to your arrival at home, usually after 6:00 P.M. You also want to hire a retail clerk in the store you own. List the qualities you will look for in each of these individuals. Can these qualities you value be taught in local schools? How?

_____

_____

_____

_____★

*H*OW IS EDUCATION CONTROLLED AND GOVERNED*?*

The three branches of government—executive, legislative, and judicial—influence the governance and finance of education at both the state and national levels. The executive branch of the national government and the federal court system exert considerable influence on education. Initially, however, state legislatures are the most influential, because they make the laws that govern education in each state. The judicial branches of government influence education policy, practice, and curriculum through court decisions and interpretations of laws. State and federal courts and the U.S. Supreme Court have ruled on many issues important to educators, parents, students, and the public. In Chapter 8, you will learn more about how federal and state laws and court decisions help determine the character of American education.

While it may seem that all control of education occurs at the local level—in the school district and school—this is not the case. The control of education really resides with state government, but the federal government also plays a major role. Much of the politics of education involves balancing the role and influence of the federal and state governments with the wishes and desires of local communities.

Roles of the National Government in Education

The national government has a long history of involvement in education. The national government operates the Military Academy at West Point, the Naval Academy at Annapolis, and the Air Force Academy at Colorado Springs. Education is a federal function in the District of Columbia, Puerto Rico, and the U.S. Territories (Virgin Islands, Northern Mariana Islands, Guam, and American Samoa). In addition, the federal government operates the Department of Defense Dependent Schools (DODDS system), which educate the children of armed services personnel and other Department of Defense employees. The armed services also operate an extensive system of child care for soldier-parents.

INTASC

Standard 10: The teacher fosters relationships with school colleagues, parents, and agencies in the larger community to support students' learning and well-being.

The U.S. government, through the Bureau of Indian Affairs (BIA), Office of Indian Education Programs, operates a school system of 185 schools in twenty-three states, serving over 60,000 students and representing 238 tribes. Sixty-five of these schools are residential schools, and the balance are day schools on reservations. Some students live in peripheral dormitories near public schools, and some attend national high schools that are off-reservation boarding schools. The BIA, for purposes of schooling, is treated as though it were the fifty-first state. This status enables Indian schools to receive federal funds that are appropriated through the states, such as support for the gifted, for vocational education, and for children of low-income families. The BIA also operates early childhood programs at thirty-two sites designed to enhance family and child education. The focus in these programs is on family and child literacy for children from birth to grade 3.[2] The Profile presents the comments of the U.S. Secretary of Education on the state of American education.

The U.S. Constitution. The word *education* does not appear in the U.S. Constitution. When the Constitution was written, responsibilities and functions not specifically given to the national government were reserved for the states. Since education is not mentioned in the Constitution, the Tenth Amendment expressly makes education a state function and responsibility. The majority of states delegate day-to-day responsibility for operating schools to local districts.

Justifications for the involvement of the national government in education come from the general welfare clause of the preamble to the Constitution and key amendments. The preamble makes it the business of the national government to promote the general welfare of its citizens. As Figure 7.2 suggests, promoting the general welfare includes making sure that states uphold the First and Fourteenth Amendments.

Federal Legislation. In addition to appropriating funds for education, the national government influences education through legislation, program initiatives, and the dissemination of information. As one example, Table 7.2 shows the programs funded through the **No Child Left Behind Act** of 2001 signed by President Bush in 2002. The act reauthorizes for five years the Elementary and Secondary Education Act originally passed in 1965. Funding for fiscal year 2004 was $56 billion. Figure 7.3 identifies

No Child Left Behind Act
Signed by President Bush in 2002, this act reauthorizes for an additional five years the Elementary and Secondary Education Act, originally passed in 1965.

The First Amendment

Congress shall make no law respecting an establishment of religion, or prohibiting the free exercise thereof; or abridging the freedom of speech, or of the press; or the right of the people peaceably to assemble, and to petition the Government for redress of grievances.

The Tenth Amendment

The powers not delegated to the United States by the Constitution, nor prohibited by it to the States, are reserved to the States respectively, or to the people.

The Fourteenth Amendment

No state shall make or enforce any law which shall abridge the privileges or immunities of citizens of the United States; nor shall any State deprive any person of life, liberty, or property without due process of law; nor deny to any person within its jurisdiction the equal protection of the laws.

The Supreme Court and other courts, when rendering decisions about educational matters, usually cite one of these amendments to justify their decision. Have these three amendments affected your educational life in any way? How might they affect you as a beginning teacher?

Figure 7.2   *C*onstitutional Amendments Relating to Education

Rod Paige was the first U.S. Secretary of Education under President George W. Bush.

First, some good news. I am pleased to report that many of our K through 12 schools are the finest in the world, with outstanding teachers, visionary administrators, and quality resources. Some schools are amazing success stories and make for great news copy, radio actualities, and TV interviews. These schools are not always in the suburbs, either. They may be in Harlem or Helena, West Chicago or East L.A., Charlotte or Charlottesville, Durham or Denver. Many of them are public schools. There is much for which we can be proud.

But that is not the full story. I wish it were. There are many schools in this same great country of ours that let students leave without teaching them anything. In those schools time passes slowly. Students attend—they sit there—but don't learn. Teachers speak, but the words are often meaningless, or they fall on deaf ears. The atmosphere of disregard confirms the students' suspicion that they have already been written off, and that no one really cares if they learn or not. For those passing through these schools, their soul withers, as their lives are wasted.

We are facing an unrecognized educational crisis in this country. Our wide and sometimes growing achievement gap confirms that there is a two-tiered educational system. For the lucky few, their education is the best in the world; virtually ensuring those students have wonderful opportunities for further education, economic security, professional rewards, and personal freedom. For others, there is an underperforming system. Students come to school but find little education. The vast majority of students left behind are disadvantaged or low income.

Effectively, the education circumstances for these students are not unlike that of a de facto system of apartheid. We can document this disparity. Last month, there were many "good news" stories about the national jump in the latest SAT scores. [But] even as the headlines say "SAT Scores Rise," closer observation reveals that the scores for African American SAT test takers didn't rise, they remained flat. And Hispanic students' scores actually went down over previous years. Thus, we celebrate by overlooking disparities, disagreeable conclusions, and disadvantaged students.

By the time they reach twelfth grade, only one in six African Americans and one in five Hispanics can read proficiently. Math scores are even worse: only 3 percent of African American and 4 percent of Hispanic students are testing at the proficient level. These statistics show that there is an education gap in this country.

There is also an education gap with other countries. Internationally, our students are falling behind students in other countries. Two weeks ago, the Organization for Economic Cooperation and Development released a disturbing report. The findings show American students are being rapidly overtaken by students in many other countries. American students read, write, and do math at rates lower than students in Asia and Europe. This is a shocking report, especially because it also documents that we spend more per student than any of the other OECD countries. Yet, we receive modest results. Our students are falling behind, and there is every indication that, if we allow the guardians of the educational status quo to have their way, we will continue to fall behind. And our nation will be left behind.

Civilizations rise and fall depending upon the quality of education. H. G. Wells said, "Human history becomes more and more a race between education and catastrophe." We face an uncertain future. Unless improvements are made, American students will not be competitive with students in other countries, dooming future generations to less opportunity, greater levels of poverty, and further disparities in health status. The OECD report shows that nearly every European country has made sizeable gains in educational achievement. What this means for the United States is that the rest of the world is catching up to us.

Today, our high school graduation rates fall short of the OECD average. These results highlight an extremely important truth about our educational system: we have become complacent, self-satisfied, and often lacking in the will to do better. The OECD report shows the urgency of our task at hand: we must improve our educational system before the rest of the world leaves us behind. Our children and grandchildren's world will be even more complex, interrelated, and global. Can anyone honestly say that our current education system is preparing them for this world?

This isn't just about jobs . . . it is also about quality of life. A sound education gives purpose. It provides companionship and solace. It enriches the mind and spirit. We cannot deny the benefits of education through shortsighted indifference or lack of will. Nor can we capitulate to the guardians of the status quo. The achievement of all our children must improve, across the board. No child can be left behind.

Education matters to all of us. The ripple effect of underachievement touches all Americans. Our citizens pay a huge economic and social price for undereducated citizens. Welfare rates rise. Poverty increases. Health status diminishes. Tax money is spent to care for those who cannot care for themselves. We find greater strains on Social Security and Medicare and Medicaid. Prices increase to cover rising costs of insurance, job retraining, job-related accidents, disability, and poor productivity. Underemployment becomes larger if workers can't hold full-time jobs. Violence, crime, substandard housing, hunger, and disintegration of the family are all linked to low educational attainment.

We live in an interconnected world. What affects one part of one community affects the entire community. We cannot be satisfied if even one child is left behind. We all must work together to solve this problem.

Forty-one years ago, Dr. Martin Luther King, Jr., spoke at this podium about the need for greater accountability—a guarantee that all Americans enjoy a full measure of the promise of the American dream. The Civil Rights Act was a landmark in extending political and economic equality to all Americans. I believe that No Child Left Behind is the logical next step, for it extends educational equality to all Americans. The American Dream begins with, and demands, a meaningful, sound education.

Quality education is a right that must be protected and fulfilled for every child in our country. Such an education is the foundation upon which we will build their future and the future of this great nation. In the months and years to come, we will travel a long and hard road. Educational reform must overcome many hurdles, just as the civil rights struggle encountered barriers and obstacles. But we can, and we will, extend the educational franchise to provide quality education to every child.

Source: You can access the full text of this address at www.ed.gov/news/speeches/2003/09/09242003.html.

Table 7.2 *Programs Funded through No Child Left Behind Act of 2001*

Description	2003 Funding	2004 Funding	2005 President's Request
Assistive Technology. These state grants increase access to and funding for assistive technology devices and services for individuals with disabilities of all ages.	$26.8 million	$25.9 million	$15 million
Charter Schools Grants. This program increases public school choice options by supporting the planning, development, and initial implementation of public charter schools.	$196.7 million	$218.7 million	$319 million
Community Technology Centers. This program creates or expands community technology centers to give technology access and training to residents living in poor urban and rural communities.	$32.3 million	$9.9 million	$0
Early Reading First. These competitive grants to school districts and non-profit organizations support activities in existing preschool programs designed to enhance the verbal skills, phonological awareness, letter knowledge, and prereading skills of children from birth through age 5. Funds are targeted to communities with high numbers of low-income families.	$75 million	$94.4 million	$132 million
Educational Technology State Grant. These grants help state, district, and school efforts to integrate technology into the classroom, ensuring that teachers have the knowledge, skills, and curricula needed to use technology effectively to improve student achievement. Districts may use funds to train teachers to integrate technology into the curriculum and serve as technology experts in their schools, develop and implement high-quality information technology courses, and purchase effective technology-based curricula.	$695.9 million	$695.9 million	$692 million
Improving Teacher Quality State Grants. This program is designed to strengthen teachers' skills and knowledge to build a high-quality teaching force. Funds also may be used to update teacher certification or licensure requirements, alternative certification, tenure reform, merit-based teacher performance systems, differential and bonus pay for teachers in high-need subject areas, and teacher mentoring programs.	$2.93 billion	$2.93 billion	$2.93 billion
Jobs for the 21st Century. The goal of this program is to improve the quality of education in the nation's high schools and colleges to better prepare students for success in higher education and the new information-age workplace.	N/A	N/A	$333 million
Literacy through School Libraries. This program helps school districts provide students with increased access to up-to-date school library materials and highly qualified school library media personnel. Increasingly, school library media centers are linked to computers in classrooms, and they can play a strategic role in enhancing the educational impact of student access to, and use of, information.	$12.4 million	$19.8 million	$19.6 million
Mathematics and Science Partnerships. This program aims to improve academic achievement in mathematics and science by promoting strong teaching skills for elementary and secondary school teachers.	$100.3 million	$149.1 million	$269 million
Preparing Tomorrow's Teachers to Use Technology. This program trains pre-service teachers to integrate technology into the classroom. The Bush administration called for the elimination of the program because its efforts duplicated activities funded by the Educational Technology State Grants and Improving Teacher Quality State Grants programs.	$62.1 million	$0	$0
Reading First State Grants. These funds are used to infuse high-quality, scientifically based reading research in school reading instruction so every child can read by the end of third grade. Funds are used to help schools and districts provide teachers professional development in reading instruction, adopt and use reading diagnostics for students in kindergarten through third grade to determine where they need help, implement reading curricula that are based on recent findings of the National Institute of Child Health and Human Development, and provide reading interventions for young grade-school children to ensure they can read at grade level by the end of the third grade.	$993.5 million	$1.1 billion	$1.1 billion
Ready-to-Learn Television. This program supports the development and distribution of educational video and related materials for preschool children, elementary school children, and their parents in order to facilitate student academic achievement. Funding has supported the development of two highly acclaimed children's shows, "Between the Lions" and "Dragon Tales," along with a bilingual newsletter that provides suggestions for books and learning activities related to PBS children's programs.	$22.9 million	$22.9 million	$22.8 million
Ready-to-Teach. This federal initiative helps public broadcasters provide educational and professional development resources to schools.	$12 million	$14.3 million	$0

Description	2003 Funding	2004 Funding	2005 President's Request
Regional Technology in Education Consortia. Federally funded programs in underserved areas designed to disseminate instructional materials and provide technical assistance in the use of improved teaching methods and assessment across grades and subject areas.	$9.9 million	$9.9 million	$0
Special Education Technology and Media Services. This program supports research, development, and other activities to advance the application of new and emerging technologies in providing special education and early intervention services.	$38 million	$39.1 million	$32.3 million
Special Education State Improvement. At least 75 percent of these funds provided to each state are reserved for professional development. The remaining funds are used to carry out state strategies for improving educational results, including efforts to hold school districts and schools accountable for the educational progress of children with disabilities, providing high-quality technical assistance to school districts and schools, and changing state policies and procedures to address systemic barriers to improving results for students with disabilities.	$51.4 million	$51.1 million	$51.1 million
Special Education Technical Assistance and Dissemination. This program provides technical assistance and disseminates materials based on knowledge gained through research and practice.	$53.1 million	$52.8 million	$52.8 million
Star Schools. This program encourages improved instruction in mathematics, science, foreign languages, and other subjects, such as literacy skills and vocational education, and serves traditionally underserved populations, including the disadvantaged, illiterate, limited English proficient, and individuals with disabilities, through the use of advanced telecommunications.	$27.3 million	$20.4 million	$0
State Assessments and Enhanced Assessment Instruments. These funds pay for the cost of developing standards and assessments required by the No Child Left Behind Act, as well as administering these yearly tests in grades 3 through 8. The funds also may be used for related professional development and for new state accountability and reporting systems.	$384.5 million	$390 million	$410 million
State Grants for Innovative Programs. This program awards grants to states and school districts that provide flexible funding for promising, evidence-based education reforms that meet the educational needs of all students. School districts may use funds to reduce class size, provide professional development, pay for Title I supplemental services, support smaller learning communities, and other activities.	$382.5 million	$296.5 million	$296.5 million
Tech Prep Education State Grants. These state formula grants link secondary and postsecondary vocational and academic instruction to prepare individuals for high-tech careers. Tech prep programs emphasize the development of (and teacher training in) applied instructional methods for academic classes; more successful entry into postsecondary education; and an increased emphasis on academics, especially math, science, and technology.	$107.3 million	$106.6 million	$0
Title I Grants to Local Education Agencies (LEAs). These grants fund supplemental programs that help poor children meet the same challenging state academic standards as other children. For example, Title I supports more individualized instruction, fundamental changes in the school to improve teaching and learning, and preschool education.	$11.75 billion	$12.4 billion	$13.3 billion
Transition to Teaching. This program addresses the national challenge of training and recruiting more than 2 million teachers over the next 10 years—owing to the retirements of long-time teachers, high attrition rates among new teachers, and booming enrollments—by supporting partnerships to train and place highly qualified professionals as teachers in America's classrooms.	$41.7 million	$45.3 million	$45.3 million
21st Century Community Learning Centers. This program establishes or expands community learning centers that provide after-school learning opportunities for students—particularly for children who attend high-poverty or low-performing schools—and related services to their families.	$993.5 million	$999.1 million	$999 million

Sources: "U.S. Department of Education Grant Programs. U.S. Department of Education, *Department of Educational Congressional Action, Fiscal Year 2004.* (Online). Available at www.ed.gov/about/overview/budget/statetables/index.html.

2002 *No Child Left Behind (NCLB) Act* (PL 107–110). Reauthorizes the ESEA, which includes increased accountability for states, school districts, and schools; greater choice for parents and students, particularly those attending low-performing schools; more flexibility for states and local educational agencies (LEAs) in the use of federal education dollars; and a stronger emphasis on reading, especially for young children.

2001 *Kids Developing Skills for Success in the 21st Century Act* (PL 107-59). Establishes a program of grants for supplemental assistance for elementary and secondary school students of limited English proficiency to ensure that they rapidly develop proficiency in English while not falling behind in their academic studies.

2000 *Reading Deficit Elimination Act* (PL 106-2452). Provides scientifically sound instruction in reading to preschool and elementary school students and reduces the number of individuals and students who cannot read.

1999 *Teacher Tax Cut Act of 1999* (PL 106-937). Amends the Internal Revenue Code of 1986 to provide a tax credit for elementary and secondary school teachers.

1998 *Healthy Kids Act* (PL 105-3474). Aimed at helping American families dramatically reduce the number of children illegally using tobacco products.

1997 *Children's Education Tax Credit Act* (PL 105-163). Amends the Internal Revenue Code of 1986 to allow a refundable credit for education expenses.

1997 *IDEA Improvement Act* (PL 105-17). Reauthorizes the Individuals with Disabilities Education Act and extends it through the fiscal year 2002.

1996 *Healthy Meals for Children Act* (PL 104-149). Amends the National School Lunch Act to permit schools to use any reasonable approach to meet certain school lunch and breakfast dietary guidelines; prohibits schools from being required to conduct nutrient analysis.

1994 *New America Schools Act* (PL 103-227). Reauthorizes previous programs such as Chapter I (now called Title I, see below); funds Even Start, a two-generation literacy program.

1992 *Ready to Learn Act* (PL 102-545). Establishes Ready to Learn Television programs to support educational programming and support materials for preschool and elementary school children and their parents, child-care providers, and educators.

1991 *National Commission on Longer School Year Act* (PL 102-62). Establishes the National Education Commission on Time and Learning.

1991 *National Literacy Act* (PL 102-73). Establishes the National Institute for Literacy, the National Institute Board, and the Interagency Task Force on Literacy.

1990 *Environmental Education Act* (PL 101-619). Promotes environmental education by establishing an Office of Environmental Education in the Environmental Protection Agency and creating several environmental education programs.

1990 *School Dropout Prevention and Basic Skills Improvement Act* (PL 101-600). Improves secondary school programs for basic skills improvement and dropout prevention.

1990 *Americans with Disabilities Act* (PL 101-336). Prohibits discrimination against persons with disabilities.

1979 *Department of Education Organization Act* (PL 96-88). Establishes the Department of Education.

1978 *Career Educational Incentive Act* (PL 95-207). Authorizes the establishment of a career education program for elementary and secondary schools.

1977 *Youth Employment and Demonstration Projects Act* (PL 95-93). Establishes a youth employment training program that includes, among other activities, promoting education-to-work transition, literacy training, bilingual training, and attainment of certificates of high school equivalency.

1975 *Indian Self-Determination and Education Assistance Act* (PL 93-638). Provides for increased participation of Native Americans in the establishment and conduct of their education programs and services.

1975 *Education of the Handicapped Act* (PL 94-142). Provides that all handicapped children have available to them a free, appropriate education designed to meet their unique needs.

1970 *Environmental Education Act* (PL 91-516). Establishes an Office of Environmental Education to develop curriculum and initiate and maintain environmental education programs at the elementary and secondary levels.

1965 *Elementary and Secondary Education Act* (PL 89-10). Authorizes grants for elementary and secondary school programs for children of low-income families.

1964 *Economic Opportunity Act* (PL 88-452). Authorizes support of education and training activities including Head Start.

Federal legislation has significantly affected how schools are funded, what is taught, and how it is taught. Of all these laws, the NCLB and IDEA exert tremendous influences on teaching. Based on the discussions of these two laws, list five ways they might affect you as a beginning teacher.

_____

_____

_____

Figure 7.3   Federal Legislation Affecting Elementary and Secondary Education

Note: Legislation is numbered for the Congress that passed it and in the order in which it was passed. For example, PL 102-545 was passed by the 102nd Congress and was the 545th piece of legislation passed during that session.

Source: J. Thomas, *Legislative Information on the Internet.* (Online). Available at thomas.loc.gov.

>>> Public Schools Pile on Fees >>>>>>>

As public schools open around the country, families are finding themselves paying steep fees for all kinds of activities and services that once came at no extra charge.

Starting this fall, middle school students in Gurnee, Illinois, must pay $145 to participate in a team sport and $60 to join the school band or choir. High school students in Harvard, Massachusetts, have to buy their own advanced placement textbooks, at $85 each. Across the country in Lake Oswego, Oregon, a family could pay as much as $900 a year for their kids to play high school sports.

The so-called user or "pay-for-play" fees, as many school districts refer to them, are an effort to make up for the shortfalls in state and local funding.

School districts have resorted to fees on families during past budget problems. But a number of districts report that their fees have reached unprecedented levels, with charges being slapped on everything from high school parking spaces to acting in the school play. And services that families already had to pay for are seeing big increases. In Arlington, Massachusetts, for example, families have to pay $1,500 to send a child to full-day kindergarten, triple the cost in 2002.

Source: Anne Marie Chaker, "Public Schools Pile on Fees," *Wall Street Journal,* September 3, 2003, p. D1. Reprinted by permission.

selected federal legislation, from 1964 to the present, that affects and influences pre-K–12 programs. As a beginning teacher, the chances are good that you will teach a program supported in some way with federal dollars. During times of budget crises, federal funding drops and schools must find other ways of making up the shortfall (see Education on the Move).

Reflect & Write

How do the First and Fourteenth Amendments (see Figure 7.2) reflect the influence of the national government on schools in your state and local district?

_____

_____

_____

_____

Department of Education. Many federal initiatives are administered and implemented through the Department of Education (DOE), which was established as a separate cabinet department in 1979. The first Department of Education was created in 1867 through the efforts of Henry Bernard and was later called the Office of Education and then the Bureau of Education. Between 1953 and 1979, the Office of Education was part of the Department of Health, Education, and Welfare.

The Department of Education collects and disseminates education statistics, awards, and grants and promotes the cause of education. Because it awards federal grants that have restrictive conditions, some critics see the department as an unnecessary intrusion of the national government into state and local affairs. However, in the first decade of the twenty-first century, the Department of Education played a more influential role in reforming and restructuring American education than at any time since its creation as a cabinet-level office.

Reflect & Write

Do you think that federal funding for education should be decreased, maintained, or increased? If you favor increasing federal funding, what programs would you earmark for increases?

_____

_____

_____

_____

Influence of the Executive Branch. National leaders advocate programs and practices they think are good for the nation's children and families. For example, President George W. Bush is an advocate of parental choice, or school choice, defined in Chapter 6 as the practice of letting parents choose the school(s) they want their children to attend. Today, many school districts have implemented choice programs that enable parents to send their children to schools within or outside a district. In addition, President Bush is a strong advocate for high and vigorous standards, testing, and accountability. First Lady Laura Bush is a powerful promoter of reading and early literacy. As governor of Arkansas, former President Clinton presided over a governor's conference that initiated America 2000 (now Goals 2000). In this program, the national government established eight goals for America's schools. These goals are shown in Figure 7.4. This effort to upgrade and reform American education demonstrates how presidential activism and political processes result in educational outcomes.

Roles of State Government in Education

The Tenth Amendment gives responsibility for education to each of the fifty states. How the states use this power depends on each state and on the political and social climate of the times. For example, in the 1980s and 1990s, in response to the public's demand for school reform, many states became more directive and prescriptive in

INTASC

Standard 10: The teacher fosters relationships with school colleagues, parents, and agencies in the larger community to support students' learning and well-being.

The Goals 2000: Educate America Act included these eight goals to be achieved by 2000:

☐ **School readiness**—All children in America will start school ready to learn.

☐ **School completion**—The high school graduation rate will increase to at least 90 percent.

☐ **Student achievement and citizenship**—All students will leave grades four, eight, and twelve having demonstrated competency over challenging subject matter . . . , and [all students will be] prepared for responsible citizenship, further learning, and productive employment.

☐ **Teacher education and professional development**—The nation's teaching force will have access to programs for the continued improvement of their professional skills.

☐ **Mathematics and science**—The United States students will be first in the world in mathematics and science achievement.

☐ **Adult literacy and lifelong learning**—Every adult American will be literate.

☐ **Safe, disciplined, and alcohol/drug-free schools**—Every school in America will be free of drugs and violence and will offer a disciplined environment conducive to learning.

☐ **Parental participation**—Every school and home will engage in partnerships that will increase parental involvement and participation in promoting the social, emotional, and academic growth of children.

Reflect & Write

Goals 2000 is not now a federal program, but it remains an example of what many view as worthy aims of education. Number these goals in order of importance, based on your beliefs about American education.

Figure 7.4   Goals 2000

Source: United States Department of Education. (Online). Available at www.ed.gov/legislation/GOALS2000/TheAct/sec102.html.

what they wanted students to achieve and in holding teachers and administrators accountable for students' achievement. This was a time of strong, top-down direction in an effort to "fix" the education system. The decade of 2000–2009 will be known as the decade of standards, tests, and accountability. All three of these areas have had strong state backing. These will be discussed in Chapter 11.

The control and governance of education at the state and local levels are shown in Figure 7.5. Figure 7.6 shows four basic models for the structure of governance at the state level. The following sections describe the governing bodies involved.

State Boards of Education. State boards of education exist in all states and generally have responsibility for education, including vocational education and in some cases postsecondary learning. Some states have two boards: one responsible for pre-K–12 and another responsible for higher education. While the scope of the boards' responsibilities is defined differently in each state, common areas of jurisdiction include:

NCATE

Elementary

Standard 5.4: Fosters relationships with school colleagues and agencies in the larger community to support students' learning and well-being.

- Setting statewide curriculum standards
- Determining qualifications for professional education personnel, including teacher certification
- Making recommendations on state education statutes
- Adopting standards to ensure equal access and due process

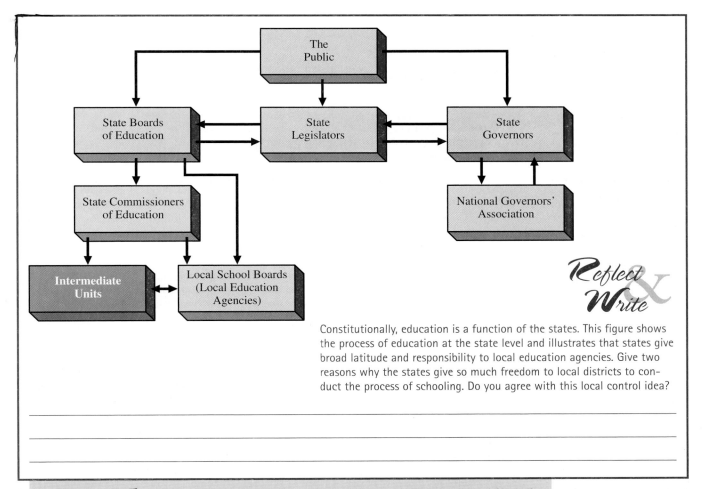

Reflect & Write

Constitutionally, education is a function of the states. This figure shows the process of education at the state level and illustrates that states give broad latitude and responsibility to local education agencies. Give two reasons why the states give so much freedom to local districts to conduct the process of schooling. Do you agree with this local control idea?

Figure 7.5   The Control and Governance of Education at the State and Local Levels

Source: Indiana Education Policy Center, *State Education Governance Structures* (Denver, CO: Education Commission of the States, 2000). Copyright 2000 by Education Commission of the States. Reprinted by permission.

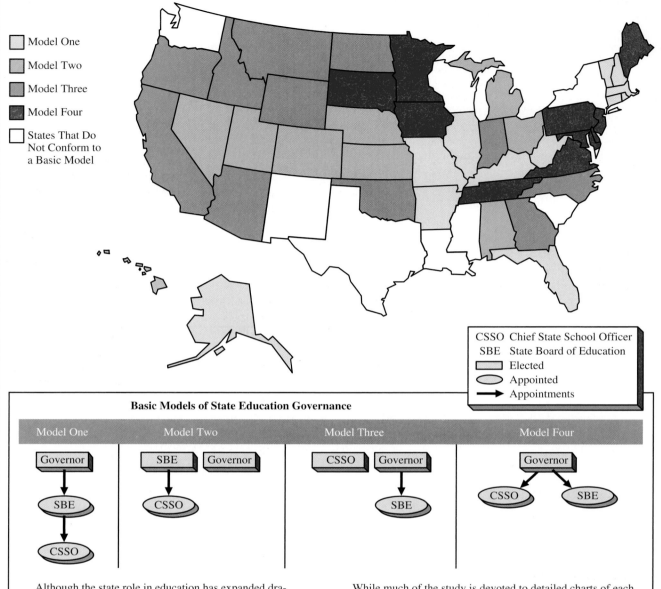

Model One
Model Two
Model Three
Model Four
States That Do
Not Conform to
a Basic Model

CSSO Chief State School Officer
SBE State Board of Education
Elected
Appointed
Appointments

Basic Models of State Education Governance

Model One	Model Two	Model Three	Model Four

Model One: Governor → SBE → CSSO

Model Two: SBE, Governor; SBE → CSSO

Model Three: CSSO, Governor; Governor → SBE

Model Four: Governor → CSSO, Governor → SBE

Although the state role in education has expanded dramatically in recent decades, most states continue to use systems of educational governance developed early in the twentieth century, according to a report prepared by the Indiana Education Policy Center at Indiana University that examines the powers and selection procedures of the chief state school officer and state board of education in each state.

The report found four basic models for choosing the state chief and board, although a number of states did not fall into any common pattern.

While much of the study is devoted to detailed charts of each state's governance structure, it also includes analyses of governance changes over time and of ongoing issues in the field, such as the tensions between centralization and decentralization and between political and professional control.

State Education Governance Structures was published by the Education Commission of the States. Copies of the report (EG-93-1) are available from the E.C.S. Distribution Center, 707 17th St., Suite 2700, Denver, Colo. 80202-3427; (303)299-3692.

Is it good public policy for each state to operate its state system of education independent from those of other states? Some school critics say that there should be much more educational unity between states. What do you think?

Figure 7.6 *H*ow States Govern Education

Source: Indiana Education Policy Center, *State Education Governance Structures* (Denver, CO: Education Commission of the States, 2000). Copyright 2000 by Education Commission of the States. Reprinted by permission.

- Undertaking quasi-legislative and judicial functions
- Administering federal assistance programs
- Formulating standards on school facilities

State boards of education are also involved in accrediting schools, disseminating information about education, and supporting and conducting research. State boards of education are very involved in creating "seamless" systems of education for pre-K–12 and pre-K–16. Florida recently reorganized its system to K–20 (kindergarten to graduate school), the first in the nation to do so. State boards promote seamless systems by setting priorities and coordinating spending. The Florida state board seeks to be the unified voice for education in the state.

The **National Association of State Boards of Education (NASBE)** is an association that represents state boards of education. The principal objectives of NASBE are to strengthen state leadership in educational policy making, to promote excellence in the education of all students, to advocate equality of access to educational opportunity, and to ensure continued citizen support for public education.[3]

State Standards Boards. All states except South Dakota have **state standards boards,** which are responsible for the governance and regulation of professional practice. These boards set the criteria for teacher certification and for entry into and dismissal from the profession. Depending on the state, the proceedings of the board can be either advisory to the state superintendent and/or the state board of education or autonomous, as in Minnesota. Membership on standards boards is usually by appointment by the state superintendent or state board of education. Teachers are included in the membership of state standards boards. For example, the Texas State Standards Board, Texas Education Agency, has the following functions:

- Administer and monitor compliance with education programs required by federal or state law, including federal funding and state funding for those programs
- Conduct research, analysis, and reporting to improve teaching and learning
- Conduct hearings involving state school law at the direction and under the supervision of the commissioner
- Establish and implement pilot programs
- Carry out the duties relating to the investment capital fund
- Develop and implement a teacher recruitment program
- Carry out powers and duties relating to adult and community education
- Review school district budgets, audit reports, and other fiscal reports[4]

State Departments of Education. When legislators and boards of education establish policies affecting education in each state, state departments of education help implement those policies. Major responsibilities of state departments of education include approving local districts' applications for federal funding and administering and monitoring the use of federal monies. For example, federal monies for specific programs and entitlements flow to local districts through the state departments of education. State departments have a stake in acquiring more responsibility and authority over federal revenues and how they are spent at the local level.

In addition to managing, monitoring, and distributing federal funding as it affects education, state departments of education have the following responsibilities:

- Overseeing public and private elementary, secondary, and vocational education
- Working cooperatively with the state legislature
- Providing for and promoting staff development
- Conducting public relations
- Monitoring school compliance with state regulations

For example, in Vermont, local standards boards have been established in each supervisory union. The boards were formed under the auspices of the Vermont Standards Board for Professional Educators (VSBPE) and its umbrella of broad standards.

National Association of State Boards of Education (NASBE)
An association that represents state boards of education; NASBE objectives include strengthening state leadership in educational policy making, promoting excellence in the education of all students, advocating equality of access to educational opportunity, and ensuring citizen support for public education.

State standards boards
Responsible for the governance and regulation of professional practice within a state and for overseeing teacher certification and entry into and dismissal from the profession.

Educators in Vermont public schools are accountable to a board of their peers, who are elected by peers in their own district or region.

Each educator in the public schools must have a recommendation from the appropriate local or regional board to be relicensed. Within guidelines established by the VSBPE, each board sets local standards for high-quality professional development and relicensure. Each educator is accountable to the local or regional board for the development of an acceptable Individual Professional Development Plan, the corresponding professional development necessary for relicensure, and a professional portfolio.[5]

In most states, the state department of education is headed by a person with overall responsibility for implementing educational policy in that state. This person is known as the State Secretary (or Director) of Education or the State Superintendent of Education (or of Public Instruction). The Profile suggests the complexities of a state superintendent's job.

National Governors' Association (NGA)

An organization of state governors devoted to addressing problems common to all the states; reflects governors' increasing leadership role in ongoing education reform and change efforts.

Influence of State Governors. The **National Governors' Association (NGA)** is an organization of state governors devoted to addressing problems common to all states. Since the 1990s, governors have played a leading role in ongoing reform in education and have called for fundamental changes in the educational system at the NGA's first education summit. In 1990, the NGA established the National Education Goals Panel (NEGP) to measure and report on state progress in achieving the goals. The panel is composed of eight governors (three from the president's party and five from the opposing party), two senior-level federal executive branch officials appointed by the president, and four members of Congress. The NEGP is a unique bipartisan body of federal and state officials who monitor, assess, and report annually on state and national progress toward achieving the National Education Goals. With the passage of Goals 2000, the NEGP became a fully independent agency charged with a variety of responsibilities to support systemwide reform.[7]

At its fourth education summit in 2001, the NGA issued a report designed to increase student achievement that focused on improving states' testing programs,

---

Profile California's Superintendent of Public Instruction Sets Priorities: Jack O'Connell

Jack O'Connell is California's State Superintendent of Public Instruction. He serves as Secretary and Executive Officer for the State Board of Education and is the chief executive officer of the Department of Education. Superintendent O'Connell's agenda for education in California is as follows:

Broaden the Base of Support for Education
- Increase parent involvement
- Strategically partner with businesses
- Create community networks supporting school sites

Increase Local Control over Decisions
- Encourage site-based management
- Reduce the Education Code
- Reduce administrative requirements

Focus Our Efforts on Results, Not Process, by Developing Standards to Measure Progress
- Develop grade-level proficiency standards
- Develop content and performance measurements
- Ensure that every child is a reader

Prepare a Skilled Work Force
- Create partnerships to provide opportunities for all students, college-bound and non-college-bound
- Strive for multilingual training for all students
- Establish lifelong positive learning patterns for all children beginning with preschool

Ensure That Facilities and Technology Are Excellent
- Expand partnerships with businesses, unions, communities, and the public sector (military, higher education, and so on) to equip schools and students with up-to-date technology and facilities
- Ensure that all schools are clean, well lighted, safe, and up-to-date[6]

---

ensuring that accountability plans are fair and effective, and raising the quality of teaching. The "statement of principles" proposed the following:

- Testing. Tests need to perform a wide variety of functions, including measuring individual students' progress from year to year and helping schools create plans to address their students' weaknesses. Schools need to be "transparent" so there is "no mystery about what is on the test." States should consider releasing test questions every year.
- Accountability. Accountability programs need to be fair, offering time so that schools can prepare for their impact and emphasizing assistance before sanctions. But if schools do not turn around, states must be prepared to take "dramatic action," such as replacing the school's leaders, hiring new staff, and allowing students to transfer to another public school.
- Teaching. States must "make the teaching profession more attractive" by offering a variety of pathways into the profession. Once there, teachers need access to "high-quality curriculum" and professional development that helps them teach what students are required to know to perform well on state tests. School officials need to take steps to make teacher salaries comparable to those of other professionals.

Roles of Intermediate Education Agencies

The governance of education involves cooperation among states and localities through the actions of intermediate agencies (see Figure 7.5). These agencies are called **intermediate educational units (IEUs),** also known as regional educational units (REUs), regional educational service areas (RESAs), or educational service agencies (ESAs). Intermediate units are designed to provide services that individual districts might not be able to afford on their own, thus maximizing existing resources and promoting interdistrict collaboration. In New York, the intermediate educational unit is the Board of Cooperative Educational Services (BOCES). A closer look at BOCES will help you understand the purposes and functions of intermediate agencies. (See the Profile, p. 244.)

Another type of intermediate agency, the **Council of Chief State School Officers (CCSSO),** is composed of state commissioners or superintendents of education and provides a forum for interstate discussion and information exchange on educational advances and issues. The chief state school officer is appointed by either the governor of a state or the state board of education. One of the programs CCSSO sponsors is the National Teacher of the Year Program.

> **Intermediate educational units (IEUs)**
> Educational service organizations that provide school districts human and material services and programs.

> **Council of Chief State School Officers (CCSSO)**
> An intermediate agency, composed of state commissioners or superintendents of education, that provides a forum for interstate discussion and information exchange on educational advances and issues.

Roles of Local Government in Education

In educational policy and issues, local government refers to local boards of education, which are the governing bodies for schools, and to municipal governments, which make decisions affecting education at the district and city levels. Boards of education, acting in their capacity as the local government, perform many functions that relate to how schools are governed and financed. Boards of education implement state regulations and policies, make and implement local policies, tax residents to raise funds, incur debt, build facilities, hire and pay school personnel, create the curriculum, and respond to community needs through special programs and initiatives.

Local city government influences education through policies relating to the support of schools and the roles it sees schools playing in the community. For example, local city government can encourage community growth and development as a means of expanding the tax base for new and improved schools. In many big cities, the local city government, represented by the mayor, has broad discretionary powers, including the hiring of the superintendent of schools. The structure of governance at the local district level is shown in Figure 7.7.

> **INTASC**
>
> **Standard 7:** The teacher plans instruction based upon knowledge of subject matter, students, the community, and curriculum goals.
>
> **Standard 10:** The teacher fosters relationships with school colleagues, parents, and agencies in the larger community to support students' learning and well-being.

BOCES began in response to the needs of small rural districts that were unable to provide their students with many of the services larger districts provide. For example, a small district might not be able to afford an art teacher or counseling services. So, BOCES was formed, in the beginning, primarily as an organization of itinerant teachers—that is, teachers who travel from one district to another teaching and providing services. Today BOCES provides services to school districts in four areas: vocational education, special education, computers and technology, and support services.

Vocational Education. In response to the needs of districts, BOCES became involved in vocational education. There is a renewed interest in vocational education, especially with the contemporary emphasis on educating students with workplace skills. Today BOCES operates many vocational centers across the state.

Special Education. With the advent of legislation such as the Education for All Handicapped Children Act, PL 94–142 (see Chapter 5), which provided for a free and appropriate education for all students with disabilities, BOCES became involved in providing such services. Today, BOCES provides educational opportunities for children with severe disabilities. While the trend is toward full inclusion—that is, education of children with disabilities in the regular classroom—there is still a need for special programs and services for children with severe emotional and physical disabilities. For example, students who need one-on-one attention, assistance with eating and toileting, and protection from injuring themselves are provided services by BOCES. In addition, BOCES also provides itinerant teachers for students

who are visually or hearing impaired. In all of these cases, and others similar to them, education can best be delivered through an intermediate type system.

Computers and Technology. BOCES houses nine regional information centers. One function of these centers is to provide technology services to districts. For example, BOCES has established an information highway linking a majority of the schools in the state with one another and with the State Department of Education. BOCES has given students access to technology that allows them to communicate with students in other schools across the country and also some in foreign countries, including Russia.

The computers and technology section of BOCES supports distance learning projects. These enable districts to electronically link up and conduct classes in which teachers and students are able to see and hear each other. The idea is to get away from putting students on buses and transporting them long distances to a class. Distance learning allows students to stay put and share learning with students in other districts. Distance learning also gives students easy access to college courses.

In addition, BOCES computer and technology support services help districts deal with fiscal and management issues and information processing.

Support Services. BOCES support services help schools with video projects, equity programs designed to make the environment hospitable to both males and females, school science projects, staff development and enrichment, automated library systems, drug education, risk management, communications, arts-in-education, and other services.

Local Education Agency (LEA)
Local school districts.

Local Education Agencies. School districts, often referred to as the **local education agency (LEA),** come in all sizes and shapes. As you can see in Table 7.3, the largest school district is for New York City schools.

The geographic area encompassed by a school district takes many forms. The state of Hawaii has one school district, although it is divided into seven administrative areas. Some states—such as Florida, Georgia, Kentucky, Maryland, Virginia, and Utah—are organized along county lines. Some cities, such as Baltimore, exist as a school district within a county system. Many big cities—such as New York, Los Angeles, Chicago, Philadelphia, Memphis, Milwaukee, Houston, Dallas, and Albuquerque—operate their own school districts.

In many states, such as Pennsylvania, the township is a common local political and administrative unit. School district boundaries are often the same as townships, with the townships operating the school districts. Sometimes the townships operate only elementary schools; junior, middle, and high school students attend schools in merged or consolidated school districts.

Since the mid 1970s, the trend has been for small school districts to merge into larger school districts that cut across township and county lines. The merging of school districts and the creation of regional schools combine resources and may serve students better. There are currently 14,859 school districts, down from 14,891 in 2001.[8]

Independent school districts cross city and county boundaries and are often the result of legislative action. Independent school districts are often regional school dis-

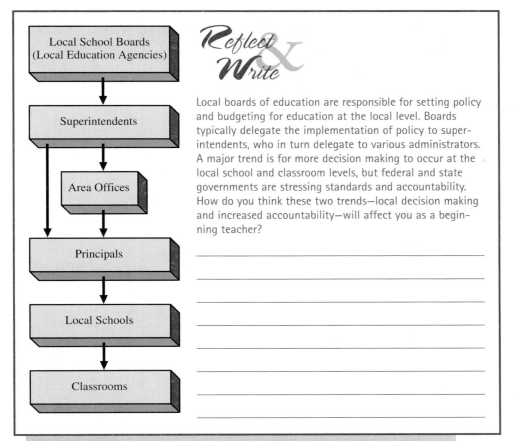

Reflect & Write

Local boards of education are responsible for setting policy and budgeting for education at the local level. Boards typically delegate the implementation of policy to superintendents, who in turn delegate to various administrators. A major trend is for more decision making to occur at the local school and classroom levels, but federal and state governments are stressing standards and accountability. How do you think these two trends—local decision making and increased accountability—will affect you as a beginning teacher?

_____

_____

_____

_____

_____

_____

_____

_____

Figure 7.7   *Control and Governance of Education at the Local Level*

tricts serving large numbers of students. Texas, for example, has independent school districts that cut across town and county boundaries.

Local Boards of Education.   Authority for education in the states resides in state departments of education, but the responsibility for education at the local level is delegated to local boards of education. Local boards are composed of five to nine members who are directly elected by voters or who are appointed by mayors or other public officials. Board politics can be highly entwined with local municipal politics. While the goal is to provide the best possible education for everyone, how to achieve this goal, how much to spend, and what to spend it on are issues of perennial contention at the local level. In reality, school boards have only the powers delegated to them by the states. In addition, they must function within local, state, and federal laws.

Individual school board members cannot act independently; rather, the board must act as a whole. This principle of the board acting as a whole applies in several ways. The board makes decisions as a body at legally called public meetings. Board members cannot make decisions for the board on their own. Furthermore, board members cannot make decisions that are in opposition to the local constituents, nor can they allow a school system to deteriorate and become ineffective.

Teachers and administrators always say that they could do a better job of educating students if they were free of many rules and regulations. Boards of education have listened and are responding. Boards of education are returning decision-making powers to school administrators and teachers by waiving district rules. **Waivers** are the temporary or permanent suspension of school board policy, union rules, and departments of education rules to enable the implementation of desired educational

NCATE

Middle Level

Standard 7: Understands the complexity of teaching young adolescents; engages in practices and behaviors that develop competence as a professional.

Waivers
The temporary or permanent suspension of school board policy or departments of education rules.

Table 7.3   *Twenty Largest School Districts*

District	K–12 Membership (2001–2002)	Expenditure per Student
New York City, NY	1,049,831	$13,566
Los Angeles, CA	735,058	8,408
Chicago, IL	437,418	9,226
Dade County, FL	375,836	7,923
Broward County, FL	262,055	7,325
Clark County, NV	245,659	8,002
Houston, TX	210,950	8,694
Philadelphia, PA	197,083	9,743
Hawaii, HI	184,546	7,394
Hillsborough County, FL	169,789	8,006
Detroit, MI	166,675	10,018
Dallas, TX	163,562	6,986
Fairfax County, VA	160,584	10,329
Palm Beach County, FL	160,223	8,349
Orange County, FL	157,433	8,204
San Diego, CA	141,599	9,092
Montgomery County, MD	136,895	10,830
Prince George's County, MD	135,039	8,737
Duval County, FL	127,392	6,843
Gwinnett County, GA	116,339	8,162

Source: National Center for Education Statistics, *Information on Public Schools and School Districts in the United States.* (Online). Available at http://nces.ed.gov/ccd/search.asp; Proximity, *Largest 100 U.S. School Districts.* (Online). Available at www.proximityone.com/lgsd.htm.

What are the powers and responsibilities of a local school board? How are the powers of local school boards limited? How do local education agencies influence education at the district and school level?

improvements. All waiver requests go to the state department of education, but a district request for a waiver does not mean it will be approved. Waivers can apply to a range of areas, including changes in instructional programs, student assessment, student discipline, organization of the school day and year, school staff positions, teacher compensation, and student transportation. For example, under the Pennsylvania Empowerment Act, each of the state's 501 school districts can seek waivers from state mandates "to improve its instructional program or to operate in a more efficient, effective, or economical manner."[9] The Altoona Area School District sought a waiver from state rules on special education class size that would require the district to hire twelve additional teachers.

Superintendents of Schools. Administration of the local school district is vested in superintendents, who are appointed or elected by the local board of education. Generally, superintendents are hired for a contracted period of time—for example, four or five years. However, superintendents serve at the pleasure of the board, so when the political makeup of a board changes or if the board is not satisfied with the job done, then their contract is terminated or bought out. Big-city superintendents in particular have demanding jobs and often have short and tempestuous tenures. (See the Profile.)

Superintendents' responsibilities include working in close consultation with the local board of education as they plan, organize, direct, control, and coordinate the activities of the school district. Superintendents also have to work collaboratively

---

 **Big-City Superintendent: Roger C. Cuevas**

Roger C. Cuevas is superintendent in the Miami-Dade, Florida, school district, which is Florida's largest.

To be superintendent of a big-city school district is to be equal parts teacher and student, business executive and social worker, activist and reactor, historian and futurist, cheerleader and critic, politician and citizen, parent and child, listener and leader. The complexities of modern life converge at your in-box, demanding to be sorted, decided, deciphered, and finessed. Focus and flexibility are your biggest challenges and your biggest assets. As a big-city superintendent, I must focus on particularly complex issues that profoundly affect our students and schools.

- **Rising Poverty.** In cities across America, more and more children are becoming poorer and poorer. The fallout affects every aspect of their lives, including their ability to learn. Schools must respond with nutrition programs that feed their hunger, pre-K programs that teach the language skills they don't learn at home, counseling that encourages them to stay in school, and career education and applied-technology programs that give them the focus and the skills they'll need to get good jobs.
- **Campus Violence.** As crime and violence rates rise in our society, so they rise in our schools. Where students once were ordered to sit in the corner for chewing gum, now they are expelled for bringing guns to class. To keep all students safe, schools today must take preventative measures, such as teaching youngsters nonviolent conflict resolution skills, and corrective measures, such as expelling the disruptive students. Some methods, such as testing

students for drugs or searching their lockers for weapons, have sparked serious debate about civil liberties in those cities where they have been tried.

- **Changing Family.** The very concept of family has changed radically since World War II. Today, many children grow up in homes with single parents or no parents at all. Many don't even have homes. School is often the one constant in their uncertain lives. More and more, the school must play the role the family once served, be it by providing free meals, offering early educational experiences parents once provided themselves, providing before- and after-school care, or offering on-campus health and social services to youngsters and their relatives.
- **Immigration and Cultural Diversity.** Once the concern primarily of a few large school districts, immigration now poses challenges and rewards for schools throughout America. Immigrant students and their families bring with them unique social and academic needs that must be met with special programs. Both they and native students often require curriculum and counseling programs to help them understand and respect their similarities and differences.
- **Inadequate Facilities.** Old buildings, scarce land, few dollars, and fast growth present many big-city school districts with a number of complex and stubborn challenges. Chief among them are overcrowding, safety concerns, and educational inequality. Traditional remedies are no longer working. Superintendents must find these old problems once and for all.

How Is Education Controlled and

and collegially with school district personnel, labor leaders, community leaders, and appointed and elected officials on local, regional, and national fronts.

More and more big urban school districts are turning to noneducators to help them address the multitude of complex problems involved in ensuring a high-quality education for all children. These new leaders come with backgrounds in law, politics, the military, and business. Alan D. Bersin, Superintendent of San Diego Public Schools, is a former U.S. Attorney General. Roy Romer, the former governor of Colorado, is Superintendent of the Los Angeles School District. Joel Klein, an anti-trust lawyer and former CEO of Bertelsmann, Inc., now leads the New York City Schools. For this new breed of school leader, education is a major challenge. As Bersin states, "Public education is what distinguishes this country, both vertically, in history, and horizontally, from other societies around the world. For the first time, there is a real belief in this country that every child has the right to a quality education. This is the most important challenge San Diego faces. It gives reality to what is otherwise the empty myth that in this country, you can do anything you want to do."[10]

SECTION SUMMARY

How Is Education Controlled and Governed?

The executive, legislative, and judicial branches of government all influence the governance and finance of U.S. education. Balancing these forces is one of the primary goals of the politics of education.

- Roles of the National Government in Education. The roles of the national government in education are to promote development and academic success, provide for national security, foster responsible citizenship, and ensure the constitutional rights of all citizens. The federal government carries out its educational responsibilities through federal courts, funding, legislation, the Department of Education, and various agencies. Presidents also shape and direct educational policy.

- Roles of State Government in Education. There are four basic models of governance of state education, depending on the traditions of individual states, which vary in the emphasis given to state boards of education, standards boards, and departments of education. The process of education varies by state, and some states do not conform to any of the four models. The National Governors' Association has been influential in setting goals and directions for education.

- Roles of Intermediate Education Agencies. Intermediate agencies maximize resources and promote cooperation across district boundaries by offering services and information exchanges that might not otherwise be available to the districts.

- Roles of Local Government in Education. Local school districts and individual schools are responsible for providing day-to-day education. Local government policies influence educational delivery. Local education agencies, or school districts, vary widely in size, configuration, and number. States delegate their responsibility for education to local boards of education, which hire local superintendents of schools.

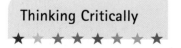

Thinking Critically

★ ★ ★ ★ ★ ★ ★ ★

Over the last decade, there has been a growing trend for state governors and legislatures to exert more control over education. Do you think this is a good trend? Why? Why not? Where do you think the responsibility for the control of education should reside?

_____

_____

_____

_____ ★

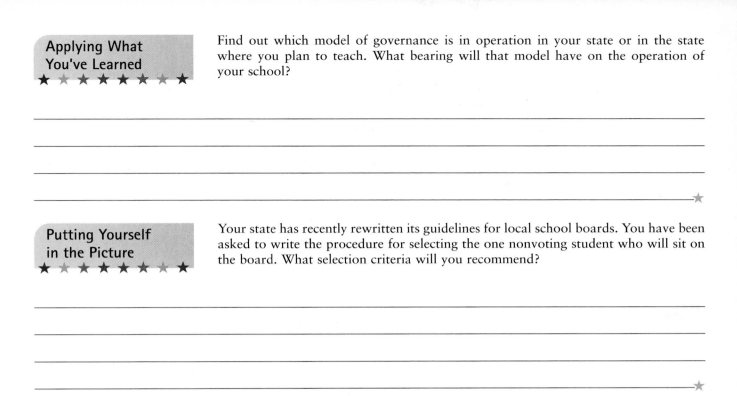

_____

_____

_____

_____ ★

_____

_____

_____

_____ ★

HOW ARE SCHOOLS GOVERNED AND ADMINISTERED?

Governance and administration at the school level are complex processes that involve principals, teachers, students, parents, and community leaders. **Administration** is the management of the affairs of the school and involves putting into everyday practice the policies established by the state legislature, state board of education, and the local board of education. The administration of a school involves, for example, scheduling classes, teacher assignments, use of facilities, and evaluation of teachers and staff. While there is always a need for administration, there is less of a tendency today to invest the sole responsibility for administration with one person. The preferred approach to administration is one that involves as many of the school's stakeholders as possible.

Administration
The management of affairs of a school or education agency based on the policies established by the state legislature, state board of education, and local board of education.

Principals and Assistant Principals

At the school level, the principal is responsible for the management of human and material resources to effectively support teachers' teaching and children's learning. Some principals manage more than one school. For example, some principals are administratively responsible for satellite schools in their districts.

How the school is organized also depends on its size and the personnel employed. While much of education is organized on a top-down linear, or hierarchical, model, there is currently more emphasis on cooperation and collaboration among principals, teachers, and parents in all matters relating to how schools function. The principal's role thus goes beyond management and administration.

Effective principals emphasize programs; set overall school directions; are concerned about building staff morale; and, even more important, provide a rationale for their priorities. Also, they employ deliberative models for problem solving and skillfully empower their staffs to develop a sense of ownership in the arrangement and direction of the school.

Today, there is less talk about managing schools and more talk about leadership. As a beginning teacher, you will be called on and looked to for leadership. When you

NCATE

Middle Level

Standard 7: Understands the complexity of teaching young adolescents; engages in practices and behaviors that develop competence as a professional.

INTASC

Standard 9: The teacher is a reflective practitioner who continually evaluates the effects of his/her choices and actions on others (students, parents, and other professionals in the learning community) and who actively seeks out opportunities to grow professionally.

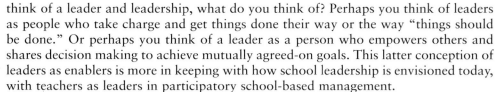

think of a leader and leadership, what do you think of? Perhaps you think of leaders as people who take charge and get things done their way or the way "things should be done." Or perhaps you think of a leader as a person who empowers others and shares decision making to achieve mutually agreed-on goals. This latter conception of leaders as enablers is more in keeping with how school leadership is envisioned today, with teachers as leaders in participatory school-based management.

For example, in characterizing the principal of an award-winning elementary school, the faculty said, "She is totally nonthreatening—she gives us a sense of our own importance. We are free to make mistakes, and we are not afraid to voice our opinion about the curriculum, the students, and school policies." Embedded in what the teachers said about their principal are attributes that Thomas Sergiovanni characterizes as moral leadership. Sergiovanni believes that moral leadership occurs when teachers and administrators are guided by professionalism and the guiding principle is not "what is rewarded gets done," but "what is good gets done."[11]

Reflect & Write

What do you consider to be good criteria for effective leadership? As a first-year teacher, how will you know good leadership when you see it?

_____

_____

_____

_____

School-Based Management

In many schools across the country, a new form of governance is changing how decisions are made and how things get done. This new form of governance is **school-based management (SBM),** also called site-based management (introduced in Chapter 6) and shared decision making. School-based management is designed to empower those affected by decisions by involving them in the decision-making process. The rationale

Who is involved in school-based management? What conditions and resources are needed for school-based management to succeed?

of school-based management is that if people are involved in the decision making, they will be more likely to carry out the decisions. In schools where school-based management has had a major impact, teachers report they use innovative practices.

As a beginning teacher, you probably will have opportunities to participate in school-based management activities. But merely making opportunities for participation is not sufficient for helping ensure the success of site-based management. Professionals at all levels need help developing skills for effective involvement.

Opportunity for participation in school-based management does not necessarily mean that all will participate or will participate with the same amount of enthusiasm. Participation takes time, energy, and commitment. How well and how much professionals use these essential resources help determine the success of SBM.

SBM depends on leadership, in particular, teachers as leaders. As the definition and role of being a professional in education continue to expand, teachers are being asked and challenged to lead—in the classroom, the school, the district, and beyond.

School Advisory Councils

A major factor in school improvement efforts is the **school advisory council (SAC)**, or **school improvement team (SIT)**. While the names of advisory organizations may be different in different school districts, their membership and functions are basically the same. SAC membership generally consists of school and community stakeholders—students, teachers, parents, community leaders, administrators, and other school staff. As you enter the profession, there is a good possibility you will be involved in some way with SAC responsibilities. The primary purpose of advisory councils is to facilitate the development, implementation, and monitoring of a **school improvement plan (SIP)**. As the name implies, the purpose of a SIP is to improve how the school functions. The intent of the SIP is to increase and enhance teaching and learning. State departments of education and local school districts often specify that each school must have such an improvement plan. A SIP often includes the following elements:

- School mission and goals
- Baseline data necessary to identify needs
- Expected student learning outcomes
- Strategies and time line for improvement
- Participatory management model
- Description of how resources will be used
- Training and technical assistance necessary to support the SIP
- Report on the status of current year's plan

Through models such as school-based management, current efforts to reform and reorganize education emphasize bottom-up, grass-roots action. School councils and improvement plans offer an important opportunity for all stakeholders to make a difference in how schools work.

INTASC

Standard 10: The teacher fosters relationships with school colleagues, parents, and agencies in the larger community to support students' learning and well-being.

School advisory council (SAC), or school improvement team (SIT) SAC membership consists of school and community stakeholders—students, teachers, parents, community leaders, administrators, and other school staff—who make decisions and recommendations regarding school operation.

School improvement plan (SIP) A plan designed to improve how a school functions and operates, with the intent of increasing and enhancing teaching and learning; often required by state departments of education and local school districts.

SECTION SUMMARY

How Are Schools Governed and Administered?

Schools are governed at the school level by principals, school-based management teams, and advisory councils. These individuals and groups put into daily practice the policies established by the state legislature, state board of education, and local board of education.

- Principals and Assistant Principals. A principal may manage one school or more than one, depending on the size of the district, the size of the school buildings, and the number of personnel involved. Effective principals do more than just manage; they are good leaders who encourage their staff to participate in problem solving and in helping determine the direction of the school.

- School-Based Management. School-based management (SBM), also called site-based management, involves teachers and other stakeholders in making decisions that affect the curriculum and day-to-day operations. Schools committed to SBM have such positive features as distribution and delegation of power, professional development, information dissemination, well-defined vision, performance rewards, and innovative practices. In addition, teachers are considered to be instructional leaders.
- School Advisory Councils. Teachers also participate in decision making through school advisory councils (also called school improvement teams). The primary purpose of such councils is to develop, implement, and monitor school improvement plans, which are designed to increase and enhance teaching and learning.

Thinking Critically
★ ★ ★ ★ ★ ★ ★ ★ ★

How comfortable are you working as a member of a team? What are some things you can do now to prepare to be an effective team member?

_____

_____

_____

_____ ★

Applying What You've Learned
★ ★ ★ ★ ★ ★ ★ ★ ★

Does your state department of education or local school district specify that schools must have a school improvement plan? Do some Internet research to see what plan is required or if one will be required in future.

_____

_____

_____

_____ ★

Putting Yourself in the Picture
★ ★ ★ ★ ★ ★ ★ ★ ★

In what roles and in what ways would you like to participate in school-based management?

_____

_____

_____

_____ ★

*H*OW IS EDUCATION FUNDED*?*

American education is funded from many sources, including the federal government, state governments, business and industry, foundations, and local taxpayers and parents and teachers. Regardless of the source, funding of education is a major and costly enterprise. In the United States, schooling is big business. The public school educa-

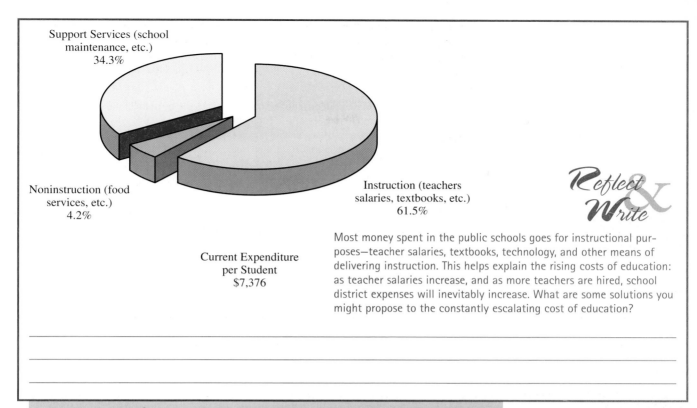

Support Services (school maintenance, etc.)
34.3%

Noninstruction (food services, etc.)
4.2%

Instruction (teachers salaries, textbooks, etc.)
61.5%

Current Expenditure per Student
$7,376

Reflect & Write

Most money spent in the public schools goes for instructional purposes—teacher salaries, textbooks, technology, and other means of delivering instruction. This helps explain the rising costs of education: as teacher salaries increase, and as more teachers are hired, school district expenses will inevitably increase. What are some solutions you might propose to the constantly escalating cost of education?

Figure 7.8 *W*here the Money Goes: Estimated Percentage of Money Spent on Pupils in U.S. Public Schools

Source: National Center for Education Statistics, *Common Core of Data, National Public Financial Survey.* (Online). Available at nces.ed.gov/ccd/.

tion enterprise is enormous, involving children and youth from birth to age 21. More than 3.4 million teachers and 2.3 million administrative and support staff in 14,859 school districts are involved in the process of educating the 52 million students in the nation's public and private elementary and secondary schools. Total expenditures for elementary and secondary schools are more than $412 billion.[12] The cost of educating American children and youth is put into better perspective when you consider that the per-pupil expenditure to educate each student in the public schools is about $7,376 per year.[13] Figure 7.8 shows how that money is spent.

The majority of financial support for public elementary and secondary schools comes from three sources: the federal government, state governments, and local communities. Other sources include businesses, industry, and foundations. Figure 7.9 shows the proportion of funding from the principal sources.

Federal Support and Mandates

Although education is a state responsibility, the national government in 2004 spent an estimated $44.5 billion on elementary and secondary programs.[14] Total federal funding for education is more than $412 billion from a variety of federal departments and agencies. In 2001, public elementary and secondary schools received 7.3 percent of their revenue from the national government, which amounted to about $22.2 billion.[15] Federal expenditures have increased from $202 billion in 1990 to $307.9 billion in 2000.

Part of the federal government's support of public schools comes through specific legislation. Some legislation is for **categorical grants,** also called block grants, designed to help particular groups of students. For example, in 1964 Congress passed the Economic Opportunity Act, which authorized the formation of Head Start in 1965

Categorical (block) grants
Federal government support of the public schools that comes through specific legislation designed to help particular groups of students; sometimes called block grants.

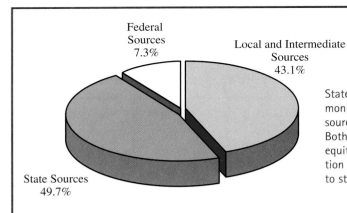

Federal
Sources
7.3%

Local and Intermediate
Sources
43.1%

State and local governments provide the overwhelming majority of monies necessary to fund education. This explains why taxes and other sources of school funding are always issues in local and state elections. Both local and state governments are constantly looking for ways to equitably fund schools at the level needed to provide a quality education for all students. What are two recommendations you would make to state legislators about how to more equitably fund education?

State Sources
49.7%

_____

_____

_____

Figure 7.9 **Sources of Public Revenue for Public Elementary and Secondary Schools**

Source: National Center for Education Statistics, *Digest of Education Statistics, 2001* (Washington, DC: U.S. Government Printing Office, 2001).

(see Chapter 3). Head Start serves about 30 percent of the nation's economically disadvantaged preschool children and greatly affects the curriculum of kindergarten and first-grade students. In 2003, Head Start had a budget of $6.7 billion.[16] Review Table 7.2 for other examples of categorical grants and their funding levels.

Regardless of how a state or school district receives federal funds, it has to comply with the federal spending guidelines attached to the funds. Recipients of federal funding also have to agree to comply with all other existing federal rules and regulations. In this way, the federal government exerts considerable influence over educational practice. When and if school districts and states do not comply with conditions of federal funding, they can lose that funding, be fined for noncompliance, or lose the right to future federal funding.

What Does This Mean for You?

If you have not thought much about school funding at the state level, consider this scenario.

In a small river town in southern Illinois, Sarah Delaney prepares to start the day in her fourth-grade classroom. Hundreds of miles away in a northern suburb of Chicago, Albert Thorpe is getting ready to greet his fourth-graders. Today, both classes will take the Illinois Standards Achievement Test. The students and teachers in both classrooms will be held accountable for the state educational performance and content standards. Both teachers worked hard to prepare their students, and both classes studied diligently. Both teachers have taught for thirty years, both graduated from a state-accredited teacher education program, and both went on to earn a master's degree.

Despite these similar backgrounds and accountabilities, when Sarah retires in another ten years, she will receive a pension of $37,000 a year; Albert's annual pension will be closer to $60,000. Over the course of their careers, Sarah will have earned about $250,000 less than Albert. This discrepancy exists because the state funding formula relies heavily on local property taxes. Almost every aspect of the education program is similarly affected in the two schools—not only salaries, but also instructional resources and physical plant. So funding really does matter.

Funding at the State Level

Historically, local property taxes were the major source of state funding for education. However, times are changing. Beginning with the 1979–1980 school year, for the first time in U.S. history more money in support of education came from the state level than from the local level. In 2001, 49.7 percent of funding came from the state level, whereas funding from local sources was 43 percent.[17]

All states have a variety of ways of collecting money to support education, including sales taxes (only Alaska, Delaware, Montana, New Hampshire, and Oregon do not have a sales tax), income taxes, inheritance taxes, various license and occupation fees, and state lotteries. One of the reasons sales taxes are popular is that they are relatively painless, since people pay in small amounts as they spend and because the state collects the revenue from businesses rather than from each individual taxpayer.

For example, the primary source of tax dollars in Florida is the 6 percent sales tax that goes into the state general revenue fund. In 2001, the state distributed $11.9 billion to the sixty-seven county school districts of the state. Of the $11.9 billion distributed, $4 billion was from this sales tax.[18] The remainder of the monies distributed to the schools came through federal funding, such as the school breakfast and lunch programs, programs for educationally disadvantaged children and exceptional children, and vocational programs.

One disadvantage of sales taxes is that they are relatively unstable. When people are earning more, they spend more, but when employment is down and wages are low, less spending occurs. Another drawback to sales taxes is that they are **regressive taxes.** Such taxes tax the poor at a higher rate than the wealthy, since the poor must spend a greater proportion of their income than do the wealthy. Personal income taxes, on the other hand, are **progressive taxes** because they tax the wealthy at a higher rate than the poor.

State Funding Formulas. States employ a variety of ways to distribute money to local districts. **Flat grants** provide equal funding based on a district's average daily attendance and calculated on enrollments in "count weeks," generally during October and February. As a beginning teacher you will be asked to help provide accurate attendance data, since student average daily attendance helps determine state funding. In addition, school districts now aggressively enforce mandatory attendance laws in an effort to improve attendance, which determines state reimbursements. Some districts threaten truants with jail time in their efforts to improve attendance. (See Chapter 8.) Some states use variable flat grants and give variable amounts of funding based on particular needs. A district with a bilingual program, for example, would receive a larger grant than would a district without such services, because such programs are more expensive to operate. **Foundation grants** guarantee each district a certain amount of funding, which varies inversely with community wealth. Poor communities with low revenues from property taxes receive more money than wealthy communities. States constantly seek funding formulas that will be effective and fair.

Regressive taxes
Taxes that tax the poor at a higher rate than the wealthy (i.e., sales taxes, since the poor must spend a greater proportion of their income than do the wealthy).

Progressive taxes
Taxes designed to tax the wealthy and poor according to amount of income.

Flat grants
Provide equal funding based on a district's average daily attendance, which is established during "count weeks," generally during October and February; some states give variable amounts of funding based on particular needs.

Foundation grants
Grants based on the property values in a school district. Funding is usually in inverse relation to community wealth; school districts in poorer communities with low property values receive more grant funding than do school districts in more affluent communities.

Reflect & Write

What state funding formula do you think best promotes both excellence and equity in schooling?

_____

_____

_____

_____

Funding at the Local Level

About 43 percent of the funding for schools comes from the local level (see Figure 7.9). The majority of local funding support for schools is raised from property taxes, which are based on the assessed value of real estate—homes, commercial land, and buildings.[19] The primary advantage of the property tax is that it is a reliable and steady source of revenue. A major problem with funding schools through property taxes, however, is the inequity it produces. In districts and neighborhoods where property values are high, property taxes provide greater funding for schools than in districts and neighborhoods where property values are low.

This means that some school districts, because of low property values, cannot support their schools at the same level as other higher-value districts, even if they tax their property owners heavily. This inability of local school districts to adequately support education is especially evident in rural and urban areas. Rural southern states tend to be poorer in terms of income and property values; therefore, the South spends less on education than does the North. Also, in inner cities, where property values are low, the ability to support schools is less than it is in wealthier suburban neighborhoods.

If professional sports teams can sell the naming rights for their stadiums and other facilities, why can't cash-starved public schools? Why not indeed! Chances are that a school stadium, gymnasium, or building near you is—or will soon be—"branded" with a corporate name. This strategy can bring in dollars. (One New Jersey school district named its new gymnasium after a supermarket chain in exchange for $100,000 and employs a director for corporate development to establish more such relationships.) But doing so also carries a price tag. Educators wonder what the message is to students who study or play in facilities named after corporations.

Another problem with raising money through property taxes is that the tax falls mainly on homeowners, who are increasingly less willing to have their taxes raised to support schools. Funding of schools at the local level can be a problem when taxpayers set "caps" on what school boards can spend on education. These limits on spending often result from propositions voted on by taxpayers in local and state elections. Given these limitations, the amount of money to operate schools may be insufficient, and students and teachers may not have the materials and resources needed for adequate teaching and learning. In some cases, if taxpayers do not vote to override spending caps, schools may close early, shortening the school year for students and teachers. Some schools find alternative ways to cut costs, as Education on the Move illustrates.

Private Funding

Foundations provide support for many kinds of educational programs. In December of 1993, for example, Walter H. Annenberg announced a $500 million "challenge to the nation" in an effort to improve public and private education. The $500 million "Annenberg Challenge" is earmarked for educational improvement projects around the country. Three Annenberg Challenge projects, in partnership with their local school districts, have been awarded grants as part of Schools for a New Society, a $60 million initiative, funded by the Carnegie Corporation of New York and the Bill and Melinda Gates Foundation, that aims to reinvigorate efforts to improve high schools around the country. The Boston Public Schools/Boston Plan for Excellence and the Hamilton County Schools/Chattanooga–Hamilton County Public Education Fund partnerships each received $8 million, while the Houston Independent School District/Houston Annenberg Challenge received $12 million (owing to its larger school district). All

>>> Four–Day Week Catches On! >>>>>>>

Aimee Kroneberger's three daughters didn't go to school on Fridays this year. And they don't have to make them up in summer school.

Along with about 1,300 other children in the East Grand school district in the Rocky Mountains west of Denver, the Kroneberger sisters attend classes just four days a week. Kylie, Tracie, and Sydnie have longer school days than when they lived in Denver, but every weekend during the school year is a three-day pass.

On Fridays, they're free to do what they want, which means in the winter they're usually tuning up their ski racing skills at Colorado's Winter Park Resort. Their school year is 146 days, compared to the norm of 180. "Our family loves it," says Aimee Kroneberger.

Begun as a money-saving experiment in 1982, the four-day school week in the mountain towns of Granby, Fraser, and Grand Lake started out as "a shock," says Superintendent Robb Rankin. But now, Rankin says, "it fits in with the lifestyle" of communities that cherish outdoor recreation and extra family time.

A small but growing number of districts across the country are switching to a four-day school schedule, mainly because of financial pressures. A survey conducted last year by the National School Boards Association found 108 districts in ten states had made the switch.

"It is typically a rural cost-saving measure," says Kathy Christie of the Education Commission of the States, an education policy center headquartered in Denver.

As with most things associated with public education, opinion can be sharply divided on whether the cost savings that come from the four-day school week are worth it.

Effect on Students

In Colorado's East Grand district, parents unhappy about the four-day week formed a charter school with a traditional schedule four years ago. Among the concerns was the effect of longer days on children in elementary school.

"Our feeling was that the students lose a full day of instruction if they don't go to school on the fifth day and that the three-day weekend every week was disruptive to the continuity of the learning process," says Tim Koepke, a mechanical engineer on the Indian Peaks Charter School board. The charter school serves about fifty children in grades K through 8.

And, says Koepke, the father of two children in elementary school, "We did not like the notion of the younger kids having to get up so early every day and spend so much time in school."

More than a quarter of Colorado's 178 school districts—but less than 2 percent of students—have a four-day schedule. Classes run for 7.5 hours a day for 144 days rather than the traditional six hours a day for 180 days.

Source: Tom Kenworthy, "Colorado Schools Give High Score to Four-Day Weeks—Effort Saves Money in Rural Areas; Kids Have Longer Days, Fridays Off," *USA Today.* (Online). Available at www.usatoday.com/usatonline/20040614/6283512s.htm. Copyright 2004 by USA TODAY. Reprinted by permission.

grants must be matched locally. The winning reform plans were selected based on a number of criteria, including having the political will and a demonstrated ability to forge broad-based partnerships that welcomed businesses, universities, parent groups, youth development agencies, and community-based organizations.[20]

In addition, a network of reform-minded public schools in the San Francisco Bay area has secured $40 million in new grants, enabling it to continue for five more years the improvement efforts it began in 1995 as part of the nationwide Annenberg Challenge. Announcing the grants in February 2001, officials with the Bay Area School Reform Collaborative (BASRC) said they planned to use the grant money from the Annenberg Foundation and the William and Flora Hewlett Foundation to leverage an additional $60 million in donations over the next five years. The BASRC intends to give the $100 million as grants to as many as 300 public schools in six Bay Area counties to use what organizers describe as data-driven methods for improving student performance and narrowing the achievement gap between disadvantaged students and their wealthier peers.[21]

The Annenberg Challenge grants and other private funding illustrate that foundations and businesses are willing to donate money to schools but only if the funding is targeted to reforming education, with particular emphasis on urban, minority, and special education. Givers want their financial efforts to have significant and measurable outcomes.

How Is Education Funded?

American education is financed primarily through federal, state, and local revenues, although businesses, industry, and foundations also contribute a relatively small amount.

- Federal Support and Mandates. The federal government contributes 7.3 percent of the money required to operate the public schools. Some of this money comes in the form of categorical, or block, grants. Federal funds require compliance with federal rules and regulations.

- Funding at the State Level. The states contribute 49.7 percent of the schools' budget, and the proportion of funding from states is increasing. States use various means to redistribute funds to local school districts, including sales taxes, flat grants, and foundation grants.

- Funding at the Local Level. Local funding accounts for 43 percent of the schools' budget. Property taxes are the main source of funding for schools at the local level. Issues relating to property taxes as a way of funding education include how to ease the taxpayers' burden, how to equalize funding among poor and wealthy districts, and how schools cope with funding limits.

- Private Funding. Foundations, business, and industry provide some funding for U.S. education. Increasingly, this support is tied to specific programs or goals.

Thinking Critically
★ ☆ ★ ☆ ★ ☆ ★ ☆ ★

Where do you stand on the liberal-conservative continuum? How do your political views affect how you believe schools should be governed and financed?

_____

_____

_____

_____ ★

Applying What You've Learned
★ ☆ ★ ☆ ★ ☆ ★ ☆ ★

Obtain a copy of the annual report for your home town school district. What were the sources of income? How was the budget spent? Did your local school receive any private funding?

_____

_____

_____

_____ ★

Putting Yourself in the Picture
★ ☆ ★ ☆ ★ ☆ ★ ☆ ★

Your school district just received a $1 million grant to "improve education at the local level." You chair the committee that will recommend to the school board how this money should be allocated. What would be your recommendations?

_____

_____

_____

_____ ★

WHAT ISSUES OF GOVERNANCE AND FINANCE AFFECT EDUCATION TODAY?

Issues of governance and finance constantly face the public. Furthermore, these issues are intertwined: Issues of governance almost always raise accompanying issues of finance; solutions to a particular finance issue almost always raise issues of governance. These issues reflect basic contradictions in the politics and economics of American education, as Figure 7.10 suggests.

Federal versus State Control

According to a 2003 public opinion survey, the American public, by a whopping 61 percent, believes the local school board should have the greatest influence in deciding what is taught in the public schools.[22]

The issues involved in national versus state control of education have to do primarily with who will decide what is best for students and what they will learn. On the one hand, some believe it is in the national interest for the federal government to set standards and specify what students should know and be able to do. On the other hand, some believe that states are most qualified and constitutionally mandated to make all decisions about learning and teaching.

State versus Local Control

States differ in the ways they concentrate power at the state level. In particular, states such as California, Florida, and Texas, more than other states, tend to concentrate

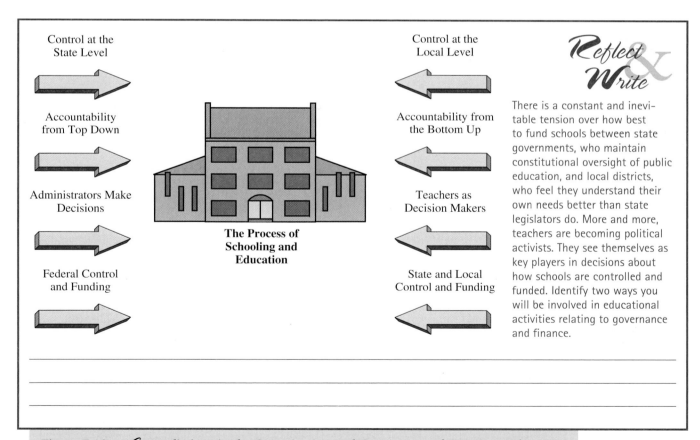

Control at the State Level

Accountability from Top Down

Administrators Make Decisions

Federal Control and Funding

The Process of Schooling and Education

Control at the Local Level

Accountability from the Bottom Up

Teachers as Decision Makers

State and Local Control and Funding

Reflect & Write

There is a constant and inevitable tension over how best to fund schools between state governments, who maintain constitutional oversight of public education, and local districts, who feel they understand their own needs better than state legislators do. More and more, teachers are becoming political activists. They see themselves as key players in decisions about how schools are controlled and funded. Identify two ways you will be involved in educational activities relating to governance and finance.

Figure 7.10   Contradictions in the Organization and Governance of American Education

NCATE

Middle Level

Standard 6: Understands the major concepts, principles, theories, and research related to working collaboratively with family and community members; uses that knowledge to maximize learning of all young adolescents.

authority and power at the state level. In fact, over the last several decades, a significant trend in American education is the continuing concentration of power and control of education at the state level.

Local control over implementing and achieving state mandates and rules leads inevitably to conflicts. For example, although states delegate responsibility for operating schools to local districts, states remain responsible for the quality and effectiveness of the educational process. If local school districts fail to do their job, the state can take over the school district. This is what happened in Philadelphia. On December 21, 2001, the state took over Philadelphia city schools. Under the agreement, a five-member commission—three members appointed by the governor and two by the mayor—replaced the school board. To date, nineteen states have taken over the operation of forty-nine school districts, including seven that enroll over 100,000 students. Under the accountability provisions of NCLB, it is likely that state takeovers of school districts will accelerate.[23]

Funding Equity

One of the problems in funding education is that great disparity can exist both between and within states for the support of education. Figure 7.11 shows per-pupil expenditures on education for each state. New York spends the most per pupil at $10,957 per year, and Utah spends the least at $4,692. These figures reflect comparative wealth and costs of living in the two states.

Funding equity issues relate to the unequal ability of school districts to pay for quality education. Districts where the property values and wages are low have a harder time raising the tax dollars they need to adequately support their schools. Similarly, rural districts have a lower tax base because agricultural land is taxed at a lower level than residential or commercial property. A recurring challenge for educators and citizens is to find ways of equalizing the support for education in all school districts.

The issue of tax equity is related to funding equity. According to a public opinion survey, a minority of respondents (21 percent) said they think using property taxes to finance schools is fair.[24] This attitude helps explain why citizen tax revolts have increased in frequency. The taxpayers' revolt began in California and spread to other states, such as Michigan and Oregon. These tax reform efforts seek to limit the amount of revenue that can be raised through property taxes, with state aid replacing lost local revenues. There has been a consequent increase of state funding to local districts over the past decade. State aid can mitigate the inequities that result from primary reliance on property taxes, especially in districts with a property tax base that is eroding due to demographic changes, declining property values, and business and industry closings or downsizing.

Privatization of Public Schools

The operation of public schools by private agencies is called **privatization.** Some agencies operate for profit, while others are nonprofit. Tesseract Group, Inc., formerly Education Alternatives, Inc. (EAI), a for-profit Minneapolis-based company whose stock is publicly traded, opened South Pointe Elementary School in Miami, Florida, in 1991. This was the first public school in the United States operated by a private company. Tesseract has a charter from the state of Arizona to operate twelve charter schools in Phoenix. Alternative Public Schools, Inc. (APS), a Nashville-based for-profit company, opened Turner Elementary School in Wilkensburg, Pennsylvania (a Pittsburgh suburb), in 1995, the first public school operated by a private firm with its own staff. Proponents of privatization cite their frustration with public education and see it as a means for reforming the schools, providing opportunities for underachieving students, and being more responsive to parents and communities about what schools should teach and how they should teach it. Local control is very much at the

Funding equity
Involves issues of equable funding; relates to the unequal ability of school districts to pay for quality education. Some states provide additional funding to compensate for school districts' inability to adequately fund education.

Privatization
The operation of public schools by private agencies; a public-private partnership.

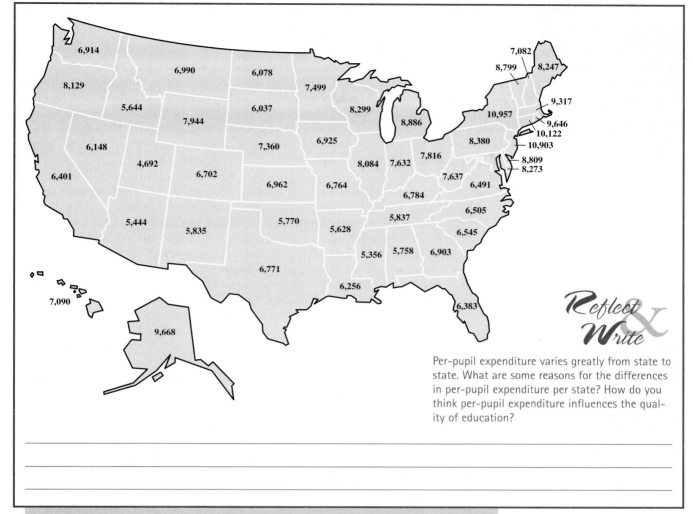

Per-pupil expenditure varies greatly from state to state. What are some reasons for the differences in per-pupil expenditure per state? How do you think per-pupil expenditure influences the quality of education?

Figure 7.11   *P*er-Pupil Expenditure, 1999–2000

Source: National Center for Education Statistics, *Common Core of Data, National Public Financial Survey, 2002.* (Online). Available at nces.ed.gov/ccd/.

heart of privatization in communities that want to find innovative ways to improve education. Local control supporters say citizens, not teachers' organizations, should set the agenda for schooling.

Opponents of privatization see it as a system for businesses and other groups to profit at the public's expense. They feel that school boards are surrendering their responsibilities to others and that privatization represents an attempt to destroy public education by tapping into public discontent. In addition, teacher organizations oppose privatization because it often leads to loss of teacher jobs and erosion of support for the teaching profession. For example, the Wilkensburg School District dismissed twenty-four teachers at Turner Elementary so that APS could hire its own teachers.

Those who favor reforming the schools without privatization believe that one of the ways they can counter the privatization movement is to forge stronger ties with parents and communities. Regardless of this debate, it is likely that privatization efforts will accelerate and that you will have many opportunities to engage in discussions about what you think make appropriate ways to use your talents and those of others in reforming public education.

INTASC

Standard 9: The teacher is a reflective practitioner who continually evaluates the effects of his/her choices and actions on others (students, parents, and other professionals in the learning community) and who actively seeks out opportunities to grow professionally.

NCATE

Early Childhood

Standard 5: Uses ethical guidelines and other professional standards; is a continuous, collaborative learner who demonstrates knowledgeable, reflective, and critical perspectives; is an informed advocate for sound educational practices.

Elementary

Standard 5.1: Understands and applies practices and behaviors that are characteristic of developing career teachers.

How Are School Governance and Finance Important to Classroom Teachers?

In seeking to change their school's discipline policy, Carol Braca and Dorrit McCormick, in the chapter opening case, are very much involved in governance issues. They recognize that issues relating to school policy affect teachers' ability to teach and how and what students learn. Carol and Dorrit also realize that in order to bring about changes they must be willing to get involved in how the school is managed as well as in school issues. Issues related to governance and finance are relevant to all teachers because they directly impact instructional potential, cooperative effort, teacher empowerment, and professionalism.

Informed Professional Participation. Knowledge and understanding of how state departments of education, school districts, and schools are organized help teachers comprehend the process of schooling. Knowledge of school governance and funding will help you understand how political and economic issues affect what you teach, how you teach, and in what conditions and environments you work. This understanding will help you become a fully functioning professional. Today's professionals are more than "just teachers." They are involved in the governance of schools through school-based management and shared decision making. Increasingly, the national government, state departments of education, and school boards are giving professionals at the local level responsibility and authority for how schools are organized and operated.

Accountability. Governance brings accountability to the educational enterprise. School board members are accountable to the public and the state for how well they provide for a district's students. Superintendents are responsible for how well school board policies are implemented, and administrators and teachers are responsible for providing evidence of what children know and are able to do. Accountability is much more of an issue now than it was several decades ago, and the public is demanding much more of schools than ever before, as is evident from the preceding discussions. Almost every dimension of education has an accountability component.

What Does This Mean for You?

The average school in the United States is forty-two years old. You may be lucky—your school may be "younger." Or it may be even older. A 2002 National Clearinghouse for Educational Facilities report (available at www.edfacilities.org/pubs/outcomes.pdf) explores the connections between the quality and kind of schoolhouse or classroom and student achievement. The report finds—predictably—that students who are too hot or too cold, or who are exposed to allergens, or who attend classrooms with inadequate fresh air, or who must read in inadequate light do not perform as well as their counterparts who enjoy better physical surroundings.

It takes money—a lot of it—to build and maintain schools. Estimates of the price tag for maintaining and building new school facilities in this country annually range from $127 to $268 billion! And many school districts are cash strapped: Needed new facilities don't get built; maintenance in older schools is put off; existing schools are overcrowded.

Even in the best-funded district, you can count on being affected by school finance. Community members may object to rising taxes—and you may find yourself playing an advocate's role in helping your district gain the funding necessary to help you do the job you were educated to do.

Teacher Empowerment. Knowledge of governance and finance also can empower you to participate effectively in the political process. Those who know, understand, and participate in the political process are better able to influence and change the teaching and learning process. Change is needed to achieve such educational goals as providing quality education for all students. Today, new forms of governance, such as site-based management and creative funding formulas, give stakeholders more power, authority, and responsibility for decision making. Empowerment gives you a voice in how your classroom, school, and education agencies operate.

Education is a political process. The idea of having people who are affected by decisions participate in decision making was not always and is still not a universally accepted approach to governance. However, empowerment is now a politically popular concept. As Dorrit so wisely counseled Carol, in the chapter opening vignette, those who know, understand, and participate in the political process are much more likely to influence and change the teaching and learning process.

Organization and governance should be changed if they interfere with or prevent the provision of quality education for all. It is most important that we not use excuses such as "We have always done it this way" to keep us from making the organizational and governance changes necessary for effective teaching and learning.

SECTION SUMMARY

What Issues of Governance and Finance Affect Education Today?

Education has been and will continue to be an instrument of social, political, and economic policy. Funding equity, tax equity, privatization, and goals and standards are major issues in education, along with issues of national versus state and state versus local control.

- Federal versus State Control. The debate over federal versus state control tends to vary with the values and political beliefs of the speaker. Issues involved in national versus state control revolve around who will decide how and what children will learn.

- State versus Local Control. States have tended to gain power and authority over education in the past decade. At the same time, however, states have tended to cede their responsibilities for education to local districts.

- Funding Equity. States are often unable or unwilling to fund education at comparable levels. As a result, the support of and opportunity for education vary from state to state and from district to district within states. Issues of tax equity are related to funding equity.

- Privatization of Public Schools. Privatization occurs when private schools operate on public funds, or when the operation of public schools and school services is taken over by for-profit private companies or not-for-profit private universities. Privatization is a controversial issue.

- How Are School Governance and Finance Important to Classroom Teachers? Issues of governance and funding are important to teachers because these areas affect teachers' ability to teach and students' opportunities to learn. These issues also have an impact on professionalism, accountability, and empowerment.

Thinking Critically
★ ★ ★ ★ ★ ★ ★ ★

How would differences in per-pupil expenditures affect you as a teacher? How would they affect students in your class?

Applying What You've Learned
★ ★ ★ ★ ★ ★ ★ ★

Controversy exists over funding of schools through exclusive licensing agreements with Coca Cola and fast food companies. Write a short paragraph pro and con on this topic.

g Yourself
he Picture
★ ★ ★ ★ ★ ★ ★

Assume you have been offered two teaching positions in two different states at your preferred grade level. Both have equal pay and benefits, but the per-pupil expenditures are unequal. What questions would you want answered before you accept either position?

_____

_____

_____

_____ ★

Applications for Active Learning

CONNECTIONS

1. Review Chapter 3 on how schools are organized and linked to society. How do aims of education and trends in schooling relate to the political and economic influences on American education described in this chapter?

_____

_____

_____

2. Think about concepts and topics introduced in this chapter. Create a picture, graphic, or figure that shows connections that are meaningful to you among this chapter's key ideas and information.

FIELD EXPERIENCES

1. Interview a superintendent or school principal about how a particular school district or school is organized and governed. Ask such questions as:
- How is school governance changing?
- What current problems or issues relate to governance and finance?
- How does the national government influence education in the district?
- What advice do you have for beginning teachers about their participation in school governance?
- What successes and failures have you observed in schools using school-based management?

2. Spend a day in a local elementary, middle, or high school visiting classrooms and talking with faculty, staff, and students. Write several paragraphs describing the basic principles of organization and governance in these schools.

PERSONAL RESEARCH

1. Attend a meeting of the local board of education or school board. Record your observations on these points:
- What issues seem to be most important? Why?
- What diverse viewpoints are expressed by various board members on particular topics?
- Is there evidence of stakeholder influence on the board's decisions?

_____

_____

_____

2. Investigate the tax and other monetary support for schools in your district.
- Where does the money come from? How do the percentages of support compare with those discussed in this chapter?
- How does the national average for per-student expenditures compare with the amount distributed in your state?

_____

_____

_____

3. Some education finance reformers believe that there should be a federal formula for equalizing funding for education among the states. Write a paragraph illustrating whether or not you support such a proposal and why.

Preparing to Teach

FOR YOUR PORTFOLIO

1. Many school districts publish annual reports. Sometimes these are called parent/community report cards. Obtain

two of these reports from school districts and answer these questions: What are the similarities and differences in how the schools are governed? Financed? How do the schools compare in teacher salaries? Student achievement? Expenditure per pupil? Total budget? What conclusions can you draw from your comparison of the two reports?

2. Use the Internet to identify three resources you think would be useful to Carol and Dorrit (in the chapter's opening vignette). Place these articles in your portfolio for use in developing governance strategies when you are a beginning teacher.

IDEA FILE

1. Write to your state department of education for information about the services that the department provides to classroom teachers.

2. Write to state agencies requesting information about their services for classroom teachers. You can place some of the information in your portfolio and other information in your idea file for use when you begin teaching.

Learning and Knowing More

WEB SITES WORTH VISITING

As you know from reading this chapter, the federal government plays a major role in funding education and determining what is taught. It is a good idea for you to keep abreast of what the federal government is doing. You can do this through their Web site at www.ed.gov. Additionally, you can reach the individual governing bodies by accessing the following Web sites: House of Representatives at www.house.gov, the Senate at www.senate.gov, and the White House at www.whitehouse.gov.

Quality Education for Minorities (QEM) Network
http://qemnetwork.qem.org
The QEM network was established in 1990 and is dedicated to improving education for minorities throughout the nation. The site provides information relating to current legal issues, current statistics and facts, and other pertinent information.

National Governors Association (NGA)
www.nga.org
The NGA is the only bipartisan national organization of, by, and for the nations' governors. Through the NGA, governors identify priority issues and deal collectively with issues of public policy and governance at both the national and state levels. The site contains publications and provides an in-depth look at the structure and levels of the NGA as well as current information relating to relevant educational and policy issues.

Board of Cooperative Educational Services (BOCES)
wswhe.boces.org
BOCES provides cost-effective shared educational programs and support services that complement component school districts in strengthening the quality of living and learning in their communities. The site provides additional links to other organizations as well as current information relating to educational issues.

National Association of State Boards of Education (NASBE)
www.nasbe.org
The NASBE is an organization representing state and territorial boards of education. NASBE principal objectives include strengthening state leadership in educational policy making; promoting excellence in the education of all students; advocating equality of access to educational opportunity; and ensuring continued citizen support for public education.

Congressional Budget Office
www.cbo.gov
CBO provides Congress with the objective, timely, nonpartisan analyses needed for economic and budget decisions and with the information and estimates required for the Congressional budget process.

Committee for Education Funding
www.cef.org
The Committee for Education Funding, a nonpartisan, nonprofit coalition of over one hundred education organizations, provides updates on federal education funding.

National Center for Education Statistics
www.nces.ed.gov
The National Center for Education Statistics (NCES) is the primary federal entity for collecting and analyzing data that are related to education in the United States and other nations.

BOOKS WORTH READING

Burrup, P. E., Brimley, V., and Garfield, R. R. (2001). *Financing Education in a Climate of Change* (8th ed.). Boston: Allyn & Bacon.
This is a comprehensive text on school finance, encompassing historical, computer/mathematical, and legal points of view. It is an excellent reference for the practitioner as well as the academic. The writing is both scholarly and student friendly, appealing to a diverse audience.

Dresan, D. L., and Gosling, J. J. (2003). *Politics and Policy in American States and Communities* (4th ed.). Boston: Allyn & Bacon.
This text combines a wealth of practical political experience and a thorough grasp of the subject to convey the excitement of the dynamics of governance. This is a text that students can appreciate. It thoroughly describes all forms of local government and details a long history of federal and local government relations, with a special focus on recent developments that strengthen the roles of states, tribes, and local governments.

Gallagher, R. R., Bagin, D., and Kindred, L. W. (2000). *The School and Community Relations* (7th ed.). Boston: Allyn & Bacon.
This text not only tells "why" but "how" to communicate with both external and internal publics. It has the answers for most communication problems school officials face and shows school officials how to put together a complete communication plan. The authors are professionals who have both academic and practical experience.

CHAPTER 8

The Legal Basis for Education and School Law

"So are you going to sue?"

Ginny Bryant is the mother of three daughters and lives in the New York City suburbs.

My daughter, Eliza, a junior in high school, was at a basketball tournament at her school, and I was home alone when the phone rang. "This is Charlene Lewis," a woman's voice said, "I'm a teacher at the high school. The first thing is, everything's fine. But Eliza got a little cut on her head. Can you come up here right away? We're in the training room behind the gym."

Whenever a conversation starts with "The first thing is, everything's fine," you know that everything is not fine. I pulled on a coat and headed for the school. I had gone to that school myself—I knew exactly where the training room was. It was full of people, and it was a minute or two before I could pick out Eliza, sitting on a training table, with her head wrapped in gauze like a mummy. Her face was pale, but she was smiling—a little wanly, but smiling. The athletics director—an old friend—rushed over.

"She's really fine," he said, taking my hand. "She was standing next to the bleachers in the gym, watching the game, and someone leaned on the railing above her, and it fell. Hit her on the head. She never passed out. There was a lot of blood, but it's really just a superficial cut." The mummy wrap didn't make it look superficial.

As I led Eliza out through the gym to our car, we passed a dozen or more of her friends, and every one of them said, "So are you going to sue?" Nothing, I assured them, was farther from my mind.

After the insertion of seven metal staples and the loss of a substantial hunk of hair, Eliza was pronounced fit to go home. There was no evidence of concussion, no serious injury—just a patch on her head that looked forlornly bare and that remained that way for many weeks. Even to this day, she can show you how the scar keeps hair from growing back along a thin line where the bleacher hit.

I went up to the school to talk about medical expenses (they offered to pay), and while I was there, I looked at the faulty bleacher. It was new, recently installed. Apparently the installers had failed to tighten a couple of screws, so that the slightest pressure on the railing pushed it over the edge. No one had tested it. The evening's chaperones—all teachers—had not been watching the game. The comments of Eliza's friends began bouncing around in my head. Eliza wasn't seriously hurt, but she was certainly hurt. And the consequences of the accident would be visible for some time. Should we sue? I wondered what the basis of such a suit would be. I even talked with a lawyer friend. We probably would have had a claim—against the school district, against the maker and installer of the bleacher. Finally, it didn't seem like the right thing to do. But in this litigious society, I suspect many parents would not have hesitated.

Negligence can be defined as "failure to exercise reasonable care resulting in harm to another person." Every day, teachers and administrators are involved in matters that relate to school law, and much of what happens in schools is based on the interpretation of laws. Learning about school law, your rights, the rights of students, and parents' rights will help you prepare for teaching.

How Will This Chapter Help You?

You will learn:

★ about federal and state laws and court cases that form the basis for school law

★ about the legal responsibilities of states and school districts

★ your legal responsibilities and rights as a teacher

★ how you can practice legal and ethical behavior

★ about students' legal rights

★ about parents' legal rights and responsibilities

*W*HAT IS THE BASIS OF SCHOOL LAW?

Laws
The principles and regulations established by governing authorities.

All public, private, and parochial schools are governed by **laws,** the principles and regulations established by governing authorities. There are basically four sources of law in the United States. The first is the Constitution, which provides the law for the nation and forms the legal basis for all the rights and protection that teachers, students, parents, and administrators have under the law. Other sources of law are federal laws, state constitutions and laws, and court decisions (see Figure 8.1).

The Constitution, federal laws, and the decisions of state and federal courts affect all who participate in the process of education—teachers, administrators, staff, students, and parents. The Constitution, laws, and court decisions influence, and in many cases determine, how students are taught, what teachers can and cannot teach, where students will or will not attend school, what students can and cannot do, and how much is spent on education.

As a beginning teacher, you will be involved in issues relating to freedom of religion, freedom of speech, desegregation, students' rights, parents' rights, teachers' rights, and discriminatory practices as they affect teaching, hiring, and dismissal. You will want to know what your legal rights are as well as the legal rights of students and parents so that you can be an informed teacher.

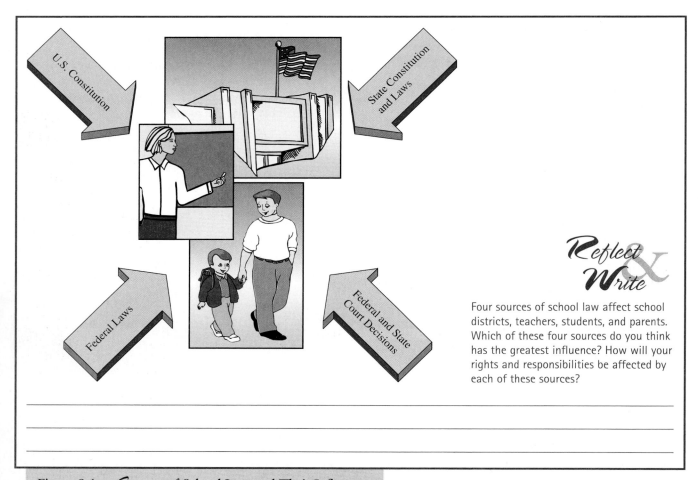

*R*eflect & *W*rite

Four sources of school law affect school districts, teachers, students, and parents. Which of these four sources do you think has the greatest influence? How will your rights and responsibilities be affected by each of these sources?

Figure 8.1 *S*ources of School Law and Their Influences

The U.S. Constitution, Basic Rights, and Education

While the Constitution does not mention education and contains no explicit provisions for education, basic rights guaranteed to individuals do affect, influence, and determine what happens in education. Individual constitutional rights are enforceable in parochial, private, and public schools. The Supreme Court and other courts frequently refer to and use provisions of the Constitution when rendering their decisions. For example, the Preamble of the Constitution contains a general welfare clause, which states:

> We, the people of the United States, in order to form a more perfect Union, establish justice, insure domestic tranquility, provide for the common defense, promote the general welfare, and secure the blessings of liberty to ourselves and our posterity do ordain and establish this Constitution for the United States of America.

Using the premise that it is promoting the general welfare, the federal government spends money and provides support for education and, at the same time, establishes certain conditions for their use. By accepting federal financial assistance and grants, state agencies and local school districts agree to comply with federal laws.

Schools and teachers promote the "general welfare" of the United States through the process of schooling in a number of ways. For example, the schools are to teach all children how to read. Give three other examples.

_____

_____

_____

_____

Three amendments to the Constitution have a great influence on educational practice.

The First Amendment. The First Amendment of the Constitution states that:

> Congress shall make no law respecting an establishment of religion, or prohibiting the free exercise thereof; or abridging the freedom of speech, or the press; or the right of the people to peaceably assemble, and to petition the government for redress of grievances.

Many issues relating to freedom of religion and speech affect what happens in schools. For example, in 1985, Bridget Mergens, a senior at Westside High School in Omaha, was denied permission to establish a Bible study group that would have the same recognition as other school groups. At issue was whether or not a school could provide an opportunity for some noncurriculum-related student groups but not for other groups to meet on school premises during noninstructional time. In the Supreme Court ruling *Board of Education of the Westside Community Schools v. Mergens*, the Court ruled that the Bible study group was denied equal access to the use of school property. The Court said the students could "form a Christian club that would have the same privileges and meet on the same terms and conditions as other Westside student groups, except that it would have no faculty sponsor."[1]

The Fourth Amendment. The Fourth Amendment provides citizens with basic privacy and security rights. It states:

> The right of the people to be secure in their persons, houses, papers, and effects, against unreasonable searches and seizures, shall not be violated, and no warrants shall issue, but upon probable cause, supported by oath or affirmation, and particularly describing the place to be searched, and the person or things to be seized.

The Fourth Amendment has particular educational implications for everyone and sometimes in ways that we might not always consider. For example, urine tests for participation in athletic programs are required in many school districts. However:

> Drug testing by urine sample constitutes a search under the Constitution. Courts have frequently found drug testing of general student populations in conflict with constitutional requirements of individualized suspicion. . . . Testing limited to potential interscholastic sports participants has met with court approval where the tests are limited in scope, provide for student privacy, and clearly state the consequences of positive tests.[2]

In 1995, in *Veronia School District v. Acton,* the Supreme Court upheld the right of the Veronia (Oregon) School District's program of random urine testing of middle and high school athletes. The district barred star football player James Acton from participating in football because his parents refused to sign a consent form for the drug testing that would have allowed him to join the seventh-grade football team. Acton's lawyer argued that urine testing constitutes an unreasonable search.[3]

While the *Veronia* case applied to student athletes, many school districts have expanded drug-testing programs to other school activities. For example, in 2002 the Supreme Court in *Board of Education of Independent School District No. 92 [OK], et al., v. Lindsay Earls, et al.,* upheld the school district's policy of mandating drug testing for all students who wish to participate in extracurricular activities, including the chess club, the honor society, and the marching band. The court ruled that the drug testing policy was "reasonable" even in the absence of an individualized suspicion or an identifiable school drug problem.

Students' rights issues have tremendous implications for teaching and learning. Some say restricting the rights of students makes them less independent and responsible and casts schools and teachers in even greater paternalistic roles. Others believe, as the Supreme Court does, that students should not leave their rights at the schoolhouse door. So, students' rights are restricted in certain regards but not in others. This is one of the reasons why studying educational law is so interesting and important and why you need to know about it.

The Fourteenth Amendment. The Fourteenth Amendment contains the due process provision and, of all the constitutional amendments, is the most frequently referred to in deciding education-related cases. This amendment states in part:

> No state shall make or enforce any law which shall abridge the privileges or immunities of the citizens of the United States; nor shall any state deprive any person of life, liberty, or property, without due process of law; or deny to any person within its jurisdiction the equal protection of the law.

Due process
The legal process that the government—or any other party—must go through before denying a person his or her rights to life, liberty, or property.

Simply stated, **due process** means that the federal, state, and local governments can deprive a person of life, liberty, or property only after following a fair decision-making process. The due process clause helps ensure that teachers and students are not deprived of life, liberty, and property without the safeguards of fair procedures and protects them from unreasonable, vague, and capricious rules. Many laws and court decisions define and spell out the rules, regulations, and procedures that must be followed in due process proceedings.

The meanings of life, liberty, and property are often interpreted by courts in ways different from what you might normally think. The courts have generally held that there is a property interest in teachers' reemployment as tenured teachers, a liberty interest in being free to enter into contracts for employment, a liberty interest as it relates to privacy (for example, personal property), and liberty interests in free speech and the exercise of religious beliefs.

Federal Laws

The federal government, in order to promote the general welfare and to uphold and promote principles inherent in the Constitution, passes laws that affect education. As discussed in Chapter 7, these laws generally relate to the constitutional requirements set forth in the Bill of Rights, which guarantees citizens certain rights.

For example, the federal government passed the Civil Rights Act of 1964. Title VI of this law states: "No person in the United States shall, on the basis of race, color, or national origin, be excluded from participation in or be denied the benefits of, or be subjected to discrimination under any program or activity receiving federal financial assistance."[4]

Title IX of the Education Amendments of 1972 prohibits discrimination on the basis of sex: "No person in the United States shall, on the basis of sex, be excluded from participation in, be denied the benefits of, or be subjected to discrimination under any education program or activity receiving federal financial assistance."[5]

The Education for All Handicapped Children Act of 1975 (PL 94-142; IDEA) is the landmark legislation that ensures the protection of the rights of students with disabilities and extends to them and their parents due process procedures in matters relating to their education. The Americans with Disabilities Act of 1990 prohibits discrimination against persons with disabilities.

State Laws

The Tenth Amendments to the Constitution states: "The powers not delegated to the United States by the Constitution, nor prohibited by it to the States, are reserved to the States respectively, or to the people."

The Tenth Amendment explains why education is a state function and why all fifty states have provisions for public education. However, education is not a nationally guaranteed right, and it can be expanded or reduced by the political process. Because states have the responsibility for controlling education, most laws affecting education are state laws that influence almost all that happens in the process of schooling. Examples of how state laws affect schooling include the following:

Teachers

- Required courses and programs in teacher preparation programs. Many states require courses in state history and multicultural education as part of preparation for teaching.
- Standards and conditions for entering the profession and gaining certification.
- Rules governing ethical practice.
- Procedures for hiring and dismissal.

Students

- Numbers and types of courses students must take to graduate (known as minimum course requirements). Some states are changing graduation requirements from courses taken to the performance and demonstration of what students should know and be able to do. As discussed in Chapter 10, required passing of state examinations frequently determines if students will graduate from high school.
- Attendance and dismissal guidelines.
- Rules of conduct.
- Residency requirements.
- Due process relating to freedom of religion, freedom of speech, searches, and urine testing.

Schools

- Regulation of the selection and purchase of textbooks.
- Curriculum and required courses. For example, some states mandate that students complete courses such as state history, the Holocaust, African American history, and so forth. Also, states specify standards they think all students should meet.
- Student and school activities.
- Mandatory achievement testing in certain grades.

Elementary

Standard 5.1: Understands and applies practices and behaviors that are characteristic of developing career teachers.

Standard 5.4: Fosters relationships with school colleagues and agencies in the larger community to support students' learning and well-being.

Middle Level

Standard 6: Understands the major concepts, principles, theories, and research related to working collaboratively with family and community members; uses that knowledge to maximize learning of all young adolescents.

State laws reflect what residents want for schools and education. State laws and local school board policies determine what is taught, the nature of the educational process, and how schools operate. States and local school districts look to education to implement policy, such as integration and equal rights; solve social problems, such as violence and teenage pregnancy; prepare students for the world of work by teaching usable and marketable skills; and teach citizenship skills, such as literacy and responsibility.

Laws reflect society's and people's beliefs and values at a particular time, and as the times change, so do how people feel about certain ideas. This explains why current laws and court decisions change and alter previous laws and court decisions. Courts are asked to interpret laws and to help explain how they apply to issues of teaching, learning, and schooling. This process of checks and balances is an important part of the democratic process and is a core value of the American democratic process.

The Courts

Federal and state courts have ruled on many topics of substantial interest to educators. Figure 8.2 lists Supreme Court cases affecting the rights of teachers and school districts. Many decisions will influence how you practice your profession. Almost daily, issues relating to students', teachers', and parents' rights are in the news. Many cases involve issues of the separation of church and state. Education is a governmental function and as such should not violate the First Amendment prohibition against the establishment of religion. States frequently pass laws that directly support or encourage such practices as prayer and Bible reading. For example, a Georgia law mandates a minute of silent reflection for all students before school begins. In response to a lawsuit, a federal appeals court ruled that "a period of quiet reflection" does not violate the U.S. Constitution's ban on government establishment of religion. Georgia's statute was the first to withstand constitutional scrutiny. The Georgia law was part of a legislative package designed to curtail crime among juveniles. The law states that students may use the moment of silence for "silent reflection on the anticipated activities of the day."[6] In another example, the Supreme Court refused to hear an appeal of a Virginia state law requiring a minute of silence of all students. The Court's refusal allows the state law to remain in effect. The state maintains that the law does not violate the issues of the separation of church and state, because students may meditate or stare out the window for sixty seconds as long as they are quiet.

Religion in the Schools. From the beginning of schooling in America, many schools have included some form of religious activity in their curriculum. Before 1962, Bible reading and prayer were an accepted part of many school-opening exercises. The reading was generally without comment, and students who objected to the reading were excused from listening. However, in 1961, the State Board of Regents of New York wrote the following twenty-two-word prayer: "Almighty God, we acknowledge our dependence upon Thee, and we beg Thy blessings upon us, our parents, our teachers and our country."

The Board of Regents believed the prayer was nondenominational and was based on "our spiritual heritage." They considered the prayer to be denominationally neutral and encouraged school districts to use it. Parents of ten pupils brought action in a New York state court and challenged the constitutionality of the use of the prayer and the school district's right to order its recitation. The case eventually went to the Supreme Court. In *Engle v. Vitale*, the Court ruled that public school officials could not require pupils to recite a state-composed prayer at the start of each school day, even if the prayer was nondenominational and pupils who so desired could be excused from reciting it. Official state sanction of religious utterances, the Court declared, is an unconstitutional attempt to establish religion. The Court declared, "It is neither sacrilegious nor antireligious to say that each separate government in this country should stay out of the business of writing and sanctioning official prayers and leave

Plessy v. Ferguson (1896). The Court ruled that a state law requiring federal railroad trains to provide separate but equal railroad cars for African American and white passengers who were traveling within one state did not infringe upon federal authority to regulate interstate commerce. This separate but equal doctrine remained in effect for fifty-eight years.

Brown v. Board of Education of Topeka (1954). The Court ruled that state-sanctioned segregation in public schools violated the equal protection of the Fourteenth Amendment.

Engle v. Vitale (1962). The Court ruled that public school officials could not require pupils to recite a state-composed prayer at the start of each school day, even if the prayer was nondenominational and pupils who so desired could be excused from reciting it.

Abbington School District v. Schempp (1963). The Court ruled unconstitutional a Pennsylvania law requiring daily recitations of Bible verses and the Lord's Prayer in public school classrooms. The Court said any practice that advances or inhibits a religion is unconstitutional.

Green v. County School Board of New Kent County (1967). The Court identified six areas in which progress toward desegregation is tested.

Epperson v. Arkansas (1968). The Court held that to forbid the teaching of evolution as a theory violates the First Amendment.

Pickering v. Board of Education (1968). The Court ruled that a teacher could not be dismissed for speaking as a citizen on matters of public concern.

Alexander v. Holmes County Board of Education (1969). The Court ordered the end to all dual systems of education.

Swann v. Charlotte-Mecklenburg Board of Education (1971). The Court ruled that involuntary busing was a legitimate means of achieving school integration.

Lemon v. Kurtzman (1971). The Court devised a three-part test that is used in considering whether government violates the establishment clause. This is referred to as the *Lemon test*.

Keyes v. School District No. 1 (1973). The Court ruled that gerrymandering results in de jure segregation.

Cleveland Board of Education v. LaFleur (1974). The Court said it was discriminatory to make pregnant teachers take mandatory pregnancy leaves at fixed periods before and after giving birth.

Ambach v. Norwick (1979). The Court held that a New York statute forbidding permanent certification as a public school teacher of any person who is not a United States citizen, unless that person has manifested an intention to apply for citizenship, does not violate the equal protection clause of the Fourteenth Amendment.

North Haven Board of Education v. Bell (1982). The Court ruled that Title IX provides protection from discrimination for teachers and students. Under Title IX, the Department of Education can investigate complaints of sexual discrimination and can curtail federal funding to programs and agencies that do so.

School District of the City of Grand Rapids v. Ball (1985). The Court held that even the praiseworthy, secular purpose of providing for the education of schoolchildren cannot validate government aid to parochial schools when the aid has the effect of promoting religion.

Wallace v. Jaffree (1985). The Court ruled unconstitutional an Alabama law authorizing a daily moment of silence in public schools for "meditation or voluntary prayer."

Edwards v. Aquillard (1987). The Court said that a state cannot require that schools teach the biblical version of creation.

Board of Education of the Westside Community Schools v. Mergens (1990). The Court ruled that a Bible study group was denied equal access to the use of school property. The Court said the students could "form a Christian club that would have the same privileges and meet on the same terms and conditions as other Westside student groups, except it would have no faculty sponsor."

Lee v. Weisman (1992). The Court ruled that prayers by a clergyman at a Providence, Rhode Island, middle school graduation violated the establishment clause.

United States v. Fordice (1992). The Court ruled that states that perpetuate policies and practices traceable to its prior de jure dual system that continue to have segregative effects violate the equal protection clause.

Lamb's Chapel et al. v. Center Moriches Union Free School District et al. (1993). The Court ruled that denying a church access to school premises to speak violates the freedom of speech clause.

Missouri v. Jenkins (1995). The Court ruled that a federal judge exceeded his powers by requiring a plan designed to attract white suburban students into the Kansas City School District.

Gebser v. Lago Vista Independent School District (1998). The Court ruled that a district cannot be held liable for a teacher's sexual harassment of a student under Title IX unless a district official with the authority to take corrective action had actual knowledge of teacher misconduct and was deliberately indifferent to it.

Santa Fe Independent School District v. Doe (2000). The Court ruled that student-led prayer at public high school football games is an unconstitutional establishment of religion.

Mitchell v. Helms (2000). The Court ruled that federal programs that put instructional equipment into religious schools is not a violation of the separation of church and state.

Goodnews Club v. Milford Central Schools (2001). The Court ruled that elementary schools must allow religious student organizations to meet on campus.

Reflect & Write

Reflect on all the cases listed. Based on the summaries of these cases, which five do you think have probably had the most impact on schools and teachers? Why?

Figure 8.2   Supreme Court Cases Affecting the Rights of Teachers and School Districts

What is the basic argument against prayer in public schools? Are private schools held to the same standards regarding prayer?

that purely religious function to the people themselves and to those the people choose to look to for religious guidance."[7]

Almost one year later, in *Abbington School District v. Schempp,* the Court ruled unconstitutional a Pennsylvania law requiring daily recitations of Bible verses and the Lord's Prayer in public school classrooms. The Court said any practice that advances or inhibits a religion is unconstitutional.

Freedom of religion is basically an issue of separation of church and state. The **establishment clause** of the First Amendment of the Constitution states: "Congress shall make no law respecting an establishment of religion." The establishment clause most often applies when schools try to initiate practices that have religious content or when state or federal aid benefits religious organizations. Schools can teach the Bible as history and literature, and religion can be part of the curriculum. Generally, schools can teach about religions but cannot promote a particular religious view or support a particular religion or denomination. In *Abbington,* the Court pronounced the following test for examining establishment clause cases:

> The test may be stated as follows: what are the purposes and the primary effect of the enactment? If either is the advancement or inhibition of religion then the enactment exceeds the scope of legislative power as circumscribed by the Constitution. That is to say that to withstand the strictures of the establishment clause there must be a secular legislative purpose and a primary effect that neither advances nor inhibits religion.[8]

The Court further stated its position as not being hostile to religion or the Bible:

> It might well be said that one's education is not complete without a study of comparative religions or the history of religion and its relationship to the advancement of civilization. It certainly may be said that the Bible is worthy of study for its literary and historic qualities. Nothing we have said here indicates that such study of the Bible or religion, when presented objectively as part of a secular program of education, may not be effected consistent with the First Amendment. But the exercises here do not fall into those categories. They are religious exercises, required by the States in violation of the command of the First Amendment that the government maintain strict neutrality, neither aiding nor opposing religion.[9]

Regarding advancement of religion, a federal appeals court upheld the policy of the Upshur County (West Virginia) School District of "passively" distributing the Bible to its 4,000 students. The court ruled that allowing a local ministers' group once a year to put Bibles on hallway and library tables did nothing more than give the group the right to use the school on equal terms with other groups. The court did not believe the distribution was an advancement of religion.[10]

In 1998, a high school in Lee County, Florida, began offering a board-approved course "Bible History." Opponents of the course sued. They argued that the course was designed to teach the Bible as fact and violated the Constitution and separation of church and state. "This course would be perfectly appropriate for Sunday school," said Lisa Versaci, the Florida director of People for the American Way. In an out-of-court settlement, the course was renamed "Introductions to Religion."[11]

In June of 2001, the Supreme Court literally unlocked the schoolhouse door for religious clubs by ruling that public elementary schools must open their doors to after-school religious activities just as they do for other clubs. (Constitutional principle already existed for high schools.) In *Goodnews Club v. Milford Central Schools,* the Court ruled that allowing the Goodnews Club to meet in rooms of a school would "ensure neutrality, not threaten it." Furthermore, the Court ruled, "We cannot see the danger that children would misperceive the endorsement of religion is any greater than the danger that they would perceive a hostility toward the religious viewpoint if the club were excluded from the public forum." The Goodnews Clubs are sponsored by the Child Evangelism Fellowship, Inc., which operates in 155 countries with 4,964 clubs in the United States.

The Lemon Test. Since 1963, many conservative organizations, such as the Christian Coalition, have sought to restore prayer and Bible reading to the public schools. In 1971 in *Lemon v. Kurtzman,* the Supreme Court devised a three-part test that is used in considering whether government practices violate the establishment clause. These are referred to as the Lemon test (see Figure 8.3). "The Lemon test requires (1) a government practice or enactment must have a secular purpose, (2) its principal or primary effect must be one that neither advances or inhibits religion, and (3) it must not foster an excessive government entanglement with religion."[12]

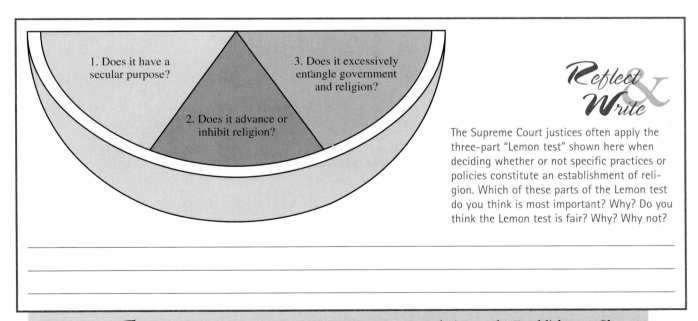

1. Does it have a secular purpose?

2. Does it advance or inhibit religion?

3. Does it excessively entangle government and religion?

Reflect & Write

The Supreme Court justices often apply the three-part "Lemon test" shown here when deciding whether or not specific practices or policies constitute an establishment of religion. Which of these parts of the Lemon test do you think is most important? Why? Do you think the Lemon test is fair? Why? Why not?

Figure 8.3 *The Lemon Test for Determining States' Practices in Relation to the Establishment Clause*

Efforts to provide for prayers in schools persist. In 1985 in *Wallace v. Jaffree*, the Court ruled unconstitutional an Alabama law authorizing a daily moment of silence in public schools for "meditation or voluntary prayer." In 1992, the Court in *Lee v. Weisman* ruled that prayers by a clergyman at a Providence, Rhode Island, middle school graduation violated the establishment clause.

In one of the biggest school prayer cases in a decade, the Supreme Court, in June of 2000, ruled in *Santa Fe Independent School District v. Doe* that prayer is a private matter and ruled that student-led prayer at public high school football games is an unconstitutional establishment of religion. At issue was whether or not it was constitutional for students in the Santa Fe (Texas) School District to have a student deliver a prayer over the public address system before every varsity home football game. The Court ruled that the establishment clause of the Constitution prohibits a school from forcing a student to endure a "personally offensive religious ritual" and that "the delivery of a pregame prayer has the improper effect of coercing those present to participate in an act of religious worship." It is likely that we will hear more about the effects of this case and others that seek to further define the barriers between church and state. However, to show how undefined or porous the separation between church and state can be, in 2000 the Supreme Court ruled in *Mitchell v. Helms* that a federal program that placed computers and other "instructional equipment" in parochial school classrooms did not violate the separation between church and state. Also, the aftermath of September 11 has created a heightened sensitivity on the matter of teaching religion in the classroom. (See Education on the Move.)

INTASC

Standard 3: The teacher understands how students differ in their approaches to learning and creates instructional opportunities that are adapted to diverse learners.

Reflect & Write

Do you think state laws requiring a moment of silence violate the Constitution? Why or why not? As a teacher, what are some ways your class could spend the moment of silence?

_____

_____

_____

_____

education *on the move* >>>>>>>>>>>>

>>> Student Teacher Says Islam Lessons Cost Him Internship >>>>>>>

A student teacher in Maine has been dismissed from his internship at a high school after students and parents contended that a unit he prepared for a world history class stepped over the line between informing students about Islam and advocating the faith.

Stephen Kent Jones, a student in the graduate teaching program at the University of Maine in Orono, was told to leave Old Town High School midway through his internship, amid complaints that the content of his lessons and his instructional approach were inappropriate.

Officials in the 1,100-student Old Town school district, where he was

fulfilling his student-teaching requirement, approved the unit, and Mr. Jones's advisers in the graduate teaching program rewarded his work with an A.

Marvin Clark, the teacher assigned to supervise Mr. Jones, said that he had "received many complaints about the student teacher's 'long rambling lectures with no point' and that the lectures seemed to have 'a strong religious angle.'" He added that Mr. Jones refused to "tone down" his lessons after the veteran teacher told him of the complaints.

Mr. Jones said he had no intention of promoting any religion. He was

merely trying to engage his students in an intellectual discussion, he said, and encourage them to think critically about a complex subject. He attributed the students' complaints to their misperceptions about Muslims, whom his students initially described as terrorists and extremists.

Source: K. K. Manzo, "Student Teacher Says Islam Lessons Cost Him Internship," *Education Week*, April 24, 2002, p. 10. Available online at www.edweek.org/ew/cwstory.cfm ?slug=32islam.h21. Reprinted by permission.

SECTION SUMMARY

What Is the Basis of School Law?

Together, the U.S. Constitution, federal laws, state constitutions and laws, and federal and state judicial decisions form the basis for school law.

- **The U.S. Constitution, Basic Rights, and Education.** The federal government's involvement is based on the Preamble and three amendments: the First Amendment protects our freedom of religion and speech; the Fourth Amendment protects our basic privacy and security; and the Fourteenth Amendment protects our right to due process. These rights are always in effect and apply to teachers, students, and others in the school setting.

- **Federal Laws.** Many federal laws influence education. The Civil Rights Act of 1964 bars discrimination on the basis of race, color, or national origin. Title IX of the Education Amendment of 1972 prohibits discrimination on the basis of sex. The Americans with Disabilities Act of 1990 prohibits discrimination against persons with disabilities.

- **State Laws.** The Tenth Amendment to the U.S. Constitution assigns responsibility for controlling education to the states, and this explains why most laws that affect education are state laws.

- **The Courts.** U.S. Supreme Court rulings have influenced educational practices relating to separation of church and state, desegregation, school financing, and other issues. Figure 8.2 lists many of these rulings.

Thinking Critically
★ ★ ★ ★ ★ ★ ★ ★

Should states accept federal funds for school buildings, equipment, and staff if accepting those funds gives the federal government more say in local decisions about educational practices?

Applying What You've Learned
★ ★ ★ ★ ★ ★ ★ ★

Supporters of school choice were pleased by the findings in both the *Goodnews* and *Mitchell* cases. Explain why the *Goodnews* and *Mitchell* rulings might provide hope for some about the future use of vouchers for religious school tuition.

A group of students has approached you to sponsor a club they will call Students for Understanding the Religions of the World. They propose that each year members will paint a mural in the cafeteria showing some aspect of a major religion and that this year's mural will focus on Islam. What will you tell them, using the Lemon test as your guide?

_____

_____

_____

_____ ★

*W*HAT ARE THE LEGAL RESPONSIBILITIES OF STATES AND SCHOOL DISTRICTS*?*

NCATE

Middle Level

Standard 1: Understands the major concepts, principles, theories and research related to young adolescent development; provides opportunities that support student development and learning.

States have the right and obligation to educate all students. As states seek to fulfill this role, they must balance the rights of students, teachers, and parents and endeavor to determine what will work best for all. As they do, laws, roles, and desires intersect and clash, resulting in efforts to find appropriate solutions. Some of these persistent issues include segregation, desegregation, and funding.

School Desegregation

De jure segregation
Segregation according to the law—that is, segregation that exists because of laws requiring or permitting it.

There has been a long history of discrimination in public schooling in the United States. Before 1955, many southern and some western states—twenty-one in all—had laws requiring or permitting segregated schools. This is known as **de jure** (according to the law) **segregation.** In addition to traditions of discrimination, the doctrine of "separate but equal" prevailed in American education. The basis for this doctrine was *Plessy v. Ferguson.* In this 1896 case, the Supreme Court ruled that a state law requiring federal railroad trains to provide separate-but-equal railroad cars for African American and Anglo-European American passengers who were traveling within one state did not infringe on federal authority to regulate interstate commerce.

De facto segregation
Segregation resulting from individual choices of neighborhoods; also known as "natural" segregation.

This separate-but-equal doctrine remained in effect for the schools until the decision of *Brown v. Board of Education of Topeka.* In *Brown,* the Supreme Court ruled nine to zero that state-sanctioned segregation in public schools violates the equal protection of the Fourteenth Amendment. In 1954, the Supreme Court ordered school districts to desegregate with all deliberate speed. While *Brown* brought an end—at least legally—to de jure segregation, it did not affect **de facto segregation**—that is, "natural" segregation resulting from individual choices of neighborhoods. This is Linda Brown Thompson's reflection on the case her father brought to the courts: "It's disheartening that we are still fighting," said Mrs. Thompson. "But we are dealing with human beings. As long as we are, there will always be those who feel the races should be separate."[13] Linda was just eleven when her father, the Reverend Oliver L. Brown, became the lead plaintiff in *Brown.*

INTASC

Standard 3: The teacher understands how students differ in their approaches to learning and creates instructional opportunities that are adapted to diverse learners.

The issue of segregation was further addressed in 1969 in *Alexander v. Holmes County Board of Education.* The Court ordered an end to all dual systems of education. From this ruling, a major implementation principle resulted in *Swann v. Charlotte-Mecklenburg Board of Education* when the Court ruled in 1971 that involuntary busing was a legitimate means of achieving school integration. Many school districts across the United States have been ordered to bus students as a means of integrating schools. However, busing has been and remains a controversial issue. Proponents of busing see it as a way to achieve equality and equity in education.

Furthermore, proponents say that the schools are the basis for an integrated society in which people live and work in peace and harmony. On the other hand, opponents see busing as a waste of valuable school resources that could be better spent on other school resources and services. Opponents also see busing as disruptive of neighborhood school patterns and say it is unfair to bus children of one race to another school to desegregate it. In September of 2001, three decades after the *Swann* decision, a federal appeals court ruled that the Charlotte-Mecklenburg School District was unitary or free from segregation.

However, as school districts integrate, busing is not always necessary to achieve desegregation goals. For example, a federal judge approved a settlement in Prince George's (Maryland) County School District that phases out mandatory busing. The plan also calls for building three neighborhood schools, maintaining magnet schools, and providing extra resources for schools whose students are predominantly African American.[14]

Busing is no longer seen as a solution to segregation. When the program began in 1971 it was effective; however, since then things have changed. Both white and African American leaders say that busing is not the answer to the current problems. The NAACP and other leaders stress that emphasis instead should be placed on improving schools in the black community. By doing so, they contend, there will be overall improvement in quality and equity. For example, Prince George's County, a predominantly white area in 1972, now has one of the largest African American populations, thus making busing no longer necessary.

The *Brown* decision did not and has not everywhere eliminated attempts at de jure segregation. For example, in the early 1970s, the Denver School District attempted to segregate through gerrymandering attendance—that is, by dividing the school district to keep some schools white and some schools African American—and by adjusting student assignments. In *Keyes v. School District No. 1*, the Supreme Court ruled that the actions of the school board resulted in de jure segregation.

Brown v. Board of Education of Topeka ended in a landmark decision against racial desegregation in the nation's schools. What are the six tests of progress toward school desegregation? Where and why is integration failing today?

Tests of Progress toward Desegregation

In 1967 in *Green v. County School Board of New Kent County*, the Court ruled that the tests of whether or not school districts are making progress toward integration consist of activities in six areas:

1. Racial balance in assigning students to attendance centers.
2. Transportation parity (for example, most students of one race should not be bused when another race is not being bused).
3. Equity in physical facilities.
4. Equal access to extracurricular activities.
5. Equitable allocation of resources.
6. Personnel placement that puts majority and minority teachers and principals in each building in proportion to their overall numbers in the system. In legal writings, these six factors are referred to as the Green categories or factors (see Figure 8.4).

While efforts to desegregate the nation's schools continue over half a century after *Brown*, some school districts may be even more segregated than ever because of increasing minority enrollments. (See the Profile.)

For example, as we have discussed, Hispanic populations continue to grow, primarily in four states: Texas, California, Florida, and New York. By 2007–2008, over 9 million Hispanics will be enrolled in the nation's public schools. Because of the continuing gains in Hispanic enrollments, white students will represent a minority of

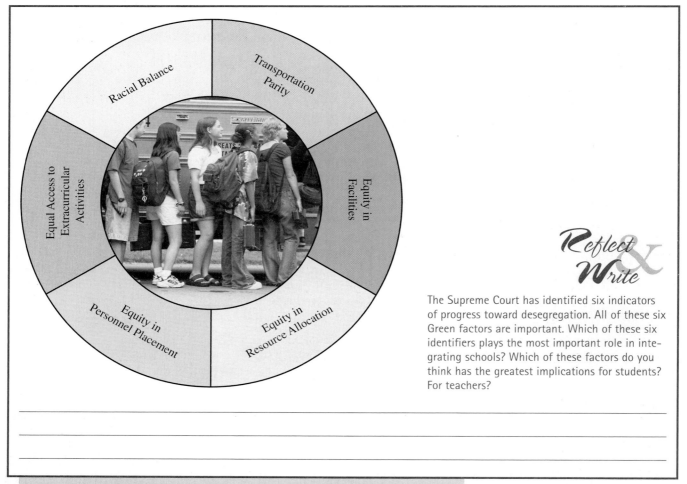

Reflect & Write

The Supreme Court has identified six indicators of progress toward desegregation. All of these six Green factors are important. Which of these six identifiers plays the most important role in integrating schools? Which of these factors do you think has the greatest implications for students? For teachers?

Figure 8.4   *The Green Factors: Tests of Progress toward Desegregation*

Profile   Fifty Years and Beyond: *Brown v. Board of Education*

Without a doubt, *Brown v. Board* is a Supreme Court decision that has fundamentally affected how schools do business. On May 17, 1954, *Brown v. Board* struck down the practice of separate but equal and replaced it with equal opportunity for all in integrated schools.

But for many, the celebrations of *Brown* ring hollow. The reason for the tarnish on the *Brown* vision is that today America's schools are more segregated than ever for African American and Latino students. In a recent study by the Civil Rights Project at Harvard University, researchers found:

- In many districts where court-ordered desegregation was ended in the past decade, there has been a major increase in segregation. The courts assumed that the forces that produced segregation and inequality had been cured. This report shows they have not been.
- Rural and small-town school districts are, on average, the nation's most integrated for both African Americans and Latinos. Central cities of large metropolitan areas are the epicenter of segregation; segregation is also severe in smaller central cities and in the suburban rings of large metropolitan areas.
- There has been a substantial slippage toward segregation in most of the states that were highly desegregated in 1991. The most integrated state for African Americans in 2001 is Kentucky. The most desegregated states for Latinos are in the Northwest. However, in some states with very low black populations, school segregation is soaring as desegregation efforts are abandoned.
- American public schools are now only 60 percent white nationwide, and nearly one-fourth of U.S. students are

in states with a majority of nonwhite students. However, except in the South and Southwest, most white students have little contact with minority students.

- Asians, in contrast, are the most integrated and by far the most likely to attend multiracial schools with a significant presence of three or more racial groups. Asian students attend schools with the smallest concentration of their own racial group.
- The vast majority of intensely segregated minority schools face conditions of concentrated poverty, which are powerfully related to unequal educational opportunity. Students in segregated minority schools face conditions that students in segregated white schools seldom experience.
- Latinos confront very serious levels of segregation by race and poverty, and non-English-speaking Latinos tend to be segregated in schools with one another. The data show no substantial gains in segregated education for Latinos, even during the Civil Rights era. The increase in Latino segregation is particularly notable in the West.
- There has been a massive demographic transformation of the West, which has become the nation's first predominantly minority region in terms of total public school enrollment. This has produced a sharp increase in Latino segregation.

For more information about the Civil Rights Project study, see G. Orfield and C. Lee, "Executive Summary: Brown at 50: King's Dream or Plessy's Nightmare?" (Cambridge, MA: The Civil Rights Project at Harvard University, January 17, 2004). (Online). Available at www.civilrightsproject.harvard.edu/research/reseg04/resegregation04.php. Reprinted by permission.

graduates from western high schools in 2013–2014.[15] As America becomes an even more diverse country, school integration will continue to be a major topic of discussion and legal battles.

Benefits of Desegregation

A major purpose of efforts to desegregate schools is to achieve **integration,** a mix of students of different races and cultures in schools and other educational programs. But there are other benefits as well, which are sometimes overlooked, such as the educational benefits desegregation provides all students. In a review of the long-term effects of school desegregation, researchers found:

> **Integration**
> A mix of students of different races and cultures in schools and other educational programs.

- Desegregated African American students set their occupational aspirations higher than do segregated African Americans.
- The racial composition of schools African American students attend largely determines whether the colleges attended by students are predominantly white or African American.
- Desegregated African Americans choose predominantly white institutions.
- Students attending desegregated elementary and high schools show higher college attainment than those attending segregated schools.[16]

School desegregation has proven to be beneficial over the years, yet it is no longer the only desired goal. Equal educational access and educational integration are goals as well. Educational integration strives for a balance of white and African American

> **INTASC**
> **Standard 3:** The teacher understands how students differ in their approaches to learning and creates instructional opportunities that are adapted to diverse learners.

students in classes. However, balance is not sufficient. All students must have equal access to curriculum programs as well. (See Chapter 12 for a discussion of access issues in relation to technology.) Many minority leaders are now concentrating on improving schools internally rather than externally through busing and other means of desegregation. For example, Nashville spent $206.8 million to eliminate most cross-county busing and has built eleven new schools, thus allowing students to attend schools in their own neighborhoods.[17]

School Accountability

NCATE

Middle Level

Standard 7: Understands the complexity of teaching young adolescents; engages in practices and behaviors that develop competence as a professional.

Administrators and teachers are held accountable for their programs and practices. States have passed accountability laws to help ensure that students who graduate with a diploma can read, write, and perform basic math skills. These laws are also in response to educational malpractice suits in which students and their parents have sued teachers and school districts because students were graduated without basic skills. Accountability laws or requirements make it mandatory that achievement tests be administered at various points in a student's career, for example, in grades 3, 5, 8, and 11. These tests are designed to assess individual progress, measure school and teacher effectiveness, and determine if students should be promoted and if they should be awarded a diploma. In Chapter 10 accountability in relation to standards and testing is discussed.

Should you and your school be held accountable when students graduate without basic skills? Why or why not?

_____

_____

_____

_____

The Law and School Finance

One of the fastest-growing and publicly popular areas of litigation and law involves states, schools, and finances. Many states, including Arizona, Kentucky, New Jersey, Ohio, and Texas, have had their K–12 funding systems ruled unconstitutional by state supreme courts. One of the most celebrated cases is *Edgewood Independent School District v. Kirby*. In this case, the Texas Supreme Court ruled that Texas's school financing system violated the state constitutional requirement and that an efficient system of public education be created to provide for the "general diffusion of knowledge."[18]

At the heart of school finance problems are three issues. One is the equitable distribution of money among affluent districts (usually suburban districts) and less affluent districts (usually inner-city districts). Because much of the funding for schools is based on property taxes, suburban districts where property values tend to be high have a broader tax base. They can raise more money to support their schools. The opposite is true in many inner-city and poor districts. It is clear that reliance on property taxes hurts poor districts. What state courts are deciding is that while school districts have local control for schooling, states are nevertheless responsible for providing for uniform education throughout the state. As a result, many states are implementing funding strategies designed to equalize funding for all students.

A second issue is the ability of wealthy districts to tax low and spend high. Poor districts, on the other hand, have to tax high in order to spend low. A third issue is the responsibility of the states to provide adequate educational opportunities for all the children of the states, not just those in affluent districts. The Ohio State Supreme Court has identified seven outcomes involved in adequate educational opportunities:

- Oral and written communication skills
- Mathematical and scientific skills
- Knowledge of economic, social, and political systems
- An understanding of government processes
- Self-knowledge and principles of health and mental hygiene in order to monitor one's own physical and mental well-being
- An understanding of the arts and one's own cultural heritage and that of other cultures
- Academic and vocational skills adequate for competing in Ohio, in surrounding states, across the nation, and throughout the world[19]

The cost of funding public education has always been an issue and will likely remain so. As more poor school districts seek to equalize funding, more states will voluntarily or through court order reexamine the way they fund schools. In all discussions of funding for education, the relationship between funding and the quality of education must be addressed. As a beginning teacher, you will have the opportunity to witness firsthand the effect of funding on the quality of education.

SECTION SUMMARY

What Are the Legal Responsibilities of States and School Districts?

States and school districts have many legal obligations and responsibilities regarding education.

- School Desegregation. *Brown v. Board of Education of Topeka* (1954) brought an end to legal segregation and systems of dual education. At the state and local levels, efforts to end de facto segregation and to provide an equal education for all of the nation's children still continue, almost half a century later. Currently, school and community leaders are challenging desegregation as the answer to all school problems of equity and access.

- School Accountability. Teachers and administrators are being held increasingly accountable for programs and practices. States are enforcing this accountability through standardized tests and other measures.

- The Law and School Finance. Funding affects the quality of education. Litigation against states has focused on three issues: equitable distribution of money between affluent and less affluent districts, unequal tax income and spending abilities between rich and poor districts, and the provision of adequate educational opportunities for all students.

Thinking Critically

★ ★ ★ ★ ★ ★ ★ ★

In what ways did different levels of funding for education affect your education?

_____

_____

_____

_____ ★

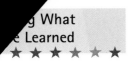

Interview some teachers in the local school system and ask them to share their views on whether the local boards' expenditure of tax dollars is done in an equitable manner.

_____

_____

_____

_____ ★

**Putting Yourself
in the Picture**
★ ★ ★ ★ ★ ★ ★ ★

Your state has a long-standing law that taxes cannot rise more than 2.5 percent each year. The schools in your state are now badly underfunded. You have no children in the school system. Will you vote to increase your own taxes to educate other people's children? Why or why not?

_____

_____

_____

_____ ★

_W_HAT ARE YOUR LEGAL RESPONSIBILITIES AS A TEACHER?

Teachers' professional practices are affected by laws and legal decisions in two ways: First, teachers have rights as citizens. Second, teachers have special responsibilities because of their positions as professional educators. (See Figure 8.2, p. 273, for legal cases affecting schooling.)

Teachers and schools are **in loco parentis,** the theory that the state, in the school context, acts "in the place of parents" in relationship to the care and education of children. Teachers act in the place of parents in many ways—for example, when they provide children with supervision and guidance as would a parent. This principle is often used to justify teachers' intervention in students' behaviors and their right to discipline them in a reasonable and appropriate manner as would a parent. How far teachers and schools should go in carrying out this parental function is a continuing matter of controversy. For example, the public is divided on whether teachers and schools should address issues of sex education and teen pregnancy, how far teachers should go in disciplining students, and whether schools should oversee students' time after school hours.

Preventing Liability

Businesses and industry are not the only agencies liable for their products, services, and actions. Schools and their employees are liable as well. This liability takes the form of **tort liability,** which is a civil wrong against the rights of others. According to tort law, a person who causes another person injury is answerable to that party for damages. There are three kinds of **torts**—negligence, intentional, and strict. Most court cases against teachers are for **negligence,** which is unacceptable conduct or care that results in the injury of another person. **Intentional torts** include assault, battery, the intent to do harm, and defamation. **Strict liability** applies to injury resulting from unusual hazards, such as when hazardous materials are not kept out of the reach of children and they are injured.

INTASC

Standard 9: The teacher is a reflective practitioner who continually evaluates the effects of his/her choices and actions on others (students, parents, and other professionals in the learning community) and who actively seeks out opportunities to grow professionally.

NCATE

Early Childhood

Standard 5: Uses ethical guidelines and other professional standards; is a continuous, collaborative learner who demonstrates knowledgeable, reflective, and critical perspectives; is an informed advocate for sound educational practices.

Elementary

Standard 5.1: Understands and applies practices and behaviors that are characteristic of developing career teachers.

Teachers must do everything they can to create a teaching and learning environment that will provide for the safety needs of all children. Field trips can pose particular challenges, but teachers must always exercise reasonable care to ensure everyone's safety. Teachers should be aware of school law, their rights, and the rights of students and parents.

Although teachers are responsible for protecting students from injury, they are not liable for every accidental injury. In determining the basis for liability,

> Courts have generally held schools or their agents liable for injuries received during the course of regular school events, which resulted from the failure to provide a reasonably safe environment, failure to warn participants of known hazards (or to remove known dangers where possible), failure to properly instruct participants in the activity, or failure to provide supervision adequate for the type of activity and the ages of the participants involved.[20]

Negligence. When a person intentionally or negligently causes an injury, they are liable for that injury. Teachers are negligent when they fail to use proper standards and care to protect students or fail to foresee and correct potential harm in a situation. Tort law is based on reasonableness. In determining liability, teachers are held responsible for doing "what a reasonable, prudent person, one of ordinary intelligence would do or should have done, in the same circumstances." The standards for judging negligence are typically based on the following four points:

- Duty and standard of care
- Breach of duty
- Proximate cause
- Injury and damages

"Duty and standard of care" means that teachers are expected to supervise students, maintain a safe environment, and give proper instruction. "Breach of duty" refers to whether or not teachers are derelict in their duties to supervise, maintain a safe environment, and give proper instruction. "Proximate cause" means that teachers' failure to do their duty resulted in loss or injury. "Injury and damages" means that a student suffered some loss or injury. The reasonable person guideline is one that teachers should follow. When this is not the case, the results can sometimes be fatal.

In loco parentis
The theory that the state, in the school context, acts "in the place of parents."

Tort liability
Civil wrong against the rights of others.

Torts
Wrongful acts.

Negligence
Failure to exercise reasonable care resulting in harm to another person.

Intentional torts
Include assault, battery, intent to do harm, and defamation.

Strict liability
Injury resulting from unusual hazards, such as when hazardous materials are not kept out of the reach of children and they are injured.

Avoiding Negligence. You should always keep the best interests of students in the forefront of your thinking and planning. These are some things you can do as a first-year teacher to avoid and prevent negligence:

- Always act in such a manner that you can pass the reasonable, prudent person test.
- Plan for what you are going to do. During your daily lesson planning, review and reflect on the activities students will participate in and what you need to do to ensure their safety and well-being.
- Make sure you know your duties and responsibilities. It is always better to know ahead of time what you are responsible for so you can make appropriate plans and take proper action.
- Be safety conscious. Part of being safety conscious is being aware of dangers and hazards in classroom and other settings. If you are teaching chemistry and there is not enough and/or the right kind of safety equipment to protect your students from harm, then you should discuss this with your principal and make arrangements for providing a safe environment for teaching science.
- Know the ages and developmental levels of your students. Third-graders will need a different kind and level of supervision than will sixth-graders.
- Do your job. Doing your job requires that you plan for what students will do and supervise their learning and behavior in a professional manner.
- Teach your students proper behavior and what is expected of them. When students know what to do and are encouraged to do it, you are providing appropriate guidance.
- Explore liability insurance provisions. The National Education Association (NEA) and the American Federation of Teachers (AFT) can provide information on liability provisions.

Reporting Child Abuse

Child abuse and neglect are serious problems in contemporary society. A survey by the National Clearinghouse on Child Abuse and Neglect estimates more than 850 thousand children are abused or neglected.[21] (Visit http://nccanch.acf.hhs.gov for more information.) The Child Abuse Prevention and Treatment Act of 1996 was amended and reauthorized in 2003 by the Keeping Children and Families Safe Act of 2003 (PL 108-36). The act defines abuse and neglect as the "physical or mental injury, sexual abuse, or exploitation, negligent treatment, or maltreatment of a child by a person who is responsible for the child's welfare, under circumstances which indicate that the child's health or welfare is harmed or threatened."

Whenever and wherever adults provide services to children and youth, issues of sexual and physical abuse inevitably arise. In today's litigious climate, more students are charging teachers with abuse.

Teachers and principals must seriously consider and weigh students' complaints, especially regarding sexual abuse. To ignore such complaints invites risk. For example:

> The U.S. Supreme Court . . . refused to disturb a federal appeals court ruling that held a high school principal potentially liable for a teacher's sexual abuse of a student. . . . In *Lankford v. Doe* (Case No. 93-1918), the Court turned down the appeal of Eddy Lankford, who has since retired as the principal of Taylor (Texas) High School. Lankford, in a lawsuit filed by a former Taylor High student, was accused of ignoring evidence that she was being sexually abused by one of her teachers.[22]

The *Lankford* ruling is particularly significant for school administrators. By allowing the federal appeals court ruling to stand, this marked the first time in legal history that a principal has been denied qualified immunity. Under the principle of qualified immunity, principals are immune from the consequences of their decisions except in cases of negligence. The *Lankford* ruling means that principals may no longer be immune from suits and are liable for all their decisions while fulfilling the role of principal.

Teachers are required by federal law to report all suspected cases of child abuse. In many cases, teachers are the frontline defense in protecting children from abuse by parents and others. Teachers see children every day and are in a special caring relationship with them. Generally, schools and school districts have procedures for how and through what channels teachers are to report suspected cases of abuse. As a first-year teacher, you will want to acquaint yourself with the procedures used in your district for reporting abuse. Furthermore, you should familiarize yourself with the signs of physical abuse and neglect, sexual abuse, and emotional maltreatment of children. You and other teachers are on the line for reporting abuse. Educational personnel report more cases of abuse than any other group.[23] While teachers are required to report cases of abuse, they are also protected from being sued for reporting suspected cases. The National Child Abuse Hotline is 1-800-4-A-Child.

Avoiding Sexual Harassment

Title VII of the Civil Rights Act of 1964 (PL 88-352) prohibits discrimination based on gender and defines sexual harassment as unwelcome sexual advances, requests for sexual favors, and other verbal or physical conduct of a sexual nature. Teachers have a responsibility to conduct themselves in such a manner that they do not sexually harass students, staff, colleagues, and parents. As a teacher, it is important that you:

- Be familiar with your school's or district's sexual harassment policy.
- Avoid situations in which you are alone with a student. If you think it is necessary and appropriate, ask another teacher or a parent to be present.
- Act appropriately at all times.
- Don't talk about sex, engage in flirtatious behavior, or tell sexually oriented jokes or stories.
- Ask your teacher-mentor or principal for advice and assistance in dealing with a difficult student or colleague.

In a recent significant case involving sexual harassment of students by teachers, *Gebser v. Lago Vista Independent School District*, the Supreme Court ruled that a school district cannot be held liable under Title IX of the Education Amendments of 1972 unless an official in a position to take corrective action knew of a teacher's harassment of a student and was "deliberately indifferent to it." As you will recall, Title IX prohibits sexual discrimination in educational programs that receive federal money. Remember also that the Supreme Court has ruled that sexual harassment is a form of sex discrimination. There has been been considerable public debate about this decision.

The Department of Education and the National Association of Attorneys General have released a guidebook, *Protecting Students from Harassment and Hate Crimes: A Guide for Schools,* recommending procedures school districts can adopt to prevent sexual, physical, and emotional abuse. The guidebook also provides guidelines for disciplining students and teachers who violate the guidelines. The guidebook has been sent to every school district in the United States and is available on the World Wide Web at www.ed.gov/offices.

Observing Copyright Law

Teachers use many and varied kinds of supplemental materials to support their teaching and to involve students in learning activities. The use of copy machines, video players, and computers is routine for the majority of teachers. As a beginning teacher, you need to know what your legal responsibilities are regarding copying and using materials. The Copyright Law of 1978 (PL 94-553) and its revisions govern what teachers and others can and cannot do regarding the copying of material. Teachers may make single copies of material for their own use and research. They may make multiple copies if each copy carries a notice of copyright, is used only for one course in the school, and meets conditions of spontaneity and brevity. Photocopying is not permitted when it replaces anthologies, is from a consumable product like a workbook, is intended to replace books, and when a charge is made beyond the actual cost of printing.

Copying software is governed by license agreements. Software designed for a single user cannot be copied without a license. School districts purchase licenses that enable them to make copies of software programs for use by staff, students, and faculty. (New copyright laws relating to electronic documents are discussed in Chapter 12.)

Teachers must receive permission in advance to copy television broadcasts. These copies can be kept for only forty-five days and must be shown to students within the first ten days of the forty-five-day period.

Practicing Ethical Behavior

INTASC

Standard 9: The teacher is a reflective practitioner who continually evaluates the effects of his/her choices and actions on others (students, parents, and other professionals in the learning community) and who actively seeks out opportunities to grow professionally.

Professional teachers conduct their practices in ways that are legally and ethically proper. Professionals want to do what is right in their relationship with students, colleagues, and parents. They base their behavior on a code of professional ethics. Many professions, such as medicine and law, have unified and universal codes of ethics that govern practice. The teaching profession does not have a unified code of ethics that governs the practice of all education professionals. However, professional organizations that represent educators, such as the NEA, have developed codes of ethics that help inform and guide professional practice.

Some states have legislated their own codes of ethics that by law are supposed to guide professional behavior. These state codes of ethics serve three purposes. First, they help establish a uniformity in ethical practice throughout the state. Second, they inform all teachers of the expectations of ethical professional practice. Third, they serve as the basis for guiding decisions of hiring and dismissal.

In your teaching, you will be involved in ethical dilemmas that will require you to think about what course of action is in the best interests of students, parents, and families. Ethical dilemmas are exactly that—dilemmas. It is hard to determine the correct course of action because of conflicting opinions of others and conflicts in your own beliefs about what is the right thing to do. Many programs of teacher preparation provide opportunities for prospective teachers to engage in an analysis of ethical dilemmas through case studies.

By devoting serious consideration to ethical behavior and how ethics relates to you as a professional you will accomplish three outcomes. First, you will be a better person and a better professional. Second, your students will benefit from your behavior. Third, the teaching profession will grow in public respect and admiration.

SECTION SUMMARY

What Are Your Legal Responsibilities as a Teacher?

Teachers have many responsibilities. Some of these include being in loco parentis, "in the place of parents," and the duty to act as "a reasonable, prudent person, and one of ordinary intelligence."

- Preventing Liability. Teachers are legally responsible for injuries caused through teacher negligence—failing to use proper standards and care to protect students or to foresee potential harm and prevent it. The "reasonable person" test is used to judge liability.

- Reporting Child Abuse. Teachers are required by law to report all suspected cases of child abuse. Although many complaints of students are unfounded, it is important to consider all charges, especially of sexual misconduct, seriously. Administrators can now be held liable for all their decisions in carrying out their roles.

- Avoiding Sexual Harassment. The law defines sexual harassment as unwelcome sexual advances, requests for sexual favors, and other verbal or physical conduct of a sexual nature. Teachers must conduct themselves so as not to sexually harass students and others in the teaching environment.
- Observing Copyright Law. Teachers must know and obey copyright laws that govern photocopying printed material or copying software, filmed, or videotaped materials.
- Practicing Ethical Behavior. Conscientious teachers base their behavior on codes of professional ethics. Some professional organizations and states have developed codes of ethics for teaching practice.

Thinking Critically
★ ★ ★ ★ ★ ★ ★ ★

The soccer coach at the local high school has a habit of slapping teenage players on the behind when the team leaves the field. Is this sexual harassment?

_____

_____

_____

_____ ★

Applying What You've Learned
★ ★ ★ ★ ★ ★ ★ ★

Obtain copies of local school district sexual harassment and abuse policies and guidelines. Also secure your state department of education guidelines for identifying and reporting child abuse. How can you use this information in your teaching?

_____

_____

_____

_____ ★

Putting Yourself in the Picture
★ ★ ★ ★ ★ ★ ★ ★

You are in your first year of teaching. One of your students, Emily, is the nine-year-old daughter of the town's leading physician, and you found her crying in the girls' rest room today. She would not tell you why she was crying. Emily seems frightened of everyone, and she frequently wears long-sleeved shirts in very hot weather. She seems to have accidents more often than other children in your class. What will you do?

_____

_____

_____

_____ ★

WHAT ARE YOUR LEGAL RIGHTS AS A TEACHER?

Teachers have many legal rights. Some relate to your rights as a citizen and also apply to you in your role as a teacher. Other rights accrue to you by virtue of your being a teacher. It is important for you to know your rights. Knowing your rights empowers you as a professional and increases the probability that you will be professional in meeting your responsibilities.

Nondiscrimination

Teachers have rights relating to nondiscrimination. School districts and school officials cannot discriminate in the hiring, dismissal, promotion, and demotion of teachers. Many cases of discrimination against teachers involve discrimination on the basis of sex, race, or disability; pay equity issues; and unequal treatment.

- Pregnancy leave. In *Cleveland Board of Education v. LaFleur,* the Supreme Court said it was discriminatory to make pregnant teachers take mandatory pregnancy leaves at fixed periods before and after giving birth. The Court said that while boards of education could set policy standards about teachers' pregnancy leaves, they could not set arbitrary leave and return dates.
- Sex discrimination. Title IX of the Education Amendments of 1972 prohibits discrimination on the basis of sex in education programs or activities that receive federal financial assistance. The Supreme Court, in *North Haven Board of Education v. Bell,* ruled that Title IX provides protection from discrimination for teachers and students. Under Title IX, the Department of Education can investigate complaints of sexual discrimination and can curtail federal funding to programs and agencies that discriminate.
- Protection of lesbians' and gay men's rights. More states and school districts are passing laws and drafting policies designed to promote and protect the rights of lesbians, gay men, and bisexual women and men. Massachusetts was the first state in the country to pass a law protecting homosexual youth from discrimination. Teachers are protected as well.

But legal protection is not enough. Schools must be proactive in their effort to provide safety and acceptance for gays, lesbians, bisexuals, and transgender students. The Gay-Straight Alliance Network is an organization that works to empower youth activities fighting homophobia in schools. This network is

a youth-led organization that connects school-based gay-straight alliances (GSAs) to one another and community resources. Through peer support, leadership development, and training, GSA Network supports young people in starting, strengthening, and sustaining GSAs and builds the capacity of GSAs to

1. Create safe environments in schools for students to support each other and learn about homophobia and other oppressions
2. Educate the school community about homophobia, gender identity, and sexual orientation issues
3. Fight discrimination, harassment, and violence in schools[24]

Contracts and Tenure

Once you have earned certification, you must find a job and enter into a contract. When you enter into a contract with a school district, you commit yourself to certain legal obligations. You should read your contract before you sign it in order to know your obligations, your responsibilities, what you need to do to earn or qualify for tenure or a continuing contract, and the grounds for dismissal.

It is surprising how many teachers don't read their contracts until something appears to be going wrong or there is a question about their continuing employment. For example, beginning teacher Marlene Mendez, who teaches high school television production, received notice from her principal that she was responsible for developing a student-produced program commemorating Dr. Martin Luther King, Jr., to be shown on district closed-circuit television. When Marlene questioned the additional assignment, her principal showed her the contract she signed, which stated that such additional assignments relating to curriculum development were permitted. Her principal further explained that it was a reasonable assignment, since it was a project she and her students could work on during class time. Generally, the reasonableness test is one often applied in determining what is appropriate in terms of teachers' duties.

Teachers are granted **tenure**, the right to permanent employment after serving a probationary period of successful teaching ranging in length from three to five years. During this time, teachers must demonstrate satisfactory teaching as measured by a district's teacher-evaluation process. The purpose of tenure laws is to prevent the firing of teachers for political or arbitrary reasons and protect teachers' academic freedom. Most states have tenure and dismissal laws that apply to all teachers. Tenure laws provide for dismissal based on certain reasons, such as negligence, and due process must be followed in dismissal proceedings. Tenure provides teachers with two important guarantees: protection from dismissal except for certain causes and the right to dismissal procedures as specified by state law.

While tenure does provide teachers with security and protection, not everyone thinks it is a good idea. Those who object to tenure maintain it protects incompetent teachers and makes it too difficult to dismiss those who should not be teaching. On the other hand, proponents of tenure argue that tenure protects competent teachers and frees teachers from the uncertainty about knowing if they will have a job from one year to the next. More important, tenure laws make it easier for teachers to practice their profession. With tenure, they are more confident about trying new methods and techniques, introducing new curricula, and taking risks in their efforts to provide the best possible education for their students.

Alternatives to career-long tenure are renewable contracts that are valid for certain periods of time, generally five years. Advocates of renewable contracts believe they can act as a safeguard for districts from hiring and then being stuck with a poor teacher forever and can also be an incentive to teachers to constantly do their best.

Tenure
The right to permanent employment after serving a probationary period of successful teaching ranging in length from three to five years.

What questions will you ask about your first-year contract before you sign it?

_____

_____

_____

_____

Evaluations and Grounds for Dismissal

As a beginning teacher, you will be evaluated from two to four times in your first year of teaching. The purpose of these evaluations is to determine your ability to teach, assess strengths and weaknesses, and provide a basis for improvement. Teachers' contracts usually specify the manner and conditions of evaluation. The collective bargaining agreement (contract) between a school district and its bargaining agent (usually a professional organization) outlines in detail the manner, content, and procedure for teacher evaluation. Due process procedures also apply to teacher evaluations.

Most states and school districts have specific causes and procedures for dismissal, which vary from state to state. Grounds for dismissal that have been upheld by various courts include contract abandonment (refusal to do the job or refusal to report to work), failing to meet continuing education and certification requirements, declining enrollments, budgetary reasons, excessive absence and tardiness, immorality, criminal conduct, falsehood, neglect of duty, incompetence, and insubordination.[25]

In addition, most states have specified the procedures to be followed in initiating and conducting dismissal proceedings against teachers. Again, these procedures are designed to protect the due process rights of teachers and to spell out what administrators and boards of education must do.

INTASC

Standard 9: The teacher is a reflective practitioner who continually evaluates the effects of his/her choices and actions on others (students, parents, and other professionals in the learning community) and who actively seeks out opportunities to grow professionally.

Collective Bargaining and the Right to Strike

Collective bargaining
The process by which terms and conditions of employment are negotiated by a bargaining agent (usually a professional organization) with the school district on behalf of all teachers.

Collective bargaining is the process by which terms and conditions of employment are negotiated by a bargaining agent (usually a professional organization) with the school district on behalf of all teachers. Many states have collective bargaining laws and agreements that provide public employees the right to organize, bargain collectively, and determine the bargaining agent that will represent them. Bargaining agreements also specify the things that can be bargained (for example, salary, benefits, working conditions, and a range of policy issues) and what happens when the parties bargaining are not able to agree. The AFT or the NEA is the collective bargaining agent for many teachers. About 75 percent of the nation's teachers are covered by a bargaining agreement. Some states, such as Georgia, hire teachers through collective bargaining.

Teachers have the right to organize and to join professional organizations. One of the first decisions you will have to make as a new teacher is whether or not to join a professional organization or labor union. Many school districts have a local teachers' organization that is affiliated with either the NEA or the AFT. Some organizations, such as the Milwaukee Teachers' Association, are not affiliated with national organizations and represent their members as a local agency. Also, Georgia, Texas, and Missouri have three of the largest independent professional organizations in the country. Membership in independent teacher organizations totals over 300,000 in over twenty-one states.

There are a number of benefits of joining and paying dues to a professional organization. One is that the organization represents—through member-elected representatives—teachers in dismissal proceedings and in disputes with the school district. When teachers believe they have been aggrieved by the board of education or administration, they can file a grievance or complaint. The bargaining agreement specifies the procedures for settling such grievances. Another benefit is that teachers may be provided with free legal advice and/or counsel and can purchase liability insurance.

Some states have laws allowing teachers to strike; other states set limitations on strikes. Some states do not allow teachers the right to strike. What rights to strike or to other work stoppages do teachers have in your state? Would you participate in a strike? Would you walk a picket line as these teachers are doing?

Participation in professional organization activities is also another way for teachers to influence local and national education policy.

At any particular time across the United States, but especially at the beginning of the school year, you will read about strikes by teachers. From Honolulu to Buffalo to Pittsburgh to Washington State, teachers strike about pay, terms of employment, and working conditions. In June 2001, Hawaii's 16,000 teachers went on strike seeking a 22 percent across-the-board raise. In September 2000, Buffalo teachers walked out in demand of a 17 percent pay raise (even though New York has a law that makes it illegal for public employees to strike). In September 2001, in Mt. Lebanon, Pennsylvania, teachers went on strike over a proposed increase in the school day from five to six periods and changes in health benefits. In 2003, Marysville (Washington) School District faculty went on strike for 49 days over salary and working conditions.

Some states have laws that prohibit strikes by public employees. One purpose of such legislation is to protect the public interest and to help ensure that settlements occur though collective bargaining agreements. Laws in other states, such as the Pennsylvania Public Employees Relations Act, give teachers the right to strike. However, the state law requires 180 days of instruction by June 30, so the number of days teachers can strike is limited.

Academic Freedom

Teachers generally have, under the principle of **academic freedom,** the freedom to teach subjects in the manner they want and the freedom to express views regarding these subjects. However, teachers cannot do or say anything they want in the name of academic freedom. Religion is one area that causes a lot of curriculum contention.

Academic freedom
The right of teachers to teach what and how they want without constraint from others.

INTASC

Standard 1: The teacher understands the central concepts, tools of inquiry, and structures of the subject being taught and can create learning experiences that make these aspects of subject matter meaningful for students.

Creationism verses Evolution. In particular, teaching about the origins of the world and humans has caused and causes much debate and legal action. The creationism point of view adheres to the account found in Genesis in the Bible. On the other hand, the evolutionary view supports the theory of evolution as articulated by Charles Darwin. A major legal conflict occurred in Tennessee in 1925. Under the state's Butler Act, it was illegal to teach in the public schools "any theory which denies the story of the Divine Creation of man as taught in the Bible, and to teach instead that man is descended from a lower order of animals." The Scopes trial, also called the "monkey trial," involved the right of John Scopes, a biology teacher who challenged the law, to teach the evolution theory. This trial pitted two legal giants of the day against each other. Clarence Darrow represented Scopes, and William Jennings Bryan, the "silver-tongued orator," represented the state as prosecutor. Scopes was found guilty of breaking Tennessee law and fined $100, but the precedent was nevertheless set for the teaching of evolution.[26]

In 1982, the Louisiana legislature passed a Balanced Treatment for Creation-Science and Evolution-Science Act. The Balanced Treatment Act, as it was called, required the teaching of creation-science whenever evolution was taught. After a number of court challenges, the Supreme Court in *Edwards v. Aquillard* ruled against the Balanced Treatment Act. The Court held that the purpose of the act was to promote religion and was a violation of the First Amendment. (See Education on the Move.)

Freedom of Expression. The First Amendment constitutes a teacher's basic guarantee of freedom of expression. The extent to which teachers may exercise their freedom of speech depends on the type of speech involved and its actual or potential effect on the school environment. Generally, challenges to teachers' freedom of expression are not an issue unless such expression is disruptive of or detrimental to the educational process.

In 1968 in *Pickering v. Board of Education,* the Supreme Court ruled that a teacher could not be dismissed for speaking as a citizen on matters of public concern. Pickering, an Illinois teacher, published a letter to the editor of the local newspaper that was critical of the board of education for the way it handled school funding. The

>>> Texas Adopts Biology Texts, Evolution Included >>>>>>

A unanimous state board of education in Texas has endorsed the concept of teaching evolution by way of adopting eleven new biology textbooks, all of which cover the politically sensitive topic.

Advocates on both sides of the issue, from within and outside Texas, had lobbied the board for months.

"Every time biology comes up, it is a very debated issue," noted Geraldine Miller, the board president. Ms. Miller said she had received between 3,000 and 4,000 e-mail messages criticizing the books in the past couple months.

In a process that is closely watched nationwide, the Texas school board approves new textbooks for public schools every fall. Districts then choose from a list of those texts. The last time biology texts were adopted in Texas was in 1997; the new ones are expected to reach classrooms in the fall of 2004.

Texas has a long history of controversial textbook adoptions. This time, the issue of evolution pitted publishers and science educators against religious organizations and conservative groups that some have accused of trying to censor the content of the books.

Because Texas is one of the largest markets in the country, the decisions made by its state board have a "ripple effect" on the rest of the country.

Source: M. Galley, "Texas Adopts Biology Texts, Evolution Included," December 19, 2003, *Education Week*, p. 5. Available online at www.edweek.org/ew/ewstory.cfm?slug=12Texas.h23.Reprinted by permission.

---

board said that Pickering's letter was defamatory and fired him. The case reached the Supreme Court, which ruled:

> To the extent that the Illinois Supreme Court's opinion may be read to suggest that teachers may constitutionally be compelled to relinquish the First Amendment rights they would otherwise enjoy as citizens to comment on matters of public interest in connection with the operation of the public schools, in which they work, it proceeds on a premise that has been equivocally rejected in numerous prior decisions of this Court. . . . Teachers are, as a class, the members of a community most likely to have informed and definite opinions as to how funds allocated to the operation of the schools should be spent.[27]

Academic freedom, as the foregoing examples indicate, continues to be a hotly debated issue. In a closely watched case, the Fourth U.S. Circuit Court of Appeals ruled that teachers have no right of academic freedom in selecting curriculum content. The 1998 case of *Boring v. Buncombe County Board of Education* involved a high school drama teacher, Margaret Boring, who was transferred in response to controversy over a play she chose for students in her acting class. Boring cleared the play with her principal. Later, when a parent objected to the contents of the play, the principal edited several scenes before the play was presented in a state competition at the end of the year. The principal gave Boring "superior" and "well above standard" ratings in all categories on her annual performance review. Nonetheless, the principal recommended that Boring be transferred to another school because of "personal conflicts resulting from actions she initiated during the course of the school year." The superintendent and the school board approved the transfer. Boring sued the principal, superintendent, and school board, claiming they violated her rights under the First Amendment. The court ruled that a high school teacher has no academic freedom to control the curriculum; therefore, "Boring's dispute was nothing more than an ordinary employment dispute."[28]

Do you agree that the Boring case was an ordinary employment dispute? Why or why not?

_____

_____

_____

_____

NCATE

Middle Level

Standard 7: Understands the complexity of teaching young adolescents; engages in practices and behaviors that develop competence as a professional.

Reflect & Write

SECTION SUMMARY

What Are Your Legal Rights as a Teacher?

You have legal rights as an American citizen and as a member of your profession. Being a teacher also gives you certain rights.

- Nondiscrimination. School districts and school officials cannot discriminate against you on the grounds of sex, race, or disability. If you are a woman, you cannot be required to take a pregnancy leave. More and more states and school districts prohibit discrimination against gays and lesbians.

- Contracts and Tenure. Before signing any contract, you should first read it thoroughly in order to understand your rights, obligations, responsibilities, and (in the case of a contract governing employment) the grounds for dismissal. Tenure is a right to permanent employment; terms of tenure vary.

- Evaluations and Grounds for Dismissal. Teachers are periodically evaluated to determine their ability to teach, assess their strengths and weaknesses, and provide a basis for improvement. Causes and procedures for dismissal vary from state to state, but they are usually stated specifically to protect due process rights.

- Collective Bargaining and the Right to Strike. Teachers have the right to organize and to join professional organizations. New teachers must decide whether they will join a teachers' union. One of the benefits is having representation in dismissal or grievance proceedings. Teachers' unions and professional organizations act as collective bargaining agents on behalf of all teachers in a school district. If no settlement is reached, teachers may strike.

- Academic Freedom. The principle of academic freedom establishes teachers' rights to teach subjects in the manner they want and to express views on those subjects. Challenges to academic freedom arise over hotly debated or politically sensitive topics.

Thinking Critically
★ ★ ★ ★ ★ ★ ★ ★

Review the Supreme Court ruling cited in the *Pickering* case. What would motivate you, as a teacher, to write such a letter to your local newspaper?

_____

_____

_____

_____★

Applying What You've Learned
★ ★ ★ ★ ★ ★ ★ ★

What are criteria for tenure in the state in which you live? Do some research on this question, using library resources and phoning some local schools. Then summarize your findings in one or two pages, ending with your opinion of the tenure rules you discovered.

_____

_____

_____

_____★

The NEA Code of Ethics says professionals "shall not unreasonably deny the student access to varying points of view." How would you enforce this guideline? Give an example of what you might do to put this idea into practice.

★

*W*HAT ARE STUDENTS' LEGAL RIGHTS*?*

Beginning in the 1960s, students became more aware of their rights. They learned that they have the same legal guarantees that their parents and others have. They also became more active in using the legal system to protect and uphold their rights. Figure 8.5 lists Supreme Court decisions affecting students and parents.

Freedom of Expression

One result of the increased concern for students' rights is that many laws have been passed and court decisions issued that define, extend, and defend students' rights. In particular, students' rights to free expression in terms of speech and dress have been and are a central legal issue.

NCATE

Middle Level

Standard 1: Understands the major concepts, principles, theories and research related to young adolescent development; provides opportunities that support student development and learning.

Free Speech. When you think about freedom of speech, what do you think of? Perhaps you think only about speaking and writing. Freedom of speech encompasses more than these two forms of expression. It includes all forms of expression—talking and writing as well as wearing items (a political button, a T-shirt, a ribbon symbolic of some organization, or an armband) or displaying items (a placard and so forth).

A landmark case relating to freedom of expression is the Supreme Court decision in *Tinker v. Des Moines Independent School District*.[29] The issue involved the high school principal who suspended two students (brother and sister John and Mary Beth Tinker) for wearing black armbands as a silent protest against the Vietnam War. The Court did not agree. It ruled that "it can hardly be argued that either students or teachers shed their constitutional rights to freedom of expression at the schoolhouse gate." The *Tinker* case is one of the most often referred to cases in legal issues regarding education.

Reflect & Write

Does a principal have the right of censorship? Write your opinion before reading the next few paragraphs.

Zucht v. King (1922). The Court upheld the requirement that a child must be vaccinated before attending school.

Pierce v. Society of Sisters of the Holy Names of Jesus and Mary (1925). The Court ruled unconstitutional an Oregon law requiring parents to send their children to public school. The Court said that such a law denied parents the right to control the education of their children.

Tinker v. Des Moines Independent School District (1969). The Court ruled that "it can hardly be argued that either students or teachers shed their constitutional rights to freedom of expression at the schoolhouse gate." Students have a right to freedom of expression. Generally, restrictions on students' and teachers' dress must have a legitimate educational value.

Wisconsin v. Yoder (1972). The Court ruled that Old Order Amish, because of their well-established beliefs, must be given some relief from compulsory attendance.

Lau v. Nichols (1974). The Court struck down a school district practice of requiring Chinese students to attend classes taught in English. This case effectively set the stage for bilingual education.

Ingraham v. Wright (1977). The Court ruled that disciplinary paddling of public school students does not constitute cruel and unusual punishment.

Goss v. Lopez (1975). The Court said that students cannot be suspended without a hearing.

Board of Education of Hendrick Hudson Central School District v. Rowley (1982). The Court defined "free and appropriate" education.

Plyer v. Doe (1982). The Court ruled that Texas could not withhold free public education from undocumented alien children in part because "education provides the basic tools by which individuals might lead economically productive lives to the benefit of us all."

Board of Education v. Rowley (1982). The court ruled that the Individuals with Disabilities Education Act's statutory entitlement to a "free and appropriate public education" for all students, including those with disabilities, means that school authorities must comply with the act's procedural requirements, which include developing individualized education programs for students with disabilities.

New Jersey v. T.L.O. (1985). The Court determined that school officials are not necessarily bound by the Fourth Amendment but by reasonable cause when engaged in searches.

Bethel School District No. 403 v. Fraser (1986). The Court ruled that school officials can restrain student speech.

Hazelwood School District v. Kuhlmeier (1988). The Court ruled that administrators have the right to censor school newspapers, and they can block "speech that is ungrammatical, poorly written, inadequately researched, biased or prejudiced, vulgar or profane, or unsuitable for immature audiences."

Franklin v. Gwinnett County Public Schools (1992). The Court ruled that Title IX authorized students who have been sexually harassed by teachers to recover damages from the school district.

Zorbrest et al. v. Catalina Foothills School District (1993). The Court ruled that the establishment clause does not prevent a school from furnishing a disabled child enrolled in a sectarian school with assistance to facilitate his/her education.

Lankford v. Doe (1994). The Court upheld a ruling that holds a principal potentially liable for a teacher's sexual abuse of a student.

Veronia School District v. Acton (1995). The Court upheld the right of the Veronia, Oregon, School District to conduct a program of random urinalysis testing of middle and high school athletes.

U.S. v. Lopez (1995). The Court said that Congress exceeded its powers in passing the Gun-Free School Zones Act, which mandated compulsory expulsion for one year for students who bring guns to school.

United States v. Virginia (1996). The Court stated that "parties who seek to defend gender-based government action must demonstrate 'exceedingly persuasive justification' for that action." To meet the burden of justification a state must show at least that the classification serves "important governmental objectives and that the discriminatory means employed" are "substantially related to the achievement of those objectives."

Agostini v. Felton (1997). The Court held that a federally funded program providing supplemental, remedial instruction to disadvantaged children on a neutral basis is not invalid under the establishment clause when such instruction is given on the premises of sectarian schools by government employees under a program containing safeguards.

Bragdon v. Abbott (1998). School districts are subject to both the Americans with Disabilities Act (ADA) and the Rehabilitation Act of 1973 if they receive federal funds. The Court ruled that "HIV infection satisfies the statutory and regulatory definition of a physical impairment during every stage of the disease," thus people who carry the HIV virus are entitled to the broad rights given to disabled people through the ADA.

Davis v. Monroe County Board of Education (1999). The Court ruled that schools are held liable if they ignore excessive sexual harassment of one student by another student.

Santa Fe Independent School District v. Doe (2000). The Court held that a district's policy permitting student-led, student-initiated prayer at football games is in violation of freedom of religion.

Troxel v. Granville (2000). The Court affirmed the fundamental right of parents to control the upbringing of their children, including their education.

Owasso Independent School District v. Falvo (2002). Students can grade each other's academic work and announce the results in class without violating a federal privacy law.

Board of Education of Independent School District No. 92 [OK], et al., v. Lindsay Earls, et al. (2002). The Court approved an Oklahoma school district's mandating drug testing for all students who wished to participate in extracurricular activities, including the chess club, the Honor Society, and the marching band.

United States v. American Library Association (2003). The Court ruled that Congress can require public libraries to install computer filters that block access to Internet pornography.

Ashcroft v. American Civil Liberties Union (2004). The Court put on hold the Child Online Protection Act, which would impose criminal penalties on commercial Web publishers who fail to restrict access by minors to sexually explicit material.

Elk Grove Unified School District v. Newdow (2004). On technical grounds, the Court preserved the phrase "one nation under God" in the Pledge of Allegiance. The Court said Michael Newdow could not sue to ban the pledge from his daughter's school because he did not have legal authority to speak for her.

Reflect & Write

Based on the summaries above, which if any of these decisions do you think might have implications for you as a teacher? Why?

_____

_____

_____

Figure 8.5 **Supreme Court Cases Affecting the Rights of Students and Parents**

Standard 5: The teacher uses an understanding of individual and group motivation and behavior to create a learning environment that encourages positive social interaction, active engagement in learning, and self-motivation.

INTASC

Sometimes freedom of speech may not seem what it is. For example, at Newman High School in Carrollton, Texas, students were set to publish an article in the *Odyssey,* the school newspaper, about the efforts of some students to start a gay and lesbian support club. But Principal Lee Alvoia pulled the article. Alvoia defended her decision based on the conservative values of the school district. "Because of the nature of the topic and because of the conservative nature of the community I didn't want a negative reaction before we even had a club. This is ot one of your normal teenage clubs. I didn't want undue controversy."[30] Principal Ken McGuire of Keller ISD canceled a school play because of its sexual content.

Principal Alvoia does have the right to pull the article from the *Odyssey,* and Principal McGuire has the right to cancel the play, based on a Supreme Court case involving the school newspaper at Westwood High School in Hazelwood, Missouri. At Westwood, students were about to publish two articles in the *Spectrum,* the school-sponsored newspaper. One article dealt with teenage pregnancy and the other with the effects of divorce on children. Principal Robert Reynolds ordered the pages containing the two articles (and four other articles) removed from the paper. The students sued, and the case ended up in the Supreme Court. The Court found in favor of the school district. In *Hazelwood School District v. Kuhlmeier* the Court ruled that administrators have the right to censor school newspapers, and they can block "speech that is ungrammatical, poorly written, inadequately researched, biased or prejudiced, vulgar or profane, or unsuitable for immature audiences."[31] The Court also held that "educators do not offend the First Amendment by exercising editorial control over the style and content of student speech in school-sponsored expressive activities so long as their actions are reasonably related to legitimate pedagogical concerns."[32] While administrators have this right, some exercise this option, others do not.

In another incident involving censorship, student Matthew Fraser, at a school assembly, nominated a student for a class office. In so doing, he used extended sexual metaphors. Fraser was suspended for three days and removed from the list of graduation speakers. In *Bethel School District No. 403 v. Fraser* the Supreme Court ruled that "the pervasive sexual innuendo in Fraser's speech was plainly offensive to both teachers and students—indeed to any mature person."[33]

Dress Codes. Generally, courts have upheld the right of school districts to set "reasonable" standards of dress and appearance for both students and teachers. However, a problem arises with the interpretation of what is reasonable. Also, as noted in *Tinker,* students have a right to freedom of expression. Generally, restrictions on students' and teachers' dress must have a legitimate educational value. What school districts must be able to show is that the regulation of student appearance is necessary for students' proper functioning and related to district and school goals. An example of a high school dress code is shown in Figure 8.6.

Gang attire is a problem in many school districts and is seen by some as one of the factors related to increasing school violence and decreasing school achievement. While some districts have drafted dress codes directed toward restricting the wearing of gang attire, other school districts are turning to school uniforms to address issues of clothing and accessories. In 1994, the Long Beach (California) School District became the first in the nation to require all elementary and middle school students to wear uniforms. School officials credit uniform wearing with a sharp reduction in school crime, but there is no research to support this connection. Philadelphia requires all students in its 264 schools to wear uniforms. Each school may select its own style of uniform, but all students must wear them every day. Most large school districts—such as New York, Los Angeles, Chicago, Miami, and Houston—have uniform policies. It is likely that in issues of required uniforms, there will be court cases filed by students and their parents who believe their constitutional rights are being infringed. Issues of the abridgment of First Amendment rights and freedom of student expression will be the basis of these suits.

There is a close relationship between high standards of dignity and pride and proper grooming. Personal appearance is important. The student and parents share in the responsibility for proper grooming of the student. The District's dress code is established to teach grooming and hygiene, instill discipline, prevent disruption, avoid safety hazards, and teach respect for authority. Students should be dressed and groomed in a manner that is clean and neat and that will not be a health or safety hazard to themselves or others. Modesty will be the dominant feature in all clothing. Behavior, attitude, and community standards take precedence over individual clothing and hairstyle. While the enforcement of the student dress code rests with the principal, teachers and other staff should be familiar with the dress code and be cognizant of student dress and grooming, referring violations to the principal. The campus principal is the final authority concerning propriety of clothes, hairstyle, and jewelry. The following dress code will be enforced:

Pants
- Pants/jeans/shorts will be worn at the natural waistline, not below or above. (No sagging/baggy will be permitted.)
- Pants/jeans/shorts must be appropriately sized, fitting in the waist, crotch, and leg. (They may not be baggy, oversized, or excessively tight.)
- Jeans must be regular/original/classic straight-legged, or boot cut. (They may not be wide legged, wide bottomed, full thigh, or loose fit.)
- Pants/jeans/shorts must be hemmed and free of holes, splits, fraying, or patches.

Shirts
- Shirts will be short or long sleeve in grades 4 through 12.
- Shirts must be appropriately sized in the shoulders, sleeves, and length. (They may not be baggy or excessively tight in grades 4 through 12.)
- Shirt/top must be cut straight across the bottom (e.g., T-shirt, sweatshirts, and Hawaiian print shirts), to be worn outside. Shirt/top cut with tails or otherwise designed to be worn tucked in, must be tucked in.
- The untucked shirt/top must cover the midriff at all times (e.g., when standing, sitting, stretching, and bending).
- The untucked shirt/top cannot be oversized/undersized and may not extend below the natural crotch on boys and girls.
- Sweaters, sweatshirts, and vests do not have to be tucked in.

Shorts, Skorts, Skirts
- Shorts are permitted in grades pre-K through 3.
- In grades 4 through 12, shorts are allowed, as follows:
- Shorts must be no shorter than 3 inches above the top of the knee.
- Shorts may not be oversized, wide legged, full thigh, or wind shorts.
- Dress and skirt length must be no shorter than 3 inches above the top of the kneecap.
- Dress and skirt slit must not exceed 3 inches above the top of the kneecap.

Shoes
- Shoes must be worn at all times.

Hair
- Hair must be a natural human color.
- A neatly trimmed mustache above the lip that does not extend beyond the lip line is the only facial hair permitted.
- Sideburns must be cut above the bottom of the ear.

Reflect & Write

Do you think the Granbury ISD dress code is reasonable? What would you add to the code? What would you delete?

Figure 8.6   *Granbury Independent School District Dress/Grooming Code, 2004–2005.*

Source: The complete dress code for Granbury Independent School District is available at www.granbury.K12.tx.us/gisd_new/docs/dress_code_2004-2005.pdf. Reprinted by permission.

Should students be required to wear uniforms? If so, who should pay for them?

_____

_____

_____

_____

Due Process

The due process provisions of the Fifth and Fourteenth Amendments and the **equal protection clause** of the Fourteenth Amendment are important parts of student discipline policies and codes. Both provisions require that no person shall "be deprived of life, liberty, or property by the government without due process of law." The due process provisions are designed to ensure that everyone is treated fairly.

The definitions of life, liberty, and property are much broader than you might think. For example, free public education is considered a form of property. So, if for some reason a student is denied a free public education, the due process clause applies. Likewise, a student's good name, reputation, honor, and integrity are considered forms of liberty.

Discipline. Managing student discipline is always an issue in the schools. Conflicts of what is and is not appropriate behavior, issues of power and control, and what is and isn't proper discipline are at the heart of guiding and managing student behavior. This is an area you as a beginning teacher will want to give special attention. There are a number of critical factors relating to school discipline. First, students must be given notice of the standards of conduct the school wishes to uphold and enforce.

Second, it is reasonable that students be given an opportunity to regulate their behavior based on standards provided by the school. Most districts have standards of conduct that are given and/or read to students. Furthermore, many districts advise teachers to talk about and discuss with students the rules of conduct that prevail in the classroom.

In *Ingraham v. Wright,* the Supreme Court ruled that disciplinary paddling of public school students does not constitute cruel and unusual punishment. On the other hand, not everyone agrees that students should be subjected to corporal punishment. In states that do permit corporal punishment, local districts have guidelines for administering it. If you teach in a district that permits corporal punishment, you should familiarize yourself with the guidelines and should do all you can to avoid using any kind of physical punishment. Many states (twenty-four of them) prohibit corporal punishment. In addition, the NEA has an official position statement against corporal punishment.

Suspension and Expulsion. As with all affairs relating to student rights, due process also has to be provided in all proceedings relating to suspension and expulsion. In *Goss v. Lopez,* the Supreme Court said that students cannot be suspended without a hearing. Commenting on the propriety of such a process, the Court said, "It would be a strange disciplinary system in an educational institution if no communication was sought by the disciplinarian with the student in an effort to inform him of his defalcation and to let him tell his side of the story."[34]

Suspensions are used to discipline students when the infractions are not of sufficient magnitude to warrant expulsion. Suspension may include the short-term denial of school attendance as well as the denial of participation in regular courses and activities. The suspension can be in-school, meaning that students are at school but not attending a class or classes. Or the suspension can be out-of-school, meaning that the student does not come to school for a period of time. Expulsion is the removal of a student from the supervision and control of the school, usually a period in excess of ten days. Generally, a student may be expelled only by action of the board of educa-

Equal protection clause
The clause of the Fourteenth Amendment that prohibits a state from denying any person within its jurisdiction equal protection of its law.

tion. Likewise, only the board of education can readmit a student after expulsion.

Right to Privacy

The Fourth Amendment is clear about the right of the people to be secure in their persons, houses, papers, and effects. All of these rights also relate to a student's right to privacy at school.

Search and Seizure. The Supreme Court in *New Jersey v. T.L.O.* ruled that the Fourth Amendment applies to searches of students by school officials. The Fourth Amendment provides that all persons have the right to be protected from bodily searches or searches of other places in which they expect privacy unless there is a search warrant or unless there are exceptional cases involved. However, the Court said:

> The accommodation of the privacy interests of school children with the substantial need of teachers and administrators to maintain order in the schools does not require strict adherence to the requirement that searches be based on probable cause to believe that the subject of the search has violated or is violating the law. Rather, the legality of a search of a student should depend simply on the reasonableness, under all the circumstances, of the search.[35]

The Court said that a reasonable search is one justified at its inception and reasonably related in scope to the circumstances that justified the initial interference. The Supreme Court has continued to let stand its decision made in *New Jersey v. T.L.O.* Recently, the Supreme Court refused to hear the appeal of two Alabama elementary school girls who allege they were strip-searched by a teacher and a counselor.[36] Federal Judge Robert G. Doumar offers the following guidelines for school officials to follow in searches for stolen property:

- When school employees want to find property (property of relatively minor value, at least, such as tennis shoes), it is possible to search more than one student so long as employees have enough suspicion to justify each search.
- Employees should ask students for voluntary consent to be searched. The Fourth Amendment does not regulate consensual searches—so long as they truly are consensual.
- Before forcing any searches, employees should investigate to determine whether individualized suspicion exists for the students who did not consent to search.[37]

Crime and Violence. Many states and local districts have laws designed to curb violence and crime in schools. Given the growth of violence in society and schools and the public's concern with reducing violence, the federal government has entered the fray. In 1990, Congress passed the Gun-Free School Zones Act, which prohibited possession of guns within 1,000 feet of a school. The act mandated that schools must expel for a year any student found carrying a firearm to school. If a state did not adopt such a mandatory one-year expulsion policy, it lost federal funding. The Supreme Court in *U.S. v. Lopez* struck down this law and ruled that Congress had exceeded its powers.

Congress passed the Gun-Free School Zones Act under its power to regulate interstate commerce on the grounds that violence near schools makes a difference in America's economic well-being and national productivity. It is common for Congress

What are students' rights to privacy? How is reasonable search and seizure defined? What are students' and parents' rights with regard to the privacy of students' school records?

INTASC

Standard 2: The teacher understands how children learn and develop, and can provide learning opportunities that support their intellectual, social and personal development.

to use its power to regulate interstate commerce as a basis for federal legislation. The Court, however, said Congress did not have such authority under the commerce clause and "that authority, while broad, does not include the authority to regulate each and every aspect of local schools."[38]

Violent crime is one of the contemporary problems with which public schools must contend. In 2000, an estimated 1.5 million violent incidents occurred in the public schools.[39] To reduce the number of guns in schools, officials are using metal detectors, surveillance cameras, specially trained dogs to sniff out guns, locker sweeps, identification tags, and a prohibition against bringing book bags to school. Some schools, such as seen in New Hampshire, conduct "bullet drills," a procedure in which teachers and students are trained to avoid being harmed by guns. These types of drills have taken place for years in the inner city, but now they are also taking place in the suburbs and rural areas. How schools' efforts to reduce violence play out in practice and in the courts remains to be seen.

A new publication, a guidebook of strategies to help schools prevent violence by the Department of Education, outlines prevention strategies, including ways to build positive relationships among students, parents, and teachers. The guidebook is being sent to all schools nationwide. It is also available on the World Wide Web at www. ed.gov/about/offices/list/osers/osep/gtss.html.

Student Records. Access to what is contained in student records and their privacy are matters of great concern for teachers and other school personnel. Under the Buckley Amendment of the Family Educational Rights and Privacy Act of 1974, schools must protect the privacy of student records while affording parents and students over eighteen years of age access to this information. If parents and age-eligible students believe student records are misleading, inaccurate, or contain information that is a violation of their rights, they can ask the school to amend the information. If school personnel refuse, parents and students have the right to a hearing.

Beyond students and their parents, access to student records is limited. Only educators with a legitimate right to examine the records may do so. Furthermore, access to students' records is not permitted without parents' written approval. However, a little-known provision of the No Child Left Behind Act requires high schools receiving federal dollars to give military recruiters the names, addresses, and telephone numbers of students.[40]

Maintenance of student records calls for particular care and attention in determining what information should go into students' records and how the records are maintained and safeguarded. For example, policies on how secure student records are and procedures for determining where and how records can be reviewed must be specified and administered by school personnel. Teachers have to be judicious about what they include in student records and about who they give access to, and what they say is in, the records.

Right to Nondiscrimination

Students are protected, as are teachers, in their right to nondiscrimination. Title IX of the Education Amendments of 1972 prohibits discrimination on the basis of sex. Many girls' school sports programs are the beneficiary of this law. Nondiscrimination means that girls' sport programs receive equal funding and girls participate in more sports programs.

Nondiscrimination of students is apparent in other areas as well. In years past, female high school students who were married or pregnant were routinely expelled. Public policy today is such that schools recognize that married and pregnant students have all the rights and privileges of other students and that marriage and pregnancy are not criteria for the exclusion of students from school or participation in extracurricular activities. However, in a much publicized case two female students—one an

INTASC

Standard 9: The teacher is a reflective practitioner who continually evaluates the effects of his/her choices and actions on others.

INTASC

Standard 3: The teacher understands how students differ in their approaches to learning and creates instructional opportunities that are adapted to diverse learners.

NCATE

Middle Level

Standard 1: Understands the major concepts, principles, theories and research related to young adolescent development; provides opportunities that support student development and learning.

unwed mother, the other eight months pregnant—sued the school district because the faculty council at Grant County High School in Williamson, Kentucky, rejected their applications to the National Honor Society. The young women charged discrimination for being disqualified for membership in the honor society.[41]

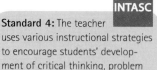

INTASC

Standard 4: The teacher uses various instructional strategies to encourage students' development of critical thinking, problem solving, and performance skills.

Bilingual Education. As immigration increases and as more of the population becomes multicultural, many students enter the public schools who are non-English speaking or who are of limited English proficiency (LEP). As you read in Chapter 4, students' home languages are many and diverse. According to the Census Bureau, about one in six residents of the United States (47.0 million) speaks a language other than English, with Spanish now the second most common language.

Title VI of the Civil Rights Act of 1964 prohibits discrimination on the basis of race, color, or national origin in programs that receive federal funds. In 1970, the Office of Civil Rights (OCR) interpreted discrimination on the basis of "national origin" to mean "[w]here inability to speak and understand the English language excludes national origin–minority group children from effective participation in the educational program offered by a school district, the district must take affirmative steps to rectify the language deficiency in order to open its instructional program to these students."[42]

How should school programs and teachers provide for the needs of non-English-speaking and LEP students? There are a number of ways. One method is bilingual education. The judicial basis for bilingual education comes from the Supreme Court. In *Lau v. Nichols* the Court struck down a school district practice of requiring Chinese students to attend classes taught in English. In this ruling, the Court said that "there is no equality of treatment merely by providing students with the same facilities, textbooks, teachers, and curriculum." Regarding what would constitute a meaningful program for such children, the Court stated, "Teaching English to the students of Chinese ancestry who do not speak the language is one choice. Giving instructions to this group in Chinese is another. There may be others."[43]

The No Child Left Behind (NCLB) Act of 2001 has had a profound influence on how schools conduct bilingual programs and how they teach English language learners (ELLs). The NCLB act

- completely changes the focus of bilingual education programs from programs teaching limited-English-proficient (LEP) children primarily in their native languages to programs focused on helping LEP children learn English
- requires accountability for results in teaching LEP children English and requires that LEP students be tested for reading and language arts in English after they have attended school in the United States for three consecutive years
- requires that *all teachers* in a language instruction class for LEP children be fluent in English, including written and oral communication skills, and any other language used by the program
- requires that parents be notified when a limited-English-proficient child is in need of English language instruction [44]

We discuss more in Chapter 11 how schools conduct bilingual programs.

Twenty-six states have official English laws that make English the official language of the state. You can identify whether or not your state has an official English law by accessing the U.S. English Home Page at www.us-english.org/.

NCATE

Early Childhood

Standard 4: Integrates understanding of children and families, of developmentally effective approaches to teaching and learning, and of academic disciplines to design, implement, and evaluate positive learning experiences for all children.

Elementary

Standard 3.1: Plans and implements instruction based on knowledge of students, learning theory, subject matter, curricular goals, and community.

Middle Level

Standard 3: Understands the major concepts, principles, theories, and research related to middle-level curriculum and assessment; uses this knowledge in practice.

Special Education. There are 6.1 million children (ages birth to 21) with disabilities served in federally supported programs.[45] Section 504 of the Rehabilitation Act of 1973 was the first piece of legislation protecting the rights of persons with disabilities. Section 504 prohibited exclusion of disabled individuals from participating in, being denied the benefits of, or being discriminated against in any program or activity receiving federal assistance.

The Education for All Handicapped Children Act of 1975 (PL 94-142), now IDEA, is the landmark legislation that provides for special-needs children. Included in its many provisions are the following:

- A free and appropriate education (FAPE) for all persons between the ages of 3 and 21.
- Education in the least restrictive environment (the environment in which a student can learn best).
- Individualization of instruction for each student, taking into consideration his or her needs, disabling conditions, and preferences as well as the preferences of the student's parents. This individualization of instruction is expressed through an individualized education program (IEP). The IEP and its preparation have had tremendous influence on curriculum for special-needs children and how that curriculum is delivered.
- Participation of the parent, and when appropriate the student, in diagnosis, placement, and the development of the IEP.
- Extending to the parents a broad range of rights regarding their children's education.

The curriculum of most middle and high schools provides students with information about wellness and healthy living. Do you think all students have a right to information about sexually transmitted diseases? Do you feel schools have a responsibility to include sex education in their curricula? At what age do you think it is appropriate to provide this information to students?

As you may have suspected by now, some of the provisions of IDEA were and are open to interpretation. The Supreme Court in *Board of Education of Hendrick Hudson Central School District v. Rowley* ruled on the meaning of "free and appropriate." The Court said it constitutes "personalized instruction with sufficient support services to permit the child to benefit from that instruction."[46]

Two other federal laws protect and define the rights of people with disabilities. The Americans with Disabilities Act (ADA) (PL 101-336) uses language similar to that of Section 504 and prohibits discrimination against persons with disabilities. The Individuals with Disabilities Education Act (IDEA) (PL 101-476) adds two additional categories of disability—"autism" and "traumatic brain injury." Furthermore, IDEA changes all references of "handicapped children" to "children with disabilities." In addition, the Handicapped Children's Protection Act of 1986 (PL 99-372) allows parents to collect attorney's fees when they prevail in suits brought for violation of IDEA.

AIDS. As the number of students with acquired immunodeficiency syndrome (AIDS) increases, the number of conflicts about AIDS-related issues between school districts and parents increases. AIDS is caused by the human immunodeficiency virus (HIV), which weakens or destroys the immune system, thus allowing diseases and infections to develop. Children and adults with HIV may not get AIDS. Some may develop symptoms not normally associated with AIDS that are referred to as AIDS-related complex (ARC), while others may develop AIDS symptoms. The manifestation of AIDS in children is different than in adults. For example, Kaposi's sarcoma, a form of cancer, is found in about 25 percent of adult AIDS cases but seldom in children. More commonly, children with AIDS develop infections such as pneumonia and central nervous system disorders. Also, some children born with HIV may have some physical problems at birth.

Some parents want policies that prohibit or limit attendance of HIV positive students in school. School officials, however, must comply with federal laws; so any person who is HIV positive is protected from discrimination by the Rehabilitation Act of 1973. Under this act, "no individual may be excluded from a program or activity receiving federal financial assistance if the individual is 'otherwise qualified' to participate."[47] Although school districts have tried to bar students with HIV/AIDS, their efforts have been unsuccessful. The Supreme Court ruled in *Bragdon v. Abbott et al.* that people who carry the HIV virus are disabled and are entitled to the rights established by the Americans with Disabilities Act. Justice Kennedy said, "HIV infection satisfies the statutory and regulatory definition of a physical impairment during every stage of the disease."[48]

Legal Issues after September 11

The tragic events of September 11, 2001, have had a number of influences on legal issues and education.

- Many states and school districts ban students from carrying cell phones while in school, but after September 11 many students want to carry phones and their parents want them to carry phones. Principal Gregory Vallone at James Monroe High School in North Hills, California, agrees. He estimates that 70 percent of his 4,600 students carry cell phones despite the ban. "Parents want to know their children are safe, and we want parents to know their kids are safe," says Teena Nations of the Norman (Oklahoma) School District.[49] More states are reconsidering their cell phone policies. States that have lifted their bans are Virginia, Arkansas, California, Indiana, Kentucky, Maryland, Nevada, Oklahoma, and South Carolina. Other states are encouraging school districts to develop a campus-by-campus policy.
- More school districts are encouraging the reciting of the pledge of allegiance. A new Michigan state law calls for a daily display of patriotism in the form of the pledge of allegiance or an instrumental version of the national anthem.[50]

SECTION SUMMARY

What Are Students' Legal Rights?

Since the 1960s, students have become increasingly aware of their rights, and more rights have been extended to them.

- Freedom of Expression. Students' rights to freedom of expression include freedom of speech and freedom to express themselves in their manner of dress. School districts may limit both, however, subject to strict guidelines that relate to pedagogical concerns and the educational process.
- Due Process. Due process provisions, designed to ensure that everyone is treated fairly, protect students in the design and enforcement of student discipline, suspension, and expulsion policies.
- Right to Privacy. The Fourth Amendment protects all Americans from unreasonable search and seizure. These protections limit schools' ability to conduct searches except under carefully defined circumstances. Given public concerns about violence, the federal government passed the Gun-Free School Zones Act, which mandates expulsion for students carrying firearms to school. The Buckley Amendment of the Family Educational Rights and Privacy Act of 1974 gives students over 18 and their families legal access to student records but restricts access by others.

- Right to Nondiscrimination. Legislation that prohibits discrimination on the basis of sex, race, color, or national origin affects many parts of school life. Some examples are funding for sports programs, programs for teenage parents, and provisions for bilingual education, special education, and education of children with disabilities or HIV/AIDS.

- Legal Issues after September 11. Many schools are reviewing cell phone policies and are encouraging displays of patriotism.

Thinking Critically
★ ★ ★ ★ ★ ★ ★ ★

Many psychologists believe that spanking children teaches them that violence is an acceptable solution to conflict. What is your opinion on corporal punishment in public schools?

_____

_____

_____

_____ ★

Applying What You've Learned
★ ★ ★ ★ ★ ★ ★ ★

What steps have schools taken to ensure safety in the schools for students and teachers? Has security been increased in response to recent stories about student violence? Interview (in person or by phone) a principal in a school near your home about these questions.

_____

_____

_____

_____ ★

Putting Yourself in the Picture
★ ★ ★ ★ ★ ★ ★ ★

You have been asked to participate on a committee that will design a program to help teenage mothers graduate from high school. What information will you want to gather, and what issues will you want to address in this program?

_____

_____

_____

_____ ★

*W*HAT ARE PARENTS' RIGHTS AND RESPONSIBILITIES*?*

Within the home and school settings, it is sometimes easy to forget that parents have rights, too. With the current emphasis on parent involvement and parents as partners in the education process (see Chapter 6), it is more important than ever for teachers to know and understand the basic educational rights and responsibilities of parents in the education arena (see Figure 8.5).

While we assume that parents have many rights relating to their children, their rights are often challenged by others. Take the case of a Washington State law that gave grandparents and others the right to petition for visits with children against the wishes of parents. In 2000, the Supreme Court in *Troxel v. Granville* ruled the law unconstitutional. The Court said that "it cannot now be doubted that the due process clause of the Fourteenth Amendment protects the fundamental rights of parents to make decisions concerning the care, custody, and control of their children."[51]

Elementary

Standard 5.3: Knows importance of establishing and maintaining positive collaborative relationships with families to promote the academic, social, and emotional growth of children.

Middle Level

Standard 6: Understands the major concepts, principles, theories, and research related to working collaboratively with family and community members; uses that knowledge to maximize learning of all young adolescents.

Parental Information and Consent

Parents have a range of rights relating to being informed about their children's school progress and behavior. Parents also have rights that require their informed consent before their children can engage in certain school activities, such as field trips, or be subjected to discipline procedures, such as corporal punishment.

In addition, many laws such as the Education for All Handicapped Children Act of 1975 (PL 94-142) provide parents with specific rights such as the following:

- The parent must give consent for evaluation of the child.
- The parent has the right to "examine all relevant records with respect to the identification, evaluation, and educational placement of the child."
- The parent must be given written prior notice whenever a change in "the identification, evaluation, or educational placement of the child" occurs.
- This written notice must be in the parent's native tongue.
- The parent has an "opportunity to present complaints with respect to any matter relating to the identification, evaluation, or educational placement of the child."
- The parent has the right to a due process hearing in relation to any complaint.
- The parent has the right to participate in development of the IEP for the child.
- Meetings to develop the IEP must be conducted in the parent's native tongue.
- Meetings to develop the IEP must be held at a time and place agreeable to the parent.

Compulsory School Attendance

Parents have broad powers for control of and responsibility for their children. Parents are responsible for feeding, clothing, and controlling the education of their children. A landmark case involving the rights of parents in relation to the education of their children was the 1925 Supreme Court case of *Pierce v. Society of Sisters of the Holy Names of Jesus and Mary.* The Court ruled unconstitutional an Oregon law requiring parents to send their children to public school. The Court said that such a law denied parents the right to control the education of their children. However, the Court made clear the role of the state in education:

> No question is raised concerning the power of the state to regulate all schools, to inspect, supervise, and examine them, their teachers, and pupils; to require that all children of proper age attend some school, that teachers shall be of good moral character and patriotic disposition, that certain studies plainly essential to good citizenship must be taught, and that nothing be taught which is manifestly inimical to the public welfare.[52]

The Court's ruling in *Pierce* did one other thing: It established the right of private schools to exist and thus enforced the tradition of public and private education in the United States.

Parents and Student Truancy

YOU DECIDE

The right to control their children's education also means that parents have the responsibility, indeed the legal obligation, to see that their children attend school. Truancy is a growing problem for most schools, and educators are not happy when students miss school for any reason. First, students don't learn when they aren't in school. Second, schools' state reimbursement is based on average daily attendance. The more absences, the fewer state dollars.

In Traverse County, Michigan, a judge sentenced Brenda Lee Hansen to spend thirty days at West Junior High School with her daughter. Ms. Hansen pleaded guilty to a misdemeanor related to her daughter's truancy. The girl had piled up thirty-seven unexcused absences in the school year.

"We hate to have these dramatic steps taken, but if it works, that's great," said Conrad Reiter, the principal of the 1,465-student school. He said Ms. Hansen was attending classes daily and having lunch in the cafeteria at her daughter's side.

In addition, Ms. Hansen, 37, spent two days in jail and must attend parenting classes, cooperate with the county family services agency, and be on probation until her daughter turns 16.

You decide: Do you think parents should be ordered to school with their truant children? Write a paragraph, pro or con. As a beginning teacher, what can you do to encourage school attendance?

For more information about this case, see A. Trotter, "Michigan Judge Orders Truant's Mother to School," *Education Week*, May 1, 2002, p. 4. Reprinted by permission.

The Supreme Court has also protected certain groups from compulsory attendance at state-sponsored schools. In 1972, in *Wisconsin v. Yoder*, the Court ruled that Old Order Amish, because of their well-established beliefs, must be given some relief from compulsory attendance. In this particular case, the defendants, Jonas Yoder and others, declined to send their children ages 14 and 16 to public school after they had graduated from the eighth grade. This was in violation of Wisconsin state law requiring school attendance through age 16. The Court said:

> Almost 300 years of consistent practice and strong evidence of a sustained faith pervading and regulating respondents' entire mode of life support the claim that enforcement of the State's requirement of compulsory formal education after eighth grade would gravely endanger if not destroy the free exercise of respondents' religious beliefs.[53]

NCATE

Early Childhood

Standard 4: Integrates understanding of children and families, of developmentally effective approaches to teaching and learning, and of academic disciplines to design, implement, and evaluate positive learning experiences for all children.

Elementary

Standard 5.3: Knows importance of establishing and maintaining positive collaborative relationships with families to promote the academic, social, and emotional growth of children.

Home Schooling

Growing numbers of parents are opting for home schooling—teaching their children at home. Reasons for the growth in home schooling are several. First, some parents are generally dissatisfied with the public schools. They object to outcome-based education, lack of individual attention to their children, school violence, and the lack of high achievement standards. Second, some parents believe home schooling is an appropriate way to inculcate the religious values of their choice into their children's value systems. In fact, the exclusion of religious advocacy from the public school curriculum and parents' perceptions that the schools completely ignore or pay little attention to the direct teaching of basic moral values are strong motivators for them to consider home schooling. Third, proponents of family strengthening see home schooling as a contributor to family stability. Finally, some parents believe children learn best when they decide for themselves what, when, and how they will learn. Conditioned by television and newspaper stories of the "hurried child," wary of some educators' efforts to "push" children, and the emphasis in the primary grades on basic education, some parents think home schooling is a natural alternative to these pressures of public schooling.

Before the advent of compulsory public schooling in 1836, home schooling was somewhat widespread. But as education became public, home schooling declined. Since the early 1990s, however, there has been a steady increase in the number of parents who are taking their children out of school to teach them at home. It is difficult to determine exactly how many parents are using home schooling, but estimates are that parents are educating between 800 thousand and 900 thousand children at home.[54] While most states permit home schooling, the conditions and restrictions for doing so vary from state to state. Some states require parents who home school to be certified. Other states do not require certification.

Critics of home schooling question whether people who are not certified teachers can do a good job of teaching their children at home. Critics also argue that home schooling denies children many social opportunities that are a part of becoming a good citizen. Home schoolers counter that their children's social needs are more than fulfilled through church groups, sports teams, community clubs and organizations, and involvement in service activities.

Tension exists among parents who believe they have the right to provide an alternative equivalent education for their children, those who believe strongly in compulsory public school attendance, and those who believe that home-schooled students should be tested to ensure that they are receiving an equivalent education. Critics think the home school movement undermines the traditional role of the public schools.

Do you think parents who home school their children limit their children's opportunities later in life? Why or why not?

_____

_____

_____

_____

SECTION SUMMARY

What Are Parents' Rights and Responsibilities?

Although their presence may be less noticeable, parents also have rights in the U.S. educational system.

- Parental Information and Consent. Parents have rights to be informed about their child's progress and behavior and to give or withhold consent for school activities and for some forms of discipline. Parents have a significant voice in decisions about the education of their children with disabilities.

- Compulsory School Attendance. Parents are responsible for feeding, clothing, and controlling the education of their children. They must observe state laws governing school attendance and immunizations of children, though the Supreme Court has made some exceptions to compulsory school attendance to protect the rights of certain groups, such as the Amish.

- Home Schooling. Many parents are educating their children at home, for a variety of reasons: dissatisfaction with the quality of public education, with the separation of church and state, with the lack of emphasis on family bonds, and with the pressures of public schooling.

If states require proof of a negative TB test only from recently immigrated students, is this a form of discrimination?

_____

_____

_____ ★

**Applying What
You've Learned**

★ ★ ★ ★ ★ ★ ★ ★

What parental consent forms does your school district require for student participation in school programs and activities? Ask some local school administrators and find out.

_____

_____

_____

_____ ★

**Putting Yourself
in the Picture**

★ ★ ★ ★ ★ ★ ★ ★

Some friends of yours tell you that they are so unhappy with the limited resources and strict policies of the local school system that they are considering home schooling their five-year-old twins. What will you tell them about home schooling and about public schooling?

_____

_____

_____

_____ ★

Applications for Active Learning

CONNECTIONS

1. In the opening case, what could the athletics director have done to avoid being sued for negligence?

_____

_____

_____

2. Think about the concepts and topics in this chapter. Create a picture, graphic, or figure that shows connections

that are meaningful to you among this chapter's key ideas and information.

FIELD EXPERIENCES

1. Interview school district administrators to determine how integration is achieved in their districts. What legal and political issues has the district addressed to achieve integration?

_____

_____

_____

2. Interview teachers, parents, and students on their views about teaching religion as a content area subject.

PERSONAL RESEARCH

1. Identify three teacher behaviors you have encountered that you think constituted unethical practice.

_____

_____

_____

2. Choose any one of the cases identified in Figures 8.2 (p. 273) or 8.6 (p. 299) and do some library research on it. Prepare a two-page summary describing the individuals, issues, and questions of constitutional rights in the case.

Preparing to Teach

FOR YOUR PORTFOLIO

1. Add to your portfolio the materials you collected on school policies regarding ethical practice, sexual harassment, child abuse, discipline codes, and safety codes. For each document, include your assessment of the points you regard as the most important for you to know.

2. Write a paragraph about why you believe it is important for the teaching profession to have a code of ethical practice.

IDEA FILE

Gather articles from daily newspapers, *Education Week*, and journals such as the *School Law Journal, School Bulletin,* and *School Law Reporter* relating to the legal rights of students, teachers, and parents. Place these in your idea file for future reference.

Learning and Knowing More

WEB SITES WORTH VISITING

The United States Supreme Court has a powerful influence on education. You can access all the Supreme Court decisions from 1937 to the present through the following Web site: www.fedworld.gov/supcourt/index.htm. Another source of United States Supreme Court cases is Oyez Oyez Oyez at http://oyez.at.nwu.edu/oyez.html.

Select one of the cases that you have read about in this chapter and research it in more detail. An interesting case to analyze is the 1987 *Edwards v. Aguillar* decision, which deals with the teaching of creation science.

National Committee to Prevent Child Abuse
www.childabuse.org
The National Committee to Prevent Child Abuse was established in 1972 to build a nationwide commitment to preventing all forms of child abuse. The NCPCA

plays a vital role in spreading the message of child abuse prevention to the public and encouraging the public to get involved. The site contains information and links to various Web pages, which give more information relating to child abuse.

National Association for Bilingual Education
www.nabe.org
The National Association for Bilingual Education was founded in 1975 to address the educational needs of language-minority students in the United States and to advance the language competencies and multicultural understanding of all Americans. The site contains current information, including information regarding California's Proposition 227.

United States Supreme Court Research
www.usscplus.com
"USSC+" data base is a searchable data base of Supreme Court decisions. The Web site contains information on

the history of the Supreme Court as well as on books and CD-ROM resources for use in researching the Supreme Court.

FindLaw Internet Legal Resources
www.findlaw.com
FindLaw is a searchable data base of Supreme Court opinions. The data base is easy to use and includes Supreme Court decisions since 1893. The site also contains information regarding the U.S. Constitution.

The Legal Information Institute
http://supct.law.cornell.edu/supct
The Legal Information Institute offers Supreme Court opinions under the auspices of Project Hermes, the Court's electronic dissemination project. This archive contains opinions of the court since 1990.

National Home Educators Research Institute
www.nheri.org
The NHERI Web site contains various amounts of information regarding home schooling. NHERI stands by its mission to produce high-quality statistics, research, and technical reports on home schooling.

National Homeschool Association
www.n-h-a.org
The National Homeschool Association works for one common purpose: the freedom of parents to choose for their children an education consistent with their principles and beliefs. The NHA Web site provides vital information for parents and families to help them with issues regarding home schooling.

Cornell Law School
www.lawschool.cornell.edu
The Cornell Law School Web site is easy to use and provides access to court decisions, news related to court cases, directories, and current awareness items.

CNN
www.cnn.com/law
CNN operates a number of useful Web sites, including Law Center, which reports on state, national, and international court proceedings.

Library of Congress
http://catalog.loc.gov
The Library of Congress Catalog provides a quick way to access the texts of government bills, including those related to education.

The American Bar Association
www.abanet.org
The American Bar Association's Web site provides access to its journal, analyses of court decisions, and a large data base of court decisions.

National Education Association
www.nea.org
The National Education Association's Web site offers legal information and a number of teaching supports for beginning teachers.

The Emory University School of Law
www.law.emory.edu
This Web site provides easy access to both Supreme Court and state court rulings on current and past school-related cases.

The National Park Service
www.nps.gov/brvb
This site commemorates the landmark Supreme Court decision (*Brown v. Board of Education*) aimed at ending segregation in public schools.

The National Clearing House on Child Abuse and Neglect Information
www.calib.com/nccanch/
The National Clearing House on Child Abuse and Neglect Information contains valuable information about these issues.

BOOKS WORTH READING

Barker, L., et al. (1999). *Civil Liberties and the Constitution: Cases and Commentaries* (8th ed.). Englewood Cliffs, NJ: Prentice Hall.
This time-honored text/casebook explores civil liberty problems through a study of leading judicial decisions—primarily those of the United States Supreme Court—and assesses the overall political-social context in which the formulation and implementation of civil liberties policies took place.

Essex, N. L. (2001). *School Law and the Public Schools: A Practical Guide for Educational Leaders.* Boston: Allyn & Bacon.
Comprehensive and practical coverage of the relevant legal issues that affect the organization and administration of public schools is found in this guide, which employs minimal legal jargon and timely court case studies.

Hinchey, P. H. (2001). *Student Rights: A Reference Handbook.* Santa Barbara, CA: ABC-CLIO.
This thorough and readable survey of the legal status of students presents a historical overview and a review of key legislation, including discussions of landmark Supreme Court decisions and their impact on school policies as well as contemporary parents' rights movements.

LaMorte, M. W. (2001). *School Law: Cases and Concepts* (6th ed.). Boston: Allyn & Bacon.
This book is written for educators with little background in school law. It focuses on an understanding of legal rationale and principles. This new edition examines the sources of law under which educators operate, the legal constraints to state action in the educational arena, the legal rights and restrictions applicable to students and teachers, the historical and legal foundations of both desegregation and recent school finance reform, the law pertaining to disabilities, and educator and school district liability.

McCarthy, M. M., Cambron-McCabe, N. H., and Thomas, S. B. (2003). *Public School Law: Teachers' and Students' Rights* (4th ed.). Boston: Allyn & Bacon.
This book provides a comprehensive treatment of the evolution and current status of the law governing public

schools. The text addresses legal principles applicable to practitioners in a succinct but comprehensive manner.

Palestini, R. H., and Palestini, K. F. (2002). *Law and American Education*. Lanham, MD: Scarecrow Press.

This text provides introductory material for educators interested in K–12 educational issues who have little or no background knowledge in school law.

Valente, W. D., and Valente, C. M. (2000). *Law in the Schools*. Englewood Cliffs, NJ: Prentice Hall.

The authors thoroughly cover the legal principles governing American schools, both public and private, and discuss the origin and development of laws pertaining to schools. The book explores the many ways in which laws influence specific educational policies, practices, and goals.

CHAPTER 9

*H*istorical and Philosophical Influences on Teaching and Learning in America

"An important part of being a professional."

Susan Santos is completing her third year as an eleventh-grade history teacher in a professional development school. (See Chapter 2 for an explanation of professional development schools.) An expert on the history of American education, Susan enjoys talking with undergraduate university students about this.

I've always been fascinated by the history of education—the undergraduates who teach at my school know that, and they often ask me to recommend books to read when they have reports due for their Introduction to Education course. A few weeks ago, one of their professors, Dr. Lepeda, asked if I would participate in a panel discussion for the course that was being taught at the school site.

"We'll be talking about the history of education, and how important it is for teachers today to know and understand it. You clearly have a lot of good ideas in that area, and my students seem to have a good rapport with you. It should be fun—and you might learn something as well! We'll have an initial planning meeting on Wednesday, after school. Can you make it?"

I was flattered and honored. I had very much enjoyed my own Introduction to Education course, and I've really benefited from reading about how influential educators have had an impact on education and teaching. But I was nervous as well. I wanted to share my own enthusiasm for both teaching and the history of education, and I wanted to provide real, useful information, and I wasn't sure I could do a good job.

Over the next week, before the planning meeting, I talked with colleagues, looked back through some of the books on the history of education that had most influenced me, and spent several hours sitting with a notepad, reflecting and clarifying my own thoughts. I decided to focus on why understanding the foundations of education forms a critical part of the knowledge base for any teacher—how that understanding helps us be better teachers.

At the planning meeting, I realized that the other two panel members were both professors, and I wondered again if I what I had to say would be as important as what they had to say. I needn't have worried! When the day came, it was clear that the undergraduates were really interested in the thoughts of someone who was out there in the classroom. Here's what I said:

Knowing the background that forms the basis of our beliefs, ideas, and practices helps us put education in perspective. If we know what happened in the past, we will have a better appreciation of what is happening today. When I was in college, I read about how those who don't know history are condemned to repeat it—and that's true in education as well.

Knowing about what happened in the past helps me understand why I do things the way I do them and why schools operate as they do. For example, because I know about John Dewey and progressivism, I can better understand student-centered practices of today—and I realize that we are not inventing something new but rather building on what came before. Because I read and learned about the impact of industrialization on schools in the last decades of the nineteenth century, I can better understand how and why schools of today are organized on an industrial or factory model.

In fact, what I've found is that almost everything we do in schools today has its roots in something that educators did before us. Isn't knowing about your profession an important part of being a professional?

How Will This Chapter Help You?

You will learn

★ about the history of education in America

★ why the history of education is important for you as a teacher

★ how American education has changed from 1776 to the present

★ why knowing about the philosophy of education is important and how it can influence education and your teaching

★ how philosophies of education are applied to curriculum and instruction

Susan's question, at the beginning of this chapter, "Isn't knowing about your profession an important part of being a professional?" opens the discussion of the historical influences on teaching and learning. How can Susan's question be answered? By asking another question: "How did we go from schools and education in colonial America to the vast network of school districts and schools that we have today?" From the time the first colonists set foot in the Americas to the present day, American education has undergone many changes and transformations. What schools are like today is a result of what schools were like in years past, just as what schools will be like in the future will be based on what schools are like today. Looking to the past helps us understand some of the basic forces that have influenced American education throughout the years. As Susan said, knowing the history of education helps us have a better appreciation of what is happening today. This knowledge helps us understand why schools function as they do and to see how ideas that originated in colonial times still influence education today. The following themes in contemporary education were shaped by the history of education in the United States:

- Universal education for all children is a powerful theme in American educational history. In the colonial period, education was limited to a wealthy, privileged few. However, through the centuries, the promise of universal education for all has influenced who and what we teach. This theme shapes contemporary educational thought and practice, even to the extent of universal public school education of three- and four-year-old children.
- Local control of schools is a hallowed principle that has developed throughout the growth of American education. A tension exists between those who advocate local control of schools and those who feel the state and the national governments need to have more authority over local education.
- Disagreement over what should be taught (the basic curriculum) and how it should be taught (appropriate methods of instruction) has existed for centuries, with changes in curriculum often reflecting the changing needs of society. Such debate continues as educational leaders search for the best ways to help all students learn to their fullest capacities.

Understanding the history of the profession you are about to enter enables you to put what is happening today into context and to better understand the forces and issues that help shape American public education today.

𝒲HAT WAS SCHOOLING LIKE IN THE AMERICAN COLONIES?

Education in colonial America was influenced by the earliest settlers who came from Europe. In this regard, all European roots influenced American education, with the result that education in the American colonies was very diverse. This educational diversity continues to influence contemporary educational organization, curriculum, and practice.

Colonial schools and the process of schooling were not organized as is schooling today.

> Colonial school arrangements were casual and the result of mere custom when not specifically adapted to local peculiarities. Many schools were not permanent or located in one place or so located that all the children could have access to a school. School terms were short, the most frequent term being three months. The attendance was irregular and there was no established curriculum in the lower or common schools. Teachers had no formal preparation in regard to how or what to teach, and they made the curriculum out of what they knew and what books they had at hand.[1]

Religion played a very powerful role in the development of colonial schools, both in how they were organized and in what they taught. Bible reading and prayer were a major part of the school curriculum well into the twentieth century. As you read in Chapter 8, these are major issues in many schools today. During colonial times, as now, religious groups wanted to rear and educate children their way and established schools to do so. The desire for religious freedom helped contribute to the doctrine of separation of church and state.[2] As you read about the development of education in the United States, keep in mind that the educational thoughts and ideas of sixteenth- and seventeenth-century Europe are the foundations of American education.

The New England Colonies

The Massachusetts Law of 1642 was the first school law relating to education in America that required parents and masters of apprentices to see that children learned to read.

> "In every towne ye chosen men" shall see that parents and masters not only train their children in learning and labor, but also "to read & understand the principles of religion & the capital lawes of this country," with power to impose fines on such as refuse to render accounts concerning their children.[3]

In 1647, Massachusetts passed the Massachusetts Act, often referred to as the **Old Deluder Satan Act,** which set the pattern for compulsory education in New England.

Old Deluder Satan Act
The Massachusetts Act (1647), which set the pattern for compulsory education in New England.

> It being one chief project of that old deluder, Satan, to keep men from the knowledge of the Scriptures. . . . It is there for ordered that every township in this jurisdiction, after the Lord hath increased them [in] number to fifty householders, shall then forthwith appoint one within their town to teach all such children as shall resort to him to write and read, whose wages shall be paid either by the parents or masters of such children, or by the inhabitants in general, by way of supply, as the major part of those that order the prudentials [affairs] of the town shall appoint; provided those that send their children be not oppressed by paying much more than they can have them taught for in other towns.[4]

These two laws made it possible for the people to have the kind of schools they needed to achieve the religious and social goals on which the colonies were founded. They also became models for laws of other states seeking to provide education for all children of both sexes.

Reflect & Write

What are some ways that religion influences the development of education in America today?

_____

_____

_____

_____

Dame Schools and Hornbooks. Typical of common school education were the **dame schools.** These were open to girls and boys and were operated by women who, for a modest fee, gave children lessons in spelling and reading. In order to learn to write and read, children went to an elementary school of some kind—a neighborhood school, private school, or church-supported parochial school.

Dame schools
A common school education open to girls and boys and taught by women.

The **hornbook** was one of the instructional devices used in the dame school. It was a frame of wood with a handle, similar in shape to a mirror. Attached to the frame was a sheet of paper containing the alphabet, Lord's Prayer, and numbers. This was covered with a transparent piece of horn that served to protect the paper.

Hornbook
An instructional device used in the dame school that was shaped like a mirror and had attached to its frame a sheet of paper containing the alphabet, Lord's Prayer, and numbers.

The New England Primer. Three books that influenced the curriculum of schooling in America were *The New England Primer*, Noah Webster's *Spelling Book*, and William

Primer
A small introductory book on a sub-ject; generally, a book intended to teach children to read.

McGuffey's *Eclectic Reader.* A **primer** is a first book, generally one intended to teach children to read. *The New England Primer,* called "the great beginning school book," served the purposes of educating children and youth in religious belief and the author-ity of God, family, and government and promoting morality. Students did not merely read *The New England Primer,* they memorized it. Through memorization and recita-tion, children learned the alphabet as they learned moral truths (see Figure 9.1).[5]

Latin Grammar Schools. The Boston Latin School, founded in 1635, was the first public grammar school in America. Typically, boys between the ages of 8 and 16 attended these schools. The purpose of the **Latin grammar schools** was college preparation.

Latin grammar schools
Colonial schools established to provide male students a precollege education; comparable to today's high school.

Since the purpose of the Latin grammar schools was college preparatory, it is understandable that the curriculum was traditional and classical in nature. The num-ber of students who attended these schools was small, and no women at all attended. The major problem with the Latin grammar school was that "it was not well adapted to the frontier. Before the end of the colonial period, a new institution, the academy, began to take its place because it was a more flexible institution and better adapted to a new country."[6]

The Middle Colonies

In the middle colonies—Pennsylvania, New York, New Jersey, and Maryland—people were more culturally and religiously diverse than they were in the New England colo-nies. Because of this diversity, schools were also more diverse. Separation of church

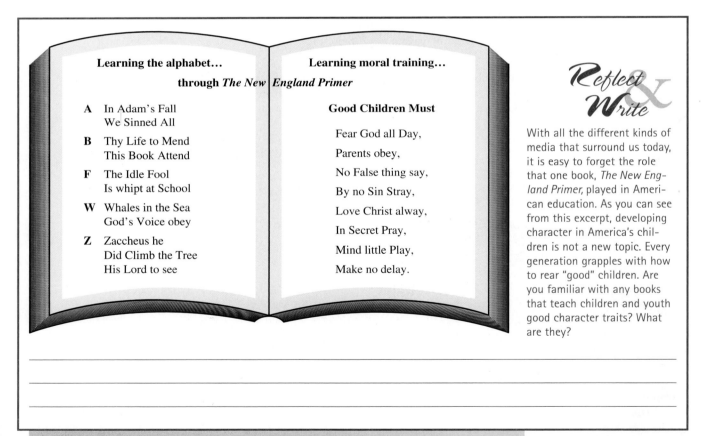

Figure 9.1 *ABCs and Moral Training in The New England Primer*

Source: P. L. Ford, *The New England Primer: A History of Its Origin and Development* (New York: Teachers College Press, 1962). Reprinted by permission.

and government was more common, and differences in religious beliefs were more accepted. All of these conditions affected school development.

Quaker Schools. In the middle colonies, education was more the responsibility of churches than government. For this reason, parochial or denominational education flourished in the middle colonies. In particular, "the Quakers were the most active group in education. George Fox, founder of the Society of Friends, believed that schools should be open to all classes and races, and he placed emphasis upon moral and religious instruction."[7]

Additionally, Quakers were strong proponents of equal education for women. The opening up of educational opportunities for women came slowly and gradually. The primary focus of women's education was providing roles for women as wives and mothers. Benjamin Rush, a tireless promoter of education, proposed a broad curriculum for women that included reading, writing, grammar, arithmetic, bookkeeping, geography, history, vocal music, dancing, and religion.[8]

Franklin's Academy. The middle colonies were involved in commerce and trade. Consequently, schools provided instruction—such as navigation, surveying, and bookkeeping—that would prepare students for work. Benjamin Franklin's Academy, opened in Philadelphia in 1751, taught these as well as traditional subjects.

> All should be taught to write a fair hand, and swift, as that is useful to all. And with it may be learnt something of drawing, by imitation of prints, and some of the first principles of perspective. Arithmetic, accounts, and some of the first principles of geometry and astronomy. The English language might be taught by grammar; in

What did students learn in the eighteenth-century school? How and why did educational aims and institutions vary so widely from one American colony to the next?

which some of our best writers, as Tillotson, Addison, Pope, Algernon Sidney, Cato's *Letters*, etc. should be classic. The style principally to be cultivated, being the clear and the concise.

Reading should also be taught, and pronouncing, properly, distinctly, emphatically, not with an even tone, which underdoes, nor a theatrical, which overdoes nature.

To form their style they should be put on writing letters to each other, making abstracts of what they read or writing the same things in their own words; telling or writing stories lately read, in their own expressions. All to be revised and corrected by the tutor who should give his reasons, explain the force and import of words, etc.[9]

The Southern Colonies

As with the other colonies, the nature and character of the southern colonies determined the system of schooling. Education in the southern colonies was characterized by three tiers or levels. At the top were wealthy landowners who hired tutors for their children and sent them abroad for higher education. Free, poor, small farmers constituted the vast majority of the population. This group had very limited access to education.

For slaves, educational opportunities were almost nonexistent. In fact, educating slaves was a felony in some states before the Civil War. Wealthy landowners were little interested in educating slaves because they thought learning and literacy would lead to rebellion. Education consisted of training for field and housework, with some provisions for apprenticeship to learn trades. Efforts of missionaries to educate slaves were largely ineffectual. By 1863 and the Emancipation Proclamation, the literacy rate among slaves was about 5 percent.[10]

Education and Native Americans

INTASC

Standard 3: The teacher understands how students differ in their approaches to learning and creates instructional opportunities that are adapted to diverse learners.

Education in the Spanish-settled lands of the Southwest was provided by Catholic missionaries. Instruction was conducted in Spanish and was designed to spread the Catholic faith and Spanish culture. In addition, education was designed to help keep territories held by Spain under Spanish control and to enculturate people into a way of life. For example:

The missions were far more than religious outposts: They were social institutions, designed to transform the Indians from scattered hunting and gathering peoples into disciplined farmers, ranchers, and cloth weavers clustered around, and faithful to the church.[11]

The history of Native American education consists of basically two phases. From the sixteenth century to the twentieth century, its aims were the neglect, full assimilation, or eradication of Indian cultures. Many people thought that Indians were not capable of being educated and civilized, so there was no need to do anything. Others thought the best policy was to use education to eradicate Native American culture and substitute European cultures and values. The second phase, self-determination, became a feature of the twentieth century.

SECTION SUMMARY

What Was Schooling Like in the American Colonies?

Education in the American colonies was influenced by European ideas and the diversity of settlers and their colonial cultures. Colonial schooling provided a common education and apprenticeships for the working class and a higher-level education for future ministers, doctors, and lawyers.

- The New England Colonies. Massachusetts passed laws requiring compulsory public education as a means of achieving the religious and social goals of the New

England colonies. Public schools developed through the Latin grammar schools, which were designed to prepare students for college.

- The Middle Colonies. In the middle colonies, schools were more culturally and religiously diverse than in the New England colonies. Separation of church and state was the accepted practice. Schools were more the responsibility of churches than of government. Quaker schools were proponents of education for women. Benjamin Franklin's Academy taught practical subjects and prepared students for work.

- The Southern Colonies. In the southern colonies, children of slaveowners were first tutored at home and later educated abroad. Small farmowners had little access to education. Education for slaves was prohibited by law in most areas.

- Education and Native Americans. In the Southwest, missionaries provided most education. Instruction was in Spanish and focused on the Catholic religion and Spanish culture. Education was part of a larger goal of conquest and eradication of native cultures.

Thinking Critically
★ ★ ★ ★ ★ ★ ★ ★

Identify several educational themes from the colonial period (for example, literacy for all) that are influencing educational practice today.

_____

_____

_____

_____ ★

Applying What You've Learned
★ ★ ★ ★ ★ ★ ★ ★

Investigate the history of education in your state, district, or school. Which of the colonial traditions is most prominent in your state? What is your evidence for your views?

_____

_____

_____

_____ ★

Putting Yourself in the Picture
★ ★ ★ ★ ★ ★ ★ ★

Imagine that you are a teacher in a colonial classroom, that you have three months in which to educate your students, and that there is no set curriculum. What will you teach, and why will you teach it?

_____

_____

_____

_____ ★

HOW DID AMERICAN EDUCATION CHANGE AFTER NATIONHOOD?

Thomas Jefferson strongly believed that the new states could not and would not long endure if people were ignorant of the laws of government and their roles in the new social order. Furthermore, Jefferson and others believed a democratic government would be only as strong as the ability of its citizenry to make intelligent choices. Jefferson remarked that "if a nation expects to be ignorant and free, in a state of civilization, it expects what never was and never will be."[12] Jefferson and others who were influenced by Enlightenment ideas believed that education was a natural right of people, just as were life, liberty, and the pursuit of happiness.

Nationhood brought a demand for education that would provide citizens who could uphold a democracy. Nationhood also brought demand for more practical and modern education. The Latin grammar schools of New England were gradually replaced by common schools devoted to universal free public education.

Two events hastened the growth and expansion of schools. The first was the Northwest Ordinance Acts of 1785 and 1787. These acts provided for the disposing of the Northwest Territories. As states were formed, they were required to set aside the sixteenth section in each township for the support of public schools. The ordinance said in part, "Religion, morality, and knowledge being necessary to good government and the happiness of mankind, schools and the means of education shall forever be encouraged."[13]

The second event was the Kalamazoo case, decided by the Michigan Supreme Court in 1873, which upheld the use of tax money to support common schools. This gave the schools, through their boards of education, the power to levy taxes to support schooling.

Do you agree with Jefferson that education is essential for a free society? How does this ideal apply to society today?

_____

_____

_____

_____

The Development of Common Schools

Common schools were designed to educate all children equally using the same kind of curriculum. The growth and popularity of the common schools were based on two basic assumptions: Schools for all could cure the major social, economic, and political problems of society, and schools for all were necessary for the survival of democratic society. Horace Mann was a champion of public education and teacher education and a strong advocate for and supporter of the common school. He believed that common schools were the best way to educate Americans. Although it is difficult to assign a specific date to the beginning of common schools, it was most likely in 1837, when Horace Mann became secretary of the Massachusetts State Board of Education.

The common school movement coincided with rapid industrialization and urbanization in the United States, along with high rates of immigration. One purpose of these schools was to "Americanize" immigrants. Another purpose was to provide skilled and semiskilled laborers for the factories. Common schools admitted young children, were free, and were open to all children.

The Spread of Education for Women

The spread of education for women is related in many ways to the growth and popularity of the common school. In rural schools, classes were mixed. In large urban areas, especially in the East, "single-sex schools were numerous, if not the norm." However, "the principles of common schooling argued against separation of the sexes."[14]

[By] the last decade of the [nineteenth] century, coeducation emerged as the dominant form of public education in the nation's cities. More conservative areas such as the South joined the older eastern cities in leaning toward separate schools for boys and girls, particularly in the high schools. Generally speaking, however, coeducation won out.

Furthermore:

Coeducation was advanced by the developing dominance of women as classroom teachers in this period. Thus, the feminization of the nation's teaching force helped to cement coeducation as a firm, if not completely dominant, presence in the nation's urban schools.[15]

Emma Willard was one of the pioneers of women's education. In 1814, Willard opened a boarding school for girls in Middlebury, Vermont, and the success of her school encouraged her to become an advocate for education for girls comparable to that of boys. Willard was named superintendent of the Kensington, Connecticut, schools in 1840, the first woman to hold such an office. (See the Profile.) Figure 9.3 highlights the events in the education of women.

Profile — Emma Hart Willard's Plan for the Education of Women

Emma Willard was one of the pioneers of women's education.

In 1814, Willard opened a boarding school for girls in Middlebury, Vermont, and the success of her school encouraged her to become an advocate for education for girls comparable to that of boys. She developed a "plan for improving female education," published in 1819, which is considered the Magna Carta of women's education. The plan had four parts: "First, an analysis of defects in the education of women; next, a statement of the principles which should regulate education; third, a description of a well-planned female seminary; and finally, an eloquent recital of the benefits the nation should reap from seminaries."

Willard published and distributed the plan at her own expense. It captured the attention of DeWitt Clinton, the governor of New York, who asked the legislature to fund "the only attempt ever made in this country to promote the education of the female sex by the patronage of government." The legislature provided a charter, but no funding.

In the meantime, the citizens of Troy, New York, purchased a building to house the school, and in 1821 Willard opened her Troy School to ninety young women from seven states. The seminary, a school of secondary or higher education for women, had a curriculum that included mathematics, geography, history, and physiology—a radical course of studies for that time. The average age of the student body was seventeen and included the daughters of many governors. Public examinations were held in February and July of each year, and noted professors conducted the tests. These examinations were a social and academic highlight of Troy and attracted large crowds of spectators to hear the young women.

In 1838, Willard left the management of her school to her son and daughter-in-law and helped Henry Bernard, Connecticut superintendent of schools, in championing the cause of education. Willard was named superintendent of the Kensington, Connecticut, schools in 1840, the first woman to hold such an office. In 1910, the Troy Seminary was named the Emma Willard School and today enrolls 289 girls in grades 9 through 12.

From the beginning of her educational endeavors, Willard encouraged her students to prepare for the teaching profession. She "stated that she sent forth from Troy two hundred trained graduates before one teacher was graduated from a public normal school."

Emma Hart Willard

MAJOR EVENTS IN WOMEN'S EDUCATION

1850 Harvard Medical School admits its first woman—Harriot Kezia Hunt, age 44. Hunt withdraws from Harvard after riots by male students protesting her admission.

1875 The Wellesley College for Women opens on September 8 in Wellesley, Massachusetts; the college began the first rowing program for women. One day later, Smith College, also exclusively for women, opens in Northhampton, Massachusetts.

1925 Florence Sabin, one of the era's foremost scientists, becomes the first woman elected to the National Academy of Sciences and the first woman elected to full membership in the Rockefeller Institute.

1975 Title IX goes into effect on June 21. Title IX mandates that all schools allocate equal resources to male and female athletic programs, opening more athletic opportunities to girls and young women.

1975 Women are admitted to the U.S. military academies under a new law signed by President Gerald Ford.

1998 The educational attainment levels of women ages 25 to 29 exceed those of men in the same age group. Ninety percent of women have at least a high school diploma and 29 percent have a bachelor's degree or more; for men, the respective percentages are 87 percent and 26 percent.

2000 More than 2.5 million girls take part in high school athletic programs during the 1997–1998 school year—triple the number that participated in 1972–1973.

Reflect & Write

Women have been making strides toward equality and empowerment for years. In the late 1990s, women's educational levels actually began to outpace men's. What differences do you think this might make to public education in the twenty-first century?

Figure 9.2 *M*ajor Events in Women's Education

Source: Created by author from data drawn from "Timeline of U.S. Women's History," *Family Education.* (Online). Available at http://familyeducation.com/article/print/0,1303,24-12688,00.html?obj_gra.

The Expansion of High School Education

The first high school in the United States was the English Classical School of Boston. Its name was later changed to English High School. This first high school was quite different from the contemporary high school you attended. It was not coeducational and served students we would now consider middle school or junior high school age—from 12 to 15. As in elementary schools, students stayed in the same room with the same teacher all day, and they studied a fixed curriculum: composition, declamation, math, history, civics, logic, navigation, surveying, and moral and political philosophy.[16]

Secondary education remained small scale until the early twentieth century; as late as 1910, only about 10 percent of American youth attended high school. Until the twentieth century, most Americans' formal education ended with elementary school, where they learned to read (especially the Bible), write, and do simple arithmetic. This was sufficient for their agrarian lifestyles. Books, magazines, and newspapers were scarce, and teenage labor was needed in the fields.

The Monitorial System of Public Education

During the 1700s and early 1800s, education remained primarily a system of private schools intended to educate the children of those who could afford to pay. This left out the children of the poor who could not afford to pay. Philanthropic schools, supported by charities and other agencies, provided education for some children, but certainly not enough and most important, not for all. A system developed by Joseph Lancaster (1753–1838), known as the **monitorial system,** offered the promise of educating more children more cost-effectively.

The monitorial system, also known as the mutual instruction system, offered the nation's school reformers an opportunity to teach moral character as a means of reforming society. It also served as a transition from private to public education. A major reason this was possible was because the monitorial system offered a cost-effective approach to education. Cost efficiency continues to be a major consideration in the funding of education.

The New York Free School Society, whose primary purpose was to provide a free education to the poor in order to create good moral character, was a major supporter of the monitorial system. The first monitorial system was opened in New York in 1806 and thereafter quickly spread to cities throughout the nation.

> Pupils were seated in rows and received their instruction from monitors, who received their instruction from the master, who sat at the end of the room. Monitors were selected from among the better students in the class, and they wore badges indicating their rank.[17]

The monitorial system was remarkably efficient and suited to educating large numbers of students for a specific purpose because so many students could be educated at once. However, this system did not lead to high-quality education because large numbers of students were educated by a few older students.

Monitorial system
A system devised for teaching large groups of students by which a master teacher instructed monitors and they, in turn, instructed younger children.

INTASC

Standard 4: The teacher uses various instructional strategies to encourage students' development of critical thinking, problem solving, and performance skills.

Textbooks for Americans

Nationhood also increased demand for American textbooks to replace European educational materials. Noah Webster, the "school master of the Republic," was a champion of public education and advocated the teaching of American language as a means of helping to unify the country. In 1783, Webster published *The American Spelling Book,* one of three in a series devoted to spelling, grammar, and reading. *The American Spelling Book,* or *Blue-Back Speller* as it is commonly referred to, was designed to teach children the "rudiments" of the English language—pronunciation, spelling, grammar, and reading. In the process, it also taught them useful truths and practical information.

William Holmes McGuffey (1800–1873) published his first *Eclectic Reader* in 1836, which provided illustrated moral stories for reading instruction. The popularity of the **McGuffey readers** increased with the growth and expansion of common schools.

McGuffey readers
A popular series of reading books for students in grades 1 through 6, produced in 1836 by William Holmes McGuffey.

The Spread of Higher Education

The first colleges in the United States were modeled after Cambridge and Oxford in England. Students were mainly children of the wealthy, and the curriculum was the liberal arts. The first college was Harvard, founded in 1636, followed by William and Mary in 1693 and Yale in 1701.

In 1862, the Morrill Land Grant University Act granted each state 30,000 acres of public land for each of its congressional representatives to establish colleges of agriculture and mechanical education. These colleges were known as **land grant colleges.** They emphasized applied studies, helped popularize higher education, and made such education available and accessible to a large part of the population.

Land grant colleges
Public colleges of agriculture and mechanical or industrial arts established by federal funds guaranteed through the Morrill Act of 1862.

How did the early normal schools help advance education in America?

Formal teacher education also developed during the nineteenth century. At the urging of Horace Mann, in 1839 the Massachusetts legislature founded the first state-supported normal school in the United States for training women as teachers.

Normal schools
A two- or four-year teacher education institution in the 1800s and early 1900s.

Following the establishment of the first normal school in Massachusetts, other states followed suit. The first **normal schools** (*normal* means "common" or "natural") were two-year programs and admitted students right out of elementary school. It was not until the early 1900s that a high school diploma was necessary for entering a normal school. The normal school curriculum was similar to a high school program of studies, with additional courses in pedagogy and student teaching that often were provided in a laboratory school connected with the normal school.

In the 1930s, many normal schools started offering four-year programs and became state teacher colleges. In the 1950s, another evolutionary change occurred, and state teacher colleges became state colleges and offered master's degrees as part of the curriculum. Today, many institutions that began as normal schools and state teachers' colleges are state universities and offer doctoral degrees. All of these changes occurred in response to the need for more teachers, the need for highly trained teachers, and the professionalization of teaching.

SECTION SUMMARY

How Did American Education Change after Nationhood?

After nationhood, education became a state responsibility. Thomas Jefferson advocated publicly supported education to preserve liberty and uphold democracy. The growth of public schools was hastened by the Northwest Ordinance Acts, which set aside land for schools, and the Kalamazoo case, which upheld the use of tax money to support schools.

- The Development of Common Schools. Horace Mann was a champion of public education, a leader of the common school movement, and an advocate for teacher education. Common schools were designed to teach a common body of knowledge to all students.

- The Spread of Education for Women. Women attended single-sex schools in urban areas, especially in the East. Coeducation in urban schools was aided by the need for educated women, since most elementary school teachers were women during this period. Emma Willard was a pioneer in women's education.

- **The Expansion of High School Education.** Boston's English Classical School was the first U.S. high school. It did not provide a transition to higher education but rather awarded a terminal degree.
- **The Monitorial System of Public Education.** In the monitorial school system, students became the instructors and were supervised by master teachers. This low-cost system of education attempted to teach moral character as well as basic skills. Like common schools, these schools were a response to industrialization, urbanization, and mass immigration.
- **Textbooks for Americans.** Nationhood increased demands for American textbooks to replace European educational materials. Noah Webster's *The American Spelling Book* and William McGuffey's *Eclectic Reader* series came into use.
- **The Spread of Higher Education.** The growth of higher education was fostered by the Morrill Land Grant University Act and the spread of normal schools. Normal schools were two-year teacher preparation schools that evolved into the teachers' colleges of today.

Thinking Critically
★ ★ ★ ★ ★ ★ ★ ★ ★

Do you think schools should "Americanize" new immigrants? Does this mean eradicating the cultural traditions they could contribute?

Applying What You've Learned
★ ★ ★ ★ ★ ★ ★ ★ ★

Do some library research and find out more about the history of U.S. high schools in the early nineteenth century. Who typically attended them? Who taught them?

Putting Yourself in the Picture
★ ★ ★ ★ ★ ★ ★ ★ ★

There have been and continue to be attempts to have separate schools for boys and girls. Would you prefer teaching in a coeducational or single-sex classroom? What advantages do you see in each setting? What disadvantages?

*H*OW DID AMERICAN EDUCATION CHANGE AFTER THE CIVIL WAR*?*

Reconstruction, the period following the Civil War, was a time of upheaval and efforts to help the South and the nation recover. Economic and social conditions in the South were much different than those in the industrialized North. The land and people were suffering from the effects of the war. The economy was in disarray, people were displaced, and civil authority was limited. Schooling was not a high priority. (See the Profile.)

Profile Life in Nineteenth-Century Schools

A Rural Elementary School. According to Nita Thurman of the Denton (Texas) Historical Commission, elementary schools in 1876 were traditional one-room schoolhouses, usually with one teacher for all grades, although schools in larger areas sometimes had more rooms and several teachers. Restrooms were out back—one for boys and one for girls. The classroom had about five rows of double wooden desks with attached seats that were screwed into the floor, and the teacher sat on a raised platform with a desk at one end of the room. There was a blackboard, and each school had one world globe, a map of the United States, and an unabridged dictionary.

The school was heated by an iron wood-burning stove that—like all other wood-burning stoves—nearly cooked the students sitting nearby while leaving those farther away out in the cold. For dark, cloudy days, there was an oil lamp hanging from the ceiling. A pail of water and a communal dipper to drink from were also available.

A standard school day began early. The teacher arrived by 7 A.M. to prepare for the day, which included starting a fire in the iron stove if it was cold weather. Students arrived at about 8 A.M. As they entered the classroom, each boy had to bow from the waist, and each girl had to curtsey to the teacher.

The first lesson was reading, so everyone took out his or her *McGuffey Readers.* Students read aloud and sometimes dramatized the *McGuffey* "pieces."

Arithmetic came next, including the popular exercise called "mental arithmetic." This was problem solving without using pen or paper. Problems from *The Common School Arithmetic* usually were practical, asking, for example: If a farmer erects 72 feet of fencing each day, how much fencing will he complete in a fortnight?

Recess was next. Children went outside to use the toilets and to play games, including hide and go seek, marbles, catch the can, and pitching horseshoes. After recess, the students settled down for a writing lesson. They may have had pens and pencils, or they may have still used slates—rectangular pieces of real slate in a wooden frame. Pupils wrote on slates with the point of a thin rod of compressed slate powder. Slates were

handy because anything could be wiped off the slate with a cloth or a shirtsleeve.

Children usually brought their lunches and ate in the classroom. Sometimes the teacher had a pot of soup simmering on the wood stove.

Afternoon lessons were in history and geography. A spelling bee would end the day, and the children left for home between 4 and 5 P.M., but not the teacher—he or she still had to clean up the classroom and sweep the floor. The teacher's contract included custodial work as well as teaching all children for a munificent sum ranging from $4 to $12 a month.

A High School. A typical nineteenth-century high school might be a three-story brick building, small by modern standards, with white ceilings, cement floors, and utilitarian furnishings. The classes were big, with at least thirty students each, and discipline might be in the form of a paddle. Half the teachers didn't have college degrees; all were poorly paid. In New York State, the average teacher's salary in 1899 was $700 (the equivalent of about $15,000 today); in 1846 in Niles, Ohio, male teachers were paid $10 a month plus a hundred pounds of iron, produced by local furnaces; female teachers earned $6 a month. (Even then, however, teachers had to pass a certification exam administered by the county to teach in Niles.)

Many teachers were responsible for more than one subject and also had other tasks to do—training the choir or cutting firewood. Lessons were prescribed by textbooks like *McGuffey's New High School Reader* or *The Normal Mental Arithmetic.* The school was open about 135 days a year, but students actually attended an average of only 86 days. For all but America's most affluent families, secondary education was irrelevant: most trades didn't require it, and colleges admitted any man who passed their exams, regardless of where or how he was educated.

Source: N. Thurman, personal communication, September 2004; C. Crossen, "In 1860, America Had Forty Public High Schools; Teachers Chopped Wood," *Wall Street Journal*, Sept. 3, 2003, p. D2. Reprinted by permission.

Education for African Americans

The education of African Americans after the Civil War was enhanced and promoted through many agencies and by the heroic efforts of many dedicated individuals. Government census records indicate:

> Prior to the emancipation of Southern blacks, school enrollment for blacks largely was limited to only a small number in Northern states. Following the Civil War, the enrollment rate for blacks rose rapidly and the beginning 20th century brought sustained increases in enrollment rates. Today, enrollment of students in schools is 64.8 percent white and 16.8 percent African-American.[18]

Individuals such as Booker T. Washington played an important role in the development of education for African Americans. Washington taught himself to read, attended normal school, and became a teacher and then a principal at the state normal school for African Americans in Tuskegee, Alabama.[19] The Tuskegee Institute, now Tuskegee University, became a leading center for the education of African Americans, especially in vocational education. Tuskegee is one of eighty-nine four-year historically black colleges and universities in the United States. Washington advocated practical education in the trades for African Americans, in contrast to another pioneer in education, W. E. B. Du Bois. (See the Profile, p. 330.)

Mary McLeod Bethune (1875–1955), the daughter of former slaves, also advocated development of educational opportunities and civil rights for African Americans. In 1904 she founded the Daytona Normal and Industrial School for Training Negro Girls in Daytona Beach, Florida. Bethune later merged her school with an all-boys school in Jacksonville, and it was named Bethune-Cookman College.

As strong advocates for civil rights, Bethune, Du Bois, and others were instrumental in establishing the National Association for the Advancement of Colored People (NAACP), which has a long history of fighting for civil rights, promoting education, and helping African Americans and others secure their rights under the Constitution.

Can you identify ways in which the views of education of Booker T. Washington and W. E. B. Du Bois are reflected in American education today? In what ways can education be reformed to further provide for the education of African American students?

_____

_____

_____

_____

The Development of Indian Schools

Following the Civil War, the prime goal of educational programs for Native Americans was to assimilate them into American life by having them give up their culture and accept middle-class American culture.[22] Three types of schools were developed to undertake the task of Americanizing Native Americans. Mission schools were run by Catholic and Protestant denominations, many under contract with the federal government. The focus of the curriculum was the three Rs, vocational and agricultural education, and religion. Although the number of Native American children educated in mission schools was never great, such schools nonetheless did provide education before there were enough schools for these children.

Another type of school was the day boarding school operated by the **Bureau of Indian Affairs (BIA)** on reservations. In addition to these schools, a number of off-reservation boarding schools were established by the BIA. This was in keeping with the belief that the best way to "Americanize" Native American children was to remove them from their tribal setting and provide them with a strict program of cultural

INTASC

Standard 1: The teacher understands the central concepts, tools of inquiry, and structures of the subject being taught and can create learning experiences that make these aspects of subject matter meaningful for students.

Standard 2: The teacher understands how children learn and develop, and can provide learning opportunities that support their intellectual, social and personal development.

Standard 5: The teacher uses an understanding of individual and group motivation and behavior to create a learning environment that encourages positive social interaction, active engagement in learning, and self-motivation.

NCATE

Middle Level

Standard 1: Understands the major concepts, principles, theories and research related to young adolescent development; provides opportunities that support student development and learning.

Bureau of Indian Affairs (BIA) Responsible for all of the management and education functions for Native American education, which is conducted through the Office of Indian Education Programs (OIEP).

Contrasting Approaches to African American Education: Booker T. Washington and W. E. B. Du Bois

At the beginning of the twentieth century, two figures stood out as preeminent leaders in the African American community: Booker T. Washington and W. E. B. Du Bois.

Washington emphasized the need for a practical education in the trades to give African Americans who were unskilled workers a higher economic base. This emphasis on practical education led him to begin Tuskegee Institute, which later became Tuskegee University in Alabama. Washington's approach to the education and social standing of African Americans was to be accommodating to the social norms of the time.

In a speech to a largely non–African American audience at the Atlanta Exposition of 1895, Washington stated the following view about the relationship between African Americans and whites: "In all things that are purely social we can be as separate as the fingers, yet one as the hand in all things essential to mutual progress."[20]

This view was criticized by W. E. B. Du Bois, among others, who felt that accepting social separation carried with it an acceptance of social inferiority. Du Bois, who was the first African American to earn a Ph.D. from Harvard University, felt African Americans should not wait for full social and political equality. His educational views focused on teaching the "talented tenth" of the African American population to the fullest of their potential. Du Bois felt that if this segment of the African American community could complete university degrees,

W. E. B. Du Bois

they could take their place among the business, professional, and intellectual elite of the nation. The "talented tenth" would then provide opportunities for other segments of the African American population.

Du Bois expressed some of his views on education in a speech delivered in 1906 to the second annual meeting of the Niagara Movement:

> And when we call for education we mean real education. We are believers in work. We ourselves are workers, but work is not necessarily education. Education is the development of power and ideal. We want our children to be trained as intelligent human beings should be, and we will fight for all time against any proposal to educate black boys and girls simply as servants and underlings, or simply for the use of other people. They have the right to know, to think, to aspire.[21]

When comparing the educational views of these two men, their philosophies must be examined within the social and political climate of the time. Both men wanted to improve the educational and economic circumstances of African Americans. They differed in the degree to which they were willing to accept racial segregation in education and other areas in order to bring about social, economic, and educational progress to African Americans.

Booker T. Washington

transformation. Off-reservation boarding schools, such as the Carlisle (Pennsylvania) Indian School, founded by Richard Henry Pratt in 1879, reflected a harsh approach to assimilation. Pratt's goal, for example, was to "Kill the Indian, and save the Man."[23] Education bore no relationship to reservation life and forced Native American children and youth to reject their families and traditional ways of life.

Today, Native American education is conducted through the Office of Indian Education Programs (OIEP) located within the BIA in the Department of the Interior.

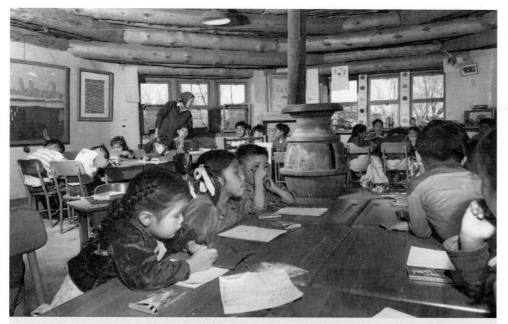

How has education for Native Americans changed between the colonial and the modern eras?

The BIA is responsible for all of the management and education functions. OIEP seeks to provide quality education opportunities from early childhood through life in accordance with Native Americans' needs for cultural and economic well-being. The education of Native Americans takes into account the spiritual, mental, physical, and cultural aspects of the person within a family and tribal or Alaskan native village contexts.[24] See Education on the Move for more information about progress in Native American education.

The Influence of European Developments in Education

After nationhood, American education continued to be influenced by developments in the European educational systems. Two important contributors to modern education were Friedrich Froebel and Maria Montessori.

Froebel's Kindergarten. Friedrich Froebel (1782–1852) devoted his life to developing a curriculum and methodology for educating young children and earned the distinction of "father of the kindergarten." Froebel's primary contributions to educational thought and practice are in the areas of learning, curriculum, methodology, and teacher training. He believed that the educator's role, whether parent or teacher, was to observe the natural unfolding of children's development and to provide activities that would enable them to learn what they were ready to learn when they were ready to learn it.

Froebel compared children to seeds that germinate, bring forth a new shoot, and grow from young, tender saplings to mature productive trees. He likened the role of educator to that of a gardener. In his **kindergarten,** or "garden of children," he envisioned children being educated in close harmony with their own natures and the nature of the universe. Children unfold their uniqueness in play, and it is in the area of unfolding and learning through play that Froebel makes one of his greatest contributions to early childhood curriculum.

Froebel developed a systematic, planned curriculum for the education of young children and was the first educator to encourage young, unmarried women to become teachers.

NCATE

Early Childhood

Standard 1: Uses understanding of young children's characteristics, needs, and interacting influences on children's development and learning to create healthy, respectful, supportive, and challenging environments for all children.

Standard 4: Integrates understanding of children and families, of developmentally effective approaches to teaching and learning, and of academic disciplines to design, implement, and evaluate positive learning experiences for all children.

Kindergarten
A program for children before they begin formal schooling at the elementary level based on the ideas of German educator Friedrich Froebel.

>>> Saving Tribal Languages >>>>>>>

Do you think much about what your world would be like if your native language—English, or Spanish, or Japanese, or Farsi, for example—simply didn't exist anymore? Probably not. But that's the situation confronting a number of Native American tribal groups. In Washington State, for example, the last two fluent speakers of the Makah tribal language died in 2002. Only ten people, all older than 65, still speak fluent Spokane. And the only skilled speakers of Lushootseed are elderly and frail and can no longer take part in their tribe's formal activities to pass on their language skills.

However, efforts are under way to save American Indian languages. In a program established in 2003, Washington State's twenty-eight federally recognized tribes will train and recommend to the state board people they deem to be qualified teachers of their languages. The state will offer a "first peoples language/culture" certification or endorsement, giving those candidates equal status with other certified teachers.

Washington's program is similar to programs in Oregon and Idaho as well as in Montana, which already has 133 teachers with such certification. On the Tulalip reservation in Washington, some eighty children are enrolled in the Lushootseed language program at Tulalip Elementary School.

Tribal languages have not always been valued. The father of Cherokee Nation Chief Chad Smith was punished for speaking Cherokee at Sequoyah High School, located at the seat of Cherokee government in Tahlequah. "If you spoke the language, your mouth was washed out with soap," Smith said. "It was an effort to destroy the language, and it was fairly successful."

But now, as in the Northwest, things are changing. In Lost City, Oklahoma, the kindergarten teacher speaks to her class in Cherokee, telling the children to pull out their mats for nap time. Using their Cherokee names, she instructs "Yona," or Bear, to place his mat away from "A-wi," or Deer. Soft Cherokee music lulls them to sleep.

These youngsters' parents were mocked for speaking Cherokee. Their grandparents were punished. But Cherokee is the only language these children will speak in their public school classroom. By immersing the youngsters in the language of their ancestors, tribal leaders are hoping to save on of the many endangered American Indian tongues.

"The language is going to be gone if we don't do something, and the best people to learn are kids in the developmental stage of kindergarten," said Annette Millard, a non-Cherokee who is superintendent of the Lost City School, with about one hundred students, two-thirds of them from the tribe. Tribal leaders say it is vital that the language survive.

"We have our medicine, our plant life, our universe, and the language the Creator has given us," said Harry Oosahwee, the tribe's language projects supervisor.

"Our medicine doesn't understand other languages but Cherokee. All this is interconnected."

Sources: M. A. Zehr, "Washington Program Strives to Sustain Tribal Languages," *Education Week*, February 5, 2003, p. 15. Available online at www.edweek.org/ew/ewstory.cfm?slug=21tribes.h.22. J. Burns, "Tribe Attempts to Save a Dying Language," (Denton) *Record-Chronicle*, September 20, 2003, p. 15, 17. Reprinted by permission.

INTASC

Standard 3: The teacher understands how students differ in their approaches to learning and creates instructional opportunities that are adapted to diverse learners.

NCATE

Early Childhood

Standard 4: Integrates understanding of children and families, of developmentally effective approaches to teaching and learning, and of academic disciplines to design, implement, and evaluate positive learning experiences for all children.

The Montessori Method. Maria Montessori (1870–1952) greatly influenced curriculum and instruction in preschool and primary education. She devoted her life to developing a system for educating children and youth, and her system has influenced all contemporary early childhood programs and many elementary programs as well. Although Montessori's first intention was to study children's diseases, she soon became interested in educational solutions for students with special needs.

Montessori believed that respect for children was the cornerstone on which all approaches to teaching should rest. She thought that because each child is unique, education should be individualized for each child. She also maintained that children are not miniature adults and should not be treated as such. Furthermore, Montessori believed that children are not educated by others but rather educate themselves. To help them achieve this self-education, she recommended a prepared environment in which children could do things for themselves. Regarding the role of the teacher, Montessori believed teachers should make children the center of learning, encourage children to learn through freedom provided in the prepared environment, and be keen observers in order to plan appropriately for children's learning.

In her first school, named the Casa di Bambini (or Children's House), she tested her ideas and gained insights into children and teaching that led to the perfection of her system. The best-known portion of Montessori's system is for children between ages 3 and 5. With contemporary interest in infant and toddler programs, applications of the Montessori method for this age group are gaining more popularity in the United States. Also, many public schools, notably in Florida, Colorado, Mississippi, and Maryland, are using the Montessori method in the elementary grades. The Montessori program was first implemented in the public schools in 1968 in Philadelphia, Pennsylvania, at Benjamin Franklin Elementary School by Patricia McGrath. To date, there are more than 3,000 classrooms in public schools that offer Montessori Programs.

 *Reflect & Write*

In addition to Froebel and Montessori, can you think of other European influences on American education, past and present?

_____

_____

_____

_____

Education Reform in the Progressive Era

The period from 1890 to 1920 was a period of great change in American society. Industrialization and urbanization continued, with accompanying economic, political, and social problems, such as poverty, poor housing, and unsafe and unhealthy workplace conditions. Cities were undergoing rapid growth, and the mostly rural economy of the states was transforming into a modern industrial society. Additionally, immigrants from Europe, with their diversity of languages and cultures, created assimilation challenges for education and the work force.

These new waves of immigrants, combined with the migration of people from rural to urban areas, produced tremendous increases in public school enrollment, which created public concern about how to address differing needs in American education. This period was known as the Progressive Era, and educators and others attempted to address these monumental social problems through innovative ideas and practices that came to be known as progressivism.

The Progressive Era was also a time of many reform efforts for workers' rights and women's suffrage. The suffrage movement sought the right of women to vote and to have greater access to economic and occupational advancement. The women's rights movement had started a century earlier. On July 16, 1848, Elizabeth Cody Stanton assembled the Women's Rights Convention at a church in Seneca Falls, New York. She called the meeting in an effort to secure equal participation by women in the trades, professions, and commerce. The movement eventually led to the ratification of the Nineteenth Amendment in 1920, which grants women the right to vote.

The needs of the Progressive Era resulted in the educational reform movement known as **progressive education,** which "revolved around . . . (1) change in the political control of education, (2) change in educational thought, (3) innovations in school curriculum and other school practices, (4) justifications of schooling in terms of professionalism, and (5) the importing of scientific management into school administration."[25]

John Dewey (1859–1952) was a leading reformer of the Progressive Era. Dewey's theory of schooling emphasized students and their interests rather than subject matter. From this student-centered emphasis come the terms *child-centered curriculum* and *child-centered schools.* The progressive movement in education also maintained that schools should be concerned with preparing students for the realities of today rather than for some vague future time. As Dewey expressed in *My Pedagogical Creed,* "Education, therefore, is a process of living and not a preparation for future living."[26] Thus, out of daily life should come the activities in which students learn about life and the skills necessary for living. Dewey believed that traditional curricula

Progressive education
An educational philosophy emphasizing change in educational thought and political control, child-centered teaching and curriculum planning, and scientific management, with the goal of making democracy work through education.

 NCATE

Early Childhood

Standard 4: Integrates understanding of children and families, of developmentally effective approaches to teaching and learning, and of academic disciplines to design, implement, and evaluate positive learning experiences for all children.

Standard 2: The teacher understands how children learn and develop, and can provide learning opportunities that support their intellectual, social and personal development.

INTASC

Committee of Ten
A high school study committee of the National Education Association (NEA) that recommended reforms for secondary education.

and methods imposed knowledge on children; instead, children's interests should be the springboard for learning skills and subject matter.

Progressive education is about educating students for democratic living, making schools democratic environments, and educating to the fullest extent every child who comes to school. Educational practices based on progressive ideas exist in many classrooms today, from the preschool to the university level. Some progressive education–based practices include students working cooperatively in groups; discovery and inquiry-based learning; assessment of students though portfolios, performances, and projects; family or multiage grouping; and flexible scheduling.

The reform of secondary education occurred primarily as a result of the recommendations by a high school study committee of the National Education Association (NEA) known as the **Committee of Ten.** In 1893, they published their study, which recommended that:

- High schools should consist of grades 7 through 12.
- The curriculum should consist of four alternative curricula consisting of classical, Latin-scientific, modern languages, and English. Students would elect one of the four curricula.
- No differences in the courses of study should exist for college-bound or non-college-bound students. Any of the four curricula would be appropriate for college-bound or non-college-bound students.
- Any of the four courses of study would be appropriate preparation for college entrance.

The recommendations of the Committee of Ten, with their emphasis on the role of high schools as college preparatory, had a tremendous influence on the shaping of American secondary education that is evident to the present time.

What specific ideas or practices in your schooling experience are traceable to progressive ideas?

_____

_____

_____

_____

SECTION SUMMARY

How Did American Education Change after the Civil War?

For most Americans, education was not a priority immediately following the Civil War, when the nation was trying to recover from the years of conflict.

- **Education for African Americans.** The education of African Americans after the Civil War was enhanced and promoted through many agencies and the efforts of dedicated individuals, such as Booker T. Washington, who founded the school that later became Tuskegee University, W. E. B. Du Bois, a Harvard Ph.D., who proposed educating the "talented tenth" of the African American population to their fullest potential, and Mary McLeod Bethune, who advocated not only education but also civil rights for African Americans and founded a school for girls that was later merged with a school for boys.

- **The Development of Indian Schools.** U.S. educational goals for Native Americans were part of a larger program of assimilation and cultural eradication and were promoted in schools operated by the Bureau of Indian Affairs. Not until the twentieth century was an educational policy of self-determination possible for Native Americans.

- The Influence of European Developments in Education. The ideas and practices of European educators such as Friedrich Froebel and Maria Montessori influenced American educational practice. Froebel founded the kindergarten, and Montessori developed a sensory-based system of education that is popular today.
- Education Reform in the Progressive Era. Education during the Progressive Era attempted to address social problems, in part through education reform. Progressive education involved changes in political control of education, educational thought, and the curriculum and emphasized schooling for professionalism and scientific management of administration. John Dewey's ideas of student-centered curriculum and schools have greatly influenced contemporary educational practice.

Thinking Critically
★ ★ ★ ★ ★ ★ ★ ★ ★

Should courses of study for college-bound students differ from those for students who do not intend to attend college immediately after graduating from high school? Why or why not?

_____

_____

_____

_____ ★

Applying What You've Learned
★ ★ ★ ★ ★ ★ ★ ★ ★

Study the recommendations of the Committee of Ten and then consider the high school from which you graduated. Were those recommendations still evident at your high school?

_____

_____

_____

_____ ★

Putting Yourself in the Picture
★ ★ ★ ★ ★ ★ ★ ★ ★

A number of teachers have had life-changing experiences as a result of teaching on an Indian reservation. Would you teach on a reservation? Why? Why not?

_____

_____

_____

_____ ★

HOW DID AMERICAN EDUCATION CHANGE AFTER WORLD WAR II?

A number of forces have greatly influenced educational thought and practice from World War II to the present, for example, the Civil Rights Movement, the Cold War, the War on Poverty, legislation for students with disabilities, the women's liberation

INTASC

Standard 3: The teacher understands how students differ in their approaches to learning and creates instructional opportunities that are adapted to diverse learners.

INTASC

Standard 5: The teacher has an understanding of individual and group motivation and behavior to create a learning environment that encourages positive social interaction, active engagement in learning, and self-motivation.

movement, the Vietnam War protest era, and conservative reaction to the 1960s and 1970s (see Figure 9.3).

Two significant events occurred almost immediately after World War II that helped create a new national interest in education from preschool to the university. The first was a series of judicial decisions and social events that shaped the contemporary Civil Rights Movement. The second event was the launching of *Sputnik* by the Soviet Union on October 4, 1957, which spurred an intensification of the Cold War between the United States and Russia (see Chapter 1).

These two events changed education practice in two important ways. First, they influenced specific policies, programs, and legislation affecting what students would learn, know, and be able to do. Second, they changed the public's attitude about what is best for the nation's children and youth and how America should educate its children and youth.

The Cold War

The 1960s and 1970s were periods of intense anticommunism dominated by a nuclear arms race between the United States and Russia and communist bloc countries. The Cold War rivalries intensified America's efforts to demonstrate its superior economic,

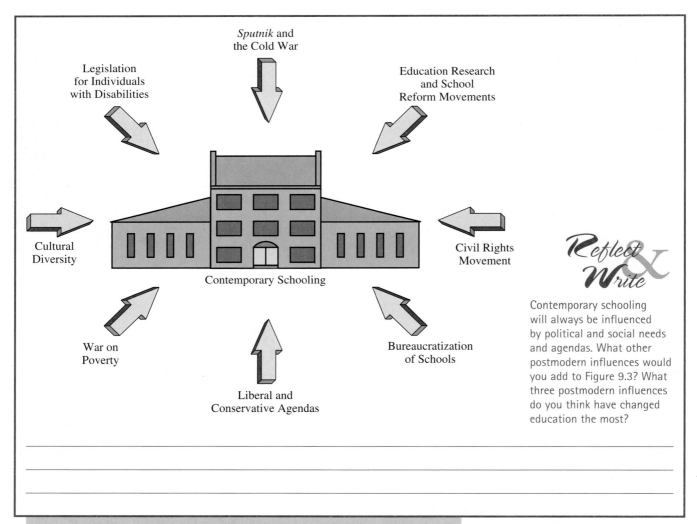

Contemporary schooling will always be influenced by political and social needs and agendas. What other postmodern influences would you add to Figure 9.3? What three postmodern influences do you think have changed education the most?

Figure 9.3   *P*ostmodern Influences on Education in the United States

political, military, and educational capabilities. Spurred by the Soviet Union's lead in space exploration, politicians and educators were determined to catch up with and surpass Russia.

In 1958, the U.S. government passed the **National Defense Education Act** to meet national education needs, particularly in the sciences. Universities received federal grants to develop national curricula in science and mathematics. Many teachers attended summer institutes at universities to learn how to implement them. Through such programs, large numbers of teachers were retrained and received advanced degrees.

National Defense Education Act
A federal law passed in 1958 to provide funds for upgrading the teaching of mathematics, science, and foreign languages and for establishing guidance services.

The Civil Rights Movement

The Civil Rights Movement began in the 1920s and 1930s and gained impetus during the 1950s and 1960s. The 1955 Montgomery bus boycott, which began when Rosa Parks refused to sit at the back of the bus, added momentum to a series of court cases and demonstrations for civil rights and human dignity. The fight for civil liberties spread quickly to the school arena. As a result, the rights of children and adults to public education were and are being clarified and extended.

The Supreme Court in *Brown v. Board of Education of Topeka* (1954) overturned the historic separate-but-equal practices of many school districts, especially those in the South. The Court ruled that "in the field of education the doctrine of 'separate but equal' has no place." The Court's decision raised many questions about educational opportunities for African Americans, Hispanic Americans, Asian Americans, and women. Equality in education soon came to mean equity, which involves adequately and appropriately addressing all students' needs. The outcomes of the *Brown* decision have included desegregation efforts, busing for school integration, and the creation of magnet schools.

Education for Students with Disabilities

Key federal and state legislation relating to the education of students with disabilities, which is essentially civil rights legislation, changed forever the way students with disabilities are educated. Three of the most important pieces of legislation in this regard were the Education for All Handicapped Children Act (PL 94-142), the Education of the Handicapped Act Amendments (PL 99-457), and the Individuals with Disabilities Education Act (IDEA; PL 101-476). These laws extend to special-needs children and their parents and families rights regarding access to educational and social services. These laws, with their tremendous educational implications, also broaden and extend civil rights. Consequently, more students than ever before have the right to a free, appropriate, individualized education, as well as to humane treatment.

INTASC

Standard 3: The teacher understands how students differ in their approaches to learning and creates instructional opportunities that are adapted to diverse learners.

Equal Rights for Women

Equal rights for women have their basis in the Fourteenth Amendment, which provides for due process and equal protection under the law. Additionally, **Title IX of the Education Amendments** of 1972 states: "No person in the United States shall, on the basis of sex, be excluded from participation in, be denied the benefits of, or be subjected to discrimination under any education program or activity receiving federal financial assistance."

The provisions of Title IX took effect in 1975 and essentially said that any gender discrimination in educational programs that receive federal funds is against the law. Title IX has had a tremendous influence on all areas of education, but particularly on physical education and athletics (see the discussion in Chapter 8). In 1987, Congress strengthened Title IX by passing the Civil Rights Restoration Act, which states that entire institutions are subject to civil rights laws and regulations if any program within the institution receives federal aid.

Title IX of the Education Amendments
Part of the Education Amendments of 1972 that prohibits discrimination on the basis of sex or exclusion from participation in an education program or activity receiving federal financial assistance.

In 1974, Congress passed the Women's Education Equity Act (WEEA), which was designed to eliminate sex discrimination and provide gender equity in education. In 1994, Congress reauthorized and strengthened WEEA. WEEA provides for programs and materials to support training in equitable practices in classrooms, the implementation of alternative assessments designed to eliminate bias in testing instruments and assessment processes, and improved representation of women in educational administration.

The War on Poverty

The Educational Opportunity Act (EOA) of 1964 was designed to reduce social class divisions and to wage a War on Poverty, the slogan President Lyndon Johnson made popular in the 1960s and 1970s. One of the main purposes of EOA was to break intergenerational cycles of poverty by providing educational and social opportunities for children from low-income families. The Economic Opportunity Act created the Office of Economic Opportunity, and from this office Project Head Start was developed and administered. The National Head Start program has a budget of over $6.5 million and serves about 900,000 children, or about 40 percent of those eligible.[27]

The **Elementary and Secondary Education Act (ESEA)** of 1965 was designed to continue the War on Poverty by providing funds to schools to improve the learning of disadvantaged children. Such federal involvement has been important for minority children, who are the recipients of ESEA programs. One major political effect of the ESEA is that it has enabled private schools to receive federal monies to support their programs.

The ESEA (now No Child Left Behind) is frequently referred to as "Title I" and currently serves about 8,125,000 children in the nation's elementary schools. Twelve percent of all kindergarten students and 24 percent of all students in grades 1 through 6 are served by Title I programs. Legislation stemming from the Civil Rights Movement and the War on Poverty led to equal opportunity and entitlement programs that have transformed American education.

Conservative Reaction to the 1960s and 1970s

Much of the conservative agenda evident in the educational community originated as a reaction against federal legislation relating to poverty and civil rights, the student protests of the 1960s, and the struggles of minorities and women to achieve equality. Many conservatives blame the public schools for social problems such as teenage pregnancy and school violence and a general decline in values and moral standards among children and youth.

The school agenda of the conservative movement in education is evident in continuing attempts to remove "objectionable" materials from school libraries and classrooms; support of home schooling as a means of providing children with an education consistent with parents' values; back-to-basics schooling, which emphasizes the basic skills; the return of school prayer to schools and classrooms; the teaching of creationism and other knowledge in keeping with biblical accounts; and the teaching of values and character traits consistent with biblical principles.

The 1990s to 2000

Seven themes dominate the educational landscape today: standards, accountability, testing and assessment, basic skills learning, emphasis on early education, increased federal and state roles in the funding and control of education, and educational reform. Standards have played, are playing, and will continue to play a major role in determining what students should learn and be able to do. The accountability movement continues to be one of the major forces driving much of educational reform. The public wants schools to be more accountable for student learning and achievement

---

Elementary and Secondary Education Act (ESEA)
A 1965 act providing funds to schools to improve the education of disadvantaged children.

INTASC

Standard 3: The teacher understands how students differ in their approaches to learning and creates instructional opportunities that are adapted to diverse learners.

INTASC

Standard 8: The teacher understands and uses formal and informal assessment strategies to evaluate and ensure the continuous intellectual, social and physical development of the learner.

and for the use of public funds and resources. Ongoing testing of all students in grades K through 12 is one means for measuring student achievement and for holding teachers accountable for student learning. Chapter 10 explores these topics in greater detail and shows how they influence the course of educational practice and, consequently, the history of education.

Over the last decade, there has been a decided return to basic skills learning and academic-based curricula. This "back-to-basics" approach is reflected in renewed emphasis on teaching of reading, math, and science. A large proportion of the public believes that a major pathway of success in school and life for their children is through a solid grounding in and knowledge of basic skills. The first decade of the twenty-first century will be known for its emphasis on an academic orientation to teaching and learning.

The 1990s were known as the "decade of the brain." At this time, the nation discovered the importance of the brain in learning, how young children learn, and the importance of early learning. With these discoveries came a renewed interest in young children and early childhood education. This, in turn, affected public educational policy. This interest in brain-based learning resulted in increased funding for early childhood programs and renewed interest in developing curricula for promoting children's cognitive development. This emphasis on children's early years will likely continue for at least the next decade, and educational historians will recognize the period of 1990 to 2010 as the golden age of early childhood education.

Beginning in 1995, state governors assumed a much more powerful role in setting education policy and crafting legislation for the reform of education. Historians will identify the migration of control from local school boards to the statehouse as one of the most significant educational occurrences of the late twentieth century and early twenty-first century. Concurrent with the usurpation of local educational control by state governors, the federal government also began to play a larger role in education matters. President George W. Bush ran on a strong education reform platform, and Secretary of Education Rod Paige is committed to expanding the federal influence over education through the funding of specifically targeted educational programs such as early literacy. The Leave No Child Behind Education Act of 2001 authorized $26.5 billion for K–12 education. Some of the requirements for receiving this federal funding include:

- Annual state tests in reading and math for every child in grades 3 through 8 beginning in the 2004–2005 school year. Schools whose scores fail to improve two years in a row could receive more federal aid. If scores still fail to improve, low-income students can receive funding for tutoring or transportation to another public school. A school in which scores do not improve over six years could be restaffed. In schools already considered poor performers, parents could receive tutoring or transportation funds as early as fall 2002.
- Schools must raise all students' reading and math proficiency in the next twelve years. Schools must also close gaps in scores between wealthy and poor students and white and minority students.
- States must ensure within four years that all teachers are qualified to teach in their subject areas. States could require teachers to pass subject tests or major in their fields in college.

The Leave No Child Behind Education Act of 2001 is significant for several reasons. First, it authorizes a huge increase in federal spending, from $18.5 billion to $26.5

INTASC

Standard 1: The teacher understands the central concepts, tools of inquiry, and structures of the subjects being taught and can create learning experiences that make these aspects of subject matter meaningful for students.

NCATE

Middle Level

Standard 3: Understands the major concepts, principles, theories, and research related to middle-level curriculum and assessment; uses this knowledge in practice.

Early Childhood

Standard 4: Integrates understanding of children and families, of developmentally effective approaches to teaching and learning, and of academic disciplines to design, implement, and evaluate positive learning experiences for all children.

What Does This Mean for You?

Throughout this book, I have continually tried to emphasize that education is a political process. In fact, it is literally impossible for me to think of any educational topic from the teaching of reading to teaching advanced placement (AP) classes that does not have political issues and implications swirling around it. What does this mean for you? It means:

- You must include politics in your life as a teacher. You must consider being involved in matters that will make a difference to how education is funded and how to best teach children and youth.
- You will need to know as much as you can about the pros, cons, and political points of view regarding the subjects you teach and other aspects of school.
- You will need to be able to explain the various educational and political points of view to parents, colleagues, and the community.
- You will need to be an articulate spokesperson for your profession.

billion, for elementary and secondary education. Second, the bill greatly expands the federal government's role in the American education system, which traditionally has been controlled by states and local districts.

If there is one word that describes the educational events of the last twenty years, it is *reform*. Educational reform has dominated the educational landscape and has touched the life of every student, teacher, and administrator in America. Educational reform is directed toward improving America's schools, increasing student achievement, and providing well-educated citizens and workers. Reform will continue to shape educational practice for years to come, and reform initiatives will shape your career as a teacher.

Education in the Twenty-First Century

Since education is an ongoing process, education inevitably undergoes never-ending change. Your career and your profession—like many others in our fast-moving times—will always be changing. We are less than a decade into the twenty-first century, but in just these few short years the educational landscape has radically altered.

Here are some of the changes that are occurring even as you are preparing to teach:

- The growing influence of the federal government in all matters and all levels of education. As we discussed above and have continually discussed in this text, the federal government continues to play a larger role in prescribing what is taught and how it is taught. The No Child Left Behind Act of 2001 is one of the most significant pieces of federal legislation in the last fifty years. It compares with *Brown v. Board* for its influence on education. The role of the federal government in the process of education will become larger and more directive over the coming decade.
- The growth of the educational industry and influence of the business community on education. Education is big business, and a lot of money is invested in and spent on education. As a result, the education industry plays a significant role in what is taught and how it is taught. This is evident in such technological programs for young children as Leap Frog; the for-profit K–12 virtual school of former Secretary of Education William Bennett; the growth of private, online for-profit colleges in higher education; and the expanded role of companies exercising control over kinds of tests students take and how they take them.
- The integration of technology with learning technology. Technology promises to change how teachers teach and how education is delivered in pre-K–12. Many schools are now discussing the elimination of hard-copy textbooks and doing all textbook-based instruction online. We will discuss the technological influences on education in more detail in Chapter 12.

While these are by no means all of the reforms that have occurred in the last decade, they are major ones and are wide ranging in their influence and effects.

SECTION SUMMARY

How Did American Education Change after World War II?

Educational thought and practice have been affected by the Cold War, the Civil Rights Movement, the War on Poverty, legislation for students with disabilities, the women's liberation movement, the Vietnam War protest era, and the contemporary conservative reaction to the 1960s and 1970s. Implementation of equity issues dealt with in some of the legislation passed since World War II continues today.

- The Cold War. Cold War rivalries during the 1960s and 1970s heightened U.S. politicians' interest in shoring up education in the sciences and mathematics and in instituting early childhood education programs.

- The Civil Rights Movement. The Civil Rights Movement overturned separate-but-equal policies for educating white and black Americans and focused attention on equal rights for other ethnic groups and for women.

- Education for Students with Disabilities. Key legislation clarified the rights of children with disabilities and the rights of their parents. Students with disabilities now participate in regular programs in many school districts.

- Equal Rights for Women. Legislation in 1972, 1974, 1975, 1987, and 1994 has helped eliminate discrimination based on sex and provide gender equity in education.

- The War on Poverty. Legislation stemming from the Civil Rights Movement and from the Johnson administration's War on Poverty led to equal opportunity and entitlement programs that transformed U.S. education.

- Conservative Reaction to the 1960s and 1970s. A conservative backlash grew up in the 1980s, evident in the "back to basics" movement, which emphasizes basic skills and education in principles and content consistent with biblical teachings.

- The 1990s to 2000. Seven themes—standards, accountability, testing and assessment, basic skills learning, emphasis on early education, increased federal and state roles in the funding and control of education, and educational reform—will continue to dominate the educational landscape during the first decade of the twenty-first century.

- Education in the Twenty-First Century. A number of reforms and changes have occurred in education since the dawn of the twenty-first century. These include the expanded role of the federal government in education. This involvement of the federal government is exemplified through the No Child Left Behind Act of 2001. The education industrial complex is exerting tremendous influence on teaching and learning through products, delivery of education online, and virtual schools. Technology is becoming more integrated with teaching and learning and is changing and will continue to change how teachers teach and children learn.

Thinking Critically
★ ★ ★ ★ ★ ★ ★ ★

Do you agree that U.S. schools should be focusing more on basics—reading, writing, and arithmetic?

_____

_____

_____

_____ ★

Applying What You've Learned
★ ★ ★ ★ ★ ★ ★ ★

History is literally all around us, and society is "making" history every day. Think back over the last five years and identify people, events, and reforms that should be included in a contemporary history of education.

_____

_____

_____

_____ ★

You are a fourth-grade teacher in a politically conservative area. The president of the parents' organization has just written to you asking to spend a day in your classroom observing and to review the books on your shelves. What will you do?

★

NCATE

Early Childhood

Standard 5: Uses ethical guidelines and other professional standards; is a continuous, collaborative learner who demonstrates knowledgeable, reflective, and critical perspectives; is an informed advocate for sound educational practices.

Elementary

Standard 5.1: Understands and applies practices and behaviors that are characteristic of developing career teachers.

Middle Level

Standard 7: Understands the complexity of teaching young adolescents; engages in practices and behaviors that develop competence as a professional.

INTASC

Standard 9: The teacher is a reflective practitioner who continually evaluates the effects of his/her choices and actions on others.

HOW IS PHILOSOPHY RELEVANT FOR CLASSROOM TEACHERS?

Just as the history of education is important to your professional practice, so too is understanding the basic philosophies of education and applying them to your own beliefs about teaching and your classroom practices. As a beginning teacher, each of your days will be filled with decisions about what to teach, how to teach it, how to best provide for the needs of all your students, and how to prepare lessons and curricula that challenge your students and enable them to learn. Your decisions about these endeavors will be guided by your beliefs about life, your students, and teaching. Professional interactions, meetings, and discussions with colleagues and administrators will be shaped by your own personal philosophy about education and learning. There is nothing that you will engage in as a teacher that will be unaffected by your own beliefs about education. Therefore, it is important to take a close look at the basic philosophies of education, examine your own philosophy of education, and then explore how the two meld.

Philosophy Is Based on Core Values

What you believe in your heart and mind about education and teaching is based on core values relating to life and living. Your philosophy of education is based on your philosophy of life. What you believe about yourself, about others, and about life infuses and determines your philosophy of education. Knowing what others believe is important and useful, for it can help you clarify what you believe; but when it is all said and done, you have to decide what you believe. What you believe moment by moment, day by day, influences what you will teach and how you will teach it.

A philosophy of life and education is more than an opinion. A personal philosophy is based on core values and beliefs. Core values of life relate to your beliefs about the nature of life, the purpose of life, your role and calling in life, and your relationship and responsibilities to others. Core beliefs and values about education and teaching include what you believe about the nature of children, the purpose of education, how people learn, the role of teachers, and what's worth knowing.

Core values and beliefs originate and have their roots in a number of sources. Primarily, these sources include culture, religion, family values and beliefs, education, political preferences, and personal experiences. These six sources and others shape who you are and what you believe. Also, as these factors have influenced and will continue to influence what you believe, so too do they influence what you believe about education and teaching.

Identify one core belief or value from each of the six sources that influences your beliefs and values as a teacher.

_____

_____

_____

_____

Philosophy Guides Decisions and Actions

Core beliefs and values that convey what you and others believe about life and teaching are based on basic philosophical questions and ideas. Understanding philosophy enables you to shape and clarify your beliefs. Philosophy forms the foundation on which educators base their practice of education.

If you have developed your philosophy of education, now is a good time to reflect, review, reconsider, and revise your beliefs. If you have not written your philosophy of education, now is a good time to begin. As you read this chapter, you will encounter many worthwhile ideas for developing your philosophy in accordance with your core beliefs.

A philosophy of education provides a foundation on which you can build a good teaching career. An added benefit of developing a philosophy of education now is that it will help you respond positively during job interviews.

A philosophy of education is basically a statement of your beliefs about the purposes of education, how children and youth develop and learn, and what and how they should be taught. Your philosophy of education is quite personal. There may be similarities between your philosophy and those of other teachers, but what you believe is unique to you. The following prompts can help you in developing your educational philosophy:

- I believe the purposes of education are . . .
- I believe students learn best when they are taught under certain conditions and in certain ways. Some of these are . . .
- The curriculum of any classroom should include certain "basics" that contribute to students' social, emotional, intellectual, and physical development. These basics are . . .
- Students learn best in an environment that promotes learning. Some of the features of a good learning environment are . . .
- All students have certain needs that must be met if they are to grow and learn. Some of these basic needs are . . . I would meet these needs in these ways . . .
- A teacher should have certain qualities and behave in certain ways. Qualities I think important for teaching are . . .

SECTION SUMMARY

How Is Philosophy Relevant for Classroom Teachers?

What you and other teachers believe influences and determines how you teach as well as the curriculum and teaching practices.

- **Philosophy Is Based on Core Values.** A philosophy of life is based on core values and beliefs. Core values originate primarily from culture, religion, family values and beliefs, education, political preferences, and personal experiences.
- **Philosophy Guides Decisions and Actions.** Your philosophy of life and of education will determine how you teach and what kind of person and teacher you are.

Your philosophy of education will be based on your own personal philosophy. What basic philosophical beliefs will you incorporate into your classroom practice?

_____

_____

_____

_____★

Your culture, religion, family values and beliefs, education, political preferences, and personal experiences will all shape your philosophy of education. In each of these areas, ask one person whose views you respect to suggest what a philosophy of education should address in American education today. Then begin drafting your own philosophy of education, using the prompts in this section.

_____

_____

_____

_____★

What teachers believe about the purposes of education makes a difference in their teaching. As a teacher in a third-grade classroom in an inner-city school with a high minority population, what goals would you find most important?

_____

_____

_____

_____★

HOW DO THE BRANCHES OF PHILOSOPHY RELATE TO EDUCATION?

Think back over the events that occurred in your life during the past week. How did philosophy influence what happened? What were the educational events that were influenced by philosophy? Every day, educational life is influenced by what people believe. Parents send their children to particular schools based on what they believe. What principals and other administrators believe greatly influences how schools function, what textbooks are purchased, and what is taught. Philosophies influence metaphors of teaching and schooling, as discussed in Chapter 1. Indeed, it is difficult to think of one area of schooling that is not affected by philosophy.

Philosophy comes from the Greek words *philo* (love) and *sophos* (wisdom). Philosophy is a love of wisdom and a pursuit of knowledge. William James (1842–1910) said this about philosophy:

It "bakes no bread" as has been said, but it can inspire our souls with courage. . . . No one of us can get along without the far-flashing beams of light it sends over the world's perspectives.[28]

By inspiring our souls with courage and by shedding far-flashing beams of light on such questions as "What is good?" "What is true?" "What is beauty?" and "What is knowledge?" philosophy influences life's decisions and course. And it becomes clear that in answering these questions, people develop their world outlook and the values they hold dear. Educational philosophy, the general theories of education, serves the practical and important purpose of influencing the daily educational decisions of parents, community members, and teachers.

Philosophy has three main branches: metaphysics, epistemology, and axiology (see Figure 9.4). Each of these branches asks questions whose answers shape core beliefs.

Metaphysics—What Is Real?

Metaphysics is the field of philosophy concerned with the nature of reality. William James wrote that "metaphysics inquires in the cause, the substance, the meaning, and the outcome of all things."[29] Metaphysics asks such questions as "What is real?" "What is the nature of existence?" "What is the meaning of life?" and "What should I do?" Metaphysics has two branches: cosmology and ontology.

Cosmology deals with the nature and origin of the universe. Cosmological questions are a part of everyday life and events. Scientists, with the use of the Hubble telescope, search for the beginnings of the universe. They want to know more about quasars, black holes, and expanding galaxies. **Ontology** examines questions and issues about existence and being. People wrestle with issues about when life begins, abortion,

Philosophy
From the Greek, *philos* (love) and *sophy* (wisdom); literally, the "love of wisdom" and the pursuit of wisdom.

Metaphysics
The field of philosophy concerned with the nature of reality; addresses such questions as "What is the self?" "What is the nature of existence?" and "What is real?"

Cosmology
The part of philosophy that deals with the nature and origin of the universe.

Ontology
An area of philosophy concerned with questions of being and existence.

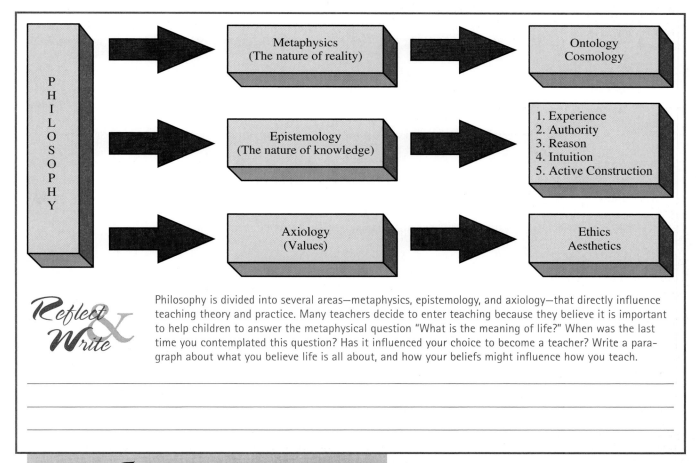

Philosophy is divided into several areas—metaphysics, epistemology, and axiology—that directly influence teaching theory and practice. Many teachers decide to enter teaching because they believe it is important to help children to answer the metaphysical question "What is the meaning of life?" When was the last time you contemplated this question? Has it influenced your choice to become a teacher? Write a paragraph about what you believe life is all about, and how your beliefs might influence how you teach.

Figure 9.4 *The Three Classical Branches of Philosophy*

capital punishment, the "right to die," cloning, and recent experiments on making human cells "immortal."

Metaphysical issues have particular meaning for teachers. For example, what teachers believe about human nature affects how they view students and interact with them. When students are viewed as basically good, teachers will see students' behavior as motivated by good rather than bad intentions.

The metaphysical question "What should I do?" shapes teacher practice. For example, when teachers see subject matter as the most important factor in education, they are likely to stress it more than other teaching areas. However, if students are considered most important, teachers will base their curriculum on student needs and interests.

How you answer these metaphysical questions will determine how you live your life. Your decision to become a teacher most likely involved questions about the meaning and importance of life, how to spend your life most meaningfully, and the importance of children and youth to society.

Epistemology—How Do We Know?

Epistemology
The field of philosophy concerned with the nature of knowledge. Epistemology asks such questions as "What is the nature of knowledge?" "How do we learn?" "What is worth knowing?"

Epistemology is concerned with the nature of knowledge and how knowledge is acquired. Basic questions of epistemology include "How does knowing take place?" "How do we define knowledge?" "How is knowledge acquired?" and "How do we decide what knowledge should be taught?" Epistemology is of great importance, since all teachers have beliefs about how students acquire knowledge and how they learn best. Other questions that affect teaching are "Is what I am teaching my students true?" and "What philosophy is guiding my teaching?" It is natural that teachers and others stress the knowledge and beliefs that support their own experiences and backgrounds. Nonetheless, it is important to consider and include knowledge that stems from other backgrounds. This is the essence of multiculturally aware teaching (see Chapter 4).

There are many ways of knowing about life and its meaning. People can come to know about the world through experience, through authority, through reason, through intuition, and by active construction. While everyone has gained knowledge from these ways of knowing, not everyone puts equal value on each way of knowing. Your approach to knowledge and learning will be based, in part, on your core values.

Empiricism
Knowledge acquired through the senses.

Knowing through Experience. One way we learn and gain knowledge about the world is through experience. Acquiring knowledge through experience and the senses is known as **empiricism.** You use the empirical approach when you base your actions on experiences and claim that "experience is the best teacher."

Knowing through Authority. The authority of a person, group, or document often serves as the basis for what is taught. Parents are authoritative sources of knowledge, as are teachers, clergy, politicians, and scientists. Documents such as the federal tax code, textbooks, and religious publications are examples of written authority of what is right and wrong and what constitutes the truth. For example, teachers often tell students that "the right answer is in the book." Thus, students come to accept textbooks as authoritative sources. However, some teachers believe it is in students' best interests to learn to challenge what is in textbooks.

Deductive reasoning
Inferring specifics from a general principle or drawing a logical conclusion from a premise.

Inductive reasoning
Thinking from the particular to the general or drawing a logical conclusion from instances of a case.

Knowing through Reason. Logic is a subfield of epistemology and deals with reasoning and the rules that govern our reasoning. There are basically two kinds of logical reasoning: deductive and inductive. In **deductive reasoning,** students use a general rule and identify examples and applications of the rule. In **inductive reasoning,** the opposite of deductive reasoning, students are taught to reason from the particular to the general, examine particular instances of a phenomenon, and arrive at a general

Nature offers many learning opportunities that cannot be duplicated in a classroom. How is knowledge being acquired by the students in this photo?

conclusion based on their observations. Leading students to learn through inductive reasoning using a process of inquiry is a skill all teachers need to possess. Inquiry learning is frequently used to teach reasoning, problem solving, and critical thinking skills.

Knowing through Intuition. Basing behavior on intuitive knowledge is necessary for creativity and invention and includes "the educated guess." Such behavior is based on accumulated learning acquired from experiences, reading and study, the advice of others (for example, parents and teachers), and the process of schooling. Teachers often use a particular teaching strategy because their educated guesses lead them to believe it will work. They did not go to a textbook first to look up the right way to teach; they just did it, relying on their past experiences and good judgment.

Knowing through Active Construction. Learning and knowing occur through mental and physical activity. As children and adults engage in activities and have new experiences, they come to know about, make sense of, and develop an understanding about the world. They literally construct their knowledge of reality. In this engagement of activity and knowing, individuals learn to organize, structure, and restructure experiences in accordance with their thoughts, ideas, and previous knowledge. In this way, we are all active participants in the development of knowledge.

As children grow and develop, they become increasingly able to act on the environment and learn from it. Acting on the environment enables them to explore, test, observe, and organize information, which they then use in their thinking processes and social interactions. Actively interacting with others also contributes to and promotes learning. What a person learns is influenced in part through learning from others. Because we learn from others, it is not necessary to reinvent all of the knowledge and information already accumulated by our culture.

Reflect & Write

Give an example from your own experience of knowing through active construction—"learning by doing."

_____

_____

_____

_____

Epistemological Questions and Teaching. There are a number of implications for classroom teachers concerning epistemological questions, or ways of knowing. First, teachers should acknowledge that there are different ways of knowing and provide opportunities for students to learn in a variety of ways. Second, teachers must respect the beliefs of students and parents about how knowledge is acquired, regardless of their own values about ways of knowing. Figure 9.5 illustrates teaching methods based on epistemology.

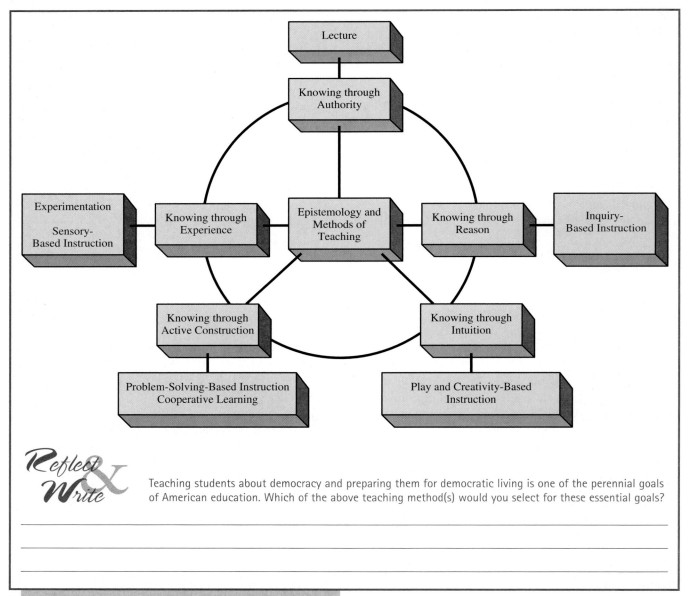

Reflect & Write

Teaching students about democracy and preparing them for democratic living is one of the perennial goals of American education. Which of the above teaching method(s) would you select for these essential goals?

_____

_____

_____

Figure 9.5 *Epistemology and Teaching Methods*

Axiology—What Is Right?

Axiology is the branch of philosophy that addresses human conduct (ethics) and beauty (aesthetics). These two areas involve questions of values, right behavior, and the quality of individuals' lives as well as the quality of human life in general. Questions axiology poses are "What values are of most importance?" "Whose values are of most importance?" "How should we relate to and get along with others?" and "What constitutes beauty?" (See the Profile.)

The education curriculum and the books included as part of the curriculum promote certain values and convey messages about what is good, true, and beautiful. What students read and discuss can enrich and expand their ideas and conceptions about the nature of beauty and the arts. Teachers who want students to exhibit certain values need to provide opportunities for students to discuss and internalize value decisions. Any presentation of values needs to be examined in the context of culture and family beliefs.

Ethics. Questions of right and wrong and good and evil are the focus of ethics. These questions relate not only to how teachers conduct their own classes but also to teachers' relationships with students, colleagues, and parents. Ethics is integral to how teachers practice their profession. Teachers are governed by their own personal ethics as well as the ethics of their profession. Ethical questions repeatedly guide personal choices and classroom discussions, particularly around such current concerns as violence, substance abuse, teenage pregnancy, and other social issues. In addition, state boards of education and professional organizations have codes of ethics for teachers to guide their professional practice (see the NEA Code of Ethics in Chapter 2).

When parents say they want schools to teach their children to be "good" citizens, they are talking about the ethical aspect of axiology. Society considers schools and teachers to be the guardians of right behavior and conduct and wants them to impart such values as honesty, respect for others, and fair play.

Axiology
A branch of philosophy that addresses human conduct (ethics) and beauty (aesthetics).

Ethics
A branch of philosophy focusing on questions of right and wrong, good and bad, and the basis for moral judgments.

INTASC

Standard 2: The teacher understands how children learn and develop, and can provide learning opportunities that support their intellectual, social and personal development.

Standard 4: The teacher uses various instructional strategies to encourage students' development of critical thinking, problem solving, and performance skills.

NCATE

Early Childhood
Standard 5: Uses ethical guidelines and other professional standards; is a continuous, collaborative learner who demonstrates knowledgeable, reflective, and critical perspectives; is an informed advocate for sound educational practices.

Profile Axiological Questions and Teaching: Nina Fue

Teachers like Nina Fue, New Jersey Teacher of the Year, are concerned about the values they convey and the ones they encourage and promote in their students' behaviors.

As always, Nina Fue starts the day by checking parental signatures. Anyone who forgot to show his homework to Mom or Dad risks a sweetly stern reminder and a demerit mark in Mrs. Fue's book.

"I'll bet you didn't forget to eat dinner last night," Mrs. Fue tells a sheepish Korey Sickler. "Well, this should be like that. Happens all the time."

Since it's Monday, Mrs. Fue chooses her student of the week. Then as every day, she asks how her fourth-graders are feeling on a scale of 1 to 10. Jillian has an earache. Stephanie feels bad but doesn't want to say why. ("That's okay. Some things are private.")

In thirty short minutes, before the academic day has even begun, Nina Fue teaches responsibility, perseverance, and the art of compassion. . . .

Values are as clearly a part of what Mrs. Fue teaches as geography, English, or math. When she mentions growing up and getting a job during a grammar lesson, she teaches the work ethic. When she explains, during reading, how the mountain changed with the help of the bird, she teaches cooperation.

Nina Fue teaches values as part of the curriculum and daily classroom activities. When teachers stress the importance of doing something for the good of all—such as meeting the goals the class has set for good behavior—they are teaching a lesson about the effects of one person's behavior on others. Teachers also teach values and character traits by how they act. Linda Bates, a New Mexico Teacher of the Year, thinks that "it is unrealistic to expect students to be better than their role models. I read somewhere that values are caught as well as taught."[30]

Aesthetics

A branch of philosophy that
addresses questions about the
nature of beauty and value in
human endeavor.

Aesthetics. The areas of beauty, art, and music are included in **aesthetics.** Aesthetics asks such questions as "What is a work of art?" "What is beauty?" and "What makes something beautiful?"

Many school districts emphasize aesthetics in their curricula, and some have established arts magnet schools that enroll students throughout a district or region. One such example is the New World School of the Arts, a unique institution operated by three agencies—the Dade County (Florida) Public Schools (which considers the arts as a basic skill), Miami Dade Community College, and Florida State University. The New World School enrolls talented students from south Florida and enables them to explore and develop their artistic talents. Topics of values as they relate to daily living are embedded in the school day and curriculum. Many of these values relate directly to what to teach students about beauty and the arts. Involving students in discussion of aesthetic issues enables them to have a deeper understanding of beauty and its nature.

Reflect & Write

What are five values that you think are the most important for teachers to convey to students?

_____

_____

_____

_____

The Impact of Culture on Philosophical Questions

INTASC

Standard 3: The teacher
understands how students differ
in their approaches to learning
and creates instructional opportunities that are adapted to diverse
learners.

The cultural background of groups and individuals, including cultural values, family styles, and religion, helps determine knowledge and behaviors that affect daily living and educational practices. For example, "Muslims in the United States feel strongly about teaching the Qur'an [Koran, Holy Book], the Arabic language, and basic Islamic beliefs to members of their communities, especially their children. Therefore, wherever there is a large concentration of Muslims, Arabic-Islamic schools have been developed."[31] These schools are designed to augment public school education.

Cultural beliefs and practices have many implications for how teachers teach children. Teaching practices and activities need to be multiculturally appropriate. For example:

The type of competence parents expect of young children may vary from culture to culture. For low-income immigrant Latino parents, expectation for their children's skill development may differ from Latinos born in the United States. That is, foreign-born Latinos perceive the behavioral capabilities of young children as developing later than do U.S.-born Latinos. It may be that immigrant Latinos have a more maturational orientation to children's development so that the early emphasis on cognitive stimulation promoted in the United States is somewhat inconsistent with their experiences.[32]

Teachers need to be culturally sensitive and incorporate into their philosophy of teaching the cultural backgrounds and needs of students and their families. For example, questions about what is beauty and what constitutes "good" art and music need to be answered in the context of culture. Thus, teachers and students have to incorporate the ideas of beauty and the criteria for judging art and music as well as the cultural contributions of other cultures.

In what ways does culture impact the core values and philosophical questions relating to teaching and learning?

Events throughout our history serve as stark reminders of the importance of and need for cultural awareness and sensitivity, particularly considering the ever-changing face of American society. The American education system, and teachers in particular, play a critical role in promoting cultural sensitivity and inclusion. We need look no further than the events of September 11, 2001, and their aftermath when there seemed certain to be an extended backlash of anger and outrage against Muslims and people of Middle Eastern descent and even those mistakenly perceived to be of Middle Eastern descent. Political, educational, and religious leaders alike addressed the public sense of outrage immediately, with educational training oriented toward understanding differences in beliefs and cultures. Many of these efforts were aimed at young people, with the intent of promoting tolerance of differences and transforming hatred. Teachers seized the opportunity to help students discuss the events in the light of known facts, separate facts from rumor, and understand that judgments about people and cultures should be based on accurate knowledge and understanding. Many teachers and schools initiated service projects designed specifically to help people from other cultures and racial backgrounds. U.S. Secretary of Education Rod Paige urged educators to take a leading role in preventing harassment and violence directed at students of particular cultures or perceived to be of particular ethnic backgrounds. Paige said, "We are all committed to making sure [all] children across America can attend school in a safe, secure environment, free from harassment and threats."[33]

SECTION SUMMARY

How Do the Branches of Philosophy Relate to Education?

Philosophy is a love of wisdom and a pursuit of knowledge. It serves the practical and important purpose of influencing the daily educational decisions of parents, community members, and teachers. Philosophy has three main branches: metaphysics, epistemology, and axiology.

- Metaphysics—What Is Real? Metaphysics inquires into the cause, substance, meaning, and outcome of all things. Metaphysics has two branches: cosmology (the nature and origin of the universe) and ontology (the nature of existence and being).

- Epistemology—How Do We Know? Epistemology addresses questions about the sources of knowledge and learning. There are a number of ways people come to know: through experience, authority, reason, intuition, and active construction.

- Axiology—What Is Right? Axiology examines questions about human conduct (ethics) and beauty (aesthetics). Ethics focuses on right and wrong, and aesthetics addresses questions related to beauty and art.

- The Impact of Culture on Philosophical Questions. The cultural backgrounds of groups and individuals help determine knowledge and behavioral/cultural beliefs and also have many implications for how you and others teach.

Thinking Critically

★ ★ ★ ★ ★ ★ ☆ ★

Metaphysical questions involve the causes and nature of the universe and ourselves. What do you believe about the origin of the universe and about the meaning of your existence? How will these beliefs influence your classroom teaching?

Epistemology relates to how we come to know things—through experience, authority, reason, intuition, and active construction. Interview friends, members of your family, and teachers about how, from whom, and where they gained their most important learnings.

_____

_____

_____

_____ ★

**Putting Yourself
in the Picture**
★ ★ ★ ★ ★ ★ ★ ★

Many Americans with European backgrounds tend to place great value on the individual. Many other Americans, such as those with Asian backgrounds, tend to place greater value on the family or society or to value the group and the individual equally. You are teaching a fourth-grade class with many Asian American children in it. How will the difference in values between Anglo-European American and Asian American students affect your teaching and your relationships with students and parents?

_____

_____

_____

_____ ★

INTASC

Standard 1: The teacher understands the central concepts, tools of inquiry, and structures of the subject being taught and can create learning experiences that make these aspects of subject matter meaningful for students.

Standard 2: The teacher understands how children learn and develop, and can provide learning opportunities that support their intellectual, social and personal development.

Standard 4: The teacher uses various instructional strategies to encourage students' development of critical thinking, problem solving, and performance skills.

Perennialism
An educational philosophy that emphasizes constancy and unchanging truth.

*W*HAT ARE THE MAJOR PHILOSOPHIES OF EDUCATION?

There are six contemporary educational philosophies that have a major influence on educational practice today: perennialism, essentialism, progressivism, social reconstructionism, humanism, and existentialism. Table 9.1 lists their characteristics.

Perennialism

Perennialism, which grows out of idealism, the belief that ideas are the only true reality, was developed by Robert Maynard Hutchins (1899–1977). As president of the University of Chicago, he developed an undergraduate curriculum based on the Great Books Curriculum. The Great Books Curriculum consists of 100 selections of literature, including Homer's *Iliad* and *Odyssey*, Melville's *Moby Dick*, Darwin's *The Origin of Species*, and other masterpieces of Western civilization. Hutchins believed:

> Education implies teaching. Teaching implies knowledge. Knowledge is truth. Truth is everywhere the same. Hence education should be everywhere the same. I do not overlook the possibility of differences in organization, in administration, in local habits and customs. These are details. I suggest that the heart of any course of study designed for the whole pupil will be, if education is rightly understood, the same at any time, in any place, under any political, social, or economic conditions.[34]

Those in the perennialist camp believe that truth is perennial—that is, enduring. They believe it is the role of education and the job of educators to focus on the search for and the dissemination of the unchanging truths that are to be found in the experiences of humans over the centuries, as reflected in their culture and literature. Perennialists are concerned that society, schools, and teachers will focus exclusively on the new and faddish and will abandon the enduring truths of the ages. They believe

Table 9.1　Six Contemporary Educational Philosophies

Goal of Education	Role of Students	Role of Teachers	Teaching Methods	Curriculum Emphasis
Perennialism				
Develop timeless virtues such as justice, temperance, fortitude, and prudence; instill knowledge for the sake of learning.	Develop and use virtues in life's decisions; acquire knowledge.	Instill virtues, know subject matter, teach subject matter to all students.	Teacher-centered; lecture	Subject matter and common core curriculum; emphasis on arts and sciences
Existentialism				
Create climate of freedom and choice where individuals can choose and be responsible for their decisions.	Accept responsibility for choices and actions; learn to set personal goals and achieve them by developing independence, making decisions, and problem solving.	Create an environment for independent action and enable students to make choices and accept responsibility for behavior.	Analysis and discussion regarding students' choices	Social studies; humanities
Progressivism				
Use student interests as a basis for understanding and ordering students' experience.	Participate in formulating the purposes that are the basis for the student-centered curriculum.	Act as a facilitator for student learning; determine student interests for developing curriculum.	Learning centers; cooperative learning; student-led and -initiated discussion	Student interests and needs; democracy; morality; social development
Social Reconstructionism				
Use education to help solve significant social problems and, as a result, make democracy more efficient and effective.	Identify social problems and use thinking skills and knowledge to solve problems.	Facilitate process of students identifying and solving community-based problems.	Facilitate cooperative learning, group problem solving; encourage students to use problem-solving skills	Integrated knowledge of and solution of social problems in the regular curriculum
Humanism				
Emphasize self-actualization, help students become self-actualized, and blend the cognitive and the affective; help students assimilate knowledge into their daily lives; stress human values.	Develop healthy attitudes toward self, others, and learning experience; become self-actualized.	Help students to become self-actualized and make sense of learning; connect individuals to their learning and help them apply curriculum to themselves, the community, the nation, and the world.	Group processes, one-on-one teacher-student interaction	Physical and emotional needs of students and development of learning experience so that students can fulfill their needs and resolve developmental crises
Essentialism				
Promote and instill cultural literacy in all students; provide a common core of cultural knowledge.	Acquire and use cultural knowledge; learn and use thinking skills.	Provide a common core cultural literacy curriculum integrated with basic school subjects.	Primarily subject- and teacher-centered methods	A uniform curriculum for all students emphasizing subject matter and cultural knowledge

enduring truths develop the intellect and form the basis for reason and rationality and that it is this process that helps separate humans from animals. For the perennialist, the goal of teachers and schools is to develop rational students grounded in and strengthened by the truths of the ages.

Mortimer Adler (1902–2001) continued Hutchins's work. Adler is often referred to as a neoperennialist, because in his Paideia Proposal he gave new life and meaning to the perennialist position. In this education manifesto, Adler proposes one common curriculum for all. As Adler stated, "The one-track system of public schooling that the Paideia Proposal advocates has the same objective for all without exception."[35]

Adler's supporters maintain that a common core curriculum is nondiscriminatory and promotes equity. It is intended for all students. They believe that one curriculum for all is more egalitarian than the current system of tracking students by ability and providing one curriculum for those who are college bound and another curriculum for those who will enter the work world after high school.

Perennialists advocate a curriculum that:

INTASC

Standard 1: The teacher understands the central concepts, tools of inquiry, and structures of the subjects being taught and can create learning experiences that make these aspects of subject matter meaningful for students.

- Develops the intellect of all learners. In this regard, perennialists advocate a standard curriculum for all that is challenging and rigorous.
- Supports the study of mathematics (because it trains the mind and develops reasoning), science, and the humanities (literature—through the study of great books—history, philosophy, and art).
- Prepares students for life rather than merely for the here and now.

From the perennialist perspective, the teacher's role is to:

- Lecture on topics relating to truth, values, and critical knowledge
- Use Socratic questioning as a means of promoting thinking and reasoning
- Coach students in strategies for problem solving and learning how to think
- Provide students with supervised practice to help ensure that learning occurs
- Set high goals and expectations for students and encourage them to achieve the goals

Perennialists believe the student's role in learning includes:

- Studying hard and learning subject matter and academic skills as a means of gaining knowledge and disciplining the mind
- Learning how to reason about human affairs and moral principles
- Learning to value the past and masterpieces of literature and art

Essentialism

Essentialism
The educational philosophy that there is an indispensable, common core of culture that should be taught to all.

Essentialism as an educational philosophy maintains that there is a common body of knowledge all students need to learn as a prerequisite for functioning effectively in society. Essentialism began as a reaction against the decline of intellectual and moral standards in the schools. In 1938, a group of professional educators met to outline the essentialist position. In part they said:

> Should not our public schools prepare boys and girls for adult responsibility through systematic training in such subjects as reading, writing, arithmetic, history, and English, requiring mastery of such subjects, and, when necessary, stressing discipline and obedience?[36]

William C. Bagley (1874–1946), professor of education at Columbia Teachers College and educational critic, founded the Essentialistic Education Society to promote essentialist ideas. Bagley felt the school curriculum was too diluted by nonessentials and should consist of essential facts and a common culture. Bagley advocated an intellectual curriculum rather than a curriculum focused on growth and development. He believed that education requires hard work and respect for authority.

Like many school critics of today, the essentialists believe schools have suffered a decline in academic rigor. Essentialists recommend that all students learn an academic-based core of knowledge that will enable them to be productive members of society. Essentialists would include vocational education—but not careerism—in the curriculum on the condition that it is practical, useful, and capable of helping students be productive members of society.

Essentialists and perennialists share many ideas, but differ in the following ways:

- Perennialists base their beliefs on realist ideas, such as that the purpose of education is to develop rational thinking. Essentialists do not.
- Essentialists believe in practical curriculum and subjects that will help students be useful citizens, such as vocational training. Perennialists do not.
- Essentialists view learning as its own goal—learning for learning's sake—while perennialists believe that education can be used to solve societal problems.
- Essentialists do not universally agree on what constitutes the "essentials" but look to the Western tradition for content.

E. D. Hirsch, Jr. (1928–), professor of English at the University of Virginia, is the contemporary articulator and proponent of the essentialist position. Hirsch outlined his essentialist position in *Cultural Literacy: What Every American Needs to Know.* He has established the Core Knowledge Foundation as a means of promoting a core-essentialist curriculum. Others who support cultural literacy include William Bennett, former Secretary of Education, author of the popular *Book of Virtues,* and founder of K–12 Inc., an online school. (See Chapter 12.) The Profile presents two views of what different schools consider essential in the curriculum.

Essentialists support a curriculum that:

- Develops cultural literacy—those things that constitute the "common core" of a literate citizenry and that form the basis of American civilization
- Teaches students, beginning in kindergarten (and even before, in the home), the names, dates, and events that constitute the foundation of our national cultural heritage
- Is practical and oriented toward citizenship and vocational training
- Views learning as a goal in itself, enabling students to function as members of society
- Teaches the basic skills—reading, writing, and mathematics—at the elementary level as well as the arts and sciences

For essentialists, the teacher's role includes:

- Imparting knowledge to students, whose job it is to learn—whether or not they feel like it or like what they are learning
- Initiating and promoting learning, motivating students to learn, and maintaining the appropriate discipline for learning. Emphasis is placed on having students learn the basics they need for success in life.
- Engaging in teacher-directed activities characterized by discipline and teacher authority

For essentialists, the student's role includes:

- Acquiring and using Western cultural knowledge
- Learning and using thinking skills
- Expending effort and being devoted to the learning process

NCATE

Early Childhood

Standard 4: Integrates understanding of children and families, of developmentally effective approaches to teaching and learning, and of academic disciplines to design, implement, and evaluate positive learning experiences for all children.

Elementary

Standard 3.1: Plans and implements instruction based on knowledge of students, learning theory, subject matter, curricular goals, and community.

Reflect & Write

What are some implications of perennialism and essentialism for culturally diverse students and multicultural curricula?

_____

_____

_____

_____

Progressivism

Progressivism
An educational philosophy maintaining that since life is ever changing, students should acquire problem-solving skills; emphasizes child-centered teaching and curriculum planning.

Elementary

Standard 3.1: Plans and implements instruction based on knowledge of students, learning theory, subject matter, curricular goals, and community.

Progressivism begins with the child rather than the subject matter. The progressive education movement developed in great measure primarily through the efforts and influence of John Dewey. Since its beginnings in the 1920s, progressivism has had a major effect on educational thought and practice.

Dewey (1859–1952) was an educational pragmatist who maintained that experience is the teacher. Thus, the instructor implementing Dewey's ideas is not a teller of facts and knowledge but rather a facilitator of problem-solving skills. Progressivism emphasizes the importance of students' interests and experiences in education. Dewey believed that to promote an interest in the intellectual—solving problems, discovering new things, and figuring out how things work—students should be given opportunities for inquiry and discovery. Dewey also believed that social interest, referring to interactions with people, should be encouraged in a democratically run classroom.

Those who embrace progressive ideas are focused on change. They believe knowledge is only tentative and not necessarily true forever. There are no lasting truths, and yesterday's values are not necessarily the ones students use today to guide their behavior. Therefore, major purposes of schooling are to educate students who can adapt to change and who can solve problems and discover new knowledge and values for themselves. Progressivists believe that students are basically good and naturally

---

Profile Two School Philosophies in Action: What Is Essential?

Longfellow School for the Visual and Performing Arts. An excellent example of the integration of the arts into the school curriculum is the Longfellow Elementary School in Kansas City, Missouri, a magnet school for the visual and performing arts. Yvonne Hatfield's kindergarteners engage in an all-day program of basic skill instruction and drama, dance, music, and movement. Visual arts include painting, sketching, modeling with clay, photography, and creative writing, and the performing arts include music, theater, and dance.

Drama plays a significant role in the curriculum and life of the kindergarten classroom. As Yvonne explains, "Drama and the other performing arts give children exposure to and experience with topics and people they would not otherwise have. Drama is in many ways a mirror of real-life events. I use drama to help children learn many important skills, concepts, and values. Drama is also a natural way of helping children learn through their bodies."

Yvonne gives these examples of drama activities in her kindergarten. "One of my groups read in their basal reader a story of the tortoise and the hare. After the reading, the children acted out the story, and we emphasized expression and how the human voice—their voices—sounds in certain situations. Also, during Black History Month in February, the children did a 'Readers Theater' of the Rosa Parks story. One group read the story, and another group acted out the events. The children had a lot of fun getting ready. They made bus-stop signs, designed and made costumes of clothing from the Salvation Army, made a bus from cardboard boxes, and used chairs for seats. I revised an existing script for the children and worked with the parents of the children who had reading parts. It was a great learning activity!"

Yvonne teaches readiness skills—reading (many of the children are reading at a first-grade level or above by the end of the school year), math, social studies, science, writing, and

creative movement—all integrated with drama. Support teachers provide instruction in art, music, physical education, computers, and Suzuki violin.

"I integrate academics into everything I do," explains Yvonne. "The visual and performing arts give children experiences on which to build their academics! The arts also give children a chance to appreciate their self-worth at many levels and in different ways. Take, for example, a child like Alex, who struggles in reading. He really excels in dance. The experiences of being good in this area are a great benefit to him."

Joella C. Good Core Knowledge School. Joella C. Good Elementary School, located in Miami, Florida, is a Core Knowledge School. The school has a population of 1,632 students in prekindergarten through fifth grade that is 55 percent Hispanic American, 28 percent African American, 14 percent Anglo-European American, and 3 percent Asian American.

The school's administration and teachers are committed to teaching a specific and sequenced content in all grades. Primary and intermediate teachers use the Core Knowledge Curriculum and other programs that emphasize the use of critical-thinking skills and higher-level questioning techniques for speaking and writing. They also incorporate math manipulatives to enhance the daily instructional program.

The Core Knowledge Curriculum provides the content for all school activities. Teachers select their own method of teaching: traditional, whole-language, or thematic units. For example, a fourth-grade teacher could integrate the Core Knowledge literature selections *Robinson Crusoe* or *Treasure Island* with critical-thinking skills and math manipulatives to create a geology project around such fourth-grade Core Knowledge geology topics as island formation, earth's layers, rocks, weathering, and/or erosion.

---

inclined to explore and inquire, that they are capable of deciding what is best for them. This helps justify why students, in a progressive curriculum, are given considerable freedom and are allowed to choose what they will learn. Progressivists believe that what students select is best for them as learners and persons.

Many educational practices used in today's classrooms are based on Deweyan progressive ideas. These include cooperative learning, multiage grouping, arranging rooms into interest and activity centers that enable children to choose what they will learn and where they will learn it, the establishment of supportive relationships with students, curricula that emphasize students' self-esteem, and the teaching of conflict resolution skills and techniques for getting along with others. Figure 9.6 shows the curriculum and instruction focus of progressivism in relation to the other educational philosophies discussed in this chapter.

Basic education principles of progressivism are:

- Education is child centered, and schooling should take into consideration the whole child; that is, students' needs and interests in all areas—cognitive, physical, social, and emotional.
- Students should have direct experience with their environments. Learning is active, not passive, and students learn best through a process of doing.
- The curriculum should be based on and built around students' interests.

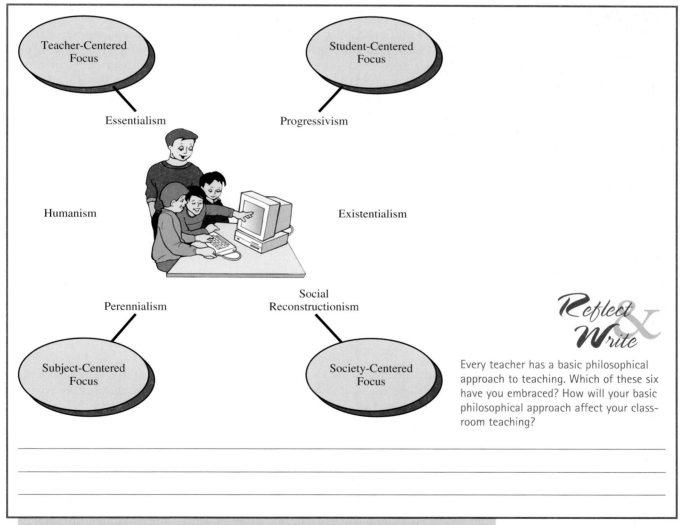

Reflect & Write

Every teacher has a basic philosophical approach to teaching. Which of these six have you embraced? How will your basic philosophical approach affect your classroom teaching?

Figure 9.6   Six Educational Philosophies: Curriculum and Instruction Focus

- Thinking and problem solving are important parts of the curriculum, since students' knowledge and values today may not be the same tomorrow.
- Problem solving, the ability to define and solve human problems, is more important than knowledge of or about human problems. Society constantly changes, so preparation for productive living includes learning how to live productively in a world of change.
- Schools should not be isolated from the community. Progressivism considers the community a rich field for both learning experiences and resources. The move to require community service as a condition for high school graduation is the result of progressive beliefs that education should have a socially useful value.

The teacher's role in the progressive classroom includes:

- Taking into account the whole child when planning and teaching
- Acting as a resource person and guiding and facilitating students' learning. For progressives, the teacher is envisioned more as a "guide on the side" rather than as a "sage on the stage."
- Asking appropriate questions to help students discover knowledge and truth for themselves
- Preparing the learning environment to enable students to experiment and engage in learning on their own
- Involving students in democratic living. For progressives, the learning environment—classroom and school—is considered a microcosm of a democratic society. Accordingly, students, teachers, and staff interact and live and learn as they would in a democratic society. Group activities, cooperative and collaborative learning, enable children to participate democratically and prepare for democratic living.
- Emphasizing methods—learning how to learn—more than knowledge or subject matter. Teachers see their role as helping children learn how to learn in any situation, time, and place. Some of the methods are reading, experimenting, interviewing, observing, and writing.
- Developing a curriculum based, in part, on the interests of children rather than solely on subject matter
- Taking into account the whole child in planning and teaching

The student's role in a progressive classroom includes:

- Learning to be an independent and self-directed learner
- Participating cooperatively with others in group work and processes
- Learning skills related to getting along with others
- Developing responsibility for helping to care for and maintain the learning environment
- Engaging in planning for what to learn and how to learn it
- Participating actively in learning-by-doing activities
- Learning problem-solving strategies and applying them to real-world problems

Social Reconstructionism

Social reconstructionism has its roots in pragmatism, the belief that the truth of ideas is tested by their practical consequences, and the progressive education movement. Social reconstructionism and progressivism are closely aligned in their beliefs. Many of the leaders of the social reconstruction movement were progressives.

As the name implies, social reconstructionists believe that teachers, students, and the schools can play a key role in reconstructing society and building a new social order resulting in more effective democratic living. Thus, they are concerned about the relationship of school curricula and activities to social, economic, and political developments. Social reconstructionists look to current social issues as a guide in determining what the schools should teach. Since schooling is a social process, sanctioned and supported by society, it is only natural that society should look to the public schools to

Standard 4: The teacher uses various instructional strategies to encourage students' development of critical thinking, problem solving, and performance skills.

Early Childhood

Standard 4: Integrates understanding of children and families, of developmentally effective approaches to teaching and learning, and of academic disciplines to design, implement, and evaluate positive learning experiences for all children.

Middle Level

Standard 5: Understands and uses major concepts, principles, theories, and research related to effective instruction and assessment; employs a variety of strategies for a developmentally appropriate climate to meet the varying abilities and learning styles of all young adolescents.

Social reconstructionism
A philosophy based on the belief that people are responsible for social conditions and can improve the quality of life by changing the social order.

help solve its problems and make society better. Thus, social reconstructionist agendas often have public support, which has implications for contemporary school curricula. (For example, see Education on the Move.)

Social reconstructionists whose thinking is influenced by Marxism believe that the schools often serve the interests of the dominant socioeconomic group of the state and tend to perpetuate the capitalistic system. Neo-Marxists are often critical of education, pointing out the social injustices that result from schooling. For example, neo-Marxists may feel that the schools are creating a generation of illiterates by not providing technological opportunities to low-income schools and children.

The social reconstructionist philosophy:

- Holds that social reform should be the goal of education. The major way that schools participate in this reconstruction or reform is by preparing students to be capable of promoting social reform.
- Advocates a curriculum that helps students develop their full potential in this and other areas.
- Believes in confronting students with the problems facing society and developing curricula that stress responsibility to self, others, and society.
- Supports student awareness of and involvement in addressing solutions to major social problems, such as violence, crime, homelessness, gender and socioeconomic inequities, substance abuse, and AIDS. Students engage in firsthand efforts to address these problems. For example, students might educate their peers about the needs of children with AIDS and help raise money for a family support center for families of children with AIDS.
- Accords with efforts to involve students in community service as a requirement for school graduation.

INTASC

Standard 3: The teacher understands how students differ in their approaches to learning and creates instructional opportunities that are adapted to diverse learners.

education on the move >>>>>>>>>>>>>

>>> Indian Schools Struggling with Federal Mandates >>>>>>>

When the No Child Left Behind Act was signed into law, it provided Bureau of Indian Affairs (BIA) schools with a strong degree of leeway in coping with some of the federal statute's toughest provisions and penalties. Yet despite the latitude provided to them under the law, BIA schools face a daunting task in meeting the No Child Left Behind Act's mandates. Administrators and tribal leaders say particularly the requirement that all students be proficient in mathematics and reading by 2014 is a challenging one.

Schools overseen by the federal bureau are not required to offer students the right to transfer out of schools repeatedly labeled as needing improvement, as is the case with those in traditional, district-run systems. Nor are BIA-financed schools obliged to offer tutoring to struggling students, a provision of the law that

has worried administrators in many rural school districts nationwide. In addition, tribes and boards that oversee BIA-financed schools can apply to the federal government for waivers that allow them to set their own definitions of "adequate yearly progress," differing from those used by the states in which they are located.

These provisions, according to federal officials and Native American leaders familiar with them, reflect the unique status of the bureau, an arm of the Department of the Interior, and its schools. Today, the Bureau of Indian Affairs oversees 185 schools serving 48,000 students in 23 states.

Many Indian students begin school with a limited English vocabulary, having heard a combination of this language and native tribal dialects at home. It follows that American Indian and Alaska Native students lag well behind other ethnic groups in

reading, in addition to mathematics, a disparity evident from the earliest grades. "All of us believe our children can learn," said Roger C. Bordeaux, the superintendent of the Tiospa Zina Tribal School, a BIA facility in northeastern South Dakota. "The difficulty we face is the ensuring that 100 percent of our students should be proficient, based on somebody else's standards."

The No Child Left Behind Act essentially treats the BIA as a fifty-first state, requiring the Interior Department to establish its own definition of "adequate yearly progress" for bureau schools by taking into account their "unique circumstances."

Source: S. Cavanagh, "Indian Schools Struggling with Federal Mandates," *Education Week,* July 28, 2004. (Online). Available at www.edweek.com/ew/ew_printstory.cfm?slug =43Bia.h23. Reprinted by permission.

The teacher's role in social reconstructionism includes:

- Confronting students with contemporary social problems
- Having students learn about social issues and guiding students in addressing these issues
- Drawing heavily on the behavioral sciences as a source for the curriculum
- Conducting classrooms based on equity and social justice and in keeping with democratic principles
- Encouraging and promoting cooperation and collaboration with community leaders and agencies
- Integrating the curriculum, directing the study of all subjects toward solving community problems

The student's role in a social reconstructionist program includes:

- Using personal interests to help find solutions to social problems
- Learning problem-solving skills as a means of addressing community-based and global problems
- Learning to value social activism

Humanism

Humanism is a philosophy concerned with human nature and the human condition. Humanism emphasizes the basic goodness of humans and our capacity for free will and self-fulfillment. Jean-Jacques Rousseau (1712–1778) clarified humanistic beliefs when he argued for a naturalistic education that is free of artificialness and does not restrict or interfere with the child's natural growth and development. Rousseau believed the true nature of children—what they are to be—unfolds as a result of natural processes of maturation.

Abraham Maslow (1908–1970) had a profound influence on humanistic philosophy. Maslow theorized that all human beings have certain basic needs, that these basic needs are interrelated, and that all of them must be met in order for individuals to become self-actualized, whereby they fully use their talents, capacities, and abilities. Maslow's *Hierarchy of Needs* identifies basic human needs in the order in which they motivate an individual to **self-actualization.** These basic human needs include physiological needs (air, food, water, clothing, shelter), safety (security, freedom from threat or physical/psychological harm), belongingness (love and affection), esteem (respect, recognition, self-esteem), and self-actualization. Maslow's hierarchy of needs has played and continues to play an important role in education today. For example, school lunch programs help meet physiological needs. Safe schools and classrooms help promote safety. Empathetic, considerate, and supportive teachers help meet love and belonging needs. Teachers who provide for individual needs and abilities and ensure achievement contribute to self-esteem needs. High expectations of teachers and administrators motivate students to do their best, thereby working toward self-actualization. Maslow's humanistic theory has been particularly influential in the self-esteem movement, which aims to provide students with a greater sense of worth and address their needs for recognition, attention, and self-confidence.

The humanistic educational philosophy:

- Encourages the development of students as persons, including their self-concepts, personal growth, and self-esteem
- Emphasizes the affective side of development; that is, how students feel about learning and learning experiences and the connections they make between learning and their lives
- Puts students at the center of learning and emphasizes "self-actualization" and "the teaching of the whole person"

Humanism
A branch of philosophy concerned with human nature and the human condition.

Self-actualization
The state in which the basic needs Maslow postulates are met so that individuals can fully use their talents and abilities.

Based on humanistic philosophy, the teacher's role includes:

- Developing meaningful relations between teacher and students
- Emphasizing the affective side of education, including aesthetics, ethics, and morality
- Helping students cope with their psychological needs
- Facilitating self-understanding of each individual student and promoting self-understanding among students

According to humanist philosophy, a student's role includes:

- Seeking independence and self-direction
- Developing greater acceptance of others
- Using talents and abilities to become fully actualized

Reflect & Write

Many conservative educational critics oppose humanistic approaches in education, feeling they interfere with the promotion of academic achievement. Discuss their argument. Which side of this argument are you on? Why?

_____

_____

_____

_____

Existentialism

Existentialism is a philosophy that focuses on the subjectivity of human experience and the importance of the individual. Meaning is determined by individuals, not by external criteria. Existentialism grew from the ideas of Søren Kierkegaard, a Danish theologian (1813–1855), and the writings of the French philosopher Jean-Paul Sartre (1905–1980). Kierkegaard believed that through education humans come to understand themselves and their destinies. He further maintained that people must recognize their responsibility for making choices and the consequences of their choices. Sartre was the leading twentieth-century articulator of existential thought and is famous for his dictums "Existence [being] precedes essence [meaning]" and "We are condemned to be free."[37] Accordingly, an individual's existence is the result of each person working out his or her own destiny and meaning of life through individual choices.

Maxine Greene, Professor Emeritus at the Teacher's College of Columbia University, is a well-known contemporary supporter of existential philosophy. As part of the humanistic educational process, Greene advocates a "new pluralism" in which "stereotypes and labels are scorned and students are allowed to develop their true identities in environments of diversity and equal regard for all cultures."[38] In order to achieve this goal, "a student must be regarded as a constantly evolving individual who is the sum of many parts."[39] An example of existentialist teaching might be to raise moral questions regarding the events surrounding September 11, 2001, and explore how individual decisions resulted in particular moral and ethical courses of action.

Existentialists believe that we cannot escape the responsibility of choosing. Individuals always have a choice and therefore should always make the most of any situation. The choices people make determine their lives, and in this sense, choices determine the future.

Existentialism as applied to education:

- Involves a quest for personal meaning. Students are encouraged to make their own decisions rather than having others make or dictate their choices.
- Encourages students to search for their own meaning in life and to identify their own values rather than to have them imposed by others.

Existentialism
A philosophy emphasizing the necessity for individuals to determine the course and nature of their own lives.

INTASC

Standard 1: The teacher understands the central concepts, tools of inquiry, and structures of the subjects being taught and can create learning experiences that make these aspects of subject matter meaningful for students.

- Views education as a process of helping students become autonomous, free think-ing, self-actualized individuals engaged in a search for self.
- Holds that education begins with the individual. Education should help students become what they want to become, not what others or society think they should become.

Based on existential philosophy, the teacher's role includes:

- Providing for and support student freedom of choice
- Providing students with experiences that will enable them to determine the mean-ing of their lives
- Engaging students in journal writing and appropriate literature and film to foster their abilities to engage in self-examination
- Providing students with individual freedom
- Engaging students in a dialogue of questions designed to promote self-reflection
- Encouraging and helping students examine institutional and societal forces that limit freedom
- Maximizing freedom of choice
- Challenging the "taken for granted," the "given," the "bound," and the "restrict-ed"[40]

According to existentialist philosophy, a student's role includes:

- Asking questions about the purpose and the meaning of life
- Being involved in inquiries and problem solving that lead to conclusions about and insight into their lives
- Being aware of and responsible for their own education and self-determination
- Being aware that their choices are theirs to make

SECTION SUMMARY

What Are the Major Philosophies of Education?

The major philosophies of education are perennialism, essentialism, progressivism, social reconstructionism, humanism, and existentialism.

- Perennialism. Perennialists see truth as eternal and unchanging. This view advo-cates the teaching of the classics and a common core curriculum.

- Essentialism. Essentialists maintain that there is a common body of knowledge all students need to know in order to function effectively in society and that this includes the content of cultural literacy.

- Progressivism. Progressivists hold that students are the center of learning and that their interests and experiences are foundational to developing and determining the curriculum.

- Social Reconstructionism. Social reconstructionists believe that the schools are a key factor in reconstructing society and building a better world. Neo-Marxist thinkers urge the use of education and schooling to bring an end to class distinc-tions, to promote equity, and to end the oppression of one group by another.

- Humanism. Humanists emphasize the humanness of existence and promote a natu-ral approach to learning. Students are seen as persons, and the affective side of their development is emphasized.

- Existentialism. Existentialists emphasize responsibility and choice as the basis for defining individuality. Applied to education, existentialism involves a quest for personal meaning.

Thinking Critically

★ ★ ★ ★ ★ ★ ★ ★ ★ ★

Do you believe the U.S. educational system trains Americans to be conformists? Was that your experience in attending school?

_____

_____

_____

_____⋆

Applying What You've Learned

★ ★ ★ ★ ★ ★ ★ ★ ★ ★

What developments in the history of education were based on philosophies that give primacy to knowing through experience? Review this chapter and find some examples. Explain how those examples were based on knowing through experience.

_____

_____

_____

_____⋆

Putting Yourself in the Picture

★ ★ ★ ★ ★ ★ ★ ★ ★ ★

Select one of the educational philosophies discussed in this section and answer the following questions.

1. How would your classroom look?
2. What would be your role as the teacher?
3. What would you expect students to learn and be able to do?

_____

_____

_____

_____⋆

WHAT ARE THE IMPLICATIONS OF PHILOSOPHIES OF EDUCATION FOR YOU AND YOUR STUDENTS?

What teachers believe makes important differences in their lives and the lives of the students they teach. There is a constant tension between philosophies of education and the educational practices that support them in the public schools. Beginning in the 1980s, the schools came under heavy criticism because they had not educated youth to the extent and degree necessary to keep the nation economically competitive. As a result, reform movements seek to change the role and scope of education (see Chapter 1). The educational philosophies discussed in this chapter are outgrowths of reform efforts directed at having schools better meet societal needs and goals.

Throughout this chapter you have read about philosophies and philosophies of education and how these affect educational practice. You are invited to reflect on and rewrite your philosophy of education. Perhaps you are in agreement with the beliefs of one of the philosophies discussed. Or you may take a more eclectic approach, drawing your ideas from several philosophies. Whatever your approach, your personal beliefs

> **INTASC**
>
> **Standard 1:** The teacher understands the central concepts, tools of inquiry, and structures of the subjects being taught and can create learning experiences that make these aspects of subject matter meaningful for students.

and philosophy of education will influence all your activities in the classroom—what you think should be taught; how to teach it; how to interact with students, parents, and colleagues; and how you conduct your professional life.

Developing your personal educational philosophy takes time, work, commitment, and a willingness to think, study, and share ideas with others. Your philosophy of education will develop from your philosophy of life and who you are. This means that as you grow and develop as a person and as a professional, your philosophy of life as well as your educational philosophy may change or be refined.

Taken together, history and philosophy provide a foundation on which you can build your teaching career. The history of education informs us of where we have been, enlightens us as to how and why we conduct current practice, and provides road maps for us to use in navigating the future of educational practice. Your philosophy of education, based on the six educational philosophies we have discussed, will enable you to confidently and proactively engage in the art and craft of teaching.

Which of the six educational philosophies do you agree with the most as a source for your philosophy of teaching?

_____

_____

_____

_____

Applications for Active Learning

CONNECTIONS

1. Review your thoughts in the first Reflection concerning the chapter opening case. Develop further your outline of points that Susan could make on the value to teachers of knowing the history of education.

2. Think about the concepts in this chapter. Create a picture, graphic, or figure that shows connections that are meaningful to you among this chapter's key ideas and information.

FIELD EXPERIENCES

1. Interview classroom teachers regarding their philosophies of education. Ask them to identify themselves according to one of the six philosophies of education discussed in this chapter.

2. Interview five veteran teachers and ask them how their roles have changed over the years. What historical events and trends have affected their careers as teachers and their classroom practice? How do they evaluate those changes?

PERSONAL RESEARCH

1. Daily newspapers are a good place to read about how philosophies of education and beliefs about education influence the curriculum and what is taught. Over a period of a week, read your local newspaper and other newspapers such as the *New York Times, Christian Science Monitor,* and *Education Week.* Select five articles and write a paragraph about each one that explains what philosophy is influencing the event reported.

2. Many historical events have influenced the process of education in the United States. Identify five events you think have been the most influential. Provide a rationale for each of your selections.

Preparing to Teach

FOR YOUR PORTFOLIO

1. Set aside some time in your daily schedule over the next several days to write, revise, and complete the "final" version of your philosophy of education. Analyze the ways in which your final version differs from your original draft.

How did you change your thinking? Why did you change your thinking?

2. Consider your own history as a learner and as a student engaged in field experiences and write a reflective essay on your own growth as a teacher.

IDEA FILE

Assess your own personal philosophy and determine your three most important educational goals. Write a paragraph on each of these goals and how you will try to achieve it.

Learning and Knowing More

WEB SITES WORTH VISITING

The history of education is extremely interesting and informative. We can see where we have been and hopefully learn where we are going as a profession. You may want to begin your research into the history of education with the History of American Education Web Project, located at ww.nd.edu/~barger/www7/. It lists Web resources, from simple to complex and from all over the world, on the history of education, and also provides texts and sources.

For a more current perspective on education, the staff of *Education Week*, with contributions from leading scholars, have written "Lessons of a Century," which examines all aspects of the educational landscape of twentieth-century America. You can access "Lessons of a Century" at www.edweek.org.

Daily life provides us opportunities to reflect on what we believe and why and how our beliefs influence our lives and the lives of others. One way you can do this is through the American Philosophical Association Web site www.apa.udel.edu/apa/index.html. The American Philosophical Association is the main professional organization for philosophers in the United States. You will find much useful information including newsletters, electronic text, and links to other sources and philosophers discussed in this chapter.

National Council for History Education
www.history.org/nche
The National Council for History Education is a nonprofit corporation whose board of trustees is dedicated to promoting the importance of history in schools and in society. NCHE links history in the schools with many activities sponsored by state and local organizations.

Society for Philosophical Inquiry
www.philosopher.org
The Society for Philosophical Inquiry (SPI) is a nonprofit organization composed of philosophical inquirers of all ages and walks of life. SPI is dedicated to helping individuals articulate and explore their philosophies of life and in the process, hopefully, cultivate a more acute social and intellectual conscience.

John Locke
www.ilt.columbia.edu/academic/digitexts/locke/bio_JL.html
This Web site offers background material on and selected essays by the English philosopher John Locke. Additionally, there are links provided to other resources on Locke and other philosophers.

Larry Shaw, *Five Educational Philosophies*
http://web.sdsu.edu/people/LShaw/F95syll/philos/phintro.html
This Web site, developed by Professor Larry Shaw, is an excellent description of key ideas competing for dominance in American education.

Philosophy of Education materials
http://commhum.mccneb.edu/PHILOS/phileduc.htm
This site contains a rich collection of further readings, including original sources on the major philosophies of education.

The Blackwell History of Education Museum
www.cedu.niu.edu/blackwell
The Blackwell History of Education Museum and Research Collection is one of the largest collections of its kind in the world. Much of the collection can be found on their Web site. The Blackwell Museum has developed a variety of instructional materials (also listed on its site) designed to help you learn more about the antecedents of American education.

BOOKS WORTH READING

Adams, D. W. (1995). *Education for Extinction: American Indians and the Boarding School Experience, 1875–1928.* Lawrence, KS: University Press of Kansas.
Based on extensive use of government archives, Indian and teacher autobiographies, and school newspapers, Adams's moving account is essential reading for scholars and general readers interested in Western history, Native American studies, American race relations, education history, and multiculturalism.

Browne, M. N., and Keeley, S. M. (2003). *Asking the Right Questions: A Guide to Critical Thinking* (7th ed.). Englewood Cliffs, NJ: Prentice Hall.
This text helps students bridge the gap between simply memorizing or blindly accepting information and the greater challenge of critical analysis and synthesis.

Jacobsen, D. A. (1998). *Philosophy in Classroom Teaching: Bridging the Gap.* Englewood Cliffs, NJ: Prentice Hall.
This book is devoted to clearly establishing the practical applicability of philosophy in classroom teaching.

Kozol, J. (1999). *Amazing Grace: The Lives of Children and the Conscience of a Nation.* Minneapolis: Econo-Clad Books.
Kozol draws a vivid picture of an urban ghetto, with its hunger, poverty, drugs, disease, and violence, using a series of interviews with the people of the Mott Haven section of the South Bronx, the poorest congressional district in the country.

Mondale, S. (2002). *School: The Story of American Public Education*. Boston: Beacon Press.

Chronologically arranged in four sections, this anthology covers much ground at a brisk, engaging pace.

Ozmon, H. A. (2002). *Philosophical Foundations of Education* (6th ed.). Englewood Cliffs, NJ: Prentice Hall.

This comprehensive survey text introduces students to various schools of thought, with due regard to historical influence and settings, and provides a balanced critical treatment of each philosophy.

Pulliam, J. D., and Van Patten, J. J. (2002). *History of Education of America* (8th ed.). Englewood Cliffs, NJ: Prentice Hall.

The authors provide a comprehensive overview of the history of American education that serves as a quick reference to the most important persons, dates, events, and movements that shaped the nation's system of education.

Titone, C. (1998). *Women's Philosophies of Education: Thinking Through Our Mothers*. Englewood Cliffs, NJ: Prentice Hall.

Unique in its contributions, this work presents the educational philosophies of seven women from a variety of times, cultures, and classes whose ideas have influenced thinking on education in the United States.

Urban, J. W., and Wagoner, J. L. (2005). *American Education: A History*. (2nd ed.). New York: McGraw-Hill Higher Education.

The authors cover the history of American education from precolonial times to the present in a comprehensive, seamless, engaging manner. They provide an objective overview of historical events along with a thoughtful analysis and integration, presenting each major period in the development of American education against the broader backdrop of national and world events.

PART FOUR

Teaching and Learning

Teachers in the twenty-first century face the exciting challenge of educating increasingly diverse students in an increasingly accountable and technological culture. Accountability is one of the most important—and high-profile—issues in education today. You will be accountable for teaching all your students so they achieve at high levels and pass state tests. Technology is changing not only how we teach but what we think of as literacy and learning. Instructional technologies are among the most important tools for teaching and learning today. Integrating technology into the curriculum and classroom practices will continue to be of crucial importance. Students will need to achieve technological literacy to be assured of employment and participation in today's and tomorrow's work world.

You as a teacher play an important role in bringing technology into the classroom and preparing students for their futures. Models for teaching and learning offer teachers a variety of approaches for integrating technological tools and addressing the varying needs of today's diverse learners. These approaches help develop the problem-solving and critical thinking skills students need to become productive and complete members of our society.

Technological and instructional advances, higher academic standards, greater accountability, and a rising demand for teachers are leading to creative ways of becoming qualified to teach. The chapters in Part Four will help you in your quest to become an outstanding teacher in this age of accountability and technology.

10 Standards, Assessment, and Accountability in Education Today: Redefining Teaching and Learning

"*All* students are challenged to meet their full potential."

Cindy Loe is associate superintendent of the Gwinnett County Public Schools. Gwinnett, Georgia's largest school district, serves more than 130,000 students.

Imagine that you had the power to predict the future of education—and to change it. Well, that's exactly what happened in Gwinnett County. In 1995–1996, our planning department predicted that the system's majority white, upper-middle-class population would rapidly become poorer and more diverse. Many assumed that, as a result, test scores would fall. In the face of these predictions, the school board and Superintendent J. Alvin Wilbanks called for a standards-based curriculum, which would be assessed by new criterion-referenced Gateway tests developed to measure student achievement.

The demographic prediction came true: in five years, poverty tripled; students whose primary language is other than English increased by more than 300 percent; and the population moved to a nonwhite majority. But the predictions of low test achievement have *not* come true. Despite overwhelming research that correlates increases in poverty and non-English-speaking students with decreases in test scores, achievement has risen to an *all-time high at every school level!*

- Eighty-eight percent of our students take the SAT, with an average score of 1036—10 points higher than the national average.
- The percentage of Gwinnett juniors passing the Georgia High School Graduation Test as first-time test takers in math, language arts, and social studies has remained even or increased.
- Gwinnett elementary and middle school students meet or exceed the state average in all subjects and all grade levels tested on Georgia's state Criterion Referenced Competency Tests (CRCT).
- And in the past five years, while our white students' SAT scores have increased by an average 18 points, the scores of our African American students have increased an average 49 points.

How did we accomplish this? First we determined content standards for every grade level and in every course. Then we implemented an assessment program to measure student learning. Students at the fourth, fifth, seventh, and eighth grades must demonstrate in a variety of ways that they have learned enough of the grade-level curriculum to be successful in the next grade in order to earn promotion.

Development of the Gateway assessment program involved teachers, parents, and community members. Each proposed test item was reviewed by groups of classroom teachers for a match of developmental appropriateness and alignment with the curriculum. A sensitivity and bias review was conducted with parents and community members, as well as English speakers of other languages (ESOL) and special education teachers, to verify that no item was inherently unfair for any group of students.

We learned that a comprehensive curriculum and aligned assessments are not enough to ensure students' success. We needed to put in place support opportunities for students having difficulty learning the curriculum as well as extensions of the curriculum to meet the needs of students seeking challenges beyond the grade-level curriculum. So teachers and administrators use the assessment data to determine where students are in their learning and to provide extensions and interventions as needed. Students are temporarily grouped for instruction based on how they score on these objectives—either in remedial groups, skill-maintenance groups, or extension groups.

In 1996, we began a summer school program for students not meeting grade-level expectations by the end of the school year. Students who fail the April administration of the Gateway take another form of the assessment at the end of summer school (more than half of these students pass), and students who fail a second time after summer school enter a transition program. Schools are provided additional personnel, staff development, and materials. More than 75 percent of the transition program students "catch up" with their on-grade-level peers during the first transition year and are not retained, and no student has needed more than one additional year in the transition program.

Thanks to a standards-based curriculum and assessment program, the Gwinnett District can proudly say that *all* students are challenged to reach their fullest potential.

How Will This Chapter Help You?

You Will Learn

★ how standards are changing teachers' roles

★ how standards are changing how and what students learn

★ about the political and educational issues associated with standards

★ about the role of tests in measuring student achievement

★ how accountability is changing teaching and learning

The New York Times
expect the world®
nytimes.com

Themes of the Times

Expand your knowledge of the concepts discussed in this chapter by reading current and historical articles from *The New York Times* by visiting the "Themes of the Times" section of the companion Web site.

HOW ARE STANDARDS CHANGING TEACHING AND LEARNING?

In school districts all across the country—from Bangor to Miami and New York to Los Angeles—standards, tests, and accountability are topics on the front burner of the educational agenda. The headlines say it all: "Exit Tests Tough on Ninth-Graders," "Teacher Woes Worst in Poor Schools," "Test Question No. 1: Why Have These Tests?", "Standards Setting Focuses Reform in Local Districts." As a beginning teacher you will be involved in all three of these educational processes—standards, tests, and accountability. Standards and tests will also influence what and how your students learn and their success in school and life. They will shape and determine how you teach, what you teach, your success as a teacher . . . and your pay.

Standards and Standards-Based Education

Standards are statements of what all students, pre-K through 12, should know and be able to do. They are goals that identify what should be learned at various grade levels. The classic example of this grade-level expectation is when President George W. Bush says that the federal government's expectation is that all children will read on grade level by grade 3. In addition, standards serve other functions and roles:

- Standards serve as expectations for what teachers should teach. When teachers make decisions about what to teach, they look to the state standards. While the standards are not and should not be the only curriculum teachers teach, they are the beginning points.
- Standards serve as a foundation for reform and accountability. Simply put, politicians and educators use standards to reform education. By promulgating standards that specify what children will know and be able to do, states play a major role in reforming education. Standards focus on essential concepts, knowledge, skills, and behaviors for children in the twenty-first century. As such, they are designed to increase achievement, one of the major reform goals of the current educational scene.
- Standards are used in efforts to increase accountability for teaching and learning. Standards become the basis for teaching and testing. Teachers and schools are evaluated and rewarded on how well children perform on local and state tests. The Texas Essential Knowledge and Skills (TEKS) specifies what Texas children K through 12 should know and be able to do. The Texas Assessment of Knowledge and Skills (TAKS) measures how well children have learned. Many other states have similar assessment systems, such as the Pennsylvania System of School Assessment (PSSA).
- Standards exert greater state and federal control of local education. Constitutionally, education is a state responsibility. Historically and traditionally, states have delegated responsibility for education to the local school districts. However, one of the educational trends of the past decade is that state legislatures and governors now play much more prominent roles in educational affairs.
- Standards provide a way of addressing the educational needs of low-achieving students. While standards represent the minimum benchmarks for grade-level achievement, they nonetheless make it clear what all students should learn and each school's responsibility in that effort. In this way, standards can be used as a means of preventing school failure and dropout.

To take some specific examples, the Florida Sunshine Standards require that all third-grade students be able to use a variety of strategies to prepare for writing. Colorado's Model Content Standards state that all middle school students should be able to identify and analyze ways in which advances in science and technology have affected one another and society. The Michigan Curriculum Framework maintains

Standards
Statements of what all students, pre-K through 12, should know and be able to do.

Early Childhood

Standard 1: Uses understanding of young children's characteristics, needs, and interacting influences on children's development and learning to create healthy, respectful, supportive, and challenging environments for all children.

Elementary

Standard 3.1: Plans and implements instruction based on knowledge of students, learning theory, subject matter, curricular goals, and community.

Middle Level

Standard 3: Understands the major concepts, principles, theories, and research related to middle-level curriculum and assessment; uses this knowledge in practice

INTASC

Standard 7: The teacher plans instruction based upon knowledge of subject matter, students, the community, and curriculum goals.

that all high school students must be able to analyze and generalize mathematical patterns including sequences, series, and recursive patterns.

A **standards-based education** is the process of basing teaching, learning, and assessment on national, state, and local educational standards. While on the surface this may seem to be a straightforward and uncomplicated process that would draw little controversy, nevertheless, standards have created and are creating a great deal of controversy, turmoil, and conflict within and without the educational arena. In fact, standards are one of the main topics of educational and political rhetoric and debate in this decade.

Searching for Accountability

A major reason for this controversy is that it is almost impossible to separate standards from assessment of student progress and teacher and school accountability. Standards specify what students will learn, and assessment measures if and what students have learned. Results of assessment often have **accountability provisions** tied to them, such as performance-based pay, school ratings and rankings, and administrator, teacher, and staff bonuses. (Recall from Chapter 2 how teachers and staff in Granbury School District in Texas received cash bonuses for increasing the state rating of their school based on student achievement data.) Supporters of standards say these accountability provisions help make schools responsible for ensuring that all students achieve at high levels. Critics claim that standards narrow the curriculum, discriminate against minorities, and erode local control of education.

The popularity of standards has grown out of two decades of political and public demand for increased accountability of teachers and schools to ensure that the nation's students learn and achieve at a high level. The standards-based reform movement began in 1983 largely in response to *A Nation at Risk: Imperatives for Educational Reform,* a report on the state of American education. This document painted a grim picture of American public education and set the tone for school reform, which still reverberates through America today. The report threw down the gauntlet of educational reform:

> If an unfriendly power had attempted to impose on America the mediocre educational performance that exists today, we might well have viewed it as an act of war. As it stands, we have allowed this to happen to ourselves. We have even squandered the gains in achievement made in the wake of the *Sputnik* challenge. Moreover, we have dismantled essential support systems, which helped make those gains possible. We have, in effect, been committing an act of unthinking, unilateral educational disarmament.[1]

(See Chapter 1 to review other reasons for current school reform movements.)

Recent national test scores underscore that the nation's students still do not achieve as well as society wants or thinks they can. For example, the 2003 results of the National Assessment of Educational Progress (NAEP)—"the Nation's Report Card"—show that only about 31 percent of fourth-graders are proficient in reading, almost the same percentage as twenty-eight years ago.[2] Figure 10.1 shows the results of the NAEP scores since 1992 for fourth-graders in reading and math and for eighth-graders for math. The modest improvement in eighth-grade math figures is encouraging, but what the figure does not show is that the gaps between top-scoring students and low-scoring students have widened, as did the achievement gaps between white students and African American and Hispanic students. This kind of data fuels the critics of public schools and drives efforts to reform schools through standards, tests, and incentives for improvement.

Supporters of standards also maintain that standards are necessary to enhance what advocates see as a stagnant curriculum that fails to challenge students or provide them with the knowledge and skills they need for living and working in the twenty-first century. The term **high and rigorous standards** is often used to convey that the curriculum can and should be more challenging for all students.

Standards–based education The process of basing teaching, learning, and assessment on national, state, and local educational standards.

Accountability provisions Performance-based pay, school ratings and rankings, and administrator, teacher, and staff bonuses.

High and rigorous standards The idea that curriculum can and should be more challenging for *all* students.

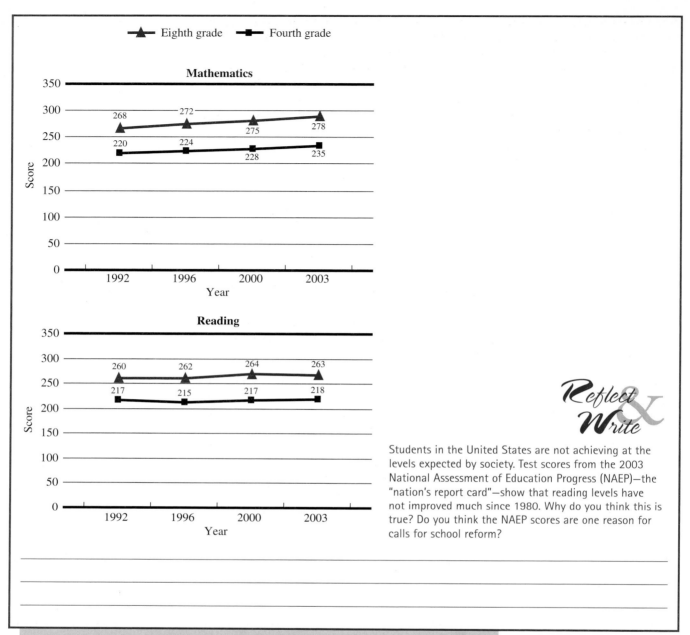

Legend: ▲ Eighth grade ■ Fourth grade

Mathematics

Eighth grade scores: 268 (1992), 272 (1996), 275 (2000), 278 (2003)
Fourth grade scores: 220 (1992), 224 (1996), 228 (2000), 235 (2003)

Reading

Eighth grade scores: 260 (1992), 262 (1996), 264 (2000), 263 (2003)
Fourth grade scores: 217 (1992), 215 (1996), 217 (2000), 218 (2003)

Reflect & Write

Students in the United States are not achieving at the levels expected by society. Test scores from the 2003 National Assessment of Education Progress (NAEP)—the "nation's report card"—show that reading levels have not improved much since 1980. Why do you think this is true? Do you think the NAEP scores are one reason for calls for school reform?

Figure 10.1 *Results of the 2003 National Assessment of Education Progress in Math and Reading for Fourth- and Eighth-Graders*

Source: National Assessment of Education Progress Web site. (Online). Available at nces.ed.gov/nationsreportcard/.

INTASC

Standard 2: The teacher understands how children learn and develop, and can provide learning opportunities that support their intellectual, social and personal development.

Additionally, those who favor standards say they are a way to increase expectations for students, teachers, and schools. As discussed in Chapter 1, one of the characteristics of good teachers and schools is that they have high expectations for all students. While many schools do have high expectations for all their students, many do not. Critics of the schools maintain that while expectations may be too low for all students, they are particularly too low for minority students. In a 2001 poll by the Metropolitan Life Foundation and the Committee for Economic Development, 56 percent of secondary school principals believed strongly that teachers have high expectations for students. However, when researchers asked students if they believed their teachers had high expectations for them, only 25 percent agreed. The poll also showed that teachers in high minority schools had lower expectations for their students than do most teachers in schools that do not have large numbers of minorities.[3] This "soft bigotry of low expectations" is one reason students do not achieve as well as they could and should. In other words, they and others believe high standards will help ensure that all students will learn at their highest levels and will learn what they need to know for college and careers.

Opinion is beginning to coalesce around the usefulness of standards. According to Reality Check 2002,[4] the standards movement continues to attract widespread support among teachers and parents, and public school students nationwide appear to be adjusting comfortably to the new status quo. Most students say they can handle the testing, and while a strong majority of teachers, parents, professors, and employers say they're worried about "teaching to the test," only one-quarter of teachers say they're actually doing it. All groups endorse standardized testing in some form, with one major caveat: majorities in all groups agree that a student's graduation or promotion should not hang on one test. The groups surveyed report tangible change in other ways. Teachers report that summer school attendance is up, and social promotion is down. Here are Reality Check's findings:

- Even as students nationwide face more testing and higher hurdles for promotion and graduation, very few seem apprehensive about school or unnerved by what is currently being asked of them.
- Even as standards are being raised nationwide, many students say they could work harder in school, and many say classmates often get diplomas without having learned what was expected.
- Broad agreement exists that local schools are moving in the right direction on standards and that testing has genuine benefits. No evidence points to a broad backlash against higher academic standards among any of the groups surveyed.
- Higher academic standards are taking root, and teachers and parents report notable changes in policies on testing, promotion, and summer school. Even so, some reforms sought by standards advocates remain more discussed than acted on.
- Employers and professors still say that too many of today's high school graduates lack basic skills.

How do these findings square with your opinions and views regarding standards? Which of the findings do you agree/disagree with the most? Why?

_____

_____

_____

_____

SECTION SUMMARY

How Are Standards Changing Teaching and Learning?

Some of the hottest discussions in American education today revolve around the need for standards, assessment, and accountability in our schools.

- Standards and Standards-Based Education. Standards are statements of what students should know and be able to do. Standards-based education arose in response to poor school performance and low student achievement.

- Searching for Accountability. Standards serve as a foundation for accountability and for the reform of education.

Thinking Critically

★ ★ ★ ★ ★ ★ ★ ★

Investigate the standards and assessment issue in your state. What are the expectations of schools in your state with regard to standards, assessment, and accountability of schools and teachers?

_____

_____

_____

_____ ★

Applying What You've Learned

★ ★ ★ ★ ★ ★ ★ ★

Why do we need standards? Reflect on this question and respond from several points of view—as a future teacher, as a parent, and as a member of the business community.

_____

_____

_____

_____ ★

Putting Yourself in the Picture

★ ★ ★ ★ ★ ★ ★ ★

Go back to your school—elementary, middle, or high school—and visit with teachers you know still teaching there. Find out how the standards movement has been affecting these school(s) and how the teachers are affected in their classrooms.

_____

_____

_____

_____ ★

_H_OW ARE STANDARDS EMPLOYED IN THE EDUCATIONAL SYSTEM_?_

A close look at standards-based education in America today reveals a multifaceted system that involves agencies at every level of decision making and affects everyone involved in determining the educational future of America's children.

Influences in the Development of Standards

National Standards. Recall from Chapter 3 that responsibility for education is a state function. Consequently, if the federal government wants to implement a particular educational program or objective, it does so through federal grants and other means of funding. Examples of national standards that relate to the curriculum include having all children read on grade level by grade 3, making the Head Start program more "academic," and the eLearning initiative, which ensures that all students have access

As technology has advanced and computers have become an integral part of our daily lives, students' knowledge and skill levels in computers and technology need to be higher as well. In response, most state and local standards now call for technology training as a part of the educational curriculum.

to and knowledge of the proper use of technology. IDEA, which was discussed in Chapter 5, mandates an individualized education plan (IEP) for every student with a special need. All these federal funding programs contain explicit required provisions that, in effect, become national standards. Consider the 2005 $57.3 billion federal Education Budget. As a condition for receiving this money, states and school districts must meet certain requirements. Some of these requirements, in effect, become the equivalent of standards. In essence the federal government is using the stick-and-carrot approach to reforming education. You want the money, then meet the standards. If standards are not met, student performance is low. If states and districts do not meet provisions of federal legislative rules and guidelines, then funding may be withheld. For example, there is strong public support for a federal role in testing, but the majority of the public opposes using tests as a basis for penalizing poorly performing public schools. Basically, the American public wants the federal government to play an active but not a punitive role in strengthening the public schools.

All national professional organizations for all the various disciplines have played and will continue to play a prominent role in developing and promoting national standards. Top scholars and respected members in each of the fields have collaborated to identify basic levels of knowledge and skills for the disciplines they consider to be appropriate and achievable by all students. In turn, developers of state and local standards are influenced by these professional standards and incorporate them into their own. A sample of national professional organizations that publish standards is shown in Figure 10.2, along with examples of their standards. Review these now and think about how they might influence your teaching.

State Standards. Currently, forty-nine states have statewide academic standards, with Iowa, home of the Iowa Test of Basic Skills (ITBS), the lone exception. All fifty states, however, have some kind of test to measure how well students are learning and, in many cases, how well students and schools are meeting the set standards. In addition,

Elementary

Standard 3.1: Plans and implements instruction based on knowledge of students, learning theory, subject matter, curricular goals, and community.

National Council for Teachers of English (NCTE)/International Reading Association (IRA)

- Read a wide range of print and nonprint texts
- Read a wide range of literature from many periods in many genres
- Apply a wide range of strategies to comprehend, interpret, evaluate, and appreciate texts
- Adjust their use of spoken, written, and visual language
- Employ a wide range of strategies as they write
- Apply knowledge of language structure, language conventions, media techniques, figurative language, and genre
- Conduct research on issues and interests
- Use a variety of technological and information resources
- Develop an understanding of and respect for diversity in language use, patterns, and dialects
- Students whose first language is not English make use of their first language to develop competency in English
- Participate as knowledgeable, reflective, creative, and critical members of a variety of literacy communities
- Use spoken, written, and visual language to accomplish their own purposes

National Council for the Social Studies (NCSS)

- Include experiences that provide for the study of culture and cultural diversity
- Include experiences that provide for the study of the ways human beings view themselves in and over time
- Include experiences that provide for the study of people, places, and environments
- Include experiences that provide for the study of individual development and identity
- Include experiences that provide for the study of interactions among individuals, groups, and institutions
- Include experiences that provide for the study of how people create and change structures of power, authority, and governance
- Include experiences that provide for the study of how people organize for the production, distribution, and consumption of goods and services
- Include experiences that provide for the study of relationships among science, technology, and society

Elementary

Standard 2.1: Demonstrates a high level of competence in use of English langauge arts; understands and uses concepts from reading, language, and child development to teach reading, writing, speaking, viewing, and thinking skills.

INTASC

Standard 7: The teacher plans instruction based upon knowledge of subject matter, students, the community, and curriculum goals.

Reflect & Write

Most discipline-specific national professional organizations have developed standards for learning and instruction. This figure shows a small sample of these. Do you think standards published by professional organizations are important? Why or why not? How might these standards impact you as a beginning teacher?

Figure 10.2   Standards of National Professional Organizations

Sources: NCTE. (Online). Available at www.ncate.org; NCSS. (Online). Available at www.ncss.org.

many states have systems in place to hold teachers and schools accountable for test results. Figure 10.3 shows selected state standards from Florida (first-grade language arts) and California (eighth-grade science).

Reflect & Write

Which of the two state standards shown in Figure 10.3 do you think are clearer? Which do you think it would be easiest to teach from?

Florida—First-Grade Language Arts

Reading

a. Uses prior knowledge, illustrations, and text to make predictions
b. Uses basic elements of phonetic analysis
c. Uses sound/symbol relationships as visual cues for decoding
d. Uses beginning letters and patterns as visual cues for decoding
e. Uses structural cues to decode words
f. Uses context clues to construct meaning
g. Cross checks visual, structural, and meaning cues to figure out unknown words
h. Knows common words from within basic categories
i. Uses knowledge of individual words in unknown compound words to predict their meaning
j. Uses resources and references to build upon word meanings
k. Uses knowledge of suffixes to determine meanings of words
l. Develops vocabulary by listening to and discussing both familiar and conceptually challenging selections read aloud
m. Uses a variety of strategies to comprehend text
n. Knows the main idea or theme and supporting details of a story or informational piece
o. Uses specific details and information from a text to answer literal questions
p. Makes inferences based on text and prior knowledge
q. Identifies similarities and differences between two texts
r. Selects material to read for pleasure
s. Reads aloud familiar stories, poems, and passages
t. Reads for information used in performing tasks
u. Uses background knowledge and supporting reasons from the text to determine whether a story or text is fact or fiction
v. Uses simple reference material to obtain information
w. Alphabetizes words according to the initial letter
x. Uses alphabetical order to locate information

California—Eighth-Grade Science

Motion—The velocity of an object is the rate of change of its position

a. Position is defined in relation to some choice of a standard reference point and a set of reference directions
b. Average speed is the total distance traveled divided by the total time elapsed and that the speed of an object along the path traveled can vary
c. How to solve problems involving distance, time, and average speed
d. Velocity of an object must be described by specifying both the direction and the speed of the object
e. Changes in velocity may be due to changes in speed, direction, or both
f. How to interpret graphs of position versus time and graphs of speed versus time for motion in a single direction

Forces—Unbalanced forces cause changes in velocity

a. Force has both direction and magnitude
b. When an object is subject to two or more forces at once, the result is the cumulative effect of all the forces
c. When the forces on an object are balanced, the motion of the object does not change
d. How to identify separately the two or more forces that are acting on a single static object, including gravity, elastic forces due to tension or compression, and friction
e. When the forces on an object are unbalanced, the object will change its velocity
f. The greater the mass of an object, the more force is needed to achieve the same rate of change in motion
g. Know the role of gravity in forming and maintaining the shapes of planets, stars, and the solar system

Structure of Matter—Each of the more than 100 elements of matter has distinct properties and a distinct atomic structure

a. Know the structure of the atom and know it is composed of protons, neutrons, and electrons
b. Compounds are formed by combining two or more different elements and that compounds have properties that are different from their constituent elements
c. Atoms and molecules form solids by building up repeating patterns, such as the crystal structure of $NaCl$ or long-chain polymers
d. The states of matter depend on molecular motion
e. In solids, the atoms are closely locked in position and can only vibrate; in liquids the atoms and molecules are more loosely connected and can collide with and move past one another; and in gases the atoms and molecules are free to move independently, colliding frequently
f. How to use the periodic table to identify elements in simple compounds

Earth Science—The structure and composition of the universe can be learned from studying stars and galaxies and their evolution

a. Galaxies are clusters of billions of stars and may have different shapes
b. The sun is one of the many stars in the Milky Way galaxy and that stars may differ in size, temperature, and color
c. How to use astronomical units and light years as measures of distances between the sun, stars, and earth
d. Stars are the source of light for all bright objects in outer space and that the moon and planets shine by reflected sunlight, not by their own light
e. The appearance, general composition, relative position and size, and motion of objects in the solar system, including planets, planetary satellites, comets, and asteroids

Most states have statewide academic standards. Notice the language in which the sample standards in this figure are written, the level at which they are written, and how specific (or vague) they are. Do you think these standards are well written? Select several and try your hand at rewriting them. Do you think writing standards is an easy or difficult task? Why?

_____

_____

_____

Figure 10.3   Examples of State Standards

Sources: Florida Department of Education, "Sunshine State Standards." (Online). Available at www.firn.edu/doe/curric/prek12/frame2.htm; California State Board of Education, "Content Standards for California Public Schools." (Online). Available at www.cde.ca.gov/be/st/ss/index.asp.

Local Standards. Local standards are in addition to, supplement, and enrich national and state standards. They express the will and desires of the local community.

Standards for Teachers

Just as there are standards stating what students should know and be able to do, there are also national, state, and local standards for initial teacher certification, recertification, and advanced certification. It comes as no surprise that these standards state what teachers should know and be able to do in order to engage in initial teaching, hold an ongoing license to teach, and gain recognition as a highly skilled and advanced teacher.

NCATE

Middle Level

Standard 7: Understands the complexity of teaching young adolescents; engages in practices and behaviors that develop competence as a professional.

Initial Teacher Certification. Initial teacher certification is tied to state standards. Examples of these standards were shown in Chapter 1 (Figures 1.1 and 1.2, pp. 6 and 7) for the states of Texas and Kentucky. Review these again and reflect how they influence what teachers should know and be able to do and the basis on which teachers are tested for initial recertification. Consider the knowledge and skills required of beginning teachers in these states. Compare these standards to the standards you will have to meet for initial licensure.

Recertification. Quite often, teacher recertification is tied to state standards. School districts and states will often formulate their own, independent recertification standards. For example, the Chicago Public Schools have initiatives in place for the following functions:

- Develop an informational brochure to educate and inform all Chicago teachers and administrators (private and public) of the tenets of NCLB.
- Disseminate information to teachers and host cluster meetings throughout the city.
- Design a template for the five-year plan that teachers can use as a model while developing their certificate renewal plans.
- Assist teachers in the development of exemplary plans.
- Establish a procedure to monitor and support teachers during the entire five-year implementation period of their professional development plans.
- Network with area colleges and universities to establish multiple, rigorous programs teachers may access to meet the state requirements for professional growth and development.
- Coordinate the efforts of the Chicago Public Schools Office with the Teachers' Academy, the Department of Curriculum and Instruction, Accountability, Specialized Services, and other units to offer joint training programs.
- Establish regional review teams and provide ongoing training to the teams to ensure consistency and rigor in the certificate renewal process.[5]

Standards and Issues

INTASC

Standard 7: The teacher plans instruction based upon knowledge of subject matter, students, the community, and curriculum goals.

As we have learned by now, education is a topic full of issues, contradictions, and concerns. Standards are no different. As educators implement standards, administer tests, and apply accountability provisions, controversies and conflicts arise. A number of issues exist and need to be considered within the context of broader-based educational issues.

Standards and Curriculum Alignment. Curriculum issues that are as old as teaching itself involve frequently asked questions such as "What should I teach?" and "What's worth knowing?" As usual, the answer is "It depends." It depends on what teachers think is important and what local districts, states, and the national government think is important. In the context of this chapter, it depends on what national, state, and local standards say are important. Therein lies the issue of how to develop curriculum that is aligned with standards.

Increasing student achievement and how to accomplish this goal are at the center of the standards movement. Policymakers believe that given appropriate standards, teaching, and rewards, student achievement will increase. Policymakers and educators view standards, tests, and teaching alignment as a viable and practical way to help ensure student achievement. **Alignment** is the arrangement of standards, curriculum, and tests so that they complement one another. The curriculum should be based on what the standards say students should know and be able to do. Tests should measure what the standards indicate.

Florida has aligned its standards (Florida Sunshine Standards), its assessment system (Florida Comprehensive Assessment Test [FCAT]), and the Governors A+ Program, which grades schools based on how well they measure on the FCAT. This alignment of state standards with curriculum, tests, and school ranking represents a comprehensive approach to educational reform.

Curriculum alignment is the process of making sure that what is taught—the content of the curriculum—matches what the standards say students should know and be able to do. One way educators achieve alignment is through the use of **curriculum frameworks,** which specify the curriculum teachers will teach. Figure 10.4 shows an example of a curriculum framework for K–2 math. In addition to aligning the standards and curriculum, some school districts also specify or suggest instructional activities and strategies for teachers to use so that the curriculum is implemented in ways to meet the standards. A related issue is how to teach the curriculum so that students learn what teachers teach. A deeper philosophical and pedagogical issue involves whether or not what standards specify is really worth knowing.

Aligning professional staff development with the state standards is one way to help ensure that teaching aligns with standards. Professional staff development in some school districts used to be fairly casual. Traditionally, many districts and schools have left decisions about staff development to teachers' preferences. Staff development is serious business and plays a major role in district efforts to increase student achievement. Staff development often includes specific training on the state and local standards, the state test, how to prepare students to achieve the standards, and how to take tests. For example, California has professional development institutes that align teacher training to the state standards.

Should teachers be told how to teach to standards? Or should teachers be told that they are to produce the results specified by the standards? A number of initiatives at the state and local level have established training programs to train teachers how to teach to the standards.[6]

- The Texas Education Agency, through its Reading Academies, has trained all of its K–4 teachers on the content of the state reading standards and how to teach reading so that students will learn what the standards specify.
- The Philadelphia public schools have developed a plan that specifies what should be taught and when it should be taught. Under this plan, K–12 teachers will be required to deliver specified curriculum in a certain sequence. The plan is designed to meet the Pennsylvania System of School Assessment (PSSA), which measures the progress of school districts.
- The Maryland State Legislature is considering a similar plan of structured teaching to the standards for the entire state. As a beginning teacher, you may not always get to teach what you want when you want. For a growing number of teachers, the state standards come first.
- Delaware is using a teacher-to-teacher mentoring program to help teachers meet standards. In this program, professional development must extend beyond one-day workshops and move into a daily learning experience. Under the five-year-old Teacher-to-Teacher Cadre program, districts identify expert teachers and assign

Alignment
The arrangement of standards, curriculum, and tests so they are in agreement.

Curriculum alignment
The process of making sure that what is taught matches the standards.

Curriculum frameworks
Specify the curriculum that teachers will teach.

Elementary
Standard 3.1: Plans and implements instruction based on knowledge of students, learning theory, subject matter, curricular goals, and community.

Standard 10: The teacher fosters relationships with school colleagues, parents, and agencies in the larger community to support students' learning and well-being.

Standard 1. All students will develop the ability to pose and solve mathematical problems in mathematics, other disciplines, and everyday experiences.

1. Use discovery-oriented, inquiry-based, and problem-centered approaches to investigate and understand mathematical content appropriate to the early elementary grades.
2. Recognize, formulate, and solve problems arising from mathematical situations and everyday experiences.
3. Construct and use concrete, pictorial, symbolic, and graphical models to represent problem situations.
4. Pose, explore, and solve a variety of problems, including nonroutine problems and open-ended problems with several solutions and/or solution strategies.
5. Construct, explain, justify, and apply a variety of problem-solving strategies in both cooperative and independent learning environments.
6. Verify the correctness and reasonableness of results and interpret them in the context of the problems being solved.
7. Know when to select and how to use grade-appropriate mathematical tools and methods (including manipulatives, calculators, and computers, as well as mental math and paper-and-pencil techniques) as a natural and routine part of the problem-solving process.
8. Determine, collect, organize, and analyze data needed to solve problems.
9. Recognize that there may be multiple ways to solve a problem.

Standard 2. All students will communicate mathematically through written, oral, symbolic, and visual forms of expression.

1. Discuss, listen, represent, read, and write as vital activities in their learning and use of mathematics.
2. Identify and explain key mathematical concepts and model situations using oral, written, concrete, pictorial, and graphical methods.
3. Represent and communicate mathematical ideas through the use of learning tools such as calculators, computers, and manipulatives.
4. Engage in mathematical brainstorming and discussions by asking questions, making conjectures, and suggesting strategies for solving problems.
5. Explain their own mathematical work to others and justify their reasoning and conclusions.

Standard 3. All students will connect mathematics to other learning by understanding the interrelationships of mathematical ideas and the roles that mathematics and mathematical modeling play in other disciplines and in life.

1. View mathematics as an integrated whole rather than as a series of disconnected topics and rules.
2. Relate mathematical procedures to their underlying concepts.
3. Use models, calculators, and other mathematical tools to demonstrate the connections among various equivalent graphical, concrete, and verbal representations of mathematical concepts.
4. Explore problems and describe and confirm results using various representations.
5. Use one mathematical idea to extend understanding of another.
6. Recognize the connections between mathematics and other disciplines and apply mathematical thinking and problem solving in those areas.
7. Recognize the role of mathematics in their daily lives and in society.

Standard 4. All students will develop reasoning ability and will become self-reliant, independent mathematical thinkers.

1. Make educated guesses and test them for correctness.
2. Draw logical conclusions and make generalizations.
3. Use models, known facts, properties, and relationships to explain their thinking.
4. Justify answers and solution processes in a variety of problems.
5. Analyze mathematical situations by recognizing and using patterns and relationships.

Elementary
Standard 2.3: Understands and uses the major concepts, procedures, and reasoning processes of mathematics to foster student understanding.

Standard 7: The teacher plans instruction based upon knowledge of subject matter, students, the community, and curriculum goals.

One way that educators achieve curriculum alignment—the process of making sure that what is taught matches the educational standards—is through the use of curriculum frameworks that specify what teachers will teach. Notice how the New Jersey math framework is generic: it applies to all grades, K–12. How would you go about applying this framework to the grade you will teach? Do you feel prepared to do this?

_____

_____

_____

Figure 10.4 *N*ew Jersey Curriculum Framework for K–2 Math

Source: New Jersey Department of Education, "Mathematics Curriculum Framework" (1996). (Online). Available at www.state.nj.us/njded/frameworks/math/math2.pdf.

them to coach peers on topics ranging from the academic content that classroom teachers are expected to teach to methods they can use to reach students. The experts split their time between offering workshops and working one-on-one with teachers by observing them at work and helping them solve problems. "We have found it very, very effective to have a peer so that [teachers] can work through the obstacles that are in their way," says Linda F. Poole, the director of learning for the Colonial School District in New Castle.

- The Lancaster (Pennsylvania) School District uses a different approach to achieve the same goal. Lancaster students take district-chosen tests in such core subjects as mathematics and language arts at the end of every marking period, or once every nine weeks. Administrators use those results, along with data collected from state tests and other assessments, to target areas for improvement. To pinpoint weaknesses at the school and classroom levels, and ensure that teachers are equipped to redirect instruction in a way that meets the identified needs, the district has assigned a master teacher, or "instructional facilitator," to each of the district's nineteen campuses. The facilitators work with teachers in their assigned schools four days a week. On the fifth day, they receive training and plot out the district's nine-week assessments with members of the support staff from the district's Office of Teaching and Learning.

- At King Elementary School (Lancaster, Pennsylvania) last year, instructional facilitator Teri Cammerata demonstrated lessons on how students can use imagery to begin writing assignments after a district assessment revealed that students were struggling to find appropriate openings to their stories. "The scoring results drove the instruction," Cammerata says. "The staff feels a sense of relief that this is something tangible we can do to make improvements." District administrators say the instructional support, along with the regular checks on student progress, has given teachers a new focus on meeting the district's standards.

Pause for a moment and consider what is worth knowing for the students you will teach. List five things you think are "nonnegotiable" for what your students should know and be able to do.

_____

_____

_____

_____

Ranking Schools. Many states rank and rate their schools on how well students achieve. Florida grades its schools much like teachers grade their students (on a letter scale from A to F),[7] while Texas rates its schools with a hierarchy of titles (Exemplary, Recognized, Academically Acceptable/Acceptable, and Academically Unacceptable/Low-Performing).[8] Ranking of schools is spreading across the country. Beginning in the 2005–2006 school year, Indiana schools will be placed in five categories based on how a school's students perform on the Indiana State Testing for Educational Progress–Plus exam (ISTEP+). The five categories are Exemplary Progress, Commendable Progress, Academic Progress, Academic Watch/Priority, and Academic Probation/High Priority.[9] As a teacher, you will be teaching in a school that is labeled and known by its rating. When you interview for a job, one of the things you will want to find out is "What is the rating of the school where I will be teaching?" In your interview you will want to ask why the school is ranked as it is and what plans administrators and teachers have for improvement. This is important information that will help you make a career decision about teaching in a particular school.

Standards and Textbook Alignment. Publishing companies, by their very nature as for-profit companies, are always engaged in keeping up with what politicians demand and what educators need. Consequently, they are continuously engaged in the task of aligning their textbooks with state standards and accompanying curriculum frameworks that specify curriculum content appropriate for teaching the standards. Frequently, curriculum frameworks include suggested and, in some cases, mandatory teaching activities. Many publishers align their textbook content to the standards of states such as Texas and California, large states that "adopt" textbooks for the entire state. In these "whole-state" textbook adoption states, school districts can use state funding to purchase only those books that are on the state textbook adoption lists. In order for a publisher to have its textbooks on the state list, it must include content that teaches to the state standards. Because Texas and California represent large revenue potential, many educators fear textbook content may be unduly influenced by the requirements of these large adoption states. Publishers, however, must appeal to a national audience and therefore work to provide a balance. In addition, for some disciplines publishers now develop state-specific texts meant to be marketed only in these large states. When selecting texts to use in the classroom, the materials available to you for meeting your state and local standards may depend on the state in which you teach.

Why might people in other states be concerned about the potential influence of Texas and California in textbook development? Which state do you think your state aligns with more closely?

INTASC

Standard 9: The teacher is a reflective practitioner who continually evaluates the effects of his/her choices and actions on others (students, parents, and other professionals in the learning community) and who actively seeks out opportunities to grow professionally.

Reflect & Write

NCATE

Early Childhood

Standard 5: Uses ethical guidelines and other professional standards; is a continuous, collaborative learner who demonstrates knowledgeable, reflective, and critical perspectives; is an informed advocate for sound educational practices.

Elementary

Standard 5.2: Is aware of and reflects on practice in light of research on teaching and resources available for professional learning; continually evaluates effects of professional decisions and actions on students, parents, and other professionals; actively seeks opportunities to grow professionally.

Middle Level

Standard 7: Understands the complexity of teaching young adolescents; engages in practices and behaviors that develop competence as a professional.

Standards and Changing Teacher Roles

Given the discussion so far, it should come as no surprise that standards have changed the art and craft of teaching. Standards and curriculum alignment have a profound impact on teachers and their teaching. Teachers have always developed their own curricula and will continue to do so, but standards have transformed (some would say reformed) teaching from an input model to an output model. As a result of standards, teachers are no longer able to say, "I taught Mario algebraic equations." Now the questions are "Is Mario able to use and apply algebraic equations?" and "Will Mario do well on algebraic equations on the state test?" Good teachers have good ideas about what and how to teach and they always will. However, the time and opportunity to do this are reduced by increasing requirements that teachers teach to the standards and teach so that students will master the standards.

Many educators admit that standards must not become the only curriculum. Teachers must have the time and freedom to supplement the content specified by the standards with material they think is important and to be able to teach to the teachable moment. Standards-based education should not hurt or interfere with teacher creativity. Figure 10.5 identifies some strategies for integrating standards and improving student achievement.

Local autonomy is another casualty of alignment. Traditionally and historically, local districts have had a great deal of autonomy over the goals of education and how to best teach to these goals. Critics assert that state and national standards erode local control. As a result, local empowerment is undermined as states mandate what all students in the state must learn. While local districts can and do teach what they think is important and always will, nonetheless, national and state standards reduce their options to do so. Critics of standards say that what should be taught and how it

Paul George, a professor at the University of Florida, visited fifty schools to determine what they are doing to raise student achievement. Here are ten strategies that work:

1. **Set urgent goals.** Focus on making a quick breakthrough in student achievement.
2. **Engage school personnel.** Develop cohesiveness and commitment among a small group of school and teacher leaders.
3. **Use school achievement data.** Skilled analysis of student achievement data has become a crucial step in breaking through the barriers of low achievement.
4. **Strengthen professional development.** Student achievement data point to the need for professional development in specific subject areas and grade levels.
5. **Align the curriculum.** The role played by standards-focused curriculum alignment stands out clearly.
6. **Increase time for academics.** Decrease the amount of time usually available for subjects that are not currently tested to increase the amount of time devoted to tested subjects.
7. **Choose instructional materials to support standards.** Use a mix of state-produced, commercial, and local curriculum materials targeted to improve achievement, focusing on those designed for new state standards.
8. **Build interdisciplinary teams.** Encourage collaboration among teachers and a more careful focus on small groups of students.
9. **Promote the test.** Target public relations efforts at students, teachers, and parents to persuade them of the importance of the standards and the state test.
10. **Redefine school leadership.** Principals now see themselves as instructional leaders, as mandated for professional survival by standards-based reform.

Reflect & Write

Which two or three of Professor George's strategies do you think are most important? How might a school district implement these strategies?

Figure 10.5 *Strategies for Integrating Standards and Improving Student Achievement*
Source: George, P. (2001). Personal Communication.

should be taught are best left to the local district, schools, and teachers. This is in keeping with the long-held tradition of local control of education. However, keep in mind that constitutionally, education is the responsibility of states, and with increasing frequency and assertiveness, state governors and boards of education are assuming a much more prominent role in education issues. Education is also becoming a major political issue at the federal level as federal candidates get more involved.

Teachers and administrators at Freeport Intermediate School (grades 7 through 8) in the Brazosport (Texas) Independent School District have developed tactics to help their students do well on the Texas Assessment of Knowledge and Skills (TAKS). The faculty has done such a good job of providing for children's social and emotional needs while increasing academic achievement that they have been named a national "Middle School to Watch." The student population consists of 12.6 percent African American, 48.5 percent Hispanic, 38.4 percent white, and 0.2 percent Asian. In addition, 65.1 percent of the student body is classified as economically disadvantaged.[10] One lesson Freeport provides is that it is possible to use state standards to provide a high-quality education for all.

A major election platform of President Bush's was his pledge to reform education based on his experience, as governor of Texas, with education reform and increasing student achievement.

SECTION SUMMARY

How Are Standards Employed in the Educational System?

State, national, and local standards have a profound influence on what students learn, what and how teachers teach, and how teachers and schools are held accountable for student learning.

- Influences in the Development of Standards. National standards are reflected in legislation and policy, which require that certain standards be met in order for states and schools to receive federal funding. Currently, forty-nine states have state academic standards; all fifty states have tests to measure how students are learning.
- Standards for Teachers. Many states have standards for initial certification and recertification.
- Standards and Issues. Issues associated with standards include curriculum alignment, professional staff development, how to redesign curriculum so that it teaches the standards, and the ranking of schools based on student tests.
- Standards and Changing Teacher Roles. Casualities of state standards include teacher autonomy and local school district autonomy.

Thinking Critically
★ ★ ★ ★ ★ ★ ★ ★ ★

Standards are very politicized, with different groups advocating standards in order to achieve a particular purpose. Why are standards and their use so highly political? Give examples for how different groups (teachers, parents, and politicians) could use standards to achieve a particular purpose.

_____

_____

_____

_____ ★

Applying What You've Learned
★ ★ ★ ★ ★ ★ ★ ★ ★

As a beginning teacher, what you teach and how you teach it will be influenced by the standards of the state in which you teach. Review the state standards of the grade and/or subject areas for the state in which you plan to teach. List some of the things you will have to begin to know and do in order to have your students meet these standards.

_____

_____

_____

_____ ★

Putting Yourself in the Picture
★ ★ ★ ★ ★ ★ ★ ★ ★

The course you are taking and your overall teacher education program have been and are being influenced by state standards. Interview your professors and have them share with you specific examples of these changes and their views, pro and con, of standards for teacher education.

_____

_____

_____

_____ ★

HOW IS ASSESSMENT CHANGING TEACHING AND LEARNING?

Tests have always been a part of teaching and the process of schooling. Over the last twenty-five years in particular, tests have assumed a major role in helping reform public education. Although tests are designed to measure student achievement, they also can be used to demonstrate or document what students know and do not know and to hold teachers and schools accountable. There are a number of reasons for the popularity of testing as a method of school reform.

INTASC

Standard 8: The teacher understands and uses formal and informal assessment strategies to evaluate and ensure the continuous intellectual, social and physical development of the learner.

1. Tests and assessments are relatively inexpensive. Assessment is cheap, compared to increasing instructional time, reducing class size, attracting more able people to teaching, hiring teacher aides, or enacting programmatic change involving substantial professional development for teachers.
2. Testing and assessments can be externally mandated. It is far easier to mandate testing and assessment requirements at the state or district level than to mandate anything that involves change in what happens inside the classroom.
3. Testing and assessment changes can be rapidly implemented. New test or assessment requirements can be implemented within the term of elected officials.
4. Results are visible. Test results can be reported to the press. Poor results in the beginning are desirable for policymakers who want to show they have had an effect.[11]

The use of tests to measure student achievement and as instruments of accountability mushroomed in response to the *A Nation at Risk* report. Since the report, federal officials, governors, and state legislators have continued to advocate and support the use of testing as a way to reform schools, teaching, and the curriculum. Commenting on the Virginia Standards of Learning (SOL) and testing, Governor James S. Gilmore says, "The whole reason you go to some measurable standards is so you can actually tell who needs help. The idea of the program is not to get some arbitrary score, it's to get kids a good education." In accord with the Virginia SOL, "Students take exams in the core subjects in the third, fifth, and eighth grades and in high school. Not only do the results count for a school's accreditation, but beginning in 2004, scores will also determine whether students receive a high school diploma."[12]

The National Test

For all intents and purposes, the National Assessment of Educational Progress (NAEP) is the national test. The NAEP, also known as "the Nation's Report Card," is the only ongoing nationally representative assessment of what America's students know and can do in various subject areas. Since 1969, assessments have been conducted periodically in reading, mathematics, science, writing, U.S. history, civics, geography, and the arts. The National Assessment Governing Board, appointed by the U.S. Secretary of Education but independent of the U.S. Department of Education, governs the program. NAEP reports information for the nation and specific geographic regions of the country. It includes students drawn from both public and nonpublic schools and reports results for student achievement at grades 4, 8, and 12. NAEP assessments are also conducted on the state level. States that choose to participate receive assessment results that report on the performance of students in that state. The state assessment is identical in content to the assessment

One of the strategic and political purposes of standards and testing is to hold teachers and schools accountable for students' achievement. Accountability for high achievement for all students is a major theme of educational practice today.

conducted nationally. When national education officials refer to student achievement, it is usually NAEP test scores they use when making comparisons and advocating reform.

Testing of Teachers

As demands for accountability grow, more legislators are paying increased attention to levels of teacher skills and knowledge. Some question how teachers who do not possess adequate and appropriate knowledge and skills can teach students so they will achieve high standards. As a response, more states and school districts are instituting tests for teachers designed to assess their level of knowledge and skills.

For the first time, Pennsylvania teachers are being tested on their basic skills in reading and math. Their scores will be reported to district and state school officials. The state will pay $7.5 million to Educational Testing Services, the company that administers the SAT, to test 115,000 teachers in the state's public schools. The testing program, called the Professional Development Assistance Program (PDAP), will be conducted over the next five years, with about 20 percent of the state's teachers participating. The first wave of tests began in November 2001 and included Pittsburgh and several suburban districts in western Pennsylvania.

"This is all for professional development," says Pennsylvania State Department of Education spokesman Jeff McCloud. "It's to help teachers and school districts decide where they need help."[13] Some schools go to great lengths to encourage student performance. (See Education on the Move.)

INTASC

Standard 8: The teacher understands and uses formal and informal assessment strategies to evaluate and ensure the continuous intellectual, social and physical development of the learner.

Testing Issues

As you might expect, a number of issues accompany the heavy emphasis on testing. Many of these issues involve questions of equality, fairness, and preparedness. (See the Profile, p. 388.)

education *on the move* >>>>>>>>>>>>

>>> What I Did for Standards >>>>>>>

Last winter, Principal Karla Onick issued a challenge to her students at L. B. Johnson Elementary School. If each grade met its goal in a book reading contest, she would eat worms. On May 21, Ms. Onick stood up in the school cafeteria and ate two eight-inch night crawlers sautéed with mushrooms and onions. The children squealed. Then Assistant Principal Alberto Reyes plucked two worms from a jar and ate them raw.

"I bit the first one and it squirted all over my mouth," he says. "So the second time, I just swallowed."

As state and federal pressure intensifies on public schools, outrageous acts by teachers and administrators are becoming increasingly popular

motivational tools. Educators have long agreed to the dunking pool and a pie in the face to raise money. But now they're turning to stunts inspired by reality TV to get students to read and perform well on tests.

Under state and federal education programs, schools face penalties if students don't continue to improve on tests. In Texas, home to one of the strictest sets of standards in the nation, the state has already closed several charter schools for failing to show adequate progress.

Last month, Charles Bruner, the principal of Forest Meadow Junior High in Dallas, let his students clip his hair with dog shears after their test scores indicated the school would

move up a notch in the state ranking system. Earlier this spring, Robert Gordon, principal of Hendrick Ranch Elementary School near Riverside, California, kissed a potbellied pig after students met a reading challenge. And in Hampton, Virginia. Principal David Gaston modeled a pink tutu for his students at Burbank Elementary after their state test scores improved.

"I even had a little tiara," said Mr. Gaston.

Source: T. Herrick. "For These Educators, the Diet of Worms Isn't Just History," *Wall Street Journal,* June 15, 2004, p. A-1. Reprinted by permission.

Equity. Should one test fit all? Generally, one state test is given to all students regardless of their backgrounds. Critics of the one-test-fits-all approach maintain that such a procedure does not take into account students' developmental levels, cultures, socioeconomic status, past education and experiences, and present circumstances. They further claim that until states provide a system of differentiated testing, policies of using one test will remain inherently unequal and discriminatory. The National Council of Teachers of Mathematics' position statement on mathematics testing outlines some of their concerns about the one-test-fits-all approach.

> The National Council of Teachers of Mathematics believes that far-reaching and critical educational decisions should be made only on the basis of multiple measures. A well-conceived system of assessment and accountability must consist of a number of assessment components at various levels.[14]

In addition, some maintain that tests are inherently unfair because they do not measure what students can and should learn. For example, some say the overriding problem with existing standardized tests is that they were designed to accomplish a totally different mission than how they are presently used. Most standardized tests currently use a multiple-choice or short-answer format that does not properly assess what a student can and should learn.[15] One of the challenges for test construction firms is to make sure tests measure what they are supposed to and to develop test questions that tap into students' full learning.

Overtesting. Overtesting is one of the outcomes of the increase in the number of states requiring more standardized tests. State tests compete with district tests tied to local curriculum and standards. Many school districts are reducing or eliminating their district tests in an effort to scale back the number of tests their students have to take. For example, Montgomery County (Massachusetts) School District has eliminated its local tests altogether, and other school districts—such as Buffalo and Rochester, New York—are doing the same.[16]

High-Stakes Testing. **Social promotion** is another casualty of standards-based education, although critics of social promotion do not decry its demise. The theory behind social promotion has always been that it is better for students to progress through the grades in the company of their social peers rather than be held back or retained. Many school districts have routinely practiced social promotion and have promoted students to the next-highest grade regardless of how well they did or did not do in course work and tests. However, with the implementation of standards and tests, fewer teachers and school districts use social promotion.[17] One such district is the Los Angeles Unified School District, which invested $82.5 million to bolster intensive education in second, sixth, and ninth grades to increase summer school attendance and to strengthen teacher training as schools move away from the practice of social promotion.[18] In Chicago, social promotion has been prohibited, and **gateway grades** have been established. Under this system, students must pass standardized tests to be promoted to the next grade. This practice is part of what is known as **high-stakes testing,** where tests act as a gate or barrier to promotion, graduation, or participation in an activity or program. Some states and school districts have no-pass, no-play policies whereby students cannot play in athletic events if they do not pass a grade. High-stakes tests also serve as a basis for compulsory participation in a program such as summer school as a requirement for promotion to the next grade.

Such testing has been used for years in early childhood education, where readiness tests are routinely used with young children as a means of determining whether they are ready for kindergarten or promotion to the first grade. However, many people argue that it is inappropriate to use such high-stakes tests with young children, since readiness is frequently a function of family education, socioeconomic background, and children's previous experiences. They argue that it is much better to have children

INTASC

Standard 3: The teacher understands how students differ in their approaches to learning and creates instructional opportunities that are adapted to diverse learners.

INTASC

Standard 8: The teacher understands and uses formal and informal assessment strategies to evaluate and ensure the continuous intellectual, social and physical development of the learner.

Social promotion
Promoting students to the next-highest grade regardless of how well they do or do not do in course work and tests.

Gateway grades
Students must pass standardized tests to be promoted to the next grade.

High-stakes testing
A gate or barrier to promotion, graduation, or participation in an activity or program.

in preschools and kindergartens where they can learn the skills they need rather than to deny them access to programs that will be beneficial or helpful.

In recent years, many states have adopted policies mandating that students pass an achievement test as a requirement for graduation. For example, Wisconsin requires its juniors and seniors to take a test that determines whether or not they can graduate from high school. Giving graduation or **exit exams** to students in tenth and eleventh grade is one way for educators to determine the areas in which students have not done well and provides an opportunity to develop programs to give students needed help in order to successfully pass the examination and graduate.

For the most part, teachers and parents alike back the use of high-stakes standardized tests as a means to motivate students and identify those who are struggling. However, parents and teachers believe that, in addition to the use of high-stakes tests to make high-stakes decisions such as promotion and graduation, there should be allowance for teacher professional judgment.[19] In other words, parents do not want their children's school and life futures based solely on one high-stakes test. (See the Profile.) Needless to say, the use of high-stakes testing to determine graduation has met resistance on many fronts. In Massachusetts, the adjustment to high-stakes testing has been rocky since the introduction of the Massachusetts Comprehensive Assessment System (MCAS). You can review the MCAS initiative at www.doe.mass.edu/mcas/.

Exit exams
Achievement tests used as a requirement for graduation.

Test Preparation. With so much riding on the outcomes of testing, critics argue that the focus of the curriculum now is more on preparation than on content. One of the most common complaints about mandatory testing is that in order to ensure that all students pass the tests, some teachers "teach the test," or as James Popham, noted test expert, says, "item teach."

In item teaching, teachers organize their instruction either around the actual items found on a test or around a set of look-alike items. For instance, imagine that a high-stakes test includes the multiple-choice subtraction item "Gloria has 14 pears but ate 3." The test-taker must choose from four choices the number of pears that Gloria now has. Suppose the teacher revised this item slightly: "Joe has 14 bananas but ate 3." The test-taker chooses from the same four answers, ordered slightly differently. Only the kind of fruit and the gender of the fruit-eater have been altered in this clone item; the cognitive demand is unchanged.

Curriculum teaching, however, requires teachers to direct their instruction toward a specific body of content knowledge or a specific set of cognitive skills represented by a given test. In curriculum teaching, a teacher targets instruction at test-represented content rather than at test items.[20]

Profile   Tests—Maps for Change: Richard Middleton

Richard Middleton is Superintendent of Northeast Independent School District, San Antonio, Texas.

Testing has always been an essential part of the educational process. In recent years, however, the tendency to use testing data as the most significant indicator of learning achievement has increased. Promotion and retention policies, graduation requirements, whole-school rankings, and even the entire standards movement rely heavily on test data to define their validity. However, educators must urge caution about policymaking based on a single measure of performance. In a volatile stock market, wise investors measure success over the long term.

Educators must do the same; our goal must be to increase test scores over time.

In education, true accountability is derived from raising student performance on increasingly higher standards. Rather than indicators for abandoning public schools, test scores present school districts with maps for programmatic change. Student performance data can provide both direction and impetus for educators to make systemic changes that will afford our diverse student population equal opportunities for learning. The education of children is vital to our democracy, and it is imperative that we now accept this challenge on behalf of our students.

Test besting, also known as test prep, occurs when schools and districts teach students how to take and pass tests. The purpose of test besting is to teach specific test-taking skills such as managing time, how to bubble, and how to identify distractions so that students will have an "edge" on test taking. Commercial programs are available to accomplish this goal, and districts and schools also develop their own programs. For years, for-profit companies have been helping students prepare for examinations. Perhaps you used a test prep company such as Kaplan or Princeton Review to help you with the SAT, ACT, or some other test as a prerequisite for college entrance. Now the students you teach are doing the same thing to prepare for state exams, many of them in their own classrooms. For example, at Point Pleasant (New Jersey) Middle School students use computer-based programs developed by SkillsTutor that seek to improve students' basic skills and prepare them for state examinations (www.skillstutor.com). The program ranges in cost from $4 to $50 per student per year, depending on school population. Homeroom (www.homeroom.com), developed by Princeton Review, is used in twenty-five Texas schools. Princeton charges $6 to $8 per student per year for use of Homeroom. The entry of test prep companies into the state testing picture only underscores that education is big business and that there is money to be made from standards and testing.

Test besting also occurs when teachers use specific content and instructional activities to teach course content. Some districts have teachers allocate a set amount of time, for instance, thirty minutes a day, to reviewing algebraic equations or teaching first-graders decoding (phonics) skills. Critics maintain that such practices take away from teaching time that could be spent on other knowledge and skills not on the test. Some parents, teachers, and administrators claim that state and national tests "hijack" time from teaching and learning. Principal Darrell Rud of Garfield Elementary School in Billings, Montana, and president of the National Association of Elementary School Principals says, "Comprehensive assessment as a key component of accountability is a vital part of our efforts to provide all students with the finest possible education. I am concerned, however, that in this current high-stakes testing environment many policymakers are frequently advocating the use of one test to determine academic capabilities without taking into consideration the extremely important social development and emotional adjustment of *all* students."[22] (See the Profile below.)

Ron Peiffer of the Maryland Department of Education says:

> Maryland's state assessment system is specifically designed for both accountability and instructional improvement. Consequently, we want to ensure that teachers understand

Test besting
When schools and districts teach students how to take tests.

Elementary

Standard 4: Understands and uses formal and informal assessment strategies to plan, evaluate, and strengthen instruction that will promote continuous intellectual, social, emotional, and physical development of each student.

Middle Level

Standard 5: Understands and uses major concepts, principles, theories, and research related to effective instruction and assessment; employs a variety of strategies for a developmentally appropriate climate to meet the varying abilities and learning styles of all young adolescents.

 **Test Prep—What Better Strategy Is There?: Sam Camacho**

For the past seven years, Sam Camacho has taught language arts at Robert J. Frank Intermediate School in Oxnard, California, an oceanside community an hour north of Los Angeles. He has coached the boys' basketball team for nearly as long. Lately, his two roles seem oddly interchangeable.

Camacho began one recent eighth-grade class by brandishing a page of the morning's *Los Angeles Times*, which listed the latest standardized test scores of all the schools in the state. "This is a competition," he told his students. "What you see here is like a box score in the sports section." The school had a sorry record for the third year in a row, ranking in the bottom 20

percent in the state. But Camacho now has a new playbook. He spent an afternoon at a tutorial paid for by the school as part of a $10,500 package designed by Kaplan, the test prep company that for the past half-century or so has taught students how to beat the SAT. From now on, his students will spend fifty minutes a week in his class and another fifty in math studying Kaplan's *Test-Taking Strategies* manual. The approach appeals to the coach in Camacho. "This class is my team, and this is the equipment they need to win this game," he explains. "What better strategy is there?"[21]

that the last thing we want is the proliferation of test prep strategies. When principals and teachers discover that the key to success is solid instruction, they migrate away from narrow prep strategies toward an emphasis on the basics and on the application of basics. And performance typically builds over time. Too frequently, schools find temporary success with easy "tricks" that have short-term impact, followed by flat performance. Because Maryland is in this for the long haul, we are going to keep our emphasis on high standards. But we are increasingly understanding that our continued success in the decade in the future depends on our attending to instructional capacity issues. While Maryland has frequently been referred to by some as a "testing state" over the past decade, we will be known as a "learning state" in the decade ahead. Our success will depend on our ability to answer the question, "What does it take to get every child to these higher levels of learning?"[23]

Tests and Discrimination. Many argue that tests discriminate against minorities and immigrants and that they perpetuate social and educational inequalities. For example, African American students have made some promising gains on Missouri's state exams, yet they still lag far behind their white and Asian peers. At every subject and grade tested, African American students had the lowest scores of any racial or ethnic group, illustrating the "achievement gap," a problem that confronts educators nationally.[24] Evidence for the racial test achievement divide is an issue in most states.

"The gap exists at the state level, the district level, and at the classroom level," says Ohio State Superintendent of Public Instruction Susan Tave Zelman. "Ohio is certainly not going to be unique in talking about it, but I would like to be unique in solving it."[25]

Are standards and testing discriminatory for minority students? Kati Haycock, director of the Education Trust and the Advocacy Agency for Minority Students, believes the following are essential in order to close the gap between high- and low-achieving students.

1. Standards are key. Historically, we have not agreed on what U.S. students should learn at each grade level—or on what kind of work is good enough. These decisions have been left to individual schools and teachers. The result is a system that, by and large, doesn't ask much of most of its students.
2. All students must have a challenging curriculum. Standards won't make much of a difference, though, if they are not accompanied by a rigorous curriculum that is aligned with those standards.
3. Students need extra help. Ample evidence shows that almost all students can achieve at high levels if they are taught at high levels. But equally clear is that some students require more time and more instruction. It won't do, in other words, just to throw students into a high-level course if they can't even read the textbook.
4. Teachers matter a lot. If students are going to be held to high standards, they need teachers who know the subjects and know how to teach the subjects.[26]

Help should be provided for all students who have difficulty mastering the standards. This help can come in the form of summer school, weekend and after-school programs, and tutoring and mentoring. (See Education on the Move.)

Anna Rios, a student at Roger L. Putnam Vocational Technical High School in Springfield, Massachusetts, dislikes the idea that she has to pass a statewide test to earn a high school diploma. Nonetheless, the slight fifteen-year-old in jeans and a baseball cap stays after school to bone up on the algebra on the Massachusetts Assessment of Comprehensive Skills, which sophomores must pass to graduate. "I know I need help," she explained, "so I decided to come for the after-school program."

Besides the after-school sessions for some sixty-four students, the school offers a breakfast club that provides academic enrichment. And there is also a support group in which upperclassmen who have already passed the exam help tenth-graders plan-

Students from Colorado's poorest families scored significantly lower on this year's state proficiency exams than their better-off peers, a review of state Department of Education data shows.

In most cases, the gaps between high-performing low-income students and all other students on the Colorado Student Assessment Program exams were more than 30 percentage points.

While the state scores are far from surprising in an era when achievement among poor and minority students is at the forefront of education policy, they underscore the desperate situation many Colorado students face in their classrooms every day.

"We know we have a problem in the state," said Jefferson County schools Superintendent Cindy Stevenson, who has studied poverty and education in Colorado. "Districts are working on it, but it's not rapid progress; it's very slow progress."

Figures from the recently released CSAP exams indicate performance gaps are prevalent at every grade level and subject, from reading to writing to math and to science.

Student poverty is defined by the federal free and reduced-price lunch program, which takes into account income levels and household size. A family of three, for example, would have had to earn $28,231 or less to be eligible for the program last school year.

More than 228,000 of the 757,000 public school students in the state were eligible to receive free or reduced-price lunches during the 2003–2004 year.

Source: Created by the author from data from R. Sanchez, "CSAP Tests Expose Gap," *Rocky Mountain News,* August 7, 2004. (Online). Available at www.rockymountainnews.com/drmn/education/article/0,1299,DRMN_957_3094699,00.html.

INTASC

Standard 3: The teacher understands how students differ in their approaches to learning and creates instructional opportunities that are adapted to diverse learners.

INTASC

Standard 8: The teacher understands and uses formal and informal assessment strategies to evaluate and ensure the continuous intellectual, social and physical development of the learner.

ning to take the test. For those ninth-graders who start high school more than two years behind in reading or math, the school has created a separate academy to bring them up to speed as quickly as possible. Summer school also awaits students who are struggling academically.[27]

Assessing and Reporting Student Achievement

Many schools are finding that traditional ways of reporting student progress are not sufficient given emphasis on standards and tests. One approach to grading is based on norm-referenced comparisons. In this approach, often called "grading on the curve," each student's achievement is compared to every other student's achievement in the class. This comparison can result in a ranking of students. Based on the **normal curve,** the teacher assigns so many As, Bs, and so forth. Grading on the curve is seen more frequently at the college level than at the K–12 level. Its critics feel this approach is inherently unfair and that there are better ways to assess student performance and achievement.

In contrast, with criterion-referenced grading, each student's performance is compared to his or her performance on the standards, regardless of how well other students perform. An issue here is how the teacher judges that achievement and how a teacher measures the level of student achievement.

Designing and implementing assessment strategies is one of the most important roles of a teacher. Assessment is a component of teaching that is necessary if learning is to occur. As discussed, testing often occurs only at the end of a course or grade, is used to compare and rank students in schools, is used to make high-stakes decisions about grade failure program exit and entry, and so forth. Teacher assessment, on the other hand, is used to guide instruction, improve student learning, improve teaching, provide ongoing feedback to students about their performance, identify students' strengths and weaknesses, and enable teachers to provide students with more enriched

NCATE

Early Childhood

Standard 3: Understands goals, benefits and uses of assessment; uses systematic observations, documentation, and other effective assessment strategies to positively influence development and learning.

Elementary

Standard 4: Understands and uses formal and informal assessment strategies to plan, evaluate, and strengthen instruction that will promote continuous intellectual, social, emotional, and physical development of each student.

Normal curve
The bell-shaped curve used for grading based on the assumption that any group of students represents a range of achievement or ability.

Teachers are the most important part of teaching and student learning. Teachers make the difference. You are the person who will make a difference with your students.

NCATE

Middle Level

Standard 3: Understands the major concepts, principles, theories, and research related to middle-level curriculum and assessment; uses this knowledge in practice.

learning experiences. This is how teacher Anthony Cody explains his changing view of assessment and how he currently uses assessment to help students learn:

> In my classroom as a beginning teacher, I first used assessments that had little connection to my classroom instruction. As a more experienced teacher, I developed my own summative assessments that were tied directly to my instruction. Now, as I deepen my practice, I am using assessment not only as a measurement of achievement following instruction, but as a tool of instruction as it unfolds, informing me and the students so that we can work together to learn from each other.
>
> There are ways of [determining] what students understand prior to a lesson, known as pre-assessment. If I know what students understand, I can build on that knowledge. I can also uncover misconceptions that research has shown are surprisingly durable and resistant to change. My lessons and activities need to challenge and overcome the students' misconceptions, giving them new understandings and models. This is called formative assessment, and this information can be used to modify my instruction.
>
> My goal is not just to measure my students' achievement, but also to help them grow. Formative assessment allows me to give feedback to my students that guides and pushes them to achieve, to close the gap between their starting point and where I wish them to be. Our real goal is to build students' capacity to judge the quality of their own work, and internalize high standards.[28]

Why do critics of norm-referenced grading feel this method is unfair? As such a critic, what would you cite in support of your stance?

_____

_____

_____

_____

Kathi Robinson is Assistant Principal at Freeport (Texas) Intermediate School.

Imagine a norm-referenced standardized test with immediate feedback for teachers! Traditionally, the two biggest complaints teachers have about standardized, norm-referenced tests is that the results do not come back until the class has moved to the next grade level and that students do not take the tests seriously. With our new TESA system, we are completely changing the impact of these tests. Our teachers see the results of the test as soon as the student pushes the "complete" button. Not only are teachers given the score, they get a breakdown of the questions and concepts the students missed. In addition, the tests are "leveled" so that if a student gets the right answers, the questions get more challenging, and if the

student is struggling, the questions become less challenging. The teachers' ability to use the scores to help inform instruction is making a big difference. Our students have commented that taking the tests using the computer is "way better" because they only see one question at a time and that they know if they do not do well, they have an opportunity to learn the concept they do not understand and take the test again when they are better prepared. Eliminating the scantron sheet and the No. 2 pencil places the focus on the questions, not on the students' ability to draw clever designs. Allowing teachers to see the results and discuss the tests with their students takes away the mystery of the test and empowers the teachers to help students succeed.

Computerized Testing

Although we think that a No. 2 pencil is the standard piece of equipment for taking a standardized test, this procedure is quickly changing in the fast-paced world of educational reform. Now, with a new model of taking required state and district tests, students stare intently at computer screens, their hands grasping the mouse. This testing model is known as the Technology Enhanced Student Assessment System, and the click of a mouse has replaced filling in a bubble with a pencil. (See the Profile.) Students in Oregon, Virginia, and South Dakota pubic schools were some of the first in the nation to engage in the national trend of taking state tests online. How long it will take for the majority of students to be online test takers is anybody's guess. As Randy Bennet of Educational Testing Service says, "This evolution is going to happen; it's going to take a while, but it's going to happen."[29]

The use of computers versus pencils and answer sheets raises a number of issues. First, if students are used to and comfortable working with computers, then they are more likely to be comfortable with taking tests online. But for students whose primary mode of learning is paper and pencil, then taking a test with paper and pencil is the mode with which they will be most comfortable. As Bennet points out, "It's very clear that as kids become used to and routinely do writing on computers, paper-and-pencil tests don't do a fair job of determining their skills. Tests that are delivered in a mode that's different from one [in which students are learning] will eventually become indefensible."[30]

Perhaps the greatest obstacle to computer testing will be access to computers. A serious digital divide exists between poor schools and affluent schools, which are more likely to have more computers and use them in the learning process. In addition, students from minority groups are less likely to have computers in their homes.

The cost of online testing is another issue. The first round of online testing cost Oregon $600,000. Can all states and districts afford what it will cost to bring their testing systems online? Only time will tell, but in a sense, states do not have a choice, because in order to test all students effectively and well, the electronic test may be their best and most cost-effective option. As time goes by, online testing will likely become more cost-effective.

NCATE

Elementary

Standard 4: Understands and uses formal and informal assessment strategies to plan, evaluate, and strengthen instruction that will promote continuous intellectual, social, emotional, and physical development of each student.

Middle Level

Standard 3: Understands the major concepts, principles, theories, and research related to middle-level curriculum and assessment; uses this knowledge in practice.

INTASC

Standard 3: The teacher understands how students differ in their approaches to learning and creates instructional opportunities that are adapted to diverse learners.

Standard 8: The teacher understands and uses formal and informal assessment strategies to evaluate and ensure the continuous intellectual, social and physical development of the learner.

What Does This Mean for You?

Accountability is one of the most visible topics in education today. You and your colleagues will be held accountable for student classroom performance and achievement, test scores, and how well your school does in relation to other schools in your district and state. As part of the accountability movement, policymakers are rewarding achievement and forcing low-performing schools and districts to redesign themselves so that all students pass state exams. This emphasis on accountability means:

- Performance is the name of the game in the schoolhouse today. You and your colleagues, faculty, and administrators will be called on to ensure that the curriculum, the instructional process, and the administrative frameworks are in place to enable all students to pass state exams.
- You will be in the public spotlight. The spotlight is the district and state report cards provided to parents and the public detailing performance. Reports of school and district performance will trigger public discussions regarding how well you, your colleagues, and your district are doing to ensure that all children learn.
- Your students will also be held accountable. An increasing number of states—currently twenty—require students to pass a test to graduate from high school. Nine states tie student promotion to test scores.

You must be prepared to help all students achieve at high levels and pass state tests. You must take your place as a member of school-based teams charged with redesigning curriculum, instructional processes, and the administrative procedures necessary to help ensure that all students learn. You will need to become an articulate spokesperson about your school's and district's performance.

Tests and Accountability

You may have guessed by now that tests play a significant role in accountability. Tests are the primary tools schools and districts use in measuring adequate yearly progress. Under the No Child Left Behind Act of 2001, every state must establish a definition of adequate yearly progress (AYP) and a plan to determine how to measure the AYP of each school district and school.

The federal government approves each state's definition of and plan for measuring AYP. Here is Connecticut's federally approved definition of AYP and their plan to measure it.

Connecticut's Adequate Yearly Progress (AYP)

The No Child Left Behind Act requires each state to define "adequate yearly progress" for school districts and schools, within the parameters set by Title I. Each state begins by setting a "starting point" that is based on the performance of its lowest-achieving demographic group or of the lowest-achieving schools in the state, whichever is higher. The state then sets the bar—or level of student achievement—that a school must attain after two years in order to continue to show adequate yearly progress. Subsequent thresholds must be raised at least once every three years, until, at the end of twelve years, all students in the state are achieving at the proficient level on state assessments in reading/language arts and math.

Initially, Connecticut will use the Connecticut Mastery Test (CMT) in Grades 4, 6 and 8 and the tenth-grade Connecticut Academic Performance Tests (CAPT) for determining the Adequate Yearly Progress (AYP) status of schools. The state will introduce spring testing with a new generation CMT in the spring of 2006 and will expand the number of grades tested to include 3 through 8, inclusive. CAPT will continue to be used as the required high school assessment.

Using the federal formula for setting AYP, Connecticut has established the following AYP standards for 2002–2003 testing:

INTASC

Standard 8: The teacher understands and uses formal and informal assessment strategies to evaluate and ensure the continuous intellectual, social and physical development of the learner.

CMT		CAPT
65%	Proficient Level in Mathematics	59%
57%	Proficient Level in Reading	62%
95%	Participation in Testing	95%
70%	Basic Level in Writing	Graduation Rate of 70%

Schools in Need of Improvement

A school or school district that doesn't meet the state's definition of "adequate yearly progress" (AYP) for two straight years (schoolwide or in any major subgroup) is considered to be "in need of improvement."[31]

Figure 10.6 shows the corrective actions and consequences for districts that fail to make adequate yearly progress.

Annual Yearly Progress (AYP)

Schools identified for improvement must receive technical assistance that enables them to specifically address the academic achievement problem that caused the school to be identified for improvement. The local education agency (LEA)—the school district—is required to provide technical assistance as the school develops and implements the plan, including specific assistance in analyzing assessment data, improving professional development, and improving resource allocation. In addition, the following must take place:

Year 1

- All students are offered public school choice.

- Each school identified for improvement must develop or revise a two-year school improvement plan, in consultation with parents, school staff, the local educational agency, and other experts, for approval by the LEA. The plan must incorporate research-based strategies, a 10 percent set-aside of Title I funds for professional development, extended learning time as appropriate (including school day or year), strategies to promote effective parental involvement and mentoring for new teachers.

Year 2

- Make available supplemental educational services to students from low-income families.

Year 3

- Replace school staff responsible for the continued failure to make AYP.

- Implement a new curriculum based on scientifically based research (including professional development).

- Significantly decrease management authority at the school level.

- Extend the school day or school year.

- Appoint an outside expert to advise the school on its progress toward making AYP in accordance with its school plan; or

- Reorganize the school internally.

Year 4

- Reopen school as a charter school.

- Replace principal and staff.

- Contract for private management company of demonstrated effectiveness.

- State takeover.

- Any other major restructuring of school governance.

Year 5

Implement alternative governance plan no later than first day of school year following year four described above.

Reflect & Write

Do you think that the consequences of failure to make annual yearly progress are appropriate? What would you change or add to the list?

_____

_____

_____

_____

_____

_____

_____

_____

_____

_____

_____

Figure 10.6 *A*ccountability and NCLB: Schools Needing Improvement

Source: U.S. Department of Education, "Key Policy Letters Signed by the Education Secretary or Deputy Secretary" (July 24, 2002). (Online). Available at www.ed.gov/policy/elsec/guid/secletter/020724.html.

How Is Assessment Changing Teaching and Learning?

Tests and assessment have always been a part of the process of schooling. All teachers have always given tests and will continue to do so. What is changing is how tests are used, the purposes for which they are used, and how they are administered. The use of tests to measure student achievement and as instruments of accountability has increased.

- The National Test. The National Assessment of Educational Progress (NAEP) is the nation's test and report card.

- Testing of Teachers. As demands for accountability increase, more states and school districts are instituting testing of teachers to assess their level of knowledge and skills.

- Testing Issues. Some issues associated with testing include whether or not one test should fit all students, overtesting, ending the practice of social promotion, high-stakes testing, teaching to the test, test besting, and discrimination. While parents and teachers support tests, they believe that other criteria should be used to make high-stakes decisions.

- Assessing and Reporting Student Achievement. Two approaches to assessing student achievement are norm-referenced comparisons, based on a comparative ranking of student performance, and criterion-referenced assessments, in which student performance is based on standards. Teacher assessment strategies play a crucial role in student evaluation.

- Computerized Testing. Testing online is the way of the future, and many for-profit companies have entered the field of providing online testing and programs to help students pass state tests.

- Tests and Accountability. Tests are used as one method of holding teachers, schools, and school districts accountable for student performance. Accountability therefore has a profound influence on the teaching process, how schools operate, and how the public views the schools. Increasingly, teachers are in the accountability spotlight as they play a central role in helping ensure that all students learn and pass state tests.

Thinking Critically

★ ★ ★ ★ ★ ★ ★ ★

Based on what you have read about tests and testing, how would you respond to the following statement? "Tests are one of the most important, if not the most important, tools of teaching."

_____

_____

_____

_____ ★

Applying What You've Learned

★ ★ ★ ★ ★ ★ ★ ★

Observe a lesson or lessons in a classroom of your choice. Following your observation, design an assessment test you believe would be fair and would measure what students are supposed to learn.

_____

_____

_____

_____ ★

You have been asked to serve on a schoolwide committee charged with the responsibility of drafting a district policy on testing. What are some policies that you think should be nonnegotiable?

Applications for Active Learning

CONNECTIONS

1. The values and beliefs you bring to the teaching profession help determine your views on the topics of standards, testing, and accountability. For each of these topics, state some of your core basic beliefs and explain how they influence your views. For example, if you believe that all students have a basic right to learning essential knowledge and skills, then you might support high and rigorous standards for all students.

2. Many high-stakes tests are given to students beginning in the fourth grade. Some fourth-grade teachers seek other assignments, saying they cannot stand the pressure of administering high-stakes tests. Do you think that administering high-stakes tests should be a reason for teachers to leave a particular grade to teach in a grade where they might not have to administer high-stakes tests? Identify the reasons for your opinion.

FIELD EXPERIENCES

1. Interview elementary, middle, and high school teachers about their views and experiences with standards-based education. Use the following questions to guide your interviews. Do you think standards are helping or hurting education? Has your teaching been affected for better or for worse by standards? Do you think it is fair to hold teachers accountable for student learning? Compare how teachers' views differ across grade levels.

PERSONAL RESEARCH

1. Given the fact that more and more teacher raises are being tied to student achievement and schoolwide performance, do you think that all teachers should be compensated in this way? Interview teachers at the elementary, middle, and high school levels to determine their opinions about whether or not raises and merit pay should be tied to increases in student achievement.

2. Standards, tests, and accountability are in the news and are frequently the subject of front-page stories. Go online and monitor the daily newspapers such as the *Los Angeles Times* (www.latimes.com), the *Chicago Tribune* (www.chicagotribune.com), the *Miami Herald* (www.miamiherald.com), and the *Washington Post* (www.washingtonpost.com). How does the implementation of standards and testing differ across the United States? What are some common problems and issues? Do any of the articles relate realistic solutions? Do the articles reflect that the reform of education through testing standards is a political process? If so, how?

FOR YOUR PORTFOLIO

1. If you have not already done so, put your state standards in your teaching portfolio.

2. Compare your state's standards with the standards from two other states.

_____

_____

_____

IDEA FILE

Select state standards for a particular subject area and grade you plan to teach. Develop a lesson plan for that standard at the beginning level. Include instructional strategies and activities that would provide for rich knowledge and understanding on the part of your students.

WEB SITES WORTH VISITING

As you begin your teaching career and begin incorporating standards into your teaching practices, you may feel somewhat overwhelmed. Remember that you are not alone. Many novice and veteran teachers are doing their best to keep up with how standards and tests are changing teaching. The following Web sites will help you integrate national, state, and local standards into your curriculum and instructional practices.

The National Endowment for the Humanities
http://edsitement.neh.gov
This site lists hundreds of lessons that align with both standards and student interests. Lesson plans cover literature and language, foreign language, art and culture, and history and social studies.

Science NetLinks
www.sciencenetlinks.org
The American Association of Science provides lessons organized by Project 2061 benchmarks, which outline what all students should know in science and mathematics by the end of grades 2, 5, 8, and 12.

PBS TeacherSource
www.pbs.org/teachersource/
You can search more than 2,000 lessons by grade, subject, and keyword and then see how the lessons match many U.S. national, state, and district standards.

Achieve
www.achieve.org
Media coverage of standards and a searchable data base of state, national, and international standards are provided in four main content areas.

National Dialogue on Standards-Based Education
www.nationaldialogue.org
Join one of the fourteen different threaded discussions on topics related to standards, such as classroom practice, local control, and information and data management.

The National Center for Research on Evaluation, Standards, and Student Testing
http://cresst96.cse.ucla.edu
This Web site is the place to find reports, policy briefs, and a newsletter on K–12 assessments, accountability, and standards.

BOOKS WORTH READING

Carr, J. F., and Harris, D. E. (2001). *Succeeding with Standards: Linking Curriculum, Assessment, and Action Planning.* Alexandria, VA: Association for Supervision and Curriculum Development.
Succeeding with Standards describes a practical, school-tested solution to the challenge of creating a curriculum. The authors describe a comprehensive process by which schools and districts can turn piecemeal initiatives into a coherent plan.

Falk, B. (2000). *The Heart of the Matter: Using Standards and Assessment to Learn.* Woburn, MA: Heinemann.
This book examines the problems of traditional standardized tests and the benefits of performance assessments, offering an overview of how performance can be created and used to serve a variety of purposes; a discussion of standards, their strengths and weaknesses; and ways to assess standards for worthy goals and opportunities for appropriate, effective practices.

Joint Committee on Standards for Educational Evaluation. (2002). *The Student Evaluation Standards: How to Improve Evaluations of Students.* Thousand Oaks, CA: Corwin Press.
These standards provide teachers and administrators with the tools they need to master every "nuance" of student evaluation, including validity, political viability, teacher biases, conflicts of interest, a student's right to privacy, and much more.

Mitchell, R., and Barth, P. (2001). *Smart Start II: Why Standards Matter.* Golden, CO: Fulcrum.

Smart Start II explores how standards are bringing about changes in elementary schools and conveys what standards-based education in elementary schools looks and feels like. This is an indispensable guide for teachers, administrators, and the community and provides a new understanding of the reforms and changes being made in the new millennium.

Popham, J. W. (2003). *Test Better, Teach Better: The Instructional Role of Assessment*. Alexandria, VA: Association for Supervision and Curriculum Development.

This "crash course" on the basic principles of instructionally focused testing explains how tests can tell you what to teach and how to teach it; what to put on a test and why, including the rules for choosing and writing good test items; how to avoid "teaching to the test"; and the five most common mistakes in test writing.

Zmuda, A., and Tomaino, M. (2001). *The Competent Classroom: Aligning High School Curriculum, Standards, and Assessment—a Creative Teaching Guide*. New York: Teacher's College Press.

Written by teachers for teachers, this book describes the cross-disciplinary journey of two high school teachers trying to align curriculum, assessment, and performance standards in their classrooms.

"When you see it happen, it's worth every minute."

Dru Tomlin, an eighth-grade teacher at River Trail Middle School, is 2003–2004 Fulton County (Georgia) Teacher of the Year. In addition to teaching, he coaches River Trail's Academic Bowl Team, which recently won first place in the state tournament.

When farmers plant seeds, they can determine fairly accurately when the seeds will germinate and when crops will rise. It takes a great deal of planning, tenderness, time, and nurturing to make crops grow—and though children are far more complex, the same kind of care and attention must be afforded them.

The difficulty with teaching and coaching students toward academic success is that the endeavor does not yield predictable—or even quantifiably measurable—results. Teachers may pour their hearts into the lives of children and get magnificent blooms, or they may get little to show for their time and effort. It is dangerously easy to become discouraged when that happens, but it is important to remember the following:

- You may see the results of your teaching only years later. I have students who write to express their appreciation for something I said to them five years ago. I may not remember what I said, but they do.
- You may *never* see the results of your actions. But you are making an impact every day you step into that classroom, every time you talk to a student or lend a student a hand.
- On the other hand, you may—unlike a farmer—see spontaneous, unexpected growth. When a student grasps a concept, it is like seeing a flower suddenly burst from the soil and blossom. There is nothing else in the world like that moment, and it can happen anytime.

I believe it is vital to remember these truths, because teaching and coaching students toward academic success is tough. The day-to-day reality of teaching is not always filled with glorious teachable moments, glowing realizations, and eager faces with congenial smiles. Rather, it can feel like an endless mountain of paperwork, assessment, and policies. It is very easy to get bogged down in the tedium of the day. But if you remember why you are really there—for the kids—then all the paperwork and minutia gradually dissolve into the background. That is definitely one way to coach students toward academic success—to make their education your paramount concern every day. In other words, remember to drop all your other baggage at the door.

It's also vital to learn about all of your students and the baggage that *they* might be carrying. To coach students toward academic success, acknowledge them first. I try to connect everything I do with their lives. Before I read anything in a language arts class, I look for the broad, universal themes so I can make the story or novel applicable to their lives. We talk about those themes and create a community of learning in which everyone has something valuable to say.

When I plan a unit, I keep in mind the various learning styles in my classroom and create lessons and assessments that meet them all. When you take that step, when you try at every turn to experience your students' lives, you will speak to them more genuinely, create assignments that better meet their individual needs, and build an educational experience for them that is authentic and responsive—not distant and prescriptive.

One of my favorite stories is about a student named J. D. J. D. arrived from his previous middle school preceded by stories of his obstinacy, his surliness, and his disobedience. When he sauntered in during third period, I decided to put away everything that I had heard about him. He was wearing a tan sweatshirt that screamed "NO FEAR" across the chest, and I took that as my motto: I refused to be afraid of J. D. or how he might behave. I felt in my heart that this kid deserved a chance. That morning, my students and I were conducting interviews with each other to get our minds going about writing topics. I grabbed my legal pad and motioned J. D. to sit next to me. I explained the activity, and he turned his head slowly to look at the other students, unconvinced. But as I asked him questions, he began to open up. He talked about his summer job tending baby chickens on a farm in Virginia. He described watching a chick hatch from its tiny egg, holding the soft, infant bird in his hands, and placing it gently back on the dusty ground. It was the start of a new J. D.—and all I did was ask him questions about his life. Our relationship wasn't all smooth sailing, but he trusted me.

That's the miracle of the teaching profession. Teachers have the power to make people grow. It takes vast amounts of time, patience, understanding, and empathy, but when you see it happen, it's worth every minute.

How Will This Chapter Help You?

You will learn

★ about the four kinds of curriculum and what students learn or don't learn in schools

★ about political, legislative, and social factors that influence curriculum today

★ about current trends in content areas

★ how education reform is changing the curriculum

WHAT DO STUDENTS LEARN IN SCHOOL?

Curriculum
All the experiences students have while engaged in the process of schooling.

Explicit curriculum
The behavior, attitudes, and knowledge schools intend to teach students.

Hidden curriculum
The behaviors, attitudes, and knowledge the school culture unintentionally teaches students.

Students come to school to learn. What should they learn? Why should they learn it? What is it that they learn? These questions and others like them are at the heart of teaching and learning. Think for a moment about what you learned in school. You learned how to read, write, and compute. You also learned about such subject areas as history, geography, and English. More than likely you acquired other knowledge, such as how to get along with others, how to participate in athletic activities, or how to help edit a school newspaper.

There is more to a curriculum than subjects and programs. What about debate, dance, and detention? Aren't these also part of the school's curriculum? Of course. What about values, vaccinations, and views of other peoples and cultures? These, too, are part of the curriculum. Consequently, **curriculum** is all the experiences students have while engaged in the process of schooling. This means that the curriculum consists of experiences while on the school bus, on the playing fields, in the classroom, in the school halls, in the cafeteria, and anywhere else students are in the school setting. As a beginning teacher, you will want to provide your students with curriculum experiences that will promote their full growth and development. Always keep in mind that schools, teaching, and learning are all about curriculum.

Kinds of Curricula

Schools and teachers seldom provide one kind of curriculum experience for students, although some educators recommend a one-curriculum-fits-all approach. As shown in Figure 11.1, there are four basic kinds of curricula: *explicit, hidden, null,* and *extra.* Each of these are examined in the following subsections to give you information for developing your own educational programs to meet the needs of your students.

The Explicit Curriculum. The **explicit curriculum,** sometimes called the official or formal curriculum, is what schools say they teach students. This curriculum consists of all the experiences relating to content and the instructional procedures and materials for teaching that content. Whatever a district, school, or teacher regards as a subject, lesson, class, or course of study is included in the formal curriculum. The explicit curriculum also includes goals, aims, policies, and guidelines issued by a state board of education or local education agency regarding what should be taught in the schools. Today, state outcome standards, which are expectations of what students should know and be able to do, play a central role in helping determine the explicit curriculum. In some schools, state standards are the curriculum, although there is much more to the curriculum than state standards.

In addition to stating the knowledge and skills that should be taught, the explicit curriculum identifies the attitudes and values to be taught, such as those regarding careers, social interaction, cultural diversity, and helping others. For example, students in Barbara Vogel's fifth-grade classroom at Highline Community School in Aurora, Colorado, formed their own antislavery organization called STOP—Slavery That Oppresses People. They raised more than $50,000 to help free more than one thousand slaves in the Sudan. According to Ms. Vogel, "The kind of people we are determines what kind of country we have. It is the school's responsibility to teach and model humanitarianism—to help children learn how to be good citizens."[1]

The explicit curriculum is also expressed in the textbooks that are chosen or adopted at the state and local level. It is also evident in a school's philosophy and in learning materials, such as computer software, course descriptions, curriculum guides, and teacher lesson plans.

The Hidden Curriculum. The **hidden curriculum** is what schools do not intend to teach but nonetheless do. For example, teacher-student relationships and the climate of

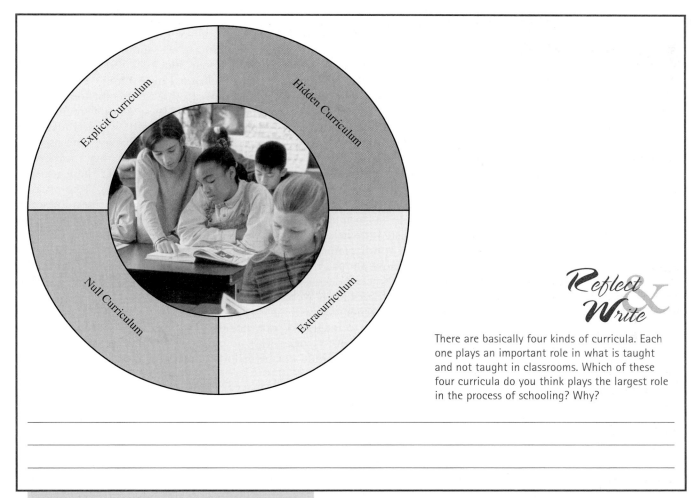

Figure 11.1   *F*our Basic Kinds of Curricula

Middle Level

Standard 4: Understands and uses central concepts, tools of inquiry, standards, and structures of content in chosen teaching fields; creates meaningful learning experiences that develop all young adolescents' competence in subject matter and skills.

expectations created by these relationships influence both positively and negatively how and what students learn. All these are part of the hidden curriculum. When students sign up to be on the staff of the school newspaper and the teacher tells them, "You better be prepared to work hard in here because we are going to print the best newspaper this school ever had," the teacher is influencing how students perceive their roles and individual efforts. In this case, students are learning that by working hard they can achieve a quality result. All the things teachers do to gain and achieve success are part of the hidden curriculum.

*R*eflect & *W*rite

What might you include in your high school curriculum that is not part of the explicit curriculum?

Null curriculum
The intellectual processes and subject content that schools do not teach.

The Null Curriculum. Have you ever thought that schools should teach something that they do not? The **null curriculum** is what is left out or not included, for whatever reasons. Elliot Eisner describes the null curriculum as "the options students are not offered, the perspectives they may never know about, much less be able to use, the concepts and skills that are not a part of their intellectual repertoire."[2] For example, students may not have an opportunity to learn how to think critically, to appreciate or participate in fine arts, or to learn career skills because these areas were intentionally or unintentionally left out of the curriculum. Additionally, when students do not have an opportunity to address or consider contemporary issues, such as those relating to September 11, 2001, gender, social class, and poverty, they may have a different perspective on these issues than do students who encounter these issues in their school curriculum. The National Institute on Drug Abuse (NIDA), a component of the National Institutes of Health (NIH), has a Web site to educate adolescents ages 11 through 15 (as well as their parents and teachers) on the science behind drug abuse. NIDA enlisted the help of teens in developing the site to ensure that the content addresses the appropriate questions and timely concerns.[3] If your middle school students do not know about or use this Web site, then they are missing a valuable antidrug resource. You can access NIDA for teens at www.teens.drugabuse.gov. You can also log on to NIDA's main Web site at www.drugabuse.gov.

As a beginning teacher, you will have opportunities to examine the null curriculum in your school and to include or not include certain subjects or topics in your teaching. Also, you will want to work with your colleagues to plan for and make decisions about what should or should not be included in the curriculum and to explain

Talking the Edutalk

At many schools, six-year-olds don't compare books anymore—they make "text-to-text connections." Misbehaving students face not detention but the "alternative instruction room," or "reinforcement room," or "reflection room." Children who once read now practice "SSR," or "sustained silent reading." And in Maryland, high schoolers write "extended constructed responses"—the essay, in a simpler time.

Jargon has been a mainstay of bureaucracy for centuries, satirized in the works of Jonathan Swift and George Orwell. Education is particularly fertile ground. At school board meetings, stakeholders gather to align curriculum to content standards. Teachers learn to "vertically articulate" and "differentiate instruction" and give "authentic, outcome-based assessments."

Now—with the teacher training industry uncommonly influential, children encouraged to think in more complex terms, and new tests and reforms each coming with its own vocabulary—the vast menu of what's called eduspeak or educationese has oozed into the classrooms. A second-grade teacher announces "modeling efficient subtraction strategies" as the task of the day, while "selected response" has taken the place of "multiple choice."

Teachers say they use the language, which varies by state or district or school, because they're told to. Administrators say they use it because it's on the tests—and besides, everyone will learn it eventually. The theory also goes that if you want students to write a paragraph in a new way, you have to call it something new, too.

"Teachers are being observed more closely than ever before, and if you're not using the right jargon, you look like you don't know what you're doing—regardless of the fact that the little kids have no clue," said Jerry Taylor, a technology teacher outside Rochester, New York.

The words change so fast, several times within a student's academic career. There are ESL (English as a second language) students, or LEP (limited-English-proficient) students, or ELL (English language learners), depending on whom—and when—you ask. The library is the "media center" and the librarian, the "media specialist," and in some schools, homeroom has become "advisory" or "achievement time" or even "time to care."

Robert Maeder, 17, a senior at Springbrook High School in Silver Spring, finds the terms demeaning, especially "learning cottage" instead of "classroom trailer" and "assessment" for "test."

So, what do you think? Has edutalk gone too far? Try writing a "brief constructed response" (paragraph in edutalk!) pro or con about whether or not you think edutalk has gone too far.

For help in figuring out where you stand on this topic, visit www.washingtonpost.com and check out the article from January 18, 2004, by Linda Perlstein called "Talking the Edutalk." (Reprinted by permission from *The Washington Post*, copyright 2004.)

YOU DECIDE

the reasons for your decisions. Whatever you and your colleagues decide, you are influencing learning. Your decisions do matter.

The Extracurriculum. Many schools have a well-developed program of **extracurriculum,** or the cocurricular activities designed to supplement, extend, and enrich the explicit curriculum. As the name implies, extracurriculum activities are seen as an addition to the academic curriculum. However, many extracurriculum activities—such as clubs, study groups, school plays, cheerleading, and band—have important educational goals and are regarded as key parts of the school curriculum.

High school activities support the educational mission of schools, are educational, and contribute to success throughout life. Some of the clubs at West High School in Madison, Wisconsin, include the Anime (Japanese animation) Club, Chess Club, Crimestoppers, Debate Club/Forensics, Drama Club, Gay/Straight Alliance, Green Earth Organization, Math Club, National Honor Society, Pep Band, Photography Club, Science Olympiad, Students for Women's Issues, and Yearbook Staff.

Influences on Curriculum Planning and Design

From colonial times to the present, school curricula are influenced greatly by religious, political, social, and economic forces and events. Forces that influence the curriculum include sociopolitical views and values concerning education—what people think is important for schools to teach and what elected officials and reformers advocate for curriculum priorities. Legislators and governors have greatly influenced what schools should teach and how they teach it, as we have seen through the provisions of the No Child Left Behind Act. This political influence on the curriculum will continue unabated over the next decade.

In addition, as discussed in Chapter 8, laws and court decisions influence the curriculum. Economic and demographic factors, such as the composition of student populations, also affect what is taught. For example, many affluent school districts emphasize curricula that are college preparatory, and many rural districts have curricula that emphasize vocational and technical skills relating to agriculture. Figure 11.2 summarizes influences on curriculum planning and design.

Social values are reflected in the curriculum in numerous ways, such as AIDS education, character education, and programs to reduce violence in the schools. Many states require curricula relating to particular issues and concerns, such as studies on environmental preservation and conservation, substance abuse, and health issues. As a beginning teacher you will be involved in debates over who decides what should be taught. Schools are accountable to local school boards, state departments of education, and federal agencies for what gets taught.

NCATE

Middle Level

Standard 4: Understands and uses central concepts, tools of inquiry, standards, and structures of content in chosen teaching fields; creates meaningful learning experiences that develop all young adolescents' competence in subject matter and skills.

INTASC

Standard 3: The teacher understands how students differ in their approaches to learning and creates instructional opportunities that are adapted to diverse learners.

The Curriculum and Scientifically Based Research

In curriculum planning meetings across America, one of the most often used and heard phrases is "scientifically based research" (SBR). The reason for this is that all schools receiving Title I funds under NCLB must spend their curriculum dollars on programs that are scientifically based. In fact, NCLB mentions SBR at least 110 times! NCLB uses seven key criteria as guidelines in determining if curricula and other reform strategies are scientifically based. Essentially, this means, Does the curriculum work? Does it increase student achievement? For example, if a publisher or program developer makes claims of effectiveness, then these should be one of the "keys" for determining if the program is based on scientifically based research.

What Does This Mean for You?

As a beginning teacher and as a member of a grade school or district curriculum committee, you will be called on to make SBR decisions. Here is one example of how decisions about scientifically based curricula will involve you.

You are teaching in an elementary school serving 500 students in grades 1 through 3. Seventy percent of the students are bilingual and are not achieving to grade-level standards. You and your colleagues are considering adopting a literacy model that claims to benefit all students, including bilingual students. Before adopting the new program, you should ask some questions about the research: Was this program tested under controlled circumstances in which some schools used the program and some did not? Was the sample size reasonable and relevant to the service provided?

Log on now to www.ncrel.org/csri/tools/gkey7/science.htm to review all seven keys involving criteria about scientifically based curricula and for other examples about how you will be involved in curriculum decision making.

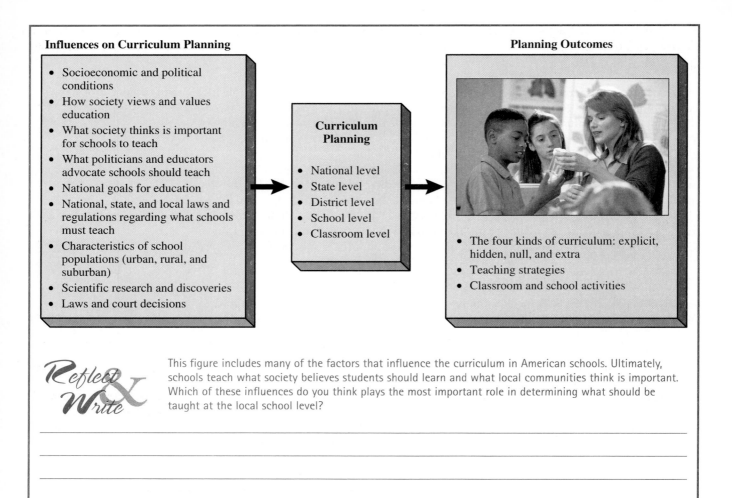

Influences on Curriculum Planning

- Socioeconomic and political conditions
- How society views and values education
- What society thinks is important for schools to teach
- What politicians and educators advocate schools should teach
- National goals for education
- National, state, and local laws and regulations regarding what schools must teach
- Characteristics of school populations (urban, rural, and suburban)
- Scientific research and discoveries
- Laws and court decisions

Curriculum Planning

- National level
- State level
- District level
- School level
- Classroom level

Planning Outcomes

- The four kinds of curriculum: explicit, hidden, null, and extra
- Teaching strategies
- Classroom and school activities

Reflect & Write

This figure includes many of the factors that influence the curriculum in American schools. Ultimately, schools teach what society believes students should learn and what local communities think is important. Which of these influences do you think plays the most important role in determining what should be taught at the local school level?

Figure 11.2 *Influences on Curriculum Planning and Design*

SECTION SUMMARY

What Do Students Learn in School?

What students learn in school makes up the curriculum—all the experiences students have while engaged in the process of school.

- Kinds of Curricula. There are four basic kinds of curricula: the explicit curriculum, the hidden curriculum, the null curriculum, and the extracurriculum.
- Influences on Curriculum Planning and Design. School curricula are influenced greatly by religious and sociopolitical views and values, laws and court decisions, economic and demographic factors, and research findings. There are many complementary and competing constituencies that determine what should be taught.
- The Curriculum and Scientifically Based Research. The NCLB Act and its requirements that Title I funds be spent on scientifically based curriculum are dramatically changing and influencing decisions about curriculum selection and implementation. You will be involved in curriculum decisions that apply selection criteria set forth in NCLB.

What are your opinions about curricula meeting scientifically based criteria? If you are in support of these criteria, explain why. If you are opposed, what three other criteria would you use?

_____

_____

_____

_____ ★

For three of the influences in Figure 11.2, write a concrete curriculum example based on your knowledge and experience.

_____

_____

_____

_____ ★

How are textbooks and other instructional materials chosen in your state or school district? How often are textbook adoptions made and by whom? What criteria are used in selecting textbooks and supplemental materials? How would you change those criteria if you had the power to do so? Would you want to participate in the textbook selection process?

_____

_____

_____

_____ ★

WHAT IS THE CONTEMPORARY CURRICULUM LIKE?

The curriculum of most public schools includes the content areas of language arts, English, mathematics, science, social studies, physical education and health, foreign languages, vocational education, and the arts. Each of these areas has an identifiable body of knowledge and skills that teachers use as the basis for selecting curriculum and planning instruction. Furthermore, professional organizations such as the National Council of Teachers of Mathematics and the National Science Teachers Association develop standards and issue guidelines and recommendations about the curriculum content of their specific areas. In times of fiscal constraint, some of these curricular areas can suffer, while others are emphasized. (See Education on the Move.)

Reading and Language Arts

Today, improving literacy is a major goal in all content areas and across all grade levels, pre-K through 12. In the last decade, there has been a decided emphasis on literacy

>>> Grade Schools Pressed to Offer Foreign Languages >>>>>>>

Even as many Florida school children struggle just to read and write English, their school districts have been ordered to submit plans by the end of the month for launching foreign language instruction in elementary schools.

Florida is one of at least nine states that have pushed to begin foreign language instruction in the lower grades, spurred by research suggesting that public schools can boost the reading and math skills of younger students, according to a national language advocacy group.

"I don't think people can deny the importance of knowing a second language any longer," said Margie Guerzon Fox, a language specialist for Orange County schools. "I don't think we can continue to be monolingual and continue to compete in the global community or even in the Florida community."

The movement has critics, many of whom question whether public schools should take on Spanish, French, and other languages when 34 percent of third-graders can't read well in English, according to 2004 statewide test scores.

Even foreign language proponents worry about finding money, space, and time for a new program when Florida already is wrestling with crowded schools and a school year dominated by preparation for the annual state proficiency test.

"If you take that time away from math and reading, are we going to have our hands slapped because we weren't doing math and reading well enough?" said Terry Golden, a consultant for the Florida Association of School Administrators.

On the other hand, while Florida is gearing up its teaching of foreign languages, other schools are gearing down. At a time when America is having trouble making friends overseas, some U.S. schools are charting a course that could make that task even tougher. Faced with gaping funding shortages, some school districts are taking the ax to their foreign language programs. The moves range from reducing the number of languages offered to eliminating entire programs in some grades. In response, some parents are organizing and funding after-school language clubs; others are sending their kids to private language schools.

The cuts are hitting students of all ages and in a broad swath of school districts. This fall, the school district of Elmbrook, Wisconsin, dropped languages such as French and German for its fourth-, fifth- and sixth-graders. Also this year, the foreign language program for seventh and eighth grades in the Roseburg Public Schools in Oregon has been scrapped. The Holland Township School District in New Jersey now uses videos for foreign language instruction in grades 4 through 7.

As budget woes have mounted in the past few years, school administrators increasingly have come to see foreign language programs as expendable. Take Russian, which saw a resurgence in the early 1990s following the excitement generated by *perestroika:* By the fall of 2001, the last year for which data are available, only 126 schools in the United States were teaching it—59 percent fewer than five years earlier, according to the Committee on College and Pre-College Russian, based at American University in Washington, D.C.

Some parents have been able to save their programs by fighting back. In Connecticut, the Glastonbury Public Schools were considering cutting Spanish for children in first and second grades but ended up keeping the program after parents spoke out at public meetings and called public officials. Parents and community organizations in Edina, Minnesota, rescued their second-grade Spanish program through different means: they donated $20,000 last spring.

Sources: D. M. Balona and T. deLusuriaga, "Grade Schools Pressed to Offer Foreign Language," *Orlando Sentinel,* June 8, 2004. (Online). Available at www.us-english. org/inc/news/use_in_news/viewArticle. asp?ID=64; A. M. Chaker, "Schools Say 'Adieu' to Foreign Languages," *Wall Street Journal,* October 30, 2003, p. D1. Reprinted by permission.

Whole language
An approach based on the idea that language development, reading, writing, speaking, and listening are interrelated processes and should be taught concurrently rather than sequentially.

Phonics
Teaching reading by letter-sound correspondence.

and reading in grades pre-K through 8. All states have adopted an educational agenda with a strong literacy focus and have set the goal of having all children read at grade level. During the 1990s, educators waged spirited battles known as the "reading wars" about how best to teach reading. One group advocated a **whole language** approach. Whole language is a philosophy of language instruction emphasizing the integration of all language skills (reading, writing, speaking, and listening), as well as reading for meaning and contextualized language learning. Another group advocated for the use of **phonics** instruction, which involves teaching letter-sound correspondence and decoding, or a "bottom-up" approach to language learning. Some whole language instructors altogether avoided reading and writing instruction based on phonics, although others included some phonics for individual students as needed.

A Balanced Approach. With the advent of the new century, the reading wars have more or less come to an end. Instead, professional efforts focus on how to achieve a **balanced** (or comprehensive) **approach to reading**, one that includes all available strategies to help children learn to read, based on their own learning styles and developmental needs.

Also, educators have supported the following changes in the reading and literacy curriculum and accompanying instructional practices:

- Giving students a more active role in the reading process. This can be done, for example, through self-directed learning. Self-directed learning involves a three-step process: modeling desired behavior, guiding students' practice in the desired behavior, and organizing the classroom environment and instructional process so that students can work independently or in cooperative learning groups.
- Emphasizing reading comprehension and activities to promote comprehension.
- Integrating reading with all content areas. This is known as "reading across the curriculum."
- Placing less emphasis on teaching reading as an isolated skill.
- Making reading more practical and tied to daily life and events.
- Using reciprocal teaching to improve students' reading comprehension. To do so, teachers employ four comprehension strategies: predicting, questioning, clarifying, and summarizing. Teachers scaffold these four strategies by modeling, guiding, and applying the strategies while reading; guide students to become metacognitive and reflective in their strategy use; and help students monitor their reading comprehension using the four strategies. Teachers use the social nature of learning to improve and scaffold reading comprehension and to strengthen instruction in a variety of classroom settings—whole class sessions, guided reading groups, and literature circles.[4]
- Integrating thinking skills into the reading and language arts curriculum.

Science

Science and the teaching of science are fast-changing enterprises. To see these changes in the role of science and in science teaching, read the Profile on the Wyoming Ethnobotany Project. The Wyoming Project provides an example of the ways teaching science in grades pre-K through 12 has changed and is changing. These changes will affect you and influence how you teach.

In addition to changing the way science is taught, the sequence of teaching the sciences is changing. For decades, the sequence of science has been ninth-grade biology, tenth-grade chemistry, and eleventh-grade physics. Now some schools are making physics the first course in the sequence and the basis for other science learning.

A leading science education reformer, Marge Bardeen, manager of the Fermi National Accelerator Laboratory Education Office, notes that what we learn in science courses could relate more to everyday life.

> Generally, I think people do not understand that science is a way of approaching problems rather than a body of knowledge. As a result, they are often unable to assess claims and counterclaims as they make choices on critical issues that face them as citizens. This is what we need to be concerned about—as we call it, scientific literacy for citizenship.[5]

Mathematics

Mathematics, like science, is being reformed. What is taught, how math is taught, and the sequence in which math skills and concepts are taught are changing. The current mathematics reform is often referred to as the "new new math" to distinguish it from the "new math" reforms of the 1960s and 1970s. The current reforms in mathematics are spurred by standards developed by the National Council of Teachers of Mathematics (NCTM) and state standards-based education. The mathematics reform movement focuses on the following initiatives:

The Wyoming Ethnobotany Project: Joel M. Kuper

Joel M. Kuper teaches science at Greybull High School in Grey-bull, Wyoming, and is a recipient of the 2003 Subaru National Science Teaching Awards. More about this project can be found at www.science.subaru.com/teaching_ideas/ b_joelkuper.shtml.

Wyoming has a rich cultural heritage that extends back to Native American influences. However, many students have little appreciation of the applications of that heritage in our current society. In looking for a way to improve the teaching of science at Greybull High School, I developed the Wyoming Ethnobotany Project. This integrated program investigates indigenous plants in northwestern Wyoming that were used by Native Americans for their medicinal properties. These plants are used to produce extracts that are tested using twenty-first-century tissue culture and biochemical analyses to evaluate their potential as medicines and supplements in today's society.

The program has been incorporated into a number of classes. The botany course does background research into plants used by the Shoshone, Arapaho, and Crow tribes from this area. Students learn to identify the plants and develop a data base on historic uses through consultation with tribal contacts and the Plains Indian Museum at the Buffalo Bill Historical Center in Cody, Wyoming. They do field work in mapping locations and collecting samples for lab evaluation. Our chemistry classes are involved with making extracts of the plant materials. Extractions are made with water, ethanol, and acetone in order to evaluate polar and nonpolar substances. The collected extracts are turned over to students enrolled in the school's research seminar course. These students select a topic for in-depth experimental research. In the Ethnobotany Project, many of these students elect to work with the native plant extracts to evaluate their effectiveness in a variety of situa-

tions. The in-depth projects are the basis of the student's research work that competes at the regional, state, and ISEF levels.

Today, there are literally no boundaries between science and other academic disciplines. The Wyoming ethnobiology project illustrates critical ways in which contemporary science teaching is changing:

- How science teaching is integrated across grades and subject areas
- How science teaching is interdisciplinary
- How science is applied to everyday life
- How science can reform cultural understanding and perspectives
- How science is applied to environmental issues
- How students are involved in projects and learn science by acting as scientists act
- How students use science to think and develop thinking skills

Source: Subaru of America, Inc. Reprinted by permission.

INTASC
Standard 1: The teacher understands the central concepts, tools of inquiry, and structures of the subjects being taught and can create learning experiences that make these aspects of subject matter meaningful for students.

INTASC
Standard 4: The teacher uses various instructional strategies to encourage students' development of critical thinking, problem solving, and performance skills.

NCATE

Elementary

Standard 2.3: Understands and uses major concepts, procedures, and reasoning processes of mathematics to foster student understanding.

- Emphasis on providing all students with meaningful mathematics experiences
- Hands-on math at all grade levels
- Less emphasis on rote learning and memorization. This deemphasis on calculation and basic arithmetic skills is a hallmark of mathematics reform. It is also one of the bones of contention with critics of contemporary math reform.
- Student-centered learning and involving students in independent and group investigations of real mathematics problems
- High mathematical expectations for all students. This equity emphasis includes students with disabilities, females, minorities, and low-income students.
- Gender equity. The emphasis here is to dismantle the stereotype that math is for males only.
- The use of differentiated instruction to achieve equity goals
- Integration of technology applications—computers, calculators, and personal hand held devices—to "do math"
- Implementation of standards-based teaching

INTASC
Standard 1: The teacher understands the central concepts, tools of inquiry, and structures of the subjects being taught and can create learning experiences that make these aspects of subject matter meaningful for students.

Within the math discipline, attention is being focused on algebra, which math educators see as the foundation for mathematical problem solving. Since the 1990s, schools nationwide have quietly begun requiring algebra for more and more students, hoping they'll develop skills for college and a changing workplace—not to mention everyday life, with its computer spreadsheets and cell phone plans. Twenty-one states now require students to pass algebra to graduate, and teachers (and textbook publishers) are being prodded to reinvent it, stressing real-world situations while minimizing calculation and theoretical concepts that dogged students a generation ago. Algebra is also being taught more and more as part of elementary and middle school curricula.

"Thirty years ago, we only taught algebra to a select group," says Linda Antinone, a nineteen-year veteran math and physics teacher at Paschal High School in Fort Worth, Texas. "If you weren't college bound, you didn't get algebra."[6] Now algebra is for everyone. When we say algebra is for everyone, this is exactly the point. Algebraic concepts are being integrated throughout the K–12 curriculum.

Social Studies

The National Council for the Social Studies (NCSS) defines social studies as "the integrated study of the social sciences and humanities to promote civic competence." (Go to www.ncss.org for more information about the association.) Within the school program, social studies courses provide coordinated, systematic study drawing on a wide variety of disciplines, including anthropology, archaeology, economics, geography, history, law, philosophy, political science, psychology, religion, and sociology as well as appropriate content from the humanities, mathematics, and natural sciences. In essence, social studies promote knowledge of and involvement in civic affairs.

The NCSS framework consists of ten themes incorporating fields of study that correspond with one or more relevant disciplines. The organization believes that effective social studies programs include the following study experiences:

NCATE

Elementary

Standard 2.4: Understands and uses major concepts and modes of inquiry from the social studies to promote students' abilities to make informed decisions as citizens of a culturally diverse democratic society and interdependent world.

Middle Level

Standard 3: Understands the major concepts, principles, theories, and research related to middle-level curriculum and assessment; uses this knowledge in practice.

- Culture
- People, places, and environments
- Individuals, groups, and institutions
- Production, distribution, and consumption
- Global connections
- Time, continuity, and change
- Individual development and identity
- Power, authority, and governance
- Science, technology, and society
- Civic ideals and practices

Social studies does not always receive the attention and recognition it deserves. It is sometimes forced to take a back seat in the curriculum to science, math, English, or language arts. This is unfortunate, because civic virtue is at the core of democratic living.

History is the leading discipline of social studies across all grades, K through 12. Many states require that state history be taught, typically between grades 4 and 8; if your state is one of these, you need to familiarize yourself with the content. In fact, some states require a state history course as a condition for obtaining a teaching certificate. History teachers are trying to keep history from being squeezed out by the emphasis of many assessment tests on reading, math, and science. History teachers are also trying to move from rote teaching and memorization of facts to other approaches that make history come alive and be meaningful to students. These include:

Creative teachers help their students connect to social studies. The Indiana Professional Standards Board (IPSB) links its standards to the INTASC Standards emphasized in this book, stating that one task of a social studies teacher is to "create and develop a dynamic learning environment that is characterized by positive, productive, and healthy interactions. The learning environment is supportive, congenial, and purposeful. Students are intellectually challenged and encouraged to learn and grow."

- Historical role-playing
- Study and use of primary sources
- Reading of historical narrative (e.g., journals, diaries, and letters)
- Use of the Internet to access primary sources

Character education
An approach to education that
emphasizes the teaching of values,
moral reasoning, and the development of "good" character.

NCATE

Middle Level

Standard 2: Understands the
major concepts, principles,
theories, and research underlying
the philosophical foundations
of developmentally responsible
middle-level programs and
schools; works successfully within
these organizational components.

Character Education. Related to civic virtue, **character education** is part of the social studies curriculum. It is an example of a curricular application of developmental approaches to learning. Programs aim to help students acquire positive character traits, such as initiative, diligence, loyalty, tact, kindness, generosity, courage, and other traits believed to be good by society in general. Georgia's Quality Core Curriculum (QCC) includes core values taught in the Georgia public schools, such as citizenship, respect for others, respect for self, self-esteem, and the work ethic. More information concerning Georgia's Quality Core Curriculum is available on their Web site at www.doe.k12.ga.us.

Character education seeks to directly teach character traits such as those in Figure 11.3. Character Education Resources, an organization based in New Hampshire, provides a wealth of information about character education on their Web site at www.charactereducationinfo.org.

Service learning, or community service, is often touted as a means for promoting character education. However, at the present time, Maryland is the only state requiring such service as a condition for graduation.

The following Calendar of Character Traits for the Duval County (Florida) Public School District was created to teach students how to take responsibility for their actions and to treat others with respect; show students that there are specific payoffs in life for doing those things; have teachers model those behaviors for students every second that they are with them during the day and expect them to do the same; and finally, create an atmosphere in the schools in which students can safely practice those behaviors until such behaviors become the norm.

August: Responsibility and Attentiveness. Responsibility—having moral, legal, or mental accountability; reliable, trustworthy. Attentiveness—being heedful and mindful of another's speech, needs, and so on.

September: Citizenship and Cooperation. Becoming an active member of the community and working within the community to achieve the common benefit.

October: Fairness. Treating others in a consistent, impartial way—free from self-interest, prejudice, or favoritism.

November: Patriotism. Showing love, devotion, and pride to one's country.

December: Kindness and Caring. Feeling interest or concern for others and being kind.

January: Courage and Initiative. Showing mental or moral strength and taking the first step to do so.

February: Respect and Tolerance. Showing regard for the worth of everyone and everything; also, respecting the individual differences, views, and beliefs of others.

March: Honesty and Trustworthiness. Practicing adherence to the facts, fairness, and straightforwardness of conduct; also being worthy of confidence.

April: Self-Control. Exercising restraint over one's impulses, emotions, and desires.

May: Patience and Perseverance. The capacity, habit, or fact of bearing pains or trials calmly or without complaint; the steady persistence in adhering to a course of action and/or a belief or purpose.

Reflect & Write

Think about the students you will teach. Develop your own Calendar of Character Traits that will guide your teaching of character. What criteria will you use to select the character traits you think your students should demonstrate? Do you think parents should have a voice in identifying character traits for their children? If yes, how would you provide for parent input?

Figure 11.3 *A* **Calendar of Character Traits**

Source: Character Education. *Duval County Public Schools.* (Online). Available at www.educationcentral.org/schools/character.

Physical Education and Health

As you know from your life experiences, things don't get done unless there is a crisis. The same applies to the field of physical education. After years of schedule cuts and playing second fiddle to reading, math, and science, physical education finds itself in the spotlight. Physical educators have a national crisis to thank for their new-found attention—childhood obesity. Physical education is no longer just for students interested in athletics. Now it is for everyone. It is for everyone because more states and schools are requiring it. Alarmed by growing numbers of overweight children and obesity-related health risks, Texas recently passed a law requiring elementary students, K through 6, to spend thirty minutes a day in physical education classes or structured physical activity; however, the "new" physical education is not what the "old" physical education was. The new physical education focuses on the whole student and relates physical fitness to all aspects of life.

Health. Encouraging and helping children lead healthy lifestyles is also a top priority of school districts today. Many districts are serving healthier food in school cafeterias and limiting students' access to junk food. For example, Francisco Macias doesn't go in much for the standard fare at the Hammocks Middle School cafeteria. But the Miami sixth-grader sure likes to chow down on treats from the school's new vending machines.

As part of a pilot program, Hammocks' two cafeterias boast dispensers filled with healthy versions of standard snacks and drinks. They range from low-fat chips to Nesquik-flavored milk and Gatorade. Francisco favors Frito-Lay's Ruffles baked potato chips. He knows they're healthier than the high-fat type, so he feels better about eating them, he says.[7]

Students' health and wellness knowledge and skills are guided by Health Education Standards, as shown in Figure 11.4. The seven standards are the same for grades K through 12; however, the benchmark for the grade levels are different. Figure 11.4 provides examples from different grades.

The Arts

Today, despite strained school budgets, treating art education as a major content area rather than as part of the extracurriculum is a trend in curriculum development. Some even suggest that art become the fourth R! Why is this trend occurring? Stephanie Perrin, the headmistress of Walnut Hill School in Natick, Massachusetts, offers the following reason:

> What is required of workers at all levels in our post-industrial society is that they be creative thinkers and problem solvers and able to work well with others or independently. Schools can no longer simply train students for specific tasks; schools must educate them in terms of broad skills, so they will be able to function in a number of capacities. Students must be active learners, they must be judicious risk-takers, they must be able to push themselves toward high levels of achievement, and they must have the courage of their convictions. Arts training develops such skills.[8]

For example, in theater students practice thinking and memory skills, problem-solving skills, and social skills. They also apply the basic skills of reading, writing, and arithmetic. Other important reasons for teaching theater include fostering student self-confidence and understanding, promoting creative thinking, developing interpersonal skills, and cultivating an understanding of human values.

As an alternative to integrating arts into the general curriculum as a content area, many school districts have established magnet arts schools that enroll students throughout a district or region. One example is the School for Creative and Performing Arts (SCPA) in Cincinnati, Ohio. SCPA is one of the older comprehensive public high schools that offers a vocational arts curriculum, and it has frequently been studied as a model by other school districts considering the establishment of a magnet arts program. It offers instruction in vocal and instrumental music, dance, acting, musical theater, creative

NCATE

Elementary

Standard 2.6: Understands and uses major concepts in health education to create opportunities for student development and practice of skills that contribute to good health.

Standard 2.7: Understands and uses human movement and physical activity as central elements to foster active, healthy lifestyles and enhanced quality of life for students.

NCATE

Elementary

Standard 2.5: Understands and uses the content, functions, and achievements of dance, music, theater, and the several visual arts as primary media for communication, inquiry, and insight among students.

INTASC

Standard 3: The teacher understands how students differ in their approaches to learning and creates instructional opportunities that are adapted to diverse learners.

Standard 1. Students will comprehend concepts related to health promotion and disease prevention.

Example K–4   Describe how the family influences personal health.

Standard 2. Students will demonstrate the ability to access valid health information and health-promoting products and services.

Example 5–8   Analyze the validity of health information, products, and services.

Standard 3. Students will demonstrate the ability to practice health-enhancing behaviors and reduce health risks.

Example 9–12   Evaluate a personal health assessment to determine strategies for health enhancement and risk reduction.

Standard 4. Students will analyze the influence of culture, media, technology, and other factors on health.

Example K–4   Explain how media influence thoughts, feelings, and health behaviors.

Standard 5. Students will demonstrate the ability to use interpersonal communication skills to enhance health.

Example 5–8   Demonstrate effective and nonverbal communication skills to enhance health.

Standard 6. Students will demonstrate the ability to use goal-setting and decision-making skills to enhance health.

Example 9–12   Demonstrate the ability to utilize various strategies when making decisions related to health needs and risks of young adults.

Standard 7. Students will demonstrate the ability to advocate for personal, family, and community health.

Example K–4   Describe a variety of methods to convey accurate health information and ideas.

Reflect & Write

What do you think are the most serious health issues facing children and youth today? Do you think schools should assume responsibility for providing students with health information, knowledge, and skills? Why? Why not?

_____

_____

_____

NCATE

Elementary

Standard 2.6: Understands and uses major concepts in health education to create opportunities for student development and practice of skills that contribute to good health

Figure 11.4   *Sample National Health Education Standards*

Source: American Association for Health Education, *National Health Education Standards.* (Online). Available at www.educationworld.com/standards/national/nph/index.shtml.

writing, and visual arts, in addition to a core curriculum of academic subjects. Enrolling students in grades 4 through 12, SCPA was the first magnet arts school to enroll elementary students.[9]

In what ways were the arts a part of your schooling? In a given grade, how could the arts be integrated throughout the curriculum?

_____

_____

_____

_____

Comprehensive School Reform and the Curriculum

Educators have made many efforts to redesign and reform schools and curricula to improve American schools. The Obey-Porter Comprehensive School Reform Demonstration program (CSRD) legislation, reauthorized under the No Child Left Behind Act of 2001, funds research-based comprehensive models designed to help ensure the

A growing number of school districts and teachers consider the arts to be a foundation for and a part of the education process. Yet a National Assessment of Educational Progress (NAEP) Arts Report Card indicated that many students lag behind in learning how to draw, dance, or play a musical instrument. Why do you think this is?

academic success of all students. Such reform models generally focus on changing all aspects of a school's operation, with an emphasis on increasing student learning, and are referred to as "whole school" and "systematic reform programs." The models are developed and implemented with federal and private funds. Many are designed to be used in low-performing schools, and their implementation is supported by Title I funds and aimed at helping low-achieving students in high-poverty schools.

These model programs are widely used in school districts across the country. Additional models can be accessed through Northwest Regional Educational Laboratory at www.nwrel.org. Some models—such as ATLAS Communities, Expeditionary Learning Outward Bound, and Roots and Wings—are supported by New American Schools (NAS). More information on NAS is available at its Web site at naschools.org.

SECTION SUMMARY

What Is the Contemporary Curriculum Like?

Recent trends in curriculum development stress addressing the standards developed by professional organizations in the discipline areas.

- Reading and Language Arts. Improving literacy and reading skills is a major emphasis across all grade levels and subject areas. After years of "reading wars," the majority of reading professionals now advocate a "balanced" or comprehensive approach to reading instruction that includes strategies from both whole language and phonics approaches and tailors instruction to individual student needs.

- Science. Science teaching is rapidly changing from a facts and rote-memory-based approach to one that utilizes a number of different approaches, including integrating science across grades and subject areas, applying science to everyday life and especially to environmental issues, incorporating cultural understanding, and emphasizing problem-solving and thinking skills. The sequence is also changing, with physics now taught first in many schools.

- Mathematics. Mathematics reform focuses on providing all students with meaningful mathematics experiences by including more problem solving and less emphasis on rote learning and memorization. Algebra is at the center of mathematics reform, and twenty-one states now require students to pass algebra to graduate.

- Social Studies. The social studies include a wide range of subjects, from anthropology to sociology. History is the leading discipline of the social studies across all grades, K through 12; teachers are using varied approaches—such as role-playing, primary sources, and technology—to help make history come alive. Character education is part of the social studies curriculum and is designed to help students acquire positive character traits. Character education is similar to moral education, which fosters moral reasoning through discussions and activities.

- Physical Education and Health. Physical education is back in vogue again, thanks to high rates of obesity and poor health of children and youth. The new physical education focuses on helping students learn skills and knowledge that will enable them to be fit for life. Health education is focused on helping children lead healthy lifestyles now and in the future.

- The Arts. Many school districts are treating art education as a major content curriculum area rather than as a part of the extracurriculum.

- Comprehensive School Reform and the Curriculum. Whole school reform models, which are funded by federal and private money, attempt to reform all aspects of a school's operation and to increase student learning. These models tend to target low-performing schools.

Thinking Critically
★ ☆ ★ ☆ ★ ☆ ★ ☆ ★

How did you learn to read? What do you consider the advantages and disadvantages of that method? Why is there so much interest in ensuring that all students know how to read well?

_____

_____

_____

_____ ★

Applying What You've Learned
★ ☆ ★ ☆ ★ ☆ ★ ☆ ★

Research the science and math requirements in high schools in your area. Are students receiving comparable educations in science and math? Do you think they should? Are all students required to take algebra? Do you think they should?

_____

_____

_____ ★

Putting Yourself in the Picture
★ ☆ ★ ☆ ★ ☆ ★ ☆ ★

Brainstorm ideas for integrating character education into your curriculum and instructional practices. Identify specific examples and the specific contexts for integrating character education appropriately. Begin by recording your first ideas here and discussing them with classmates.

_____

_____

_____ ★

HOW DO TEACHERS PLAN AND DELIVER INSTRUCTION?

INTASC

Standard 1: The teacher understands the central concepts, tools of inquiry, and structures of the subjects being taught and can create learning experiences that make these aspects of subject matter meaningful for students.

Standard 7: The teacher plans instruction based upon knowledge of subject matter, students, the community, and curriculum goals.

NCATE

Elementary

Standard 3.1: Plans and implements instruction based on knowledge of students, learning theory, subject matter, curricular goals, and community.

Middle Level

Standard 1: Understands the major concepts, principles, theories and research related to young adolescent development; provides opportunities that support student development and learning.

Of all of the many roles of a teacher, planning and providing instruction are the most essential. How you teach determines to a great extent how successful you are—that is, how well your students learn. The instructional methods you use will have a major effect on the way you interpret the curriculum and address curriculum goals. Your planning will also determine to a large extent if what you teach is interesting, understandable, and integrated with what students already know.

Instructional Goals and Learning Objectives

When you plan for implementing the curriculum, one of the tasks is to identify standards and **instructional goals**—statements regarding what students will learn. As we learned in Chapter 10, national, state, and local standards are the starting place for instructional goals. In addition, you need to consider the objectives and outcomes of the instructional process.

One of the first persons to provide a model for curriculum planning was Ralph Tyler, who called the purposes of education **learning objectives**. Tyler's influence led to an emphasis on stating learning objectives in behavioral terms that specify what students should master in each subject at each grade level. Traditionally, this kind of planning results in a scope-and-sequence approach to curriculum and instruction. For example, students might master the correct use of capitalization and end punctuation in grade 1 and then go on to more complex punctuation rules in grades 2 and 3. Robert Mager developed a widely used system for writing instructional objectives. He maintained that a well-stated learning objective has three parts: a description of what students should do, the conditions under which the student will perform, and how the student's performance will be evaluated.[10] Teachers who use formulas such as Mager's need to write many specific objectives to cover all of the behaviors they want students to demonstrate.

Learning Domains. Learning objectives have been classified according to the domains of knowledge they address. For example, Benjamin Bloom proposed a taxonomy of educational objectives for the cognitive domain. Bloom believed that cognitive learning should progress from simple to complex and from factual to conceptual.[11] Types of learning objectives in the cognitive domain are shown in Table 11.1, along with examples from a secondary-level science curriculum.

Instructional goals
What students will learn; what they will know and be able to do.

Learning objectives
Purposes of education stated in behavioral terms and specifying what students should master in each subject at each grade level.

Table 11.1   Learning Objectives in the Cognitive Domain

	Type of Objective	Example
More simple and factual ↑ ↓ More complex and conceptual	Knowledge	What are the bones of the human skull?
	Comprehension	What functions do the bones of the skull serve?
	Application	What can scientists learn by looking at skulls?
	Analysis	How does this skull reveal human traits?
	Synthesis	What might the owner of this skull have looked like in the flesh?
	Evaluation	What are some problems in interpreting skeletal evidence scientifically?

Outcome-Based Education

Outcome-based education (OBE) An educational approach that focuses on developing students' ability to demonstrate mastery of certain desired outcomes or performances.

A contemporary approach based on learning objectives is called **outcome-based education (OBE)**. In OBE, broader outcomes of learning are evaluated rather than the mastery of specific behavioral objectives. For example, a student's science project might demonstrate broader outcomes such as concern with environmental stewardship, participation in local affairs, and personal accomplishment. At the same time, the project might demonstrate an array of curriculum goals, such as being able to apply the scientific method, to measure accurately, and to communicate learning. William Spady, an influential proponent of OBE, defines outcomes as "high quality, culminating demonstrations of significant learning in context."[12]

Some critics of outcome-based education favor step-by-step teaching and evaluation of basic skills. Others claim that demonstrations of student learning are often difficult or impossible to assess and report to parents and that training teachers to assess outcomes is costly and time consuming. However, advocates claim that outcome-based education offers an opportunity for all students to succeed because they have more time to achieve mastery before products of their learning are evaluated. Students also can demonstrate their learning in relation to real-life situations. (See Education on the Move.)

Prepared Curricula

INTASC

Standard 5: The teacher uses an understanding of individual and group motivation and behavior to create a learning environment that encourages positive social interaction, active engagement in learning, and self-motivation.

One of the oldest and most discussed curriculum issues centers around a teacher's right to use the curricula and materials they want and to teach in the ways they want. This chapter and this book stress the theme that high-quality teachers make high-quality decisions and deliver high-quality instruction resulting in student achievement. However, teachers also teach from textbooks that have a particular approach, content, and sequence. In addition, more textbooks are becoming highly scripted—that is, they come with detailed teacher guides that outline daily lessons and teaching scripts. These kinds of textbooks will become more common, and teachers will be expected to follow them.

education *on the move* >>>>>>>>>>>>

>>> Making Sure Everybody Learns Math >>>>>>>

If you get your first job as a math teacher at Del Valle High School in El Paso, Texas, you really will have little choice in what to teach or how to teach it. For example, you will never have to write a test again. The math department chairwoman writes them all for you, along with your entire curriculum and what you'll be teaching every day of the year. Want some leeway to do your own thing? "You can be one day ahead of the plan or one day behind—that's it," said Patty Lucero, the department chairwoman.

"The idea of academic freedom is truly a thing of the past," said principal J. R. Guinn. "We've got

a curriculum, and everybody's going to learn it. That's how we're going to be able to set the academic bar every other school will try to reach."

That sort of academic centralization and a single-minded focus on success have helped Del Valle become one of the state's rarest stories: an excellent urban high school.

Dell Valle is by all appearances a standard, traditional high school, filled with about 1,800 students. Eighty-five percent are poor enough to qualify for free or reduced-price school lunches. It's barely a mile from the Zaragosa Bridge and the Mexican border, and many of its students are recent immigrants.

When Ms. Lucero became department chairwoman, she centralized and standardized so that every teacher would be teaching and testing the same material at the same time.

"That way you know exactly what kids should know at every point in the year," she said.

It also made it easier to compare how teachers were doing. After a test, passing rates for each teacher are distributed among the math faculty.

Source: Created by the author from data from J. Benton, "Success Driven by a Singular Focus," *Dallas Morning News*, December 2, 2002, p. 1A, 9A.

SECTION SUMMARY

How Do Teachers Plan and Deliver Instruction?

Teachers' instructional methods and models affect their interpretations of curricula and their ability to attain goals as well as how their students learn.

- Instructional Goals and Learning Objectives. When teachers plan for and provide instruction, they identify instructional goals that students will know and be able to do. Instructional goals relate to educational philosophy and also speak to specific learning. Ralph Tyler was one of the first persons to develop learning objectives as a means of guiding instruction. Educational objectives have been classified according to the domains of knowledge they address, such as those for the cognitive domain or the affective domain.

- Outcome-Based Education. Outcome-based education is a contemporary approach that specifies broader learning outcomes and emphasizes the demonstration of learning.

- Prepared Curricula. In efforts to increase student achievement, many schools are using prepared curricula. These prepared curricula are in the form of highly scripted textbooks and other learning materials that provide teachers with detailed instructions about what to teach and how to teach it. It is likely that more teachers will be using prepared curricula in the decades to come.

Thinking Critically
★ ★ ★ ★ ★ ★ ★ ★ ★

What are the dangers of having state standards be the primary source of learning objectives in your classroom? What would be the advantages for you and students?

_____

_____

_____

_____ ★

Applying What You've Learned
★ ★ ★ ★ ★ ★ ★ ★ ★

The high school textbooks of today are different from the textbooks you used. Review the teacher editions of textbooks in the subject areas in which you plan to teach. What will you have to do to prepare yourself to teach from them?

_____

_____

_____

Putting Yourself in the Picture
★ ★ ★ ★ ★ ★ ★ ★ ★

The school in which you teach will have a particular approach to the curriculum and testing. What are some questions you will ask about the curriculum and your "freedom to teach"?

_____

_____

_____

_____ ★

Direct instruction
Highly structured, teacher-centered strategy that capitalizes on such behavioral techniques as modeling, feedback, and reinforcement to promote basic skill acquisition, primarily in reading and mathematics.

In **direct instruction,** as the name implies, teachers determine what students will learn and how they will learn it by directly transmitting information, skills training, and concepts. Direct instruction is used primarily and most often successfully to teach students basic skills and structured knowledge, such as phonics, reading vocabulary, grammar rules, math computation, and science facts. Teaching practices most associated with direct instruction are lectures, teacher-prepared lessons, and demonstrations. The following section explores some of the models for delivering knowledge through direct instruction.

Explicit Instruction

Explicit instruction
Instruction that is directly focused on the improvement of learning through the mastery of basic skills.

Barak Rosenshine refers to direct instruction as **explicit instruction** and identifies the following six basic teaching functions that guide teaching practice:

1. Review and check the previous day's work.
2. Present new material.
3. Provide guided practice.
4. Give feedback and correctives.
5. Provide independent practice.
6. Review weekly and monthly.[13]

These teaching functions serve as a framework in which to teach basic skills using explicit instruction.

Examples of curriculum that employ direct instruction are:

- Open court reading, which uses systematic, explicit instruction of phonemic awareness, phonics and word knowledge, comprehension skills and strategies, inquiry skills and strategies, and writing and language arts skills and strategies.[14]

This teacher is giving a lesson through direct instruction. What factors did she consider in planning the lesson? What steps does she take to deliver the instruction effectively?

- Distar Language: Language for Learning provides practice in vocabulary, word and sentence variety, and development of precise word knowledge and in hard-to-teach concepts such as some/all/none and same/different.[15]

Mastery Teaching

Another model of direct instruction, called **mastery teaching,** was developed by Madeline Hunter. It includes the following five steps:

1. Anticipatory set—that is, using techniques to get students' minds ready to learn
2. Instruction or providing information, including modeling and checking for understanding
3. Guided practice
4. Closure or checking for performance
5. Independent practice[16]

Mastery teaching
Teaching designed to help ensure that students learn particular skills and concepts.

SECTION SUMMARY

What Are Some Models of Direct Instruction?

In direct instruction, teachers determine what students will learn and how they will learn it by directly transmitting information skills training and concepts. Direct instruction is used to teach basic skills and structured knowledge.

- Explicit Instruction. Rosenshine's explicit instruction views teaching as a framework of six functions that guide teaching practice in imparting basic skills.
- Mastery Teaching. Hunter's mastery teaching is a five-step model in which more specific instructions are grouped.

Thinking Critically
★ ☆ ★ ☆ ★ ☆ ★ ☆ ★

Some critics say that direct instruction stifles student and teacher creativity because it is systematic and scripted. What do you think? Support your answer with some examples.

_____

_____

_____

_____ ★

Applying What You've Learned
★ ☆ ★ ☆ ★ ☆ ★ ☆ ★

Interview a teacher in a local school and find out what methods of direct instruction are used. Ask the teacher to share personal views on the strengths and limits of direct instruction.

_____

_____

_____

_____ ★

Assume you are teaching third-grade students. Choose one of the following four situations: (1) making a watercolor painting of a bowl of apples, (2) writing a thank-you note for a birthday present, (3) playing a game of ping-pong, or (4) performing a science experiment (your choice of experiment). Break the situation down into (1) basic skills and structured knowledge that seem best suited to learning through methods of direct instruction and (2) other knowledge or skills that would not benefit from direct instruction.

_____

_____

_____

_____ ★

*W*HAT ARE SOME MODELS OF NONDIRECT INSTRUCTION*?*

Nondirect instruction is any form of instruction that is not transmitted directly to the students by the teacher. The teacher's role is to structure opportunities for students to advance their own learning. Thus, nondirect instruction includes learning that students acquire on their own through reflection, experimentation, or discovery. It also includes learning that students acquire through interaction with other students in peer-mediated instruction, such as group investigation and cooperative learning.

Nondirect instruction is used primarily and most often successfully to provide opportunities for students to learn higher-level thinking and problem-solving skills and to assimilate content-area knowledge that is open-ended rather than basic. Further development and testing of teaching models based on nondirect instruction is a current trend in education.

Discovery Learning

A classic example of nondirect instruction is **discovery learning**. Discovery learning was developed during the 1960s by Jerome Bruner[17] and reflects Jean Piaget's and Lev Vygotsky's principles of instruction. Piaget advocated children's active involvement in learning activities as the primary means of promoting cognitive development. Vygotsky's theory of learning is presented in the Profile on "Teaching in the Zone" on p. 424.

In discovery learning students are allowed to experiment with materials to gain new understandings and to discover information for themselves through active participation. For example, students provided with various classes of objects to roll down ramps can discover and state principles of friction and velocity.

Teaching and Learning through Social Interaction

Students' cognitive development and learning are facilitated and enhanced through their interactions with others. When students work collaboratively with more competent peers, teachers, and adults, they learn more than when they work on their own. Cooperative learning and scaffolding are ways to facilitate students' social interaction as a basis for promoting student learning.

Cooperative Learning. In cooperative learning, as noted in Chapter 1, students work together in small mixed-ability groups, sharing responsibility for their learning. Students are responsible for their own learning, for helping other group members, and for overall group success. There are now many different kinds of cooperative learning programs that have been formally developed and researched, such as Teams-Games-Tournaments (TGT), Jigsaw II, Learning Together, and Student Team Learning (STL).[18]

Nondirect instruction
Any form of instruction that is not transmitted directly to the students by the teacher.

Discovery learning
Learning that occurs from students' efforts to discover knowledge for themselves rather than from being taught directly by a teacher.

INTASC

Standard 1: The teacher understands the central concepts, tools of inquiry, and structures of the subjects being taught and can create learning experiences that make these aspects of subject matter meaningful for students.

Standard 2: The teacher understands how children learn and develop, and can provide learning opportunities that support their intellectual, social and personal development.

Standard 5: The teacher uses an understanding of individual and group motivation and behavior to create a learning environment that encourages positive social interaction, active engagement in learning, and self-motivation.

In a cooperative learning group, students are assigned certain roles and tasks. For example, in one program a group leader announces the learning task or problem, a praiser praises group members for their answers and work, and a checker assesses results. Group responsibilities and membership rotate as the group engages in different tasks. Students are also encouraged to develop and use interpersonal skills, such as addressing classmates by their first names, saying, "Thank you," and explaining to their group-mates why they are proposing an answer. Listening and communication skills are also enhanced. (See the Profile below.)

Research suggests that five basic elements are needed for cooperative learning to be successful:

- Positive independence. Students have to believe that they are in the learning process together and that they care about each other's learning.
- Verbal, face-to-face interaction. Students have to explain, argue, elaborate, and connect what they are learning now to what they learned previously.
- Individual accountability. All members of the group have to realize that they are responsible for their own learning.
- Social skills. Students must learn appropriate leadership, communication, trust-building, and conflict-resolution skills.
- Group processing. Group members have to assess how well they are working together and how they can do better.[19]

Research on cooperative learning is overwhelmingly positive, and cooperative approaches are appropriate for all curriculum areas.[20] Cooperative learning activities enable students to learn how to cooperate rather than compete and how to respect and learn from one another. Students also gain opportunities to learn the cooperative skills they will need later in life in the family and in the workplace. Also, cooperative learning groups are low-risk contexts in which lower-ability students can improve their skills. During cooperative learning, teachers can provide one-on-one instruction. As a teaching method, cooperative learning may not be appropriate for all learning tasks or all students. Cooperative learning activities usually require large blocks of time and must be carefully planned and evaluated to work well.

Scaffolding. **Scaffolding** is another approach for facilitating learning through social interaction. It is based on the learning theory of Lev Vygotsky. (See the Profile on p. 424.) There are several ways of scaffolding students' learning. You can choose activities that interest students and prepare students for activities before presenting them. You can actively monitor activities in progress by providing immediate guidance and

Scaffolding
The teacher builds a structured learning environment that supports modeling and learning.

Profile **The Classroom "Familia": Rosa E. Lujan**

Texas Teacher of the Year Rosa E. Lujan participated in a long-term national research project on the effectiveness of cooperative learning with fifth- and sixth-grade Hispanic American students at Ysleta Elementary School in El Paso, Texas. The cooperative learning program used was Cooperative Integrated Reading and Composition (CIRC). The study showed that CIRC is an effective method for bilingual and second-language instruction as well as for monolingual instruction.

In CIRC, cooperative learning is used to follow up reading group instruction. Students work in teams containing two pairs of students from two different reading-level groups. The students take turns reading stories to one another; answer questions about the characters, setting, and plot of each story; practice new vocabulary together; help each other with read-

ing comprehension skills and spelling; and write about the stories they have read. While the students are working in teams, the teacher provides one-on-one instruction and feedback as needed.

Rosa Lujan found many benefits of cooperative learning, including more effective use of her instructional time and of students' time on task. She adds:

The greatest result, though, has been the increased self-esteem and achievement of my students. Even the most reluctant learner becomes actively involved in learning. Students know they are important, a part of the classroom familia. Academically, they are now reading and writing in two languages.

Teaching in the Zone: Lev Vygotsky

Lev Vygotsky (1896–1934), born the same year as Piaget, increasingly inspires the practice of educators. Vygotsky, a Russian psychologist, developed a theory of learning that is particularly useful in describing children's cognitive, language, and social development.

Vygotsky believed that children's mental, language, and social development is enhanced by learning that occurs through social interactions. "Learning awakens a variety of developmental processes that are able to operate only when the child is interacting with people in his environment and in collaboration with his peers. Once these processes are internalized, they become part of the child's independent developmental achievement." This is a "contextual" view of cognitive development in which learners are embedded in social contexts such as family, home, friends, and school.

Vygotsky developed the concept of the **zone of proximal development,** which he defined as "that area of development into which a child can be led in the course of interaction with a more competent partner, either adult or peer. The zone of proximal development . . . is not some clear-cut space that exists independently of the process of joint activity itself. Rather, it is the difference between what the child can accomplish independently and what he or she can achieve in conjunction with

another, more competent person. The zone is thus created in the course of social interaction." The more skilled adult builds on the competencies the child already has and presents him or her with activities that support a level of competence slightly beyond where the child is now.

In guiding children's classroom learning within the zone of proximal development, the metaphor of scaffolding comes into play. The teacher builds a structured learning environment through communication and provides opportunities for interaction that support modeling and learning. These supports act as scaffolds on which the learner reaches new heights in intellectual development.

Vygotsky believed that as a result of teacher-learner collaboration, the learner uses concepts acquired in the collaborative process to solve problems independently of the teacher.

Social interaction and collaboration are part of many current instructional practices, such as cooperative learning, joint problem solving, coaching, mentoring, peer-mediated learning, and other forms of assisted learning. According to Vygotsky, "Learning is a necessary part and universal aspect of the process of developing culturally organized, specifically human, psychological functions."[22]

Zone of proximal development
The area of development a child can achieve through social interaction with another, more competent person.

Middle Level

Standard 1: Understands the major concepts, principles, theories and research related to young adolescent development; provides opportunities that support student development and learning.

Standard 3: Understands and incorporates young adolescent development in the school context.

Differentiated instruction (DI)
Providing different learning opportunities for differing student needs.

feedback. And you can follow up activities with opportunities for review and reflection. Providing information as needed, suggesting where students can find information and resources, and giving hints and clues to help students think through their ideas are also good methods for scaffolding. For older students, lecture outlines and study guides can serve as scaffolds for their learning. Pairing more competent learners with less competent learners, as in cooperative learning, is an application of Vygotsky's theory of scaffolded learning in social context.

In cross-age tutoring, for example, older students tutor younger students in their zone of proximal development. In elementary grades, fifth- and sixth-grade students might tutor kindergartners, first-graders, and second-graders. Studies show that cross-age tutoring improves the attitudes and academic achievement of both the tutor and the tutee.[21]

Individual Differences—Differentiated Instruction

You know from your own classroom experiences that all students are different. Think, for a moment, about the students that were with you in first grade, eighth grade, and twelfth grade, and the differences they demonstrated. All students are different, have particular learning needs, and learn differently. It makes sense to meet the different learning needs of students. But, as with many things, some things are easier said than done. How do you provide for the individual learning needs of students? One approach is through **differentiated instruction (DI)**, a process of providing different learning experiences to meet students' learning needs. There are a number of approaches to differentiating instruction:

- Differentiate the content. Ways to vary the content are to let students work at their own rates and have students who know the content go directly to application activities.

- Differentiate the process/activities. This is a process of varying learning activities.
- Differentiate the product. The product that students create to demonstrate mastery of the concepts can be varied according to student interest and choice.
- Differentiate the environment and accommodate individual learning styles. One way to differentiate is according to different students' learning styles.

In effective differentiated classrooms

- Teachers and students accept and respect one another's similarities and differences.
- Assessment is an ongoing diagnostic activity that guides instruction. Learning tasks are planned and adjusted based on assessment data.
- All students participate in respectful work that is challenging, meaningful, interesting, and engaging.
- The teacher is primarily a coordinator of time, space, and activities, rather than a provider of information. The aim is to help students become self-reliant workers.
- Students and teachers collaborate in setting class and individual goals.
- Students work in a variety of group configurations, as well as independently. Flexible grouping is evident.
- Time is used flexibly in the sense that pacing is varied based on student needs.
- Students often have choices about topics they wish to study, ways they want to work, and how they want to demonstrate their learning.
- The teacher uses a variety of instructional strategies to help target instruction to student needs.
- Students are assessed in multiple ways, and each student's progress is measured, at least in part, from where that student begins.[23]

Data–Driven Instruction

Standardized tests and other forms of assessment provide a great deal of data regarding student achievement and how students learn. One of the administrative and teaching challenges is how to capture and effectively use these data to focus teaching and increase student achievement. Data-driven instruction refers to the practice of using student outcomes on various measures to plan curriculum and instruction. Teachers can use data to plan diverse instructional strategies in response to the differences in how students think and learn. Data-driven instruction is being used to reform how teachers plan, teach, and assess. As a beginning teacher, it is highly likely that you will be involved in processes related to using student data to tailor-make plans and instructional activities designed to ensure that all children learn and meet state and national standards. For an interesting look at how Leadmine Elementary School in Raleigh, North Carolina, implemented a program of data-driven instruction, go to www.infotoday.com/MMSchools/mar03/decker.shtml.

Reflect & Write

Which models of direct and nondirect instruction appeal to you the most at this time? What are your reasons?

_____

_____

_____

_____

SECTION SUMMARY

What Are Some Models of Nondirect Instruction?

Nondirect instruction is any form of instruction that is not transmitted directly to students by the teacher. This type of instruction is used to develop higher-level thinking and problem-solving skills and to differentiate instruction.

- Discovery Learning. Bruner's discovery learning is based on Piaget's and Vygotsky's principles of instruction and encourages active experimentation and learning.

- Teaching and Learning through Social Interaction. Practices include cooperative learning and scaffolding. Students in cooperative learning situations are responsible for their own learning, for helping other group members, and for overall group success. Scaffolding is a metaphor referring to a learning environment that provides opportunities for social interactions that support learning.

- Individual Differences—Differentiated Instruction. Providing different learning activities for students enables teachers to meet individual learning needs. DI is widely used as an effective instructional strategy.

- Data-Driven Instruction. Data-driven instruction refers to the practice of using student outcomes on various measures to plan curriculum and instruction. Teachers can use data to plan diverse instructional strategies in response to the differences in how students think and learn.

Thinking Critically
★ ★ ★ ★ ★ ★ ★ ★

Today's workplace often relies on teamwork. How will classroom experiences with cooperative learning help prepare students for working in teams? Will that training stifle individuality and creativity?

Applying What You've Learned
★ ★ ★ ★ ★ ★ ★ ★

Interview teachers about the teaching methods and materials they prefer to use. How did they decide which instructional methods and curriculum materials to emphasize?

Putting Yourself in the Picture
★ ★ ★ ★ ★ ★ ★ ★

Refer to the section on differentiated instruction. Explain how and why you would or would not enjoy utilizing this strategy. Which of the differentiated instructional approaches would you use in your classroom? Why?

CURRICULUM INFLUENCES FOR THE TWENTY-FIRST CENTURY

As a result of reading this chapter and other chapters in this book, you are aware that educational reform has created and will continue to create many changes, innovations, and new approaches regarding how teachers teach and students learn. As a beginning teacher, you will stand in the eye of the hurricane of educational reform. Without a doubt, politicians, educators, and society are radically reforming and changing education. The majority of these reforms and changes will find their permanent place in schoolhouse practice. Some of these reforms and their influences that will continue into the future are:

- The rapid pace of radical school reform is here to stay. The first decade of the twenty-first century will be known as the decade of reform. Indeed, more educational change has occurred in the past ten years than in the previous fifty. Teachers' roles are rapidly changing and will continue to change. For example, teachers of the recent past were able to say "I taught Mario reading." Teachers of today and tomorrow will say "I taught Mario to read, he met district and state standards, and achieved at a high level."
- The three Rs of reading, writing, and mathematics are the crown jewels in the curriculum crown. They will continue to be the major benefactors of instructional time, funding, and testing for grades pre-K through 12.
- Standardized testing at the district, state, and national levels is here to stay. Tests will be used to assess student achievement, hold teachers and schools accountable, and drive instructional planning and decision making.
- Accountability is and will be a way of life for teachers and school districts. Accountability for all facets of the educational process will be a hallmark of education in the years to come.
- The accountability movement has created competition among schools. This competition for students, for performance-based dollars, and for recognition will continue. More "market-driven" approaches—such as outsourcing of services, privatizing of schools, and choice—will be applied to schoolhouse practices.

All of these reforms are designed to make education for all children a better and more meaningful experience. You should not be fearful or apprehensive about participating in any of these activities, as they will enhance your life as a professional and add value to your future as a teacher.

WHAT WORKS IN THE CLASSROOM?

Teachers work hard and spend a lot of time and effort developing plans, activities, and instructional resources to continue instruction in reading and writing effectively in the middle and secondary grades. They bring different styles and approaches to the classroom.

But, as you know from your school experiences, some teachers do a better job than others. Why is this? Judith Langer at the National Research Center on English Learning and Achievement studied a range of middle and high school English classrooms, and came up with an answer. In fact, she came up with six answers—six features that occur in effective middle and secondary English teaching. These features seem applicable to most classrooms.

1. Students learn skills and knowledge in multiple lesson types. Teachers use a variety of different teaching approaches based on student need. For example, if students need to learn a particular skill, item, or rule, the teacher might choose a *separated* activity to highlight it. Students would study the information as an independent

NCATE

Early Childhood

Standard 4: Integrates understanding of children and families, of developmentally effective approaches to teaching and learning, and of academic disciplines to design, implement, and evaluate positive learning experiences for all children.

Elementary

Standard 3.1: Plans and implements instruction based on knowledge of students, learning theory, subject matter, curricular goals, and community.

lesson, exercise, or drill without considering its larger meaning or use (e.g., they might be asked to copy definitions of literary terms into their notebooks and to memorize them). To give students practice, teachers prepare or find *simulated* activities that ask students to apply concepts and rules within a targeted unit of reading, writing, or oral language. To help students bring together their skills and knowledge within the context of a purposeful activity, teachers use *integrated* activities. These require students to use their skills or knowledge to complete a task or project that has meaning for them. Teachers of higher-performing students use all three of these approaches. See the Profile of Gail Slatko for an example of bringing all three approaches together.

NCATE

Middle Level

Standard 5: Understands and uses major concepts, principles, theories, and research related to effective instruction and assessment; employs a variety of strategies for a developmentally appropriate climate to meet the varying abilities and learning styles of all young adolescents.

2. **Teachers integrate test preparation into instruction.** In higher-performing schools, the knowledge and skills for performing well on high-stakes tests are made overt to both teachers and students. Teachers, principals and district-level coordinators often create working groups of professionals who collaboratively study the demands of the high-stakes tests their students will take. This reflection helps teachers understand the demands of the test, consider how these demands relate to their current practice, and plan ways to integrate the necessary skills and knowledge into the curriculum, across grades and school years. In addition, students learn to become reflective about their own reading and writing performance. Teachers provide students with ways to read, understand, and write in order to gain the abilities that are necessary for being highly literate for life, not merely for passing a test.

3. **Teachers make connections across instruction, curriculum, and life.** Teachers work consciously to weave a web of connections within lessons, across lessons, and to students' lives in and out of school. They make connections throughout each day, week, and year. And they point out these connections so that students can see how the skills and knowledge they are gaining can be used productively in a range of situations. Teachers also work together to redevelop and redesign curriculum. They share ideas and reflect on their work.

4. **Students learn strategies for doing the work.** It is important for students to learn not only subject matter content, but also how to think about, approach, and do their work in each subject. In higher-performing schools, teachers divide new or difficult tasks into segments and provide their students with guides for accomplishing the task. They provide strategies not only for how to do the task but also how to think about it. These strategies are discussed and modeled, and teachers develop reminder sheets for students to use. In this way, students learn the process for completing an assignment successfully.

Profile   **Using Multiple Lesson Types: Gail Slatko**

Gail Slatko teaches English at Reuben Dario Middle School in Florida.

Gail Slatko uses three approaches—separated, simulated, and integrated activities—to empower her students to be better readers, writers, and editors. For example, she often teaches vocabulary skills within the context of literature and writing, but she also asks students to complete practice workbook exercises designed to increase their vocabularies. And they create "living dictionaries" by collecting new words as they come across them in books, magazines, and newspapers. To provide practice with analogies, Gail goes beyond merely providing

examples: she requires that students discuss their responses and explain the rationales for their answers. Later, students design vocabulary mobiles that she displays in the classroom. Gail uses the same approach when she targets literary concepts, conventions, and language. Students integrate literary vocabulary, alliteration, and story telling through words and pictures. During one recent school year, five books were entered in the county fair competition, and one of them was awarded first prize. Gail's lessons are models for her students to use in their own reading and writing as well as when they are editing and responding to the writing of their classmates.

5. **Students are expected to be generative thinkers.** All of the teachers in the higher-performing schools take a generative approach to student learning. They go beyond students' acquisition of skills or knowledge to engage students in creative and critical uses of their knowledge and skills. Teachers provide a variety of activities from which students will generate deeper understandings. For example, when studying literature, after the more obvious themes in a text are discussed, teachers and students together explore the text from many points of view, both from within the literary work and from life.

6. **Classrooms foster cognitive collaboration.** In higher-performing schools, students work in communicative groups, and teachers help students participate in thoughtful dialogue. Students engage in the kind of teamwork that is now so highly prized in business and industry. They bring their personal, cultural, and academic knowledge to these interactions, in which they play the multiple roles of learners, teachers, and inquirers and have opportunities to consider issues from multiple perspectives. Minds bump against minds as students interact as both problem generators and problem solvers.

Reflect & Write

As you can see, high-quality teaching involves many new skills along with the skills you have already learned. Langer's six features are not necessarily applicable only to teaching English. What can you do now to prepare yourself to incorporate Langer's six features of effective teaching?

_____

_____

_____

_____

Applications for Active Learning

CONNECTIONS

1. Review Dru Tomlin's vignette about coaching. Consider how you could apply Dru's approaches using the curriculum content of this chapter.

_____

_____

_____

2. Select one curricular emphasis and/or one teaching model described in this chapter and say how it will make a difference in how you teach.

_____

_____

_____

FIELD EXPERIENCES

1. Observe some classrooms and identify uses of the instructional concepts described in this chapter. Record examples of teaching practices you think best represent each instructional model you identify.

2. Ask teachers about their experiences with cooperative learning. What do they see as the benefits and drawbacks of this model?

PERSONAL RESEARCH

1. Find out about the curriculum in your state or district for the grade level or content area you plan to teach. What instructional goals are expressed in this curriculum? To what extent and in what ways is the curriculum integrated or interdisciplinary? How will you prepare to implement this curriculum? Are there parts of it that you might wish to augment, eliminate, or change? If so, how could you begin to go about doing so?

2. Add to your clipping file articles on curriculum controversies and curriculum reform initiatives in your state or in your content area. What spheres of influence have an impact on the curriculum? What concerns do public protests and reform efforts represent regarding the curriculum?

FOR YOUR PORTFOLIO

1. Add to your portfolio artifacts from your personal research, such as curriculum guidelines and textbook selection criteria.

2. Revise your position statement on your teaching philosophy to reflect information you've gained through reading this book. Keep both versions in your portfolio as a record of your development as a beginning teacher.

IDEA FILE

Brainstorm ideas for authentic assessments you might use that are appropriate for a content area you might teach as well as developmentally appropriate for your future students.

Learning and Knowing More

WEB SITES WORTH VISITING

Accountability is one of the major themes of schooling of the new millenium. Schools are making greater efforts to be accountable to the public for what they teach and the achievement of their students. How well schools do is a matter of public record. For example, many community newspapers make local school district report cards and analysis of student achievement results available on the World Wide Web. Access the following three newspaper Web sites:

www.latimes.com/news/education
www.phillynews.com/mld/philly/living/education
http://seattletimes.nwsource.com/html/education

Compare how the three school districts involved report to the community. Which of the three do you like the best and why?

About the National Science Teachers Association
www.nsta.org
The National Science Teachers Association is the largest organization in the world committed to promoting excellence and innovation in science teaching and learning for all.

Teaching K–8 IdeaSite
www.Teachingk-8.com
Teaching K–8 is a monthly professional magazine for kindergarten through eighth-grade teachers. This IdeaSite highlights articles in the current issue and provides new ideas and resources spanning the curriculum.

Teacher Connections Home Page
www.nytimes.com/learning/teachers/index.html
Contains the latest news featured in the *New York Times* as part of the *New York Times* Learning Network.

"What Works Clearinghouse" Office of Educational Research and Improvement, U.S. Department of Education.
www.w-w-c.org
The What Works Clearinghouse was established by the U.S. Department of Education's Institute of Education Sciences to provide educators, policymakers, and the public with a central, independent, and trusted source of scientific evidence of what works in education.

ERIC Clearinghouse Digest
http://eric.uoregon.edu/publications/digests/digest167.html
This digest describes the generally accepted characteristics of scientifically based research and anticipated implications for school leaders.

Curriculum Archive
www.buildingrainbows.com/CA/ca.home.php
The Curriculum Archive is a central repository for free lessons and classroom projects. It is intended to be a forum for creating, distributing, and archiving education curricula for all grade levels and subject areas.

PBS Teacher Source
www.pbs.org/teachersource
This source aids teachers in using PBS resources to teach lessons and activities to their students.

BOOKS WORTH READING

Ciaccio, J. (2004). *Totally Positive Teaching: A Five-Stage Approach to Energizing Students and Teachers*. Baltimore: Association for Curriculum Development.
The author of this text presents a five-part approach to positive teaching in school situations where resources are limited and students aren't always ready and eager to learn. There are several tips and sample lessons that will help you build trusting partnerships with students and create positive learning experiences.

Dougherty, E. (2001). *Shifting Gears: Standards, Assessments, Curriculum, and Instruction*. Golden, CO: Fulcrum Publishing.
Designed to help educators make the necessary changes in the curriculum. As a companion to *Front-End Alignment* (Education Trust) and *Learning in Overdrive* (Fulcrum Publishing), *Shifting Gears* aims to connect the operative parts of standards-based education—standards, assessments, curriculum, and instruction—in order to ensure the success of students and schools.

Drake, S., and Burns, R. (2004). *Meeting Standards through Integrated Curriculum*. Alexandria, VA: ASCD Books.
This is an important learning resource for teachers wanting to know how to further use a standards-based integrated curriculum. You can learn how to identify

the connections in your standards that provide the basis for interdisciplinary units and understand how to create interdisciplinary units that provide data-based evidence of student learning.

Herrell, A., and Jordan, M. (2003). *Fifty Strategies for Teaching English Language Learners* (2nd ed.). Baltimore: Association for Curriculum Development.

In this book, you can explore fifty research-based, classroom-tested strategies that English-speaking teachers can use to help English language learners understand content materials while they acquire English language skills.

Morrison, G. R. (2000). *Designing Effective Instruction* (3rd ed.). New York: John Wiley.

This practical approach to the instructional design process features applications to a variety of settings and situations. The models presented are applicable to both K–12 classrooms and higher education. The author incorporates both behavioral and cognitive approaches.

Ornstein, A. C., and Behar-Horenstein, L. S. (1999). *Contemporary Issues in Curriculum* (2nd ed.). Boston: Allyn & Bacon.

This edition offers forty articles by the major thinkers in curriculum study. Balanced yet eclectic in its approach, it reflects the emergent trends in the field of curriculum.

Taylor, R., and Doyle-Collins, V. (2003). *Literacy Leadership for Grades 5–12*. Alexandria, VA: ASCD Books.

This book provides the leadership strategies and practices you need to rise to the challenge of ensuring that elementary students achieve the reading skills they need to succeed in middle and high school while standards call for maximizing students' literacy achievement.

Tomlinson, C. A. (2001). *How to Differentiate Instruction in Mixed-Ability Classrooms* (2nd ed.). Alexandria, VA: ASCD Books.

This is a valuable resource for how to succeed in today's increasingly diverse classrooms using differentiated instruction. The author presents proven ideas for how to match instructional approaches to the readiness, interests, and talents of all students.

Tomlinson, C. A., and Cunningham-Eidson, C. (2003). *Differentiation in Practice: A Resource Guide for Differentiating Curriculum, Grades 5–9*. Alexandria, VA: ASCD Books.

This book illustrates the five differentiated units of study focused on the core subjects in the middle grades. Each unit includes annotated lesson plans, worksheets, assignments, rubrics, and other tools to allow you to design your own differentiated curriculum.

Wiles, J. W. (1999). *Curriculum Essentials: A Resource for Educators*. Boston: Allyn & Bacon.

This text covers the most important basic ideas for understanding the area of curriculum. It contains compilations of important dates and events, definitions of curriculum, names to know in curriculum study, and an introduction to the philosophies and theories influencing curriculum development.

Zmuda, A., Kuklis, R., and Kline, E. (2004). *Transforming Schools: Creating a Culture of Continuous Improvement*. Baltimore: Association for Curriculum Development.

This book shows you how to ensure that plans of school improvement will lead to continuous improvement that gets all staff members involved. Using a fictional school setting with representative characters, the authors reveal essential principles of continuous improvement, systems thinking, collective accountability, and the change process.

CHAPTER 12

Technology, Teaching, and Learning

"Technology should always enhance sound teaching."

Kim DiBaise teaches social studies at Herndon High School in Herndon, Virginia.

Teachers at Herndon High School provide an excellent model for incorporating technology into a standards-based classroom. In Virginia, the core curriculum is based on the Virginia Standards of Learning, and many of these classes have an end-of-course test. Students in social studies must pass three end-of-course tests (World History and Geography I, World History and Geography II, and Virginia/United States History) in order to graduate. Despite the intense focus on covering the material, the teachers here are extremely successful in making the curriculum meaningful for their students. Technology is a big part of this success.

Each classroom in our school is equipped with a teacher workstation connected to a 36-inch monitor. Having this kind of technology available in every classroom makes it easy to incorporate presentation programs—for example, we can use the wealth of digital images that have been made available for use in social studies teaching by the Library of Congress, the National Archives, and other government and educational institutions. I use the images in PowerPoint presentations as springboards for discussion and to enhance lectures. It is a more convenient and less expensive method than making transparencies from the same images. At the end of the year, I use the same images in review games and quizzes. I've had many positive student responses about using this kind of technology support.

We are fortunate in that Herndon is also equipped with two computer labs for student use. Many of my colleagues and I use the Internet to help our students master the standards of learning. For example, in U.S. History, my students complete an Internet scavenger hunt to answer questions about the Civil War. The assignment is challenging and gives them the opportunity to read battlefield stories from a variety of sources, to read and interpret primary sources, to see original maps, and to view some of the first photographs of warfare. All of this has a deeper meaning for the students than the same information would have if it came in a lecture from me. My students do a similar assignment for World War I. It would be difficult for me to reproduce the amount of material that my students are exposed to by using the Internet.

Students at Herndon High School also have many opportunities to produce assignments themselves using technology. My colleagues and I have come up with a variety of projects that engage students actively in the learning process. Assignments and projects that use technology often hit on many different modes of learning; they provide multiple ways for students to process information and process knowledge. For example, students create their own presentations using PowerPoint, and they create newspapers using word-processing or publication programs—and often they are asked to do this collaboratively. In my classes, students have seen my presentations throughout the year so they are eager to know "How did you do that?" In other classes, my colleagues have had students with a great deal of experience in using presentation software teach their classmates (and the teacher) the process. I find collaborative projects an exciting part of teaching. The best ones have clearly defined problems to be solved and/or goals to be achieved.

I think that the most important thing to keep in mind when incorporating technology into the classroom is that technology should always enhance sound teaching techniques—never be asked to replace them. In my school, technology has become one more way to help students master the standards of learning.

INTASC

Standard 6: The teacher uses knowledge of effective verbal, nonverbal, and media communication techniques to foster active inquiry, collaboration, and supportive interaction in the classroom.

How Will This Chapter Help You?

You will learn

★ about technology and its applications to teaching and learning

★ about technology literacy and information literacy

★ about technology standards

★ how technology contributes to community and worldwide education

★ how technology supports parent involvement in education

★ about issues associated with technology and its use

★ how to integrate technology into the curriculum and your teaching

The New York Times
expect the world®
nytimes.com

Themes of the Times

Expand your knowledge of the concepts discussed in this chapter by reading current and historical articles from *The New York Times* by visiting the "Themes of the Times" section of the companion Web site.

*W*HAT IS TECHNOLOGY?

Technology is the application of scientific, mechanical, material, and human resources to address human needs. Using this definition, technology goes beyond computers and video games.

Every area of society is affected and influenced by technology. Computers and computer-based technology are widely used in business and industry, the government, and the military. Many consumer goods, from automobiles to crayons, depend on computers. Computer use in the home has grown in popularity during the last decade. A host of computer manufacturers have introduced computers targeted for the home market. Manufacturers design software to entertain and educate adults and students at home. Publishers of educational software for school use now design many of their newest titles with families in mind as well. The Internet is only a little over thirty-five years old, personal computers about thirty years old, and the World Wide Web is fifteen years old. Computers and other forms of technology have come a long way in the last half a century, and if the past is any prediction of the future, the technological changes to come will be even more rapid, widespread, and influential in changing how schools operate, teachers teach, and students learn.

The use of computers and other technology is widespread in schools today. Nearly three-quarters (74 percent) of students in grades 7 through 12 use school computers to do research for assignments.[1] But there is more to learn about technology than merely using it to get class assignment information off the Internet. This is where you enter the picture. Perhaps you are wondering what your role will be as a teacher in the technological future and how you will use technology to help you and your students learn. One thing is certain: technology is playing a major role in how students learn and what they learn.

Today's teacher must be technologically literate and capable of integrating technology into the teaching-learning process. (See the Profile.) Thousands of teachers use desktop and laptop computers with built-in modems, faxes, and CD-ROM drives as well as camcorders, optical scanners, laser printers, and digital cameras. They also use software for e-mail, word processing, desktop publishing, presentation graphics, spreadsheets, data bases, and multimedia applications. Are you prepared to use technology to enhance your teaching and your students' learning? Assess your technology skills using Figure 12.1.

*W*HAT IS TECHNOLOGICAL LITERACY?

We cannot speak or think about technology as though it is separate from what goes on in the everyday world. Many students are very knowledgeable about technology and its use, while others are less so. (See Education on the Move.)

As a society, we increasingly feel that **technological literacy**—the ability to understand and apply technology to meet personal goals—is as important as the traditional components of literacy—reading, writing, speaking, and listening. With today's technology it is possible for students and teachers to access and have available a great deal of information. How to use this information is also part of being technologically literate. Figure 12.2 outlines six ideas for what is necessary for you and your students to gain information literacy.

Advocates of technological literacy maintain that students need (1) to be able to read and write online as well as with books and paper and pencil, (2) to be able to speak on the phone and with voice mail, (3) to be able to participate in video conferencing as well as in face-to-face conversations, and (4) to develop skills in presenting their own knowledge and products with multimedia.

Profile   Using Robots to Inspire Young Minds: James Distler

James Distler is an engineering teacher at Montgomery Blair High School in Maryland.

James Distler believes students need options—options for how to spend their time and educational options to hook kids into learning. "You'll either get them into the positive stuff, or they'll get into the negative," he explained. To help open doors for students in Montgomery County, Distler started a program that teaches children about engineering by designing robots built out of Legos.

Distler brought the program to South Lake Elementary School in Montgomery Village and Monocacy Elementary School in Poolesville as summer programs this year. He said he hopes to have five or six elementary schools participate next summer.

Eighteen rising third-graders through rising sixth-graders are part of the South Lake enrichment program.

The program uses Lego Mindstorm robotics kits, which cost about $200 each. The cost for the two-week program is $210, which helps pay the student and adult supervisors and buys some equipment and snacks, Distler said. The robots are self-contained battery-operated computers that can be programmed to do a variety of tasks, such as going up ramps, climbing walls, and catching and throwing balls. Once the task is chosen, a nearby corresponding desktop computer sends out directions from a remote-controllike transmitter.

Students at South Lake were programming their trucklike robots to follow a path outlined on a table with masking tape. The robots used lasers to determine where the line was and then follow it.

Nivetita Ravi, a rising fourth-grader at South Lake, said the program has taught her about gears, programming, and building and has helped teach her new vocabulary words. Janhvi Barthwal, a rising sixth-grader, said she decided to participate because she was interested in robots and how they work. She said she enjoys programming them to do what she tells them.

Despite the fact that all of the children in the program at South Lake are gifted and talented students, Distler emphasized that the program is open to everyone. The engineering program is about much more than just how to build and program robots. Distler said he makes a point of talking to the kids about school and how to treat others with respect.

The program is an offshoot of Distler's Career Exploration and Mentoring Program, which he started ten years ago when he was a teacher at Takoma Park Middle School. There, Distler helped get the school's technology program off the ground and began teaching industrial arts to students after school. The group learned how to use tools and build birdhouses, among other skills; the program grew from five or six students to 180.

Distler left Takoma Park Middle School to begin teaching at Blair in 2000, and it was then he decided to train high school students in both robotics and mentoring skills and let them teach younger students. This way, Distler said, younger children will get an enrichment option and older kids can earn a little money.

"I want to spread the joy—I want to spread the enthusiasm," Distler said.[7]

Standard 1—Technology Operations and Concepts
Teachers demonstrate a sound understanding of technology operations and concepts.

Standard 2—Planning and Designing Learning Environments and Experiences
Teachers plan and design effective learning environments and experiences supported by technology.

Standard 3—Teaching, Learning, and the Curriculum
Teachers implement curriculum plans that include methods and strategies for applying technology to maximize student learning.

Standard 4—Assessment and Evaluation
Teachers apply technology to facilitate a variety of effective assessment and evaluation strategies.

Standard 5—Productivity and Professional Practice
Teachers use technology to enhance their productivity and professional practice.

Standard 6—Social, Ethical, Legal, and Human Issues
Teachers understand the social, ethical, legal, and human issues surrounding the use of technology in pre-K–12 schools and apply that understanding in practice.

Compare your skills with those listed in this figure. How do you stack up? What technology skills will you have to work on to be prepared to integrate technology in your classroom?

Figure 12.1   Technology Standards for Teachers

Source: International Society for Technology in Education, *National Education Technology Standards for Teachers—Preparing Teachers to Use Technology* (Washington, D.C.: International Society for Technology in Education, 2002). Reprinted by permission.

>>> Technology Can Make the Difference >>>>>>>

Students in Tim Comolli's electronic arts class at South Burlington High School have won awards for their 3-D graphics designs. They've sold computer-generated logos to businesses in their South Burlington, Vermont, community, and they've taught teachers how to use Internet search engines and sophisticated multimedia software.

Yet many of the students who are drawn to Comolli's class are teenagers who are struggling in most of their other classes. Once they see what they can do with technology, they begin to appreciate the importance of doing well not only in his class, but in their other subjects as well, Comolli said. "We've found that technology becomes the great equalizer [for struggling students]," said the

English teacher, who began offering the course three years ago. "Kids who are having trouble in school have as good a success rate in my class as the advanced students, even more so."

In some of Chicago's toughest neighborhoods, professional artists are showing urban youngsters how to use technology to express themselves through video and Web art. In Massachusetts, a special digital divide project is harnessing the powers of the World Wide Web to help teachers find lessons linked to state academic standards. Meanwhile, in Charlotte, North Carolina, community activists are providing public school students with special computer training after school.

In a remote area of New Mexico, Central Consolidated Schools is struggling to get a workable connection

to the Internet for all its schools. The 7,500-student district, with seventeen schools, straddles a Navajo reservation. The district's five schools that are not on the American Indian reservation, plus one that is, have a fast and robust connection to the Internet. But eleven of the schools on the reservation have a lousy connection, so slow that it can take half an hour to download a few e-mail messages.

"Not only is there a digital divide, but we live on it," says Rick Nussbaum, the director of technology support services for the district.

Source: Education Week, 2001, 20(35): "Technology Counts 2001: The New Divides"; K. K. Manzo, "Academic Record, p. 22; A. Trotter, "Projects Offer Access, Training," p. 39; M. A. Zehr, "Rural Connections," p. 24. Reprinted by permission.

Reflect & Write

How do you measure up to the standards for technological literacy? Could you stay ahead of your students in this area? If your answer is no, what could you do to improve?

_____

_____

_____

_____

Changing Concepts of Literacy

NCATE

Elementary

Standard 2.1: Demonstrates a high level of competence in use of English langauge arts; understands and uses concepts from reading, language, and child development to teach reading, writing, speaking, viewing, and thinking skills.

Technology is changing society and in the process has changed the goals of education, what it means to be educated, and the meaning of literacy. Literacy now has added dimensions. Students not only have to read, write, listen, and speak, they also have to learn to use technology to be truly literate. Students need keyboarding skills—that is, how to type—to be literate. Literacy is considered to be the foundation of American democracy and fundamental to making decisions related to democracy such as being an informed voter and participating in community interchange. The following are some of the many dimensions of technological literacy:

- Knowing navigational strategies. These strategies are necessary for accessing and finding information.
- Staying literate. In the technological context, being literate is not a one-time thing, nor is it static. The challenge for today's students and teachers is to constantly keep up with technological changes in order to stay literate.
- Developing critical thinking and analytical skills. The abilities to sort fact from error, truth from fiction, and clarity from distortion are necessary to assess and evaluate the information that almost anyone can publish on the Internet. Remember: Just because information is online doesn't mean it is valid or true. Figure 12.3 presents some critical thinking guidelines for using the Internet and other sources.

1. *Collaboration should be part of the learning process.* Teaching interdependence is natural in the process of information literacy. Students as well as teachers must learn how to use technology as a tool for communication, creation, and collaboration. Learning as a team and how to work in partnerships are key.

2. *The teacher's role as guide is essential.* Teachers must take on the roles of motivator, mentor, and colearner if they want to produce information-literate students. Acting as a mentor is critical.

3. *Ethics play a role in the development of information literacy.* Students must understand the ethical issues raised by the use and misuse of the Internet. In addition to plagiarism, slander, and pornography, ethical issues include unlicensed copying of software (theft); flaming via e-mail (poor netiquette); hacking into school records (unlawful entry); and creating viruses that corrupt files (destruction of property).

4. *Technology must become part of the curriculum.* Students must develop an understanding of how technology influences our lives. Much of the material included in courses on communication, transportation, or production (tech ed) can be useful to students in a college prep curriculum that has little or no reference to technology. Unfortunately, many schools see tech ed and tech prep as a separate curriculum to be kept strictly apart from the college prep curriculum.

5. *Students must learn communication skills, including presentation and motivation skills.* They should be able to communicate with technological media—text, graphics, video, and sound. They must learn how to arrange information and motivate learners with more than the written and spoken word. Understanding the motivation of providing and receiving information will be one of the great challenges of information literacy.

6. *Visual literacy is essential.* This includes knowing how to create, organize, and display print, video, audio, and graphics. Learning how to use color, style, placement, and font size are important. Once they understand specific content, students must learn to articulate their knowledge both visually and verbally.

Elementary

Standard 3.5: Uses knowledge and understanding of effective verbal, nonverbal, and media communication techniques to foster active inquiry, collaboration, and supportive interaction.

Review the six features that support literacy. How would you rank their importance? What are some things that you can do now to prepare yourself to ensure that you will integrate these themes into your teaching?

Figure 12.2   Six Interacting Themes Supporting Information Literacy

Source: Gerald D. Bailey and Dan Lumley, "Fishing the Net," January 1999, p. A22. (Online). Available at www.electronic-school.com. Copyright 1999, National School Boards Association. Reprinted by permission.

- Comprehending and managing dimensions of information presentation. Information is supplied on CDs, at Web sites, in digital photographs, and in any number of ways.[2]

These dimensions of the new technological literacy not only affect how students learn, but also affect how students will conduct their future lives. Technological empowerment, or the lack of it, may well mean the difference between employment and unemployment.

Computers, computer programs, television, videodiscs, tape recorders, cassettes, and assistive technology are some of the forms of technology that will affect your curricula and teaching applications. You must consider the full range of technology available in your classroom, learning centers, and activities. To become technologically literate, students must have experiences with the full range of available technological resources and be conversant with the terminology.

Technological Divides

There are increasing discussions about the "great divide" that exists between the technological haves and the technological have-nots. The metaphor that comes to

☑ Who provided this information? Why?

☑ Is someone trying to sell us a product or a point of view?

☑ How is the source coded (e.g., .com = commercial; .gov = government; .edu = educational institution; .org = nonprofit organization; .mil = military, etc.)? How might this influence evaluation of its accuracy? Can we assume that everything from an educational institution, for example, is necessarily true? How about from a government source?

☑ What possible biases may be detected here (e.g., an organization dedicated to environmental protection or a business selling a product)?

☑ If quotes or data are provided, are they appropriately referenced?

☑ How can we find other information with which to compare and evaluate accuracy (e.g., call sources, check authorized print sources)?

☑ Does this information represent theory or evidence? What is the difference between these terms? How can we distinguish one from another? (Even undergraduate university students in the United States have difficulty with this question.)

☑ Why might some sources be more accurate than others (e.g., many professional journals are "vetted" or reviewed by experts before publication)?

☑ How do the visuals influence the way we receive this information? Is emotion a part of the design? Are sound effects intended to influence our thinking?

☑ Do the visuals and the text convey the same message?

Reflect & Write

The Internet provides massive quantities of information, but not all this information is appropriate, useful, or accurate. How can you use the guidelines shown here to help you and your students evaluate the information they have access to on the Internet? How might you apply these guidelines in your teaching?

_____

_____

_____

Figure 12.3 *Guidelines for Using the Internet for Teaching and Learning*

Source: J. M. Healy, "Failure to Connect: Naïve Excitement vs. Information Literacy," September 1998. (Online). Available at www.electronic-school.com. Copyright © 1998 by Jane M. Healy.

INTASC

Standard 3: The teacher understands how students differ in their approaches to learning and creates instructional opportunities that are adapted to diverse learners.

mind is a gulf we must bridge by laying optic cables to connect one side to the other. This conception of the "great divide" is incomplete; there is not one digital divide but rather many technological divides that separate students from teachers, teachers from students, schools from schools, and communities from communities. A more appropriate metaphor to explain the technological disparities and inequalities that exist is a split computer cable with many different wires representing different technological divides. The goal is to connect the breaks in this metaphoric cable by providing high-quality equipment, software, Internet access, and appropriate use for all students.

In addition, there are other important factors that promote technological inequalities. One of these issues relates to the quality of the technology available to particular students. For example, at Oliver High School in Pittsburgh, many of the computers that students use are older than the students themselves and cannot be repaired when they break down because no parts are available.[3] While we may think Oliver High's antiquated technology is only an occasional occurrence, it is not. Across the nation, other schools struggle to keep up with new technology. Financial issues are a major factor in this struggle. Schools in low socioeconomic areas generally have less money to spend on technology. Other issues of the digital divides involve teacher training, schoolhouse leadership, and the importance of the role of technology in a school district. All of these help account for why some schools and districts are farther ahead, while others lag behind.

However, there are hopeful indications that school districts are doing their best to provide computer and Internet access for all students. For example:

- Mississippi has connected all of its 32,354 public classrooms to the Internet, becoming the first state in the country to achieve this goal.[4]
- Vijay Sonty, information officer of the Broward County Public School District, the nation's fifth-largest with 270,000 students, just ordered 4,500 laptops for the upcoming school year. His purchase is part of an ongoing initiative geared to eventually give every high school student a notebook computer.[5]
- Maine has given fully loaded laptops—valued at $1,300—to all 33,000 students and 3,000 teachers in 241 schools.[6]

Tables 12.1 and 12.2 show students' computer use at home and school. Note how computer use varies by gender, culture, and socioeconomic background. These demographics of technological ownership, availability, and use have important implications for students, families, and professionals. For example, even though the number of schools connected to the Internet is increasing, low-income minority students are less likely to attend schools that have Internet access. In addition, students from upper-income families are more likely to have computers in the home. Access to computers and the Internet at school will help ensure that all students will have the opportunity to learn at their highest levels.

Today's world is fast-paced and technology-dependent, making technical fluency necessary. How technologically fluent do you consider yourself? Do you think most schools are prepared to address today's technology needs?

Technology and Standards of Learning

Technology has its own set of standards, and students must master these skills in order to become technologically proficient. For example, students are not considered

Table 12.1   Students' Computer Use at Home

Household Income	Prekindergarten and Kindergarten (%)	Grades 1 to 8 (%)	Grades 9 to 12 (%)
Less than $5,000	23.4	22.2	31.5
$5,000 to $9,999	14.8	24.1	24.4
$10,000 to $14,999	23.4	28.2	44.7
$15,000 to $19,999	28.6	34.3	44.7
$20,000 to $24,999	32.0	43.4	45.2
$25,000 to $29,999	44.8	41.7	55.5
$30,000 to $34,999	45.2	57.7	59.6
$35,000 to $39,999	52.6	62.4	64.9
$40,000 to $49,999	56.6	72.3	77.2
$50,000 to $74,999	68.6	76.8	85.5
$75,000 or more	78.2	87.1	92.9

Source: National Center for Education Statistics, *Digest of Educational Statistics, 2002* (Washington, DC: U.S. Government Printing Office, 2002).

Table 12.2   Students' Computer Use at School

Group	Prekindergarten and Kindergarten (%)	Grades 1 to 8 (%)	Grades 9 to 12 (%)
Male	55.8	85.2	87.9
Female	56.3	85.6	88.2
White	55.6	88.2	89.2
Black	56.9	83.6	89.0
Hispanic	57.1	77.3	83.8

Source: National Center for Education Statistics, *Digest of Educational Statistics, 2002* (Washington, DC: U.S. Government Printing Office, 2002).

INTASC

Standard 9: The teacher is a reflective practitioner who continually evaluates the effects of his/her choices and actions on others (students, parents, and other professionals in the learning community) and who actively seeks out opportunities to grow professionally.

competent in math or in reading unless they meet certain standards. (See the earlier discussions of standards in Chapters 2 and 10.) The International Society for Technology in Education (ISTE) has created six broad categories of standards for technological proficiency, which are listed in Figure 12.4.

After reviewing this listing, ask yourself if your school or classroom curriculum meets these standards. The ISTE standards are not necessarily universally accepted, nor should you think that every student must master them. People in different school districts, organizations, and communities have differing opinions as to the standards of technology their students should meet. Contrast Figure 12.4 with Figure 12.5, which shows the technology standards of Acalanes Union High School in Lafayette, California. What similarities and/or differences do you notice in these standards compared to the standards set by the ISTE?

- **Basic operations and concepts.** Students demonstrate a sound understanding of the nature and operation of technology systems and are proficient in the use of technology.

- **Social, ethical, and human issues.** Students understand the ethical, cultural, and societal issues related to technology; practice responsible use of technology; and develop positive attitudes toward technology uses that support lifelong learning, collaboration, personal pursuits, and productivity.

- **Technology productivity tools.** Students use technology tools to enhance learning, increase productivity, and promote creativity and to collaborate in constructing technology-enhanced models and producing other creative works.

- **Technology communication tools.** Students use telecommunications to collaborate, publish, and interact with peers, experts, and other audiences and use a variety of media formats to communicate information and ideas effectively.

- **Technology research tools.** Students use technology to locate, evaluate, and collect information from a variety of sources; use technology to process data; and evaluate and select new information resources and technological innovations.

- **Technology problem-solving and decision-making tools.** Students use technology resources for solving problems and making informed decisions and employ technology in the development of strategies for solving problems in the real world.

Reflect & Write

These standards are foundational—that is, they represent both the essential and the minimum that students need to have meaningful technological learning experiences. What are three other standards that you would add to this list? For example, what about an ethical use of technology standard?

Figure 12.4   Technology Foundation Standards for All Students

Source: International Society for Technology in Education, *National Educational Standards for Students* (August 2004). (Online). Available at http://cnets.iste.org. Reprinted by permission.

NETS for Students

1. Basic operations and concepts
   - Students demonstrate a sound understanding of the nature and operation of technology systems.
   - Students are proficient in the use of technology.
2. Social, ethical, and human issues
   - Students understand the ethical, cultural, and societal issues related to technology.
   - Students practice responsible use of technology systems, information, and software.
   - Students develop positive attitudes toward technology uses that support lifelong learning, collaboration, personal pursuits, and productivity.
3. Technology productivity tools
   - Students use technology tools to enhance learning, increase productivity, and promote creativity.
   - Students use productivity tools to collaborate in constructing technology-enhanced models, prepare publications, and produce other creative works.
4. Technology communications tools
   - Students use telecommunications to collaborate, publish, and interact with peers, experts, and other audiences.
   - Students use a variety of media and formats to communicate information and ideas effectively to multiple audiences.
5. Technology research tools
   - Students use technology to locate, evaluate, and collect information from a variety of sources.
   - Students use technology tools to process data and report results.
   - Students evaluate and select new information resources and technological innovations based on the appropriateness for specific tasks.
6. Technology problem-solving and decision-making tools
   - Students use technology resources for solving problems and making informed decisions.
   - Students employ technology in the development of strategies for solving problems in the real world.

Grades Pre-K–2 Performance Indicators

All students should have opportunities to demonstrate the following performances.
   Prior to completion of Grade 2 students will:

1. Use input devices (e.g., mouse, keyboard, remote control) and output devices (e.g., monitor, printer) to successfully operate computers, VCRs, audiotapes, and other technologies. (1)
2. Use a variety of media and technology resources for directed and independent learning activities. (1, 3)
3. Communicate about technology using developmentally appropriate and accurate terminology. (1)
4. Use developmentally appropriate multimedia resources (e.g., interactive books, educational software, elementary multimedia encyclopedias) to support learning. (1)
5. Work cooperatively and collaboratively with peers, family members, and others when using technology in the classroom. (2)
6. Demonstrate positive social and ethical behaviors when using technology. (2)
7. Practice responsible use of technology systems and software. (2)
8. Create developmentally appropriate multimedia products with support from teachers, family members, or student partners. (3)

continued

INTASC

Standard 6: The teacher uses knowledge of effective verbal, nonverbal, and media communication techniques to foster active inquiry, collaboration, and supportive interaction in the classroom.

NCATE

Elementary

Standard 3.5: Uses knowledge and understanding of effective verbal, nonverbal, and media communication techniques to foster active inquiry, collaboration, and supportive interaction.

NCATE

Early Childhood

Standard 4: Integrates understanding of children and families, of developmentally effective approaches to teaching and learning, and of academic disciplines to design, implement, and evaluate positive learning experiences for all children.

Figure 12.5   *N*ational Education Technology Standards of the International Society for Technology in Education (ISTE)

Source: International Society for Technology in Education, National Education Technology Standards. (Online). Available at http://cnets.iste.org/students/pdf/NETSS_Standards.pdf. Copyright 2000. Reprinted by permission. All rights reserved.

9. Use technology resources (e.g., puzzles, logical thinking programs, writing tools, digital cameras, drawing tools) for problem solving, communication, and illustration of thoughts, ideas, and stories. (3, 4, 5, 6)
10. Gather information and communicate with others using telecommunications, with support from teachers, family members, or student partners. (4)

Grades 3–5 Performance Indicators

All students should have opportunities to demonstrate the following performances.
Prior to completion of Grade 5 students will:

1. Use keyboards and other common input and output devices (including adaptive devices when necessary) efficiently and effectively. (1)
2. Discuss common uses of technology in daily life and the advantages and disadvantages those uses provide. (1, 2)
3. Discuss basic issues related to responsible use of technology and information and describe personal consequences of inappropriate use. (2)
4. Use general purpose productivity tools and peripherals to support personal productivity, remediate skill deficits, and facilitate learning throughout the curriculum. (3)
5. Use technology tools (e.g., multimedia authoring, presentation, Web tools, digital cameras, scanners) for individual and collaborative writing, communication, and publishing activities to create knowledge products for audiences inside and outside the classroom. (3, 4)
6. Use telecommunications efficiently and effectively to access remote information, communicate with others in support of direct and independent learning, and pursue personal interests. (4)
7. Use telecommunications and online resources (e.g., e-mail, online discussions, Web environments) to participate in collaborative problem-solving activities for the purpose of developing solutions or products for audiences inside and outside the classroom. (4, 5)
8. Use technology resources (e.g., calculators, data collection probes, videos, educational software) for problem solving, self-directed learning, and extended learning activities. (5, 6)
9. Determine which technology is useful and select the appropriate tool(s) and technology resources to address a variety of tasks and problems. (5, 6)
10. Evaluate the accuracy, relevance, appropriateness, comprehensiveness, and bias of electronic information sources. (6)

Elementary

Standard 3.5: Uses knowledge and understanding of effective verbal, nonverbal, and media communication techniques to foster active inquiry, collaboration, and supportive interaction.

Grades 6–8 Performance Indicators

All students should have opportunities to demonstrate the following performances.
Prior to completion of Grade 8 students will:

1. Apply strategies for identifying and solving routine hardware and software problems that occur during everyday use. (1)
2. Demonstrate knowledge of current changes in information technologies and the effect those changes have on the workplace and society. (2)
3. Exhibit legal and ethical behaviors when using information and technology, and discuss consequences of misuse. (2)
4. Use content-specific tools, software, and simulations (e.g., environmental probes, graphing calculators, exploratory environments, Web tools) to support learning and research. (3, 5)
5. Apply productivity/multimedia tools and peripherals to support personal productivity, group collaboration, and learning throughout the curriculum. (3, 6)
6. Design, develop, publish, and present products (e.g., Web pages, videotapes) using technology resources that demonstrate and communicate curriculum concepts to audiences inside and outside the classroom. (4, 5, 6)
7. Collaborate with peers, experts, and others using telecommunications and collaborative tools to investigate curriculum-related problems, issues, and information, and to develop solutions or products for audiences inside and outside the classroom. (4, 5)

Middle Level

Standard 5: Understands and uses major concepts, principles, theories, and research related to effective instruction and assessment; employs a variety of strategies for a developmentally appropriate climate to meet the varying abilities and learning styles of all young adolescents.

Figure 12.5 *Continued*

8. Select and use appropriate tools and technology resources to accomplish a variety of tasks and solve problems. (5, 6)
9. Demonstrate an understanding of concepts underlying hardware, software, and connectivity, and of practical applications to learning and problem solving. (1, 6)
10. Research and evaluate the accuracy, relevance, appropriateness, comprehensiveness, and bias of electronic information sources concerning real-world problems. (2, 5, 6)

Grades 9–12 Performance Indicators

All students should have opportunities to demonstrate the following performances. Prior to completion of Grade 12 students will:

1. Identify capabilities and limitations of contemporary and emerging technology resources and assess the potential of these systems and services to address personal, lifelong learning, and workplace needs. (2)
2. Make informed choices among technology systems, resources, and services. (1, 2)
3. Analyze advantages and disadvantages of widespread use and reliance on technology in the workplace and in society as a whole. (2)
4. Demonstrate and advocate for legal and ethical behaviors among peers, family, and community regarding the use of technology and information. (2)
5. Use technology tools and resources for managing and communicating personal/professional information (e.g., finances, schedules, addresses, purchases, correspondence). (3, 4)
6. Evaluate technology-based options, including distance and distributed education, for lifelong learning. (5)
7. Routinely and efficiently use online information resources to meet needs for collaboration, research, publications, communications, and productivity. (4, 5, 6)
8. Select and apply technology tools for research, information analysis, problem-solving, and decision-making in content learning. (4, 5)
9. Investigate and apply expert systems, intelligent agents, and simulations in real-world situations. (3, 5, 6)
10. Collaborate with peers, experts, and others to contribute to a content-related knowledge base by using technology to compile, synthesize, produce, and disseminate information, models, and other creative works. (4, 5, 6)

Standard 6: The teacher uses knowledge of effective verbal, nonverbal, and media communication techniques to foster active inquiry, collaboration, and supportive interaction in the classroom.

Reflect & Write

Many school districts have developed technology standards based on these ISTE standards. The ISTE standards are widely used and are very influential in determining what students should know and be able to do in the field of technology. Why do you think these technology standards are so influential? Look up on the Internet the technology standards for two school districts and compare them with the ISTE standards. What conclusions can you draw?

Figure 12.5 Continued

Reflect & Write

Do you think it is unrealistic for all students to meet the ISTE standards?

SECTION SUMMARY

What Is Technological Literacy?

Computers have modified the concept of literacy for American students and teachers.

- Changing Concepts of Literacy. Technology is changing how society and educators view literacy. In addition to knowing how to read, write, listen, and speak, students now must also learn to use technology. Mastering the dimensions of technological literacy will have a major impact on how students learn and on their future lives.

- **Technological Divides.** Instead of one "great divide" between the haves and have-nots, there are many technological divides that separate students from teachers, teachers from students, schools from schools, and communities from communities. Some programs and schools are finding ways to address these divides.
- **Technology and Standards of Learning.** Although schools have lagged behind the rest of society in integrating technology into daily experience, professional organizations and societies are developing standards for technological proficiency in education. For example, the ISTE standards offer guidelines for teaching and specifying what students should know and be able to do.

Thinking Critically
★ ★ ★ ★ ★ ★ ★ ★

In the text I state that "to become technologically literate, students must have experiences with the full range of available technological resources." Is this a realistic goal for all students? Why or why not?

_____

_____

_____

_____ ★

Applying What You've Learned
★ ★ ★ ★ ★ ★ ★ ★

Interview K–12 teachers in a local school district. What barriers must they contend with in their efforts to include technology in the curriculum? What implications do these barriers have for what you may be able to accomplish as a teacher?

_____

_____

_____ ★

Putting Yourself in the Picture
★ ★ ★ ★ ★ ★ ★ ★

In an interview for your first teaching job, you are asked to give three examples of how you will integrate technology in your teaching. Write your three examples here.

_____

_____

_____

_____ ★

HOW IS TECHNOLOGY CONTRIBUTING TO COMMUNITY-BASED AND WORLDWIDE EDUCATION?

Internet
A vast telecommunications network consisting of a group of internationally interconnected computers that communicate electronically.

The **Internet**, the World Wide Web electronic superhighway started by the Department of Defense in 1969, offers tremendous learning opportunities for teachers, students, and others. The Internet is a vast telecommunications network consisting of a group of internationally interconnected computers that communicate electronically. The Internet comprises more than 40 thousand smaller networks interconnected with more than 179 million host computers offering resources and services that afford you, your students, and their parents access to a vast array of information and learning opportunities. More than 797 million individuals have access to the Internet through educational, corporate, public-provided, and private accounts. The United States has the highest number of Internet users, followed by China, Japan, Germany, and the United Kingdom. With a personal computer, a **modem** (a device that enables computers to communicate over telephone lines), and the appropriate access software, you and your students can be on the Internet. You and others gain access to the Internet through university links, commercial agencies, regional networks, state networks, and freenets. Most colleges and universities are connected to the Internet and give students and faculty access through personal accounts. Often, these accounts are free or provided to certain users at a modest cost per semester. Enrolled students generally have access through their institutions. In addition, some colleges and universities provide access to local school districts.

Commercial companies—such as America Online, IBM, CompuServe, Prodigy, Microsoft, Apple, and Norton—provide software that provides access to the Internet for a monthly fee. It is through these companies that many parents and students have Internet access in their homes. Many large school districts, governmental agencies, and corporations have **networks** whereby they provide access to the Internet. More than half of the states—including Michigan, Virginia, Kansas, California, North Dakota, and Texas—have statewide networks. For example, the Texas Educational Network (TeNet) is a network of colleges and secondary, middle, and elementary schools that provides access to the Internet as well as to many educational resources. Networks such as TeNet charge an annual membership fee.

Many communities provide **freenets** for use by educators and community members. These freenets are generally operated and supported by local and regional libraries and are paid for out of local tax revenues. For example, Fernnet is operated by the Broward County (Florida) library system and provides free access by dialing a special telephone number. Contact your local library system to determine if there is a freenet in your area.

Often commercial networks will offer additional services to their subscribers. For example, America Online (www.aol.com) offers education discussion groups; online homework help for students; software library with programs in science, mathematics, language arts, and social studies; and access to National Geographic's educational resources. To log onto these Web sites, connect to the Internet and type in the Web address of where you want to go. If you don't know the Web address, you may use a search engine such as Yahoo (www.yahoo.com) or Google (www.google.com) to find the Web address you want. Internet search engines aid users in finding Web sites based on key words entered by the user. Some commercial firms partner with schools to offer technological services. (See Education on the Move.)

E-mail, the sending and receiving of electronic messages, is the most widely used of all Internet applications. Through e-mail, you and your students can communicate with teachers and students in your district and other school districts and at schools across the country and around the world. You will also be able to communicate with some of your students at home. Some teachers provide help with homework and other class work via e-mail. You and your students can also participate in newsgroups, a cross between a bulletin board and a discussion group. In fact, you can start a discussion group on a particular classroom topic and invite other teachers and students to participate. You can set up "chat rooms" for your students in each of your classes. Students enjoy talking with each other, and it is a great way to share information and ideas.

Since September 11, 2001, many teachers and students are using e-mail to help their students develop multicultural awareness and international understanding.

> "I have no grudge with you about the incident that happened on September 11, 2001," e-mailed a New York sixth-grader to a schoolkid in Cairo. "The reason I

Early Childhood

Standard 4: Integrates understanding of children and families, of developmentally effective approaches to teaching and learning, and of academic disciplines to design, implement, and evaluate positive learning experiences for all children.

Modem
A device that enables computers to communicate over telephone lines.

Elementary

Standard 3.5: Uses knowledge and understanding of effective verbal, nonverbal, and media communication techniques to foster active inquiry, collaboration, and supportive interaction.

Networks
Systems of computers, terminals, and data bases connected by communication lines that provide access to the Internet.

Freenets
Networks that can be used free or with minimal charge.

Elementary

Standard 5.4: Fosters relationships with school colleagues and agencies in the larger community to support students' learning and well-being.

E-mail
The sending and receiving of electronic messages.

Middle Level

Standard 6: Understands the major concepts, principles, theories, and research related to working collaboratively with family and community members; uses that knowledge to maximize learning of all young adolescents.

>>> Tech Firms Go to School in Search of Customers >>>>>>>

At the ripe age of 18, Jonathon Tanner is learning about leadership, people management, and project management—not to mention high-level technical support. Tanner, an incoming senior at Zion-Benton High School in north suburban Zion (Illinois), heads up the school's student-operated technical-support department, called TechCrew. About forty-five students are involved each year and handle nearly every computer glitch, crash, and virus on the school's 1,000 Dell personal computers.

And while many of today's teenagers are technically inclined, the volunteers at TechCrew also handle such human resources issues as hiring, training, disciplining, and firing fellow students. "My son is running a business," said Tanner's mother,

Cheryl. And the other students are working their way up "the chain of command," as Jonathon described it.

"Programs like TechCrew are the result of partnerships with [technology] vendors, which really create win-win situations for everybody," said Dave Lemon, a network administrator at Zion-Benton.

"Look, we don't have the resources [of other school districts with more money]," Lemon said. In fact, just 34 percent of Zion-Benton's students go on to a four-year college or university, according to a school spokeswoman. But nearly all TechCrew volunteers go on to college, with some getting full scholarships.

Technology companies know that school kids are not only big high-tech buyers, but also that they affect what

their parents and grandparents purchase as well.

"It's a huge market for us," said Karen Bruett, director of education and community initiatives at Dell. "Young people are increasingly influencers on their parents' decisions. Kids today are savvy consumers."

Which is why deals between schools and the technology industry are extending beyond personal computers and stretching into wireless networks, MP3 players, and music download services.

Source: A. L. Goldfayn, "Tech Firms Go to School in Search of Customers," *Chicago Tribune*, August 9, 2004. (Online). Available at www.chicagotribune.com. Reprinted by permission.

brought this up is so that we can speak to each other openly, and hopefully learn about each other's culture and everyday life."

"I want the ideas of many people who think Arabs and Muslims are terrorists to change," replied the Egyptian youngster.

This is e-mail conversation is an example of a White House–initiated e-mail exchange program linking U.S. students whose schools were directly affected on September 11 with students in the Middle East.[8]

Other applications of networks include accessing data bases that provide useful information. For example, the U.S. Department of Education supports the Educational Resources Information Center (ERIC), which provides access to literature in the field of education: www.eric.ed.gov/.

Reflect & Write

Think about how you can use e-mail and chat rooms to help you and your students learn.

_____

_____

_____

_____

INTASC

Standard 10: The teacher fosters relationships with school colleagues, parents, and agencies in the larger community to support students' learning and well-being.

Increased Opportunities for Parent Participation

Parents live with their children 365 days a year, twenty-four hours a day. Their questions about and concerns for their children go well beyond the capability of teachers and school personnel to provide help within the time limits of the school day. In addition, many parents face constraints of time and mobility for getting to the school for parent conferences, programs, and assistance. Technology offers a rich assortment of ways parents and teachers can exchange and gain information and get help and assistance.

Growing numbers of preschools and day-care programs are installing cameras and systems that enable parents to access secure Web sites so they can monitor how their children are doing. A special user I.D. and password give parents access. Presently, these programs offer silent still pictures that are periodically updated from a few seconds to minutes.

Proponents of such access to preschool programs contend that they ease parents' minds about how their children are doing, promote communication between parents and programs, create closer bonds between parents and children, and are a safeguard against possible child abuse. On the other hand, critics say that it is another example of the intrusion of technology into the lives of children and families and that unauthorized people could get access to the system if parents are careless about their passwords or if they give them to others.

This student is using e-mail, the most widely used of all Internet applications. Through e-mail, students can communicate with other students in their home town, in their state, across the nation, and throughout the world. You as a teacher can provide help with homework via e-mail and can set up discussion groups, or "chat rooms," for your students to share information and ideas with each other.

Reflect & Write

If you could choose between a child-care center with technology that enabled you to see your child at work and at play and another equally good and equally convenient center that had no such technology, which would you choose? Why?

_____

_____

_____

_____

One reality of children's use of technology is their increasing use of computers. Another reality is the challenge of trying to screen out the good from the bad on the Internet. In a November 2002 report, the Pew Internet and American Life Project found that more parents are concerned about what their kids encounter online (38 percent) than what they view on television (16 percent). Furthermore, according to the Pew Project, parents have concerns about the people and material their children will encounter on the Net. "These worries prompt many parents to impose rules on Internet use, to monitor their children's online activities, and to install software to prevent their children from accessing objectionable material."[9] One way to monitor is through the use of a **filter,** a computer program that denies access to sites parents specify as inappropriate. One such program, Cyber Sentinel, blocks access to chat rooms, stops instant messages, and can be programmed to stop questions such as "What is your phone number?" Parents who use America Online can specify three levels of access—Kids Only (under 12), Young Teen (13–15), and Mature Teen (16–17). While many of these solutions are helpful, none can be considered 100 percent effective. In an effort to help ensure a safe and enjoyable Internet experience for children, Belkin Corporation, the leading manufacturer of connectivity solutions, offers its Parental Control Web Content Filter. Easy to set up and operate, Parental Control is an advanced Web-filtering system that blocks and filters offensive or unwanted Web pages using a data base of more than 4 million sites.[10]

NCATE

Early Childhood

Standard 4: Integrates understanding of children and families, of developmentally effective approaches to teaching and learning, and of academic disciplines to design, implement, and evaluate positive learning experiences for all children.

Filter
A computer program that denies access to sites parents specify as inappropriate.

Communication and interaction with parents is a primary goal of schools and teachers. District and school Web pages are an excellent way to inform, involve, and collaborate with parents and families. Web pages such as these provide important information about the district itself, its schools, faculty, and students. Good Web pages present a positive image of the district, explicitly state the mission of the schools, have e-mail features enabling parents to communicate with administrators and teachers, provide Web resources (e.g., help with homework), and publish student work. Web sites also contain school "report cards," as required by No Child Left Behind.

The Internet is also a valuable tool for parents who home school their children. Through the Internet, parents have access to educational information and resources and can be in contact with other parents and home-schooled children. Web sites for parents are becoming more numerous and contain curriculum resources, list names of organizations and individuals offering help with home schooling, and provide advice on legal matters.

In 1998 Congress passed the Children's Online Privacy Act (COPA), which was designed to ensure privacy rights of children and protect them from unscrupulous individuals and firms. This would have required World Wide Web operators to secure parental permission before they receive children's e-mail or home address. However, the law never took effect because of legal challenges. In 2004, in *Ashcroft v. ACLU,* the court blocked enforcement of the law, saying it was unconstitutional. In *Privacy Online: A Report to Congress,* the Federal Trade Commission reported that of 212 children's Web sites, 90 percent collected personal information and only 1 percent obtained parental permission.[11] Federal Trade Commission Chairman Robert Pitofsky believes collecting information from children without parental permission is not acceptable. To alleviate any privacy concerns, many businesses, such as America Online, use mail-in parental notifications whereby parents can fill out an information card and mail it back in to the company. Congress also passed the Child Online Privacy Protection Act (COPPA), which calls for commercial Web site operators who offer "harmful" material to check the I.D.s of visitors. It is likely that Congress will continue to legislate ways to protect the privacy of children age 12 and under.

NCATE

Elementary

Standard 3.2: Understands how elementary students differ in development and approaches to learning; creates instructional opportunities that are adapted to diverse students.

Reflect & Write

How do you feel about legislation meant to protect privacy? Do you believe it limits freedom of access?

_____

_____

_____

_____

Home Schooling Online

YOU DECIDE

The Internet has become a valuable tool for parents who home school their children. Through the Internet, parents have access to educational information and resources and can be in contact with other parents and home-schooled children. Web sites for parents are becoming more numerous and contain curriculum resources, list names of organizations and individuals offering help with home schooling, and provide advice on legal matters. Former Secretary of Education William Bennett launched one such site, K12, Inc., a for-profit company that uses the Internet to deliver a "classical" education.

Home-schooled students who enroll directly in K12 pay about $325 per course, or $1,495 for an entire school year's program, which they access on the company's Web site. The content and approach of the K12 program are based on the core knowledge curriculum, developed by University of Virginia English professor E. D. Hirsch, Jr.

It emphasizes phonics-based reading instruction at the K–2 levels, a "Great Books" approach to literature, and a general commitment to understanding Western culture and history.

The online resources consist of learning activities, daily assessments, planning tools, and instructions for parents on how to guide their children's learning. Shipments to students of other materials—including books, tambourines, music CDs, and videotapes—augment the online resources.

How do you feel about parents educating their children with online "schools" such as K12, Inc.? For more information about K12, Inc., visit its Web site www.k12.com. For more general information about home schooling online, try a search on those keywords.

Educational Software for Very Young Children

As indicated earlier, technology is part of the world of young children. Computers and other technology have a great deal to offer, and there is much that young children can learn via technology in all domains—cognitive, social, emotional, and linguistic. Software is being designed for children as young as 9 months. This software is often referred to as **lapware**, because children have to crawl onto parents' laps in order to use it and it is intended to be used by parents and children together. Jumpstart Baby (www.etoys.com) and BabyWow (www.babywow.com) are aimed specifically at children 9 months to 2 years. Jumpstart Baby leads children through eight activities, including wood-block puzzles and nursery rhyme sing-alongs. BabyWow has 300 pictures and corresponding vocabulary words in eight languages. Preschool Workshop emphasizes matching colors, shapes, and sizes; Alphabet Playhouse focuses on reading readiness; Reader Railway is a beginning reading program; and Mathopolis is devoted to mathematics. (See the Profile.)

The market for infant, toddler, and preschool software is growing, with an estimated $50 million spent each year. Programs designed for children under 5 represent the fastest-growing educational software market. Not everyone believes that such software is developmentally appropriate, and the debate rages on in early childhood circles about how much time children should spend on computers and what kind of

Lapware
Software designed for children as young as 9 months.

NCATE

Early Childhood

Standard 4: Integrates understanding of children and families, of developmentally effective approaches to teaching and learning, and of academic disciplines to design, implement, and evaluate positive learning experiences for all children.

Profile   Integrating Technology in the Primary Grades

In an active primary classroom, the teacher and children use a mix of traditional materials and new technology tools. The children in the class work in groups scattered throughout the room.

Some students draw crayon pictures that are then scanned into a word processor or authoring program such as KidPix, while others create pictures directly on the computer. Later, they will dictate stories to accompany their pictures. Another group uses a digital camera to take pictures of each other. The pictures will illustrate their biographies. Other children build

designs with pattern blocks. Using yarn, they mark lines of symmetry and take photos of the completed designs. Meanwhile, in a quiet corner, a parent volunteer tape records a student reading aloud a story. This activity will happen several times during the year with each child so that students can hear their own progress as they listen to the recordings. Yet another group is "reading" a talking book on the computer, listening to the spoken words as the speech synthesizer turns letters into sounds.[12]

software they should use. See Figure 12.6, which contains highlights of the position statement on technology and young children of the National Association for the Education of Young Children.

Standard 3: The teacher understands how students differ in their approaches to learning and creates instructional opportunities that are adapted to diverse learners.

INTASC

Supporting the Learning of Students with Special Needs

Public Law 100-407, the Technology-Related Assistance for Individuals with Disabilities Act of 1988 (Tech Act), defines **assistive technology** as "any item, device or piece of equipment, or product system, whether acquired commercially off the shelf, modified, or customized, that is used to increase, maintain, or improve functional abilities of individuals with disabilities."[13]

Assistive technology covers a wide range of products and applications from simple devices, such as adaptive spoons and switch-adapted battery-operated toys, to

Assistive technology
Any item, device, or piece of equipment or product system used to assist individuals with disabilities.

Although there is considerable research that points to the positive effects of technology on children's learning and development, the research indicates that, in practice, computers supplement and do not replace highly valued early childhood activities and materials, such as art, blocks, sand, water, books, exploration with writing materials, and dramatic play. Research indicates that computers can be used in developmentally appropriate ways beneficial to children and also can be misused, just as any tool can. Developmentally appropriate software offers opportunities for collaborative play, learning, and creation. Educators must use professional judgment in evaluating and using this learning tool appropriately, applying the same criteria they would to any other learning tool or experience. They must also weigh the costs of technology with the costs of other learning materials and program resources to arrive at an appropriate balance for their classrooms.

- In evaluating the appropriate use of technology, NAEYC applies principles of developmentally appropriate practice and appropriate curriculum and assessment. In short, NAEYC believes that in any given situation, a professional judgment by the teacher is required to determine if a specific use of technology is age appropriate, individually appropriate, and culturally appropriate.

- Used appropriately, technology can enhance children's cognitive and social abilities.

- Appropriate technology is integrated into the regular learning environment and used as one of many options to support children's learning.

- Early childhood educators should promote equitable access to technology for all children and their families. Children with special needs should have access when this is helpful.

- The power of technology to influence children's learning and development requires that attention be paid to eliminating stereotyping of any group and eliminating exposure to violence, especially as a problem-solving strategy.

- Teachers, in collaboration with parents, should advocate for more appropriate technology applications for children.

- The appropriate use of technology has many implications for early childhood professional development.

NCATE

Early Childhood

Standard 4: Integrates understanding of children and families, of developmentally effective approaches to teaching and learning, and of academic disciplines to design, implement, and evaluate positive learning experiences for all children.

Reflect & Write

This position statement of the NAEYC makes the point that technology such as computers should have a support role and not be used in place of other early childhood activities. How would you use computers in teaching young children so that they enhance but not dominate the learning experience? What activities do you feel are crucial to young children's development?

Figure 12.6 **N**AEYC Position Statement on Technology and Young Children

Source: National Association for the Education of Young Children, "NAEYC Position Statement: Technology and Young Children, Ages 3 through 8," *Young Children* (February 1998). pp. 11–16. Copyright © 1998 by the National Association for the Education of Young Children. Reprinted by permission from the National Association for the Education of Young Children.

complex devices, such as computerized environmental control systems. You will have opportunities to use many forms of assistive technology and modified educational software with all ages of students with special needs.

Assistive technology is particularly important for students with disabilities who depend on technology to help them communicate, learn, and be mobile. For example, closed circuit television can be used to enlarge print, a braille printer can convert words to braille, and audiotaped instructional materials can be provided for students with vision impairments. Closed captioned television and FM amplification systems can assist students who are deaf or hard of hearing. (See Education on the Move.) Touch-screen computers, augmentative communication boards, and voice synthesizers can assist students with limited mobility or with disabilities that make communication difficult. In addition, computer-assisted instruction provides software tools for teaching students at all ability levels, including programmed instruction for students with specific learning disabilities. (See also the discussion in Chapter 5.)

Closing the digital divides also includes providing appropriate technology applications for students with disabilities. According to Bill East, the executive director of the National Association of State Directors of Special Education, school administrators have to be more rigorous in evaluating how technology is used for students with disabilities. "The problems of the haves and the have-nots are just magnified when we

Early Childhood

Standard 4: Integrates understanding of children and families, of developmentally effective approaches to teaching and learning, and of academic disciplines to design, implement, and evaluate positive learning experiences for all children.

Middle Level

Standard 1: Understands the major concepts, principles, theories and research related to young adolescent development; provides opportunities that support student development and learning.

education *on the move* >>>>>>>>>>>>

>>> Miking Teachers >>>>>>>

Teachers of kindergartners through third-graders at Gosnell Elementary School will be wearing microphones this school year as part of the school's effort to increase learning by making teachers heard.

Talking neighbors, air conditioning, squeaking desks, and noise outside the classroom can all distract students. To help improve the situation, the district has invested in a sound field amplification system for each K–3 classroom to help students hear no matter where a teacher is located in the classroom.

"Basically, it is a PA system for each individual classroom that amplifies and focuses the teacher's voice," Bart Branum, psychological examiner/school psychology specialist for the district, said. "In the classroom you have a lot of auditory distractions, along with teacher's voice, and that is a big distraction for the kids. With this there is a constant sound in a particular location minimizing the distraction. This will help kids with attention deficit disorder and those with hearing problems."

"We had a young man that was in the first grade last year that wore

a hearing aid, and this will help amplify his hearing aid," Wendy Evans, special education supervisor for the Gosnell district, said. "We had two teachers try it last year, and they really like it. What the research has shown is that when these systems are in the classroom, it reduces special education referrals and helps kids learn because the sound is better. They use this in a lot of different schools but usually not in this many classrooms. We had some extra special education money, and so we purchased the system to see if it would make a difference."

Evans said the district has been seeing an increase in hearing-impaired students and students who have attention deficit disorder. By utilizing the system, Evans said she hopes students can benefit more from regular classroom instruction instead of having to go to a special education environment.

Studies show that children in grades K through 6 spend 45 to 60 percent of the school day engaged in listening activities. Also, a teacher's voice drops by 75 percent for a child twelve feet from the teacher.

"Teachers can walk around to all corners of the room or even turn their back to the students to write something on the board, and the sound quality will be the same," Branum said. "Research shows that oral comprehension and grades go up by using this system, and behavior problems go down. Teachers also won't have to raise their voices to make sure everyone hears them. They can talk in a normal tone."

With the system, teachers wear a headset microphone that plugs into a wireless microphone receiver with an amplifier, which looks like a small battery pack, that will clip onto their belts or pockets. The wireless microphone receiver with amplifier picks up an FM signal and plays it through the loud speaker for the class to hear. The speakers have to be kept six feet away from computers to prevent feedback.

Source: C. Benhan, "Gosnell Will Be Miking Teachers This Year." *Blytheville Courier News*, July 2004. Retrieved August 18, 2004, from source. Reprinted by permission.

Today's students come from an increasingly diverse range of backgrounds and have many varied special needs. Assistive technology is particularly important for students with physical and learning disabilities. Technology not only can provide the means to expand these students' physical capabilities—such as speech, hearing, and mobility—but can play a crucial role in helping them learn and interact socially.

talk about disability," East says. "Technology can be a great equalizer, but when the playing field is not leveled, students with disabilities will have even greater problems." East believes that states must work hard to close that gap. When education officials deal with technology grants and programs, he says, they must always consider the needs of such students: "They should not be an afterthought."[14]

SECTION SUMMARY

How Is Technology Contributing to Community-Based and Worldwide Education?

The Internet, a worldwide electronic superhighway, provides access to a vast array of information, enabling students and teachers to expand and enrich teaching and learning.

- Increased Opportunities for Parent Participation. Technology is providing parents with information and the ability to monitor their children in child-care programs, keep in touch with school activities, exchange information, get assistance, and communicate with teachers. In order to help parents and teachers, Congress has passed laws to help protect children from illicit and other potentially harmful information.

- Educational Software for Very Young Children. Children use technology at ever younger ages. Professional organizations such as the National Association for the Education of Young Children have adopted position statements about what is and is not appropriate use of technology in teaching and learning.

- Supporting the Learning of Students with Special Needs. Assistive technology, which ranges from simple devices to complex systems, is playing an even greater role in helping students with disabilities learn. This area of technology is especially important to students with disabilities who depend on technology to communicate, learn, and be mobile.

Thinking Critically

★ ★ ★ ★ ★ ★ ★ ★

How will you ensure that software aimed at helping you teach a diverse population will respect and help preserve that which is unique and special about your students' ethnic heritages and cultural differences?

_____

_____

_____

_____★

Applying What You've Learned

★ ★ ★ ★ ★ ★ ★ ★

You will be teaching in an inclusive classroom. What might be some technology you could use to help your students with a reading disability learn better?

_____

_____

_____

_____★

Putting Yourself in the Picture

★ ★ ★ ★ ★ ★ ★ ★

What are your opinions regarding technology that enables parents to observe their children without a caretaker's knowledge? Would you want parents to have online access to your classroom? State your reasons, both pro and con.

_____

_____

_____

_____★

$\mathcal{W}$HAT ISSUES ARE ASSOCIATED WITH THE USE OF TECHNOLOGY?

As a beginning teacher, you will be faced with a number of issues related to the uses of technology and will be involved in many decisions regarding how to use technology. You will likely play an advocacy role in promoting access to technology for you and your students. (See the Profile.)

Ensuring Equitable Access to Technology

All students must have equitable access to technology that is appropriate for them. While some may think it a worthy goal to have all students spend the same amount of time on a computer, students' needs and abilities vary. Some students may have to spend more time to master the objectives of their particular grade and subject, while others may not need as much time or may prefer other ways to learn.

Equity issues affect how you as a teacher approach your students' needs to learn how to use relevant technology to become technologically literate. If one group, socio-economic class, or gender is more comfortable with, skillful with, and proficient in

INTASC

Standard 3: The teacher understands how students differ in their approaches to learning and creates instructional opportunities that are adapted to diverse learners.

Tony Vincent teaches fifth grade at Willowdale School in Omaha, Nebraska.

"Handhelds" are fully functional computers that can fit in the palm of a student's hand—and I am fortunate to teach in a classroom where every student has one! The one-to-one computing ratio helps students enjoy school and learning; these devices have brought my teaching and my students' learning to a higher level. Kids collaborate, create quality products, and look forward to completing assignments at home. And get this—my students are often sad to leave school at the end of the day!

Every one of my fifth-graders has a Palm m515 handheld computer and keyboard. They quickly learn the basics of the Palm operating system. In fact, Palms are so intuitive that the focus is always on the task or curriculum, not the technology. And handhelds are a versatile tool, so I've been able to infuse handheld technology into all curriculum areas.

With the advantages of technology, however, comes the challenge of management. But I find that with a few simple rules and procedures, management has not been a problem. Students have a routine for turning in their handhelds at the end of the day (if they are not going to be taken home) and a routine for charging their Palms. Additionally, students know that their handhelds will be taken away for a day if they are used inappropriately. My fifth-graders rely on their Palms so much that they would never risk losing them, even for a day!

I could fill the pages of a large book with all of the engaging and meaningful activities that take advantage of handheld technology, but let me give three brief examples.

- Sketchy is an animation application in which students animate vocabulary words, stories, diagrams, and more. Animating a long division problem is my favorite! Students show step-by-step the process of solving a long division problem. They create "thought bubbles" that explain what they've done at each step, and since Sketchy allows students to move objects on the screen, the number actually moves down when a student "brings down" a number when dividing! Because of the great learning that takes place while creating the division animation sequence, students learn the division algorithm much more quickly than simply practicing problems from a math book.
- "Roving reporter" is another of our frequent activities. Each day, one student is designated as the roving reporter. The reporter's job is to take photos throughout the day using a digital camera that attaches to and stores the photos on the handheld. That evening, the reporter takes his or her handheld home to compose an article about our day of learning. The reporter uses WordSmith, a word processor for the Palm. If the reporter can't remember what to write about, the photos will provide instant memories. The article and photos are synced to a classroom computer the next morning, and I combine them into a Web page, which is immediately added to the daily log on our class Web site. The daily log contains photos and a narrative for every day of the school year, accessible not only to students but also to parents, friends, administrators—and the world. At the end of the school year, I put the daily log on CD-ROM and send a copy home with each student, who then will always have a copy of the fifth-grade experience—thanks to handheld technology!
- Finally, there is the "Million Dollar Project." As part of learning accounting and the value of money, students are given the task of spending one million dollars. Each student's project must have a theme, and all purchases must relate to that theme. Using a Palm application called MyCheckbook, students deposit $1,000,000 into their accounts, research what they need to buy to complete the project (including land, labor, materials, and supplies), input prices, and make "purchases." MyCheckbook categorizes all purchases and instantly calculates the remaining money in the account. Purchases may be edited or deleted later as students reach their spending limits and begin to prioritize. After spending their million dollars, students create a pie chart showing their final purchases by category.

These are just a sampling of the dozens of activities my students have completed using handhelds. Using handheld computers is so engaging that I absolutely love to teach, and students love to learn. My students and I have discovered that handhelds are small devices that can do big things for learning!

NCATE

Elementary

Standard 3.5: Uses knowledge and understanding of effective verbal, nonverbal, and media communication techniques to foster active inquiry, collaboration, and supportive interaction.

---

the use of technology, inequities and technological illiteracy can result. Teachers must avoid helping create a generation of technology "have-nots."

Income level and socioeconomic status also affect technological equity. Although the overall number of schools connected to the Internet is increasing, schools with predominantly low-income and minority student populations are still less likely to have computer access than are schools with affluent, mainstream student populations. Students from families with high income and socioeconomic status are almost three times as likely to own a computer than are lower-income students. Seventy-three percent of white students have computers. Forty-one percent of African American students have computers.[15] Table 12.3 shows the percentage of public schools having

Table 12.3 *P*ercentage of Public Schools Having Access to the Internet

School Characteristics	1997	1999	2001
All Public Schools	78%	95%	99%
Instructional Level			
Elementary	75	94	99
Secondary	89	98	100
Size of Enrollment			
Less than 300	75	96	99
300 to 999	78	94	99
1,000 or more	89	96	100
Metropolitan Status			
City	74	93	97
Urban fringe	78	96	99
Town	84	94	100
Rural	79	96	99

Source: National Center for Education Statistics, *Digest of Education Statistics, 2002* (Washington, DC: U.S. Government Printing Office, 2002).

access to the Internet. The percentage of public schools with Internet access is now almost 100 percent, as Table 12.3 shows.

Bridging the Gender Gap

Ashley Weagraff doesn't worry about the boys anymore. She is the exception. One of the few girls taking technology-related classes at G. Ray Bodley High School in Fulton, New York, the fifteen-year-old fought back her initial anxiety and now works well with male students in a computer-enhanced technical drawing, design, and production class. But she still knows well the fear that keeps many girls from taking similar courses that feature a heavy dose of technology. "A lot of the time, girls steer clear of technology classes because they are intimidated by the majority of males in the classes," she says.[16]

A study by the American Association of University Women (AAUW) reports that technology represents a new gender gap between girls and boys. "Girls have narrowed some significant gender gaps, but technology is now the new 'boys club' in our nation's public schools," says AAUW's executive director Janice Weinman. "While boys program and problem solve with computers, girls use computers for word processing, the 1990s version of typing."

While there is progress in certain areas, gaps persist. "The gender gaps we see are evidence that public schools are failing to fully prepare girls for the twenty-first century. High schools still tend to steer girls and boys into School-to-Work programs that prepare them for traditional occupations for their gender," says Sandy Bernard, president of the AAUW. "We are in the midst of profound change," says Maggie Ford, president of the AAUW Educational Foundation. "As student diversity changes the face of public education, and technology changes the workplace, schools must work smarter and harder to ensure that girls graduate with the knowledge and abilities they need to compete and succeed in the twenty-first-century economy."[17]

Many programs are in place in schools and communities to help ensure that girls are encouraged and supported to be involved in technology and to pursue technologically based careers. For example, Techbridge in Oakland, California, introduces girls to various applications of technology and encourages them to consider technology-related careers. Techbridge is a "bridge" for girls between middle school and high school and provides girls with academic guidance, role models, and training for

INTASC

Standard 3: The teacher understands how students differ in their approaches to learning and creates instructional opportunities that are adapted to diverse learners.

NCATE

Elementary

Standard 3.2: Understands how elementary students differ in development and approaches to learning; creates instructional opportunities that are adapted to diverse students.

Equitable access to technology means that all students, regardless of gender, background, or ability, are provided equal opportunity to use technology in the schools. Many school districts have programs that ensure access for all children to computers and other technological tools, such as calculators and interactive video. As a teacher, you will need to continually assess the appropriateness of software and the availability of technology for your students.

teachers, and works with families.[18] Girlstart, in Austin, Texas, is designed to empower middle school girls and encourage them to excel in math, science, and technology. Girlstart offers after-school programs and Saturday and summer camps.[19]

It has been a stereotype that boys are adept at technology and girls are not. Now that technology has entered the classroom, this stereotype has once more gained sway. Although girls have proven themselves equal competitors in the areas of academics and athletics, it seems they will once again have to prove themselves, this time in the technological arena. This gender gap is reflected in the fact that computer and technology classes are mainly attended by boys rather than girls. If girls do enroll in computer classes, they most likely will enroll in a class such as data processing, whereas boys will enroll in advanced computer science courses.

The gender gap in technology is serious, but will not be around forever. The past shows that gender gaps shrink and often become nonexistent. Women have made tremendous gains in the last century. They have become leaders in math and science, have flown on space shuttle missions, and are successful leaders in all walks of life. The same will hold true regarding the technology gender gap.

Integrating Technology into the Curriculum and Teaching

A decade ago, educators discussed technology integration as something that would occur in the future. That future is now. Technology integration has moved from wishful thinking to public policy to reality. Under the No Child Left Behind Act of 2001, states that request educational technology funds must describe how they will promote and support technology integration into curricula and instruction by December 31, 2006.

As with so many things educational, money drives change. School districts are not going to let federal technology funds remain unclaimed. So, efforts to integrate technology will be fueled by federal, state, and local funding. School technology integration will also be championed by parents and the public, who think it is a good idea. They see how technology is integrated into daily life, and they want the same for schools.

A number of other events and processes promote technology integration. Certainly, the widespread use of the Internet and its availability to schools and classrooms has encouraged teachers to be innovative and try different approaches. A generational change has helped also, as more and more children who are technologically literate and savvy come to school. They are not content to engage in nontechnological approaches to learning. Students in and of themselves encourage their teachers—indeed, in many cases, tutor teachers—in technology use and applications. Widespread funding for the use of school-based technology through E-rate and business and industry development of new technology applications also make integration more attractive.

Technology integration can transform teaching. As a beginning teacher, you will want to examine your beliefs about teaching and learning and your beliefs about how technology can be applied to the curriculum. If you have not already thought about how you will transform your teaching to include technology then you must begin that process now. Ideally, you will have opportunities to view classrooms that integrate technology and use technology for delivering curriculum and activities. You will need to think about how to use technology to enhance student learning, to engage students in problem-based learning, and how students can use technology cooperatively to solve curriculum-based problems.

Integration of technology assumes that there is technology available to integrate. This assumption is not necessarily a safe one or a good one. You will have to recommend to administrators the kind of hardware and software you want and justify how you will use it to enhance teaching and learning. In addition, you will have to become adept at and comfortable with project-based learning and student self-directed learning. You will use technology to prepare and present classroom material. Your use of technology as a teaching tool is one dimension of technology integration. However, technology integration is really all about having students use technology to support their own learning. In other words, students are not only involved in learning activities using technology, they are using technology to learn, to collaborate with others, to engage in research, to learn how to think, to become self-directed learners, to achieve at high levels, and to pass state standard assessment tests. One of the transforming qualities of

Early Childhood

Standard 4: Integrates understanding of children and families, of developmentally effective approaches to teaching and learning, and of academic disciplines to design, implement, and evaluate positive learning experiences for all children.

Elementary

Standard 3.1: Plans and implements instruction based on knowledge of students, learning theory, subject matter, curricular goals, and community.

Standard 3.2: Understands how elementary students differ in development and approaches to learning; creates instructional opportunities that are adapted to diverse students.

Technology has an increasing impact on every facet of modern life, and education is no exception. Children and youth today are technologically oriented, and more and more teachers, like the one in this photograph, realize the importance of incorporating computers into the curriculum. You as a teacher in the new millennium will play an important role in helping your students become technologically literate.

technology integration is that it has the ability to extend learning beyond the traditional curriculum. Another is that it can transform you as a person and as a professional.

Balancing Drill-and-Practice with Discovery

A major controversy among early childhood professionals involves the purpose of computers in the classroom. On one hand, some say that drill-and-practice programs that emphasize helping children learn colors, numbers, vocabulary, and skills such as addition are not vitally important to the curriculum. These critics maintain that only software that encourages learning by discovery and exploration is appropriate. On the other hand, some professionals see drill-and-practice software as a valuable means for children to learn concepts and skills they need to succeed in school.

Of course, as with so many things, a middle-ground approach seems an appropriate course of action. Many students like drill-and-practice programs and the positive feedback that often comes with them. However, not all students like or do well with skill-drill programs. Technological aids, as with other learning materials, require that teachers identify and address students' learning styles. What is important is that all students have access to a variety of software and instructional and learning activities that are appropriate for them as individuals. (See the Profile for an example of a discovery learning approach.) This is what a developmentally appropriate curriculum is all about, and this concept applies to technology and software as well.

Profile   Project SMART: Alan Horowitz

Alan G. Horowitz is Chairman, Technology Education Department, Clarkstown Central School District, West Nyack, New York, and a part of the USA Today *All-USA Teacher Team.*

I have found that large-scale, hands-on projects for all students, including those with learning disabilities and in special education, can be very successful as a teaching tool. Students seem to learn better from the "big stuff" as long as it piques their imagination and interests. I use an integrating approach in my teaching, trying to link mathematics, science, and technology education as much as possible. With the growing shortage of engineering graduates and data pointing to our education system not keeping up with the demands in math, science, and technology education, I have found that the introduction of the large-scale special projects enhances my students' interest and enthusiasm in pre-engineering programs.

The first large-scale activity I did with the sixth-, seventh-, and eighth-grade students in my school was a full-size solar-powered vehicle called SPARC (for Solar Powered Advanced Research Car). The fully equipped, completed car has rack-and-pinion steering, hydraulic disk brakes, digital metering, coil-over-shocks suspension, turn signals, brake lights, a horn, and even a rear-view TV camera and screen. The students designed and built the car from scratch over a four-year period. This was very challenging for the youngsters but equally as rewarding. The looks on their faces as they drove the finished car around in the school parking lot for the first time said it all. SPARC, like most of my projects, was funded by grants and donations from all over the country and cost approximately $12,000 in supplies and material. The solar car has since been on display at shopping malls, science fairs, professional conferences, and even in the legislative office building in Albany, New York.

In September 2000, after the huge success of project SPARC, the math, science, and technology students of the Felix V. Festa Middle School began constructing a two-passenger, full-size, RotorWay International Exec 162F helicopter. This exciting, multiyear, interdisciplinary activity, called "Project SMART" (for science, math, and rotorcraft technology), continues to pilot the large-scale approach to math, science, and technology education. The purpose of this ambitious math/science/technology (MST) project is to give as many as 2,100 middle school students the opportunity to advance their mathematical, engineering, scientific, and technological interests, skills, and knowledge while building an advanced design rotorcraft vehicle.

As you can imagine, this project has been received with great interest and enthusiasm from students, parents, the Board of Education, and school district administrators. I had to raise over $80,000 in parent and corporate donations, fellowships, and grants toward the purchase of the helicopter kit and needed components. This took a lot of letter writing and grant applications to reach our goal. All in all, the fundraising wasn't that difficult, and after the project began, I found additional support and encouragement from many sources to keep Project SMART moving along. In May 2001, I earned my helicopter pilot's license in preparation to fly the aircraft when it's complete.

In addition to large-scale projects, other activities used with students in the technology education program include magnetic levitation (MagLev) vehicle design, rocket and rocket launcher construction, CO_2-powered vehicle design, and bridge construction and testing. Wind and smoke tunnels, an earthquake simulator, flight simulator, boat hull tester, CAD/CAM machine, and computers are also used with students to enrich their engineering experiences. These activities, along with Project SMART, make math, science, technology, and engineering education fun, interesting, and enjoyable for students . . . key ingredients for successful learning.

How Can Schools Pay for Technology?

Unfortunately, many schools do not have current technological capabilities due to funding and finances. To help solve this problem, Congress created the educational rate, or **E-rate**, to assist schools in attaining new technology, such as computers and Internet connections, by providing them with a technology discount. The E-rate was part of the federal Telecommunications Act passed in 1996 (PL 104-104) and is administered by the Schools and Libraries Corporation, which is part of the Federal Communications Commission (FCC).[20] The E-rate follows the 1934 tradition of universal service, which states that everyone should have access to telephone service. The E-rate extends the tradition by saying that telephone service includes "advanced" telecommunications. To apply for the E-rate, schools and libraries must develop a technology plan that should specify how they will integrate technologies into their curricula and programs. Specifically, plans should address the following five criteria:

> **E-rate**
> Educational rate—a technology discount given to schools to assist them in purchasing new technology such as computers and the Internet.

- Goals. The plan must establish clear goals and a realistic strategy for using telecommunications and information technology to improve education or library services.
- Staff. The plan must have a professional development strategy to ensure that the staff knows how to use these new technologies to improve education or library services.
- Needs. The plan must include an assessment of the telecommunication services, hardware, software, and other services that will be needed to improve education or library services.
- Budget. The plan must provide for a sufficient budget to acquire and support the nondiscounted elements of the plan: hardware, software, professional development, and other services that will be needed to implement the strategy.
- Evaluation. The plan must include an evaluation process that enables the school or library to monitor progress toward the specified goals and make midcourse corrections in response to new developments and opportunities as they arise.[21]

SECTION SUMMARY

What Issues Are Associated with the Use of Technology?

Technology and its use raise many issues in the schools.

- Ensuring Equitable Access to Technology. Equity is an important issue in ensuring that all students are computer literate. Poor and minority students have less access to equipment and less instruction in the use of technology, which means that they often lack the technological skills of their more advantaged peers. Technology can either narrow or widen the gap between the haves and the have-nots.

- Bridging the Gender Gap. Girls have one more hurdle to clear in sharing equal opportunities with boys. As a teacher, you will need to take care to encourage female students to take an active role in learning about information processing and using technology.

- Integrating Technology into the Curriculum and Teaching. Technology should be an integrated part of learning, not a game or reward for students who do tasks well or finish them expeditiously. Such integration takes careful planning and consideration of issues that affect teaching practice.

- Balancing Drill-and-Practice with Discovery. There is an ongoing and unresolved debate about the extent to which technology places too much stress on drill-and-practice at the expense of other activities that encourage discovery and exploration. As with most issues, a middle-ground approach seems appropriate.

- How Can Schools Pay for Technology? A section of the federal Telecommunications Act extends discounted or E-rate telephone service to cover advanced telecommunications networks for schools that apply.

What evidence of the technological gender gap have you experienced (or are you experiencing) in your own education? What can you do as a beginning teacher to try to ensure that the technological gender gap between boys and girls is eliminated?

_____

_____

_____

_____ ★

Applying What You've Learned

★ ★ ★ ★ ★ ★ ★ ★ ★

Visit classrooms in your local school districts. What evidence of the integration of technology into the curriculum can you find? What conclusions can you draw?

_____

_____

_____

_____ ★

Putting Yourself in the Picture

★ ★ ★ ★ ★ ★ ★ ★ ★

You have been selected to serve on a committee that will apply for aid from software and hardware companies to set up programs similar to Techbridge and Girlstart. Develop the basic components of a school-based program to involve elementary schoolgirls in technology. Then, contact the public relations departments of local companies of your choice. Ask for information about applying for a corporate grant to set up such a program.

_____

_____

_____

_____ ★

*W*HAT ARE THE LEGAL ISSUES IN TECHNOLOGY*?*

Copyright legalities and censorship are matters of concern to the general public as well as to educators (see the discussions on both topics in Chapter 8). The rapid acceleration of technological innovations such as the Internet has presented thorny issues in both these matters. There are no easy solutions to many of these issues, which await future determinations by the legislature and the courts.

Copyright Law and the Use of Technology

The United States has had a copyright law since 1790. The law protects eight types of works: literary works; musical works; dramatic works; pantomimes and choreographic works; pictorial, graphic, and sculptural works; movies and other audiovisual works; sound recordings; and architectural works.

A main issue in copyright law is the idea of fair use. **Fair use** is a concept that allows individuals to reproduce copyrighted material, with some limits, as long as it does not harm the market. Congress has no precise definition of fair use, but the law does cite four issues to consider in determining if fair use does exist:

Fair use
A concept that allows individuals to reproduce copyrighted material, with some limits, as long as it does not harm the market.

- The purpose or the character of the use
- The nature of the copyrighted work
- The amount used
- The effect on the work's potential market value

Guidelines for fair use were approved in 1996 at the Conference on Fair Use (CONFU). For example, the guidelines say that teachers and students may use 10 percent or 1,000 words of a book (whichever is less). Many of the guidelines have come under criticism from educational organizations that believe the guidelines to be overly restrictive and a hindrance to interdisciplinary instruction.

With regard to the Internet, copyright law may not be specific, but it still applies. The same rules that apply to print, recordings, and videotape also apply to the Internet. "Copyright's the kind of thing you've got to kind of parade out before your staff every year and go over," says Ted Czajkowski, assistant superintendent of the Bellingham (Washington) School District, whose Internet site (www.bham.wednet.edu) contains an extensive copyright policy. Refer to Figure 12.7 for an idea of Bellingham School District's copyright policy.

Many teachers may have an informal—and inaccurate—understanding of the issue, says Czajkowski: "Their memory is, 'As long as it's for educational purposes, you can do anything.' And, of course, that isn't the case."[22] Since the advent of the Internet and online publication, the public has often violated the copyright law. Instead of practicing the principle of fair use, many people copy documents, Web pages, and other materials

INTASC

Standard 9: The teacher is a reflective practitioner who continually evaluates the effects of his/her choices and actions on others (students, parents, and other professionals in the learning community) and who actively seeks out opportunities to grow professionally.

Copyright law and district policy do not allow the republishing of text or graphics found on the Web on the district Web sites or file servers without explicit written permission.

1. For each republishing (on a Web site or a file server) of a graphic or a text file that was produced externally, there must be a notice at the bottom of the page crediting the original producer and noting how and when permission was granted. In many cases, that notice should also include the URL (Web address) of the original source.
2. Students and staff engaged in producing Web pages must provide library media specialists with e-mail or hard-copy permissions to file before the Web pages are actually published. In case of "public domain" documents, printed evidence must be provided to document the status of the materials.
3. The failure of a site to display a copyright notice may not be interpreted as permission to copy the materials. Only the copyright owner may provide the permission. If the materials have been improperly and illegally displayed by a Web site, the manager of that Web site may not be considered a source of permission.
4. The "fair use" rules governing student reports in classrooms are less stringent and permit limited use of graphics and text.
5. Student work may only be published if there is written permission from both parent and student.

Staff members and students with questions regarding these guidelines are advised to check with the library media specialist in their building before proceeding with the collection of images and text.

Schools and nonprofit organizations may copy and make use of these materials within their own school districts or may republish the pages on their Web sites provided that a clear notice of source is included on the Web page.

_____

_____

_____

Reflect & Write

You will want to ask for a copy of your school district's copyright policy and review it to make sure that you and your students are in compliance. Review this copyright law policy. How would its provisions apply to you and your students if you were teaching in this school district?

Figure 12.7   Copyright Policy of Bellingham School District
Source: Bellingham Public Schools, Bellingham, WA (August 19, 2004). (Online). Available at www.bham.wednet.edu/technology/copyrule.htm. Reprinted by permission.

Middle Level

Standard 3: Understands the major concepts, principles, theories, and research related to middle-level curriculum and assessment; uses this knowledge in practice.

from the Internet, which, in some cases, is a direct violation of copyright law. However, legally there has been no violation, because until now there was no specific copyright law for the Internet. In 1998 Congress passed the Digital Millennium Copyright Act, which imposes new safeguards for software, music, and written works on the Net and outlaws technologies that can crack copyright protection devices. Although the act has been long overdue, it has come under criticism from academics, computer researchers, and librarians, who say that it will allow companies to build digital tollgates, thus hindering fair use rights that let educators copy and share material with certain limitations. The Library of Congress will set rules for exactly who is allowed exemptions from the new act, and with the help of the Commerce Department will determine if the new act blocks fair use access to copyrighted materials.[23]

What Does This Mean for You?

I'm sure that in response to the question "What does this mean for you?" one of the conclusions you have come to is that technology means a lot, and you're right about that. You will be involved in integrating technology into your teaching and administrative duties. You will use computers, the Internet, digital cameras, scanners, printers, voice amplification systems, assistive technology, video cameras, whiteboards, projectors, and many and varied kinds of software. You will use technology to prepare lesson plans; track student attendance; retrieve student data from state and local data bases to make instructional decisions (see data-driven instruction in Chapter 11); participate in staff development training; communicate with other teachers via chat rooms, online forums, and message posting boards; communicate with parents about school activities, student progress, and your teaching plans and activities; engage students in project-based activities and independent work; and generally participate in a culture of technology.

You will want to approach your teaching with an air of confidence and a willingness and ability to be a leader and innovator in integrating technology and creating a technological climate that enhances and supports student achievement and success.

Censorship and Control over Students' Web Pages

Another legal issue involves schools' control over students' Web pages. Chapter 8 mentioned that a school has the right to censor a school paper if the paper is vulgar and profane (refer to the Supreme Court case of *Hazelwood School District v. Kuhlmeier*). The problem that school districts and teachers face now is whether they have the right to censor a student-made Web page if it contains vulgarity, profanity, and other derogatory and threatening statements. "Schools need to be very careful before disciplining for anything students do outside school grounds," says Michael McGuire, a school lawyer in Minneapolis. "Unfortunately there is no case law on Web site issues to guide schools."[24]

With the advent of the Internet and cyberspace comes a whole set of issues for teachers and administrators. Principals have a legal right to censor student publications if they are produced as part of the curriculum. Many teachers hope that this authority can extend to student-owned Web sites, but this may not be the case. For example, at Westlake High School in Westlake, Ohio, a junior who posted a Web page on the Internet that mocked his teacher was paid $30,000 by the school after he was suspended.[25] Although such cases may be few in number, they pose serious questions as to the extent of the power that schools have over student use of the Internet. When students misbehave in class, they are usually disciplined for their actions. Regarding the Internet, the school can exert little disciplinary action.

Some schools have come up with codes of conduct for dealing with Internet issues in an attempt to alleviate any student pranks. For instance, Howard L. Pitler, principal of L'Ouverture Computer Technology Magnet School in Wichita, Kansas, provides this advice: "Respect yourself, respect others, be where you're supposed to be when you're supposed to be, and do not do anything that will keep others from learning—it's the same attitude that applies to cyberspace."[26]

Reflect & Write

As a teacher, can you think of any suggestions for a code of conduct on the Internet? Do you think a code of conduct that cannot be legally enforced will limit students' tendencies to play pranks on the Internet?

_____

_____

_____

_____

SECTION SUMMARY

What Are the Legal Issues in Technology?

The two major legal issues that you as a teacher will confront in using technology are copyright law and censorship.

- **Copyright Law and the Use of Technology.** As a teacher, you will be responsible for understanding the concept of fair use—the extent to which one person may use work created by another person. Copyright law governs your use of material posted on Web sites and on the Internet. Your role as an educator does not protect you from prosecution for violating copyright laws.

- **Censorship and Control over Students' Web Pages.** The extent to which school administrators and teachers can discipline students for material they post on their Web sites is not yet clear.

Thinking Critically
★ ★ ★ ★ ★ ★ ★ ★ ★

If you spent the better part of a month planning design and navigation steps, researching and writing content, finding graphics, and proofreading and fine-tuning a Web site, would you allow others to reproduce it without giving you credit for your work?

_____

_____

_____

_____ ★

Applying What You've Learned
★ ★ ★ ★ ★ ★ ★ ★ ★

You just bought a new computer and added the latest virus protection software to be sure your files will be protected. Does fair use give you the right to copy that software onto computers owned by your family members? Could you copy it onto the school computers your students use? Go to the library and do some research on copyright laws and find the answers to these questions. Share your findings with your classmates.

_____

_____

_____

_____ ★

Putting Yourself in the Picture
★ ★ ★ ★ ★ ★ ★ ★ ★

You are teaching a high school English class, and your students have just completed their final writing assignment for the year. You want to post the best and worst examples of their writing on a new Web site you're designing. Do you have a legal right to post their work without their permission? Do you have an ethical right to post their work without their permission?

_____

_____

_____

_____ ★

Applications for Active Learning

CONNECTIONS

1. After reading the Profiles about technology in this chapter, reflect on how you can teach literacy to your students. Make a list of five ideas sparked by these profiles.

2. Think about all the possible uses of technology described in this chapter. Create a picture, graphic, or figure that shows connections that are meaningful to you among those uses.

FIELD EXPERIENCES

1. Visit classroom programs that provide services to students with disabilities. Cite five ways in which technology is used to implement curriculum, help teachers teach, and promote learning.

_____

_____

_____

2. Some teachers and parents think children should not be introduced to computers at an early age. List reasons why they might feel this way. Then interview five parents and teachers. Ask them the following questions:

• Should young children be introduced to computers?

• At what age should young children be introduced?
• Why do you feel this age to be the best?

_____

_____

PERSONAL RESEARCH

1. I have provided you with many Internet resources and links. Select five of these and, as you explore them, make notes of ideas for use in your teaching.

2. Choose a particular theme and write a lesson plan to show how you would integrate technology relating to that theme into a subject you plan to teach.

Preparing to Teach

FOR YOUR PORTFOLIO

In the first section review, you made a list of some things you thought you could do to make yourself more technologically literate. Review this list now and develop plans for how you can accomplish your goals.

IDEA FILE

In Chapter 10, you wrote a paragraph on each of your three most important educational goals. Write another

paragraph here, describing how your mastery of technology could help you achieve those goals.

_____

_____

_____

Learning and Knowing More

WEB SITES WORTH VISITING

As you begin your teaching career and incorporate technology into your teaching, other teachers can help you meet your technology literacy goals for you and your children. A good place to begin is with the International Society for Technology in Education (ISTE). ISTE is the largest teacher-based, nonprofit organization in the field of educational technology. Its mission is to help K–12 classroom teachers and administrators share effective methods for enhancing student learning through the use of new classroom technologies. You can reach the ISTE at www.iste.org.

Another excellent resource to extend technology learning for you and your students is the Global SchoolNet Foundation (GSN). GSN is a nonprofit corporation and is a major contributor to the philosophy, design, culture, and content of Internet-based learning. Their mission is to "harness the power of the Internet" to provide ongoing opportunities to support learners both inside and outside of the school environment. You can find more information about the GSN at www.gsn.org.

Many professional organizations recommend that colleges of education incorporate technology in their curriculum so teachers are prepared to provide their students with valuable technology skills. See, for example, the NCATE's report

Technology and the New Professional Teacher: Preparing for the 21st Century Classroom. You can access this report at www.ncate.org/accred/projects/tech/tech-21.htm. After reading the report, consider how your teacher preparation program is or is not meeting the report's recommendations.

The CEO Forum on Education and Technology was founded to help ensure that America's schools effectively prepare all students to be contributing citizens and productive workers in the twenty-first century. You can review their *Year 4 Report* (2001), which assesses how well American schools are incorporating technology into their curricula, at www.ceoforum.org.

Hands-On Universe™ (HOU) is an educational program that enables students to investigate the Hands-On Universe while applying tools and concepts from science, math, and technology. HOU is currently developing activities and tools for middle school students, designing informal education centers, and implementing HOU in regional high school networks across the world, including Department of Defense dependent schools. Access their Web site at http://hou.lbl.gov and determine if you could use these activities in courses and subjects you plan to teach.

Milken Exchange on Education Technology
www.mff.org/edtech/
Offers online discussions, research analysis, and background data on a range of technology issues. Also offers up-to-date information about the use of technology in education.

National Council of Teachers of English
www.ncte.org
Offers teaching ideas that include technology and a forum for online conversations among teachers.

Logo Foundation
http://el.media.mit.edu/logo-foundation
The Logo Foundation supports a "constructivist" approach to teaching math skills and other subjects through the use of "Logo programming environments," which educators have used since the late 1970s. Includes current information and tips.

IBM Education
www.ibm.com/software/info/education/
Offers current information relating to the use of technology in education. Provides information on how to get help from IBM to incorporate technology into the curriculum. Shows profiles of schools currently working with IBM.

KidzOnline
www.kidzonline.org
Kidz Online is an educational organization dedicated to reducing the widening gap between the "information haves and have-nots." The members feel this can best be accomplished by having kids teach kids. The organization brings kids together electronically to share ideas, exchange viewpoints, and learn from each other.

Assistive Technology, Inc.
www.assistivetech.com
Assistive Technology, Inc., was founded in 1995 to develop innovative hardware and software solutions to increase the opportunity and enhance the quality of life of people with disabilities. This corporation provides innovative solutions to help people with learning, communication, and access difficulties lead more independent and productive lives.

Stanford University Libraries
http://fairuse.stanford.edu
This site contains a searchable data base for up-to-date information relating to copyright law and fair use.

The Virtual High School
www.wondertree.org/wondertree/virtualhigh.html
This is an example of a private school that uses Internet technology to provide an alternative to the traditional school.

Eisenhower National Clearinghouse
www.enc.org
This site offers links to outstanding math and science sites and free publications on topics related to teaching math and science. It provides information on assessment, conferences, grants, online courses, and school reform.

California Technology Assistance Project
www.ctap.k12.ca.us
Provides information relating to becoming a digital high school. Digital high schools focus on integrating technology into the curriculum so that students can meet the challenges of the twenty-first century.

SuperKids Educational Software Review
www.superkids.com
This site offers teachers and parents objective reviews of educational software. Also has online activities for children.

The Global Schoolhouse
www.globalschoolhouse.com
The site is for the well-connected educator. It contains articles and features on educational technology. Also, teachers are welcome to submit their favorite Web sites.

Blue Web'N
www.kn.pacbell.com/wired/bluewebn/
An online library of Blue Ribbon learning sites.

Classroom Connect
http://corporate.classroom.com
Classroom Connect is a dynamic Internet site that provides many "connections" to the classroom. Check out the searchable GRADES Internet links.

Federal Resources for Educational Excellence (FREE)
www.ed.gov/free
This site offers quick access to learning and teaching resources from the federal government.

BOOKS WORTH READING

Bitter, G. G., and Pierson, M. (2004). *Using Technology in the Classroom* (6th ed.). Boston: Allyn & Bacon.
Includes the most current information on the use of technology in the classroom: online educational resources, the latest in educational software, electronic communication, and emerging technology, as well as how to create Web-based instruction and utilize each of these elements in implementing a technology-based curriculum.

Desberg, P., and Fisher, F. (2001). *Teaching with Technology* (3rd ed.). Boston: Allyn & Bacon.
Teaching with Technology uses state-of-the-art technology to introduce educational technology to teachers. As an interactive CD-ROM disk, it combines the best aspects of books and software. It uses text and graphics to present information, but also uses technology to make the experience interactive. Students learn by doing and participating rather than through passive description.

Grabe, M., and Grabe, C. (2004.) *Integrating Technology for Meaningful Learning* (4th ed.). Boston: Houghton Mifflin.
This is an informative text, with practical examples of integrated applications of technology.

Means, B., Penuel, W. R., and Padilla, C. (2001.) *The Connected School: Technology and Learning in High School.* Hoboken: Wiley.
Reformers have long found that high schools are more difficult to change than elementary schools. It is especially interesting to read the stories of urban high schools that used technology to achieve their education goals.

Provenzo, E. F. (2002). *The Internet and the World Wide Web for Preservice Teachers* (2nd ed.). Boston: Allyn & Bacon.
This handbook serves as an excellent resource to help beginning teachers use the Internet and the World Wide Web. By following the National Council for the Accreditation of Professional Teacher (NCATE) guidelines on Technology and the New Professional Teacher, the author provides a practical and engaging introduction to using the Internet and the World Wide Web.

"Analyze data. Get uncomfortable. Make trouble."

Andrea S. Libresco is special assistant professor in the Department of Curriculum and Instruction at Hofstra University (New York), where she teaches social studies methods to preservice and inservice teachers at the graduate and undergraduate levels.

Since 1982, I have taught kindergarten through graduate school. When I need guidance as a teacher and a human being, I often turn to teachers in children's literature for advice. Three of them continue to help me practice the art and science of teaching.

First, Albus Dumbledore, headmaster of Hogwarts School of Witchcraft and Wizardry. Near the end of the second Harry Potter book, *Chamber of Secrets,* Harry questions whether he has ended up in the right Hogwarts house, or whether he should instead have been assigned to the house that Voldemort, the villain of the series, had lived in during his Hogwarts days. But Dumbledore reminds Harry that, although he could have ended up in Slytherin with the bad eggs, Harry had in fact requested of the Sorting Hat that he not be assigned there. Dumbledore reassures him, "It is our choices, Harry, that show what we truly are, far more than our abilities."

Teaching is *all* about choices. Choosing to listen to and learn from kids, all kinds of kids. Choosing materials that acknowledge the varied experiences of children in your community and beyond. Choosing to educate yourself in unfamiliar content so that you will have more choices in and out of the classroom in terms of planning—even if it's content you may have thought boring in your own school days. (After all, scientist Richard Feynman points out, "Everything is interesting if you look deep enough.") Choosing to acknowledge that you are a role model and that all of your choices are messages to the children in your class. Choosing to carry around a book at all times and share interesting ideas from it so that you show how much you gain from your own reading. Choosing to carry around and read a newspaper so that you model the behaviors of a good citizen for yourself and for your students. Choosing to check out a variety of sources until you're satisfied you've found the truth. Choosing to talk with veteran and new teachers about their curricular choices, their room set-up, the materials they select, how they communicate with children, with parents, and so on. Choosing to observe the world around you and make

transparent to your students that you delight in doing so—for its beauty and for what you learn from it. Choosing to notice and think about *everything*.

This puts me in mind of the second children's book that has teachers as role models for us: *Math Curse*. The book begins with the protagonist explaining about his teacher: "On Monday, Mrs. Fibonacci says, 'You know, you can think of almost everything as a math problem.' On Tuesday, I start having problems." The rest of the book is all about noticing how everything can relate back to math in some way, and it ends with, "Life is just great until science class, when Mr. Newton says, 'You know, you can think of almost everything as a science experiment. . . . '" I hope that everything you look at becomes a teaching and, by extension, a societal problem. I hope this for you in your personal lives and your political lives, which is really rather redundant, for I hope that you live your lives with the knowledge that the personal is political. And I hope that this knowledge will cause you constant discomfort.

One of the main characters in Herb Gardner's play *I'm Not Rappaport* goes through his life in constant discomfort, saying, "The only proper response to the outrageous is outrage." We live in outrageous times. If you're outraged by events in your school, in the profession as a whole, in the government that has an effect on your school and your profession, then get outraged and make trouble. But first we all need to know what to make trouble about. Go forth; gather data in your personal and political lives.

In your quest to gather data and make change, you'll certainly make some mistakes along the way. The final fictional role model I think of is the outrageous science teacher, Ms. Frizzle. Her continual charge to her students is, "Take chances. Make mistakes. Get messy." Good advice for students *and* teachers.

So, as you embark upon your teaching career, keep the maxims of Albus Dumbledore, Mrs. Fibonacci and Mr. Newton, and Ms. Frizzle in mind. Over time, you are sure to build on theirs with your own maxims. I leave you and your students with mine: "Analyze data. Get uncomfortable. Make trouble." Nothing less than our lives and the lives of our students are at stake.

How Will This Chapter Help You?

You will learn

★ how you can become qualified to teach

★ how to find your first teaching job

★ about what you can expect as a beginning teacher

★ how to collaborate with colleagues, parents, and the community

★ how you will be evaluated as a beginning teacher

The New York Times
expect the world®
nytimes.com

Themes of the Times

Expand your knowledge of the concepts discussed in this chapter by reading current and historical articles from *The New York Times* by visiting the "Themes of the Times" section of the companion Web site.

WHAT CAN YOU DO TO PREPARE FOR TEACHING?

Like all beginning teachers, you are engaged in the challenging process of becoming a professional. You have read a lot about teaching and are looking forward to your first year of teaching. Chapters 1 and 2 covered many of the factors involved in becoming a good teacher. This chapter continues the discussion of the themes of becoming a professional teacher in the context of looking forward to and getting ready for your first year of teaching.

As you prepare for your first teaching job, you will want to reflect on and make your own decisions about the experiences and advice of teachers like Andrea and others you've read about in this and other chapters. (See the Profile.) Your course work, field experiences, and other involvements are helping you prepare for teaching as you think about the many routes to getting a teaching license and becoming a teacher. This chapter provides additional ideas for what you can do now to ensure that your quest of becoming a highly qualified teacher is successful.

Reflect & Write

Make a list of some things you can do now to prepare for your first year of teaching. Add to your list other things you read about in this chapter.

_____

_____

_____

_____

Observe, Observe, Observe

Observation is an excellent way to prepare yourself for teaching. You will want to engage in a lot of observation of students, teachers, classrooms, schools, and communities. Observe students. Students are the focus of teaching and are the reasons schools exist. It makes sense for you to learn as much as you can about students, and observing them is one way to do this. **Observation** is an "authentic" means of learning about your students and about what they know and are able to do, especially as it occurs in more *naturalistic settings* such as classrooms, activity centers, child-care centers, athletic fields, playgrounds, and homes. Observation is the intentional, systematic looking at the behavior of a student or students in a particular setting, program, or situation. Observation is sometimes referred to as "kid watching" or "student watching" and is an excellent way to learn about your students' behaviors and learning.

Purposes of Observation. Observation is designed to gather information on which to base decisions, make recommendations, develop curriculum, plan activities and learning strategies, and assess your students' growth, development, and learning. For example, sometimes teachers and parents are more concerned with whether students are safe and orderly than with what students are doing or why they are engaged in a particular behavior or activity. However, students' behaviors provide insight into their learning. The significance and importance of critical behaviors go undetected if observation is done casually and is limited to "unsystematic looking." Through observation, you are able to

- Determine the cognitive, linguistic, social, emotional, and physical development of students. A good way to learn about students in general is to observe a student in particular. One method you can use is to develop a "portrait" of a student. Through your observation, you can assess and record your student's cognitive, linguistic, social, emotional, and physical development.
- Identify students' interests and learning styles. Today, teachers are interested in developing learning activities, materials, and classroom centers based on students'

Thoughts on the First Year: Fred Hutchinson

Fred Hutchinson has just completed his first year as a fifth-grade teacher at Ann Beers School in Washington, D.C.

I always wanted to have an influence on children. Every day, I felt like I was reaching children's lives and having an impact on their future. Every day, I dealt with people, and that felt good. A lot of my students don't have positive male role models in their lives. For many of them, I was the first—and that was fulfilling.

One of the things that made my year so satisfying was that my fifth-grade team of four teachers was very supportive. We met every day for lunch and had formal meetings once a week. We talked about lesson planning, curriculum development, discipline, integrating the curriculum—everything. My colleagues really helped me improve. Without them, the first year would have been difficult. I think all first-year teachers—all teachers, really—should have the opportunity to join with other teachers to collaborate and work together.

My administration was supportive also. When I had a problem, I felt comfortable going to my principal and other administrators. That's important for success, too, that the administration helps you when you need help and not just send you into the classroom and act as though you weren't there.

I also was lucky. I had five students with parents or families who were very involved. One was the PTA president, and he gave me tremendous support. Before I started teaching, I really didn't understand how important parents were in helping children learn and making teaching more meaningful and effective. All the parents had my home phone number, and a few of them called me regularly. Some teachers think that giving out your home phone number is a bad idea, but it worked for me, and I plan to do it again.

I did have some real challenges my first year. Keeping up with the paperwork was one of them. Grading all the students'

work was tough at first, but I expected that. It was the documentation of grades, behavior, and classroom activities that was almost overwhelming. At the beginning of the year, I was told to document everything, because parents want to see everything in writing. I took it literally! But eventually I learned what I did or didn't have to write down. Even more frustrating sometimes was the additional amount of paperwork—forms and requests—that the administration wanted in writing.

Last week my principal asked me to meet with a group of field experience students from the local university and talk about what I'd learned in my first year. I told them to do some soul searching and to consider their motivations for wanting to teach—to be sure they knew why they were choosing this career. I think it's important that people know why they want to do something, and this applies to teaching more than any other career, because you won't be a good teacher unless you understand why you're there.

I also said they should work on their lesson planning and ask their professors for suggestions about how to get the paperwork done. And to think about classroom management. You have to have a plan before you go into the classroom—you need to know how to handle transitions between subjects and other activities.

But the biggest thing I told them was to know and remember that they're not alone and to not be afraid to ask questions. Find a good teacher as a mentor. That helps more than anything. But also realize that there are limits to what you can accomplish. Idealism can take you only so far. You do touch lives, but you are not going to change every life in one school year. For that, there's next year—and I'm looking forward to it!

---

interests, preferences, and learning styles. Students' interests provide a channel for motivation and learning.

- Facilitate intentional planning. The professional practice of teaching requires planning on a daily, ongoing basis. Observation provides useful, authentic, and solid information on which you can base your intentional planning for activities.
- Meet students' individual needs. Meeting the needs of individual students is an important part of teaching and learning. Observation provides information about these individual needs. For example, a student may be advanced cognitively but be overly aggressive and lack the social skills necessary to interact cooperatively with others. Through observation, you can gather information to develop a plan for helping the student gain these skills.
- Determine students' progress. Systematic observation, over time, provides a rich, valuable source of information about how individual students and groups of students are progressing in their learning and behavior.
- Provide information to parents. As a teacher, you will report to and conference with parents on an ongoing basis. Observational information adds to other sources of data, such as test results and student work samples. Observation will provide you a fuller and more complete picture of individual students' learning and abilities.
- Develop self-insight. Observational information can help professionals learn more about themselves and what to do to help children.

Elementary

Standard 1: Knows, understands, and uses the major concepts, principles, theories, and research related to development of children to construct learning opportunities that support individual students' development, acquisition of knowledge, and motivation.

Middle Level

Standard 1: Understands the major concepts, principles, theories and research related to young adolescent development; provides opportunities that support student development and learning.

- Gather additional information. A great deal of the consequences, causes, and reactions to students' behaviors can only be assessed through observation. Observation enables you to gather data that cannot be assessed by formal, standardized tests, questioning, or parent and student interviews.
- Learn about students' prosocial behavior and peer interactions. Observation can help you plan for appropriate and inclusive activities to promote the social growth of students. Additionally, your observations can serve as the basis for developing multicultural learning activities.
- Provide a basis for assessing developmental stages. Many learning skills are developed sequentially. Through observation, you can determine whether students' abilities are within a normal range of growth and development.
- Assess performance over time. Documentation of daily, weekly, and monthly observations of students' behaviors and learning provides a data base for the cumulative evaluation of each student's achievement and development.

In summary, intentional observation is a useful, informative, and powerful means for informing and guiding teaching and helping you prepare for teaching and to ensure that all students will learn.

The steps involved in the process of systematic, purposeful observation are shown in Figure 13.1. You can use these steps to help prepare yourself for teaching.

Talk to and Observe Teachers. Talking to teachers and observing them in action is a great way for you to learn firsthand from the professionals what teaching is really like. Seasoned teachers can give you tips about these important matters:

- How to prepare for your first day
- Classroom management
- Managing stress
- Classroom organization
- Handling and staying on top of paperwork
- Planning and time management
- What is expected of teachers

Observe in Schools. Observing in a variety of different schools can be a real advantage for you as you prepare to teach. I recommend to my students that they observe in at least six schools in addition to their field placement schools and the school where they will student teach. These six schools should be two elementary, two middle, and two high schools. Students planning to teach in the elementary grades often question why they should observe in middle and high schools. My reply is always the same: "Education is about students, pre-K–12. In order to do a good job in your grade, you need to be familiar with all grades."

Make the Most of Your Field Experiences

School classrooms are only one setting in which you can gain field experiences. Other sites that provide experience and knowledge of students and families include private schools, homes, public agencies (for example, the March of Dimes), child-care centers, and social service agencies serving children, youth, and families.

Field experiences help you gain knowledge, skills, and insights not usually available in the college classroom. These experiences help you bridge the gap between theory and practice and give you firsthand experience with students and teachers. As Figure 13.2 suggests, participating in field experiences brings you, early in your career, into contact with the reality of teaching and allows you to test your ideas, reconsider your beliefs, and clarify your values about teaching and the professional role.

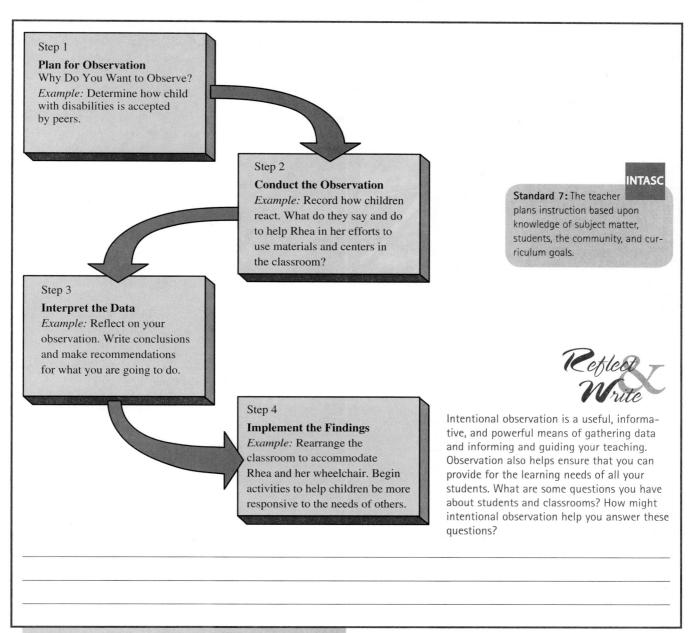

Step 1

Plan for Observation
Why Do You Want to Observe?
Example: Determine how child with disabilities is accepted by peers.

Step 2

Conduct the Observation
Example: Record how children react. What do they say and do to help Rhea in her efforts to use materials and centers in the classroom?

Step 3

Interpret the Data
Example: Reflect on your observation. Write conclusions and make recommendations for what you are going to do.

Step 4

Implement the Findings
Example: Rearrange the classroom to accommodate Rhea and her wheelchair. Begin activities to help children be more responsive to the needs of others.

INTASC

Standard 7: The teacher plans instruction based upon knowledge of subject matter, students, the community, and curriculum goals.

Reflect & Write

Intentional observation is a useful, informative, and powerful means of gathering data and informing and guiding your teaching. Observation also helps ensure that you can provide for the learning needs of all your students. What are some questions you have about students and classrooms? How might intentional observation help you answer these questions?

Figure 13.1 *Four Steps for Effective Observation*

Reflect & Write

In what field experiences will you be participating? What do you anticipate learning from each experience?

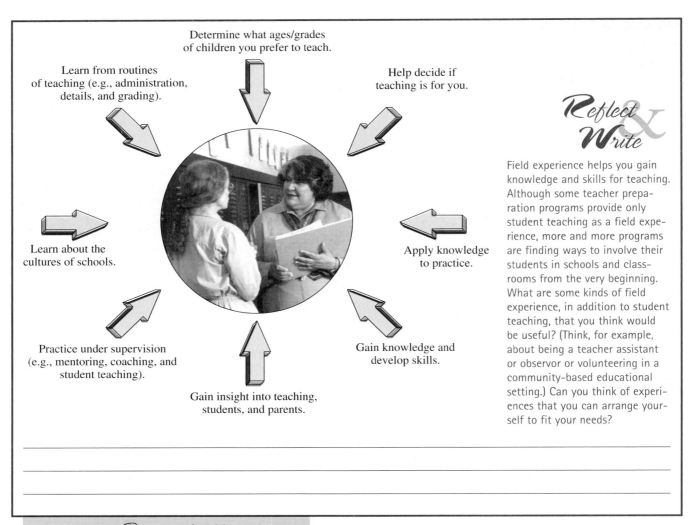

Determine what ages/grades of children you prefer to teach.

Help decide if teaching is for you.

Learn from routines of teaching (e.g., administration, details, and grading).

Apply knowledge to practice.

Learn about the cultures of schools.

Gain knowledge and develop skills.

Practice under supervision (e.g., mentoring, coaching, and student teaching).

Gain insight into teaching, students, and parents.

*R*eflect & *W*rite

Field experience helps you gain knowledge and skills for teaching. Although some teacher preparation programs provide only student teaching as a field experience, more and more programs are finding ways to involve their students in schools and classrooms from the very beginning. What are some kinds of field experience, in addition to student teaching, that you think would be useful? (Think, for example, about being a teacher assistant or observor or volunteering in a community-based educational setting.) Can you think of experiences that you can arrange yourself to fit your needs?

Figure 13.2 *P*urposes of Field Experiences

Participating in a PDS Program

NCATE

Middle Level

Standard 7: Understands the complexity of teaching young adolescents; engages in practices and behaviors that develop competence as a professional.

Chapter 2 introduced professional development schools (PDSs) and their role in the reform of teacher education. Professional development schools are intended, in part, to give preservice and inservice teachers opportunities to reflect on and talk about their practices, to engage in action research designed to test best practices, and to develop new teaching strategies. In professional development efforts, PDSs have four critical functions:

- Preparing teachers and other educators
- Providing continuing education for professionals
- Conducting inquiry
- Providing an exemplary education for all pre-K–12 students enrolled[1]

You may do part or all of your preservice training in professional development schools. Not all university teacher preparation programs have developed a PDS relationship with local districts. Some states, such as Texas, mandate by law that all teacher education programs establish and conduct preservice teacher education activities in professional development schools.

Pathways to Teaching

One of the ways to prepare for your first year of teaching is by completing requirements for certification. *Certification* and *licensure* are two terms people use synonymously and interchangeably. Simply put, **certification** is a voluntary process through which the profession recognizes individuals meeting high qualifications. The National Board of Professional Teaching Standards is responsible for the advanced certification of teachers. A teaching certificate specifies that you have met certain requirements and completed a program of skills training preparing you to teach.

"**Licensure** is a mandatory process whereby individuals interested in practicing the teaching profession must meet predetermined state qualifications."[2] The licensing process in the fifty states is administered through state organizations such as professional state standards boards (PSSBs), state standards boards, and departments of education. These agencies set standards that require teacher education candidates to successfully demonstrate that they are ready to teach. Thirty-four states now have standards for certification that conform or are comparable to the Interstate New Teacher Assessment and Support Consortium (INTASC) standards. The following specifics about licensure will assist you in planning for your first year of teaching:

Certification
A voluntary process whereby the profession recognizes individuals meeting high qualifications. The NBPTS is responsible for advanced teacher certification.

Licensure
The mandatory process whereby individuals interested in practicing the teaching profession must meet predetermined state qualifications.

- States have specific academic and education course requirements for obtaining a license. Some common course requirements include foundations of education, special education, bilingual/multicultural education, computer education, and drug abuse prevention. In addition, courses such as state history, American history, and psychology may be required.
- Most states require teacher candidates to pass a state examination as a condition of licensure. On the Praxis (see Chapter 2), individual states set their own passing scores.
- Some states provide a provisional teaching license that requires further study and/or the successful completion of a beginning teacher program before issuing a "permanent" license to teach. Most states issue a license with certain provisions such as further study and testing.
- Some states and school districts require fingerprinting and drug tests as part of the licensing process.
- Many states belong to the NASDTEC Interstate Contract, which enables teachers and other education professionals to have their licenses recognized in more than one state. Even within the IC, various states only have reciprocity with certain other states. For instance, Pennsylvania has reciprocity agreements with forty-five states, whereas New York has reciprocity agreements with only thirty other states. In Pennsylvania all candidates for certification must pass the Praxis test. Figure 13.3 lists certification requirements that states have in common. Reciprocity agreements are arrangements among states to honor one another's teacher certifications.

Performance–Based Licensure. Many states are implementing a system of performance-based licensure (PBL), a process that requires beginning teachers to demonstrate their knowledge and ability to teach. This is part of the PBL process in North Carolina:

1. A first-year teacher in North Carolina is an ILT (initially licensed teacher) and has three years to earn performance-based licensure (PBL). In essence, these three years are an apprenticeship period, a common practice in other trades and professions.
2. Each beginning teacher is assigned a mentor teacher, who acts as a coach, consultant, and mentor.
3. Over the three years, beginning teachers convert their initial licensure into a performance-based licensure through the completion of a performance-based product.
4. The performance-based product is based on the standards of the Interstate New Teacher Assessment and Support Consortium (INTASC). Material relating to the INTASC standards is identified in the margins of this text.

- B.A. or B.S. degree
- Completion of an approved program of teacher preparation
- Screening for moral character
- Recommendations from the college or previous employer
- Passing score on a basic skills and/or pedagogical knowledge and/or content knowledge test, such as Praxis or a state exam
- Minimum age (usually 18)
- Application fee (ranging from $165.00 in Alaska to $2.00 in Ohio)
- Ten states have a loyalty oath
- Course work in special education
- Sixteen states require fingerprinting
- Disclosure of prior license invalidation, dismissal, prior arrest, and prior conviction
- Recertification after the initial teaching certificate

For you to receive a teaching certificate, you need to complete all of the requirements in the state in which you plan to teach. Although specific requirements vary from state to state, most states share the twelve shown here. What does your state require? How prepared do you feel to meet those requirements?

_____

_____

_____

Figure 13.3   **Typical Features of States' Requirements for Certification**

Source: National Association of State Directors of Teacher Education and Certification, *NASDTEC Manual,* 1998 (Mashpee, MA: Author). Reprinted by permission.

5. The performance-based product is developed in the second year of teaching and is designed to demonstrate the ability to teach. Examples of evidence and artifacts that constitute the performance-based product are:
   - Unit and daily lesson plans
   - Teacher-made assessment materials
   - Classroom management plan
   - Parent communications log
   - Samples of student work
   - Photographs of student activities, classroom, etc.
   - Student, parent, and colleague surveys
   - Record of professional activities
   - Awards, recognitions, etc.
   - Publications

6. Salary increases are tied to the completion of the performance-based licensure and the earning of tenure in the fourth year. This process is in keeping with the national trend of tying pay to performance.

Quality assurance programs (or warranty programs)
Colleges and universities ensure the success of their teachers by providing mentoring and specialized assistance to those who do not meet school district standards.

Quality Assurance Programs. Some colleges of education are instituting **quality assurance programs**—guarantees or warranties for their new teachers in order to provide for quality assurance. For example, Figure 13.4 shows the Quality Assurance Guarantee of the Georgia State University Professional Education Faculty (for more information, visit them online at www.gsu.edu).

Would you want to be a beginning teacher who is "guaranteed"? Why? Why not? What could be some issues with such a guarantee?

_____

_____

_____

_____

Georgia State University's Professional Education Faculty guarantees that each individual recommended for initial educator certification . . .

1. Has completed an educator preparation program that is accredited by the National Council for Accreditation of Teacher Education (NCATE), Georgia Professional Standards Commission (GPSC), and the Southern Association of Colleges and Schools (SACS)
2. Has passed or exempted Praxis I (knowledge of basic skills) and has passed Praxis II (in certification area[s])
3. Has successfully completed a supervised capstone student teaching or practicum/internship experience in an accredited school setting
4. Has demonstrated knowledge of subject matter required to teach Quality Core Curriculum objectives in the specialization field of preparation at Georgia State University
5. Will demonstrate success in bringing students from diverse cultural, ethnic, international, and socioeconomic groups to high levels of learning
6. Will use telecommunication and information technologies as tools for learning when appropriate

Georgia State University will guarantee educators during the first two years immediately following graduation from Georgia State University or following recommendation by Georgia State University for initial certification, whichever occurs first. Any educator in a Georgia school who fails to demonstrate the essential skills will be provided additional training by Georgia State University's Professional Education Faculty at no expense to the educator or employer. That training will consist of an individualized plan agreed upon by the school district and the university that includes specific learning outcomes. Georgia State University assumes no responsibility for the educator's employment contract with the employer.

As the movement for accountability grows, even universities that train teachers are responding to the pressure for "quality control." Do you think such warranties of new teacher quality are worthwhile? Do you think a program can ensure items like 5 and 6 on this guarantee from Georgia State University?

Figure 13.4 *Quality Assurance Guarantee of the Georgia State University Professional Education Faculty*

Source: Georgia State University, *Educator Preparation.* (1999). (Online). Available at www.gsu.edu/~wwwedu/framework/guarantee.html.

Alternative Certification. Traditionally, the only route to teacher certification has been the completion of a bachelor's degree, including specified education courses in a college or university teacher education program approved by a state department of education. However, now another means is through **alternative certification,** the process whereby those with a bachelor's degree in any field can become licensed to teach. Alternative certification (AC) is a growing trend, and a number of factors contribute to its popularity:

Alternative certification
The process whereby those with a bachelor's degree in a field other than education become licensed to teach.

- An overall teacher shortage, especially in certain fields such as mathematics, science, and exceptional student education. Many school districts recruit mathematicians and scientists from business and industry to fill the need for teachers in these areas.
- Teacher shortages in inner-city and rural areas.
- The number of people seeking to enter teaching as a second career. For example, many unemployed turn to teaching as a second career. Alternative certification is one way to help the unemployed enter the teaching profession.

Emergency certification Temporary certification to teach granted to individuals without formal credentials, typically in hard-to-fill specialties.

- Dissatisfaction with the ways colleges of education have trained teachers. As discussed in Chapter 2, criticism of teacher training has led to new ways of educating and licensing teachers. One of the outcomes of teacher education reform is the desire of school districts, especially big-city school districts, to play a greater role in teacher education and certification. State departments of education are taking a more active role in helping design and implement alternative routes to certification. For example, the New Jersey Provisional Teaching Program provides training for candidates with bachelor's degrees before and during teaching as part of its certification process.

Across the nation, alternative certification programs are growing by leaps and bounds. For example, in Texas, for the first time, a majority of first-year teachers came from nontraditional sources. In fact only 46 percent of new teachers came from traditional college teacher training programs.[3] What seems to be clear is in the coming decade, the primary source of new teachers will be from some type of alternative certification program. I use the phrase "some type" intentionally. Many alternative programs are what are called "hybrids." They combine many features of certification into a particular model. In addition, more alternative certification programs are being conducted by for-profit companies, such as Sylvan Learning System.

Emergency Certification. In addition to alternative certification, many states and school districts provide **emergency certification** in areas of teacher shortage. Emergency certification is given to someone who lacks the skills and knowledge necessary for teacher certification. Emergency certification is usually valid for a period of two to three years. School districts may have particularly hard-to-fill areas owing to special circumstances; for example, higher rates of immigration may create a need for more bilingual teachers. As the demand for teachers continues to rise and as colleges of education fail to fully meet demand, alternative certification and emergency certification programs will increase. Other alternative routes, such as Teach For America, provide an inviting way to enter the teaching profession. (See the Profile and Education on the Move.)

Bilingual teachers are in great demand. Many school districts actively recruit both beginning and experienced teachers with bilingual abilities. Additionally, some districts pay higher salaries for bilingual teachers or offer signing bonuses to those teachers in short supply, such as bilingual teachers. The demand for bilingual teachers and for teachers to work with minority students will continue to increase.

Preparing for Teacher Examinations

The majority of states require the completion of the Praxis series of professional assessment for beginning teachers (see Chapter 2). Other states require their own state initial certification tests. Praxis I (Academic Skills Assessment) covers the areas of reading, writing, and mathematics, often referred to as "basic skills" and "enabling skills." Praxis II (Subject Assessments) tests students' knowledge of the subjects they will teach. Praxis III (Classroom Performance Assessments) is a performance-based assessment system for first-year or beginning teachers.

More than likely, you will participate in and successfully complete a beginning teacher program (BTP) that involves Praxis III–type assessment. The requirements of a BTP vary according to state and school district, but generally include the help of a **mentor teacher**—an experienced teacher judged highly effective and professional by colleagues and administration—the development of a

I grew up in Dallas, went to Princeton, and in my senior year was searching for a way to make a difference in the lives of others and in the world in general. I intuitively felt other college students were also looking for the same thing—a way to have an impact on society. It was this that led me to think of a teacher corps, and I became obsessed with the idea of inspiring some of the nation's most talented seniors to compete for teaching jobs in urban and rural schools.

I was rather naïve, and I really thought someone—some agency—would give me money for a teacher corps, so I progressed and it worked! The first year we inspired more than 2,500 people to apply, and we selected 500 to participate.

Teach for America is the national teacher corps of outstanding recent college graduates who commit two years to teach in urban and rural public schools. It seeks to build a corps of outstanding individuals who have an immediate impact in the lives of underserved children and who go above and beyond throughout their lives in pursuit of educational excellence and equity. We recruit aggressively from more than 200 colleges and universities. In 2004, we had 14,000 applicants apply for 2,000 teaching positions. Since 1989, when this program started, we have placed 12,000 teachers in everywhere from Los Angeles to the rural South to South Bronx.

The selection process is rigorous. We ask each participant to teach a sample five-minute lesson to a small group of other applicants. Applicants participate in small group discussions, and each is personally interviewed by Teach For America staff. Trained recruiters use these sessions to select people to participate in Teach For America. Teach For America seeks candidates who demonstrate leadership traits such as past demonstrated leadership, personal responsibility for success, critical thinking skills, the ability to influence and motivate others, and a desire to work relentlessly in pursuit of our particular mission. Once candidates are selected, they participate in a summer-long training program and then are placed in one of twenty-one school district sites across the United States that are part of the Teach For America network. The candidates commit to teach for two years in the school districts where they are placed as beginning teachers; during this time, they receive support and ongoing professional development. Then they join an alumni force of individuals working from within and outside of education to effect fundamental change.

All of us in Teach For America are unified by a common vision that one day all children will have an equal opportunity for an excellent education. We aim to build a truly effective movement among our nation's most promising future leaders to expand opportunities for children.

Corps members have exceeded traditional expectations, going above and beyond to impact their students' life prospects. Through their teaching experience, they have also gained the insight and added commitment necessary to be a lifelong leader for change. They are already running successful urban schools, serving as board members and legislators and working to improve health services, legal services, and more for their students. More information about Teach For America is available at our Web site www.teachforamerica.org.

education on the move >>>>>>>>>>>>

>>> Troops to Teachers and Spouses to Teachers >>>>>>>

Spouses to Teachers, the Defense Department's latest endeavor to help military spouses interested in teaching, is serving a similar purpose as the popular Troops to Teachers program.

Department of Defense (DOD) officials established Troops to Teachers in 1994, and responsibility for the program was recently transferred to the U.S. Department of Education. Troops to Teachers was created to help recruit quality teachers for schools that serve low-income families throughout America.

"Troops to Teachers laid the groundwork for Spouses to Teachers in providing individual state information," said Michael Melo, director of a Spouses to Teachers pilot program in Virginia and director of Virginia's Troops to Teachers program. Spouses to Teachers is currently a pilot program in six states: California, Colorado, Florida, Georgia, Texas, and Virginia. "The program was prompted by military spouses who were already teachers or interested in teaching but were facing difficulties finding certification requirements and job information when they moved," said Gary Woods, acting director of DOD educational opportunities.

The program offers information, counseling, and guidance to eligible, interested individuals. Initially, eligibility is limited to those with a bachelor's degree who are spouses of active-duty service members and members of the selected reserve or individual ready reserve on extended duty.

It also offers limited financial assistance to help defray the costs of meeting state certification requirements in the pilot states.

Source: S. L. Quig\ley, "Program Aims to Help Military Spouses in Teaching," *Air Force Link,* August 23, 2004. (Online). Available at www.af.mil/news/story.asp?storyID=123008473. Reprinted by permission.

Is Teacher Testing the Best Way?

After three years of preparation, Jessica Halstead got the first big test to fulfill her dream of becoming a first-grade teacher in her home state of Wisconsin. In March, Halstead took the Praxis II, one of the nation's leading exams for prospective teachers. The testing requirement, one of many long-awaited changes to the state's educator certification system, adds Wisconsin to a growing list of states requiring public school teachers to pass exams for subjects they will teach.

Opinion is divided about the usefulness of having potential teachers demonstrate their knowledge on a test. Some educators think there are better ways to determine who will be a good instructor. "There is no evidence that any teacher test by any company can accurately or fairly assess who is and is not likely to be an adequate first-year teacher," said Robert Schaeffer, public education director for the National Center for Fair and Open Testing (FairTest) in Cambridge, Massachusetts.

But Wisconsin Representative Luther Olsen, who headed the Wisconsin Assembly committee that oversaw the teacher licensing changes, pointed out that many professionals are required to pass tests before they can receive licenses. "Teachers are professionals, and if we're going to raise the quality of teaching in the state, we have to make sure teachers have at least some minimum standard of competency in what they're teaching," he said. "Testing may not be the best way to do this," Olsen conceded. "But it's one of the ways, and I think it's better than no test."[4]

What do you think? Is testing a good way to set minimum standards for teachers? Is it the best way?

You may want to find out more about the Wisconsin testing debate at www.isonline.com/news/state/aug04/249804.asp or visit an ongoing debate on teacher certification exams in Virginia at www.kimberlyswygert.com/archives/001746.html.

Mentor teacher
An experienced teacher—leader, guide, role model, supporter, and sponsor—who mentors beginning teachers.

Reflect & Write

portfolio, and evaluations by principals or other district personnel. Completion of the beginning teacher program can also include a performance-based assessment system such as Praxis III that covers planning and implementing instruction, classroom management, and evaluating student progress and instructional effectiveness.

You should check with the state agency responsible for teacher licensure to be certain you are taking the proper tests required for your beginning teacher's license. The Praxis Web site—www.ets.org/praxis—has a comprehensive list of each state's required exams. Sample items from the Praxis are available on the Praxis Web site.

Identify three specific actions you can take to begin preparing yourself for your certification exam.

_____

_____

_____

_____

SECTION SUMMARY

What Can You Do to Prepare for Teaching?

The courses you take, the fieldwork you participate in, and your interactions with experienced professionals all lay the foundation for a successful teaching experience.

- Observe, Observe, Observe. Observing teachers and students provides many opportunities to determine students' levels of development and their progress; to identify students' interests, learning styles, and individual needs; to provide a basis for planning; to convey information to parents; to gain insight and to reflect on practice and on your ideas and beliefs. Intentional systematic observation has a number of advantages and is carried out in four steps. Talking to teachers and observing them in action is a great way to learn firsthand from the professionals what teaching is really like. Observe in a variety of schools to get a real feel for what teaching is like. At a minimum, you should observe in six different kinds of schools at all levels from pre-K–12.

- Make the Most of Your Field Experiences. Field experiences play a significant role in preparing you for teaching. There are several options that can provide useful, practical knowledge of students and families (see Figure 13.2 on p. 472).

- Participating in a PDS Program. A professional development school (PDS) is meant to provide the following opportunities to preservice and inservice teachers: preparing teachers and other educators, offering continuing education for professionals, conducting inquiry, and providing an exemplary education for enrolled pre-K–12 students.

- Pathways to Teaching. All states have guidelines and requirements for teacher licensure and/or certification. Many states are implementing performance-based licensure, which requires beginning teachers to demonstrate knowledge and ability to teach. Some states also issue warranties of quality training of new teachers. Other routes to certification, or alternative certification, are increasingly available and becoming more popular and used. Emergency certification is also a possibility.

- Preparing for Teacher Examinations. Before you are licensed to teach, you may have to take and pass a teachers' examination such as Praxis. Working with a mentor teacher can be part of the preparation process.

Thinking Critically
★ ★ ★ ★ ★ ★ ★ ★ ★

Do you think that licensure exams such as Praxis are a good idea? Why or why not?

_____

_____

_____

_____ ★

Applying What You've Learned
★ ★ ★ ★ ★ ★ ★ ★ ★

Observe in a grade level or subject area you would like to teach. Observe specifically the characteristics of students, how learning occurs, and specific methods used by teachers. Explain how your observation will be helpful to you in your first year of teaching.

_____

_____

_____

_____ ★

Putting Yourself in the Picture
★ ★ ★ ★ ★ ★ ★ ★ ★

Ask your education professors or director of certification what tests you will have to take and pass in order to meet state licensure requirements. Also ask if you will participate in a beginning teacher program and what it will involve. Find out if your teacher training program is involved in a PDS or similar program and how the program works.

_____

_____

_____

_____ ★

How can you find your first teaching position?

Standard 9: The teacher is a reflective practitioner who continually evaluates the effects of his/her choices and actions on others (students, parents, and other professionals in the learning community) and who actively seeks out opportunities to grow professionally.

As you progress through your teacher education program, you can engage in a continuous process of searching for the job you want. Too often, students wait until the end of their program or after graduation to start the job hunt. There are a number of things you can and should do now.

Know Yourself

Your job search begins with you—who you are, your hopes and dreams, your strengths and weaknesses, the subjects you want to teach, and the students you want to teach. Ask yourself, "Am I a flexible person who is willing to try new things?" You should honestly analyze each of these areas. Review the self-assessment you completed in Figure 2.12 (p. 71) in answer to the question, "Is teaching for you?" Now that you have finished this course, what items in the self-assessment might you answer differently, and why? Also, review the self-assessment you completed in Chapter 9 on your philosophy of education and reflect on your responses. You might be surprised to find how your capacity for professional reflection and self-knowledge has grown. This capacity will help you be a better teacher and be clear about your priorities and goals as you look for your first teaching job. (See the Profile.)

Reflect & Write

From your knowledge about yourself, what are the three most important factors that will guide your job search?

_____

_____

_____

_____

Profile   **A Home-Schooled Teacher in a Public School: Sara Erickson**

Sara Erickson never played her flute in the pep band or sang in the school choir. She never even went to high school.

This fall, she will be a high school teacher.

Erickson, who was home schooled through twelfth grade, will be teaching music to both high school students and elementary students in the Kensal public school.

"It was just something that I wanted to do since I was 7 years old," she said.

Erickson, 25, graduated with a music education major from Union College in Lincoln, Nebraska, in May, married in June, and settled with her farmer husband near Cleveland, North Dakota, about an hour from Kensal.

She was delighted to find a job in her field.

"It was pretty nice, because I wasn't thinking that I would be able to use my major," she said.

She is one of four new teachers, the most the district with about 65 students has hired at one time since Superintendent Tom Tracy came to Kensal fourteen years ago.

He believes the school has a "teacher-friendly" interview process. He interviews teachers first and asks them questions

similar to ones they will face when they meet with the school board. "The board asks serious questions but also keeps things light," he said.

Erickson is preparing, nervously, to start her first year as a music teacher.

"It's hard to take a program from someone else," she said. "It's really hard to pick out music."

She believes she knows what to expect from life at a public school, after student teaching in schools in Lincoln. "The flexible part of it is way different," she said.

She is sprucing up her new classroom, which has pale blue walls, a semicircle of gray metal folding chairs, and a few decorations hung by the last teacher.

"It's kind of dull for me," she said.

She plans to add new posters to brighten the walls and perhaps some new music. She purchased a CD player for the music room, and she has been going through music selections for her students.

"I would like them to enjoy music most of all, but I would also like them to learn discipline," she said.[6]

Prepare a Portfolio

Developing and compiling a portfolio is both a process and a product that will help you be a better teacher and also will help you get your first job. A **teacher portfolio** is a selected collection of data that describe your expertise and proficiency in areas associated with effective teaching. Your portfolio can be used as a record of authentic assessment and as an overall evaluation of your performance. As a portrait of you, it is an invaluable tool for interviews and other situations in which you need to provide evidence of your abilities.

A portfolio serves many other useful purposes as well. It helps you reflect on and evaluate your performance over time and provides a record of your past accomplishments as a benchmark against which to constantly improve your performance. You can also continually add to your portfolio as you progress toward certification. Many colleges and universities use portfolios in their teacher preparation programs as one measure of assessment to augment standardized tests and classroom observations. Many teachers continue to develop their professional portfolios throughout their careers.

What you include in your portfolio depends on the specific purposes for which you will use it. You can add to and delete from your portfolio according to circumstances. A portfolio is not a collection of all your work, only the best and most relevant. Some artifacts to consider for inclusion are:

- Videotapes of yourself presenting lessons with different students in a variety of situations
- An up-to-date resume
- A statement of your philosophy of teaching
- Photographs documenting and illustrating your performance, student products, and so forth (for example, you with students, your classroom, classroom activity outcomes, and bulletin boards)
- Your teaching journal or samples from it demonstrating how you have reflected on and improved your teaching (Your responses to many of the reflection write-ins in this textbook would be suitable for inclusion in your portfolio.)
- Examples of lesson plans
- Observations by supervising teachers, college instructors, and colleagues
- Examples of students' work and specific examples of how you have evaluated students' work and made suggestions for improvement
- Letters and notes from parents and others commenting on your performance and efforts during your field experiences and student teaching
- Summaries and commentaries of professional development activities in which you have participated

The For Your Portfolio feature at the end of each chapter of this textbook gives you more ideas for what to include in your portfolio. You will find that your portfolio can be an invaluable tool to help you grow as a professional. In addition, it can help you get the job you want.

Analyze Job Opportunities

Knowing yourself as a teacher helps you establish your personal and professional criteria for evaluating job opportunities. Finding a match between what you want and what is available is the central task of any job search, and this includes knowing where the jobs are.

Review the information in Chapter 2 about teacher supply and demand nationwide. Part of your analysis of job opportunities would include finding areas where demand is high or where there are teacher shortages. Demand is greatest, for example, in urban and rural areas and in areas of greatest population growth, such as in the southeastern and southwestern United States.

Matching your qualifications with areas of critical shortage is another consideration in analyzing job opportunities. If you have training in special education,

Teacher portfolio
A selected collection of data that describe a person's expertise and proficiency in areas associated with effective teaching.

Early Childhood

Standard 5: Uses ethical guidelines and other professional standards; is a continuous, collaborative learner who demonstrates knowledgeable, reflective, and critical perspectives; is an informed advocate for sound educational practices.

Elementary

Standard 5.1: Understands and applies practices and behaviors that are characteristic of developing career teachers.

bilingual education, or science, for example, you can expect to find a greater number of job opportunities to investigate. In addition, teaching jobs may be more plentiful at certain times of the year. Teachers seeking local positions, for example, take advantage of last-minute vacancies that appear in the Help Wanted sections of newspapers near the end of every summer and at the beginning of school breaks.

You can find information about teaching opportunities through a variety of sources and agencies, described in the following sections.

Recruiters and Job Fairs. Your first job in teaching and your teaching career may begin with the visit of school district recruiters to your campus. Many large school districts actively recruit all across the United States to get the teachers they need. For example, the Dade County (Florida) public schools hire over 2,500 new teachers each year. The school district has more than thirty trained recruiters who visit colleges and universities all over the United States. Recruiters search for the best teachers in all areas and especially focus on recruiting minorities and teachers in critical shortage areas such as special education. At a recent job fair in Carrolton-Farmers Branch (Texas) School District, 825 prospective teachers showed up, the best ever turnout. Hiring at the job fair is no-nonsense. Dr. Hopkins, the executive director of personnel for Carrolton-Farmers Branch School District, had this to say: "Principals have the final decisions on hires, and if they agree on a recommendation, they fill out a form and submit it. We do extensive background checks and if everything checks out, we call with an offer to the applicant."[5]

College Placement Services. Many colleges have a placement service that helps college graduates find jobs. Placement services provide help with resume writing and developing interview skills and act as clearinghouses for prospective employers by assisting them in setting up and conducting on-campus interviews. Placement services also have lists of vacancy notices from school districts across the country. Check with your placement agency to see if these vacancy announcements are available online.

Job fairs provide an excellent opportunity to learn where the teaching jobs are. Many job fairs are an employment smorgasbord: Districts showcase a wide range of positions— some you might not even have thought about! In addition, you have an opportunity to talk with school and district administrators, who can explain what their districts and schools are looking for. And you have an opportunity to "sell" yourself. Many job seekers walk away from a job fair with interviews scheduled—or even their first teaching job!

Many placement services operate a credential service, which is a clearinghouse for sending your files to prospective employers. Credential files usually include a resume, copies of transcripts, letters of recommendation, and information on the type of position sought. Placement services send a fixed number of credentials—usually three—and then charge a fee for each additional one they send.

When asking people to write letters of recommendation for you, select people who are very familiar with your abilities and performance. These are usually professors, a supervising professor, and a teacher. Be sure to tell your recommenders the kind of positions you are applying for and share with them significant facts about you that they can include in their letter. You want your letters of recommendation to set you apart from other candidates. Letters of recommendation state your significant achievements and describe your personality and character traits. It is important that a letter of recommendation emphasizes your ability to work with many kinds of students and parents, and states your ability to work well with others.

State Departments of Education. State departments of education have continually updated lists of teacher vacancies throughout their state. Contact the state where you are interested in teaching and request a list of job openings. Use a search engine to find the Web site of state departments of education.

Networking. There is probably no better way to find a teaching job than through personal networking and networking on the computer. Often it is whom you know that counts. As a prospective teacher, you will want to network with the people who can tell you about job openings and school district needs and/or who can get you connected with those who do know where the jobs are or have the authority and responsibility for hiring. Make your availability and preferences known, and do not hesitate to ask others to help you find a job. The more others know about your job search, the more likely that someone will help you make the right connection.

School District Contacts. Contacting school districts that interest you is another good way to find out about available vacancies. A letter of inquiry asking for a list of position vacancies will provide current information that you can get directly from the source. Also, job announcements published by a district usually have much information that is good to know, including starting salary, where to send letters of application, and a job description. Most school districts have Web sites that you can access to find out about employment opportunities. For example, when you visit the Dallas Independent School District's Web site at www.dallasisd.org, you can click on their "employment" button to access the district's current job openings. In addition, there are numerous job search engines on the Web, including Career Builder (www.careerpath.com) and the Monster Board (www.monster.com), both of which allow you to post your resume and search job listings geographically. (See Education on the Move.)

Reflect & Write

In analyzing job opportunities, what information about a school or school district would be most important for you to know?

_____

_____

_____

_____

Teacher Salaries. Part of analyzing job opportunities is to also analyze the salary you will receive. When teachers identify their reasons for teaching, love of money is not one of them. And, I'm sure you know that teaching is not going to make you rich, dollar wise. Nonetheless, you need to be realistic and consider the teaching salaries.

>>> Live Talent Search for New Teachers >>>>>>>

What's quick, easy, and sorts applicants for teaching jobs by how much promise they show?

Until recently, that riddle was perplexing. Putting prospective teachers though standardized interviews about their approach to the job might fulfill a sorting function, but it was time consuming on both sides. Online applications, though they can be relatively quick and easy, tend to give a school district too little information about the real-world potential of candidates.

But with the latest in technology, some district hiring experts and their partners in the private sector say they've got the answer. By giving candidates a short online talent assessment that returns results to the district almost immediately, a school system has a better chance of snagging the best people at a cost it can afford—a practice that is gaining ground.

"We're working a lot smarter by using the screen[ing test]," said Cordelia G. Harris, the recruitment manager for the Cleveland schools, one of the first districts to sign up for the Gallup Organization's latest teacher assessment. "And the price is very reasonable."

Another sign that the tests are gaining popularity is the entry into the field of Kenexa Technol-ogy, a human resources manage-ment company that makes more than fifty job aptitude tests for private employers. Kenexa recently partnered with the Wake County (North Carolina) school district to design the company's first such tests for schools.

Not only does the 109,000-student district hire about 1,200 teachers a year, but it's also trying to improve its retention rate by ensuring a good fit from the start.

The test, which takes about thirty minutes, can be accessed from any Internet-connected computer, anytime. "The district receives the score almost immediately," said Ame Creglow, the director of operations for Kenexa's assessment division.

The convenience of online applicant screening has even lured districts into devising their own tools. Pennsylvania's Lower Merion district requires a "preliminary interview" as a part of its online application. That instrument asks candidates about their education and experiences inside schools and out, but it also poses questions of belief and judgment. One, for example, tries to ascertain the test taker's attitude toward assessments.

Source: Excerpted from B. Keller, "Schools Employing Online Talent Tests to Screen Prospects," *Education Week,* May 19, 2004. Available online at www.edweek.org/ew/articles/2004/05/19/37hiring.h23. Reprinted by permission.

Look back at Figure 2.11 (p. 67), and then look at Figure 13.5 for a better idea of what you can expect.

Apply for a Teaching Position

Applying for a job is one of your most important responsibilities as you finish your program of teacher preparation. It is also one of the most rewarding experiences of your life, for you will always remember your first job and how you got it. One of your first jobs will be to prepare a resume, which is a clear summary of you, your education, experiences, and accomplishments. When writing your resume, use the KISS principle—keep it short and sweet—one page is usually enough and is about all a prospective employer wants to read. Have one of your professors review your resume and advise you on content and format. Your goal is to have an error-free resume that will persuade an employer to hire you. The following list suggests some information to include in your resume:

- Educational background
- Honors, recognitions, and awards
- Experiences (Make sure you include all that might be of interest to a future employer. The fact that you volunteered in an inner-city literacy program may make the difference between getting and not getting an interview.)
- Professional memberships
- Activities, interests, and involvements in organizations (A good background of extracurricular activities is important.)

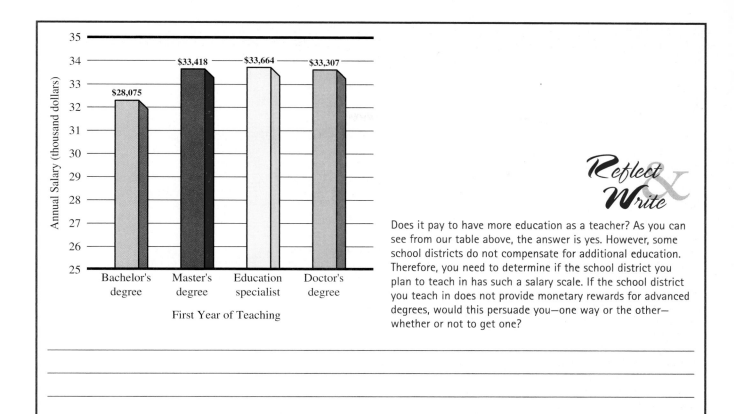

Figure 13.5 *A*verage Teacher Salary by Degree for First-Year Teachers

Source: U.S. Department of Education, National Center for Education Statistics. Schools and Staffing Survey (SASS). (2002). (Online). Available at http://nces.ed.gov/programs/digest/d02/tables/dt079.asp.

The preceding items in a resume can also serve as a guide for what you should be doing now to ensure that you have qualifications and experiences to include in your resume when applying for your first teaching job. The figures on the next several pages provide examples of some of the documents you will need to prepare when seeking a teaching job and other information that can help you prepare for potential interviews. The better prepared you are, the greater your chance of finding the right job. The process begins with the resume. Figure 13.6A is the resume of Maria del Carmen Lopez, which you can use as a model. Be sure to personalize your resume so that you are "putting your best foot forward."

When applying for a job, you will be writing three kinds of letters: a letter of inquiry, a letter of application, and a follow-up thank-you letter. Your letter of inquiry introduces you, states the positions you are seeking, inquires about the procedure for applying, and requests an application. Maria del Carmen's letter of inquiry is shown in Figure 13.6B.

Your letter of application officially makes application for a particular position and states your qualifications. Your letter should state your specific qualifications for the position and why you are an excellent candidate. This is the letter that sells you and is the one that often determines if you will get an interview. Your resume should accompany this letter. Also indicate if you are having your credentials sent by the placement office. Figure 13.6C shows Maria del Carmen's letter of application.

Your third letter is a thank-you and follow-up letter to either your letter of application or an interview. In it, you should still "put your best foot forward" and

Maria del Carmen Lopez
1234 South 56th Avenue
Miami, Florida 33133
(305) 555-7890

OBJECTIVE
Employment as an elementary school teacher in Dade County

COLLEGE EDUCATION
Bachelor of Arts in Elementary Education, 2005
    Minor in Psychology   GPA: 3.7
    Florida International University
        —Phi Delta Kappa
        —Alpha Phi Omega Service Fraternity

PROFESSIONAL AFFILIATIONS
Member of National Association for the Education of Young Children
Member of Florida Association for the Education of Young Children

TEACHING EXPERIENCE
Spring 2005   Coral Reef Elementary School, Miami, Florida
                 Third-Grade Student Teacher

                 Banyan Elementary School, Miami, Florida
                 Kindergarten Student Teacher

Fall 2004   South Miami Heights Elementary School, Miami, Florida
                 Practicum Student in Fifth-Grade Classroom

2002–2004   Upward Bound, Miami, Florida
                 Volunteer Reading Tutor

OTHER EXPERIENCE
Volunteer Work: Big Brothers and Big Sisters Program
                 Special Olympics Coach
                 Pee-Wee Soccer Coach

References Available upon Request

Figure 13.6A   Sample Resume

continue to sell yourself as the best candidate for the position. In any event, common courtesy dictates that you thank people for helping you.

Have a Successful Interview

Your interview is one of the most important parts of getting your first job. In many respects, it is the make-or-break part of job hunting. It is important that you be well prepared for the interview by anticipating what will be asked and how you will answer specific questions. Figure 13.7 gives guidelines for preparing for your interview. The purpose of the interview is twofold: to enable the school district to decide if they want to hire you and for you to convince the school district they should hire you. Maria del Carmen Lopez may be asked questions like those shown in Figure 13.8. You should be prepared for interview questions such as these.

1234 South 56th Avenue
Miami, Florida 33133
(305) 555-7890

March 15, 2005

Ms. Barbara Thune
Dade County Public Schools
2800 Thames Drive
Miami, Florida

Dear Ms. Thune:

In two months I will be graduating with a Bachelor of Arts degree in elementary education from Florida International University.

My formal education program included a fifth-grade teaching practicum at South Miami Heights Elementary School and a kindergarten student teaching position at Banyan Elementary School. I am currently involved in a third-grade student teaching position at Coral Reef Elementary school. As you can see I have worked in a variety of schools and a good range of grade levels.

My primary objective is to start working in my field as soon as I graduate, so I am flexible enough to accept whatever position may be available for either the summer or fall of 2005.

I believe my extensive field experiences and my enthusiasm for teaching make me an excellent addition to any elementary school staff.

Please send any application material I may need to the address above.

Sincerely,

Maria del Carmen Lopez

Maria del Carmen Lopez

Figure 13.6B **Sample Letter of Inquiry**

SECTION SUMMARY

How Can You Find Your First Teaching Position?

Your first stage of becoming a teacher is your teacher preparation program. As you progress through it, you will become increasingly more engaged in identifying and searching for the type of teaching position you want.

- Know Yourself. Finding your first job involves knowing yourself. You started this process when you considered taking this course. Reflect on how you have grown in your thinking about being a teacher since the course started.

- Prepare a Portfolio. Preparing a portfolio is an ongoing process in which you compile data that describe your expertise and proficiency. Your portfolio presents a portrait of you as a teacher. Others will use your portfolio as a record of authentic

1234 South 56th Avenue
Miami, Florida 33133
(305) 555-7890

May 9, 2005

Ms. Barbara Thune
Dade County Public Schools
2800 Thames Drive
Miami, Florida

Dear Ms. Thune:

Enclosed please find a completed application, along with references and resume, for employment as an elementary teacher in the Dade County Public Schools.

I graduated from Florida International University (FIU) in April with a Bachelor of Arts degree in Elementary Education. My training at FIU included a fifth-grade teaching practicum at South Miami Heights Elementary School. As a student teacher, I was placed at Banyan Elementary School in Kindergarten and Coral Reef Elementary School as a third-grade teacher. I have worked in a variety of school settings and a range of grade levels.

I believe my extensive field experiences and my enthusiasm for teaching make me an excellent addition to an elementary school staff.

I am available for an interview on Mondays and Wednesdays and can be reached at home after 3:00 p.m. at (305) 555-7890.

I look forward to meeting you soon.

Sincerely,

Maria del Carmen Lopez

Maria del Carmen Lopez

Figure 13.6C   Sample Letter of Application

assessment and to evaluate your teaching performance. You can use it to measure your own growth and to help you evaluate and improve your teaching practice.

- **Analyze Job Opportunities.** To find a match between your special qualities, skills, and training, and the job opportunities available to you, you will need to do some intensive research. Resources you may want to consult include recruiters and job fairs, college placement services, state departments of education, personal and computer networks, and school districts that interest you.

- **Apply for a Teaching Position.** To apply for a teaching position, you will need an up-to-date, one-page, error-free, personalized resume that reflects your best qualities. You will also be writing letters of inquiry, letters of application, and—assuming you gain an interview—a follow-up thank-you letter.

Before the Interview

Your successful interview starts long before the interview itself. Here is what you can do to prepare for the interview.

- **Anticipate what questions will be asked.** You will be asked questions about classroom discipline, a typical day in your classroom, why you chose teaching as a career, and your philosophy of education.
- **Write out your answers to potential interview questions.**
- **Practice interviewing with a colleague.** You can use your prepared answers from simulated interviews to help answer the real questions in an interview.
- **Complete all the paperwork that accompanies an application and the interview.** Many districts have an application process that includes many forms. All paperwork needs to be completed thoroughly and neatly. Your application is you. If the application requests all official transcripts, make sure you have requested them, and that they are with the application.
- **Develop a short list of questions you want to ask the interviewer.** It is important for you to ask questions so that you have the information you need to make an informed decision and to demonstrate that you are genuinely interested in the position. Some questions you may want to ask are:
  1. What are some important characteristics of the school district and the student population?
  2. What is the philosophy of the district or school? (Ask for a copy of the district's mission statement.)
  3. What is the curriculum in the grades and subject areas I will be teaching?
  4. What does the district do to support professional development? Does the district reimburse for graduate study?
  5. Will I be assigned to a school and grade level, or will I get to choose the school and grade level I want? (A question such as this depends on the local school district. In smaller school districts, you are generally interviewing for a particular job. In large districts, after

a general interview, you may be sent to local schools to interview with principals.)
  6. What other assignments are included in the job?
  7. What is the starting salary? What are the benefits?
  8. How does the beginning teacher program work?

During the Interview

- **Dress professionally.** While the law does not allow for discrimination on the basis of dress or hair, appearance does matter to professionals, students, and parents.
- **Speak clearly and forthrightly and answer the questions asked.** Avoid answering just "yes" or "no" to a question. Expand on the questions you are asked.
- **Be positive and enthusiastic.**
- **Don't limit yourself to a particular age group, grade level, or subject area.** You may be able to teach things you never thought you could before. Many principals want teachers who are willing to try different things and get involved. If in the interview you say you are willing to consider teaching more than one grade level and to be involved in after-school activities, you will make yourself more desirable as a candidate and more valuable to the school and district. Principals and hiring committees are looking for teachers who can help get the job done.
- **Be prepared to respond to a number of people during the interview.** In addition to the principal, you may also be interviewed by teachers, parents, and community members.
- **Talk about the satisfaction you have gained from teaching.** Hearing your feelings and thoughts gives interviewers insight into your attitudes and goals.
- **Describe how you and others assess your effectiveness as a teacher.**

After the Interview

- **Write thank-you letters to all involved.**
- **Reflect on the interview process.** Analyze what went well and how you can improve.
- **Make necessary changes.** Revise your responses, and plan how you will approach your next interview.

Asking questions is always a good thing to do at a job interview. Can you think of other questions you might want to ask besides those listed here?

_____

_____

_____

Figure 13.7 *A* Successful Interview

- Have a Successful Interview. If your letter of application and your resume lead to a job interview, you will have the opportunity to convince the school district to hire you. To make your interview as successful as possible, you should anticipate questions that are frequently asked, such as those in Figure 13.8. You should dress and act professionally and remember to ask the questions you want to have answered. After the interview, you should follow up with a thank-you letter as soon as possible.

- **Your Education and Background:** Briefly describe your education background and explain how it has prepared you to teach.

- **Work Experiences:** What work and volunteer experiences have you had, and how have they helped prepare you for teaching?

- **Strengths and Weaknesses:** What do you consider to be your particular strengths as a beginning teacher? What are your weaknesses, and how do you plan to strengthen them?

- **Teaching:** Why did you select teaching as a profession?

- **Meeting Special Needs:** How do you plan to meet the special needs of students in your classroom? Give an example of how you would plan to meet the special needs of a student in your classroom with a disability.

- **Curriculum:** What kind of curriculum do you think is appropriate for the students you will teach? What was your most successful lesson?

- **Preparation and Planning:** What are things you will do to prepare and plan for instruction? What kind of planning have you done?

- **Instruction:** What instructional strategies do you think are most effective?
  How will you meet the individual needs of your students?

- **Evaluation:** What techniques will you use to evaluate student learning?

- **Classroom Management:** What kind of classroom management techniques do you plan to use?

- **Parent/Family/ Community Involvement:** Describe how you plan to involve and communicate with parents.

- **Philosophy/Beliefs:** What are your core values and beliefs about education? About students? What is your philosophy of education?

- **Collaboration:** Do you get along well with others? What are some people skills that you use when collaborating with others?

- **Extracurricular Activities:** What extracurricular and community activities have you participated in? What extracurricular activities would you be able to supervise?

An interview is one of the most important steps in helping you get the job you have always wanted. Which of these interview questions would you have the most difficulty in answering? Which of these interview questions will you have to prepare for the most?

_____

_____

_____

Figure 13.8   Typical Interview Questions

Thinking Critically
★ ☆ ★ ☆ ★ ☆ ★ ☆

From your knowledge about yourself, what are the three most important factors that will guide your job search?

_____

_____

_____

_____

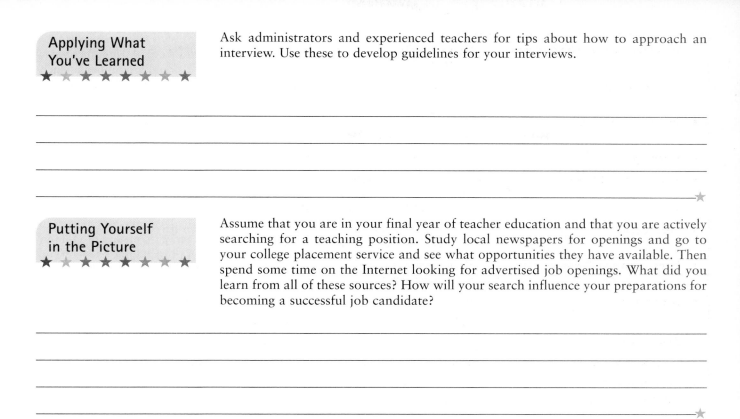

Applying What You've Learned

★ ★ ★ ★ ★ ★ ★ ★

Ask administrators and experienced teachers for tips about how to approach an interview. Use these to develop guidelines for your interviews.

_____

_____

_____

_____★

Putting Yourself in the Picture

★ ★ ★ ★ ★ ★ ★ ★

Assume that you are in your final year of teacher education and that you are actively searching for a teaching position. Study local newspapers for openings and go to your college placement service and see what opportunities they have available. Then spend some time on the Internet looking for advertised job openings. What did you learn from all of these sources? How will your search influence your preparations for becoming a successful job candidate?

_____

_____

_____

_____★

$\mathcal{H}$OW CAN YOU BENEFIT FROM BEGINNING TEACHER PROGRAMS?

The first year of teaching is a formative time in a teacher's life and career. First-year teachers are under close scrutiny and must prove they are good teachers and are able to help students learn. Also, as a beginning teacher you will be entering a social system with a particular culture and climate. You will need to get along and fit in with students, faculty, staff, parents, and the community. Proving one's worth, fitting in, and getting along are important tasks associated with the first year of teaching. Helping beginning teachers successfully accomplish these tasks is the primary purpose of beginning teacher programs.

INTASC

Standard 10: The teacher fosters relationships with school colleagues, parents, and agencies in the larger community to support students' learning and well-being.

Participating in an Induction Program

As a novice or beginning teacher, you will probably participate in a program of induction and mentoring. **Induction** is a planned program that focuses on providing teacher training, assistance, support, and retention for two or three years. Two important processes of induction programs that are supported by research are mentor teachers and ongoing opportunities for learning.

Induction programs help bridge the gap between theory and practice and enable novice teachers to reflect about and develop new insights into the teacher's role. In this regard, the beginning teacher program is very much an ongoing professional development process.

Induction
A planned program intended to provide some systematic and sustained assistance, especially to beginning teachers, for at least one school year.

Learning through Development Programs

Many teachers, including the teachers who have shared their experiences with you in this text, all agree that they benefited from or would benefit from having a skilled pro-

In a job interview, you need to be well prepared to answer questions about yourself, your philosophy of teaching, and how you will be a contributing member to the district. The America's Job Bank Web site (www.ajb.dni. us:80) may help you prepare for and find a teaching position.

fessional teacher provide them with help and assistance. (See the Profile.) You will want to establish a mentoring relationship with such a professional as you begin teaching. A mentor teacher can help you "learn the ropes" and support you as you develop your own distinctive teaching style and approach. A mentor provides moral support, guidance, and feedback as you progress toward your goal of becoming a good teacher.

Although professional development is a lifelong process, becoming a professional involves participating in programs and activities that will provide you opportunities to continually grow, learn, and become more expert in your work. As staff development opportunities become available, use them as a means of collaborating with your colleagues and of taking risks—trying new things, experimenting with new ideas. Many school districts list staff development opportunities on their Web sites. You can access the Web sites in local districts near you and evaluate the nature and quality of their staff development programs. In addition, many companies provide training and support for teachers in the use of their products and technology. For example, Apple Computer is offering a series of staff development workshops to help teachers integrate technology into their curriculum. For more information, see www.apple.com/education/k12/leadership/acot/.

Mentors. There is a good chance that as a novice teacher you will be assigned to a mentor teacher—a teacher, leader, guide, role model, supporter, and sponsor. While not new, mentoring is a growing trend and represents a major professional responsibility. Mentors are usually chosen by administrators, colleagues, and in some cases, teacher unions.

Profile California Beginning Teacher Support and Assessment Program

The California Beginning Teacher Support and Assessment Program (BTSA) is a key initiative for providing a supportive induction for beginning teachers. Each year, almost 10,000 beginning teachers in California face overcrowded classrooms and are challenged by serious academic, social, and physical needs of many of their students. BTSA provides beginning teachers with important formative assessments of their teaching practices and professional development in order to promote teacher effectiveness with students, retention in teaching, and satisfaction with the occupation.

BTSA programs vary in organizational design and include individual districts, districts in collaboration with colleges and universities, and large consortia in which districts, colleges, universities, and county offices of education work together. About 80 percent of the state's new teachers receive such support through the 132 projects that are part of BTSA.

One such project is the Santa Cruz New Teacher Project, which began in 1988 as a BTSA model program, with about

forty advisors who work with 450 beginning teachers. The idea was to give new teachers job-specific training and support, beyond their internships as students, similar to the extra training medical residents receive as new doctors. In the Santa Cruz program, veteran teachers meet weekly with novices to observe and coach them. The veterans offer advice on planning and classroom management, teach demonstration lessons, and provide emotional support. Together, each advisor and novice keep a portfolio to help assess the new teacher's progress. Advisors also videotape new teachers working with students and analyze students' course work with the novices.

The project is overseen by the University of California–Santa Cruz, whose education department works with sixteen school districts in three counties. It costs $5,100 to train each beginning teacher in the Santa Cruz program, with $3,000 provided by the state and $2,100 from the local districts. This may seem like a sizable investment, but it is an investment in the future.

Qualifications for mentor teachers and their responsibilities in the Arlington (Virginia) public schools are that the teacher

- is recognized as an outstanding teacher by his/her school community
- has at least three years of successful teaching experience in Arlington public Schools
- reflects positive peer relations
- has knowledge of adult learning theory/working with adults (Priority is given to lead teachers, teachers who have taken the Best Practices Course, or teachers who have taken a mentoring course.)
- demonstrates knowledge and leadership in the area of Best Instructional Practices
- is willing to maintain a year-long commitment to his or her mentee(s)
- provides assistance and support for up to three new teacher hires
- serves as a coach for teachers new to Arlington public schools
- maintains confidentiality between the mentor and the mentee(s)
- works with new teacher hires who are near the same grade level and/or subject area as the mentor when possible
- works with the countywide teacher mentors in supporting new teacher hires
- participates in a mentor training program
- attends mentor meetings throughout the school year
- meets regularly with new teachers to support/model Best Instructional Practices
- conveys the culture of the school system to new teachers
- develops instructional strategies with new teachers that might include topics of immediate need, such as classroom organization and management, planning, pacing, and delivery of the curriculum
- keeps a log or record of time and activities spent with new teachers (to be turned in monthly to the Office of Staff Development)
- models lessons of Best Instructional Practices within his or her classroom[7]

INTASC

Standard 9: The teacher is a reflective practitioner who continually evaluates the effects of his/her choices and actions on others (students, parents, and other professionals in the learning community) and who actively seeks out opportunities to grow professionally.

NCATE

Elementary

Standard 5.1: Understands and applies practices and behaviors that are characteristic of developing career teachers.

What qualities would you prize in a mentor? How might you use a partnership with a master teacher to develop professionally? How would you be contributing to your mentor's professional development?

Mentors act as coaches. In their role of coaching, they promote interactions that support reflection and develop professional capacity. Mentors are also consultants, sharing their experiences and providing technical assistance. In all their roles, mentors collaborate through shared planning and problem solving.

The mentoring function is designed to support novice teachers, facilitate their induction into the profession, and promote collaboration and leadership as part of a teacher's career development. Mentoring can improve the quality of your beginning teacher experience and be a positive process for all involved. Furthermore, mentoring increases the possibility that you and other mentored novice teachers will remain in the profession.

Staff Development Programs. Staff development is an important part of reforming educational practices, making schools function well, and professionalizing teaching. Staff development "includes considerations of curriculum content, instructional strategies, and the ways in which the staff interact with each other and with students. Staff development is ongoing education, training, and study designed to help you and your colleagues improve skills, attitude, knowledge, and performance. The ultimate goals of staff development are to have high-quality teachers who achieve the school's mission, implement its programs, and help students achieve at high levels. As a novice teacher you will participate in ongoing staff development throughout your career. School districts invest a great deal of money in staff development. For example, the Chicago Public Schools spend over $200 million a year, or about $6,500 per teacher, on staff development.[8]

Part of your staff development will be directed toward earning advanced certification such as National Board for Professional Teaching Standards certification that was discussed in Chapter 2. Part of your professional staff development will be in the context of small learning communities where you and other teachers meet to address common concerns and achieve common goals. Part of your staff development may occur online. (See Education on the Move.)

NCATE

Middle Level

Standard 7: Understands the complexity of teaching young adolescents; engages in practices and behaviors that develop competence as a professional.

NCATE

Early Childhood

Standard 5: Uses ethical guidelines and other professional standards; is a continuous, collaborative learner who demonstrates knowledgeable, reflective, and critical perspectives; is an informed advocate for sound educational practices.

Elementary

Standard 5.4: Fosters relationships with school colleagues and agencies in the larger community to support students' learning and well-being.

Becoming a Part of Your Learning Community

Your success during your first year of teaching and beyond will depend in part on people who make up your learning community. Everyone who can be a source of help to you is part of your learning community; however, a number of significant groups play a particularly important role. These include members of the administration and staff, peers, specialists and service providers, students, parents and families, and community leaders.

You will want to establish friendly, cooperative, collaborative working relationships with everyone you work with in your learning community. You will want to convey the feeling that you are a team player, a member of the learning community who is willing to seek help and give help to others. Guidelines for achieving this goal are:

- **Ask for help.** Administrators are interested in your success. Your being a successful teacher means the school is successful. Make sure you establish a good working relationship with the administration. Usually, the principal, assistant principals, and your mentor will evaluate your work, so seek their advice and guidance. You can also request assistance from colleagues. You will be surprised how helpful your colleagues can be when they recognize that you are willing to ask for help. Many of the ideas mentioned above for administration and staff apply equally to peers.

- **Be a teachable person.** You will want to give the impression that you are open to new and different ways of planning and teaching and that you can learn from your more experienced colleagues. It is important to avoid giving the impression that you have all the answers because you have recently graduated from college.

>>> Teaching Teachers Online >>>>>>>

Jackie Lunz was looking for a way to take courses to help hone her teaching skills while continuing to teach third grade at Baltimore County's Carroll Manor Elementary School. But making it to evening classes presented a challenge when she had to grade papers and prepare lesson plans for the next day. So she turned to the county school system's growing online course program. More and more, Baltimore County public school teachers are taking advantage of a program designed to provide a convenient way for them to take professional development courses. "The program, which began in 2001 with 100 students, now has more than 700," said Barbara Dezmon, assistant to the superintendent for equity and assurance. "The school system has also tripled the number of classes. It offers up to thirty free, year-round online courses that can help teachers get graduate school credits and gain and maintain their certification," she said. "When you have 8,000 teachers and 1,000 staff, there has to be a way to take courses to the people," she said. "We're thinking about service and convenience when we offer these courses."

Source: A. Balakrishnan, "Online Courses Build Teachers' Skills," *Baltimore Sun,* August 16, 2002. (Online). Available at http://baltimoresun.com/news/education/bal-md.online;16aug16,1,6966576.story. Reprinted by permission.

- Be willing to take on responsibilities. Being positive and professional about your job, career, and the people you work with is a lifelong habit you will want to develop. Let others know that you are a "can do" person willing to help with activities, sponsor clubs, and serve on committees.
- Participate in school governance and professional activities. Get involved in professional activities and special events, such as American Education Week, open-house activities, and other events that help advance the profession and the school.
- Work toward making the school a success. If your colleagues have decided to implement a new initiative, such as block-scheduling or a special reading curriculum, be part of the team to work toward making these programs successful.
- Be friendly with everyone. You will develop friendships with many people in the school and others whom you are particularly close to, but be friendly to all the school staff, including custodians, front office staff, and support staff.
- Be collegial and sociable with teachers and other professionals and staff members. Colleagues can validate your feelings about what you are experiencing. The social dimension of the teaching world—and your friendly relations with those in it—can contribute to your success and happiness. Collegiality is the process of identifying with and interacting with colleagues as esteemed peers.
- Develop trusting relationships. As we discussed in Chapter 7, trust is a cornerstone of successful teaching. You will want to develop a trusting relationship with your students, colleagues, administration, and parents. Remember that at the heart of trust is the belief that people can depend on you.

INTASC

Standard 9: The teacher is a reflective practitioner who continually evaluates the effects of his/her choices and actions on others (students, parents, and other professionals in the learning community) and who actively seeks out opportunities to grow professionally.

Some colleagues will have more enthusiasm for teaching than others. Those who are positive and dedicated to doing their best for students and the profession are good models for you to follow. Through observing, listening, and questioning, you will soon learn who are the leaders of your school. These are the colleagues with whom you want to associate.

Other colleagues include specialists and service providers, such as itinerant teachers, guidance counselors, speech pathologists, special educators, psychologists, social workers, home visitors, and parent-involvement specialists. Support staff might also include librarians; technology resource staff; and specialists in music, art, and physical education. Make a point of finding out who all your colleagues are, how their work fits in with yours, and how, together, you can best meet the needs of students and their families. In the Profile, an expert teacher gives advice on becoming a part of the learning community.

Constance Slaughter–Jordan is a Kentucky Middle School Teacher of the Year. She and her team at Winburn Middle School in Lexington provide the following suggestions:

- **Don't worry about being popular and well liked by students.** Classroom management and discipline come first. Develop a plan of fair discipline, stick with it, and students will respect you. Follow through with reasonable and attainable consequences. If you say you are going to do something, do it. Don't take students' behavior personally. Stay objective and consistent, and deal with the actual behavior. Remember, you are a professional and must always act as one.

- **Save everything before you begin teaching and everything you do the first year of teaching.** Begin now and develop a file system of ideas, concepts, and materials relating to topics and activities that you can use in your classroom. Sometimes you don't have all the materials you want or need when you need them. Your materials file gives you a resource to draw from that is immediately accessible.

- **Get in touch with the interests of your students and make assignments around their interests.** For example, if some students are particularly interested in baseball, make math assignments and projects that involve baseball statistics and so forth.

- **Be a multicultural teacher in knowledge, attitude, and practices.** For example, we have had an influx of Japanese into our community because of the Toyota plant, and we needed to provide for their culture. We held Saturday classes for the Japanese students because their parents

expected classes six days a week. Today's classrooms are very diverse, and you have to enable students to express their feelings and ideas from their cultural point of view while at the same time incorporating cultural ideas into your lessons.

- **Make initial, positive contact with parents.** For example, at the end of July, we make visits to the homes of our incoming sixth-graders. Last year, we made 121 visits to homes. As teachers we have to get in touch with families. Our team of six teachers visits homes in groups of three. We go to the homes, meet, and talk with the students and parents. We leave information about the initial school orientation, the curriculum, and what we expect of sixth-graders and their parents. When we visit, some parents invite us in, some talk to us outside, and others talk to us through the screen door. The important thing is that we visit them. The ones we can't visit in person, we call. (See Chapter 6 for more information on involving parents and families.)

- **Develop friendships with everyone: teachers, staff, and parents.** You need to be a friend and make friends; you can't be antisocial in the teaching profession.

- **Have a plan for dealing with stress.** Stress comes with the job. You need a way to relax and relieve stress, such as aerobics, walking, or whatever method you want to work out for yourself.

- **Have a motto for yourself and, if appropriate, others whom you teach with.** Our team motto is "Look past the mess and see the mind—look past the hassle and see the heart."

Establishing Relationships with Students and Parents

NCATE

Early Childhood

Standard 2: Understands and values complex characteristics of families and communities; creates respectful, reciprocal relationships that support and empower families; involves families in children's development and learning.

The relationships you establish with students are among the most important in your teaching career. As discussed in Chapter 4, you will establish relationships with a variety of students from all cultural and socioeconomic backgrounds and ability levels. Students are your allies in the teaching-learning process and also can be a valuable resource in the classroom. For example, they can help identify and clarify rules, routines, and procedures and provide insight into school culture and the expectations they have for themselves and the school.

Parents hold one of the keys to the academic and social success of their children. You hold another. For these reasons and others, as discussed at length in Chapter 6, you will want to involve parents in your program. Most parents and other family members want the best for their children. They look to you and the schools to assist in achieving this goal. Many parents will assist you in making your first year and all your years of teaching successful if you provide them with the opportunity. Parents and other family members differ in the time they have to be involved. While it is unrealistic to think that all parents will be involved, it is not unrealistic to try to encourage the involvement of all parents.

Others from the community have a wealth of talent and abilities to share. Many are waiting for you to contact them for help and assistance. For example, an engineer from a local industry might be an ideal person to assist you with your math project and to mentor students for participation in the local science fair.

Many businesses support the participation of their employees in school activities through release time and monetary support. Your school and school district probably have a directory identifying individuals and businesses and how they want to be involved in the schools. Some school districts have parent-community involvement specialists who can link you with sources of help. Businesses offer grants to teachers for special projects and often match money raised by students and parents for the support of learning.

As discussed in Chapter 1, one of the major changes in education over the past decade is the increased direct involvement of the community in education. You should make every effort to solicit the support of the community in making you a successful teacher.

SECTION SUMMARY

How Can You Benefit from Beginning Teacher Programs?

After preparing to become a teacher, getting certified, and applying for and obtaining a teaching position, your next stage is the first year of teaching, which is a time of challenge and opportunity.

- **Participating in an Induction Program.** As a beginning teacher, you more than likely will participate in an induction program, which is a program meant to bridge the gap between theory and practice. Induction programs involve two important processes: working with a mentor teacher and observing and being observed by other colleagues.

- **Learning through Development Programs.** The administration in your school will probably appoint a mentor to work with you. A mentor's most important functions include encouraging reflection, directing and supporting action plans, providing assistance and information, offering encouragement and support, supplying professional advice, and mediating conflicts. During your first year, you will attend staff development programs and develop a professional support network.

- **Becoming a Part of Your Learning Community.** Part of the success of your first year will depend on how well you develop friendly relationships with those in your learning community. This includes administration and staff, peers, specialists and service providers, students, parents, families, and community members.

- **Establishing Relationships with Students and Parents.** You will want to encourage the parents of your students to become involved in your teaching and learning program. Your students may be able to offer a great deal of help as you become acquainted with your new school.

Thinking Critically
★ ★ ★ ★ ★ ★ ★ ★

What role do you expect your mentor teacher to play? What do you think will be the most difficult part of working with a mentor?

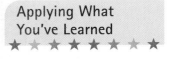
Arrange to interview some experienced teachers who are teaching at a grade level you would like to teach. Ask them if they went through an induction program during their first year of teaching. Do they now function as teacher mentors for new teachers? What did they learn from their induction program? If they did not participate in such a program, what took its place?

Putting Yourself in the Picture
★ ★ ★ ★ ★ ★ ★ ★ ★

What are the most important things you can do to prepare for your first year? What are your major concerns as you look forward to beginning teaching? What can you do now to address these concerns?

INTASC

Standard 7: The teacher plans instruction based upon knowledge of subject matter, students, the community, and curriculum goals.

Standard 10: The teacher fosters relationships with school colleagues, parents, and agencies in the larger community to support students' learning and well-being.

NCATE

Elementary

Standard 1: Knows, understands, and uses the major concepts, principles, theories, and research related to development of children to construct learning opportunities that support individual students' development, acquisition of knowledge, and motivation.

Standard 3.1: Plans and implements instruction based on knowledge of students, learning theory, subject matter, curricular goals, and community.

*H*OW CAN YOU SURVIVE AND GROW IN YOUR FIRST YEAR?

One of the primary things you can do to help ensure your success as a first-year teacher is to begin now to do those things that lead to success. The Profile presents two views of the first year of teaching.

Preparing for Your First Year

Just as preparation for a successful teaching career begins now, so too does preparation for a successful start to the school year begin now. Figure 13.9 shows a first-year teaching checklist that should be of help to you in getting off to a good start and completing the year successfully. In addition, reread the advice of teachers, such as the following Profile and other Profiles in this chapter, about what to do to make your first year successful.

Preparing for Your First Day. Preparing for your first day is an important part of being successful in your first year. The following guidelines will contribute to that success and will ease some of the anxiety that comes with starting a new year as a new teacher.

- Know your school. If possible, visit the school ahead of time and find out about the layout and facilities—where the library, gym, cafeteria, and other rooms are located. If you are slated to teach students who are new to the building—for example, kindergartners or an entering class of middle or high school students— you will want to orient them to their new surroundings, so it is important to be familiar with the building. Ask someone to give you a tour of the school.
- Get to know your students, families, and community. A good way to do this is to spend some time in the community, walking or driving, to learn what is in the community and where things are. Knowing the community is also beneficial to your

Interviews

____ First-year teachers

____ Experienced teachers

____ Administrators

____ Students

____ Parents

Volunteering

____ Tutoring

____ Family Service Agency

____ Child care

____ Other education related

Portfolio Preparation

____ Video of "best teach"

____ Samples of student work

____ Lesson plans

____ Teaching philosophy

____ Resume

____ Interview Qs and As

Observations

____ In classrooms

____ Mentor or master teachers

____ Students

____ School life

____ Community survey

Networking

____ Contact teachers in other cities and states.

____ Visit schools in other cities and states.

____ Investigate government resources for teachers.

____ Investigate computer networks for teachers.

Exam Preparation

____ Plan and complete required course work.

____ Take electives to fill teaching needs.

____ Review state and subject area standards.

____ Review state teachers' exams.

____ Review Praxis.

Reflect & Write

As you complete this course and continue through your teacher education program, you can do many things to help prepare for your first year of teaching. Keep this checklist handy and develop a timeline for completing it. Look it over now. What can you check off right now? What steps can you take now to allow you to continue checking off items as you move through your teacher preparation program? Completing this checklist will help ensure that you are well prepared to begin your first year of teaching.

_____

_____

_____

Figure 13.9 *Preparing for Your First Year: A Checklist*

students because you can relate classroom activities to community places and events.

- Organize your classroom before school begins. Consider decorating bulletin boards, arranging desks, chairs, and tables, and setting up learning centers.
- Ask other teachers for advice. Find out what you can plan for before the opening of school. This is where your mentor teacher can help. If you don't have a mentor teacher, ask the principal for the names of teachers you can call on for guidance.

Jennifer Lasher teaches in Phoenix, Arizona.

"My first year—I was in for a pleasant surprise." I was an English literature major in college, and I never thought that during my first year I would teach special education in grades 1 through 3! But exceptional student education is an area of extreme shortage, and as a result of my involvement with Teach For America, I got the chance. I didn't know I was teaching special education until three days before school opened, but I was in for a pleasant surprise. It was one of the most enjoyable years I could ever spend. I learned a lot during my first year, but the most significant thing I learned was that children are differently abled and how to address all children's learning styles.

I also learned that some children are dealing with a lot of home problems, more than I ever thought children dealt with. You hear all these statistics and your professors tell you about children's problems, but you don't believe it until you see it. I visited in all of the homes of my children. A lot live with aunts, uncles, brothers, and sisters. Trying to help provide stability for my children has been difficult, but in spite of this I have had a lot of success.

I do a lot of project-based learning activities. For example, we did a two-month project on "Around the World," based on Scholastics' the "Magic School Bus." Students can really learn and draw connections. I integrated skill-oriented multisensory reading, and that helped provide a lot of success. I was glad it worked so well because my students were frustrated and hadn't done much for years. It was a juggling act to teach to all their needs and learning styles, but it was worth all the hard work and effort.

I don't want you to get the impression that there weren't any challenges—there were, many. It was really hard with all the students I had, more than sixty students, and it is hard to meet all of their intellectual and emotional needs. I did a lot of self-esteem projects and tried to enhance my students' self-esteem as much as I could, but it was hard. I had to be parent, psychologist, and doctor—and it is hard to play all these roles. I took on so much that for a while I was spreading myself too thin. I was trying to do too much. You have to pick what you want to work with, but at the same time never lose hope with anybody. All kids are capable of learning but they don't know that. You have to help them learn that they can learn.

Another challenge for me was trying to meet all the needs of teachers, administrators, and parents. There was a lot of paperwork and regulations working with special education students. I was the teacher in a resources classroom, and I found it hard to create my own community and culture because all the children were coming from their classrooms to mine. This was also one of the reasons it was challenging to work with other teachers, to coordinate all the schedules.

It was challenging working with parents and trying to get them involved. I encouraged them to work with their children at home and would constantly ask parents what I could do to help them. Creating a community with parents was difficult. One of the reasons for this is because there is a high transient rate in the neighborhood. The students don't know what a community is. There is a lot of violence in their neighborhood, and they have a lot of fear in them when they come to school.

After finishing my first year, my advice to beginning teachers is to slow down and don't try to do everything the first year. As a beginning teacher, you want to take on the world, but there is always the next year and the years after that, too.

I also suggest that teachers take students out into the community to meet different people and to learn there. The community has a lot of resources and a lot to teach. Students' education can't be just within the four walls of their school. I also feel that I personally need to get more involved in helping others and the community. I think I will be a better teacher as a result. This is one of my goals for the coming year.[1]

Jennifer Barger teaches at Winburn Middle School in Lexington, Kentucky.

"What I wish I had known before my first day of school." I was hired on a Friday and I started on Monday. The school district didn't know how many teachers they needed until right before school began, so I was anxious all summer not knowing if I had a job or not. I had done all my teaching in first grade, and I was hired to teach sixth-grade special education part of the day and eighth-grade special education the other part, so you can imagine how I was feeling a few days before school began.

I asked some other teachers what I should do, and they advised me to introduce classroom rules and routines, and it worked.

I wish I had known the names of other teachers, where to get materials, and what the school was like. Knowing these kinds of things would have made my life easier. I also needed to know more about the parents, the neighborhood, and the community.

Needless to say I wish I would have had a better discipline plan. I was very concerned about discipline, because when I told people I got a job and where I was going to teach, they replied how rough it was going to be and how bad the kids were. Everything worked out all right in the long run, but I could have planned more.

I wish I could have known more about how to find out about the kids and their interests, what motivates them, what their families are like, and so forth. If you are going to do a good job of teaching, you have to know your students and parents. I wish I would have done a better job of having more contact with parents for good and bad things. I was pretty good about it at the beginning of the year, but I kind of slacked off, and that was a mistake.

Another thing I wish is that I hadn't started out the year as lenient with the students as I did. I got a lot of disrespect, and some kids took advantage of me. I am a young-looking person. I felt I didn't get the respect I wanted because I was young and new. It was difficult for some students to realize I was in a position of authority. I'll start out a little stricter next year.

Developing a Leadership and Management Plan

Chapter 1 identified and analyzed metaphors for teachers and teaching. Teacher as manager is a metaphor often used to describe teachers' approaches to classroom management. This metaphor implies that teachers focus on exercising authority and control over students. The teacher is strong and assertive, and students are expected to be loyal and obedient. While the manager view of the teacher's role is widely held, there is currently a shift toward more student-centered approaches in which power is shared and students are involved in decision making. Teachers act as guides to help students be responsible for their own behavior.

The following guidelines can help you develop a plan for leading your students and maintaining a learning-oriented classroom:

- Develop a philosophical basis for classroom management and how you will implement it.
- Make a list of "best practices." Base this list on your observations of how successful, experienced teachers manage their classrooms and encourage students to be responsible for their own behavior.
- Observe how classroom environment influences behavior and learning. Environment includes such conditions as seating arrangement, placement of workstations, and traffic patterns, among others.
- Consider how your beliefs affect your teaching approach. Your ideas about how students learn and your role as a teacher influence the way you manage the learning environment.
- Understand that leadership, classroom management, and instruction are interrelated and integrated. For example, when teachers plan for instruction and make decisions about how time and resources will be used and how the classroom will be arranged, they are making decisions about classroom management.
- Take as many opportunities as you can to work directly with children. During your field experiences, and in as many settings as possible, gain experience managing children's learning and behavior. The problem many beginning teachers encounter is a lack of experience in applying the theories and ideas they have about classroom management.
- Anticipate potential management problems and develop preventive approaches. For example, developing routines and making smooth transitions from one learning activity to the next can help prevent misbehavior. Times that need special attention and planning include when students enter the classroom, the beginning of class, transitions from one topic or activity to another, changing from whole-group to small-group activities, and getting, distributing, or collecting materials.
- Think about how students' behaviors are influenced by their prior experiences and home background. Students come to school with many needs—for example, the need for acceptance—and home environments. Developing classrooms where students are accepted, valued, and respected affects how they behave in school.
- Consider ways students can be encouraged to control and manage their own behavior. A primary goal of classroom management is to have students manage their own behavior and learning activities.

Developing a Teaching Identity

In your journey from a novice to a veteran teacher, you will be involved in creating your teaching identity. (See the Profile.) You will be creating your image, your reputation, and your outlook on teaching. You will want to make sure that your teaching identity will stamp you as highly qualified and one of the best teachers. Your teaching identity includes these things:

- Learning what to teach. Learning what to teach is important, because student achievement hinges on whether or not you teach students what they need to know and what states' and districts' standards indicate they should know and be able to do. Being a good teacher means that students learn.

INTASC

Standard 9: The teacher is a reflective practitioner who continually evaluates the effects of his/her choices and actions on others (students, parents, and other professionals in the learning community) and who actively seeks out opportunities to grow professionally.

NCATE

Elementary

Standard 5.4: Fosters relationships with school colleagues and agencies in the larger community to support students' learning and well-being.

Middle Level

Standard 7: Understands the complexity of teaching young adolescents; engages in practices and behaviors that develop competence as a professional.

Evelyne Ng has just completed her first year as a special educa-tion teacher at Hollywood Park (Florida) Elementary School. She works with third-grade students with mental disabilities. Student names have been changed in this Profile.

11/21/03. Week 13. I started off this week with an IEP meet-ing. In college, I learned that IEP meetings included many par-ticipants: the ESE specialist, the ESE teacher, the parent(s), the general education teacher, the psychologist, the speech pathol-ogist, and/or the assistant principal. I now find this unrealistic; the IEP meetings that I have had so far were mostly what I call "informal." Most of my IEP meetings include me, the ESE spe-cialist, and the parent, if he or she can make it. I wonder if IEP meetings are like this everywhere. Maybe the number of people depends on the severity of the case. My IEP meetings seem just like regular parent conferences.

The reading specialist also notified me that four of my students will participate in the Benchmark Assessment for the FCAT in March, even though they didn't participate in the first one in September. I have no idea what this is—the reading spe-cialist will train me how to administer the tests next week.

The beginning of this week was quite rough. On Monday and Tuesday, Ralph (who hadn't shown any aggressive behaviors for several weeks) started biting, kicking desks, and spitting at his peers. I used the book to try to control his impulsive behavior, but it didn't seem to work, so I had my aide put him on time-out. I've always preferred to modify student misbehaviors by using more positive measures, but I think sometimes I need to implement time-outs when behaviors risk physically harming other students. On Wednesday and Thursday, Ralph was calmer. My instructional coach explained that students with MH often have a hard time transitioning from home (weekend) to the classroom (weekdays), so Mondays and Tuesdays can be tough days. Students forget classroom procedures and rules. I think she's right. I've also noticed that I need to repeat classroom rules and procedures more on Mondays than the rest of the week.

At the end of the week, I attended a SAC meeting, where they talked about the school improvement plan. It seemed like the goals were mostly applicable for general classrooms, not for the MH clusters (there are five of these in my school). I wonder if school improvement plans should put their focus on the general education programs because that's where real progress can be made.

12/19/03, Week 17. I began thinking about what I've accom-plished since the beginning of this school year. It's amazing how fast time has passed—I never thought that I would be able to make it through December! I have seven students. Six are making good progress, including one girl who regressed at first but now is improving again. But one boy has been a real challenge. It's been hard for me to reach him, to talk to him, to praise for his good work, and to even have him look at me. Since the beginning of the year, he has been hiding under desks, refusing to work and participate in class. Interestingly, he did start improving—but only when a male teacher aide started in our classroom a few weeks ago. This is something I

need to explore—when a student works with males but not with females. I do know that he has improved, so next year, I will keep reaching him because I believe I can touch his life, too.

I feel proud that I have accomplished something with my students in my first four months of teaching. I still remember the other teachers telling me on my first week that I should not expect to TEACH them because their behaviors will not allow me to. Every time my two readers read the word flashcards to me, some teachers open their mouths in disbelief. They prob-ably thought that Ralph and Dey might be able to read at some point in their lives, but I don't think they thought they could learn to read in four months! I might be exaggerating, but I cannot hide my pride and the effect that these two students have made in my career as a teacher. Just knowing that I have made a difference with even one student has taught me that I can make another difference for another student and so on. The change I could make in these students' lives is endless.

Teaching the academics is hard if the class is disorganized. The first two months were really a challenge to me. I wasn't able to teach much because I had to deal with students hitting, calling out, spitting, kicking, running around, etc. But I have learned to be firmer with what I say and do. I reread one of my journal entries and found this rhetorical question:

"Throughout my college years, I always thought that I should use praise and positive reinforcement more than punishment. I still want to keep that thought and apply it more frequently, but would that help me manage my students' misbehaviors?"

I don't have the complete answer to this question, but I think I have learned something. I still believe that praise and positive reinforcement are important tools to modify students' behaviors, but I also realize I need to be firm and apply consequences. I have been doing more of this, and I have noticed that this has stopped some of the calling out and kicking and even encouraged on-task behaviors. I also look straight at their eyes when I am talking to them, something I didn't do before. December was a nice month because I finally was able to get my class's attention when I needed it and get them to work when I told them to.

The week ended with the notice that each ESE cluster teacher can spend up to $500 for materials to use with stu-dents. This money comes from IDEA funds. I think this is great because I can buy some materials (e.g., games, leap pads) that will help me add more stuff to my learning centers. I'm sure my students will be very happy!

2/6/04, Week 24. The Florida Alternate Assessment Report (FAAR) was a big thing this week. Our ESE specialist handed out the FAAR manual and the students' FAAR forms so that we could go over them and fill out the forms based on the required standards and benchmarks. I extended this brief meeting by going to the MH Cluster Network workshop, where I learned more about filling out the FAAR—determining the student's level and finding the most appropriate rating for each benchmark. I thought this workshop was more helpful than the meeting held at my school, because I was able to hear other teachers' concerns and questions.

On Thursday, I learned that I would be getting another student from the 4–5 grades cluster, because the teacher had had an argument with the student's mom, who then demanded that her son be placed with another teacher. This student is famous for being an instigator, violent, and verbally aggressive. I was very nervous—I was concerned about managing my classroom, where I have worked so hard to gain control and where my students are learning nicely, and I was concerned that I might have to lose a student to another cluster to make room for this boy. I tried to appear confident and positive, but when the ESE specialist told me that the boy would not be coming into my classroom after all, I have to admit I was relieved. And here was one of the lessons I learned: how much my seven students mean to me. The thought of moving any of them to another cluster made me very sad. I wanted so much to finish teaching what I had planned for them. I was nervous about the student who might come into my classroom not because I didn't want him or the challenge of teaching him, but because I was concerned for the students I had already watched make progress.

3/05/04, Week 28. This was the first week of FCAT. Three of my students participated in this test. For the reading sessions, I was not allowed to read anything to them, so instead I prompted them to turn the pages and look at the questions and choices so they could fill in the bubble for the best answer. One student didn't know how to use the bubbles, so I had to let him circle the answer on the booklet. For math, I was allowed to read the prompts. I transcribed the test for one student, whose IEP allowed this accommodation. I have to say that even though having these students take this test was seen as an "opportunity" for them, I believe it was actually very draining. I'm not sure it was a positive experience.

But in the math section, they were able to identify shapes—something I had taught them. They seemed to have retained this learning! Simply put, this means that these students can learn regardless of their disability. The difference is that the teacher must know how to teach it, such as turning the abstract into concrete as in the case of math: showing them the total number of things a digit depicts; reiterating constantly a single concept; connecting this concept to other things that have a relationship to their lives; praising, motivating, and encouraging for their correct answers. The teacher must work harder and squeeze out all of her creativity. I think that we as teachers must be very expressive and show pride in every accomplishment, whether small or big. The students need to rely on other people to confirm that they are doing the right thing so that they can be confident that they can learn. That's why I love to challenge them by introducing them to new things, because this feeling of challenge gives them a sense that they are thinking and being productive.

4/23/04, Week 35. My goal is to have at least 40 percent of my students improve their readiness skills (phonemic aware-

ness, counting, colors, shapes) by the end of the 2004 school year. I have been carrying this goal in my mind since the beginning of the school year, and it has encouraged me to work hard to help my students learn more. In fact, I think I have taught them more than just the readiness skills. I have introduced my students to vowels and consonants, which five out of seven of them know very well now. I have taught them how to recognize and read a fraction, how to sound out the letters. They can identify a pentagon, parallelogram, trapezoid, octagon, quadrilateral, and semicircle. Three students can read sentences. I am very happy with the results, and as a first-year teacher, I couldn't ask myself more than that. I feel very accomplished, and for me, this is a great success!

Even though my PGP goal didn't include anything related to behavior, indirectly, behavior was a very big part of it to accomplish the goal. If my students continued spitting, biting, kicking, and hitting, it would have been harder for me to continue teaching them the academics. I would have needed to focus more on behavior to make my class less chaotic. Thankfully, my students learned to cooperate and work together as a team, so today, I am pleased to say that my students know how to behave themselves most of the time. In fact, many times, I forget that I am teaching a group of students who are diagnosed as mentally handicapped. I guess this is why I am able to teach them—because I just see them as individuals who want to learn and have fun.

5/7/04, Week 37. I had a very rewarding week. At parent conferences, all the parents said they were happy with their children's progress over the school year. One parent told me that she is so happy that her son can now read simple sentences and understands the concept of addition. Now that I am almost officially done with my "first year" of teaching, I can say that what matters most to a dedicated teacher is not really the salary that a teacher gets, but the outcome and impact I can make in the lives of these children. Even before I became a teacher, I knew that I was not going to make a lot of money; however, knowing that the result of teaching always brings a daily reward made me understand the importance and value of this career.

On Thursday, my principal came around 9:00 A.M., during the reading block, to do a final observation. I started with a computer alphabet game, then a rhyming words activity, and finally, a story. The students were engaged in all three activities, and I praised them frequently with handclaps and treats for their efforts. Afterward, I talked with my principal. She said that during her thirty-five years in education, she has rarely seen such an energetic, positive, and excellent teacher! I am so happy to know that my efforts are recognized and appreciated—as a first-year teacher, I could have not asked for more than that!

I have also begun to develop final evaluations for my students. Even though my two lowest students didn't make as much progress as the others, they learned some skills that they hadn't known at the beginning of the year. This month, I'll finish up the assessments and also write two IEPs for next school year.

continued

I'll also evaluate whether or not I have accomplished my goal of having "at least 40 percent of my students improve their readiness skills (phonemic awareness, counting, colors, shapes) by the end of the 2004 school year."

I've had a number of professional staff development opportunities this year. I attended several workshops—the ERI (Early Reading Intervention) workshop, which is helping three of my students acquire and retain phonemic awareness skills, and the Four Blocks of Literacy—and I've finished my first ESOL course, a cross-cultural course, which reinforced the importance of having an open mind and understanding that sometimes what I see as a "misbehavior" might actually be a correct behavior in the student's culture. I've signed up for two workshops during the summer, one for reading strategies and another about autism, and will also take two more ESOL courses. There's so much more to learn!

6/4/04, Week 41. It's the end of the year—and I've learned many things I did right and many that I could do better. I implemented a behavioral plan for all my students, where students earn happy/fair/sad faces based on their behavior after each class period. Students who earn all happy faces in a week get to watch a movie or to go for a treasure box, treat bucket, or snacks during the last class period. This plan has worked very well, since students understand that good behavior will earn them these rewards. I also use a lot of verbal reinforcement. Every time they finish a project, I take time to show them to all the other students, pointing out what they did right and what they did wrong. After this, I have the whole class clap for the student, so that he or she gets a sense of appreciation and reward. I also ask the students to clap for themselves whenever they participate nicely in an activity or game. The "Weekly Note Home" is another thing I did right. Every day, I spend time after school writing notes about each student's behavior for that day. Then, on Fridays, I send this note home to parents and ask them to return it to me on Monday. Another thing I did right was the IEP documentation. I created a documentation log so that I could collect data for the IEP goals, and I put everything in a binder for easy access and proof. My rapport with the students was also good. They show respect for me, but they are not scared of me.

I would do some things differently. I would be very firm at the beginning of the year and assign consequences every time the student breaks a rule or does not follow my directions. This year, I was too lenient with the students, and I allowed them to control me. Thankfully, after reflecting on how I was behaving in the classroom and talking with my ESE specialist, I realized that I needed to take more control, and my students began to learn that I meant what I said. I would also assign more tasks to my aide, such as helping me prepare my lesson materials and collecting data for IEP goals and behavior plans. For my nonverbal students, I would try more to integrate them by having them point and match the things that we work on during teacher-directed activities. I would also like to try to integrate more technology. I did a little bit of this, but there's lots more I could do.

Altogether, I'm very happy with my first year. I can't think of anything else I would rather be doing!

- **Learning how to teach.** Knowing yourself as a teacher is important. Part of your self-knowledge as a teacher includes knowing what methods and activities to use; knowing what teacher roles to assume to reach the goal of being an effective teacher; and constructive and personal teaching style.
- **Knowing the school and community.** Knowing the environment in which you teach is important. Part of your teaching identity involves learning what the school and the community expect of you as a teacher. Schools and communities shape teaching identity. Some schools and communities give teachers much more freedom than others do to be instructional leaders and play significant roles in the school and community organizations. For your personal and professional happiness, you will want to select a school and community that give you the freedom to construct an identity that will characterize you as a high-quality and high-worth teacher.

Looking Beyond the First Year

Figure 13.10 provides some suggestions for ways you can enhance your first-year experience, and beyond. In addition, there are other larger issues to consider. As you progress through the early stages of your teaching career, a legitimate question to ask is What does the future hold? In the teaching profession, the future appears to be challenging and exciting. A number of themes will dominate the teaching profession in the coming years. Some of these are:

- **High-quality teachers.** The term *high-quality teacher* is one that resonates with the profession, parents, and the community. There is no doubt that all parents want

To Do *during Your First Year*

_____ Participate in a beginning teacher program.

_____ Serve on a committee.

_____ Help sponsor a student activity.

_____ Work with a mentor teacher.

_____ Involve parents and community.

_____ Delegate to helpers.

_____ Develop your professional network.

_____ Attend a professional meeting or conference.

_____ Attend an in service workshop.

_____ Exhibit professionalism.

_____ Reflect on practice.

To Do *after Your First Year*

_____ Reflect and write about what went well.

_____ Compile suggestions for beginning teachers.

_____ Develop plans for making the second year even more successful.

Reflect & Write

Once you get your first job, there are many things you can do to make yourself more comfortable and to gain knowledge and skills. Which five strategies in this list seem most important to you? Why?

_____

_____

_____

Figure 13.10   *Your First Year and Beyond*

high-quality teachers to teach their children. So, throughout your career, there will be an ongoing emphasis on how to be sure that all teachers are of high quality. You will want to make sure that you are.

- New kinds of teachers. Today's teacher and tomorrow's teacher are vastly different from Miriam Tupper, my first-grade teacher. Ms. Tupper was a "spinster," a life-long teacher who devoted her whole life to the process of teaching. Today's and tomorrow's teachers represent a new breed. Many come to the teaching profession after having successful careers in other fields. Many teachers have had two or three careers by the time they come to teaching. Other teachers will use teaching as one of their two or three careers over a lifetime. As teachers enter teaching from other careers, they bring different viewpoints to the educational environment and decision making and help create a different culture for schools and classrooms. (See the Profile.)

In this chapter, you have learned about preparing for and being successful in your first year of teaching. Getting your first job, getting ready for the first day and the school

Barb Vogel and her fifth-graders are the founders of Slavery That Oppresses People (STOP). (See Chapter 11 for more information.)

"I am a life sentence! You don't get Barb Vogel for a year, you get her for life!" That has been the trademark of my twenty-six years teaching elementary school children. For me, teaching is a chance to make a friend for life. My motto is "Today a teacher, tomorrow a friend." I have stayed in contact with more than 85 percent of my former students and their parents over the years. I have been matron of honor in their weddings, sat by their side in the delivery room because their own parents were in jail, held them in my arms after they lost a parent, and brought them to my home to spend the weekend when times were tough in their homes. I have clothed them, car pooled them, and fed them—and what a joy it has been!

I also try in all that I do with children to recognize the importance of balancing their hearts and minds. I have found that once you touch the heart of a child, the mind easily and willingly follows. While teaching a diverse, mobile, and too often troubled group of children, it has become clear to me that given challenging, consistent, and loving expectations, all children will thrive. Children want to succeed, and I feel blessed to be able to show them the way to success.

One way that I help children reach their highest potential is by providing a loving environment. I expect my students to respond to each other in a caring and respectful manner. Once children feel safe and loved, they will more easily take risks in their thinking and learning. We call ourselves a "school fam-ily," and we meet each other morning and afternoon in a family group. Here we sit together on the floor to discuss our plans, feelings, and goals for our day. I meet individually with all the children as they arrive and before they leave at the end of the day. I know this extra time spent meeting their personal needs pays off. I see it reflected in their test scores year after year. We continually receive the highest scores in our school. Last year, our class average was in the eightieth percentile, and all these children's test scores greatly increased.

Another method I use to help balance the minds and hearts of my students is to place before them guidelines that I feel are unique to our classroom. For example, our guidelines include:

- Do small things with great love.
- Do unto others as you would have them do unto you.
- Never doubt that a small group of thoughtful, committed people can change the world: Indeed it is the only thing that ever has!
- The pen is mightier than the sword.
- Be a part of the caring majority.
- The greatest sin of our times is not the few that have destroyed but the vast majority who have sat idly by.

Many of these precepts are drawn from famous humanitarians like Martin Luther King, Jr., Mother Teresa, and Margaret Mead. Over the years, we have put into practice the beliefs that run our classroom through community projects. We work monthly with the elderly, collect food and clothing for the needy, and we volunteer to help the homeless in our city.

year, and teaching students to the fullest extent of your abilities offer significant professional challenges. The checklists and guidelines presented here can be of real assistance in helping you become the best teacher you can be. Preparation and forethought can help you achieve success. Good luck and all the best for a successful teaching career.

SECTION SUMMARY

How Can You Survive and Grow in Your First Year?

There are a number of things you can do to ensure success in your first year. Advice from experienced teachers provides a basis for planning that can help make your teaching experience a positive one.

- Preparing for Your First Year. A checklist of specific tips for teaching in your first year can be found in Figure 13.9 (p. 499). Preparing for your first day is important to making your first year of teaching a success. Preparation includes being familiar with your students, parents, school, and community; getting organized by using a checklist of things to do your first day; and getting advice from other teachers.

- Developing a Leadership and Management Plan. The metaphor of teacher as guide is displacing the metaphor of teacher as manager in many classrooms. Guidance requires careful planning for classroom management. A classroom management plan is a major contributor to success in the first year of teaching.

- Developing a Teaching Identity. You need to make sure you develop an identity as a qualified teacher. Doing this includes learning what to teach and how to teach and knowing your community and school.

- Looking Beyond the First Year. Themes that will dominate the teaching profession in the years to come include the need for high-quality, accountable teachers and the need for new kinds of teachers, including converts from other careers.

Thinking Critically
★ ☆ ★ ☆ ★ ☆ ★ ☆ ★

How will your values and views of your and your students' roles in the classroom influence how you manage your classroom?

_____

_____

_____

_____ ★

Applying What You've Learned
★ ☆ ★ ☆ ★ ☆ ★ ☆ ★

Interview three classroom teachers and ask them for their top five tips about effective classroom management. Combine these tips into one list. Discuss these with your professors and peers to determine their appropriateness. When you have the opportunity, try these ideas out in your work with students. Place this information in your portfolio.

_____

_____

_____

_____ ★

Putting Yourself in the Picture
★ ☆ ★ ☆ ★ ☆ ★ ☆ ★

With groups of students, develop rules and procedures to be used in the classroom. Rules identify what students can and cannot do. Procedures specify how things get done. Add these ideas to your developing model of classroom management.

_____

_____

_____

_____ ★

Applications for Active Learning

CONNECTIONS

1. What advice did Fred Hutchinson give in the opening vignette that is most helpful to you? What did Fred learn during his first year of teaching that he could only learn by doing?

_____

_____

_____

2. Think about the concepts in this chapter. Create a picture, graphic, or figure that shows connections that are meaningful to you among this chapter's key ideas.

FIELD EXPERIENCES

1. Interview teachers in a PDS to determine what they think are the values and benefits of professional development in a PDS.

2. Teachers who have recently completed their first year of teaching can give you helpful ideas and insights for your

first year. Ask second-year teachers the following questions and use their answers to develop a personal action plan for your first year of teaching:

- What did you do to plan for your first year?
- What went well for you in your first year?
- What did not go as well as you expected?
- What would you do differently if you were starting now?
- What were your major challenges?
- How have your beliefs about teaching changed since your first year?
- What areas of teaching do you plan to strengthen now?
- On what committees and sponsorships do you serve?

- In what professional development activities have you participated?

PERSONAL RESEARCH

Certification information from all fifty states is available in the NASDTEC Manual on Certification 2004. Certification information and information about reciprocity agreements among states are available on the Internet and through the U.S. Department of Education. Explore electronic sources of information to find out more and to talk online to other preservice teachers who are seeking certification.

Preparing to Teach

FOR YOUR PORTFOLIO

Write your philosophy of classroom leadership and develop a model for managing students' learning and behavior. Incorporate ideas from the profiles in this chapter, tips you gathered from experienced teachers, the rules and procedures you developed with students, and the thoughts you wrote down from other exercises in this book.

IDEA FILE

By now you may feel overloaded with ideas about how to prepare for and survive in your first year of teaching. And I'm sure that you have thought of some additional things you need to do and some tasks you need to prepare for. Make your own personal "To do" list regarding what you want to do in the next two months to get ready for your first teaching job.

Learning and Knowing More

WEB SITES WORTH VISITING

As stressed throughout this text, technology can play a powerful role in your professional development. As a beginning teacher and throughout your teaching career, you can use the Internet as a source of knowledge and information regarding your journey toward licensure, tenure, advanced certification, and advanced degrees. You can begin that journey now by accessing the wealth of information on the following Web sites.

National Council for Accreditation of Teacher Education
  www.ncate.org
  NCATE is a coalition of thirty-three specialty professional associations of teachers, teacher educators, content specialists, and local and state policymakers. This Web site includes detailed descriptions of the organization and its standards, history, and role in the quality assurance continuum.

Beginning Teacher's Tool Box
  www.inspiringteachers.com
  This site offers an "Ask Our Mentor a Question" section, where you can e-mail questions or concerns to a veteran teacher, and a "Tips for New Teachers" section, which

includes inspirational and humorous quotes and a top-10 "to do" list before school starts.

Teachers Helping Teachers
  www.pacificnet.net/~mandel/index.html
  Educators provide basic teaching tips to beginning teachers at this site. Teachers can immediately implement these ideas in the classroom and can download lesson plans and such features as "Poem of the Week" and "This Week's Stress Reduction Moment."

Teachers.net
  www.teachers.net
  Teachers.net brings together educators in category-specific chats, including a chatboard specifically for beginning teachers. Also available are lesson plans, live meetings, a resource list, and a newsletter.

What to Expect Your First Year Teaching
  www.ed.gov/pubs/FirstYear/index.html
  The U.S. Department of Education offers this free online book (in PDF format, requiring Acrobat Reader) that is a compilation of award-winning first-year teachers' experiences, challenges, and successes.

The National Center for Education Information
  http://ncei.com
  The National Center for Education Information (NCEI) is a private, nonpartisan research organization in Wash-

ington, D.C., specializing in survey research and data analysis. NCEI is the authoritative source of information about alternative teacher preparation and certification.

Teachnet
http://teachnet.org
Teachnet is a nationwide, educational, nonprofit organization that supports innovative teachers who exemplify professionalism, independence, and creativity in public school systems.

BOOKS WORTH READING

Feirsen, R., and Weitzman, S. (2004). *How to Get the Teaching Job You Want: The Complete Guide for College Graduates, Returning Teachers, and Career Changers.* Sterling, VA: Stylus Publishing.
Specifically written by school administrators, this book offers insights and experiences from two authors who do the hiring. A detailed, step-by-step program for taking charge of your teaching career is offered.

Gordon, S.P., and Maxey, S. (2000). *How to Help Beginning Teachers Succeed* (2nd ed.). Alexandria, VA: ASCD Publications.
The authors provide clear steps for creating an effective beginning teacher assistance program.

Heller, D.A. (2004). *Teachers Wanted: Attracting and Retaining Good Teachers.* Alexandria, VA: Association for Supervision and Curriculum Development.
The public school system in the United States faces a perpetual challenge in attracting and retaining well-qualified teachers. Heller provides an insider's view of the sources of this ongoing problem—and powerful suggestions for resolving it.

Johnson, S.M. (2004). *Finders and Keepers: Helping New Teachers Survive and Thrive in Our Schools.* San Francisco, CA: Jossey-Bass.
This book highlights the cases of ten teachers whose stories vividly illustrate the joys and disappointments of new teachers in today's schools. It documents why they entered teaching, what they encountered in their schools, and how they decided whether to stay or move on to other schools or other lines of work.

Kopp, W. (2003). *One Day, All Children . . . : The Unlikely Triumph of Teach For America and What I Learned Along the Way.* New York: Public Affairs.
This book tells the remarkable story of one young woman's tenacious grasp on a seemingly impossible dream. It reveals the struggles of an organization created by and for young idealists, but more important, it explores the growth of a new civil rights movement, a movement that demands educational opportunity for all Americans. Wendy Kopp's dream is that one day all children across the nation will have the opportunity to receive an excellent education.

Martin-Kniep, G.O. (2000). *Becoming a Better Teacher: Eight Innovations That Work.* Alexandria, VA: ASCD Publications.
The author provides guidance in using the eight innovations most apt to support a student-centered classroom and then explores the rationales for the innovations, what is needed to implement them, and how to adapt them to different classrooms.

Newman, J. (2001). *America's Teachers: An Introduction to Education* (4th ed.). Boston: Allyn & Bacon.
The author provides an updated look at information on several current issues affecting educators in today's schools, examines the job market for teachers, and provides an analysis of the National Commission on Teaching and America's Future. The text covers such issues as immigration, Ebonics, bilingual education, assimilation, diversity, academic freedom, AIDS/HIV, and child abuse, among others.

Roe, B., and Ross, E. (2001). *Student Teaching and Field Experiences Handbook.* Upper Saddle River, NJ: Prentice Hall.
This handbook reviews essential educational theory, fills in some gaps that are often not covered by methods courses, offers practical suggestions for handling a full range of classroom concerns, and provides a setting for critical analysis of teaching activities.

Endnotes

CHAPTER 1

1. Good, T. L., & Brophy, J. E. (2003). *Looking in classrooms* (9th ed.). Boston: Allyn & Bacon.
2. Zehm, S. J., & Kottler, J. A. (2000). *On being a teacher: The human dimension.* Newbury Park, CA: Corwin Press, pp. 5–15.
3. Knobloch, N. A., & Whittington, M. S. (2003). Novice teachers' perceptions of support, teacher preparation quality, and student teaching experience related to teacher efficacy. *Journal of Vocational Education Research* 27(3).
4. Hoy, A. W. (2002). *The influence of resources and support on teachers' efficacy beliefs.* Paper presented at the annual meeting of the American Educational Research Association, session 13:82, April 2, 2002. New Orleans, Louisiana.
5. Soodak, L. C., & Podell, D. M. (1993). Teacher efficacy and student problems as factors in special education. *Journal of Special Education* 27(1), 66–81.
6. Goddard, R. D., Hoy, W. K. & Hoy, A. W. (2000). Collective teacher efficacy: its meaning, measure, and impact on student achievement. *American Educational Research Journal* 37(2), 482–486.
7. Cooper, J. M. (2003). The teacher as decision maker. In J. M. Cooper (Ed.), *Classroom teaching skills* (7th ed.). Lexington, MA: Houghton Mifflin.
8. Weinstein, C. S., Woolfolk, A., Dittmeier, L., & Shanker, U. (1994). Proctor or prison guard? Using metaphors and media to explore student teachers' thinking about classroom management. *Action in Teacher Education* 15(1), 43. (Reprinted with permission of the Association of Teacher Educators.)
9. Stapler, T. (2004). Personal communication.
10. Nieto, S. M. (2003, May). What keeps teachers going? *Educational Leadership* 60(8), 14–18.
11. Bemis, A. E., & Palmer, E. A. (1999). *Year-round education.* (Online). Available at www.extension.umn.edu/distribution/familydevelopment/components/7286-09.html.
12. National Commission on Excellence in Education. (2000). *A nation at risk: The imperatives for educational reform.* (ERIC Ed 279603). Washington, DC: U.S. Government Printing Office, p. 1.
13. National Center for Education Statistics. (2002). *Internet access in U.S. public schools, fall 2002.* (Online). Available at http://nces.ed.gov/surveys/frss/publications/2004011/2.asp.
14. Louis Harris and Associates (2003). *Metropolitan life survey of the American teachers*, p. 10.
15. Marquis, D. M. (1990). *I am a teacher: A tribute to America's teachers.* New York: Simon & Schuster, p. 101.

CHAPTER 2

1. National Council for the Accreditation of Teacher Education. (2003). *NCATE standards, procedures, and policies for the accreditation of professional education units.* Washington, DC: Author. (Online). Available at www.ncate.org. (Reprinted by permission of NCATE.)
2. Goldhaber, D., & Anthony, E. (2004). *Can teacher quality be effectively assessed?* Seattle, WA: Center on Reinventing Public Education, Daniel J. Evans School of Public Affairs, University of Washington. (Online). Retrieved March 22, 2004, from http://www.crpe.org/workingpapers/pdf/NBPTSquality_report.pdf.
3. Ibid.
4. Brophy, J. (1998). The uses and abuses of educational research. *Educational Research Network* 2(1), 12–15.
5. National Center for Education Statistics. (2002). *Digest of education statistics, 2002.* (Online). Available at http://nces.ed.gov/pubs2002/digest02.
6. Rockburn Elementary School homepage. (Online). Available at www.howard.k12.md.us/res/default.html.
7. American Federation of Teachers. (2004). *Mission statement.* (Online). Available at http://www.aft.org/about/index.html.
8. Reprinted with permission from the March 2004 "Where We Stand" monthly column of the American Federation of Teachers.
9. Weaver, R. (2003, April 30). Diversity's opportunity. *A commentary by the NEA president.* (Online). Available at http://www.nea.org/columns/rw030430.html.
10. Carnegie Forum on Education and the Economy. (1986). *A nation prepared: Teachers for the 21st century.* Report of the Carnegie Task Force on Teaching as a Profession. Washington, DC: Author.
11. Holmes Partnership homepage. (Online). Available at www.holmespartnership.org/origins.html.
12. The Chief Council of State School Officers homepage. (Online). Available at www.ccsso.org/intasc.html.
13. American Council on Education. (1999). *To touch the future: Transforming the way teachers are taught.* (Online). Available at http://www.acenet.edu/resources/presnet/teacher-ed-rpt.pdf.
14. Grant, C. A. (1994, Fall). Best practices in teacher preparation from urban schools: Lessons from the multicultural teacher education literature. *Action in Teacher Education* 16(3), 13. (Reprinted with permission of the American Teacher Association.)
15. National Center for Education Statistics. (2003). *Digest of education statistics, 2003.* Washington, DC: U.S. Government Printing Office, table 68.
16. National Center for Education Statistics. (2003). *Digest of education statistics, 2003.* Washington, DC: U.S. Government Printing Office.
17. Miami-Dade County Public Schools. (2003, October). *Statistical highlights, 2002–2003.* (Online). Available at http://drs.dadeschools.net/Highlights/.
18. NEA Today Online Topic. (2001, July). The disappearing minority teacher. (Online). Available at www.nea.org/neatoday/0105/cover.html.
19. Podgursky, M. (2002, August 14). *The single salary schedule for teachers in K–12 public schools.* Discussion paper prepared

for the Center for Reform of School Systems. (Online). Available at http://www.missouri.edu/~econ4mp/teacher_salary_schedules.pdf.

20. Carroll, T. G., Fulton, K., Abercrombie, K., and Yoon, I. (2004). *Fifty years after Brown v. board of education: A two-tiered education system.* (Online). Available at http://www.nctaf.org/documents/nctaf/Brown_Full_Report_Final.pdf.

21. McCollum, S. (2001, February). Educational leadership: How merit pay improves education. *Association for Supervision and Curriculum Development 58(5),* 21–24.

22. Helping teachers feel at home. (2001, June 23). *Dallas Morning News,* p. 16A.

23. Sandham, J. L. (2000, July 12). California sweetens pot to ease teacher shortage. *Education Week,* p. 24.

24. National Teacher Recruitment Clearinghouse (2004). Teacher shortage areas. (Online). Available at http://www.rnt.org/channels/clearinghouse/becomeateacher/121_teachershort.html.

25. National Center for Education Statistics. (2002). *Digest of Education Statistics, 2002.* Washington, DC: U.S. Government Printing Office, table 68.

CHAPTER 3

1. Commission on the Reorganization of Secondary Education. (1918). *Cardinal principles of secondary education.* (Bulletin 1918). Washington, DC: Bureau of Education, U.S. Department of the Interior, pp. 12–13.

2. Paige, R. (2001, August). High standards for all. School accountability and more frequent tests can lead to improved student performance. *District Administration.* (Online). Available at http://www.districtadministration.com/page.cfm?p=113.

3. National Center for Education Statistics. (2002). *National digest of education statistics, 2002.* (Online). Available at http://nces.ed.gov/programs/digest/d02/.

4. Gross, L., Kentucky Department of Education. (2001, October 12). Personal communication.

5. National Institute of Out-of-School Time. (2003). Wellesley centers for women. (Online). Available at www.niost.org.

6. National Center for Education Statistics. (2002). *National digest of education statistics, 2002.* (Online). Available at http://nces.ed.gov/programs/digest/d02/.

7. Shugart, K. (2004, May 27). Pros, cons of year-round class calendar weighed in Dooly. *Macon Telegraph.* (Online). Available at http://www.macon.com/mld/macon/news/local/8769186.htm.

8. National Center for Education Statistics. (2002). *National digest of education statistics, 2002.* (Online). Available at http://nces.ed.gov/programs/digest/d02/.

9. Pinzur, M. (2003, July 25). Fast track graduation may affect thousands. *The Miami Herald.* (Online). Available at http://www.miami.com/mld/miamiherald/news/local/6379395.htm.

10. National Center for Education Statistics. (2002). *National digest of education statistics, 2002.* (Online) Available at http://nces.ed.gov/programs/digest/d02/.

11. Ibid.

12. Oxley, D. (1994). Organizing schools into small units. Alternatives to homogeneous grouping. *Phi Delta Kappan 75(7),* 521.

13. National Center for Education Statistics. (2002) *National digest of education statistics, 2002.* (Online). Available at http://nces.ed.gov/programs/digest/d02/.

14. Ibid.

15. Rural School and Community Trust. (2003). School size, poverty, and student achievement. (Online). Available at www.ruraledu.org/states/tx.htm.

16. Lear, R. J., and Wasley, P. A. (2001, March). Small schools, real gains. *Educational Leadership,* pp. 23–24.

17. Head Start Bureau. (2004). *Head start program fact sheet.* (Online). Available at http://www.acf.hhs.gov/programs/hsb/research/2004.htm.

18. National Education Association. (2003, July 4). *NEA delegates call for universal pre-K and full-day kindergarten.* (Online). Available at http://www.nea.org/newsreleases/2003/nr030704b.html.

19. Rose, L. C. and Gallup, A. M. (2002, September). The 34th annual Phi Delta Kappa/Gallup poll of the public's attitudes toward the public schools. *Phi Delta Kappan.* (Online). Available at http://www.pdkintl.org/kappan/kimages/k0209pol.pdf.

20. Alianza Charter School. *Mission statement.* (Online). Available at http://www.alianza.pvusd.net/mission.html.

21. Manzo, K. K. (2001). Missed opportunities. *Education Week.* (Online). Available at www.edweek.org/ew/ewstory.cfm?slug=05mscurric.h20.

22. Shafer. R. (2001, September). Personal communication.

23. Schmidt, P. (1994, February 2). Magnets' efficiency as a desegregation tool questioned. *Education Week,* pp. 1, 16.

24. Reading High School. (2003). Personal communication.

25. Richardson, L. (1994, October 26). Little country school copes with change. *New York Times,* p. A12.

26. Lindsay, D. (1994, August 3). E. D. report hails rural schools as a "model of strength." *Education Week,* p. 3.

27. Stern, J. (1994). *The condition of education in rural schools.* Washington, DC: U.S. Government Printing Office.

28. Johnson, D. (1994, September 21). Study says small schools are key to learning. *Wall Street Journal,* p. B12.

29. American Legislative Exchange Council. (1993). *The report card on American education.* Washington, DC: Author.

30. Association for More Effective Schools. *Correlates of effective schools.* (Online). Available at www.mes.org/correlates.html.

CHAPTER 4

1. Oakes, J. (1987, April). *Race, class and school responses to ability: Interactive influences on math and science outcomes.* Paper presented at the annual meeting of the American Educational Research Association, Washington, DC, p. 3.

2. U.S. Bureau of the Census. (2002). *Current population surveys, 1972–2002.* (Online). Available at http://www.census.gov/population/www/socdemo/school/cps2002.html.

3. Abedi, J., & Dietel, R. (2004, June). Challenges in the No Child Left Behind Act for English-language learners. *Phi Delta Kappan 85(10),* 782.

4. Greene, J. P., & Forster, G. (2003). *Public high school graduation and college readiness rates in the United States.* New York: Manhattan Institute for Policy Research.

5. Gibbs, N. (1995, October 2). The E.Q. factor. *Time,* p. 6.

6. Miller, G. (2004, May 26). Muslim student just one of many reported harassments at area schools. *Reno Gazette-Journal.* (Online). Available at http://www.rgj.com.

7. Banks, J. A. (1993). *Multiethnic education: Theory and practice* (3rd ed.). Boston: Allyn & Bacon, p. 147.

8. National Council for Accreditation of Teacher Education. (1987). *Standards, policies, and procedures for the accreditation of professional education units.* Washington, DC: Author. (Online). Available at http://www.nces.ed.gov.

9. Northwest Regional Educational Laboratory. (2003, May). *The implications of No Child Left Behind for the mainstream teacher.* (Online). Available at http://www.nwrel.org/request/2003may/implications.html.

10. Ruiz de Velasco, J., and Fix, M. (2000, December). *Overlooked and underserved: Immigrant students in U.S. secondary schools.* Washington, DC: The Urban Institute. (Online). Available at http://www.urban.org/pdfs/overlooked.pdf.

11. General Accounting Office. (2001, February). *Public education: Meeting the needs of students with limited English proficiency.* (Online). Available at http://www.gao.gov/new.items/d01226.pdf.

12. ERIC Clearinghouse on Urban Education. (2001, August). Gender differences in educational achievement within racial and ethnic groups. *ERIC Digest No. 164*. (No. ED455341). New York: ERIC Document Reproduction Service.

13. Campbell, D. (1996). *Choosing democracy: A practical guide to multicultural education*. Englewood Cliffs, NJ: Merrill/Prentice Hall, p. 113.

14. Kleinfeld, J. S., & Yerian, S. (Eds.). (1995). *Gender tales: Tensions in the schools*. New York: St. Martin's Press, p. 4.

15. Hickman, S. (2004, May 20). AHS separates boys, girls for some classes. *Littleton Independent* 116(21), 1, 4.

CHAPTER 5

1. Public Law 105-17, 1997.

2. Elam, S. M., & Rose, L. C. (1998, September). The 30th annual Phi Delta Kappa/Gallup Poll of the public's attitudes toward the public schools. *Phi Delta Kappan*. (Online). Available via FTP at www.pdkintl.org/kappan/kp9809-a.htm.

3. National Center for Education Statistics. (2000). *Digest of education statistics, 2000*. Washington, DC: U.S. Department of Education, table 170.

4. National Center for Education Statistics. (1997). *Public elementary and secondary education statistics: School year 1996–1997*. Washington, DC: U.S. Department of Education, table 169.

5. IDEA of 1997. (1997). Washington, DC: U.S. Senate and House of Representatives. (Online). Available at www.ed.gov/offices/osers/Idea/Idea.pdf.

6. Individuals with Disabilities Act Amendments of 1997, Sec. 602 (26), p. 13.

7. Weiner, H. M. (2003). Effective inclusion: Professional development in the context of the classroom. *Teaching Exceptional Children* 35(6), 12–18. (Online). Available at http://journals.sped.org.

8. Council for Exceptional Children. (1995). *Creating schools for all our students*. Reston, VA: Author, p. 58.

9. Raskind, M. (1996). *Assistive technology for children with learning disabilities*. San Mateo, CA: Parents Educational Resource Center.

10. Ross, P. O. (1993). *National excellence: A case for developing America's talent*. Washington, DC: Office of Educational Research and Improvement, U.S. Department of Education.

11. Bintrim, L. (2001). Mentoring taps talent. *Education Update* 43(6), 2.

12. Hess, M. (1999). Teaching in mixed-ability classrooms. Wisconsin Education Association. (Online). Available at www.weac.org/kids/1998-99/march99/differ.htm.

13. Wehrmann, K. (2000, September). Baby steps: A beginner's guide. *Education Leadership*, pp. 21–22.

14. U.S. Census Bureau. Poverty, table A. (Online). Available at www.census.gov/hhes/poverty/poverty99/pv99est1.html.

15. National Center for Education Statistics. (1997). *The condition of education 1997*. Washington, DC: U.S. Department of Education.

16. National Center for Education Statistics. (1997). *The pocket condition of education 1997*. Washington, DC: U.S. Department of Education, p. 1.

17. U.S. General Accounting Office. (1995). *Health insurance for children: Many remain uninsured despite Medicaid expansion*. Washington, DC: Author, p. 18.

18. National Center for Education Statistics. (2002). *Digest of education statistics, 2002*.

19. Carnegie Council on Adolescent Development. *Great transitions*, p. 39.

20. Ibid., p. 97.

21. U.S. Department of Health and Human Services. (2003). *Public health service centers for disease control and prevention HIV/AIDS surveillance report*. (Online). Available at www.cdc.gov/huv/stats/hasr1402.htm.

22. National Center for Education Statistics. (2000). *Digest of education statistics, 2000*, table 379.

23. National Center for Education Statistics. (1999). *Education Statistics Quarterly*.

24. Hamilton, B. E., Mathews, T. J., & Ventura, S. J. (2001). Births to teenagers in the United States, 1940–2000. *National vital statistics reports, 49(10)*, 1–2.

25. Ibid., p. 1.

26. Center on Adolescent Sexuality, Pregnancy, and Parenting. (Online). Available at http://outreach.missouri.edu/hes/impact/impact99/centeraspp.htm.

27. U.S. Dept. of Health and Human Services. The Child Abuse Prevention and Treatment Act of 1974. Washington, DC. (Online). Available at www.utk.edu/~orme00/PowerPoint/cw/tsld001.htm.

28. U.S. Department of Health and Human Services. (2001). HHS reports new child abuse and neglect statistics. (Online). Available at www.hhs.gov/news/press/2001pres/20010402.html.

29. National Center for Education Statistics. (2000). Indicators of school and crime safety. (Online). Available at nces.ed.gov/pubs2001/crime2000/.

30. U.S. Centers for Disease Control. (2001). Deaths: Preliminary data for 1999. (Online). Available at www.cdc.gov/nchs/data/nvsr/nvsr49/nvsr49_03.pdf.

31. The Challenge of School Violence. (Online). Available at http://www.crf-usa.org/violence/school.html.

32. Carnegie Council on Adolescent Development. Great transitions. (Online). Available at www.carnegie.org/reports/great.transitions/gr_intro.

33. Schweinhart, L. J. (1994). Lasting benefits of preschool programs. (Online). Available at ericps.ed.uiuc.edu/eece/pubs/digests/1994/schwei94.html.

CHAPTER 6

1. American Youth Policy Forum. (2003, May 9). *A new wave of evidence: The impact of school, family, and community connections on student achievement*, (Online). Available at www.aypf.org/forumbriefs/2003/fb050903.htm.

2. U.S. Department of Education. (2002). *No Child Left Behind Act of 2001*. (PL 101-110). Washington, DC: Author, Sec. 1118.

3. Florida Information Resource Network. (2004). *Florida statutes and State Board of Education rules: Excerpts for special programs* (rev. ed.). Tallahassee, FL: Bureau of Instructional Support and Community Resources, Florida Department of Education.

4. U.S. Department of Education. (1994). *Strong families, strong schools: Building community partnerships for learning*. Washington, DC: Author, p. iii.

5. District of Columbia Public Schools. (1999). *Even Start Family Literacy Program*. Retrieved July 23, 2004, from source. (Online). Available at www.k12.dc.us/dcps/evenstart/esdescription.html.

6. National Center for Family Literacy. (2004). PACT time with school-aged children and their parents. (Online). Available at www.famlit.org.

7. Generations United. (n.d.). *Linking youth and old through intergenerational programs*. Washington, DC: Author.

8. U.S. Department of Education. (2002). *No Child Left Behind Act of 2001: Parental Involvement—Title I, Part A, Nonregulatory guidance*, p. 3.

9. National Network of Partnership Schools at Johns Hopkins University. Available at http://www.csos.jhu.edu/p2000/default.htm.

10. *Zelman, Superintendent of Public Instruction of Ohio, et al. v. Simmons-Harris et al.* Available online at http://supct.law.cornell.edu/supct/html/00-1751.ZS.html.
11. Rose, L. C., & Gallup, A. M. (2003, September). The 36th annual Phi Delta Kappa/Gallup poll of the public's attitude toward the public schools. *Phi Delta Kappan.* (Online). Available at www.pdkintl.org/kappan/k0409gal.htm.
12. U.S. General Accounting Office. (1995). *Charter schools: New model for public schools provides opportunities and challenges.* Washington, DC: Author, p. 4.
13. National Center for Education Statistics. (2001). *Overview of public elementary and secondary schools and districts: School year 1999–2000.* (Online). Available at nces.ed.gov.
14. Rose, L. C., & Gallup, A. M. (2003, September). The 36th annual Phi Delta Kappa/Gallup poll of the public's attitude toward the public schools. *Phi Delta Kappan.* (Online). Available at www.pdkintl.org/kappan/k0409gal.htm.
15. Governor's Work-Based Learning Board, School-to-Work. (Online). Available at http://www.dwd.state.wi.us/gwlbl/stw.htm.
16. Hardiman, P. M., & Fortune, J. C. (1998). School-linked services. *American School Board Journal, 185(9),* 37–40.

CHAPTER 7

1. U.S. Department of Labor, Bureau of Labor Statistics. (2004, February 11). *Civilian labor force projections to 2012.* (Online). Available online at www.bls.gov.
2. Office of Indian Education programs. (Online). Available at www.oiep.bia.edu/news.htm.
3. National Association of State Boards of Education. (1998). (Online). Available at www.nasbe.org.
4. Texas Education Agency. (Online). Available at www.tea.state.tx.us.
5. Vermont Department of Education, Local standards boards. (Online). Available at www.state.vt.us/educ/localsb.htm.
6. California Department of Education. (2004). *Agenda for education in California.* (Online). Available at goldmine.cde.ca.gov/eo/da/da/deptagendahome.asp.
7. National Education Goals Program. (1998). *National education goals: Building a nation of learners.* (Online). Available at www.negp.gov.
8. National Center for Education Statistics. (2001). *Digest of education statistics, 2000.* (Online). Available at nces.ed.gov.
9. Chute, E. (2000, September). School districts look for ways to avoid rigid state regulations. (Pittsburgh) *Post-Gazette,* p. 3.
10. Lewin, T. (2000, June). Educators are bypassed as school system leaders. *New York Times,* p. 2-B.
11. Sergiovanni, T. J. (1996). *Moral leadership: Getting to the heart of school improvement.* San Francisco: Jossey-Bass.
12. National Center for Education Statistics. (2003, October). *Projections of Education Statistics to 2013.* (Online). Available at http://nces.ed.gov/programs/projections/tables/table_31.asp.
13. National Center for Education Statistics. (2003). (Online). Available at nces.ed.gov/fastfacts.
14. Ibid.
15. Ibid.
16. Almanac of Policy Issues. (2004, May 18). Head Start Program fact sheet. (Online). Available at http://www.policyalmanac.org/education/archive/Head_Start_Fact_Sheet_2004.shtml.
17. National Center for Education Statistics, *Digest of education statistics, 2001.* Available online at nces.ed.gov.
18. Ibid.
19. Ibid.
20. The Annenberg Challenge. (Online). Available at www.annenbergchallenge.org.

21. Gewertz, C. (2001, February). California group receives $40 million for school improvement. *Education Week.* (Online). Available at www.edweek.com.
22. Rose, L. C., & Gallup, A. M. (2003, September). The 36th annual Phi Delta Kappa/Gallup poll of the public's attitude toward the public schools. *Phi Delta Kappan.* (Online). Available at www.pdkintl.org/kappan/k0409gal.htm.
23. Cook, G. (2002, December). Leading city schools—Challenge and change in urban education. *American School Board Journal.* (Online). Available at http://www.asbj.com/specialreports/1202Special%20Reports/S1.html.
24. Rose, L. C., & Gallup, A. M. (2003, September). The 36th annual Phi Delta Kappa/Gallup poll of the public's attitude toward the public schools. *Phi Delta Kappan.* (Online). Available at www.pdkintl.org/kappan/k0409gal.htm.

CHAPTER 8

1. *Board of Education of the Westside Community Schools, Petitioners v. Bridget C. Mergens, Daniel N. Mergens, et al.* 58 L.W. 1720 (1990).
2. *Deskbook encyclopedia of American school law.* (1994). Eagan, MN: Data Research, Inc., p. 480.
3. Students' rights in drug testing divide court. (1995, March 29). (Miami) *Herald,* p. 4A.
4. United States Code, Title 42, Sec. 2000d.
5. Kay, H. H. (1981). Sex-based discrimination text, cases and materials (2nd ed.). St. Paul, MN: West, p. 1010.
6. Jacobson, L. (1997, May 14). Appeals court allows moment of silence in Georgia schools. *Education Week.* (Online). Available at www.edweek.org/we/vol-16/33ga.h16.
7. *Steven I. Engle et al., Petitioners v. William J. Vitale, Jr. et al.* 370 U.S. 421 (1962).
8. *School District of Abbington Township, Pennsylvania v. Edward Lewis Schempp et al.* 374 U.S. 203 (1963).
9. Ibid.
10. Court allows Bible handout. (1998, September 9). *Education Week,* p. 4.
11. Walsh, M. (1998, January 14). Lawsuit challenges Bible-history curriculum. *Education Week,* p. 16.
12. *Deskbook encyclopedia of American school law,* p. 51.
13. Celis, W. III. (1994, May 18). Aftermath of '54 ruling disheartens the Browns. *New York Times,* p. B8. (Copyright © 1994/95 by the New York Times Company. Reprinted by permission.)
14. Hendric, C. (1998, September 9). Judge's vote ends busing in suburban Maryland county. *Education Week,* p. 4.
15. Hispanics boost enrollment in high school. (2004, January 29). *USA Today.* (Online). Available at http://www.usatoday.com/news/education/2004-01-29-hispanics_x.htm.
16. Wells, A. S., & Crain, R. L. (1994, Winter). Perpetuation theory and the long-term effects of school desegregation. *Review of Educational Research,* pp. 531–555.
17. Manzo, K. K. (1998, October 7). Curtain falls on desegregation era in Nashville. *Education Week,* p. 3.
18. *Edgewood Independent School District v. Kirby.* 777 S. W. 2nd 391 (1989).
19. Pipho, C. (1994). Stateline: The scent of the future. *Phi Delta Kappan, 76(1),* 10.
20. *Deskbook encyclopedia of American school law,* p. 12.
21. Summary of child maltreatment, 2002. (2004). *Administration for Children and Families.* (Online). Available at http://www.acf.hhs.gov/programs/cb/publications/cm02/summary.htm.
22. Walsh, M. (1994, October 12). Supreme Court refuses "duty to protect" case. *Education Week,* p. 18. (Reprinted with permission from *Education Week,* Vol. 14, No. 6, October 12, 1994.)

23. Summary of child maltreatment, 2002. (2004). *Administration for Children and Families*. (Online). Available at http://www.acf.hhs.gov/programs/cb/publications/cm02/figure2_1.htm.

24. Gay-Straight Alliance Network. (2002). About the network. (Online). Available at www.gsanetwork.org/about/index.html.

25. *Deskbook encyclopedia of American school law*, pp. 251–302 (1994).

26. *Epperson v. Arkansas*. 393 U.S. 97(1968).

27. *Pickering v. Board of Education*. 391 U.S. 563 (1968).

28. Dowling-Singer, B. (1998, June). A matter of fairness. *American School Board Journal*, pp. 14–15.

29. *Tinker v. Des Moines Independent Community School District*. 393 U.S. 503 (1969).

30. Bensman, T. (1998, June 8). Censorship or caution? *Dallas Morning News*, pp. A13, A15.

31. *Hazelwood School District v. Kuhlmeier*. 86–836 S. Ct. (1988).

32. Ibid.

33. *Bethel School District v. Fraser*. 478 U.S. 675 (1986).

34. *Goss v. Lopez*. 419 U.S. 565 (1975).

35. *New Jersey v. T.L.O.* 469 U.S. 325 (1985).

36. Walsh, M. (1997, November 19). Supreme Court lets stand ruling on alleged student strip search. *Education Week*, p. 18.

37. Dowling-Sendor, B. (1998, April). Before you search that locker. *American School Board Journal*, pp. 24–25.

38. *U.S. v. Lopez*. 64 F.3rd 1425. 9th Cir. (1995).

39. National Center for Education Statistics. (2001). *Digest of education statistics, 2000*. (Online). Available at nces.ed.gov/pubs2001/2001033.pdf.

40. High schools must give student info to military. (2002, December 27). *The Rocky Mountain News*, p. 18A.

41. Hoff, D. J. (1998, November 25). Venerable national honor society catching flak from some quarters. *Education Week*, pp. 1, 12.

42. Office of Civil Rights. (1970). *Identification of discrimination of denial of services based on the basis of national origin*. 35 Fed Reg. 11, 595.

43. *Lau v. Nichols*. 414 U.S. 563 (1974).

44. No Child Left Behind Act bill summary. (2004). *House Education and the Workforce Committee*. (Online). Available at http://edworkforce.house.gov/issues/108th/education/nclb/billsummary.htm.

45. National Center for Education Statistics. (2001). *Digest of education statistics, 2000*. (Online).

46. *Board of Education v. Rowley*. 102 S.C. 3034 (1984).

47. *Deskbook encyclopedia of American school law*, p. 123.

48. Supreme Court gives "disabled" status to HIV diagnosed people. (1998, June 26). *Christian Science Monitor*. (Online). Available at www.csmonitor.com.

49. Galley, M. (2001, October). Cellphone bans get a second look. *Education Week*. (Online).

50. Patriotism and the law. (2001, October). *New York Times*. (Online).

51. *Troxel v. Granville* (99-138) 530 U.S. 57. (2000). 137 Wash. 2d 1, 969. P. 2d 21, affirmed. (Online). Available at supct.law.cornell.edu/supct/html/99-138.Z5.html.

52. *Pierce v. Society of Sisters of the Holy Names of Jesus and Mary*. 268 U.S. 510 (1925).

53. *Wisconsin v. Yoder*. 406 U.S. 219 (1972).

54. National Center for Education Statistics. (2001). *Digest of education statistics, 2000*. (Online).

CHAPTER 9

1. Good, H. G. (1962). *A history of American education* (2nd ed.). New York: Macmillan, p. 37.

2. Pulliam, J. D. (1991). *History of education in America* (5th ed.). New York: Macmillan, p. 18.

3. Cubberley, E. P. (1948). *The history of education*. Cambridge, MA: Riverside Press, p. 326. (Copyright © 1948 by Houghton Mifflin Company. Reprinted by permission.)

4. Cohen, S. S. (1974). *A history of colonial education: 1607–1776*. New York: Wiley, pp. 47–48. (Copyright © 1948 by John Wiley & Sons, Inc. Reprinted by permission.)

5. Ford, P. L. (1962). *The New England primer: A history of its origin and development*. New York: Teachers College Press.

6. Good, *A history of American education*, p. 386.

7. Gwynne-Thomas, E. H. (1981). *A concise history of education to 1900 A.D.* Lanham, MD: University Press of America, pp. 151–152.

8. Cremin, L. A. (1980). *American education: The national experience*. New York: Harper & Row.

9. Cohen, *A history of colonial education*, pp. 188–189.

10. Ibid., p. 146.

11. Fogel, D. (1988). *Junipero Serra, the Vatican and enslavement theology*. San Francisco, CA: ISM Press, p. 53.

12. Ripp, S. A. (1984). *Education in a free society*. New York: Longman, p. 43.

13. The Northwest Ordinance. (Online). Available at earlyamerica.com/earlyamerica/milestones/ordinance/text.html.

14. Urban, W., & Wagoner, J., Jr. (1996). *American education: A history*. New York: McGraw-Hill, p. 73.

15. Ibid., pp. 168–169.

16. *From here to there: The road to reform of American high schools*. (2004). Issue paper of the High School Leadership Conference, sponsored by the Office of the U.S. Secretary of Education. (Online). Available at http://www.ed.gov/about/offices/list/ovae/pi/hsinit/papers/history.doc.

17. Spring, J. (1990). *The American school 1642–1990* (2nd ed.). New York: Longman, p. 56.

18. National Center for Education Statistics. (1997). *Digest of education statistics*. Washington, DC: U.S. Government Printing Office.

19. Washington, B. T. (1963). *Up from slavery: An autobiography*. Garden City, NY: Doubleday, pp. 1, 2, 5, 18–20.

20. Banks, J. A., & Banks, C. A. (1978). *March toward freedom: A history of black Americans* (2nd ed.). Belmont, CA: Fearon Pitman, p. 84.

21. Foner, P. S. (Ed.). (1970). *W. E. B. Du Bois speaks: Speeches and addresses 1890–1919*. New York: Pathfinder Press, p. 172.

22. Butts, R. F. (1973). *The education of the West*. New York: McGraw-Hill., p. 464.

23. Ibid.

24. Office of Indian Education Programs. *Information brochure*. Washington, DC: Bureau of Indian Affairs, U.S. Department of the Interior.

25. Urban & Wagoner, *American education*, p. 190.

26. Archambault, R. D. (Ed.). (1964). *John Dewey on education—selected writings*. New York: Random House, p. 430.

27. Head Start (2000). (Online). Available at www.acf.hhs.gov/programs/hsb.

28. James, W. (1908). *Pragmatism: A new name for some old ways of thinking*. New York: Longmans, Green, p. 6.

29. James, W. (1948). *Some problems of philosophy: A beginning of an introduction to philosophy*. New York: Longmans, Green, p. 31.

30. McLarin, K. (1995). Curriculum or not, teachers teach values. *New York Times*, p. A13. (Copyright 1995 by the New York Times Company. Reprinted by permission.)

31. Al-Ani, S. H. (1995). Muslims in America and Arab Americans. In *Comprehensive multicultural education: Theory and practice* (3rd ed.). Boston: Allyn & Bacon, p. 137.

32. Morrison, G. S. (1998). *Early childhood education today* (7th ed.). Columbus, OH: Merrill, pp. 542–543.

33. Murphy, R. D. (2001). School officials urged to prevent harassment of muslim and Arab-American students. United States Department of Education. (Online). Available at www.ed.gov/news/pressreleases/2001/09/09092001c.html.

34. Sartre, J. P. (1978). Existentialism. In J. M. Rich (Ed.), *Readings in the philosophy of education*. Belmont, CA: Wadsworth, pp. 98, 101.

35. Shea, C. (1993). *Reporter, 23*(6). (Online). Available at wings.buffalo.edu/publications/reporter/vol25/vol25n6/5a.txt.

36. Ibid.

37. Shaw, R. P. (2000). The educational theory of Maxine Greene. (Online). Available at www.newfoundations.com/GALLERY/Greene.html.

38. Hutchins, R. M. (1936). *Higher learning in America*. New Haven: Yale University Press, p. 166. (Copyright 1936 by Yale University Press. Reprinted by permission.)

39. Adler, J. M. (1982). *The Paideia proposal*. New York: Macmillan, p. 15.

40. Myer, A. E. (1949). *The development of education in the twentieth century*. Englewood Cliffs, NJ: Prentice Hall, p. 149.

CHAPTER 10

1. Barksdale-Ladd, M. A., & Thomas, K. F. (2000, November/December). What's at stake in high-stakes testing: Teachers and parents speak out. *Journal of Teacher Education, 51(5)*, 384–397.

2. National Center for Education Statistics. (2003). The nation's report card. (Online). Available at http://nces.ed.gov/nationsreportcard/reading/results2003/natachieve-g4.asp.

3. Metropolitan Life survey of the American teacher. (2001). (Online). Available at www.metlife.com/Companyinfo/Community/Found/Docs/ed.html.

4. Public agenda reality check 2002. (Online). Available at www.publicagenda.org/specials/rcheck2002/reality.htm.

5. Chicago Public Schools, Office of Teacher Recertification and Professional Standards. (1999). (Online). Available at www.cps.k12.il.us/AboutCPS/Departments/OTRPS/otrps.html.

6. **Texas:** UTCRLA, "Teacher reading academies." (Online). Available at http://www.texasreading.org/tra/; **Philadelphia:** Snyder, S. (2001, October). Philadelphia teaching plan to offer more structure. *Philadelphia Inquirer*, p. B1; **Maryland:** Libit, H. (2002, October). Uniform teaching program advances. *Baltimore Sun*, p. 1A; **Delaware:** Olson, L. (2001, January). Examples of promising practices. *Education Week, 20*(17), 50; **Pennsylvania:** Olson, L. (2001, January). Driven by data. *Education Week, 20*(17), 62.

7. Florida Department of Education. (Online). Available at www.firn.edu/doe/schoolgrades/.

8. Texas Education Agency. (Online). Available at www.tea.state.tx.us/perfreport/account/2001/manual/.

9. Zehr, M. A. (2001, October). After long debate, Indiana adopts plan for ranking schools. *Education Week on the Web*. (Online). Available at www.edweek.com.

10. Freeport Intermediate homepage. (Online). Available at www.brazosport.isd.tenet.edu/schools/FIS/FIS.html.

11. Barton, P. E. (1999, March). Too much testing. Educational Testing Service. (Online). Available at www.ets.org.

12. Seymour, L. (2001, October). Schools making headway on SOL. *Washington Post*, p. B1.

13. Elizabeth, J. (2001, November). Teacher test begins with many questions. *Pittsburgh Post-Gazette*, p. A1.

14. National Council of Teachers of Mathematics. (Online). Available at www.nctm.org/about/position_statements/highstakes.htm.

15. Students are chafing under "test stress." (2001, August). *American School Board Journal*, p. 9.

16. Galley, M. (2001, September). Districts beginning to scale back on tests to lighten school burden. *Education Week*, pp. 1–14.

17. Public Agenda Online. (2001). Reality check 2001. (Online). Available at www.publicagenda.org/specials/rc2001/reality.htm.

18. Giordani, S. (2001, November). Social promotion's end may be in sight. (Online). Available at www.tomorrow.org/csnewsarticles10.htm.

19. Public Agenda Online. (2001). Reality check 2001. (Online). Available at www.publicagenda.org/specials/rc2001/reality.htm.

20. Popham, J. (2001, March). Teaching to the test? *Educational Leadership*, pp. 16–17.

21. Mores, J. (2002, February 4). Test drive. *Time*, pp. 53–54.

22. Rud, D. (2001, November 15). Personal communication.

23. Peiffer, R. (2001, November 6). Personal communication.

24. Hacker, H. K. (2001, October). Racial gap persists in standardized testing. *STL Today*, p. B4.

25. Ohlemacher, S. (2001, April). Test scores reveal width of racial gap. *Plain Dealer*. (Online). Available at interversity.org/lists/arn-1/archives/Nov2001/msg00170.html.

26. Haycock, K. (2001, March). Closing the achievement gap. *Education Leadership*, pp. 6–14.

27. Olson, L. (2001, April). A quiet crisis: Unprepared for high stakes. *Education Week, 20*(31), 1.

28. Cody, A. (2001). How can assessment serve our students? Cody's Science Education Zone. (Online). Available at tlc.ousd.k12.ca.us/~acody/assessment.html.

29. Testing computerized exams. (2001, May). *Education Week*, pp. 1–17.

30. Ibid.

31. Connecticut's Adequate Yearly Progress (AYP) and how it is applied. (2003). *CBIA Education Foundation*. (Online). Available at http://www.cbia.com/ed/NCLB/ayp.htm.

CHAPTER 11

1. For more information, visit www.iabolish.com.

2. Eisner, E. W. (1985). *The educational imagination: On the design and evaluation of school programs* (2nd ed.). New York: Macmillan, p. 107.

3. About NIDA. *National Institute on Drug Abuse*. (Online). Available at http://teens.drugabuse.gov/about.asp.

4. Reciprocal teaching focuses on four strategies: predicting, questioning, clarifying, and summarizing. (2003, August/September). *Reading Today*, p. 12.

5. Pattanayak, V. (2003, February). Physics first in science education reform, *Journal of Young Investigators*. (Online). Available at http://www.ivi.org.volumes/volume6/issue7/features/pattanayak.html.

6. Toppo, G. (2004, August 12). Algebra's for everyone now—Expectations are rising; 21 states require it for a high school diploma. *USA Today*, p. 1A. (Online). Available at http://www.usatoday.com/news/education/2004-08-11-algebra_x.htm.

7. Much, M. (2004, May 24). A lesson in selling healthy snacks. *Investor's Business Daily*, p. A12.

8. S. Perrin, Walnut Hill School, Natick, Massachusetts. (1996). Personal communication.

9. Corathers, D. A. (1989, November). The fame factory. *Journal of Basic Education*, pp. 9–10.

10. Mager, R. F. (1975). *Preparing instructional objectives* (2nd ed.). Belmont, CA: Fearon.

11. Bloom, B. S. (1969). *Taxonomy of educational objectives: The classification of educational goals by a committee of college and university examiners* (2nd ed.). New York: McKay.

12. Spady, W. G. (1994). Choosing outcomes of significance. *Educational Leadership 51*, 18.
13. Rosenshine, B. (1988). Explicit teaching. In D. Berliner & B. Rosenshine (Eds.), *Talks to teachers*. New York: Random House, pp. 75–92.
14. Open court reading. *Science Research Associates*. (Online). Available at http://www.sraonline.com/index.php/home/curriculumsolutions/reading/ocr/622.
15. Direct Instruction. *Science Research Associates*. (Online). Available at http://www.sraonline.com/index.php/home/curriculumsolutions/di/languageforlearning/106.
16. Hunter, M. C. (1982). *Mastery teaching*. El Segundo, CA: TIP Publications.
17. Bruner, J. S. (1960). *The process of education*. Cambridge, MA: Harvard University Press.
18. Slavin, R. E. (1994). *Educational psychology: Theory into practice* (4th ed.). Boston: Allyn & Bacon.
19. Madden, N. A., Slavin, R. E., & Stevens, R. J. (1986). *Cooperative integrated reading and composition: Teacher's manual*. Baltimore, MD: Center for Research on Elementary and Middle Schools, Johns Hopkins University.
20. Brandt, R. (1987). On cooperation in schools: A conversation with David and Roger Johnson. *Educational Leadership, 45*, 14–19.
21. Good, T. L., & Brophy, J. E. *Looking in classrooms* (6th ed.). New York: HarperCollins, p. 304.
22. Vygotsky, L. (1978). *Mind and society*. Cambridge, MA: Harvard University Press. (Online). Available at www.hup.harvard.edu/web_Backlist/Backlist_categ/Mind_Society.html; Tudge, J. R. H. (1992, December). Processes and consequences of peer collaboration: A Vygotskian analysis. *Child Development 63*(6), 1365; Vygotsky, L. (1987). *The collected works of L. S. Vygotsky*: Vol 1. *Problems of general psychology*. New York: Plenum, p. 216.
23. NCATE. (2000). Program standards. (Online). Available at www.ncate.com/standards/programstds.htm; INTASC. (1995). INTASC core standards. (Online). Available at www.ccsso.org/intascst.html.

CHAPTER 12

1. Education Week/MDR/Harris Interactive Poll of Students and Technology. (2001). (Online). Available at www.edweek.org/svcreport/tc03/lc2003.
2. Leu, D. J. (1997, September). Caity's question: Literacy articles on the Internet. *Reading Teacher 81*(1), 62–67.
3. Bushweller, K. (2001). Beyond machines. Technology count 2001: The new divides. *Education Week, 20*(35), 31.
4. Associated Press. (2003). Mississippi puts computer in every classroom. *CNN.com*. (Online).
5. Salkever, A. (2004). Apple's back-to-school blast. *Business Week Online*. (Online).
6. Nebraska State Science and Technology Institute. (2004). Maine laptop program paying benefits. (Online.) Available at www.nitc.state.ne.us.
7. Stanley, B. W. (2004). Robot-building program helps to inspire young minds. *Gazette.net*. (Online). Reprinted by permission.
8. Thomas, K., (2001). Kids in USA, mideast exchange e-mail, ideas. *USA Today*, p. D03.

9. Belkin, J. (2003). Parental control from Belkin protects children and families from objectionable websites. (Online). Available at www.belkin.com.
10. Ibid.
11. Thibodeau, P. (1998, September 23). Senate weighs online privacy rules for tots. *Online news*. (Online).
12. Northwest Regional Education Library. (2002). *Learners, language, and technology: Making connections that support literacy*. (Online). Available at www.ncrel.org.
13. Public Law 100-407. *Bill summary and status for the 100th congress*. (Online). Available at Thomas.loc.gov.
14. Fine, L. (2001). Special-needs gaps. *Education Week, 20*(35), 26.
15. National Center for Education Statistics. (2002). *Digest of education statistics*. Washington, DC: U.S. Government Printing Office.
16. Gehring, J. (2001). Not enough girls. Technology counts 2001: The new divides. *Education Week, 20*(35), 18.
17. AAUW. (1998, October 14). Technology gender gap develops while gap in math and science narrow. AAUW foundation report show. (Online). Available at www.wccusd.K12.ca.us.aauw.htm.
18. Techbridge: Encouraging girls in technology. (Online). Available at www.chatbotspace.org/visit/programs/techbridge.asp.
19. Girlstart—Empowering girls in mathematics, science, and technology. (Online). Available at www.girlstart.org.
20. Zehr, M. A. (1998, September 9). Policy battles leave e-rate funds on hold. *Education Week*, p. 41.
21. USAC Schools and Libraries Division. (2002). Program description—funder year 5. (Online). Available at www.sl.universalservices.org/reference/.
22. Macavinta, C. (1998, October 28). Digital copyright bill becomes law. *NCET News.com*. (Online).
23. Schools police home web sites. (1998, June). Available at www.electronic-school.com.
24. Trotter, A. (1998, May 13). Administrators confounded by internet pranks. *Education Week, 17*(35), 1.
25. Ibid.
26. Ibid.

CHAPTER 13

1. National Education Association, Center for Teaching and Learning. (n.d.). Professional development. In *The profession builder*. Washington, DC: Author, p. 4.
2. National Education Association. (n.d.). Professional state standards boards. In *The profession builder*, p. 1.
3. Stutz, T. (2004, June 11). More Texans taking new path to teaching: Majority of state's rookie educators are now alternatively certified. *Dallas Morning News*. (Online). Extracted from www.dallasnews.com. Retrieved June 15, 2004.
4. Hetzner, A. (2004, August 8). Teacher certification will face its own test. (Online). Extracted from www.jsonline.com/news/state/aug04/249804.asp.
5. Morales, K. (2002, May 5). Teaching prospects flock to job fair. *Denton County Morning News*, p. 21.
6. Domaskin, A. (2004, August 22). Teacher shortage: Home-schooled teacher starts new year in public school. *Grand Forks Herald*. (Online). Available at http://www.grandforks.com/mld/grandforks/news/local/9464266.htm. Reprinted by permission.

Index

Bernard, Henry, 59, 237, 323
Bernard, Sandy, 455
Bersin, Alan D., 248
Bethel School District No. 403 v. Fraser, 297–298
Bethune, Mary McLeod, 329
Bethune-Cookman College, 329
bilingual education, 303
    definition of, 132
    legislation on, 132
Bilingual Education Act, 132
block grants, 253
block scheduling, 85
Bloom, Benjamin, 417
Blue-Back Speller (Webster), 325
Board of Cooperative Educational Services (BOCES), New York, 243–244
Board of Education of Hendrick Hudson Central School District v. Rowley, 297, 304
Board of Education of Independent School District No. 92 (OK), et al., v. Lindsay Earls, et al., 270, 297
Board of Education of the Westside Community Schools v. Mergens, 269, 273
boards of education
    local, 245–247
    state, 239–241
Bordeaux, Roger C., 359
Boring v. Buncombe County Board of Education, 294
Boston Latin School, 318
Bott, Don, 105
Braca, Carol, 225
Bragdon v. Abbott, 297, 305
branding, 256
Branum, Bart, 451
breach of duty, 285
Brown v. Board of Education of Topeka, 273, 278, 281, 337
Bruett, Karen, 446
Bruner, Charles, 386
Bruner, Jerome, 422
Bryan, William Jennings, 293
Bryant, Ginny, 267
bullet drills, 302
Bureau of Indian Affairs (BIA), 329–331
    NCLB and, 359
    Office of Indian Education Programs, 232
Bush, George W., 228, 232, 238, 334, 383
Bush, Laura, 238
business and industry
    and funding, 256
    partnerships with schools, 189, 215–216, 446
    as stakeholders, 228–229
busing for desegregation, 278–279
Butterfield, Karen, 213

Cahill, Michele, 91
California

Beginning Teacher Support and Assessment Program (BTSA), 492
    eighth-grade science standards, 377
Camacho, Sam, 389
Cammerata, Teri, 381
Canada, Geoffrey, 216
Cantrell, Tina, 79
Cardinal Principles of Secondary Education (NEA Commission on the Reorganization of Secondary Education), 76
Cardinez, José, 189
Carlisle Indian School, 330
Carnegie Corporation of New York, 256
Carnegie Council on Adolescent Development, 180
Carnegie Task Force on Teaching as a Profession, 55
    A Nation Prepared: Teachers for the 21st Century, 55
Carnegie Unit, 85
Casa de Bambini, 332
Casimir Pulaski Elementary School, 90
categorical grants, 253
Catholic missionaries, and Native Americans, 320, 329
censorship, of students' Web pages, 462
Center for the Study and Prevention of Violence, 175
Center on Adolescent Sexuality, Pregnancy, and Prevention, 175
Centers for Disease Control and Prevention (CDC), 171, 174–175
certification, 473
    alternative, 475–476
    emergency, 476
    initial, 378
    national, 41
    Praxis, 38–39, 476, 478
    requirements for, 474
    testing for, 38–39
character education, 412
charter schools, 97–98
    parent involvement and, 212–213
    and schedules, 257
Cherokee language, 332
child abuse
    definition of, 286
    reporting, 286–287
Child Abuse Prevention and Treatment Act, 177, 286
child-centered curriculum, Dewey and, 333–334
child-centered schools, Dewey and, 333
Child Online Privacy Protection Act (COPPA), 448
Children's Online Privacy Act (COPA), 448
child study team, 151
choice
    existentialism and, 361
    school, 96, 210–212, 238
Christie, Kathy, 257

Circle of Inclusion, 165
Civil Rights Act, 271
    Title VI, 303
    Title VII, 287
Civil Rights movement, 337
Civil Rights Restoration Act, 337
Civil War, and American education, 328–335
Clark, Marvin, 276
classrooms
    climate of, 16
    collaboration in, 429
    inclusive, 158, 160–164
Cleveland Board of Education v. LaFleur, 273, 290
Clinton, DeWitt, 323
Clinton, William J., 238
clothes, and learning, 178
coaches, teachers as, 20
Cody, Anthony, 392
coeducation, development of, 322–324
Cold War, 336–337
collaboration, 161–163
    in classroom, 429
    definition of, 160
    in family involvement, 203
    in high school, 94
    and inclusive classrooms, 160–164
    knowledge base on, 4
collective bargaining, 292–293
collective teacher efficacy, 9–10
college placement services, 482–483
colonies, schooling in, 316–321
Colorado, Model Content Standards, 370
Commerce Department, 462
Committee for Economic Development, 372–373
Committee of Ten, 334
The Common School Arithmetic, 328
common schools, 322
communication, in family involvement, 201, 204
communities, 214–220
    high schools and, 94–95
    and teaching and learning, 190–195
    working with, 32
    See also learning communities
community agencies
    directory of, 215
    working with, 217
community-based education, technology and, 444–453
community groups, as stakeholders, 229–230
community-school partnerships, 215
community service, 412
Comolli, Tim, 436
compensatory programs, 181–182
comprehensive high schools, 94
comprehensive school reform, 414–415
compulsory school attendance, 307–308
computerized testing, 393
computers
    balance in use of, 458

staff development
  programs for, 494
  See also professional development
stakeholders, 226–230
standards, 368–384
  and contemporary education, 338
  definition of, 370
  development of, influences in, 374–378
  effects of, 370–374
  employment in educational system,
    374–384
  high and rigorous, 371
  integration of, strategies for, 383
  issues with, 378–382
  in knowledge base, 4
  state, 241
  for teacher education, changes in, 56–58
  for teachers, 378
  on technology, 435, 439–442
standards-based education, 77–78, 370–374
  definition of, 371
Stanton, Elizabeth Cady, 333
Stapler, Theresa, 23
state(s)
  legal responsibilities of, 278–283
  standards boards of, 241
state government
  and contemporary education, 338–339
  and education, 238–243
  versus federal, 259
  and funding, 254–255
  and law, 268, 271–272
  versus local, 259–260
  and standards, 375–377
  and teacher placement, 483
Steiner, Rudolf, 3
stereotypes, 108
Stevenson, Cindy, 391
Stewart B. McKinney Homeless Assistance
    Act, 172
Stoneham, Joyce, 168
strategies, for learning, 428
strict liability, 284
strike, right to, 292–293
structure. *See* organization
student(s)
  computer use at home versus school,
    439–440
  cultural backgrounds of, 119–121
  legal rights of, 296–305
  relationships with, establishing, 496–497
  as stakeholders, 229–230
  teachers as, 20
  Web pages by, control of, 462
student records, privacy of, 302
student roles
  essentialism on, 355
  existentialism on, 362
  humanism on, 361
  perennialism on, 354
  progressivism on, 358

social reconstructionism on, 360
students with disabilities, 148
  educational service options for, 156
  education for, history of, 337
  laws on, 303–304
  technology for, 450–452
student-teacher progress, 82
Student Team Learning (STL), 422
subject-area content, in knowledge base, 4
substance abuse, 173–174
suburban schools, 100, 103–105
summer school, 84
superintendents of schools, 247–248
suspension, 300–301
*Swann v. Charlotte-Mecklenburg Board of
    Education,* 273, 278–279

talented students, definition of, 166
Tanner, Jonathon, 446
tax equity, 260
taxes, and education funding, 254–255
Taylor, Jerry, 404
teacher(s), 2–35
  characteristics of, 62–63
  as decision makers, 14–15
  first year as, 466–509
  functions of, 14–22
  high-quality, 504–505
  itinerant, 161
  job opportunities for, 65–72
  and learning environments, 16–18
  legal responsibilities of, 284–289
  legal rights of, 289–296
  motivation of, 22–26
  observation of, 471
  as planners, 15–16
  professional organizations for, 50–53
  qualifications of, 4–14
  as researchers, 20–21, 49
  resource, 161
  as stakeholders, 229
  standards for, 378
  supply and demand for, 68
  technology standards for, 435
  testing of, 386
teacher accountability. *See* accountability
teacher certification testing, 38–39
teacher education
  educational reform movements and,
    55–62
  history of, 59, 326
  programs in, changes in, 59–60
  reform in, politics and, 58
  standards for, changes in, 56–58
Teacher Education Accreditation Council
    (TEAC), 41
teacher effectiveness, 6–8
teacher efficacy, 8–10
  collective, 9–10
teacher empowerment, school governance
    and, 262–263

teacher examinations, preparation for,
    476–478
teacher in-service education. *See*
    professional development
teacher preparation, 468–479
  for examinations, 476–478
  for first day, 498–500
  for first year, 498–501
  home schooling and, 480
  for multicultural education, 60
  observation as, 468–470
teacher/researchers, 5
teacher roles
  essentialism on, 355
  existentialism on, 362
  humanism on, 361
  perennialism on, 354
  progressivism on, 358
  social reconstructionism on, 360
  standards and, 382–383
Teach For America, 476–477
teaching
  changes in, 26–34
  diverse students, 12–14
  extrinsic rewards of, 25
  historical influences on, 314–366
  intrinsic rewards of, 23–25
  love of, 23
  metaphors for, 19–20, 510
  National Governor's Association on, 243
  pathways to, 473–476
  performance-based, 10–11
  philosophical influences on, 314–366
  as profession, 5, 36–73
  professionalization of, 39–40
  rewards of, 22–26
  self-analysis for, 69, 71
  technology and, 456–458
  as way of life, 3
  See also instruction
teaching identity, development of, 501–504
teaching methods
  educational reform and, 31
  epistemology and, 348
  variety in, 427–428
teaching positions
  applying for, 484–486
  finding, 480–491
Teams-Games-Tournaments (TGT), 422
Techbridge, 455
technological divides, 437–439
technological literacy, definition of, 434–444
technology, 432–465
  assistive, 165–166
  and community-based and worldwide
    education, 444–453
  definition of, 434
  funding for, 459
  instructional, 31–32
  issues with, 453–460
  in primary grades, 449

Credits

Page 2, 8, Jim Cummins/CORBIS; 5, Ed Bock/CORBIS; 10, 415, Ellen Senisi/The Image Works; 19, Nita Winter/The Image Works; 23, 347, Elizabeth Crews/Stock Boston; 32, 191, 375, 403, David Young-Wolff/Photo Edit; 36, Will Hart/Photo Edit; 40TL, LWA-Sharie Kennedy/CORBIS; 40TM, 40TR, 40BR, 406, Comstock Royalty Free; 40BL, 400, 420, 472, 492, 493, Lindfors Photography; 40BM, 447, Royalty-Free/CORBIS; 46, ThinkStock LLC/IndexStock Imagery; 49, Laura Dwight Photography; 51, Rick Friedman/Black Star Publishing/PictureQuest; 59, 63, 392, Will Hart; 74, Rachel Epstein/Photo Edit; 80L, HIRB/IndexStock Imagery; 80R, Rick Berkowitz/IndexStock Imagery; 89, 174, 250, Will Faller; 91, 246, Robert Harbison; 95, Kathy McLaughlin/The Image Works; 102, Julie Habel/CORBIS; 105, Rob Lewine/CORBIS; 112, 168, Jim Cummins/CORBIS; 120, Mary Kate Denny/Photo Edit; 128, 196, Prentice Hall, Inc.; 132, Robert Finken/Photo Researchers; 136, 466, Peter Hvizdak/The Image Works; 146, Bob Daemmrich Photography; 151, 285, Elizabeth Crews/The Image Works; 177, Shepard Sherbell/CORBIS SABA; 188, Elizabeth Crews; 204, Amy Etra/Photo Edit; 211, 301, 368, 476, Bob Daemmrich/The Image Works; 224, 331, Bettmann/CORBIS; 229, Bob Daemmrich/Stock Boston; 256, AP/Wide World Photos; 266, Michael Newman/Photo Edit; 274, Journal-Courier/Valerie Berta/The Image Works; 279, Library of Congress; 280, Stephen Simpson/Getty Images; 292, AP/Wide World Photos; 304, Jeff Greenberg/The Image Works; 314, CORBIS; 319, 323, 330B, North Wind Picture Archives; 326, Minnesota Historical Society/CORBIS; 330T, Library of Congress; 350, PhotoDisc/Getty Images; 383, AFP/Getty Images; 385, Barbara Rios/Photo Researchers; 403; 411, Gabe Palmer/CORBIS; 432, LWA-Dann Tardif/CORBIS; 439, GDT/Getty Images; 448L, Farmington Municipal Schools; 448R, courtesy of Nashville Public Schools; 452, Richard T. Nowitz/Folio; 456, Lawrence Migdale/Photo Researchers; 457, Bill Aron/Photo Edit; 482, Spencer Platt/Getty Images.